The
System

The
System

The American Way of Politics
at the Breaking Point

by Haynes Johnson
and

David S. Broder

Little, Brown and Company
BOSTON NEW YORK TORONTO LONDON

First Edition

The authors are grateful for permission to include
the previously copyrighted material:
Excerpt from *The Congressional Quarterly*
by Bob Merry. Reprinted by permission
of *The Congressional Quarterly*.

Library of Congress Cataloging-in-Publication Data
Johnson, Haynes Bonner
    The System : the American way of politics at the
breaking point / by Haynes Johnson and David S. Broder.
        p.   cm.
    Includes bibliographical references and index.
    ISBN 0-316-46969-6
    1. Health care reform — United States. 2. United States — Politics
and government — 1993– I. Broder, David S.   II. Title.
RA395.A3J64   1996
362.1′0973 — dc20   95-26477

10   9   8   7   6   5   4   3   2   1

MV-NY

*Published simultaneously in Canada
by Little, Brown & Company (Canada) Limited*

Printed in the United States of America

For our families
And their American future

*Victory has one hundred fathers
and defeat is an orphan.*

— John F. Kennedy,
after the failure of the Bay of Pigs invasion

*There is nothing more difficult to carry out,
nor more doubtful of success, nor dangerous to handle,
than to initiate a new order of things. For the reformer
has enemies in all these who profit by the old order,
and only lukewarm defenders in all those who would profit
by the new order . . .*

— Machiavelli

Contents

To Our Readers: *A Moment in History*   ix
Sources   xiii
The Players   xv

Book One

The Delivery Room   1

1   On His Own   3
2   Launch   14
3   The Players   32
4   The Delivery Room   48

Book Two

The Plan   55

5   The Clinton Connection   57
6   The Task Force   96
7   Loose Lips and Missed Deadlines   137
8   The Moral Imperative   164

Book Three

The Debate   179

9   Hillary on the Hill   181
10   The Interests   194
11   The Void   225
12   Beyond the Beltway   256
13   Waves of Whitewater   254
14   The Playmaker Fails   300
15   Make a Deal   345

16   The Baron Falls   396
17   To the Rescue   437
18   The Phony Express   460
19   Summer of Discontent   476
20   Pulling the Plug   511
21   The Country   533
22   Earthquake   545
23   Aftershocks   560
24   Lessons: Lost Opportunities   601
     Epilogue: *The System*   636
     Notes   643
     Bibliography   647
     Acknowledgments   649
     Index   651
     About the Authors   669

To Our Readers
A Moment in History

BEFORE BEGINNING THIS CHRONICLE, we owe readers a statement about our motives and goals. In the years we have reported on American politics and government, the United States has advanced from a segregated society to a freer, fairer, more prosperous nation. For all its failings, over those years The System of government and politics — the presidency, the Congress, the political parties, the lobbyists, the press — and the men and women who served in it have forged a proud record of progress for the American people. But by the nineties, faith in The System had been seriously shaken. We see a System buffeted by divisive political forces, a people deeply disillusioned with their government, a country experiencing radical change, a society less fair in dealing with its poor, its ill, and its disabled. Against that background we undertook a deeper examination of the way The System really works. We asked ourselves and all those we interviewed to reflect on this historic moment and to address a greater question at the heart of our story: In these closing years of the century, a time of unprecedented stresses on government, growing cynicism about politicians and institutions, rising clamor for third parties and independent presidential candidacies, and increasing power of private interests to manipulate public opinion and political events, how well does The System serve the people?

To illuminate that question, for three years, from 1993 through 1995, we watched as an epic battle was waged in Washington and around the country. When it was over, the nation's political system had been shaken to its foundation and the forces of reform routed. Politically, America veered sharply to the right, setting the stage for a historic debate in the 1996 presidential election, the last of the century, about the role and purposes of government as significant as any since the New Deal. The consequences of this battle were felt in the lives of each American family and in the U.S. economy. They will continue to affect all parts of The System.

What follows is our narrative account of this extraordinary political episode. It is the story of how the attempt to provide affordable, lifelong health insurance for all Americans led to the electoral earthquake of 1994 and the aftershocks that continue to roll over The System, producing remarkable political changes and explosive new social and economic conflicts. The Clinton effort was the largest domestic reform attempt in sixty years, prompting the most heavily financed and sophisticated lobbying in America ever. It set off tremors of public fear and anger that, when exploited by opponents and combined with long-boiling frustrations about government and politics, enabled Republicans to end forty years of Democratic dominance of Congress. Once in power the Republicans began the most dramatic assault in decades on operations of the federal government — a struggle that will continue until Americans and their political representatives decide what role government should play in their lives.

In the summer of 1995, President Bill Clinton and the new Republican Speaker of the House, Newt Gingrich, offered us starkly differing interpretations about the meaning and lessons of the battle they had fought — and were still fighting.

President Clinton conceded, as he reflected from his end of Pennsylvania Avenue, that despite a lifetime of study and practical experience in governance, nothing had prepared him for how difficult the attempted reform proved to be. "It was an enormous undertaking, and there's no example since the Depression and the war when something that sweeping was done in as short amount of time as I was trying to do," he said. "We thought we had a little window of opportunity, a needle we could thread."

He had wanted to enact a bipartisan health reform to "prove that the government could do something positive" and redeem the promise for which Presidents since Theodore Roosevelt had fought: to provide health security for all Americans. But all the powers of his presidency, backed by Democratic majorities in Congress and public opinion surveys showing Americans overwhelmingly wanted universal health insurance, could not enable him to thread that needle. A historic opportunity to improve the lives of all Americans was lost.

When we talked to President Clinton in the summer of 1995, he placed full responsibility on himself for the failure of the effort that most defined his first two years in the White House.

He was correct in accepting blame, but, as our narrative will show, that responsibility also rested on weaknesses in the Democratic Party, defections among its allies, and especially on the ability of well-financed opponents to fan public fears of Big Government and bureaucracies. Nor was the President expressing the despair of defeat. "We're having debates in this Congress about the role and the responsibilities of government that are more profound than the ones we had at the dawn of the Depression," he said during our Oval Office conversation. "We are ending this century with debates about who we are as a people and what our public purposes are that are as profound as the ones with which we began the century."

In that same summer of 1995, Speaker Gingrich, seated on his Capitol balcony commanding a view of the Washington Mall and the national monuments stretching west before him, explained that he had anticipated and planned for this battle a full year *before* Bill Clinton even decided to announce his campaign for the presidency in 1992. He said he had realized health care reform would be the next great battleground in the political struggle and anticipated that denying Democrats victory on health reform would pave the way for Republicans to win back control of Congress. Vanquishing Democrats in the health care battle would become, in the words of a key Gingrich strategist, "their Stalingrad, their Gettysburg, their Waterloo." Then Gingrich would lead a historic period in which the role of government in American life would be dramatically reduced.

As he spoke, the revolution he led was rapidly dismantling basic functions of the liberal welfare state established over the last sixty years. The Speaker proudly cited how his strategy of blocking the Clinton reform had provided this historic opportunity to pulverize the old order and establish a new one. "The Founding Fathers' greatest fear was tyranny," the Speaker reminded us. "The price of freedom is frustration. So in a very real sense I look back on the negative achievement of not imposing an obsolete health model as one of the crowning glories of The System. It worked. The country didn't want it. It wasn't the right thing to do, and despite all the efforts of the President of the United States, it failed."

At the same time, both the Speaker and the President knew the story wasn't over. "As the Republicans have found out," the President said, referring to the second stage of this battle at the end of 1995, "you can't balance the budget unless you can slow the rate of health care costs."

So the struggle continues, with these men still representing diametrically opposing views of government. The stakes have risen and promise to be even more fateful for The System and the American future.

Sources

A T THE BEGINNING of this struggle, we enlisted the co-operation of the major players in the drama from the White House and Capitol Hill and many of the competing interest groups. For nearly three years, we conducted repeated lengthy interviews with these participants, and with many others involved, both in Washington, D.C., and around the country. All were done with the understanding that the words and views expressed would be used only for this book and only after the political battle ended. Each interview was tape-recorded and transcribed. In addition, in the course of our research we obtained access to numerous closely held official and private documents, memoranda, notes of meetings, and even diaries of participants. Whenever possible the players are identified and quoted directly. In some cases, at their request, we have granted the privilege of anonymity. But in every instance, the descriptions in our narrative derive from accounts given us by participants, often as they were occurring, supplemented by our own reporting. Where people's thoughts and feelings are recalled in the narrative, they come from what people said they *remembered* thinking or feeling at the time or shortly thereafter.

While great care has been taken to ensure accuracy, conflicts arise between accounts of the players in these events and especially their interpretations of them. That is inevitable in such a complicated story as this, a story that despite its fateful conclusion in this narrative remains a story without an end.

The Players

THE WHITE HOUSE

President Bill Clinton
First Lady Hillary Rodham Clinton
Bob Boorstin, Health Care Communications Coordinator
David Gergen, Presidential Counselor
Stan Greenberg, Presidential Pollster
Pat Griffin, 1994 Chief of Legislative Affairs
Mandy Grunwald, Presidential Media Consultant
Harold Ickes, Deputy Chief of Staff
Chris Jennings, Legislative Aide
Ira Magaziner, Health Care Policy Chief
Howard Paster, 1993 Chief of Legislative Affairs
Steve Ricchetti, Legislative Aide
George Stephanopoulos, Senior Presidential Adviser

THE CLINTON ADMINISTRATION

Roger Altman, Deputy Secretary of Treasury
Lloyd Bentsen, Secretary of Treasury
Judy Feder, Health Policy Analyst
Alice Rivlin, Office of Management and Budget
Bob Rubin, National Economic Council Director
Donna Shalala, Secretary of Health and Human Services
Laura D'Andrea Tyson, Council of Economic Advisers Chairman

CONGRESSIONAL BUDGET OFFICE

Robert Reischauer, Director

THE SENATE

Democrats	Staff
Majority Leader George Mitchell, *Maine*	
President Pro Tempore Robert Byrd, *West Virginia*	
John Breaux, *Louisiana*	
Tom Daschle, *South Dakota*	
Ted Kennedy, *Massachusetts*	Nick Littlefield
Bob Kerrey, *Nebraska*	
Pat Moynihan, *New York*	Lawrence O'Donnell
Jay Rockefeller, *West Virginia*	
Harris Wofford, *Pennsylvania*	

Republicans	
Minority Leader Bob Dole, *Kansas*	Sheila Burke
Bob Bennett, *Utah*	
John Chafee, *Rhode Island*	Christy Ferguson
Dave Durenberger, *Minnesota*	
Phil Gramm, *Texas*	

THE HOUSE

Democrats	Republicans
Speaker	Minority Leader
Tom Foley, *Washington*	Bob Michel, *Illinois*
Majority Leader	Minority Whip
Dick Gephardt, *Missouri*	Newt Gingrich, *Georgia*
Jim Cooper, *Tennessee*	Michael Bilirakis, *Florida*
John Dingell, *Michigan*	Fred Grandy, *Iowa*
Sam Gibbons, *Florida*	Nancy Johnson, *Connecticut*
Peter Hoagland, *Nebraska*	Bill Thomas, *California*
Jim McDermott, *Washington*	Fred Upton, *Michigan*
Dan Rostenkowski, *Illinois*	
Roy "Doc" Rowland, *Georgia*	
Jim Slattery, *Kansas*	
Pete Stark, *California*	

THE LOBBYISTS AND CONSULTANTS

CONSUMERS:
Arnold Bennett, *Families USA*

LABOR:
Lane Kirkland, *AFL-CIO*
Ellen Globocar, Gerald McEntee, *American Federation of State, County and Municipal Employees*

REFORM PROJECT:
Robert Chlopak, *Chlopak, Leonard, Schechter and Associates*

SENIOR CITIZENS:
John Rother, *American Association of Retired Persons*

DEMOCRATIC PARTY:
David Wilhem, *Democratic National Committee*

BUSINESS CONSULTANT:
Deborah Steelman, *Law Offices of Deborah Steelman*

HEALTH INSURANCE:
Bill Gradison, Chip Kahn, *Health Insurance Association of America*

REPUBLICAN PARTY:
Haley Barbour, *Republican National Committee*
William Kristol, *Project for the Republican Future*
William McInturff, *Public Opinion Strategies*

SMALL BUSINESS:
Jack Faris, John Motley, *National Federation of Independent Business*

BEYOND THE BELTWAY

LOS ANGELES:

Julie Delgado, *Social Worker at L.A. County General Hospital*
Ed Edelman, *Head of L.A. County Board of Supervisors*
Christine Klasen, *Physician at L.A. County General Hospital*
David Langness, *Head of the L.A. Hospital Council*
Tom Priselac, *Chief of Beverly Hills's Cedars-Sinai Hospital*
Reed Tuckson, *President of Watts's King/Drew Medical Center*

MINNESOTA:

Duane Benson, *Republican State Senator*
Arne Carlson, *Republican Governor*
Curt Johnson, *Governor's Chief of Staff*
Mary Jo O'Brien, *State Health Commissioner*

BOOK ONE
The Delivery Room

1

On His Own

HE SENSED SOMETHING WRONG when the President began to speak. Uh-oh, Jay Rockefeller of West Virginia thought, he seems to be stumbling.

Never had Senator Rockefeller identified more with a fellow politician, never had he felt so great an emotional pull to will a presidential success. He tensed even more as he leaned forward, his eyes riveted on the rostrum rising above the marble dais set against the backdrop of a huge American flag and a clock that has been ticking away historic moments there in the Congress of the United States since before the Civil War. It was 9:10 P.M., September 22, 1993.

His senatorial colleagues, Democrats Harris Wofford of Pennsylvania and Ted Kennedy of Massachusetts, felt nothing amiss. They were seated nearby in the packed chamber of the House of Representatives ablaze with lights and astir with excitement. The lights reflected off the glazed and paneled skylight bearing the seals of fifty states, the arabesque shields, and marble relief portraits of great lawgivers from antiquity — Hammurabi, Moses, Solon, Gaius, Justinian — to founders of the Republic — Thomas Jefferson, George Mason. Illuminated above the gallery door were Webster's words, graven in marble, imploring those who convene there to "see whether we also in our day and generation may not perform something worthy to be remembered."

Wofford was especially swept up by the emotions of the moment. Only minutes before he had led the President into the chamber. More scholar than politician, a college president who had studied the passive resistance tactics of Gandhi in India, Wofford instinctively took his place at the back of the line as befits a most junior senator. No, no, Majority Leader George Mitchell of Maine commanded. We want you up there. So Wofford, whose stunning election upset two years before symbolized the power of the issue the President was about to address, made his way beside the President down the crowded aisles, through the rising chorus of sound. Their passage was recorded by television cameras beaming the scene into a hundred million American homes and, by satellite, around the world.

A generation ago in time, but eons when it comes to changes in America, Wofford affected history. In the closing days of the 1960 presidential campaign, the closest in the century, he persuaded John F. Kennedy to make the critical phone call to Martin Luther King Jr.'s wife, Coretta, after King was arrested in Georgia and threatened with six months' hard labor for leading a civil rights sit-in. That call led to an outpouring of black support at the polls, strongly contributing to Kennedy's victory by one-tenth of a percentage point.

Now, caught up by the excitement of a new drama, Wofford reflected on how extraordinarily fortunate he was to be given, at this stage of his life, a second chance to be present when history was being made, and to influence it. It was fitting that he found himself near the old lion of the Democratic Party, the last of the Kennedy brothers and the leading exemplar of the old liberalism, a man whose gray hair and girth more resembled a senator of the past than the slim young figure who first took his seat there some thirty years before. As the President began to speak, Wofford heard Ted Kennedy say, "Just look at him there. He's the coolest person I've ever seen. I'd be so nervous if I were giving the speech of my life, and look at him. Completely calm."

But something *was* wrong, even if hardly anyone else was aware.

The President made the discovery as he stood at the rostrum gazing over the scene below. There, gathered, were the members of House and Senate. Allies and foes alike occupied the semicircular rows of seats before him; among them were more doubters than believers in his leadership. To his immediate right front were members of the cabinet, chosen so laboriously and at times at such cost to him politically. Some in that group had serious private reservations about the magnitude and wisdom of the action he was about to announce.

Near them were members of the Joint Chiefs of Staff, resplendent in their uniforms and campaign ribbons. He knew some of those men harbored grave doubts about him. As his eyes roamed the chamber, he could see invited dignitaries filling every seat in the galleries.

The President then glanced at the TelePrompTer and was astonished.

In the most important speech of his life, the moment that would launch a titanic battle affecting the lives of every citizen and a seventh of the U.S. economy, that could define his presidency, restore badly eroded public faith in the political system's ability to serve the people, and redeem a promise more than sixty years in the making to provide universal health care, the President found the wrong speech displayed on the TelePrompTer.

Not only that, he didn't even have his reading glasses to help with the written text in the binder resting on the rostrum. To compound his problem, that text was not the easily readable big-type script customarily provided on such major occasions; the President's own big-type version was a casualty of the chaotic round of strategy meetings and draftings and redraftings that had lasted virtually until the last seconds before he left the White House.

It was as if, the President thought, God were testing him. For a moment, he was seized with sharply conflicting emotions. Is God trying to tell me I shouldn't be doing this? Is this a message to change the subject?

The President turned and whispered urgently to the vice president standing behind him, still leading the applause reverberating throughout the room. They've got the economics speech up, he said. You've got to be kidding, the vice president, Albert Gore of Tennessee, replied. Take a look, the President said. Gore leaned forward and saw the words "President William Jefferson Clinton: A New Beginning." Yes, it was the economics speech, the same one Bill Clinton had delivered to a joint session of Congress seven months earlier, only weeks after taking office as the forty-second President of the United States.

Gore stepped to the side and gestured vigorously toward George Stephanopoulos, the President's most trusted young aide.

Stephanopoulos was standing below, to the right of the podium.

When the vice president beckoned, signaling him to come talk to him, Stephanopoulos shook his head no. There's no way I'm going to go up there in front of a hundred million people, he thought. Gore beckoned again, more urgently. Then Gore moved halfway down the podium. Reluctantly, Stephanopoulos moved halfway to meet him. Check the TelePrompTer, the vice president ordered. They've got the wrong speech up.

A sense of dread enveloped Stephanopoulos; he felt as if the blood had drained out of his body. He hurried back down the steps, trying to be as unobtrusive as possible. As he did, he could hear the President's familiar drawl filling the chamber.

By then, the President was riven no longer with doubts. His confidence surged. He knew what he wanted to say and told himself: If I can't convince these people that I know this cold, and that I care about it and they can trust what I say about it, I don't have a prayer anyway. So, as he recalled later, "I just sort of whipped back and did it."

Stephanopoulos heard Clinton begin by asking those present to bow their heads for a moment of silent prayer in memory of those who died or were injured in a train wreck that day in Alabama. At least he's still in the introductory remarks, Stephanopoulos thought. Thank God we worked up a few applause lines at the beginning.

He quickly turned the corner into the Speaker's lobby. "We've got a problem," he snapped at the military aide operating the computer that worked the TelePrompTer. The aide was startled. As far as he was aware, everything was perfect.

Stephanopoulos looked at the screen bearing the President's speech and experienced one of the most frightening moments of his life. It was the wrong speech, all right — the old one, the economics address from last February. It was horrible. It couldn't be true. He suddenly had a flashback to that time, after his eighth-grade graduation, when he awakened from a deep sleep and the unshakable memory of a nightmare, convinced that he hadn't graduated after all. He remembered the feeling of terror then. Now, he had the same feeling. In desperation, Stephanopoulos turned to his friend and fellow presidential aide, David Dreyer.

Dreyer had joined Stephanopoulos after traveling separately in the presidential motorcade to Capitol Hill. Not only had Dreyer been a principal final drafter of the speech, but he was an expert on computers. He had made three copies of the final version of the speech barely half an hour before, placing each copy on a clean diskette. He had given two of the diskettes to presidential assistant Andrew Friendly, who accompanied Stephanopoulos in the President's and First Lady's limousine, and had put the last one in his coat pocket before riding in another vehicle in the motorcade to the Hill.

When they had arrived at the Capitol, it was dark and rainy. Stephanopoulos had found the military aide operating the TelePrompTer computer and handed him one of the diskettes. The aide popped it in, read it into the computer's memory, then, as instructed by Stephanopoulos, scrolled through the text to type in final handwritten revisions the President had made in the car. That completed, the computer operator hit SAVE to maintain the material. Then he hit the key to move the cursor to the very beginning of the speech.

All done. all ready for the President. He sat back, the speech glowing before him both on his screen and on the TelePrompTer screens positioned on either side of the rostrum.

The operator had been especially pleased because this was not the way major presidential addresses were handled in prior administrations. Then, speeches would be completed long before the final moments before delivery. This time, aware the text was not completed, the operator had gone to the Hill earlier that day to set up the TelePrompTer and make sure everything was ready. As an extra precaution, he had called up an earlier presidential address still residing in the computer's memory and displayed it on the prompter.

Satisfied all was in order, he made a fatal mistake. He punched YES to save that file in memory instead of punching the prompt to purge it. When the right speech was entered into memory, and its additions completed later that day. he again punched SAVE, unwittingly appending the health care speech to the economics address residing on the screen. The new health care reform speech was below it.

Now, as the presidential aides huddled around the computer operator, their fears intensified as they saw him scroll down the screen. It couldn't be, but there it was; it was all economics text. They didn't think to move the cursor to the end, where they would have found health care.

Watching the whirring words on the screen, Stephanopoulos felt even more sickened. God, he said, I hope the President isn't seeing that text moving up and down. No, the operator assured him. He'd already cut the feed to the TelePrompTer screen.

The President was on his own.

Before leaving the White House Dreyer had picked up his shoulder bag containing his laptop computer. Thinking of history, and wanting to have a final version for his personal record, he had fortuitously decided to transfer the diskette bearing the speech onto the hard disk of his own laptop computer. He did so, on battery power, while proceeding in the motorcade down Pennsylvania Avenue to the Capitol building.

When he and political consultant Paul Begala arrived at the Hill before the speech, they were met by Howard Paster, the chief presidential liaison with Congress. Paster was furious that he and his staff hadn't been provided advance copies of the speech to give Democrats as they entered the chamber so they could anticipate applause lines and show their support for the President. After Dreyer handed over his shoulder bag to an aide for safekeeping, he and Begala had raced to find an office with a printer that could process the final text. After trying to find the right printer in three congressional offices, they settled in the office of Majority Leader Richard Gephardt of Missouri.

As the speech began printing, Dreyer left Begala in charge and went to find Stephanopoulos in the Speaker's lobby, just outside the House chamber, where Stephanopoulos was overseeing the military aide's placement of the President's last-minute additions of his text into the computer. Dreyer had remained in the Speaker's lobby next to the military operator before the computer screen while Stephanopoulos stepped into the House chamber to stand below the podium just before the President began speaking.

When the disaster of the wrong speech struck, Dreyer told an aide to find the assistant carrying his shoulder bag with the laptop computer and retrieve it. He then ordered the computer operator to wipe out all the data on the TelePrompTer and give him a clean diskette. Taking up his laptop, he transferred the text from his personal hard drive onto the freshly formatted — and now clean — diskette. Hurriedly, he handed it back to the operator, who slapped it in. After another moment that seemed an eternity, Dreyer and Stephanopoulos saw the correct address displayed before them. Finally, success.

Listening to the words of the President out front as Clinton delivered his speech, largely improvising and occasionally glancing at the text on the podium, Stephanopoulos and Dreyer watched anxiously as the computer operator quickly scrolled the text to catch up with the President. That occurred at the point where the President had earlier written, in his small scrawl slanting backward on the final draft, his tribute to his wife, Hillary: "When I launched our nation on this journey to reform America's health care system, I knew we needed a talented navigator, someone with a rigorous mind, a steady compass, a caring heart. Luckily for me, and for our nation, I didn't have to look very far. Over the last eight months, Hillary and those working with her have talked to literally thousands of Americans to understand the strengths and the frailties of this system of ours . . ."

Thunderous applause. A standing ovation. As those in the chamber rose as one, the lights shifted to the galleries above and to the left of the President. They picked out the figure of the young First Lady wearing a midnight-blue dress.

Hillary Rodham Clinton had already played a critical role in the shaping of this moment, but her influence was far greater than that. In terms of wielding power and determining crucial policy making, she had forged a place unlike any other American President's wife. She stood and acknowledged the cheers, appearing at ease and confident. In fact, she always felt nervous when her husband spoke. This night she was even more nervous, a feeling intensified by the importance of this address. As she waved in response to applause, the correct text flashed back on the TelePrompTer.

Seven minutes had elapsed, the longest seven minutes in the lives of George Stephanopoulos, David Dreyer, and the military TelePrompTer operator.

Dreyer and Stephanopoulos, too drained emotionally even to feel relief, and still fearing disastrous consequences, waited a few more minutes, listening to a rising crescendo of repeated applause. Maybe it wasn't so bad after all.

They hurried back to the Democratic cloakroom to check reaction to the speech. There they found Rahm Emanuel, one of the President's chief political aides, intently engaged in a phone conversation with Stan Greenberg, the President's pollster, who was relaying information from inside the White House War Room in the Old Executive Office Building.

Greenberg, a political scientist and former college professor who had become Clinton's chief pollster and one of his most influential advisers, had set up a special citizen focus group called a "dial group" in Dayton, Ohio, to gauge instantaneous public reactions. Each person had a lever in his or her hand to register positive or negative responses to specific words, phrases, and passages as the President spoke.

Emanuel was ecstatic. Greenberg reported the Dayton dial group thought the President was doing fabulously well. The speech was a smash, the presidential delivery superb, powerful, compelling. Never had the President been better. Response to his words was overwhelmingly favorable.

What none of them knew — or could imagine — was that this was the high point of the battle for the Clintons and their plans. The bobbles that plagued the President and his unhappy TelePrompTer operator were but a small symptom of the problems that would continue to bedevil the project. And no rescue squad would be standing by to solve these crises in seven minutes flat.

Already, the health plan was dangerously behind schedule. Clinton had promised in the campaign to have his proposal ready within the first hundred days, but even as he spoke, five months after he had hoped to begin, there was no bill for Congress to see. The task force headed by Hillary Clinton had labored in secrecy for months — sometimes employing as many as six hundred people to analyze what should be done. But the President's own decision making had been delayed until the last minute, just like the speech revisions. Another two months would elapse before the Clinton bill — all 1342 pages of it — would be sent to Capitol Hill.

There, many traps awaited. Despite the cheers that filled the House chamber on the night of the speech, the Democrats were deeply divided over what constituted real reform. Some wanted government-run health care, financed by an addition to the payroll tax. Others would rely on market competition. And on the Republican side, some key leaders came with a steely determination to deny Clinton the political and policy victory he was seeking.

None was more determined than Newt Gingrich of Georgia, the second in command of House Republicans. Gingrich already had devised a private strategy to kill the Clinton plan. His idea was to maintain his party rank and file in a holding action, something he called "coagulation": "You want to clot everybody you can away from Clinton," he told his troops. "I don't care what you clot onto, just don't let it be Clinton." This was not passive resistance, as Gingrich's words seem to imply. His troops operated like a guerrilla army, lying in wait to spring what Gingrich himself described as an "ambush" that would destroy the Clinton forces.

Much more than political gamesmanship over defeating a rival's most cherished policy was at stake in Gingrich's battle plan. To Gingrich, defeating health care reform was essential to making himself the first Republican Speaker of the House of Representatives in forty years. He planned to ride to power on the crest of a new Republican wave. Republicans would win control of Congress and then reshape the American political, social, and economic future. Killing the Clinton reform was a critical means to achieving that end. Had *any* part of the Clinton plan passed that Congress in *any* form, Gingrich and his closest conservative allies believed, their dreams for forging a militantly conservative future would "have been cooked," as a key Gingrich strategist later explained. It would have been the final nail in the coffin of the American marketplace resulting in a social-welfare state like Britain and Canada, creating greater public dependency on government and a government-run plan, and a stronger allegiance of voters to majority Democrats, who provided them their benefits. Only by controlling Congress with a new conservative Republican majority could the final goals of their "Republican Revolution" be achieved: to break the public dependency on Democratic tax-funded government programs; "defund the government," as they put it, and in so doing, destroy the liberal constituency groups; and permit the flowering of an antigovernment, antitax, entrepreneurial nation. All these aims were threatened by the Clinton plan.

Nor was such determined political opposition the only obstacle to passage of reform. Perhaps most daunting of all was the very complexity of the health care industry. As House Majority Leader Richard Gephardt of Missouri would say, much later in the battle, "There are a hundred cul-de-sacs where you can ride into the issue and drive around in it for days, with people just shooting at you and screaming at you about what they have to have — and never come out."

But for the moment, the lobbyists representing this trillion-dollar American industry were, like the members of Congress, impressed with Clinton's selling job. Some of them had already begun working to undercut public support for his program. Others were just mobilizing. All of them knew they were in for a long, hard fight.

The ambivalence of public attitudes — to say nothing of the underlying doubts about Clinton and the Congress — underscored the political risks involved in this eagerly awaited public launching. *All* the players in The System were on trial. *All* would be judged by how well they rose to the occasion. But if risks were present, so were opportunities. They were potentially historic, and everyone in that chamber and countless Americans watching on television understood them, not least the President of the United States.

No wonder the President had listened attentively months earlier as the leader of organized labor, Lane Kirkland, president of the AFL-CIO, ill and aging but still capable of summoning genuine passion, urged upon him the strongest possible action on reform. If Clinton succeeded in passing a national health insurance system, Kirkland told the President, generations yet unborn would thank him as they had thanked Franklin Roosevelt for Social Security. It would be the hallmark of his administration and would elevate the Clinton presidency into the realm of historic success. "We're prepared to do everything we can to help you," Kirkland told Clinton. "We want to be your storm troopers on it."

Now Kirkland was among those who watched with anticipation as the President formally began that fight. All others with direct stakes in the outcome were also either present or watching. So was the entire country, for the stakeholders in this battle were everyone, everywhere.

2

Launch

THE SCRAMBLE to get the right speech into the TelePrompTer was but an aftermath to the struggle to get the speech written. As always in the Clinton White House, the battle over the text pitted competing clans — political consultants versus policy experts, outsiders versus insiders, campaign veterans versus newcomers. It almost didn't get done.

Late in August the President's speechwriting team began work on the address. This needs to be "the Clinton version of 'I have a dream,'" one speechwriter wrote another, referring to Martin Luther King Jr.'s famous 1963 civil rights address on the steps of the Lincoln Memorial. Its delivery should produce next-morning front-page headlines saying, "Health Reform Will Lead to Next Chapter in American Greatness," said another. It must be "bigger than health care," was the advice from still another, and "must define, symbolize, the fundamental concepts of the Clinton presidency."

At the end of August, Ira C. Magaziner, who worked directly with the First Lady to develop the plan, wrote a lengthy strategy memo to Hillary Clinton about the September speech.

By then, Magaziner had already become a lightning rod for criticism. Members of Congress found him arrogant, aloof, rigid, impractical. This plan — and its enactment — had become his obsession, the consuming interest of his life. Magaziner was forty-five, a tall, thin man with unruly curly hair and a prominent beak of a nose who sometimes wore thick-lensed tortoiseshell glasses, and was at times painfully shy and insecure, at times brusque and intellectually arrogant. He was depicted as a Rasputin-like figure, mesmerizing the Clintons and their young staff and leading them down a path toward political disaster. He was aware of this criticism and acutely conscious that he was not a Washington political insider. His fervent commitment was to the Clintons. He was determined that their success with this reform would be his vindication.

Magaziner had kept in close contact with Clinton in the years since they were Rhodes scholars together at Oxford, and he had impressed both of the Clintons during a 1991–92 New Year's Eve Renaissance Weekend gathering in Hilton Head, South Carolina, of prominent public officials, academics, journalists, and business executives, many of whom were also assiduously networking baby boomers. At that gathering he described a Rhode Island health project he was completing. From that weekend grew his ever more important strategic role, accompanied by his equally characteristic penchant for displaying even greater boldness and complexity. Those traits, and the controversies that had been the hallmarks of his career as a consultant, came into even stronger play during the health plan battle. The plan he put together for the President was nothing if not complex. Leaked drafts had already stirred huge controversy.

But in his strategy memo that August about the speech, Magaziner urged a moderate, centrist approach — "we're all in this together" — stressing political flexibility, openness to new ideas, and a true bipartisan spirit emphasizing this is "not the Clinton plan, but the work of many, including many Republicans over many years." All of this provides a way of "winning in the middle," Magaziner concluded. "Almost all agree that something has to be done to fix the health care system; less agreement exists about what the reform should look like."

A great irony emerges from this advice. While the Clinton planners privately were stressing a conciliatory, middle-ground approach for reform, the public and many on Capitol Hill were beginning to form a different impression of their intentions. That public portrait, painted in part by opponents and in part by the Clinton team's own actions, depicted the administration plan as a liberal Big Government scheme, secretly concocted, that would dictate how people got their health insurance and medical treatment.

Already, an insurance industry TV advertising campaign had

begun airing around the country. It featured Mr. and Mrs. Average American Couple, "Harry and Louise," expressing fears that the Clinton plan would restrict their freedom to choose and result in "government-run" health care. "There has to be a better way," Louise says to Harry, in a punch line that was beginning to become familiar to Americans assessing how the Clinton reform would affect them.

In his strategy memo to the First Lady, Magaziner spelled out six main points to counter the growing opposition to the plan:

1. The U.S. has probably never done anything as big or comprehensive as what we are proposing.

2. At this point in time, no one can win an "us" versus "them" fight on comprehensive health care reform. It doesn't matter who the "us" or "them" is.

3. Our best themes are: security, cost control, prevention, quality, choice: these are non-threatening, non-aggressive, middle-class themes.

4. We cannot win with the liberal coalition alone. We must win some real, not just token, support from Republicans, businesses and provider groups.

5. We need to lead a search for consensus rather than a political fight. Our themes must be positive and consensus-building rather than negative and divisive. A divisive approach will be out of touch with a security and national consensus theme.

6. We need to turn complexity into an asset — or at least make people see that simplicity won't do the job.

Hillary Clinton endorsed the ideas. Three weeks later, and just two days before the President's speech, that memo crossed Clinton's desk. It included a suggestion for public issue forums where they would campaign for their program. When he read it, the President scrawled a note on top to his wife. It was revealing not only of their strategy but even more so for the glimpse it offers into their political partnership:

H — Speech writers
should see this if
they haven't — also
I like the idea of

having series of issue
events — but I'll defer
to you & yr team on what.
Love
B

The speechwriters *had* seen that Magaziner memo — and numerous others. On September 14, eight days before the scheduled address, the President's pollster, Stan Greenberg, gave his advice on themes and language. The speech should bring "a substantial lift" to the President, he wrote, echoing the views of the First Lady. "Our surveys as late as last night show rising support on health care. This speech can change the mood of the country."

Underlying those remarks was a concern about the increasingly negative feelings about Bill Clinton after less than eight months in office. Though voters were supportive of reform, Greenberg warned they were in "a skittish mood and only now coming to a more positive view of the President." His concern was the public impression of a President buffeted by one problem after another, many of his own making: the bungled drive to force the armed services to acknowledge and accept homosexuals; two failed nominations for attorney general, Zoë Baird and Kimba Wood, and a crawlback from his first choice, Lani Guinier, for the top civil rights enforcement post; defeat at the hands of a Senate Republican filibuster of the first piece of his economic plan. And more snafus and contretemps within the White House staff than anyone could remember.

All the more reason, Greenberg counseled, that the tone and text of this speech be exactly right. It should convey a sense of history and, most important, of simplicity. "We must set out a simple, core idea that captures the whole complicated exercise," the pollster wrote. Greenberg thought he had found the perfect device. It would be a Health Security card that everyone would carry, just as every American had a Social Security card. Greenberg had tested that idea in his focus groups and found that people liked having a universal Health Security card that guaranteed them comprehensive benefits that could never be taken away. The health card "outdistanced everything else in the [Clinton] plan by about 4:1."

Like Magaziner, Greenberg urged the need for humility and caution in what the President proposed. Americans must be constantly reassured "against the serious doubts that lie just below the surface."

Two-thirds of voters surveyed were dissatisfied with the health care system as a whole. But most were satisfied with their personal health care and insurance. The Clinton goal thus must be to reassure citizens that reform would "preserve and protect what is valued." Greenberg warned, however, "As many people fear that the government will screw up reform as fear that change will not happen." The key, he stressed, was that voters wanted Congress to take its time in making major changes. While an overwhelming majority of Americans believed the Clinton plan to be "a risk worth taking," he wrote, they needed to be reassured that the President was determined to "get it right." That meant emphasizing the reform process would be deliberate and inclusive, that it would embrace other ideas, that it would be bipartisan, that it would stress "we do not have all the answers."

Two days later, the first set of speechwriters delivered their first formal draft. Greenberg's reaction, as relayed in a faxed memo to the White House, was scathing. The draft was "pretty flat," it lacked passion and language to engage the public and the Congress. Discussion of the plan itself was "stilted and fragmented," the historical section "strange," raising all the anxieties about a system that people were coming to believe wouldn't be there when they needed it. Applause lines should be peppered throughout the speech. Pithy language should characterize the present system as "anti-business, anti-jobs, anti–middle class." Furthermore, he added, displaying the cynical art of the political media world: "When the President thanks HRC [Hillary Rodham Clinton], there should be a crafted line because there is a good chance this will be the sound bite."

Greenberg was not alone in offering caustic criticisms. The critiques came from the top down. The President was feeling badly pressured, but even more so was his staff. As time for the speech approached, staff members directly charged with developing the plan and seeking the best way to launch it reeled with fatigue and frustration. They already had spent months of wearying planning sessions; at times, Magaziner himself had slept on the couch in his Old Executive Office Building suite overlooking the Mall.

The two weeks leading up to the address were a nightmare. An entry in a diary kept by one staff member captured the feelings of many. Referring to the Clintons, this person wrote:

> I wonder how much Mr. and Mrs. think about the staff, about all the long hours, about all the people who are ready to be bruised, even trampled, in the name of the cause. Both of them can be faulted. He because of his conflict aversion, which leads to hands-off for personnel and hands-on for policy; it's easier to knock an idea or a plan than a person. She because of her drive and capriciousness. It sounds sexist but it's also very true. Every decision is changed at least twice and she bounces up and down before setting her answer in concrete. An unerring conviction that she is right. I can't imagine that they would be where they are today without these traits, but the impact on the staff cannot be underestimated.

Relentless pressure continued as the staff struggled to prepare for the speech and the launch. Political strategy meetings on how best to employ the President's and the First Lady's appearances after the speech produced even more conflicts and irresolution. Decisions were made and revised about what TV shows cabinet members and Democratic members of Congress would appear on — and then remade again. The result, one of those involved said sardonically, was "piss-poor planning and disastrous conflicts."

The carefully crafted plans for a two-week prespeech launch quickly collapsed as other events intervened. Nine days before the speech, Clinton's attention and the staff's efforts were suddenly shifted to arranging the historic peace-signing ceremony on the White House lawn between Israeli Prime Minister Yitzhak Rabin and Palestine Liberation Organization Chairman Yasir Arafat. At the same time, the White House was mobilizing for another highly promoted political event in which the President had great stakes. This was the gathering of three former Presidents — Ford, Carter, and Bush — whom Clinton had called to the White House to help win congressional approval for the hotly controversial North American Free Trade Agreement (NAFTA). That nationally telecast event was staged the very next day after the Israel-PLO ceremony, further diverting attention from health care.

Intense pressures affected everyone, not least the President. Twice in the few days leading up to the speech, he erupted in anger. The first time came when, visibly weary, he appeared in an early-morning drizzle in the White House Rose Garden, where he was to preside over a prespeech gathering of health care reform supporters. A tent had been placed on the grounds; when he walked inside he found aides had failed to provide a podium for him. Clinton launched into what an aide described as "a pissing fit." Many hours later, after an intensive round of meetings, the presidential temper surfaced again, this time as he stood behind his desk in the Oval Office. He lashed out angrily, his face flushed and his arms waving, at not having been given adequate background information for a media interview about to take place.

The President's temper was explosive. One of his aides who repeatedly witnessed it remarked, "He can really explode — blow, blow." Clinton's outbursts came suddenly. With reddened face and furious gestures, he would loudly inveigh against the culprit; then he would subside. He did not hold grudges or seek retribution. He did not keep score. He needed to vent; he did not want to confront.

Friday, Saturday, and Sunday before the President's Wednesday speech produced even greater pressures: 7:30 A.M. communications meeting; 8 A.M. War Room meeting; 8:30 A.M. Oval Office briefing; 8:45 A.M. "countdown" meeting in the office of Chief of Staff "Mack" McLarty, Clinton's boyhood friend and now White House overseer; 9 A.M. senior staff session on health care.

On and on the meetings went. At one session where the chief economic advisers tried to decide which taxes to put in the plan, a quip by Treasury's Roger Altman broke the tension. He said, "The last time I checked, the President was upstairs having a drink, smoking a cigar, and trying to make up his mind."

A meeting Sunday night was supposed to settle the speech questions. Gathered in the solarium on top of the White House above the family quarters to discuss the latest draft were key members of the President's team: the cabinet secretaries, the political consultants, the speechwriters, the White House chief of staff, and, of course, the First Lady and members of her team. When that skull session was over, most of the advisers thought it had gone well. But the President didn't like this draft. He thought it pedestrian. The First Lady agreed. By the next morning, both Clintons were determined to start over. Figuratively, the speech was thrown in the trash basket. The search for a new one, and a new speechwriter, began.

About eleven o'clock on the morning of the day before the speech, David Gergen, presidential counselor, called Jeremy Rosner, a young aide on the National Security Council who served as the President's principal speechwriter on foreign policy and defense.

Gergen was an anomaly among the top Clinton aides. Hardly any of them had ever worked in a White House, and all were chosen out of a background of belief in Clinton; they were, virtually without exception, idealistic young Democrats convinced that in serving this ambitious new President they were going to change America. Gergen was a stranger in their midst, personally and philosophically. He had worked in the campaigns or administrations of four Republican Presidents — Nixon, Ford, Reagan, and Bush — as a speechwriter and public relations, or "communications," adviser, and always with what appeared complete agreement with their political and ideological views.

To the dismay and resentment of the other Clinton aides, Gergen was recruited in early May by Mack McLarty for a rescue effort on the presidential image. Gergen and the Clintons had become acquainted at the annual New Year's Eve Renaissance Weekend gathering. When he agreed to help out, Gergen was given a special charter to improve the President's effort to communicate effectively with the American people, the press, and the political players in Washington. Now, he became the latest of the many aides, advisers, and consultants trying to take control of the stumbling White House effort to launch the reform battle.

He had just talked with the President and the First Lady, Gergen told Rosner. Both of the Clintons were upset with the draft they had been given. They wanted Rosner to take over and write the speech. So, Gergen urged, did he.

Rosner demurred. That wasn't his department, and besides, it wasn't fair to his friends on the President's speechwriting staff who had been laboring for days, weeks even, on the draft. Gergen pressed. The President and First Lady *really* wanted him to do this. They liked the well-received presidential remarks Rosner had prepared only days before for the Israel-PLO peace accord ceremony. Now Rosner had a chance to help forge a domestic policy triumph, Gergen said.

Finally Rosner agreed, but only if he could share the responsibility with his friend on the communications team, David Dreyer, with whom he had worked closely when both served Gary Hart on Capitol Hill in the mid-1980s, Rosner as Hart's chief speechwriter, Dreyer as his legislative director. Within the hour Rosner and Dreyer were summoned to meet the First Lady.

As they hurried to her West Wing office, another phase in the public relations strategy to begin the battle was under way. Outside, on the White House lawn, hundreds of radio talk show hosts from around the country, who had been invited to the White House to generate greater media attention for the launch, were setting up behind long tables covered in microphones and wires. It gave the White House grounds a country fair atmosphere. The talk show hosts had been invited to interview leading administration officials. Vice President Gore, Treasury Secretary Lloyd Bentsen, Health and Human Services Secretary Donna Shalala, and White House aides George Stephanopoulos and Robert Rubin, among many others, moved from table to table offering views about the plan.

The buzz of sound rising in the languid Indian Summer air, the administration and congressional officials lining up to be interviewed, the movement about the grounds all conveyed the sense of an extremely active presidency about to undertake something historic. But inside the White House, a state of chaos was rapidly approaching over this speech.

Come on in, you guys, the First Lady said to Rosner and Dreyer. Hillary Rodham Clinton knew exactly what she wanted. The speech has to be different, she told them, and here's how. We have to portray this as a voyage, a journey, for all Americans. Give it more lift, more vision. We have to stick to six principles: Quality. Responsibility. Choice. Savings. Simplicity. Security. These are the things I've been saying in my own speeches, she went on. She handed them a folder. It contained twenty to thirty pages of segments from her speeches, carefully organized into categories, complete with her handwritten notes. Included were full transcripts of what she'd been saying for months before general audiences and interest groups around the country.

Go through each segment, the First Lady said. Weave a little bit of this and a bit of that. Go to it.

Rosner and Dreyer left their session with the First Lady and went to Rosner's office on the third floor of the Old Executive Office Building overlooking the White House, where the foreign-policy experts were housed in distant isolation from the political operatives. They were a matched pair, two slim, dark-haired young men in their mid-thirties. Both exuded energy and confidence. Dreyer was the more flamboyant — his earring, ponytail, and loud ties had become trademarks during his days on the Hill — though Rosner had his own emphatic personality. He was an adventurer; he had scaled the Himalayas and was known among his friends for his quick, sharp witticisms. He was devoted to his family and so passionate a believer in democracy that he and his wife gave their young son the middle name "Mandela."

Once inside Rosner's office they disconnected the phones, told their staffs they were not to be disturbed, and closed the doors for six hours. "David and I had one of our usual sessions of writing," Rosner remembers. "He'll suggest something and I'll yell at him, and then he'll suggest something and I'll yell at him again, and we'll yell at each other for about ten minutes and then come up with a great sentence. We've got creative tension."

While this increasingly hectic scene was taking place behind closed doors, the President and First Lady appeared at ease and in good humor at an elaborate luncheon they gave for Washington-based national columnists and media commentators, many of whom had been critical of what they knew about the Clinton plan.

The setting was formal: the mirrored splendor of the Old Family Dining Room in the White House. After cocktails in the State Dining Room, the journalists filed next door and found their places marked by name cards graced by the fine art of White House calligraphers.

Luncheon began at 12:55 P.M. Before all the guests were served, the President opened a dialogue that lasted nearly an hour and a half. "As many of you know, this is a rather busy day at the White House," he said, drawing laughter. "We just had a wonderful signing ceremony for the national service bill, and we've got a couple of hundred radio talk show hosts here. Have you been over to see them yet?"

"I have," the First Lady, seated beside him, replied, recalling her meeting with the talk show hosts shortly before in an Executive Office Building auditorium.

"Was Limbaugh there?" the President asked, referring to Rush Limbaugh, the best known of the conservative talk radio hosts, and the most harshly critical of the Clintons.

"He didn't come," the First Lady answered, to more laughter. "In fact, I read somewhere that he said it was a plot to have been invited at a time when he couldn't be there. Or something. I don't know. I wish we could be that clever." More laughter.

Then the President, continuing to speak extemporaneously, got to the point of the meeting.

"I thought it might be helpful if we just had a little time to discuss the health care initiative," he said, "and if, at the end of the hour or hour and a half or however much time we have here, you want to ask a few other things, I think that would be fine with me.

"I'd like to make two points to open the discussion, one general and one specific. The general point I want to make is that I think profound change has happened in societies when essentially people understand that the cost of staying with the present course of action is greater than the cost of change; that the risks of staying with the present course of action are greater than the uncertain risks of any change.

"Franklin Roosevelt proposed the first bill to provide national security in health care in 1943, fifty years ago."

Hillary Clinton immediately spoke up. "In 'thirty-three," she corrected.

"In 'thirty-three," the President continued, " — sixty years ago.*

---

*The year the President originally cited was correct. The first insurance coverage bill was introduced in 1943, during FDR's third term.

And we've been debating this ever since. But I believe very strongly that this is a moment when it is likely to occur, because I think there is a shared consensus that the problems with the system and the escalating costs, and the escalating dysfunctions, with more and more losing their health insurance every month, are greater than the costs of change."

For the next hour and twenty minutes, the Clintons fielded a wide range of questions, a number of them quite critical in tone, as they alternated in responding to questions and expanding on each other's replies about their belief they would get a reform bill passed sometime in the next year.

The First Lady offered examples of how others outside Washington were already accomplishing significant cost reductions and improvements. "The average Medicare patient in Minnesota," she said, "is cared for at one-half the cost of the average Medicare patient in Philadelphia."

There shouldn't be that kind of differential, she went on. In Pennsylvania, she said, a coronary bypass operation ranged from $21,000 to $84,000, with no difference in quality of medical procedure or outcome for the patient. "Why do we pay eighty-four thousand dollars for an operation that can be performed very well with good outcomes for far less than that?" she asked, adding, "See, most people who are out there on the front lines of trying to make these health care decisions have been very supportive of what we're trying to do. When I was at [Minnesota's] Mayo Clinic last Friday night, [they told me] they've gotten their costs down to 3.9 percent."

Back and forth the Clintons went. They poured out a wealth of facts and figures; they seemed entirely comfortable, highly informed, and responsive; there were no fumbles. It was a tour de force. Even their strongest critics in that room were impressed, if not persuaded.

It was early evening before Rosner and Dreyer finished their draft. By then, George Stephanopoulos was feeling frantic. He had left message after message, each time imploring, Where's the draft? Where's the draft?

Rosner had a printout distributed to all involved — among them

Stephanopoulos, for the President; the First Lady; Magaziner; Gergen; and other key aides, chief among them the outside political consultants who played so prominent, if not extraordinary, roles in the Clinton White House after helping him win the presidency. Though they were unelected and unappointed, the consultants had virtually unlimited access to all the President's and the First Lady's decision-making sessions. They were the equals, if not the superiors, of Clinton's top appointed aides.

Stan Greenberg, the President's pollster, was foremost among them. A small man with a small moustache, he appeared mild and thoughtful, as befits a former political science professor who had profitably turned to political consulting and polling. But Greenberg was a tough, formidable fighter: Clinton aides had learned to cross him at their peril. That was even more true of Mandy Grunwald. Tall and angular, intense and chain-smoking, she was nothing if not aggressive. Grunwald was the thirty-four-year-old Harvard-educated daughter of Henry Grunwald, the former editor in chief of *Time*. Nearly everyone who dealt with her found her arrogant and confrontational. But not Hillary Clinton, who highly valued Grunwald's counsel on how to frame and deliver the White House message on controversial questions. Both Bill and Hillary Clinton respected the third outside consultant, Paul Begala, a liberal Democrat whose style was to respond to any criticism of the Clintons by launching political attacks. Another in that group was Bob Boorstin of the White House communications office.

All of them had a great personal stake in winning reform, but none more so than Boorstin. He had even more reason to feel a special sense of anticipation about that outcome, and his contribution to it.

Bob Boorstin suffered from manic-depressive illness. In the summer of 1987, while working as a reporter for the *New York Times*, he was hospitalized after a manic episode. He left the paper, then joined the presidential campaign staff of Michael Dukakis in Massachusetts. In the midst of that campaign, while in Boston, he had another manic episode and was admitted to Massachusetts General Hospital, where he found himself strapped to a gurney. When contacted, Boorstin's psychiatrist recommended he be transferred to McLean Hospital, specializing in mental illness treatment. Before McLean approved his admittance, they said they had to check Boorstin's insurance.

Several years before, Boorstin had purchased a personal insurance policy that supposedly provided the best, most comprehensive coverage: Major Medical 100, with a $100 deductible. It covered everything, or so Boorstin thought. He was wrong. Boorstin had reached his limit on mental health coverage; McLean wouldn't admit him unless an astronomical advance payment was guaranteed.

Bob Boorstin, Harvard graduate, former editor in chief of the school's daily *Crimson*, holder of a master's degree in international relations from Cambridge, nephew of Daniel J. Boorstin, distinguished historian and former Librarian of Congress, son of Hannah Cohn Boorstin, also a gifted writer, who was married to the film director Alan Pakula, was strapped to a hospital gurney with no place to go.

Unable to reach his parents immediately, McLean called his twin brother, Louis, on the trading floor of Lehman Brothers. To get his brother admitted, Louis had to guarantee a payment of $18,000.

Bob Boorstin emerged from that experience an advocate for those suffering from mental illness. He sued his insurance company on grounds they had discriminated against him because of his illness. Eventually, he won. From there, he began studying insurance practices worldwide. When he joined the Clinton campaign, he said he wanted to be an adviser to Clinton on health issues. Since then, his work inside the White House had made him even more determined to fight for real reform.

As the time for the speech approached, Boorstin found himself working harder, sleeping less. On the morning of the speech, he was up at 5:15, jogging in the cool late-September air. As he ran, he reflected on the palpable sense of history he, and others, felt this day. Renewed by that spirit, he spoke about his hospital experiences at the White House early-morning staff meeting, telling his colleagues how proud he was to work with them and apologizing for any irritable behavior he might have displayed.

Meanwhile, at breakfast in the White House family quarters, Clinton handed over his heavily edited version of the Rosner-Dreyer draft to his principal advisers. They found it studded with his hand-written notes, suggestions, even symbols — Clinton had inked triangles, his favorite symbol for change, wherever he wanted a change in the text: " — Δ — Dislocation — uncertainty-Future w/Fear — in trust gov't — Central goal: Dynamic Soc — create new jobs. . . . Compare to — Δ — reg. Security . . . Confid in Future —" He had also drafted completely new passages.

Where the speechwriters had begun "Tonight, those of us in this room, and those of you in your homes, have come . . ." he had edited the text to read "Tonight, we come together . . ." Where they had written that the American story started over 350 years ago, he had drafted "Our forebears enshrined the American Dream: life, liberty, the pursuit of happiness. Every generation of Americans has worked to strengthen that legacy . . ."

Once again, a unique speech-writing process began. "I don't know how to describe it," one White House staff member said, "but that whole group assembles. You can sense the vibrations. They buzz around each other. Depending where the President is, the action moves to various rooms. Everyone becomes the speechwriter, everyone has an opinion, everyone has an equal say. They move together in this frantic little bevy. First they go to Dreyer's office, then move to the First Lady's office, then to the Oval Office. You'll see them crossing West Executive Avenue together. They move as a pack."

Now the pack began to move again. They descended on Rosner's office, where the rewriting — and rerewriting — was under way. Long before, Clinton's aides had learned to tape his words at these final speech-strategy sessions. Now, transcripts of the President's verbatim remarks at breakfast were being faxed to Rosner's office, directed toward either Rosner or Dreyer.

To: Jeremy
From: POTUS [President of the United States]
"We haven't always known exactly how we would get there, but we've always known where we are going. This is a time of

profound change, profound opportunity, and profound dislocation and uncertainty. A lot of people are facing the future
with fear. They don't know if they can trust their government . . ."

To: Jeremy
Faxed to Dreyer 1:27 P.M.
"Five years ago, three-fourths of the American people were
able to choose between more than one health insurance plan.
Today, fewer than half of us have the freedom to choose our
health plan. Under the present system, your choices are eroding. Under our system, your choices will be expanding . . ."

Other faxes from POTUS followed.

To: Jeremy
Faxed to Dreyer P.M.
[Where he refers to his mother . . .]
"My mother was a nurse. I grew up around hospitals. The
first professional people I ever looked up to were doctors and
nurses. And doctors and nurses were the first to tell us there is
a lot wrong with the system . . ."

After three o'clock now, approaching four. Five hours to go.
Stephanopoulos calls. The President's waiting for the draft so he can
practice his delivery in the White House family theater, a small auditorium in the East Wing opposite the First Lady's sculpture garden.
It resembles a movie theater with rows of seats rising from the floor
level, where the President stands to try out his speech.

Sometime after five o'clock, the pack moves into the theater. The
First Lady is wearing her sweatsuit. Of all those in the room, the
President seems most calm. He's in a good mood, relaxed. As with
previous speech practices, the President stands at the lectern, the
TelePrompTer off, as he reads aloud sentence by sentence. Often, he
challenges what he's read. Why are we framing it this way? he says.
The people in the packed room respond. Changes are made.

Standing behind the last row of seats, watching this chaotic scene
in amazement, a military cameraman from the White House whis-
pers to a presidential aide. He can't believe what he's seeing, he says.

When Ronald Reagan was President, he would come into the theater by himself a few days before his scheduled address, read the text from the prompter twice without changes, then walk out.

Not Clinton. He approaches his speech as a performance artist rather than as an orator or writer. The advantage is he becomes more intimately involved in the sinews of the text and makes it his own. That will stand him in good stead this night.

The clock continues to tick. After six now. Later and later the hour hand moves. The theater practice goes on.

Finally the First Lady tells the speechwriters, Look, you guys have to fold these changes into the text.

Some of the aides peel off and head for the first-floor West Wing office of White House communications director Mark Gearan, a political operative and veteran of Capitol Hill, the Michael Dukakis presidential campaign, and the Democratic Governors' Association, where he first worked closely with Bill Clinton. Near bedlam now. Some huddle around the computer, frantically incorporating changes. Others scramble to check anecdotes the President or First Lady has suggested for inclusion that day, some only a few minutes earlier. Clinton is especially effective in citing personal examples. Two that he recalled in the family theater involved a recent visit he and Hillary made to Children's Hospital in Washington, D.C., "where they do wonderful, often miraculous things for children." The President spoke of his dismay at hearing a nurse in the cancer and bone marrow unit say she had to leave the side of a child during chemotherapy treatment because she had been instructed to attend a class on how to fill out another form. A doctor there told the Clintons she didn't go into medicine to spend up to twenty-five hours a week filling out forms. And the President recalled how doctors applauded when he told them the administration's reform research demonstrated that cutting paperwork requirements in that one hospital would permit staff doctors to see ten thousand more children a year. How can we fact-check that Children's Hospital story? an aide shouts. Can we verify that now? They do so, placing quick last-minute phone calls. It goes into the text.

In the family theater the remainder of the President's team listens as Clinton continues to read aloud and make changes. Each time a page from the text is completed, an aide takes it and runs from the ground floor of the residence, where the theater is located, to Gearan's first-floor office to enter more changes in the final text. The sounds of heels clicking on marble floors echo through the mansion.

After eight o'clock now, approaching eight-thirty, only half an hour before time for the nine o'clock national telecast in the Capitol. Many of the President's aides begin moving toward the presidential motorcade forming outside on the south lawn driveway. Among them is Bob Boorstin. He finds himself sitting next to an exhausted Ira Magaziner, who has been without sleep for nearly sixty-five hours preparing for this moment. As Magaziner waits for the motorcade to depart, he is seized by two conflicting feelings: sheer exhaustion and excitement.

Five minutes later, Dreyer enters the final speech changes into the computer, makes the three copies of the diskette bearing the text, then races for the motorcade just as it leaves for Capitol Hill.

3

The Players

JAY ROCKEFELLER relaxed. His initial concern over Clinton's beginning passed; now, as he listened, he became excited. Clinton was giving the best speech on a major public-policy issue that Rockefeller had ever heard a President deliver.

Rockefeller's interest was far from academic. Few senators were as passionately committed to reform, few had worked harder to achieve it. On the surface, his passion appeared somewhat curious. He was, after all, a Rockefeller, the fourth generation to bear the name of John D. Rockefeller, the original robber baron. The advantages his name and fortune provided had shaped his life. But there was no doubting his sincerity on this issue. More than thirty years before, he was a Peace Corps aide in the Kennedy administration. During the Johnson presidency, he became a VISTA poverty program volunteer in West Virginia, where he later became governor. Now that he was a senator, health care was a major concern.

More than do-goodism or political ambition motivated him. To Rockefeller, reform was an imperative. His mother died of Alzheimer's disease, a long, lingering terrible decline that affected him profoundly.

He would speak of this from time to time, and once brought a room filled with burly union members to tears as he recalled how over years he watched his mother lose control and become another person. It reached the point where she would get up at two o'clock in the morning, put on two dresses, go into the kitchen and say she wanted breakfast, without remembering anything that happened.

On trips to see her in New York, sometimes he would lie in her lap, sobbing, as he looked into her eyes and found her staring vacantly, showing no recognition of her only son. "What makes me so angry and what is unfair," Rockefeller told the union members, "is that there are four million people here in America who have Alzheimer's today. And they don't have the luck that my three sisters and I have. They can't afford a fifty-thousand-dollar nurse for eight hours a day. . . . So, sure, I've got personal reasons why I am passionate about health care. And I don't apologize for them. But it makes me angry to see congressmen and senators who will not make the hard votes, who are afraid of criticism, who won't stand up and make a hard vote and have PACs [political action committees] . . . throw money against them in their next election."

He felt especially involved with the Clintons and their attempt to achieve real reform; he had, in fact, been largely responsible for creating the coalition of pro-reform groups to campaign for passage of the Clinton plan and had opened his mansion in Rock Creek Park (with the John Singer Sargent portrait of his dour great-grandfather hanging in the hallway) to them for their first strategy meeting.

To Rockefeller, what was finally being launched this night was the most massive, controversial, and important social legislation in American history, one that made, as he said, Social Security look like "an add on, de minimus." Medicare, which took a decades-long struggle to enact, was another add on, de minimus. Aside from the personal stakes of everyone involved, he believed health care reform to be an issue that represented nothing less than the economic health and future of the United States.

From his personal dealings with the President, Rockefeller knew those early months in the White House came as a real shock to Clinton. They were hurtful, bewildering. The President was still fundamentally upbeat, but fully aware of the new doubts about him. That's why this moment was so critical. If Clinton does it right, it's his second term, his legacy, his resurrection, Rockefeller said shortly before the speech, adding,

My understanding of Bill Clinton starts with the fact that he's the first person who's ever been President of the United States who was an abused child. If you are an abused child, you can withdraw into yourself, be angry, be vicious. Or you can want everyone to like you. Obviously, he's of the second school. He wants people so much to believe in what he's doing. Health care expresses not only his youth, but expresses his success — he cut the infant mortality rate in half in Arkansas — and it expresses his love of people. It's basic. It combines everything. It's justice, it's fairness. It's making the economy work, it's giving us a future. I think the two of them — he and Hillary — will be brilliant at it.

That hope could be fulfilled, he thought, only if Clinton did well this night. No, he must do better than well. The President would succeed only if he connected emotionally with the American people. In effect, Clinton must re-ignite the rising public anger that had swept Harris Wofford into office two years before. Though he would never acknowledge it publicly, Rockefeller believed the prospects for passage of major reform were at best little more than fifty-fifty. The prospect of defeat was, as he said privately then, "very real." All the more reason that this moment be seized and its opportunity fulfilled.

Now he was on his feet cheering. It was going even better than he could have hoped.

Edward Moore (Ted) Kennedy of Massachusetts was no less involved. More than any other senator, he was identified with health care, and better than anyone in that chamber he knew how strong opposition was. Three times over past decades he had tried to pass national health insurance. Each time his bills had failed. Like Rockefeller, he greatly admired both Clintons. Clinton, he thought, was the first President who really understood the immensely complicated issue, the first who could articulate it publicly. The same was so, he felt, with Hillary Clinton — a "superstar," he called her privately — with whom he had spent hours in conversation through these early presidential months. Like Rockefeller, Kennedy believed this was a moment of historic opportunity, the most favorable in all his years in Congress. It was not easy, of course, and he knew that many of his fellow Democrats were deeply doubtful about prospects for real reform.

Daniel Patrick (Pat) Moynihan of New York was one of them. With his trademark bow tie, arching eyebrows, pink cheeks, high-pitched voice with slight stammer, and pixie demeanor, Moynihan was unlike anyone in that chamber of strong wills and highly developed egos. No one understood the theoretical principles of government better than this former Harvard professor who emerged out of the poverty of New York's Hell's Kitchen to serve Presidents as different as John Kennedy and Richard Nixon on domestic policy in the cabinet and on foreign affairs as U.S. ambassador to India and to the United Nations. As new chairman of the powerful Senate Finance Committee, Moynihan would have a critical role in the passage of any reform bill.

Now, as he listened to Clinton, he thought, America faces many troubling questions, but health care is not that serious. It's immensely complex and probably too much for us. But he was a loyal Democrat and would do his best. In the end, he believed, they would get something done. He thought that because he was convinced he would strike a deal with Bob Dole, the Republican leader in the Senate.

Many eyes were on Robert J. Dole of Kansas this night.

Of all the complex political figures present, Dole was surely among the most complicated, as Bill Clinton already had learned. The President, like Moynihan, thought he would be able to strike a deal with the Republican leader. It was not just wishful thinking on Clinton's part, and the President knew that Dole was a potential presidential rival. But Clinton also believed Dole to be a blunt straight shooter. The President remembered Dole telling him privately in Clinton's first week in the White House that the Republicans had already decided that there would not be any votes from their ranks for Clinton's critical first budget. There was no use for the President to try to compromise with the Republicans, the President heard Dole say; they had met and decided not to vote for the new budget after the President sent it to Congress. But that same intransigence did not apply to health reform, Clinton believed. In the months leading up to this speech whenever the President saw Dole, the Republican leader would tell him, "We'll work something out."

Though already seventy that night, having celebrated that mile-stone exactly two months before, Bob Dole had a youthful bearing. He bristled with energy. Tall, slim, dark-haired, he was one of the most skilled legislators in that chamber. He also had long been in the forefront of those working for reform, but that desire collided with another: He wanted to be President and was weighing one last presidential attempt in 1996. Would he hurt his chances by helping Clinton pass a bill whose general goals he himself believed to be in the national interest? Or would he work to defeat it, permitting him-self to lead that fight another day and be credited as the leader who accomplished reform?

Presidential ambition was also a factor in the thinking of another major Republican player, Phil Gramm of Texas.

Gramm was hot, emotional, one of the bloc of erstwhile conserva-tive Sunbelt Democrats who had rejected the northern and west-ern liberal wings of their party to become Republicans. His thick drawl, slightly owlish look as he squinted through rimless specta-cles, and his stridently ideological phrases had made him an in-creasingly familiar figure on TV and radio talk shows. Now, as he intently watched Clinton, Gramm found himself eager to talk to his "mama," as he always referred to her, because Clinton had touched on one of Gramm's mother's pet peeves in life, the high costs of pharmaceutical bills. The President, Gramm felt, was scoring public points.

As a Civil War buff — he kept a Confederate pistol and rawhide holster with the initials "C.S.," for Confederate States, displayed in his Senate office — Gramm recalled the line that Joshua Lawrence Chamberlain used at Gettysburg in the critical defense of Little Round Top. "We've got to be stubborn today," Chamberlain had said to himself. Gramm felt much the same. They would have to be stubborn, he thought, to defeat this onslaught. Gramm knew that many Republicans thought the Clinton reform was a runaway train about to roar through the station. It made them either want to get on it or wave flags in support as it passed. Gramm was seized with a different determination. This train has to be stopped, he thought. "We have to blow this train up."

John Chafee of Rhode Island had no such destructive thoughts.

If Gramm was the new version of the Republican Party — "the rancorous right," a fellow Republican said of the increasingly aggressive "brook no compromise" GOP conservatives — Chafee represented the old. His was the traditional Republican Party, careful, moderate, neither liberal nor conservative, but progressive in spirit and action. This wing of the party was rapidly declining; Chafee perfectly reflected the best of its diminishing ranks.

In personal conversation, Chafee was mild and wryly self-deprecating. But he knew who he was, and once convinced of a position would defend it tenaciously. On health care, Chafee was determined. Chafee knew that other Republican senators were counseling hands off. Let Democrats go out into that minefield, they would say in their private strategy meetings. Why should we help them and give Bill Clinton another ticket to the White House? Chafee disagreed. And, he was convinced, so did other Republicans who wanted to achieve reform in this Congress. "It is of momentous importance to our country and we want to be key players in a constructive way trying to solve these problems," Chafee said, assessing legislative prospects just before the speech.

Such admirable political selflessness was not shared by other key Republican strategists. One was Haley Barbour, the portly and drawling — and shrewd — national party chairman from Mississippi. Barbour saw in Clinton's political weakness an opportunity to score big Republican gains.

Throughout Clinton's first year, as the health care issue moved to center stage, Barbour's greatest fear, and one he shared privately with other conservatives, was that Clinton would publicly embrace a reform bill proposed by a Republican moderate like Chafee. The bill would pass. Democrats and Clinton would profit politically, dashing Republican chances for gains in the 1994 midterm congressional elections and beyond. "We'll be sitting there like bumps on a log," Barbour said. "We'll be cooked."

Barbour's belief that a number of Republican supporters would combine with the Democratic majorities to pass a bill was held by many in that chamber. But private doubts also ran high.

George Mitchell of Maine shared them.

Publicly, the Senate majority leader expressed strong confidence that this Congress would pass major reform. Privately, he had doubts whether a bill could pass. The odds for passage would have been zero, he would say, had it not been for the intense public efforts of the President and the First Lady. "No President in my time here has taken on an issue of such significance," he would say. "The Presidents I've served under are Carter, Reagan, Bush, and Clinton. Certainly none of them has gotten so deeply involved in this issue personally, acquired the knowledge, and pursued it with such doggedness as Clinton."

But if reform was to succeed, it would not occur without the determined efforts of the Senate majority leader. George Mitchell was nothing if not determined. He would need that persistence to lead the fight, especially when confronted by an increasingly polarized Senate.

Barely a glimmer of bipartisanship animated the House. With each passing session of Congress, relations between House Democrats and Republicans had grown more embittered and divisive. Frustrated and angry at their long decades as members of what seemed a permanent minority, and by what they fairly regarded as contemptuous mistreatment by overbearing Democrats in power, Republicans more and more turned to tactics of defiance and warfare. They targeted not only Democratic rivals; with equal fervor, they attacked older, more moderate, leaders of their own party.

A new, more combative Republican House was emerging. This session would mark the last in which Robert H. Michel of Peoria, Illinois, a seventy-year-old mainstream midwesterner shaped by World War II infantry service, with a reverence for traditional political institutions, would lead House Republicans. Michel's retirement plans were known to all present and would be formally announced two weeks after Clinton's address.

In actuality, Michel's power long since had shifted to the de facto leader of the House Republicans, Newt Gingrich of Georgia. Of all those present in the House chamber, Gingrich was perhaps the most interesting and quixotic — and, to his many foes, the most infuriating. Fifty years old, tall and plump, with a shag of prematurely white hair surrounding his round face like a helmet, with his rumpled suits and theatrical manner Gingrich resembled what a critic once said of the playwright and columnist Heywood Broun: He was an unmade bed. But there was nothing casual about this aggressive former history professor. He was ebullient and cocky, sternly ideological and combative, a politician always in motion and always on the attack. His mobile face, with crooked smile exposing small teeth, gave him a terrierlike appearance; the comparison was apt. He was persistent, he was dogged, he was snarling. He never let go.

Gingrich differed from his older colleagues in both parties in an important respect. Where they tended to have great respect for the traditions and practices of their institution in The System, often preferring the quiet and unspectacular — but necessary — work of private negotiation and consensus-building, Gingrich directed his attention at the public beyond the Congress. His sharp tongue and flamboyant attacks on his Democratic opponents were becoming familiar, through television, to Americans beyond the Washington Beltway. He viewed himself as a political visionary, indeed, as a revolutionary, and reveled in attacking, always before the cameras, what he constantly referred to as a corrupt and arrogant Democratic Congress out of touch with ordinary Americans. His very outrageousness, his contemptuousness toward those who criticized or opposed him, led some either to underrate or dismiss him. They thought he was too hot and too controversial to become a major player in The System. That was a mistake.

Newt Gingrich's goal was to forge a new System, one that he would construct out of the wreckage of the old. A Democratic health reform plan of the kind Bill Clinton was now proposing was anathema to Gingrich. And now, as he watched the President deliver what Gingrich thought was a superb speech, Gingrich took comfort in having foreseen this moment — and having already taken steps to oppose it. In the spring of 1991, more than a year before the Democrats nominated Clinton, Gingrich was discussing long-term political strategy with a friend as they strolled around the Washington Monument at about six o'clock one morning. In a moment that he recalled vividly, Gingrich was seized by the conviction that the "next great offensive of the Left," as he put it, would be "socializing health care," because the Left, as he put it, was "gradually losing power on all other fronts, and they had to have an increase in the resources they controlled. We had to position ourselves in the fight before they got there or they might win."

From that moment until this night nearly two and a half years later, Gingrich prepared to defeat the very kind of plan now being proposed. No support would come from Gingrich and the restive Republicans he led, especially support for a President of Gingrich's own post–World War II generation who possessed, Gingrich believed, formidable political gifts with potential for becoming another FDR.

House Democrats knew they could not expect a single Republican vote. They would have to win this by themselves. So they could. They had the control, they had the votes, they had the power. The question was whether Democrats had the unity of purpose and the urgency to act.

In the Speaker's chair, directly behind Clinton as the President spoke, was Thomas S. Foley of the state of Washington.

Foley was the mirror-opposite of Gingrich: self-effacing, collegial, a public servant who believed in comity and a search for political consensus. Even his demeanor set him apart from Gingrich. A tall, rangy man, with a long face marked by creases and large ears and a solemn, at times almost mournful look, at the age of sixty-four Foley seemed serious to a fault. In private, he was a wry and delightful teller of stories; in public, he maintained a more subdued manner as befit, he seemed to think, his responsibilities not only as leader of House Democrats but as the Speaker, who stood third in constitutional succession to the presidency. However reserved his public manner, Foley was a passionate believer in The System and proud of the record Democrats had made in expanding, through government, rights and entitlements to all citizens.

But he had also experienced the recent public backlash against the glut of Great Society legislation, and it made him cautious about pushing for big breakthroughs. Too cautious, said some of the younger Democrats, who thought Foley had lost the fire and drive a Speaker needed. But the widespread respect — shared by many of the veteran Republicans, as well — for his personal integrity and decency quelled any rebellion against Foley.

Personally, Foley had serious doubts about the scope and timing of the Clintons' sweeping effort, but did not, of course, express them publicly.

He turned over the management of the project to Majority Leader Dick Gephardt of Missouri, the hard-driving milkman's son and Eagle Scout with an earnest Howdy Doody look, who was accustomed to being in the legislative engine room while Foley stayed up on the bridge.

Gephardt was no newcomer to the issue. In 1977, back in the Carter administration, when he was a thirty-six-year-old House freshman from St. Louis, Secretary of Health, Education and Welfare Joseph A. Califano Jr. had been pressing for an administration bill to slow the growth of hospital costs. Gephardt had helped derail that bill, an action he later publicly recanted. In more recent years, the failure to reform health care was his great political frustration. As early as 1991, Gephardt got large numbers of Democratic members to hold town meetings in their home districts, setting the stage for what he hoped would be a big legislative push. He thought that if the Democrats could agree on a measure and send it to the White House, where President Bush was likely to veto it, then the issue would be at the center of the 1992 campaign — a race he was contemplating making himself but ultimately turned down.

But in 1991 he couldn't get the Democrats into line. "We came very close," he told the Clintons when they launched their effort, "but I was never able to get them to see any agreement on this."

Still, Gephardt, as upbeat as Foley was inclined to be skeptical, also told the Clintons early in the presidency that the earlier discussions had "cleared away a lot of misunderstandings" and "prepared the ground" for what they were going to do. On the night of the speech, he was not alone in thinking the time had arrived for the Democrats to deliver on one of their oldest unfulfilled pledges. Gephardt and Foley both understood that House passage of reform would rest more in the hands of the old barons, whose grip on critical committees represented the real balance of power in that chamber. As Clinton spoke, the TV cameras panned the room, focusing briefly on some of those barons.

There was Dingell of Michigan — "Johnny" Dingell, as labor's

Lane Kirkland called him privately out of long familiarity over years of joining him in political battles.

Tough and blunt, with the solid build of a Mack truck and the stern steamroller manner to match, Dingell at sixty-seven was secure in his exercise of power. His Energy and Commerce Committee was critical in passage of reform legislation, and he ruled it with an iron hand. Helping pass this reform would be a crowning point of John D. Dingell's congressional career, and a matter of intense family pride. His father, for whom he was named, had also been a congressman from Michigan and had sat in that same chamber when Franklin Roosevelt proposed Social Security. The senior Dingell became an ardent battler to provide Americans universal coverage. Now the son, after thirty-eight years in Congress, ranking sixth in seniority of all members, was in a position to fulfill that personal legacy. He was determined to do so.

In the House seats nearby was another prototype of a powerful Democrat pol. With his craggy face, square jaw, gravelly voice, and the frame of a meat packer, Danny Rostenkowski of Chicago was a chip off the old block of the urban school of politics that for decades had been a centerpiece of the Democratic Party.

Dan Rostenkowski, or "Rosty," as everyone called him, came to Congress four years after Dingell. Now, at sixty-five, he ranked eighth in seniority. The Clintons courted him assiduously, and for good reason. They counted on him to deliver the crucial support of his powerful Ways and Means Committee. As a consummate deal maker among deal makers, Rosty loved the power-broker role. And he was committed to the Clintons, whose backgrounds and age were so different from his own; he sometimes referred to them affectionately as "the kids." Bluff and gregarious, almost brutal at times in his outspokenness, he was also capable of expressing strong reservations about them, sometimes directly to them.

But reservations aside, Rosty was a team player. When the time came to deliver, he would do so. The problem was that he was under investigation by a federal grand jury in Washington, D.C., looking into his use of congressional office funds and payroll accounts. Leaks from the prosecutors suggested Rosty might be charged with converting his official vouchers for House post office stamps into cash, of having "ghost payrollers," of mingling personal and official funds. The investigation had begun under the Bush Justice Department; rumors this night were that an indictment could come down at any time.

Another player in the chamber as Clinton spoke was the bearded James McDermott, fifty-six, of Washington state, leader of the "single-payer" bloc of House Democrats, who supported the federal government–financed universal program modeled on that of Canada. On this night, a single-payer bill had the names of eighty-nine Democratic supporters; only the Republican alternative, assembled by Bob Michel's task force the year before, had more.

Of the 535 members of Congress, Jim McDermott was one of a relative handful who could claim real expertise in the debate. A physician himself, and a practicing psychiatrist, McDermott represented the Vietnam-era generation of Americans whose experience with that war changed their lives.

In medical school, his goal was to become an academic — either dean of a medical school or head of a department of psychiatry. Then Vietnam. McDermott finished his medical training in the midst of the war, with a two-year obligation to serve. From 1968 to 1970, he was on active duty at the Long Beach Naval Station dealing with the rising number of casualties then pouring back from Vietnam. Until then, he had had only minimal interest in politics. Vietnam changed that. "Essentially, I became radicalized politically," he would recall. "I was very angry about the war and thought about leaving the country. Ultimately, I served my two years but decided that, as a psychiatrist, you either have to try to get people to live with the world as it is or try to change it."

From that came his decision to enter public life. Immediately upon leaving the service, he ran for the Washington state legislature. He won. Two years later he ran for governor on a platform of getting America out of the war. He lost. "I didn't know anything about politics," he said. "I was green as grass and got my ass kicked." All that time he was also practicing psychiatry at the University of Washington in Seattle.

McDermott's gubernatorial defeat brought him to another career decision: He was going to be serious about politics and treat it like a profession. For six years, while continuing to serve in the legislature, he studied his new craft. Finally, in 1980 he won his party's gubernatorial nomination from the sitting governor, then, along with other progressives, was wiped out by the Reagan conservative tide.

That was it for politics, McDermott thought. He spent several years in Africa with the U.S. State Department until, in 1989, he learned that a "safe" congressional seat had opened up in his home district of Seattle. He ran for only one reason: to go to the capital to work on national health reform. "I've always been ashamed and mad at the health care professionals for allowing this system to exist where we have all these inequities and waste and craziness that's in it," he explained. "Especially when you can see other systems that work." He won.

Once in Congress, he immediately began putting his reform ideas into practice. Convinced that Clinton was embarking on the greatest social change in America since 1934, McDermott began reading histories of the Roosevelt New Deal era. The lessons he drew were not reassuring. FDR had planned to accomplish national health insurance in 1935 when he introduced Social Security, and was overwhelmed by organized opposition to it. He dropped health reform as too controversial and proceeded with Social Security. In decades since, other Presidents had tried and failed.

Clinton's approach was fundamentally flawed, McDermott thought. The President was trying to achieve universal coverage mainly by controlling costs. That was fine; costs had to be contained, but the reality of reform was much more complicated. And Clinton was beginning this battle with his forces seriously doubtful and divided.

Privately, McDermott thought this effort doomed. "We're not going to pass anything," he said two and a half months before Clinton's speech. "Now you'll never hear me say that publicly. You'll see me out there cheering."

There were many reasons for his pessimism, but he was most concerned about two factors: division and doubts about the Clinton plan — and doubts about Clinton himself — among Democrats.

Of even greater concern was the powerful opposition of organized interests.

"Everybody ought to go out and see the movie *Gallipoli*," McDermott said in his office before Clinton's speech, "because we are like the colonials in *Gallipoli*. The British generals have sent the Australians and the New Zealanders and the Irish and all the rest out there to get themselves chopped up. And they've [the Clintons] pulled the rug out from under us on other controversial issues. So you've got wounded, bruised troops who are not so sure they trust their officers. They've got to look at where their troops are before they run us out into the kind of fire this is going to be."

He leaned forward in his chair, and said emphatically, "We're taking on the medical industrial complex. I'm talking about a terribly complicated, highly sophisticated economic power, the sixth-largest economy in the world, in fact. Yes, the U.S. health care industry, the nine hundred fifty billion dollars that we're fiddling with here. And they're sending raggedy-ass troops out there led by officers that nobody's quite sure we trust."

Now, listening to Clinton speak, McDermott was reassured. Several times during the address, he felt overwhelmed by emotion. This was one of those rare moments, he thought, when you really are part of history. It's just dumb Irish luck that I'm present at such a moment after being in Congress for only four years, he said to himself.

Looking around the chamber, McDermott saw John Dingell. He remembered reading about how Dingell's father had fought for reform, and wondered how Dingell must be feeling now. McDermott had sensed the President's initial nervousness. When the President stumbled there at the beginning, McDermott thought Clinton seemed overcome with emotion. But the President had quickly recovered.

McDermott's respect for the President rose. However it comes out, the President's willing to lay his political career on the line, he thought. We wouldn't be here if it weren't for his courage in bringing the issue up. Once the ball's in our court, we'll do the massaging from behind the scenes. It will still be extremely difficult to pass a major piece of legislation. But the odds have improved.

Now we have about a fifty-fifty chance, he thought. Maybe even better.

A block away, in the massive Rayburn House Office Building on Capitol Hill, S. Jackson (Jack) Faris, fifty-one, was thinking similar thoughts, but from a different political perspective.

It was obvious to Faris that something was wrong with the TelePrompTer when the President began speaking. Clinton seemed to be tentative, feeling his way. Faris wondered if it was possible the President was going to ignore his text and speak off-the-cuff.

Yes, Faris thought, it was possible. He'd seen Clinton do that at the fiftieth-anniversary celebration of the organization Faris headed, the National Federation of Independent Business, the powerful lobbying group representing six hundred thousand small businesses across America. NFIB was already mobilizing in opposition to Clinton's proposal to impose a so-called "employer mandate" requiring every business owner to have insurance for every employee. So threatened by the Clinton reform were Faris and his NFIB that he had left a conference in Europe and flown to Washington to watch it and respond.

As he watched, Faris saw Clinton become impassioned, speaking with confidence. It was absolutely wonderful, he thought. Those six points he made about what he wants for America are wonderful. The problem is the President's giving broad generalizations upon which everyone can agree. Wouldn't you like everyone to have health insurance? Yes. Wouldn't you like everyone to have a Fortune 500 plan? Yes. But there was a disconnect, especially when you tried to simplify something this complex. If you ask people if they want to pay for their insurance or have their employer pay it, naturally they'll want somebody else to pay for it. But wait a minute, Faris said to himself. Who really pays for it? The consumer pays for it. *I* pay for it.

Another lobbyist in that Rayburn Building room felt equally concerned about the direction this fight seemed headed. Willis (Bill) Gradison knew the Clinton White House was upset with him and the organization he represented, the Health Insurance Association of America (HIAA), for the "Harry and Louise" ads HIAA was running nationally.

Gradison was one of those familiar Washington figures, a former member of Congress turned lobbyist. A respected moderate Republican from Cincinnati, where he and his father had been leaders of city government, he knew the players, public and private. And he knew The System, and how to maneuver in it. He was concerned about White House criticism of the Harry and Louise ads, he had told Richard (Dick) Celeste, a former governor of Ohio whom Clinton had named to lead the Democratic National Committee's efforts to win reform. They had talked briefly on the phone just before Clinton began speaking. Gradison believed the Harry and Louise commercials to be accurate and appropriate, he told Celeste, but he had decided unilaterally to discontinue them as of that day.

The insurance companies he represented stood to lose between $300,000 and $400,000 by that decision because they had already paid for the ads, Gradison told Celeste. HIAA was discontinuing the ads as a goodwill gesture, in the hope they'd be able to meet privately later with top administration officials to discuss their differences with the Clinton plan.

All these lobbyists had gathered before a TV screen in a Rayburn Building room where they would later be interviewed by Dan Rather and Connie Chung on the CBS-TV program *48 Hours*. Whatever goodwill about the Clinton reform they had brought with them into that room swiftly dissipated during their TV interviews immediately after the President's speech. Small businesses' Faris condemned the President's remarks. Requiring every business owner to have insurance for every employee would cause "tremendous dislocation of employees," he said. "About a million and a half the first year."

The insurance industry's Gradison was not inhibited by the occasion or by the national audience watching. When the television interviewers turned to him for his reaction to the speech, Gradison tore into Judy Feder, a Clinton health policy aide sitting nearby. Despite Feder's denials, Gradison repeatedly charged that the Clinton plan would prevent American families from keeping their health care plans. It was not the first time — or the last — that Bill Gradison left the White House puzzling about what his real game was.

4

The Delivery Room

THE HOUSE CHAMBER rang with applause. During the address, Democrats began standing and waving small American flags, borrowing a device employed to great effect two years before when President George Bush spoke before Congress about the Persian Gulf War. Now, as then, the waving of the flags acted as prompt lines for the opposition party. As Democrats stood and cheered, so did Republicans.

It was over. The President made his way from the podium back through the packed aisles. Toward the rear of the chamber, George Stephanopoulos was waiting with other presidential aides. Stephanopoulos was still anxious over the TelePrompTer debacle, and worried how the President would react to the incredible slipup. Once, during the speech, Stephanopoulos turned to an aide and said, "This is the worst thing that ever happened." "I don't know," Mike Feldman, who was Jewish, replied. "The Holocaust was pretty bad." Stephanopoulos laughed; but he was still not reassured.

Now, watching the clamorous response to Clinton as the President walked triumphantly up the aisle accepting praise from members of both parties who told him how great a speech he had given, the TelePrompTer didn't matter anymore. It might even be better, the President's aide thought cynically. When the press learns about Clinton having the wrong speech displayed on this critical night, his stellar performance will make him appear even better.

In the crush of lawmakers following the President up the aisles of the Capitol chamber toward the glaring lights of the TV cameras was Robert Bennett, a GOP freshman senator from Utah. Bennett had listened intently to the President, and thought he had just heard "the most comprehensive, brilliantly presented analytical dissection of everything that is wrong with the present health system." I could have given that speech, he told himself; indeed I wish I had, at some point.

As Bennett moved up the aisle, he began thinking about having to face "all the vultures" his press secretary had gathered to listen to his reaction to the President's speech. The sound bite for the TV news popped into his head; it was a theme he would repeat over and over again: "This is all diagnosis and no prescription. He did not give us any view of what he was going to do to fix it. He just told us how sick we are. All diagnosis and no prescription."

In the galleries, they were still applauding Hillary Clinton.

The First Lady's party stood and began to leave. Seated directly behind her, next to Ira Magaziner, was Bob Boorstin.

Clinton, Boorstin thought during the speech, always gave his best speeches at night, always in a crowded hall, always when he was under pressure. He had done so that night. Boorstin was thrilled; he could feel history being made. Magaziner, too, wanted to savor the moment, but his eyes kept closing.

The glow continued. Boorstin wandered through the Capitol with a group of presidential aides, heading for the motorcade that would take them back to the White House. In crowded Statuary Hall, where Senator Bennett was delivering his "all diagnosis, no prescription" sound bite for the TV cameras, Boorstin almost ran into the vice president. He and Al Gore embraced with bear hugs, grinning and celebrating the success of a mental health benefits line Gore had ordered inserted in the speech. Gore told Boorstin that he had passed the word to three Democratic senators and some thirty House members, asking them to applaud wildly at that line. They did.

Boorstin made it into the motorcade, but Magaziner and his wife did not. Somehow, their car and driver were not there. The architect of the Clinton health policy found himself standing outside the Capitol in the dark, rainy night with no way back to the White House. Eventually, he hailed a cab.

The celebration was already under way at the White House. In the East Room, underneath four massive crystal chandeliers and before the solemn Stuart portrait of Washington, a special group of supporters had gathered earlier to watch on theater-size television screens as the President spoke. Among them was John Rother, chief lobbyist for the American Association of Retired Persons (AARP), the largest single special-interest group in America, representing more than thirty-three million senior citizens nationally. At forty-six, Rother not only directed AARP's lobbying on Capitol Hill and across the country; he also headed the new coalition group of labor and health interests called the Health Care Reform Project, formed with Jay Rockefeller's assistance. Representatives of all the coalition groups sat around Rother, watching the President launch a battle many of them had been involved in for years, even decades.

With his salt-and-pepper beard, his glasses, his quiet and serious manner, Rother resembled a gentle professor instead of one of the nation's chief lobbyists. He was a specialist in the field of health. A lawyer by profession, for years he had worked for Republicans on select committees in the Senate, first with Jacob Javits of New York on labor and health, then with John Heinz of Pennsylvania on aging. In recent months, Rother had become increasingly concerned over the time it had taken to reach this launching moment, and over the ability of the Clinton administration to operate successfully. "Everyone in the White House understands that this is the Clinton presidency," he remarked a few days before the speech. "This is not only their moment in history. This is their political future as well."

Rother's anxiety level rose when Clinton began speaking. He, too, sensed something amiss. The East Room fell silent. Oh, my God, Rother thought, the President seems nervous. Then he relaxed. He thought the President was powerfully communicating the emotional intensity people felt and that Rother knew millions of Americans shared. Rother felt proud. Finally, they had turned the corner. Now they would begin to act. Something was really going to happen. He, too, felt part of history.

That feeling was contagious. The other supporters in the East Room rose from their seats, applauding and cheering. Among them was Ellen Globocar, political director of one of the fastest-growing and most aggressive labor unions, the American Federation of State, County and Municipal Employees (AFSCME).

Globocar had been exhausted, and also apprehensive. Now after months of frustrating attempts to coordinate political planning for this moment, she was excited, and relieved. Some day after they pass health care, she said to herself, I'm going to remember I was in the White House this night and how exciting it was. It must have been like this, she thought, for those who were involved in passing Social Security.

When the motorcade got back to West Executive Avenue, Bob Boorstin dashed ahead of the President and First Lady to the War Room on the first floor of the Old Executive Office Building adjoining the White House. There, inside Room 108, seventy-five young Clinton aides had been working virtually around the clock for the last two weeks preparing for the speech.

The room was a replica of the Little Rock nerve center of the Clinton presidential campaign, headed by Stephanopoulos and James Carville, where all the political scheduling and media operations were coordinated. In the Washington version, staff members were drawn from the White House policy, public and congressional liaison, communications, scheduling, and intergovernmental relations offices. From early morning until late at night, they gathered around a horseshoe of folding tables and chairs, surrounded by a network of fifteen computers, news wire machines, fax machines, telephones, and four TV sets. From there, they monitored the media, orchestrated responses to attacks on the Clinton plan, and scheduled administration and congressional visits to the forums being held around the country.

In time, the War Room became the center of their lives, and the place itself the most familiar aspect of their existence. They debated giving themselves a different name to distinguish theirs from the campaign War Room. A contest was arranged. Call it the ICU, one person suggested — not for Intensive Care Unit, but for Interdepartmental Communications Unit. Make it the Special ICU, someone else said: Special-Interest Combat Unit. Others came up with less bureaucratic-sounding names: Emergency Room, Health Security Room, Triage. None stuck; War Room it remained on the night of the speech.

The crowded room had been remarkably quiet during the speech; the young aides watched the President intently while eating a $300 order of take-out Chinese food arranged by Jeff Eller, the White House communications aide and computer wizard in charge of the War Room. Then, after initial tension over Clinton's delivery, the sound of cheers and applause had filled the room.

Now Boorstin stuck his head inside. The President and First Lady were coming to express their thanks, he warned them. They're on the way now. Then he ran back to greet the Clintons.

Hillary Clinton was beaming as she walked down the long, dim hallway, the sound of footsteps echoing off the vaulted walls and high ceilings. She turned to Boorstin. She hated calling their health care room a War Room, the First Lady said. We should call it the Delivery Room, Boorstin replied. Hillary laughed. A cheer greeted her when she entered the War Room. From now on, the First Lady said, we're going to call this the Delivery Room.

A mile from the Capitol, lights burned on the seventh floor of an otherwise darkened downtown Washington office building. Michele Davis, a health economist for Citizens for a Sound Economy and former aide to President Bush, turned away from her conference room TV set, which was still broadcasting sounds of applause for the President throughout the Capitol chamber, and rapidly began typing out a message on her laptop computer. She was alone.

Hours later, in its coverage of the speech, the *New York Times* reported Davis's critical reaction to the plan Bill Clinton had just presented to Congress and the American people. It would, she charged, "force insurance companies and HMOs to ration care in order to survive under federally established premium caps." Within days, the conservative lobbying group she worked for became the first to label the Clinton health approach government-run health care, a term that became a mantra of reform opponents, repeated again and again in the months to come. Soon that seventh-floor conference room, located three blocks from the White House, became the nerve center for strategy sessions with a loose confederation of special-interest groups nationwide. They united for one purpose — to kill what they termed derisively "Clintoncare."

From a handful of conservative groups, starting with the Christian Coalition and the National Taxpayers Union, at times the meetings expanded to include more than thirty diverse organizations, ranging from the Health Insurance Association of America (HIAA) to the National Federation of Independent Business (NFIB).

Privately, they called themselves the "No Name Coalition" and kept their conferences "off the record" and hidden from public scrutiny. But their combined efforts to influence The System resulted in what became the most costly and intensively waged lobbying battle in U.S. history.

In Blue Ash, Ohio, a Cincinnati suburb in the congressional district once represented by Bill Gradison, two *Washington Post* reporters sat with a dozen voters watching the Clinton speech. For an hour before the President came on, the voters had discussed their own experiences. They quickly found common ground, swapping horror stories about their encounters with insurance companies, hospitals, and doctors. They talked of indecipherable and, they suspected, inflated bills, of "greedy" practitioners who sometimes treated them "like dirt." Real estate agent Cathy Ratliff said, "The whole country is being held hostage by medical care," with employers using its cost to resist granting wage increases, workers with illnesses in the family afraid to change jobs because they might not get a new insurance policy, and grandparents driven out of their homes by the cost of prescription drugs.

As they listened to the early portions of Clinton's speech, outlining the need for major reforms, they glanced and smiled at each other. It was as if the President had been eavesdropping on their earlier conversation; he was giving voice to exactly their deepest concerns. Around the table, murmurs of agreement grew into an amen corner of assent.

Clinton carried them with him all the way to his final plea to Congress to "answer the call of history and meet the challenge of our time." Then, over Cokes and cookies, they exchanged reactions.

Those reactions were surprising. The President's main prop — the plastic Health Security card that his consultants had assured him would bring the guarantee of coverage vividly to every viewer — was more puzzling than reassuring. "Where did he get that?" asked Thomas Dean, a data systems technician. "Was that a credit card or what?" No one was sure.

That one question seeded many more. Group members confessed that the President had left them uncertain about where unemployed people would go to get their insurance. If free care was available to everyone who was not working, they wondered, why would anyone leave welfare? Someone asked whether illegal aliens could "freeload" on the system. Another person asked whether this meant friends in insurance company offices would soon be looking for jobs. And they debated whether this would prove to be just another expensive government boondoggle — like "welfare hotels." "Why should we trust The System to implement something like this?" asked housewife Christine Harrison.

Then it emerged that this unusually attentive audience had noticed a piece missing from the President's speech. Bill Clinton had outlined the problem; he had stated his principles; but he hadn't adequately explained the plan.

"I heard a lot of thoughts but no solutions," said Jamarkus Rucker, nineteen, a recent high school graduate who had just started a job with no health insurance. "It's like telling us we're going to take a trip to the moon without telling us how we're going to get there," Mrs. Harrison agreed.

"If he has a plan, he should have submitted it," said Carol Templeton, a mother of two, and a manager for Mary Kay cosmetics.

The President did have a plan. It had been almost two years in gestation. He understood it perfectly. The country understood it not at all.

BOOK TWO
The Plan

5

The Clinton
Connection

BILL CLINTON could have leapt straight from the pages of a
Dickens novel. Charming and articulate, he entered political
life with superlative credentials. His academic background was enviable: undergraduate studies at Georgetown University, postgradu-
ate work at Oxford on a Rhodes scholarship, law degree from Yale,
constitutional law professor at the University of Arkansas. So was
his practical preparation. His two-year Capitol Hill internship for
Senator J. William Fulbright gave him a window on Washington
at a moment of historic turmoil over civil rights and the Vietnam War. He spent two years as attorney general of Arkansas and
twelve years as its governor, working on education, economic development, and the myriad other concerns of a state trying to escape from chronic poverty and gain a foothold in a rapidly changing
world.

Clinton's career was unusually favored; mentors, seeing in him ex-
ceptional intellect and political talent, were always at hand to move
him forward. Contemporaries were drawn to him, convinced he had
the makings of a future President. Indeed, his upward path appeared
almost effortless, just as he himself seemed supremely at ease and
confident in confronting difficult challenges.

This portrait is not inaccurate, but it fails to convey the am-
biguities and darker shadows that marked his upbringing. Like
Ronald Reagan before him and like his generational contemporary, Newt Gingrich, Bill Clinton was forced by circumstances to

reinvent himself. Reagan was born to an alcoholic father, an orphan who later drifted from one poorly paying job to another. Gingrich was born Newton Leroy McPherson to a father, born out of wedlock, who abandoned his sixteen-year-old wife days after their marriage ended in a violent fight. Bill Clinton came into the world as Billy Blythe, born three months after his traveling salesman father, William Jefferson (Bill) Blythe, drowned in a ditch after a nighttime automobile crash. In his childhood, he experienced poverty, difficulty, and abuse. His stepfather, Roger Clinton, who adopted him and gave him his name, was an alcoholic who beat his wife, who eventually divorced him.

Young Bill Clinton was raised by his grandparents after his mother left Arkansas for New Orleans to become a nurse anesthetist. His strongest early influence was his grandmother Edith Cassidy, also a nurse, who wore a white starched uniform, white stockings, and a blue cape on her private rounds in Hope, Arkansas. One of the legacies of those two strong women was a concern about health care that Bill Clinton carried into his public life, making him more knowledgeable on the issue than those outside his immediate circle understood.

When he was governor, health care had not been high on Clinton's agenda, and he did not personally make it an issue in the 1992 presidential campaign. The public, the dynamics of his fight for the Democratic nomination, and fate did.

It began with an accident.

On Thursday afternoon, April 4, 1991, a small private plane and a helicopter collided in the air near Philadelphia. One of the seven victims was Senator John Heinz of Pennsylvania, heir to the ketchup and pickle fortune and a moderate Republican regarded as the most popular politician in the commonwealth. Seven months later, on November 5, a special election was held to fill the Heinz Senate seat.

Republicans selected their strongest potential candidate, Dick Thornburgh, twice a popular governor of Pennsylvania, most recently U.S. attorney general under President George Bush. Democrats chose Harris Wofford, whom the Democratic governor, Robert

P. Casey, had appointed earlier to fill Heinz' Senate seat until the special election.

Harris Wofford was then sixty-five years old and had never run for public office. His governmental career, however, extended back to the Eisenhower administration, when he was counsel to the Reverend Theodore Hesburgh, the president of Notre Dame, on the U.S. Commission on Civil Rights. He subsequently taught law at Notre Dame, then joined the Kennedy administration, leaving government service to become the founding president of the State University of New York's College at Old Westbury. For eight years, he was president of Bryn Mawr College outside Philadelphia. Wofford also served as Pennsylvania's Democratic Party chairman and as the state's secretary of Labor and Industry.

Wofford was not a likely political candidate. He seemed better suited to political theory and philosophy than to the rough-and-tumble of the campaign trail. Nor was Wofford the governor's first choice to fill the Heinz vacancy; the position had been turned down by Chrysler chairman Lee Iacocca and by other ambitious Democrats convinced they could not defeat Thornburgh. Few gave Wofford much chance. When the campaign began, he trailed Thornburgh three to one in the polls.

In the campaign, Thornburgh seemed more intent on parading his Washington credentials than addressing concerns of voters about Pennsylvania's chronic economic problems, then intensified by the continuing deep recession. Harris Wofford knew that health care was one of those worries. His wife had a chronic medical problem, and every time he changed jobs they worried that she would be denied insurance. As the state's Labor secretary, he had seen, as he recalled, that "increasingly, every labor dispute, every strike, turned in whole or in part on the issue of health care. Increasingly, companies were trying to reduce costs, limit choices, cut benefits. Unions were fighting them."

Early in his campaign, Wofford met with Dr. Bob Reinecke, a Philadelphia ophthalmologist and potential contributor. After an hour-long conversation, Reinecke picked up from his desk a copy of the U.S. Constitution. "Take this Constitution, Senator," the doctor said, "and tell people that the Constitution says if you're charged with a crime, you have a right to a lawyer. Every American, if they're sick, should have the right to a doctor."

Wofford was so impressed he tried out that argument in a campaign appearance that night. The response was immediate. Loud applause. He tried the line in black churches. Loud amens. "I think I know what Jefferson meant by self-evident truths," Wofford said to an aide.

When he went to film the first of his political ads, Wofford told his consultants he had found a strong applause line. One who was skeptical was James Carville, the campaign consultant he had inherited from Governor Casey's winning campaigns, who would later become famous as the "Ragin' Cajun" who masterminded Bill Clinton's presidential campaign. "Senator," Wofford remembers Carville drawling, "that's so theoretical, only you academics would think something like that would make sense."

But Carville humored his candidate. The TV spot was made. Wofford looked earnestly into the camera and proclaimed: "If criminals have a right to a lawyer, I think working Americans should have the right to a doctor."

In a stunning upset, Harris Wofford defeated Dick Thornburgh by a 55- to 45-percent margin. He was the first Democrat to win a U.S. Senate seat in Pennsylvania in thirty years. Though subsequent Republican polls in Pennsylvania indicated economic issues had been far more damaging to Thornburgh than the TV spot, Wofford's victory attracted national attention and convinced Democrats they had found a powerful issue to use against President George Bush in the upcoming 1992 campaign.

George Mitchell, the Senate majority leader, invited Wofford and Carville to brief the Democratic caucus. A task force of about a dozen senators, including Wofford, was charged with developing a Democratic bill. Mitchell's idea was to present something so big and bold that Bush would veto it. But Wofford was troubled. "Only a certain number of senators had done enough homework that they had some grasp of what the factors were," he said. "I also think there was exaggerated fear of what the costs of a universal-coverage package would be."

As with the earlier effort that Dick Gephardt had led among House

Democrats, Mitchell found consensus to be elusive. Lloyd Bentsen of Texas, the conservative chairman of the Senate Finance Committee, thought a modest health insurance reform bill could attract bipartisan support. Bentsen's bill never passed.

The Democrats wanted an issue, not a law. Harris Wofford seemed to have given them that.

In the annals of the American political system, four challenges emerge as the greatest the nation faces: war and the threats from foreign enemies; race and the dreadful heritage of slavery; economic instability and the ravages of periodic and often severe joblessness; and the social safety net, protecting the most vulnerable in their times of need. Within that fourth category, nothing has challenged the American system more seriously or proved more daunting than ensuring that every citizen has access to good and affordable health care. It is an issue that is at least a match in significance and complexity for any The System faces. It's also the most personal of all issues. Whatever their political or policy disagreements, no one in government in 1993 was indifferent to the need to find a way to bring greater health security to all citizens. These officials were emotional about it, because the problem had touched them, and all they knew or served, intimately.

By economic terms alone, soaring health costs represented a grave threat to the nation's security and future. By the nineties, health care was consuming $1 out of every $7 of the goods and services produced in America, a higher proportion by far than any nation in the world. And those costs were rising rapidly. By the time Clinton became President, they were almost twice those of leading industrialized nations; Germans, to take one example, paid on average only half what Americans paid. Even in the boom years of the eighties, when real household median income of Americans rose by $1500, health cost increases virtually wiped out the economic gains enjoyed by families, growing by $1400. Every business battled rising expenses in order to provide employee health insurance, and increasing numbers of firms were compelled to reduce those benefits.

Those covered were among the fortunate Americans. Thirty-seven million Americans, 15 percent of the population, had no insurance at all. An additional seventy-two million people lacked coverage for prescription drugs. This meant that providers — insurance companies, hospitals, and doctors — passed on the costs of medical treatment for the uninsured and underinsured to those with insurance, who paid ever higher rates to cover those without.

These inexorably rising figures also placed an enormous burden on federal, state, and local budgets and on every taxpayer whose money financed them. Behind these statistics lay a deeply disturbing fact: In a nation burdened by historic levels of rising debt, unless health costs were controlled, there would be barely *any* money left to spend on *any* other governmental effort to improve the quality of American life.

None of this came as a surprise to anyone in Congress when Clinton launched his fight. For years they, too, had been debating the issue. Countless hearings had been held. Expert testimony, covering every aspect of the issue, had been taken from every interest involved. Both Democrats and Republicans had formed special task forces. Poll after poll had been commissioned to fathom public attitudes. Legislation had been drafted, introduced, and subjected to intense scrutiny and lobbying. Yet only once did a bill providing universal national coverage ever pass a single congressional committee.

Despite this record of repeated failure, the prospect for reform appeared the brightest ever when the Clinton effort began. Not only were costs continuing to rise, but Americans were experiencing a troubling new sense of vulnerability.

The recession of the early nineties forced a fundamental restructuring of the American economy, resulting in permanent loss of hundreds of thousands of high-paying jobs, white-collar as well as blue-collar, management as well as clerical. With this restructuring, or downsizing, of corporate America, came reductions in or loss of health and pension benefits. Suddenly, members of the shrinking American middle class found themselves feeling highly insecure. Benefits previously taken for granted now were at risk. A *Washington Post*/ABC News survey, taken just before Clinton's health care reform speech to Congress, showed that nearly half of employed Americans said their bosses had either cut back in the past two years or made them pay a greater percentage of insurance costs. Increasingly anxious Americans worried that illness could cause them to lose everything. If they changed jobs and had a preexisting medical condition, even one previously covered by insurance, they might be denied coverage.

Nor were these fears unfounded. In the last year alone, one million two hundred thousand American families had lost their insurance, and they were by no means the poorest citizens. A million of those families earned between $25,000 and $50,000 a year. Many others were discovering painfully that their coverage was inadequate when they became seriously ill. All this contributed to a gnawing sense of insecurity on the part of millions of Americans who no longer could count on having coverage.

All these factors combined to focus intense public attention on the way American health care was provided, and on how The System should improve it. The public clearly did not want government to take over running all the hospitals and clinics or intrude on the private relationship between doctor and patient. But there were so many loose ends in that system — uninsured people, underused facilities — that it clearly needed fixing.

America's health care system had developed more by accident than by rational design. By the 1990s, the debate mirrored the complexity of the system itself. Terms of the debate were so arcane, so filled with bureaucratic jargon, that few politicians could knowledgeably define or explain them (as we will attempt to do in the course of this book): HIPCs. Community rating. Global budgets. Premium caps. Cost shifting. Cost containment. Capitation. Co-payments. Managed competition. Managed care. Single-payer. Pay-or-play. Catastrophic. Long-term care.

If the politicians were confused, the public was even more so. But there was no confusion about one central fact. The nation's system needed reform.

As far back as the presidential election campaign of 1912, in the flowering of the Progressive era, both Theodore Roosevelt and Woodrow Wilson pledged to improve the nation's health. In his inaugural address that next March, Wilson promised to attend to "safeguarding the health of the nation, the health of its men and women and its children. This is no sentimental duty," the new President declared. "These are matters of justice."

Every subsequent Democratic President — and some Republicans — made similar unequivocal commitments. All came to naught.

While repeated reform attempts failed, and while other industrial nations expanded health guarantees for their citizens, the American system continued to evolve far beyond its traditional boundaries.* In the words of Sheila Burke, the registered nurse who became Bob Dole's top Senate aide, in the beginning "people took care of people. It was the old country doc, the family physician. People stayed at home; they didn't go to hospitals. That's where people died."

From that time, the system burgeoned into one encompassing sixty-five hundred hospitals, fifty-four thousand pharmacies, six hundred thousand physicians, two million two hundred thousand nurses, and millions of other workers. In addition, there were hundreds of outpatient surgery centers and thousands of nursing homes, mental health organizations, and rehabilitation facilities.

At first, hospitals were largely charitable institutions in which indigents and orphans could be isolated. There, they would be given moral training as well as medication. As science professionals moved in, philanthropists and universities endowed hospitals for research and training of physicians. Religious and ethnic groups established their own hospitals, enabling them to serve their special constituencies and permit doctors within their communities to have internships and residencies denied them elsewhere. Local politicians put their own stamp on the system. Using taxpayer funds, they set up county and municipal hospitals for those unable to afford private care. They received their rewards at the polls. Not to be outdone, the federal government began building facilities, clinics as well as hospitals, for veterans. Soon, entrepreneurs discovered the lucrative potential of for-profit hospitals, primarily surgical centers.†

---

*German Chancellor Otto von Bismarck inaugurated that country's compulsory health insurance program in 1883, creating the model used by other nations to cover their citizens.
†Paul Starr's Pulitzer Prize–winning *The Social Transformation of American Medicine* (New York: Basic Books, 1982) is the best account of this history.

Quality of care improved, but at a heavy price in access to the system. The wealthiest Americans enjoyed the best care in the world; the poorest were increasingly excluded. By the late 1920s, on the eve of the Great Depression, the problem was serious enough that a group of medical professionals and scientists created the Committee on the Costs of Medical Care. The committee called for a massive reorganization of the fee-for-service medical system, urging patients to join together in a nationwide network to insure against the risk of large medical bills and for doctors to form networks around hospitals to provide needed services.

When the committee report was issued on October 31, 1932, the *Journal of the American Medical Association* condemned it. The committee economist who helped draft that report was Wilbur J. Cohen, a lifelong advocate of national health insurance and later secretary of Health, Education and Welfare under Lyndon B. Johnson. Referring to the opposition that greeted the committee's report, Cohen's disgusted reaction would echo in every attempt to create a national health insurance system. "Anyone who advocated national health insurance," Cohen said, "was usually tarred with the epithet of being a socialist, or a communist, or a radical."

Doctors were not about to yield control to any form of government intervention. So fierce was their opposition that in 1935 Franklin Roosevelt was forced to remove medical benefits from his first Social Security bill. He vowed to reinstitute them — but never did.

Eight years later, in 1943, three liberal Democrats with strong backing from organized labor, Senators Robert Wagner of New York and James Murray of Montana and Representative John Dingell Sr. of Michigan, introduced the first compulsory national health insurance bill. With Roosevelt preoccupied with the burdens of World War II, the bill fell before the strong opposition of America's doctors, now joined by the nation's pharmaceutical and insurance industries.

The war did bring about a major change. In order to lure critically needed workers, industries barred from offering higher wages by wartime price controls promised instead to provide workers' medical benefits. Thus was born an employer-financed health insurance system. Over the following decades, this system mushroomed until it became the principal source of medical coverage for most American families. Despite later mythology about medical benefits being a purely free-enterprise operation, the federal government was deeply involved: The U.S. tax code encouraged formation of the employer-financed system, permitting employers to deduct cost of benefits while workers did not have to report them as income.

In the postwar years, Blue Cross and Blue Shield and such private insurance giants as Mutual of Omaha entered the greatly expanding field. Thousands of smaller insurance companies found they could make money by "cherry picking," by marketing their coverage only to individuals or groups believed to be good risks.

These developments made it harder and harder for reform advocates to win congressional approval of a plan. When Harry Truman became President in 1945, he promoted a "new economic bill of rights," which, he said, "should mean health security for all, regardless of residence, station, or race." Stymied by what he called the "good-for-nothing, do-nothing" Republican-controlled eightieth Congress, Truman made health care a major issue in his 1948 presidential campaign. Despite Truman's classic upset victory that fall, which brought a surge of public goodwill for him, his health plan was crushed.

Immediately after the election, the American Medical Association (AMA) launched a four-and-a-half-million-dollar "national education" campaign, warning that "national health insurance would lead to federal control of health care." Joining the doctors in opposition were the U.S. Chamber of Commerce, the American Farm Bureau Federation, and even the social welfare arm of the American Catholic Church.

More than a decade passed before health care again emerged on the national agenda. In 1960, at the very end of Dwight Eisenhower's second term, a Rhode Island Democratic representative named Aime Forand drafted a bill to expand Social Security and provide hospital and nursing home care for senior citizens. Forand could not get his bill approved by his House Ways and Means Committee. In his presidential campaign that fall, Senator John F. Kennedy took up the fight for Medicare — as Forand's new program was called — but Kennedy's narrow victory left him without the political power to pass it. Two years later, in his 1962 midterm campaign, Kennedy renewed the fight.

In a nationally televised speech before an enthusiastic crowd of labor union members and senior citizens at New York's Madison Square Garden, Kennedy said, "This is not a campaign against doctors. The people of the United States recognize that this is a problem whose solution is long overdue."

John Kennedy was dead when in 1965 Medicare became law, along with a companion program called Medicaid, which set up a joint federal-state program for welfare recipients and their children and provided long-term care for the indigent elderly and the disabled. The key to that 1965 success was Lyndon Johnson's landslide triumph over Barry Goldwater the year before. Flush with his victory, which produced the biggest Democratic majorities in Congress since the early 1930s — Republicans were left with only 140 House and 32 Senate seats — Johnson pushed Congress to pass Medicare, Medicaid, and a host of other "Great Society" domestic legislation. In a symbolic act of homage, he traveled to Harry Truman's hometown of Independence, Missouri, to sign the law.

The expectation then was that Medicare would be expanded, step-by-step, year by year, until it covered the entire American working population. Once again, history intervened to dash those hopes. Johnson's Great Society dreams ended in the ashes of the divisive Vietnam War, and he decided not to seek reelection in 1968.

Richard Nixon took a different approach. The first health care bill he introduced in 1971 would have facilitated expansion of health maintenance organizations, or HMOs — voluntary associations of hospitals and doctors that provide, for a preset fee, all medical benefits an individual or family needs. HMOs, which had begun to develop in California, Minnesota, and a few other places, were seen as a way to provide care to more people at a lower cost. The companion measure would require employers to provide a basic minimum package of benefits to all their employees. The HMO bill passed; the benefits bill, opposed by the AMA and the insurance industry, did not.

Jimmy Carter's presidency gave the Democrats control of both the White House and Congress for the first time since Lyndon Johnson was driven from office. Carter, too, had promised during his 1976 presidential campaign to offer a "comprehensive national health insurance system with universal and mandatory coverage." Because of his narrow victory, like John Kennedy's sixteen years before, Carter postponed any attempt to fulfill his campaign promise until faced in 1979 with a renomination challenge from Senator Ted Kennedy. Kennedy favored a government-run, tax-financed system; Carter, one that preserved a role for private insurance. Neither had the votes to pass.

For the next twelve years, with Republicans Ronald Reagan and George Bush in the White House, there was much talk but almost no significant action — with one notable exception that left a lasting mark on everyone involved in reform. That exception was the enactment, in the summer of 1988, of a law that would expand Medicare to protect its recipients against the costs of catastrophic illness — a critical omission in the original law.

Here, at last, was a major reform that seemed to have every political advantage. It would make a difference in the lives of millions of Americans, and it had something previously lacking in all the dreary record of past failed reforms. It enjoyed the most impressive of bipartisan support.

Dan Rostenkowski, the chairman of the House Ways and Means Committee, hailed it as "the most significant and far-reaching expansion of Medicare protection since the program was enacted in 1965." Lloyd Bentsen, then chairman of the Senate Finance Committee, said it would give Medicare beneficiaries and their children "the peace of mind they deserve." Huge bipartisan majorities passed the law: 328 to 72 in the House; 86 to 11 in the Senate. In signing the bill into law, Reagan added his own popular imprimatur. "It will remove a terrible threat from the lives of elderly and disabled Americans," he said.

Yet, despite this acclaim, the Medicare catastrophic-insurance program became a political casualty. Seventeen months after becoming law, and before any of its major benefits took effect, the catastrophic-insurance provision was repealed by Congress. It was a victim of a loud protest from the very people it was supposed to help.

Inflamed by reports — some accurate, some exaggerated — of

the costs catastrophic insurance would impose on them, many intended beneficiaries told their members of Congress they were being asked to shoulder an unfair burden for something many of them
did not want. Retirees who could afford it had purchased private
"Medigap" policies to cover expenses not reimbursed by Medicare.
Now they were being asked to pay supplemental premiums to provide similar coverage for other retirees. In an attempt to satisfy
the protesters, Congress tried to amend the program. The protests
continued. In the end, Congress abandoned it. Catastrophic was
dead.

One provision of the bill had created a commission on broader
health questions, and that commission was allowed to complete
its work. The first chairman was Representative Claude Pepper of
Florida — a tireless battler for senior citizens since his days as a New
Deal senator. After Pepper's death, his place was taken by Senator
Jay Rockefeller of West Virginia. In March of 1990, the commission
issued a final report that again illustrated how contentious and polarizing the issue was. Although eleven of the fifteen members of the
bipartisan commission endorsed a proposal to add long-term care
coverage to the menu of government-guaranteed benefits, the panel
was hopelessly deadlocked on other critical questions. The commission split, eight to seven, on a proposal to require all employers in
firms with more than one hundred workers to provide insurance for
their workers. More crucially, it made no recommendation on a key
question: how to finance the estimated $23 billion a year it would
cost to insure those who would *not* otherwise be covered.

Foreshadowing events to come, even as Rockefeller was claiming
that the commission report was a breakthrough, two of the dissent-
ing commissioners were separately telling journalists, as Rockefeller
later put it, "This is dead on arrival, so forget it." The chairman and
the two dissenters, House members Pete Stark, a California Democrat, and Bill Gradison, an Ohio Republican, would replay their roles
three years later in the greatest health reform attempt of the century.

In 1993, when Clinton began his effort, the fiasco of catastrophic
insurance was very much on the minds of members of Congress. Both
the President and the First Lady directly questioned, in private, leading participants in the fight for catastrophic-insurance reform about

the lessons of that disaster. Architects of the Clinton plan received memos cautioning them to avoid the same mistakes. Be sure the benefits are greater and more visible than the costs, they were told. Don't try to disguise taxes behind some euphemistic phrase. Don't believe that altruism will outweigh perceived self-interest. Despite all the warning flags, many of the same errors were to be repeated.

In the fall of 1991, an early "Friend of Bill," Anne Wexler, a savvy Democratic lobbyist and public relations executive, found the Clinton campaign vacant rooms on the ninth floor of a downtown Washington office building, just above the space her firm occupied, two blocks from the White House. Bruce Reed, the newly named issues director of the campaign, was one of the first to arrive. A Rhodes scholar from Idaho, he was only in his early thirties but already had spent four years on the staff of Senator Albert Gore Jr. of Tennessee, soon to be Clinton's running mate, and two years as policy director of the Democratic Leadership Council, the middle-road group that Clinton headed.

When Reed arrived, he was introduced to Bruce M. Fried, a Wexler Group executive vice president with extensive experience on health care issues. One of Fried's earlier projects was running the National Health Care Campaign, an attempt to put the issue on the agenda for Democratic candidates in the campaigns of the 1980s. Fried offered Reed a memo on the current thinking among liberal-oriented policy experts. He also volunteered to bring together a small group of people who would be available for consultation.

Thus was born the Blueberry Donut Group — in honor of the repast Fried would invariably buy from Reeves Bakery for their Tuesday morning conferences. The other key players included Judy Feder, most recently executive director of the Pepper-Rockefeller Commission; Marilyn Moon of the Urban Institute; and Ken Thorpe, a University of North Carolina at Chapel Hill health economist. Seven others — lawyers, physicians, lobbyists — became part of the group.

While these consultants were beginning work early in 1992 in Washington, Clinton was being hammered in New Hampshire by two of his rivals for the Democratic nomination for his lack of a specific health care proposal. One of them, Senator Bob Kerrey of Nebraska, already had staked out the issue as his main concern. Kerrey had good reason. When he was a Navy SEAL in Vietnam, Kerrey's right foot and lower leg were blown off by an enemy grenade. He endured months of painful hospitalization and rehabilitation, eventually using his prosthesis so well that he could run marathons.

When Kerrey came to the Senate in 1988, he attracted unusual media attention. He was that rare figure, a member of the baby boomer generation who was a genuine war hero — he won the Medal of Honor for bravery in Vietnam — and a colorful character. A successful small businessman who had been a popular liberal governor of a conservative midwestern state, Kerrey was an intriguing personality who would not conform. A loner, the divorced father of two children, he seemed unconcerned about public opinion; he dated movie actresses, inviting one to stay with him in the governor's mansion. After only one term as governor, Kerrey dropped out of political life, then reappeared as a successful Senate candidate. Bob Kerrey was quixotic, even quirky, in the eyes of some critics who found the logic of his positions hard to track. But he was a high-risk political player who attracted and fascinated many followers.

Kerrey introduced his own comprehensive plan in July of 1991, a full year before the Democratic convention was scheduled to assemble in New York. It bore a close resemblance to the "single-payer" system adopted in Canada, Great Britain, and most European countries. The governments of those countries, using tax dollars, are the sole source, or "single-payer," of all medical bills. Supporters of this centralized system often called it the Canadian-style plan, suggesting that a neighboring country much like the United States had already tested it and found it workable. Private insurance companies and many others opposed the single-payer system because it would convert private insurance premiums into taxes and expand the share of the economy and society that is directly regulated by the government. In Kerrey's version, Washington would set the benefits package and the annual budget. In order to stay inside their assigned budgetary limit, the states would set physician and hospital fees; when the budget limit pinched, doctors and hospitals would have to accept less. It would be expensive; but, unlike most politicians, Kerrey did not shrink from stating that fact clearly. To pay for universal coverage, he proposed a 5 percent payroll tax, plus a new top-bracket income tax, and higher taxes on cigarettes and alcohol. In the long run he believed, as did other single-payer advocates, Senator Kennedy and Representative Dingell among them, that the system would save money because it was more efficient. Critics claimed the savings would come at a heavy cost in terms of government controls and lower-quality care.

In the same week that Bill Clinton entered the presidential race in Little Rock, Bob Kerrey announced his candidacy in Lincoln. Then they both headed for New Hampshire, bypassing the first delegate caucuses in Iowa, since that state's U.S. Senator Tom Harkin had monopolized activist Democratic support there. Waiting for them in New Hampshire, the home of the first presidential primary, was former Senator Paul Tsongas of Massachusetts, a near-favorite son who had been making the rounds of his neighboring state for months.

If Kerrey staked out the "maximalist" position on health care with his government-financed, government-run plan, Tsongas adopted the most conservative position in the Democratic spectrum. The soft-spoken Tsongas, a friend of Harris Wofford since their Peace Corps days, had left the Senate in 1984 because he was battling a rare and severe form of cancer. His life was saved by a radical, experimental treatment at Massachusetts General Hospital. That experience, supplemented by business dealings with major insurance firms based in Massachusetts, gave Tsongas an early introduction to some of the newest work being done by providers and insurers to slow exploding medical costs and provide better coverage at a lower price.

When Tsongas launched his long-shot presidential campaign, he asked friends from the worlds of insurance and medicine to develop policy. They came back with the newly minted notion of managed competition, which had been developed by Stanford business school economist Alain C. Enthoven and made public in a pair of 1989 articles in the *New England Journal of Medicine*. As he continued to flesh out his theory, Enthoven met regularly with a group of academics and businesspeople in Jackson Hole, Wyoming, where a Minneapolis physician and managed care proponent, Paul Ellwood, had a vacation home. Thus, the theory of managed competition came to be known as the Jackson Hole Plan and the people who contributed to it as the Jackson Hole Group.*

The proponents of managed competition envisioned a health system relying largely on market forces of supply and demand. In this essentially private system — under which employers would pay a portion of their workers' coverage but not necessarily be required to provide the whole insurance — the government would have a limited role. It would set minimum standards for the benefits insurers would have to offer. It would also help organize customers — individuals or small businesses — into health insurance purchasing cooperatives (HIPCs — pronounced "Hippicks"). Insurers would compete for HIPC business on the basis of the price and quality of their benefit packages. The HIPCs would monitor the hospitals, doctors, and other providers to assure the consumers that quality standards were being met. Competition for customers would force the providers to control their costs; wasteful paperwork and procedures would be eliminated by market forces. It was assumed that many of the providers would, for efficiency's sake, shift into managed care plans, offering all services for a fixed fee. Thus, managed competition would restructure the health care market so that the leverage of insurance companies over consumers would be reduced and cost containment would be achieved with a minimum of direct government controls.

In "unmanaged competition," insurance companies can decide which people to insure and which to exclude because their medical risks are too high. For all but the largest customers, insurers can for

---

*Managed care differs from managed competition. In managed care plans, which have been operating for twenty or more years with some roots extending even back into the 1930s, an insurer or network of hospitals and doctors called a health maintenance organization, or HMO, agrees to provide all health care services for a flat fee for those who enroll. Managed care emphasizes preventive medicine and relies mainly on family physicians. Specialists on its roster are used only in cases where the primary care physician decides there is a clear need. HMO members are limited in choice of physicians and hospitals. Members of an HMO usually pay less for health insurance than individuals relying on traditional fee-for-service providers. People argue fiercely over whether there is a difference in the quality of care the two plans provide.

the most part dictate what the policy premiums are. In the managed competition marketplace, all insurers would have to accept all customers in the HIPC, rather than avoiding people with high-risk, and costly, health problems. In turn, insurers would be compensated for accepting high-risk people through some form of standardized risk adjustment or "community rating," under which each individual would pay a premium representing the average cost of insuring each member of the group. The goal of this system is to reduce, hopefully to eliminate, the spread between insurance costs of the easily insured and the hard-to-insure.

This market-oriented reform concept appealed to some Republicans and conservative Democrats, like Tsongas and Tennessee Representative Jim Cooper, and to many in business. But it faced skepticism and engendered much disagreement because it was essentially untested in the real world.* Managed competition proponents themselves voiced significant differences over what additional elements were needed to make it effective. Enthoven and some colleagues argued for taxing high-benefit plans and requiring significant co-payments from individuals in order to drive home cost-consciousness among consumers. To many of the politicians, that was political poison.

Some of Enthoven's early allies — and some politicians — broke from him and suggested backup cost controls were needed to enforce marketplace discipline. To guarantee that promised savings would be achieved, they advocated two differing approaches: adopting either "global budgets" or "premium caps." Under global budgets, a ceiling would be established on what the nation, and each state, could spend each year. Under premium caps, price controls would be imposed on insurance policies. To Enthoven, such fiddling with the marketplace was anathema. And this conflict of principles would prove significant in the debate to come.

---

*In California, where Enthoven lived, the state employees' and retirees' pension fund, called CALPERS, had organized a purchasing cooperative to bargain for good-value insurance coverage for its eight hundred thousand members. That experience showed that a cooperative of health consumers of that size could indeed bargain down rates charged by insurers competing for business. Firms and groups in Rochester, New York, enjoyed similar success. But the concept had not been tested in enough places, with varieties of populations, for anyone to be certain how it would work.

*   *   *

With early polls showing Tsongas and Kerrey as his main rivals in New Hampshire, Clinton began searching for a policy that would be distinctive. Typically, he sought a policy that would occupy the middle ground between Tsongas's reliance on the restructured marketplace and Kerrey's dependence on Big Government. He found the pay-or-play health proposal favored by George Mitchell and other Senate Democrats suited his middle-ground campaign strategy. A relative newcomer to the debate, the pay-or-play plan was devised as a way to keep much of the existing insurance system intact while also expanding coverage. The basic provision was simple: Each business would be given a choice of providing insurance for its own workers, with part of the cost deducted from their pay and part from the employer, as is the current practice, or contributing to a national health care insurance fund that would be administered by the government.

While simple in concept, pay-or-play entailed serious political problems. Many predicted that low-risk companies, with healthy young workers, would choose to provide their own insurance, while those with aging or injury-prone workforces would not. Thus, the government's new insurance fund would be saddled with a disproportionate share of the high-cost cases. Proponents of the plan had great difficulty deciding how and by whom the government insurance fund should be run, and how it would avoid the financial problems plaguing Medicare. (Advocates of pay-or-play generally assumed that federal taxes would pay for the unemployed or the needy not already covered by Medicaid.)

Just an hour before the Democratic candidates were to meet in one of the New Hampshire primary debates on January 19, the Clinton campaign issued a health care white paper. Ten pages long, it was drafted mainly by Clinton and Bruce Reed, his presidential campaign issues director. The paper achieved its political goal. As Richard A. Knox wrote in the next day's *Boston Globe*, Clinton's "timing blocked Kerrey and Tsongas from accusing him once again of dodging the health care issue, and it also prevented them from examining the proposal in detail."

In fact, there wasn't much detail to examine. As Knox accurately observed, the Clinton statement did not say "how he would pay for universal health care or how quickly he would move to cover all Americans' medical expenses." Clinton's paper claimed that when fully implemented, his program would save "far more than it costs to extend comprehensive coverage to all Americans." But it conceded there would be extra costs, for both business and government, for at least two or three years. A five-step plan to achieve universal coverage was advanced, with the first step aimed at controlling costs by simplifying paperwork.

Clinton appeared to think the pay-or-play system would be only a transitional arrangement. In a health care forum in Nashua, the day before his position paper was issued, the *Globe* quoted him as saying, "We have to begin, make a commitment now to go to universal coverage, no matter what. We can at least start with an employer-based system with universal coverage, with a view toward moving toward a single-payer system."

The January 19 position paper was the opening round in what became an eight-month internal struggle to get Bill Clinton to define his approach to reform. Such battles are commonplace in The System, as rival groups of presidential campaign advisers struggle to get their ideas — and themselves — accepted by the man who may be President. The ideological issues frequently become personal, and they certainly did in this case. Much of the infighting takes place without the participation — or even the knowledge — of the candidate, who is busy raising money, wooing voters, making TV spots, and taking care of other urgent chores. But the ideas and the people who win the fight inside the campaign turn out to be critically important in the subsequent administration. The Clinton plan took its essential form during the 1992 internal struggle — and never much changed thereafter. Although Clinton maintained in our 1995 interview with him that "our health care bill, if you look at it, was basically the legislative embodiment of the principles that I laid out in my New Hampshire campaign," those principles evolved and changed significantly between January and October of 1992. The changes had important consequences for the fate of the Clinton plan.

Despite his reference to a "single-payer system" in that Nashua

comment. it made no sense for Bill Clinton to sign on to the most liberal of the existing Democratic policy alternatives. The whole premise of his campaign was that he was a "New Democrat," unenamored
of big, bureaucratic government and fully aware of the need for
spending discipline. His political base lay in the Democratic Leadership Council, a group of moderate-to-conservative officeholders with
no ties to organized labor, the chief proponent of the Canadian plan.
His allies were the governors, who had had bitter experience with
the government-financed Medicaid program. Many of them found
that the state share of Medicaid was the fastest-rising part of their
budgets, crowding out spending for schools, roads, and other needs.
The notion that Clinton would embrace a Canadian-style proposal
that called for big payroll taxes and a giant expansion of the welfare
state was a non-starter.

Like all governors, Bill Clinton had been forced to deal with exploding costs of Medicaid payments in his state, and he worked on
that issue for the National Governors' Association. But he was barely
aware of the concept called "managed competition." It first came to
his attention in conversations with his California campaign chairman, state insurance commissioner John Garamendi. Garamendi
was a contemporary of Clinton and as ambitious to rise as the man
he was supporting. As the first elected insurance commissioner since
California became a state, he had waged politically profitable battles
against the auto insurers and was preparing to run again for governor, an office he had sought unsuccessfully before. Garamendi's
deputy, Walter Zelman, had put together a health insurance advisory panel that included people who were developing the managed
competition theory at Stanford.

When Clinton went to Los Angeles for a fund-raiser in January
1992, he spent the better part of an hour talking health policy with
Garamendi and Zelman. A week later, Garamendi introduced his
state version of a managed competition plan and saw it praised on
the editorial page of the *New York Times*.

Traveling with Clinton on the governor's frequent fund-raising
and political forays to their mega-state, Garamendi and Zelman began to introduce him to the idea. Clinton had also heard it advocated
by Tsongas, who in mid-March, short of money and states he might

win, had followed Harkin and Kerrey in being forced to withdraw from the presidential campaign.

Separately, Ira Magaziner had begun to pay closer heed to some of the same Boston and Cambridge business and economic advisers who had steered Tsongas to managed competition. Magaziner had been working on economic policy for the campaign as one of a group of academics including a Rhodes scholar classmate of his and Clinton's, Robert Reich of Harvard. Later, Magaziner would say of managed competition, "[I] actually didn't bump into it until I had come to a lot of the same conclusions myself. I came across some of the stuff that Walter Zelman had been doing with Garamendi in California, and, as I read it, I said, Boy, this fits a lot with what we've been thinking."

During the winter and spring of 1992, Clinton himself was much too preoccupied with politics to worry about doctrinal debates on health care policy. His passage through that modern torture chamber called the presidential primaries had been exhausting. Every time he seemed to be making headway some new peril presented itself: Gennifer Flowers, who claimed to have been his mistress for many years, released torrid tapes of their phone conversations. New documents appeared casting doubt on his previous explanations of how he avoided the Vietnam military draft. After many denials that he had ever tried marijuana, he retreated to the claim that he had "never inhaled." His integrity and veracity were under constant challenge. No sooner did he dispose of rivals Harkin, Kerrey, and Tsongas than Jerry Brown, the former governor of California, popped up, running a "guerilla campaign" that provided a convenient haven for Democratic voters worried that Clinton could not beat President Bush. And then, finally, just when Clinton clearly had the Democratic nomination in sight, there came Ross Perot, the eccentric but media-brilliant Dallas billionaire businessman, whose populist appeal as an independent dwarfed that of the incumbent President and pushed Clinton into third place in the polls. In June 1992, with the nomination in hand, Clinton was reading daily reports that Perot had a massive team of researchers preparing a platform for his campaign. Clinton felt that he was under immense pressure to spell out his own general election campaign proposals before Perot did. Bruce Reed's policy staff in Little Rock began a crash project on a booklet that would be called *Putting People First*. The health care section gave the contestants for Clinton's mind a chance to test their strengths. It came down to a contest between the Blueberry Donut Group, representing the Democratic establishment in Washington, and Magaziner, leading the Cambridge-California alliance attracted to the new theory of managed competition. As they battled, the crucial question that emerged was whose numbers could be trusted.

After much preliminary jousting, the battle heated up in a conference call on Saturday, June 20, with Fried and his Donut allies at their office in Washington; Magaziner at a miniature golf course in Massachusetts, where he was taking his kids on an outing; and Clinton at the Governor's Mansion in Little Rock, where, according to Bob Woodward in *The Agenda*, he was paying fitful attention to the health care debate while watching the U.S. Open golf championship on television. It was a contentious conversation.

Magaziner had come up with a set of financing numbers. The Blueberry Donut Group was skeptical of their authenticity, and Clinton was wary of being challenged about their accuracy. Until the financing was more firmly tested, Clinton seemed to be leaning toward dropping the health care section entirely. In the end, Bruce Reed found a compromise: Keep the outline of the proposal, but eliminate the numbers

As Magaziner recalled, Clinton said, "Well, I want to be honest, but what we can do is just assume it's deficit-neutral regardless. Just say we're going to get universal coverage without specifying a date."

The decision was a draw, leaving both sides free to fight again. The resulting four-page chapter on health care in *Putting People First* was bare-bones indeed; heavy on rhetoric and short on details. It boldly declared that "we are going to preserve what's best in our system: your family's right to choose who provides care and coverage, American innovation and technology and the world's best private doctors and hospitals. But we will take on the bureaucracies and corporate interests to make health care affordable and accessible to every American."

It promised expansive basic benefits. Preventive care and prescription drugs were included. Medicare would be expanded to include long-term care and establishment of more community centers. Insurance reform was mentioned, including a pledge to ban denial of coverage to anyone with a preexisting condition such as cancer or heart disease. Community rating — the young and healthy would pay the same premiums as the old and ill — was advocated, and proclaimed without proof to be a boon to small business.

Little was said about the most controversial, and difficult, question: how to pay for these reforms? Magaziner's hand showed in the promise to "shut down the 'paper hospital' " with a single claim form, end billing fraud, and stop drug price–gouging by pharmaceutical companies. He had argued in the internal debates that savings from these moves would be enough to slow medical inflation and pay for the added coverage. But others in the campaign were skeptical, so *Putting People First* also called for the establishment of a national board to set an annual medical budget for the entire nation — an idea lifted from Kerrey's single-payer plan. The pamphlet also referred vaguely to "local health networks," the HIPCs, or buyers' clubs of managed competition, which would be given "the necessary incentives to control costs." The plan was hard to decipher because the battle for Clinton's mind had not yet been resolved.

The only hint that new money might be needed came in a pledge to "phase in business responsibilities, covering employees through the public program until the transition is complete."

Nowhere was that public program described.

But by June 19, when interviewed at a convention of radio talk show hosts in Washington, D.C., Clinton was beginning to use the jargon of the new approach pushed by Magaziner and Garamendi. "The government," he said, "instead of trying to regulate the health care business, would set up an environment of managed competition in which we would really do a lot more to hold costs within inflation." He was beginning to lean away from the pay-or-play system he had borrowed from the Washington establishment at the beginning of the campaign and toward the new notion of managed competition. But he wasn't there yet.

*   *   *

After the infighting over *Putting People First*, Magaziner decided it was time to take on the Blueberry Donut Group. He arrived from Cambridge, and immediately made clear that he had his own agenda and way of working.

To Fried, Magaziner seemed "arrogant, all-knowing and dismissive." At one point, Fried recalled, "Magaziner turned to Judy Feder and said, 'It's you people in Washington that created this problem.' And Judy just lost it and said, 'How dare you? I have spent my life trying to improve the health quality of the people in this country.' " Another person present at that encounter remembers Feder interrupting a Magaziner presentation with the comment, "That would be a tad disruptive." Magaziner's response, this person recalls, was a curt: "That's the trouble with you people. You don't want to disrupt anything."

Other unsettling signals followed. As Fried recalled, Magaziner was so sure he knew how to squeeze out the wasted dollars that he claimed, "We don't have to raise any taxes and we'll fix the whole health care system." Anne Wexler remembered "another stunning remark: 'We can convert everyone to HMOs in a year.' "

Despite their reservations, Fried said, "We knew we were going to have to deal with this guy." And Magaziner understood he would have to out-flank or coopt them. "My sense was that there was a certain Washington Democratic thinking on this thing," he said. "It was in a pay-or-play mode and not very serious about cost containment. To them, cost containment was controls; it wasn't trying to reorient the system." Karen Ignagni of the AFL-CIO was worried that Magaziner's approach would leave the insurance companies still "gaming the system." Henry Aaron of the Brookings Institution was skeptical that competition would contain costs much. "And so I tried to bring in, I did bring in — no joy to some of the people there — a group from outside, people who had experience in industry," Magaziner recalled, "people who were working in Hawaii, Minnesota, California, and other places."

In Madison Square Garden, on July 15, when Clinton accepted the Democratic presidential nomination, he vowed to "take on the health care profiteers and make health care affordable for every family." Deliberately, his rhetoric was general; there was more risk than reward in getting specific, his political advisers counseled. Polls taken by Stan Greenberg for the campaign showed that while voters wanted the system changed, they weren't certain what changes would help them. They understood that question was crucial; therefore, they wanted politicians to be careful in making those changes. The Clinton campaign prepared a number of TV commercials. It aired none. Every time the reform message became specific, the consultants found as many voters were disturbed by it as attracted.

Clinton was not permitted to campaign only in platitudes, however. From its polling, the Bush campaign knew Clinton enjoyed a real advantage on the health issue. A Kaiser Family Foundation–Harris poll taken after both political conventions that summer showed Clinton holding a 55- to 27-percent edge over Bush when voters were asked which candidate would do more to provide affordable coverage for all Americans. President Bush, who had introduced modest proposals earlier in the year, had to fight back. In September a friendly lobbyist tipped off Susan Brophy, a Democratic National Committee operative, to expect a concerted attack from the Bush camp. Within days, Bush was charging that "Clinton's for universal coverage, but doesn't say how to pay for it or how to contain health care costs."

The Clinton team was nervous. In Arkansas the Medicaid program for poor people had run out of money. Clinton was forced to furlough employees of the state's human services department for five days without pay and to cut reimbursements to doctors and dentists by 20 percent. New restrictions were placed on doctor's visits, hospital stays, and access to prescriptions. As Robert Pear noted in a *New York Times* article that October, the situation was dire enough for a federal district judge to block the reimbursement cuts to obstetricians and pediatricians. The judge acted out of a perceived emergency: So many doctors were threatening to stop serving Medicaid patients that the health of mothers and infants was in jeopardy.

Political reaction was inevitable. Prompted by the Bush White House, Health and Human Services Secretary Louis W. Sullivan, a physician himself, charged, "Bill Clinton can't even control Medicaid costs in his own state. The thought of him trying to reform the nation's health care system is certainly enough to make me sick."

Publicly, Clinton replied that Arkansas, like other states, was a victim of inaction by the Bush administration. He vowed to redouble his efforts to control health care inflation. Privately, Atul Gawande, a young aide who would become influential in shaping Clinton policy, bluntly warned in an August 9 memo that he and Magaziner feared "the campaign's position on health care was too unstructured to defend ourselves well. . . . As it stands, the plan does not hang together and it is not clear. For anyone who knows anything, our current writeup is singularly unsatisfying. . . . We rely too much on the complexity of the issue to lead people to trust Clinton-the-policy-wonk."

On leave from Harvard Medical School, Atul Gawande was then twenty-six years old, a younger-generation reincarnation of Bill Clinton — a precociously bright Rhodes scholar, fascinated by politics and public policy, ambitious, determined to make a difference. Greyhound lean, with black hair, dark eyes, an intent look, Gawande had the kind of impressive academic credentials and boundless self-confidence, unsullied by much workaday experience, that later came to characterize much of the Clinton White House staff. Born in Athens, Ohio, Gawande was the child of two physicians from India — his father a urologist, his mother a pediatrician — who met while studying in the United States. At Stanford, Gawande had pursued a double major in biology and political science, combining an interest in public policy and in research into drugs, genetics, and AIDS. He continued those interests at Oxford on his Rhodes scholarship, studying political science and classical philosophy with the idea of applying what he learned to medical research. With that background, Gawande was accepted by Harvard Medical School but deferred admission in order to gain practical experience in his other consuming interest — politics.

At Stanford, he had worked on the 1984 presidential campaign of Gary Hart. Four years later, after Oxford, he was involved with then-Senator Al Gore's bid for the Democratic presidential nomination. When Gore dropped out of the race, Gawande decided to spend a year in Washington working on health care policy before taking up his medical studies at Harvard. He applied for jobs with congressmen holding junior positions on committees dealing with health care legislation. "I'm young, I'm cheap, and I'm interested in working a lot on health care," Gawande would tell them. Then he would add, with no little hubris: "And I'll give you a name on health care if you let me work with you on it."

Gawande accepted an offer from a thirty-four-year-old congressman from Tennessee, Jim Cooper, who had also studied at Oxford. He immediately became part of a network of bright, young advocates that met and exchanged ideas in the basement of a Capitol Hill restaurant, talking about the managed competition theory and staying in touch with its Jackson Hole designers. They called their meeting place "Jackson Holey."

They were the "best and brightest" of their generation. In the 1960s, the Vietnam "best and brightest" had been animated by an unshakable belief that American power could solve a political struggle in a distant land that they thought threatened American security. The health planners of the next generation, while perhaps not as inflated with self-assurance, nonetheless believed that rational planning and new ideas could solve a domestic problem they saw threatening U.S. economic security in the 1990s.

Many of them were, as Gawande described himself, believers in "progressive social policy within fiscal bounds." In Gawande's eyes, the culprit could be named in one of two ways: "Waste is the political way of putting it," he would say, "but inefficiency is the economic way of putting it."

After two years of working on Capitol Hill, Gawande resumed his medical studies at Harvard but was drawn back into the presidential politics of 1992, first as a Clinton volunteer, then as a campaign staff member, and eventually as the Little Rock campaign headquarters' resident expert on health policy.

Gawande brought with him to Little Rock the managed competition concepts he had developed while working with Jim Cooper. He and Magaziner had worked out what the younger man called a "good cop, bad cop" routine. "When we'd hold meetings, Ira would lose his temper and say to the Washington people, 'Now, you've got to get your act together and stop thinking like Washington people and realize what's going on out there.' And I would come in and say, 'Well, what about this managed competition thing?' "

Magaziner further urged the campaign to stress what had become his own mantra: "The Clinton health care plan will insure everyone out of the cost savings which will be achieved. . . . There will be no new taxes in our system. Our plan for universal coverage can be financed from savings from cost controls in four years."

The advice, and warnings, to Clinton continued. In an August 16 memo, Gawande cautioned Clinton that while "we start with a huge lead in public trust on health care . . . the last two weeks of Bush attacks may threaten that lead." Gawande's analysis identified what he saw as the six dangers then facing the Clinton campaign health position. Although the plan was soon to be modified significantly, Gawande's points anticipated what eventually became fatal vulnerabilities in the Clinton presidential health program:

> *Vagueness and lack of thematic integration.* They charge that the plan does not yet hang together with a focused program and resonance to core values. This has allowed partisans to depict us in the most unfavorable light and experts to withhold active support.
>
> *Hidden payroll tax charge.* People believe there is waste and fraud at the heart of our health care mess, but are skeptical that it all can be solved without an extra dime. Bush/Quayle see this as an opening for claiming we have a hidden payroll tax.
>
> *Small business fears.* Our story is not coming through, so they believe that mandated health benefits will hurt their business and that there will be a payroll tax hike in play-or-pay.
>
> *The dumping threat.* Republicans will argue that play-or-pay opens workers to getting dumped by their employers out of private coverage and into a public program that turns out to be like a giant Medicaid program.
>
> *Rationing.* Bush/Quayle charge that we will create rationing.
>
> *Bureaucracy.* We are portrayed as in the old liberal tradition of creating a giant-like Medicaid bureaucracy which will be inefficient and without compassion.

* * *

By the end of August, partly as a result of political pressures from Bush and partly out of the internal debates among the rival advisers, a major effort was under way to reposition Clinton's health policies. The objective was to form a merger of Democratic positions from Left and Right, and also to shed the pay-or-play label that had come under increasing Republican attack. Bringing everyone into an insurance pool would please the Left; letting private insurers and providers compete for business in that pool would please the Right. Letting market forces discipline inflation would please the Right; having a ceiling on overall spending, as a backup, would reassure the Left. The hope was that in blending these opposing views, the single-payer advocates, including the unions, and the managed competition folks, including parts of business, would find enough common ground to be supportive.

Jay Rockefeller, a strong pay-or-play supporter, got wind of what was happening and fired off a memo to Clinton on August 30, arguing against any change of direction. "This is not the time to reinvent the wheel," he told Clinton. "There may be some within your organization, right now, who are arguing that a better policy option could still be crafted which could win more unanimous support. After six years of exhaustive effort, I do not believe any major stones have been left unturned. . . . More importantly, even if a silver bullet is still waiting to be discovered, this is not the time to be looking. With weeks to go, take the plan you have (it is damn good) and beat Bush over the head with it."

But the revisionists were now in control. In Washington, Magaziner convened a meeting of advisers to discuss shifts in policy. It lasted nearly seven hours. "I was trying to make the point that we really had to be more private-sector oriented," Magaziner said, "and more reliant on competition."

As was often the case when Magaziner was involved, the session was hard on everyone's nerves. Magaziner saw it as a "clash of cultures" between federal and state dominance and the private sector. "There were still some single-payer people there," he observed, notably Karen Ignagni of the AFL-CIO. Magaziner was the outsider — and felt resented. "I mean," he recalled, "these people were the kind of community that knew each other quite well, and none of these people knew who I was. There was some tension."

Only a shared sense of political danger kept it from blowing up. "We know we're not going to get anything done if we don't get Clinton elected," Magaziner said. "We can talk about some of these other things afterwards. Let's get him elected first."

Out of those staff conferences in Washington and Little Rock came a memorandum Gawande prepared that summarized the internal agreements on policy, and became, in turn, the basic text for briefing Clinton on September 22, the date of the first scheduled presidential debate. These were the key elements of the new approach:

- All workers and their families would receive health insurance through their jobs, with employers paying most of the premiums. The economic costs to small business would be cushioned by direct subsidies and a slow phase-in.
- Every American would be covered; those outside the workforce would have their premiums paid by the government.
- Networks of hospitals, physicians, and other medical professionals would be organized in every community to compete in this expanded health care marketplace, charging flat fees for a standard package of benefits for everyone who signed up. The government would set the top fee; market forces might undercut it.
- States would organize health insurance purchasing groups [the HIPCs, later rechristened alliances] through which small firms, the self-employed, and other individuals could buy policies at better rates than they would otherwise get. The alliances would put competitive pressure on the health care networks to improve quality and reduce costs.
- To be sure that the anticipated savings were realized, the federal government would set an overall national health budget, and both insurance premiums and providers' fees would have to stay under that ceiling.

The Clinton campaign had given birth to its version of managed competition.

"Sticking with employer-based coverage is the right way to go,"

Gawande assured the candidate. "As we protect businesses from unpredictable costs, we will ask employers not now covering their workers to do their fair share. They must buy coverage for their workers or opt to buy through their regional purchasing group. . . . We must not embrace a payroll tax. Although it is a guaranteed ceiling on the costs of coverage for businesses, they find this concept anathema. Instead, a substantial tax credit should be provided to limit employer costs."

The conclusion of that memo captures the essence of what the Clinton advisers thought they were offering the candidate — and the country:

"The plan will secure basic health care as a right for every American and it will take a giant stride in securing a strong economy and the public health." Gawande argued that the plan did not "nationalize medicine," but did help small business and consumers. "Doctors and hospitals are sheltered from micromanagement, paperwork and bureaucracy [and freed] to care for patients. . . . In this system, responsibilities are to be evenly distributed. Whether it is business or the consumer, everyone will be doing their fair share. No burden is too heavy, but no one is freeloading on the system either."

They thought they had reached the policy version of the promised land.

Bill Clinton walked into a room in Lansing, Michigan, the morning of September 22, 1992, with a huge cup of coffee and an expression clearly suggesting, as Bruce Fried remembered, "that he did not want to be at this meeting with yet another group of goddamn health policy experts." The look of distaste on his face, the stiffness of his posture as he lowered himself into a chair, conveyed an unspoken cry: Can't you leave me alone on this stupid issue?

His reaction was not surprising. The hard-fought presidential campaign would be decided just six weeks from that day, and Clinton had gone to Michigan for the first scheduled presidential debate — a debate that George Bush had refused. Taking advantage of his opponent's absence, Clinton had scheduled a set of rallies in the swing state and had sandwiched in this meeting.

But as the Lansing briefing began with a rundown of the points in the Gawande memo, "a quite visible change" came over the candidate. "You could see him lighten, sort of begin to get it: 'Gee, if this really works, this fits in with my whole public-private partnership in government.' He began to get very engaged in the discussion, challenging people," Fried recalled. "By the end of the session, he was very enthused." Gawande had the same impression: "He quickly understood not only the policy but how to make these [supporting] arguments. And his face literally brightened up and he was out of his chair, walking up and down, talking out loud. It was just a great meeting. You felt like you'd just hit a home run."

Two days later, the results of that briefing were codified in a speech that unveiled Clinton's final health reform policies. He delivered it before some two thousand employees of Merck Pharmaceutical Co., in Rahway, New Jersey. The site was a natural — in a swing state with a company that had voluntarily decided to keep increases of its prescription drugs below the inflation rate, headed by a chairman, Dr. P. Roy Vagelos, who was an active Democrat.

Without ever using the term "managed competition," Clinton contrasted his policy approach with that of President Bush, who proposed tax subsidies of private insurance companies. "Throwing good money after bad," Clinton said, castigating the Bush position. His own plan, Clinton explained, "is a private system. It is not pay-or-play. It does not require new taxes. It will preserve what is best about the present health care system, but it will also incorporate what we have learned about what is wrong." Emphasizing the market aspects of his plan, Clinton added, "We've got to quit having the federal government try to micromanage health care and instead set up incentives for the private sector to manage the cost down within limits, beyond which we absolutely must not go in spending."

Clinton's speech received favorable coverage. Only the *New York Times* reported a disconcerting note: After his speech, while he mingled with the crowd, an admiring mother held up her baby before the candidate. The baby threw up on Clinton's suit jacket. "That's what babies do," the paper quoted Clinton as saying cheerfully.

* * *

Thus, Bill Clinton's presidential campaign both determined the basic substantive approach he would take to health care as President, and, equally important, established the political strategy he would pursue in office to achieve his reforms.

In early discussions, Bruce Fried recalled, Clinton's political advisers referred to public opinion research published in April of 1992 by the Public Agenda Foundation, *Faulty Diagnosis: Public Misconceptions About Health Care Reform*, which asked both policy experts and ordinary citizens what they thought was the health care system's main problem.

Experts defined the problem as unendurable escalation of costs. The citizens polled, on the other hand, wanted the government to spend more on health, but also have their own bills reduced. Experts knew the uninsured were mainly the working poor. The citizenry thought they were the elderly or the very poor — people already protected by government programs. Experts designed complex solutions. People wanted simply to punish those profiting from the system. In a prophetic statement, John Immerwahr, the report's principal author, said, "Until these differences are fully understood, and until leadership and media take steps to address them, the debate on health care will likely result in continued political gridlock — with the public and leaders talking past each other and genuine long-lasting consensus elusive."

In the campaign period, Fried recalled, Clinton's political advisers focused mainly on the message that for "the plain folks, it's greed — greedy hospitals, greedy doctors, greedy insurance companies. It was an us-versus-them issue, which Clinton was extremely good at exploiting."

Clinton's political consultants — Carville, Begala, Grunwald, Greenberg — all thought "there had to be villains," Anne Wexler remembered. "It was a very alarming prospect for those of us looking long term at how to deal with this issue. But at that point, the insurance companies and the pharmaceutical companies became the enemy."

Wexler, it should be noted, was not an entirely disinterested party. Her firm represented the Health Insurance Association of America; Upjohn, the pharmaceutical giant; the American Dental

Association; the Catholic Hospitals Association; the National Association of Community Health Centers; and others with large economic stakes in the battle. Such groups like to have lobbyists with access not only to the current administration but to the one that may be elected next.

For Clinton, both political rhetoric and policy seemed to be working. The combination of the free-market theory of managed competition and an overall budget-spending ceiling threw the Republicans off. By early October, Clinton had widened his health-issue margin over Bush from twenty-eight percentage points in late August to forty-two points in another Kaiser Family Foundation–Harris poll.

On Election Day, the final poll in that series disclosed a thirty-four-point Clinton lead over Bush. Still, voters ranked health care only third in importance to them, far behind the economy and slightly behind the budget deficit. Public support for Clinton's plan was even less impressive. When three alternatives were described to voters, one-third of those polled favored Bush's subsidy plan for insurance and another third the single-payer plan. Only 28 percent picked Clinton's still-unfamiliar managed competition scheme with national budget caps. As Harvard expert Robert J. Blendon wrote in his analysis of the poll, "Clinton has a general mandate for health reform which will expand coverage and contain costs. He does not, however, have a mandate for a particular plan and he faces the formidable challenge of building consensus on a specific health reform program."

Other clear warning signs existed. The Public Agenda Foundation, analyzing its polls and focus groups, concluded ominously that "the apparent consensus" is a "house of cards that will fall apart with the first gust of reality. . . . The American public believes that the country's health care system is riddled with waste and greed. Consequently, they are not eager to talk about hard choices, or to consider solutions that will increase their own costs or reduce the services they get. Nor are they ready to relinquish the miracles of modern medicine."

Republican pollster Bill McInturff had found the same attitudes in his surveys. The public's idea of "radical reform," he said, was not radical at all. It meant getting rid of bureaucratic waste, allowing people to get insurance even if they had a disease, not having their premiums raised when they became ill. A post-election poll showed that Clinton's real advantage over Bush on the issue stemmed simply from the fact that twice as many people thought the Democrats had a plan. And when McInturff asked what they thought Clinton would do, the overwhelming response was "make their own health care more affordable." Guaranteeing insurance for the uninsured was a distant second.

But the most striking critical appraisal — especially considering its source — came in the August memo Jay Rockefeller sent to candidate Bill Clinton. Rockefeller's reading of public psychology and the politics of the issue was blunt. Fear, he said, will dominate this debate much more than hope or altruism: "Cost control is the reform Americans most need, want and are willing to pay for. . . . Peace of mind follows cost control. Voters fear losing coverage from loopholes, job changes, layoffs or catastrophic illness. Reform that makes insurance more affordable helps allay this fear, but voters want stronger safeguards. Fear, much more than compassion, drives support for universal guarantees of coverage."

Then Rockefeller offered Clinton his own checklist of propositions that the public would accept — or reject: "Voters believe insurance companies, drugs and equipment manufacturers, doctors and hospitals are raking in obscene profits at their expense. Voters are skeptical of any politician's promise of reform 'for free.' But they do believe there is so much money being wasted and gouged that reform could reap substantial returns. . . . If cost control is the major focus, financing reform from savings wrung from the system is credible."

The West Virginia senator turned then to a catalogue of broader biases that he thought Clinton should note: "Voters like choosing their own doctor and believe the current system is the best in the world in terms of research technology and quality of care. Americans worry that any fix of what they hate will ruin the aspects they like. Voters have deep unease about government's ability to manage complex health reform . . . but they do want government to clear the kudzu out of the system — restore competitive conditions that keep prices down and stop abuses that leave them at the mercy of profiteers and market forces run amok."

Despite these cautions, Rockefeller told Clinton he was optimistic about building a broad coalition of support, both during the campaign and later. "From my years of work on this issue," he wrote, "I know firsthand what an extraordinary range of leaders and groups can be brought together — from consumer advocates to the AMA, big business to big unions, barrio social workers to Park Avenue doctors and everyone in between. Bringing their support together behind your health care plan would be a dramatic demonstration of your ability to 'heal this nation' and get us working together to solve the real problems of average families."

But Rockefeller also raised a warning that was to be ignored by Clinton — with serious consequences.

The statement that "Americans deserve or have a right to health care is a dead-end approach," he wrote. "Although many Americans may initially react positively to this statement, over time it can make them uneasy. Before long they will be asking: How would we pay for all that care for all those people? Won't it require a huge new government bureaucracy? Is every American deserving?"

The importance of Rockefeller's message cannot be overstated. He was cautioning Clinton not to read too much into the Wofford victory in Pennsylvania. He was recalling the lesson of Congress's battle over catastrophic insurance — that voters will calculate carefully whether any promise of new health benefits is really in their personal financial interest. He was saying, Be very careful of the rhetoric you use — or it may turn on you.

Coming from a man who had well-established credentials as a crusader for universal health insurance, these were amazingly pointed warnings. Their significance would not be seen until it was too late.

Atul Gawande had been up all night but still felt wired. Along with other Clinton campaign aides, he felt incredibly lucky to have stood only a few feet from the steps of the Arkansas State House, surrounded by thousands of screaming people in Little Rock, when Bill Clinton finally announced he had won the election and would become the next President of the United States. "We were all just electric with excitement," Gawande said later, remembering the emotion that swept the crowds late that night, touching off a celebration that lasted till dawn.

He was still exultant later that morning when he went to Clinton campaign headquarters to begin packing. There, he encountered George Stephanopoulos. "You did a great job, Atul," Stephanopoulos told him. Then, in words that suddenly made Gawande feel a sense of foreboding, Stephanopoulos added, "You're going to wish you never did, because health care is now on the agenda."

In the few hours he had left before flying home to Cambridge, Gawande sat amid the packing boxes in his crowded campaign cubicle and wrote a memo addressed no longer to the governor of Arkansas but to President-elect Bill Clinton. In Gawande's mind, this was his last chance to shape the Clinton reform policy. It was critical that Clinton and his advisers understand how important the issue would be and the real challenge they faced. "In my mind," he said later, "the issue was cost containment — cost, cost, cost — and leave it at that."

What he wrote next was broader in concept, broad enough to foreshadow the battle to come. Reform, Gawande advised Clinton, is "at once our most ambitious and most treacherous task. . . . If health reform is passed and successful, it would be an indelible symbol of achievement and of your ability to create needed change in the face of special interests. . . . It also would be an accomplishment on the scale of Social Security and, in combination with a strong economy and a strong America abroad, could restore a Democratic lock on the middle class.

"At the same time," his memo continued, "getting health reform passed will be enormously difficult. We are at great risk of defeat. As you know, health reform involves restructuring spending in a sector that occupies 15 percent of our economy. We will have to take on extremely powerful and entrenched interests, and navigate through a deeply divided Congress (and that's just the Democrats)."

In words that would become ever more meaningful, he warned the President-elect: "The difficulty is compounded by the fact that we have won a mandate for change, but not one for any specific policy." Gawande was saying exactly what Harvard's Bob Blendon and the Public Agenda Foundation had extracted from their polls.

After a year of campaigning, after debating the issue with his rivals for the Democratic nomination and with George Bush, after months of briefings with Magaziner, Gawande, and the Blueberry Donut Group, Clinton had worked out in his own mind a specific blueprint for reform. But he had given only one major speech — the one at Merck — outlining the plan. Most of the public had only the fuzziest notion of what he had in mind, and some who knew were skeptical.

Bill Clinton's inaugural day was bracingly fresh and brilliantly clear. Long after that day passed into history, one of the young aides who had labored long on the policy during the campaign and would play a role in trying to pass the reforms into law was struck by the unrealistic euphoria that swept the inaugural throngs at the Capitol. Here, he remembered thinking, was their chance to affect history. "What was missing then was the same thing that had been missing in the campaign," he said. "That was an opinion from the President about how extravagant and elaborate a reform you want. Nobody in January of 1993 was thinking about the fact that Bill Clinton only got 43 percent of the votes. He was on top of the world. He was young, he was good-looking, he gave a good speech. The world was full of hope. That inflates in your mind what actually can be done."

6

The Task Force

I T WAS FIVE DAYS after the inauguration. In the Roosevelt
Room of the White House, down the corridor from the Oval Office, members of the cabinet, top White House aides, and First Lady
Hillary Rodham Clinton assembled behind closed doors to hear the
President discuss his national health plan. After an hour of conversation, the press was summoned to hear the President describe "the
massive task ahead."

"The message is pretty simple," Clinton told the reporters, after
detailing examples of the problems people had told him about during
his presidential campaign. "It's time to make sense of the American
health care system."

With that he announced formation of the President's Task Force
on National Health Reform. Its job would be to "prepare health care
reform legislation to be submitted to Congress within one hundred
days of our taking office."

The President had another announcement of critical importance.
His wife, Hillary Rodham Clinton, would head the new task force.
Named its day-to-day operating head was Ira Magaziner.

"I knew from the beginning it was a very big thing, something no
one had ever been able to do before," President Clinton told us in the
summer of 1995. "I knew that it was an issue with a lot of downside
and a high probability of failure. It turned out to be even more difficult than I thought it would be," the President confessed. Many of
the specific problems that damaged his project were unforeseeable,
but he knew even as he announced the task force and the timetable

that "it was just an enormous undertaking and there was no example since the Depression, the war, and the early pressures of the Cold War when something that sweeping was done in as short amount of time as I was trying to do it."

Why then attempt it — especially after the election results had left him with a shaky hold on public support, when he was also committed to push through a controversial budget, and when his administration had yet to test its working relationship with Congress?

Campaign promises were part of the answer. Clinton had scorned Bush's indifference to health care and had pledged swift action. The hubris of a hard-fought victory was also at work. But there were also solid policy reasons for attempting it. "It seemed to me," he said, "that the problems of ordinary families, the problems of the economy at large, the problems of specific businesses, and the problems of the government's finances were all caught up in the health care inflation and in the fact that we were the only advanced country that couldn't figure out how to cover everybody."

But why attempt to do it all in one piece of legislation? Why not take it a step at a time, as many in both parties on Capitol Hill and in the health care community were recommending? The answer to that lies in the way Bill Clinton's mind works. As James Carville, his campaign consultant, once remarked, "He is blessed — or cursed — with a mind that sees the connectedness of things."

A politician looking for an easy victory might have taken the least controversial and most broadly popular piece of health care reform — say, a standardization of claim forms or a guarantee that people who changed jobs could keep their insurance — and secured a nice win. But Clinton, as he said, "was afraid that if we took it on piece by piece, we might solve some problems but we might make others worse." The popular insurance reforms — like guaranteed portability — would help some people, he said, but "might raise insurance costs so much" that young people and small businesses could be forced to drop or cut back their coverage.

Similarly, he said, reducing payments for Medicare and Medicaid might cut government costs dramatically, but unless at least some of those savings were recycled into the system, some hospitals and clinics that were already "really strapped" might be forced into bankruptcy.

In chess and in campaigns, it is a great advantage to be able to see how the board might look several plays ahead. In government, as Carville suggested, it can be a curse. In some instances, like human rights in China, it can paralyze you from acting. In others, like health care, it can cause you to attempt too much — trying to ward off problems that others might not have seen.

"It seemed to me," Clinton said, "that all aspects of this problem were sufficiently interrelated that we ought to try to have a comprehensive solution." That was his mandate to his task force — make it comprehensive. Not just the big pieces like Medicare and Medicaid but rural clinics, Native American medical services, the research hospitals, the nursing schools — be sure all the pieces fit.

Why Bill Clinton picked his wife to lead the health care reform effort remains a subject of endless speculation. The decision grew out of a number of conversations the Clintons had after the election about what role Hillary Clinton would play in the new administration. There was consideration of giving her a broader policy role. An insider remembers participating in serious internal arguments that Christmas after hearing that "Hillary was going to be made principal domestic adviser." This person remembers arguing with others, "You can't do that. It'll destroy her. It'll destroy us. It'll mean she's co-President. It's wrong. And we won that battle, but there was blood on the floor." Others say she had other roles in mind. One longtime friend, who discussed the decision with the First Lady, says many of Hillary Clinton's friends "were very concerned that she'd be seen as the co-President." Therefore, this person adds, "the decision that she take one subject and run with it" made a lot of sense.

As Hillary Clinton recalled in one of our interviews, the President's decision to vest formation of health policy in a White House task force came out of his desire to avoid the infighting he expected would occur among the cabinet secretaries with a claim to significant jurisdiction. Only later did the President decide to appoint her to head that effort.

"Instead of having to referee fights because somebody thought their turf had been taken," she said, describing that decision, "he wanted to try to set up a system so that everybody had to participate, but it would be run out of the White House." The President echoed that thought and added another explanation. As a governor who had had his own severe problems with Medicaid, the joint federal-state program for the poor, he shared the view of many state and local officials that the federal agency responsible for administering that program and Medicare — the Health Care Financing Agency (HCFA) — had "big troubles." If word got out that HCFA (pronounced "Hickfa") and its parent department, Health and Human Services (HHS), were designing the Clinton health care plan, he said, the governors, whose support would be vital, "would be hard to bring" along.

The President told us that he picked Hillary because he thought "she cared enough about it, had enough talent, and had enough understanding that if anybody had a chance to do it, she would have the best chance." Besides, he added, she was the only one around the White House who "could devote full time to it."

His last statement is questionable. Obviously he could have appointed someone else as full-time coordinator. At the time, people in Washington widely suspected that Clinton had promised his wife the generalship in return for her support when he faced accusations of infidelity during his presidential race. We were never able to substantiate those rumors. Clearly, both of the Clintons thought of his public offices as a shared responsibility. In Arkansas, she had led the commission that framed his proposals for education reform — the keystone of his agenda as governor. As she reminded reporters when her role as the head of the President's task force was announced, she had led the rural health care task force for two years in Arkansas and served as her husband's representative on a regional task force on infant mortality. She had also served on the board of the Arkansas Children's Hospital and chaired the national board of the Children's Defense Fund.

Hillary Rodham Clinton brought other qualifications to her new Washington position. From the beginning of their relationship, back in Yale Law School, Bill Clinton had recognized in this daughter of a suburban Chicago businessman — a Republican, incidentally — and spokeswoman of her Wellesley graduating class a will to lead and a reformist zeal that was at least a match for his own.

He also recognized she possessed many qualities he lacked. Where he was dilatory, open-hearted, diffuse, she was disciplined, tough-minded, focused. Because of her work on the Arkansas education reform, the President told us, "I knew that she could manage a long, complex, highly contentious process [involving] something people care a lot about." From his first, losing campaign for Congress in 1974, and especially when he plotted his comeback from the bitter 1980 loss after his first term as governor, Clinton had acknowledged that Hillary was probably better than he in managing big and difficult enterprises. Bill Clinton knew how to charm people; Hillary Rodham Clinton knew how to get things done.

During the presidential campaign, Clinton had told audiences, in what reporters quickly recognized was not a joke, "Buy one, get one free." Early in the primaries, she would sometimes speak as long, and at least as effectively, as he did. When her off-the-cuff comments in Chicago about not wanting to "stay at home and bake cookies" were taken as a put-down of traditional homemakers, her public profile was deliberately lowered. But she remained a strong voice in campaign strategy meetings — and obviously a powerful influence on his thinking.

Hillary Rodham seemed to put the steel in Bill Clinton. She was aggressive enough in his last campaign for governor, in 1990, that when Clinton's Democratic primary opponent scheduled a news conference in the capitol, the state's First Lady broke in unannounced. Quoting the opponent's earlier praise of her husband, Hillary raised her voice and berated him for his apostasy. "You have a very short memory," she told the astonished challenger. When he tried to respond, she cut him off: "Give me a break!"

That kind of toughness would be needed in the upcoming fight, and especially in guiding the new task force toward the goal Clinton announced of submitting legislation to Congress "within one hundred days of our taking office."

The President's estimates of Hillary's skills were widely echoed. Philip Lee was sixty-nine years old and happily teaching at the University of California at San Francisco in January of 1993 when

Donna Shalala asked him to be her assistant secretary for Health. It was in essence the same job that Lee had held thirty years earlier in the Johnson administration, when he was one of the architects of Medicare. He was not eager to resume a government career, but he agreed to take a short leave and help Shalala get organized. She took him to some of the early White House meetings and he found the First Lady "so impressive that I said to myself, 'Hey, wait a minute, why did I turn this down?' " Shalala asked again, and he said yes. By April, he was on the road with Hillary to Nebraska and Montana; his respect for her ability soared. "I've never seen anybody who grasped the complex issues of health care as well as she did and who could explain them as clearly to the public."

The appointment of Hillary sent one other message, the President thought. "People would know that I was really serious about trying to do this. I thought if we were going to take this on against all the odds, we had to give it our best shot. We had to stretch to the last degree."

That was certainly true. But the appointment of the First Lady also created problems. As one person watching from close range put it, the decision to name someone as close to and influential with the President as Hillary sent two major signals. It made clear to all in his administration, and to the players in both parties on Capitol Hill, the importance he placed on health care. It also served instantly to limit how far cabinet secretaries and White House aides could go in pressing for *their* views.

"They went about this exactly in the right way," this same official said, "with one exception: The person who's in charge shouldn't sleep with the President, because if you sleep with the President, nobody is going to tell you the truth." Underscoring the point, he added that the key economic advisers to the President had 'grave reservations about the direction this thing was going right at the beginning," but were reluctant to express them after asking themselves, "Do I want to take on the President's wife?"

After the battle, Clinton said he had underestimated this problem. "That's where being a President and a governor is different," he said. "There was a sense that some people felt that they were somewhat constrained by [Hillary's role]. I was surprised by that, since I have gone out of my way to make people feel that they should say what is on their mind." As governor, he said, he knew his aides and they knew him — and few things were held back. But as President, "they have to work for you for a year or two before they're really sure how far they can go." Some, including men and women who had been around Presidents for many years, did not want to test the limits of Hillary Clinton's patience.

Other risks of the assignment were evident to both Clintons, but, as Hillary told friends, "We had heard it before and we had survived it and we had been able to produce something."

Later, when the plan encountered strong opposition and some of the critics turned it into a personal assault on the ideology and character of the First Lady, she said, "I also understood — as many people never tired of telling me — that this could be a disaster, that I could get blamed. But I can only be true to myself. That didn't bother me. Heat comes with anything. If I had done nothing, I would have gotten heat. So better to get heat trying to do something important for people."

At the time of her appointment, a friend sent her an article about the controversies Eleanor Roosevelt had stirred with her advocacy of favorite New Deal programs. Mrs. Roosevelt, Hillary Clinton read, ignored the criticism and continued speaking out on issues she cared about. That strengthened the First Lady's resolve. When Doris Kearns Goodwin completed her Pulitzer Prize–winning book about the Roosevelts during World War II, *No Ordinary Time*, Hillary Clinton invited the author to stay over at the White House while they discussed the problems that earlier First Couple had encountered.

Later, both Clintons would reflect that their belief in Hillary's ability to walk this fine line, sensing what was acceptable and what was unacceptable for an extremely activist First Lady, was perhaps naive. "The reaction was more negative than I thought," the President said. "I will admit, I underestimated this." And, the First Lady said, "I really did not appreciate what a firestorm this decision would create." She blamed it on "the incredible personal investment that people had in health care as an issue." But it also reflected the reluctance of the public to abandon their traditional notion of what the First Lady should — and should not — be.

Even more than Eleanor Roosevelt, Hillary Clinton was a political trailblazer. If Bill Clinton was the representative of the post–World War II generation come to power in the 1990s — the first President born after that war, the first born after the advent of the atomic age, the first to come of age protesting the military policies of the U.S. government, the first to exercise American leadership in a world where the old fears of a communist threat neither existed nor produced national unity at home, the first to govern an America experiencing growing doubts about the previously unquestioned promise of an American Dream in which tomorrow would always be better than today — so Hillary Rodham Clinton exemplified a new generation of American women fully coming into their own. "A friend told me I've turned into a gender Rorschach test," she told Hilary Stout of the *Wall Street Journal*. "People are not really often reacting to me so much as they are reacting to their own lives and the transitions they are going through." She was not only America's first career professional First Lady; she had also been given authority never previously granted a President's wife to shape policy. She had not been elected to anything or confirmed to any position, but here she was, exercising real and visible power. Controversy over her role was inevitable.

Ira Magaziner was the obvious choice to be Hillary Clinton's chief collaborator. He was chosen, a close friend of the Clintons said, "because they had confidence in him, they knew he would be loyal, they knew he would be thorough, and they knew he wouldn't play games."

Like most of the campaign workers and advisers, Magaziner had been waiting anxiously during the transition to learn what he would be doing in the new administration. In a conversation with the President-elect in the kitchen of the Governor's Mansion, a number of possibilities were discussed: secretary to the cabinet; coordinator of technology policy. . . or defense conversion . . . or competitiveness programs . . . or worker training. Nothing was settled. It seemed to Magaziner that the Clintons were moving people around as if they were pieces on a chessboard. Every option seemed to place Magaziner on someone else's square. Washington veterans warned Magaziner that "the idea of sitting in the White House and running an inter-departmental effort among secretaries who were going to have their own turf was crazy."

Not until early January did Magaziner hear from the President-elect that he would be asked to work on health reform. Clinton gave him assurances that he would be in charge of coordinating all health matters, including those involving the President, the vice president, and the First Lady. He would have their backing.

The pledge was given unstintingly because Clinton had developed great confidence in his fellow Rhodes scholar. As the President said in our interview, "First of all, he was one of the few people I knew that I thought understood the health care system and could render it intelligible to people who weren't in health care. Secondly, because he worked with me in the campaign, he understood what I thought had to be done. Thirdly, I thought Ira understood big systems, be-cause he made quite a lot of money, several million dollars, advising corporations about what kind of changes they ought to make to meet the demands of the global economy. So I thought there was some evidence that he had pretty good judgment."

When Magaziner learned that Hillary Clinton would direct the effort, he felt no qualms. She had not been a significant player in the health policy debates during the campaign, but they had established an easy working relationship during the time they served together on a national job-training commission. "And from my point of view," Magaziner said, "it gave me a backup that I needed to have a shot at it and not get killed in the process."

Nonetheless, the assignment was worrisome. Magaziner's friend Harrison Wellford, a Washington lawyer who had been through the same battles as an aide to Jimmy Carter and later worked on Clinton's transition team, told him that serious reform would take "at least four years, maybe longer." The issues were too complicated, he warned, the interest groups too strong, too powerful. "The divi-sions of public opinion about it are too great," Wellford cautioned. "You'll never be able to bridge the chasms, and you'll tear apart the Democratic Party."

Kirk O'Donnell, Magaziner's Brown University classmate and former aide to Speaker Thomas P. (Tip) O'Neill, who was now a

Washington lobbyist, warned of another problem: the difficulty of managing such an undertaking from a White House staff position. Other experienced Washington hands told Magaziner that the President's stated intention of passing reform in his first year — or even during his first Congress — was utterly unrealistic.

"The common wisdom," Magaziner recalled at a time when he still had high hopes of proving all the Cassandras wrong, was "try to do something simple so you can say you've done health. Then get away from it as fast as you can."

But Ira Magaziner, at age forty-five, loved challenges that others found too daunting. He grew up on Long Island and crossed the sound to Providence, Rhode Island, for college. The summer of his sophomore year at Brown, in a pattern he was to repeat often, he produced a four-hundred-page plan to reconstruct the entire curriculum. This was in the heady 1960s, when academic improvisations were sprouting across America's campuses. Magaziner's proposed new curriculum — it waived many course requirements and eliminated letter grades in others — became a cause among activist students. In 1969, it was largely adopted by Brown's faculty, attracting national attention. It is still in effect today.

After graduating as valedictorian, Magaziner began studies as a Rhodes scholar at Oxford. There, he met Bill Clinton and organized antiwar protests; Clinton was later criticized for participating in some of them. When Magaziner returned to the United States, he tried to become a community organizer. For two years he and other former fellow students attempted, with little success, to create neighborhood organizations pressing for changes in the government of Brockton, Massachusetts. His organizing efforts produced few reforms and did nothing to cushion the economic blows of major factory relocations. Feeling frustrated and rebuffed, he moved to the private sector, joining a business consulting group, working for industrial clients, and, in one case, for the government of Sweden. A friend from that period says Magaziner did not abandon the goals of sixties activism, but came to believe that working from inside the business system, and using market forces rather than relying solely on government, were likely to produce more results.

Boldness and complexity were hallmarks of his work; his audacity and originality appealed to some in business. Amo Houghton, who became a Republican member of the House from New York, found Magaziner the most valuable consultant his family firm, Corning Glass Co., ever hired. Most consultants just repackage old ideas and tell you what you already know, Houghton said. Magaziner had original ideas. Mitt Romney, the Republican businessman who later opposed Ted Kennedy in the 1994 Senate race, worked as a colleague of Magaziner in the BCG consulting firm during this period and echoed Houghton's praise.

But Romney added an important caveat. "You have to understand what consultants do," he said. "They analyze an operation and come up with dozens of ways to change it. Then the management has to judge what the ideas are worth. Usually, they'll say I have to discard this set because our customers don't want or expect that of us; this set, I'm going to forget, because my people aren't capable of doing these things in this way. But these others — the remainder — I may be able to use. Ira generated lots of ideas. But he had no sense of which were usable and which were not."

By 1979, Magaziner was ready to leave BCG and form his own firm. Three years later, he began his most ambitious project to date — what came to be called "The Greenhouse Compact," a comprehensive economic plan for the entire state of Rhode Island. It applied many of the industrial-policy concepts Magaziner had developed in collaboration with Robert Reich, his Cambridge neighbor and friend, in their 1982 book, *Minding America's Business*. His blueprint called for providing investment and government support for industries judged to have the best growth potential. "Losers" would be liquidated.

The Greenhouse Compact, a massive eleven-hundred-page document, became the center of a huge public debate. Supporters included key Democrats running the state government and some business executives. They were not enough. The plan was defeated four to one in a statewide referendum.

Undeterred, Magaziner took on two more public-policy projects that produced large and complex blueprints for projects that never materialized. One was a 1990 design for a national apprenticeship and training program. It would have reorganized America's high school curriculum and imposed a mandatory training fee on companies lacking their own training programs. Hillary Clinton was on that board. His second project was a four-hundred-page study of the Rhode Island health care system.

Although Magaziner had a successful business career and could point to several small-scale successes as a consultant to government, his track record on big public-policy programs might have caused another President to look for someone else to manage his most important initiative. Clinton knew of these projects and had thought particularly about the implications of the Greenhouse Compact fiasco. "That was the one negative I had," because "it was thought of as too complicated — a Big Government plan," the President said. But he decided that "Ira got kind of a bum rap as being some kind of wild-eyed, left-wing social engineer. I don't think that's a fair rap on him." Besides, he and Ira had discussed what went wrong there and were determined that what they would present would be a plan they "simplified as much as possible."

Afterward, Clinton ruefully admitted that Magaziner's "development plan for Rhode Island was defeated basically with the strategy that defeated the health care plan" — by attacking it as a big, complicated, new government endeavor. In other words, the lesson went unlearned.

Throughout Magaziner's career, associates discovered that it took an enormous effort to produce these massive studies on the tight timetables Magaziner set for himself. Mark Patinkin, a Rhode Island journalist who worked with him on the Swedish project, recalled that when they got off the plane back in Providence, "I had about a hundred pages of notes in my portable computer. As we parted at the airport, he asked, 'Do you think I could see a first draft of the chapter tomorrow afternoon?' He was surprised when I said no."

For many, Magaziner was a difficult, frustrating, intimidating figure, someone to be avoided. But he had support where it counted most. The Clintons liked him — a lot. Their conversations on health care had begun at the New Year's Eve Renaissance Weekend of 1992, where Magaziner, responding to an invitation to describe a "meaningful experience" of the past year, reported on the Rhode Island health care project he was completing. He told how "we literally followed nurses and doctors and technicians around on their shifts, recording what they did with their time, understanding how costs got built up, analyzing inefficiencies in the system." Bill Clinton liked what he heard. He asked Magaziner to send him his thoughts.

In the new Clinton administration, the First Lady and Magaziner complemented each other. Magaziner was the quintessential policy wonk. While he lacked her public talents — her effectiveness as a speaker, her skill at cultivating allies, perhaps acquired from watching her husband beguile other politicians — Magaziner was well suited to do the heavy behind-the-scenes policy lifting. She was perfectly positioned to become the public symbol.

They resembled, and possibly reinforced, each other in other ways. As Connie Bruck noted in "Hillary the Pol," her 1994 *New Yorker* profile, "Each had long evinced an extraordinary self-confidence (coupled with a tendency to be dismissive of others) and a conviction that no social problem, however complex and seemingly intractable, could resist his or her applied power to solve it. . . . Ira and Hillary not only possessed these qualities but were vivified by them; and this project provided the greatest opportunity either one of them had ever had to give full expression to them."

They also admired each other's courage. In the early days of the administration Magaziner wrote a note to Hillary Clinton describing the great forces they would contend with in the coming weeks. But after a discussion, "we just kind of joked about how crazy we both were to try it." Noting the more public role Hillary Clinton would have, Magaziner said it was "a tremendously gutsy thing to have the First Lady, fully aware of all this, step up to it and put her own reputation on the line."

Certainly, Magaziner recognized the risks. Everyone, from family to friends, warned him about them. "So I went in with my eyes open about it," he would say. "But when the President of the United States says, 'I want you to do this,' you do it."

Magaziner and the First Lady did not have to start from scratch. More than a year's time had been invested already in formulating a Clinton health plan, starting with the Blueberry Donut Group and climaxing in the East Lansing briefing and the Merck speech. There, Clinton had formulated a quite specific outline of his approach, and work on drafting a more detailed plan actually began, in secret, even before Election Day. A month before the election, Bruce Fried, organizer of the Blueberry Donut Group, was asked by campaign aide John Kroger to "put together the outlines of what a health care reform bill would be like." He prepared a twenty-page outline for Atul Gawande and the Little Rock team.

During the two-and-a-half-month presidential transition period, a critically short time to staff and plan for any incoming administration, especially for a party out of power for twelve years, the health care portfolio was given to Judy Feder. Along with Gawande and others from the original policy-planning group, she developed recommendations for the new President. On January 10, they were called to Little Rock to meet with Clinton, Magaziner, and others, including Carol Rasco, soon to be named White House domestic policy adviser.

The night before she flew to Little Rock, Judy Feder unburdened her fears to her friend Jay Rockefeller, her former boss on the Pepper-Rockefeller Commission. After the excitement of campaign policy work, the prospect of returning to teaching at Georgetown was not enticing to Feder. She wanted to work on health care. She wanted to be in the White House. But she was worried. In developing policy recommendations for the new President, she told Rockefeller, she and her group had reexamined economic assumptions they had made about the impact of reform on the budget deficit. Economists among the working group argued strongly that their work must not be tainted by the kinds of "rosy scenarios" that had marred other administrations' cost projections. When their work was completed, the cost estimates Feder had been asked to prepare for Clinton came in with "very high numbers." Feder confided to Rockefeller that she didn't think they were going to like them. "This is expensive to do," she said.

"Be honest," Rockefeller counseled her. "It might work." But, he later reflected, "Of course, I was wrong. She got crushed. They were furious at her. Clinton personally was furious at her, because he couldn't do what he wanted."

The memo Feder and her team gave Clinton that day certainly

did contain bad news. It concluded that the costs of universal care would be felt long before significant savings could be achieved from reforms — a gap that could blow the federal budget wide open. Specifically, the report warned Clinton that "even if your plan is passed at the end of 1993, the earliest that significant Medicare and private sector savings will be realized from competition within global budgets is probably 1997. . . . [But even] if universal coverage is phased in over four years, these costs could reach ninety-one billion dollars by 1998."

Feder's team said "most experts agree that health insurance purchasing cooperatives [the structures for managed competition] would require at least two to three years to set up across the country." The only way to avoid huge additional deficits during the startup period of four to five years, the report stated, would be "all-payer price controls."

No wonder Clinton didn't like the alternatives he was offered. Every one was dismal. He faced either the prospect of further exploding deficits or adopting a gradual step-by-step approach that would delay universal coverage until well beyond the 1996 presidential election. If he balked at those options, he would have to impose rigorous, cumbersome price controls on one-seventh of the American economy.

This report should have raised the most serious questions in Clinton's mind about the political and fiscal hazards in pursuing the comprehensive approach he had outlined in the campaign. But instead of heeding the message, he sent the messenger home in disgrace.

The meeting left Feder, as she later told friends, feeling "devastated, treated abominably." In time, she came to believe she had been regarded as a mere "placeholder" for the Magaziner-run task force to come, a process Feder learned was already in the works by the time of the Little Rock meeting. As she feared, her star declined. Magaziner's rose even higher.

In conversations with Magaziner about his possible role in the new administration, Clinton often expressed discomfort with the "traditional Washington views on health care." The Beltway experts like Judy Feder were, Clinton believed, either too government-oriented or too insensitive to the need for getting costs under control. These were views Magaziner already shared; so did the First Lady. In recalling Clinton's negative reaction to the recommendations from the Feder policy group, one of the President's closest counselors said, "He found them, frankly, too conventional in their thinking about how to deal with this. Although they did a lot of very good work, he was not satisfied he would get what he wanted out of this approach." So he proceeded down a road that was even more hazardous.

The formal announcement of the task force on January 25 unleashed Hillary Clinton on Washington. That very afternoon and evening the First Lady made a round of calls to congressional leaders. One after another, she engaged them in conversations for the better part of an hour. It was 10:30 at night when Don Riegle of Michigan, a member of the Senate Finance Committee, got his call. "It was clear to me that she was absolutely focused on this issue," Riegle said, "and I am delighted that she has that assignment."

That was the general reaction on Capitol Hill, at least in public. Privately, Dan Rostenkowski said, "I couldn't do that to my wife." And commentator George Will said handing Hillary the health care assignment was a form of spousal abuse.

In time, people working with Hillary Clinton would recognize that they had made two mistakes right at the start — one trivial, the other more consequential. Bob Boorstin, the thirty-three-year-old War Room veteran who ran White House communications on health reform, said months later that one mistake he made in that announcement was "having the President urge people to write in and tell us about their health care problems. About eight hundred thousand letters later, I'm on a wanted poster in the correspondence department."

The more serious error, he said, was that he "named it the task force. What a mistake! That got us into all this lawsuit bullshit." He was referring to a challenge from a group of conservative physicians who contended that the task force violated federal open-meeting laws. Because of that lawsuit, Hillary Clinton — who was not formally a government employee — never attended a single task force session after the suit was filed. Eventually, to the embarrassment of some officials, the administration was compelled to divulge more than 250 boxes of task force memoranda. And still later, after the reform plan was dead and buried on Capitol Hill, Magaziner and his aides were forced to spend months assembling evidence that eventually convinced prosecutors there were no criminal violations serious enough to merit action. "If I'd called it a working group, there never would have been a question about Hillary," Boorstin said. "We were young and stupid and we didn't check with legal counsel."

The biggest mistake of all may have been the President's decision that the way to handle this issue was with a White House task force headed by his wife and his Oxford classmate. He decided to short-circuit The System's conventional policy-making process, and The System rebelled. Had Clinton not chosen to give his wife and Magaziner the charter and instead awarded the job to the Health and Human Services Department, which desperately wanted it, the process would probably have followed traditional Washington patterns. Political appointees — many with extensive backgrounds in health policy — would have hooked up with the career officials in the department to assemble the options for review by the secretary. The "policy networks," as political scientist Hugh Heclo called them, of which these officials were a part, would have sprung to life. Think tank authors, academics, congressional staffers, and others would have put their ears to the meeting room walls and slipped their memos under the doors. So would staffs of the myriad interest groups with a stake in the policy.

As the process moved along, the drafts would have been shown to officials of other departments — Treasury, Veterans, Labor, Defense — who would have been called on to carry the ball on Capitol Hill and run the program if it were passed. The Office of Management and Budget would have double-checked the policy and financial assumptions. Members of the President's staff would have been shown the ideas and asked for their reactions to the political feasibility. And, at some point well before any final sign-off, the key players on Capitol Hill and in the affected interest groups would have been brought in to discuss both the policy and the politics of the measure. By the time the President acted, the policy would have undergone multiple layers of scrutiny by a wide spectrum of people — and the coalition of support would have been put in place.

Magaziner set up a very different design. He wanted the specialized expertise, but he didn't want special interests to write the policy. Instead he wanted outside experts to challenge the conventional views of the health care bureaucrats and force them to document their assumptions. He wanted to keep the veteran policy-network players from taking over this exercise. Most important, he wanted to preserve the final key decisions for three people — Bill and Hillary Clinton and himself. And that is what happened.

What emerged was a process that Magaziner himself jokingly called "managed chaos." As he said, "We recognized that it was an enormously complicated policy process. And so we knew we had to do something broad. The kind of team we'd have to pull together would have to be big, and would have to move quickly."

Originally, he envisaged a task force of ninety-eight people, including members of the congressional committee staffs that would be handling the reform legislation. But the White House congressional liaison staff urged that Democratic House and Senate members be allowed to designate aides to work on the project. And the cabinet departments, just beginning to organize for the new administration, said they had additional people who could contribute. Magaziner's attitude was "Heck, why piss them off? Let's be inclusive."

The task force grew. Eventually more than six hundred thirty people, broken down into eight "cluster teams" and thirty-four "working groups," were slaving away. Depending on their own areas of expertise and responsibility, they began drafting policy options and proposals. About a thousand other people later vetted their decisions.

This extraordinary, burgeoning decision-making process was borrowed from Magaziner's corporate practice. It involved a series of deadlines or "tollgates," meetings at which each of the working group leaders would make a presentation to Magaziner on a set of policy questions. One might ask, for example, Who really pays for employer-provided health insurance, the employer, the workers, or the consumers? Is there cost-shifting involved? Does the tax code encourage overconsumption of benefits? These hours-long meetings were supposed to help Magaziner and other members of the task force make decisions about the design and the details of the plan. As Magaziner outlined the operational method to all task force members, "the first tollgate would develop a work-plan or methodology; the second and third tollgates would expand the list of possible options; the fourth and fifth would narrow them to preferred possibilities; and the sixth and seventh would be auditing sessions, where outsiders — lawyers, health professionals, consumer representatives — would critique the proposed plan."

Magaziner thought that the designers of Medicare and Medicaid had not been systematic enough in their work. They had taken too narrow a focus, and because of that shortsightedness, both programs were constantly exceeding their budgets and frustrating both the administrators and the beneficiaries. Employing the jargon of the consultants' world from which he came, he said his intention was "to take the full-system approach, where we could try to look at the various interactions." That was quite an undertaking, to put it mildly, for a system as complex as American health care. Hillary Clinton remembers Jay Rockefeller remarking to her then, "I don't think that there's been this kind of effort since they planned the invasion of Normandy."

And all this was to be done in one hundred days.

In an internal organization memo he distributed to cabinet members and White House staff the day after he was appointed, Magaziner set forth a week-by-week schedule that he said would enable them to meet their deadline. Bob Boorstin would say later that the deadline "was hubris. There was no understanding of how long it takes to do things."

Another aide, Walter Zelman, later reflected, "The process was more cumbersome and chaotic than it needed to be. It was a tremendous spinning of wheels and relatively little opportunity for reflection."

At that point, reality had not sunk in at the White House. Determined, confident, driven, Magaziner began the task force meetings by passing out sheets detailing the schedule for the next three months. A few of the task force members said that they had planned to get home occasionally on weekends, but Magaziner didn't bend. The deadline must be met, he said. If it meant "eighteen-hour work-days seven days a week," he would not complain — and neither should they.

But some inside the administration were concerned. Donna Shalala, the secretary of Health and Human Services (HHS), and her close friend Alice Rivlin, then deputy director of the Office of Management and Budget (OMB), went to both Clintons and voiced their qualms about the process Magaziner had outlined. Shalala, a former political science professor, said she and Rivlin thought it was "an interesting intellectual exercise on a set of subjects [but] it wasn't a disciplined policy-development process that would result in a piece of legislation that was fully vetted by experts and political people."

Shalala and Rivlin were old friends, fellow members of a "smart women's club" that got together from time to time during the Republican years to discuss politics and policy and to take venturesome rafting, climbing, and hiking trips. Both of them were short, energetic, Washington-savvy, and eager to make their mark in this new administration.

Rivlin, ten years the elder at sixty-two, was the daughter of an Indiana University physicist. Armed with her Harvard economics Ph.D., she moved to Washington in 1957 and for much of the next three and a half decades was a mainstay of the Brookings Institution, the city's leading liberal think tank. She worked in the Health, Education and Welfare Department under Lyndon Johnson and was best known as the first director of the Congressional Budget Office, from 1975 to 1983. Having thought about — and written on — almost all the domestic policy problems on Clinton's agenda, including the deficit, she was a strong favorite for the job of budget director. When Clinton picked Leon Panetta instead, Rivlin agreed to be his deputy. (In 1994, she got the top job in a White House staff reshuffle.)

Unlike Rivlin, Shalala did not have a health policy background. Her strength was as a longtime friend and admirer of Hillary Clinton, with whom she had worked for years on the board of the Children's Defense Fund. She was named to her cabinet post in no small part because she could be expected to give strong support for the new First

Lady's effort at reforming the health care system. A Clevelander who served in the Peace Corps after college and held a series of academic posts, culminating in being chancellor of the University of Wisconsin at Madison, Shalala was no stranger to Washington. In the late 1970s she served in the Carter administration as assistant secretary for policy development and research of the Department of Housing and Urban Development (HUD).

The two officials thought they knew how policy should be made — and Magaziner's approach did not much resemble it. At OMB, Rivlin would almost be guaranteed a look in on the task force process, but Shalala's people at HHS feared they were going to be bypassed, or relegated to menial assignments. The two of them were allowed to make their case to the Clintons, but were turned down, they thought, because both Clintons were committed to Magaziner as the project manager and "were intrigued" by the way he proposed to draft the plan.

Rivlin and Shalala were not the only doubters. Watching the process unfold from his post as director of the Congressional Budget Office, Robert Reischauer was struck that while Magaziner had large numbers of Capitol Hill staffers involved in the task force, "most of the big-time players in the health game didn't join in."

In fact, many of them took a deeply skeptical view of the whole process — as did Reischauer himself. And Reischauer would be a critical player in the game. Then fifty-two, Reischauer came from a distinguished academic background. His father, Edwin O. Reischauer, was a noted Asian scholar at Harvard, where Bob Reischauer did his undergraduate work before earning his master's and Ph.D. at Columbia. He was steeped in economic analysis, having developed his skills over two decades of work at such think tanks as the Brookings Institution and the Urban Institute and at the Congressional Budget Office, which he was named to head in 1989. It was Reischauer's office that would have to make the vital dollars-and-cents assessments of every plan presented to Congress. Though a Democrat, Reischauer enjoyed wide bipartisan support on Capitol Hill. A negative assessment from his office would be a major, if not fatal, blow to the Clinton proposal.

Early on, Magaziner paid a call on Reischauer in the director's office. There the two policy experts spent most of an afternoon discussing Magaziner's approach.

Reischauer's message to Magaziner, as he recalled it later, was, "It's a lot more complicated than you think it is. I would urge caution. Despite everything you people are saying and what the public opinion polls seem to show, when the details of any plan come out, you're going to find these guys [the members of Congress] running away from it."

Reischauer did not share all his doubts with Magaziner. He was privately convinced the Clinton health care reform would not pass congressional muster. Reform was needed, he knew, but the political obstacles to achieving it were enormous. Nothing this big could get done in the time frame they had established. In the last half century, he reflected, there had been three great governmental undertakings that required the talents and cooperation of all elements of the society: the Manhattan Project, which created the atomic bomb; the Marshall Plan, which saved and rebuilt a ravaged Europe after World War II; and the space program, which put men on the moon in the 1960s. Each of these took years to accomplish. Later — after much political blood had been shed — Bill Clinton himself would come to realize that he had grossly overestimated his ability to move The System. But in 1993 neither the President nor Magaziner knew that yet.

New Presidents, Reischauer thought, were always seized with the dream of being another FDR: In their first hundred days, they want to pass thirty-five major pieces of legislation. But even FDR could not have accomplished his New Deal reforms without a 27 percent unemployment rate and a populace that demanded dramatic governmental action to resolve the worst crisis since the Civil War. And FDR faced nothing like the accumulated power available to the organized interest groups that would mobilize for the health care fight in the Washington of the 1990s. FDR was forced to feel his way in a very naive world, Reischauer reflected. The world isn't like that anymore.

He did tell Magaziner that it would be better if the Clintons made clear to the American people that their effort was only a beginning; that, like the famous Kennedy promise to send men to the moon before a decade was out, they told the public they were building only the first stage. They were erecting a launching pad, as it were, that in later years would result in a change benefiting all Americans.

Reischauer feared the Clintons would run the government in a campaign mode, in which policy was defined by thirty-second applause lines and slogans about "ending welfare as we know it" and "universal coverage that can never be taken away from you." He had heard of that pre-inaugural Little Rock meeting where Judy Feder was sent to the salt mines for telling the Clintons about the slim possibilities of cost control. To Reischauer, that was a signal the Clintons weren't going to face the real-world problems of the economic and political costs of reform.

Now, in his private meeting with Magaziner, Reischauer said, "It's better to do it right over a fifteen-year period, Ira, than to try to stuff it all into a few years. I know when you run for President you have to promise results within your four-year time span, but you'd better get this right for Chelsea's presidency than screw it up by trying to make The System swallow more than it can."

He also warned Magaziner: "If this is the way you feel, then make it a four-year enterprise. One hundred or two hundred days or whatever is absolutely crazy. It shows no appreciation for the magnitude of what you're trying to undertake or of our institutions. Our institutions were created to stop things from happening, and they're very good at it."

Many others had tried and would try again to impart this wisdom to Magaziner and the Clintons, but no one put it more succinctly and directly than the CBO director. Reischauer was right, of course. The System *was* designed so that its checks and balances would make major changes difficult to achieve. But the newcomers in the White House and the Executive Office Building were determined they could prove the conventional wisdom wrong. They would show the doubters — they thought.

That was before they came across that living embodiment of checks and balances, Senator Robert C. Byrd.

The Clintons had a plan to meet their hundred-day deadline and win swift congressional passage. They would fit their proposal into the President's budget and pass it all in one gigantic package. The idea had been hatched very early in the administration. Five days after the inauguration, in the private meeting before the task force was announced, both Vice President Gore and Secretary of Treasury Lloyd Bentsen — the two Senate veterans — expressed their concerns about whether health care reform and deficit reduction could go forward simultaneously on separate tracks. The President appeared to be stunned. "If they can't," he asked, "how are we going to get them done?" The answer was "reconciliation."

The reconciliation bill is the final step in the annual congressional budget process, as it has operated over the last two decades. "Reconciliation" does not imply political harmony, but rather assures that the policy steps necessary to make the budget numbers work have actually been taken. Early in each year, overall congressional spending and budget targets are set in a nonbinding budget resolution. Those targets guide the work of congressional committees on annual appropriations bills and on legislation that controls other spending. After all that is done, the reconciliation bill locks the necessary spending cuts and legislative changes into place to guarantee the budget targets are met. It is the capstone — the most important single piece — of each year's work on Capitol Hill.

Ronald Reagan used the budget reconciliation bill in 1981 to achieve the huge shift in spending priorities and social policies at the heart of his "Reagan Revolution." It was that bill that locked in the myriad individual actions that moved billions of dollars from domestic spending into the Pentagon's buildup. The Clintons saw reconciliation as a way to put their stamp indelibly on a different direction for the national government. The procedural rules for consideration of the budget reconciliation bill made it a most appealing vehicle. No filibuster could derail it in the Senate. It could be passed by a simple majority in both houses of Congress.

In their early conversations, Hillary Clinton and Magaziner agreed that "time was of the essence," Magaziner recalled. "If we did not get it done in 1993, it would have the danger of being politicized in 1994. Opposing interest groups would mobilize, and our chances would lessen dramatically."

With that 1993 goal in mind, Hillary Clinton and Magaziner met with the majority leaders of Senate and House, George Mitchell and

Dick Gephardt, respectively. Getting health care reform into the reconciliation bill would be a good strategy, they agreed, *if* it could be done. Gephardt was particularly emphatic on the subject when he met Ira and Hillary for lunch on February 3 in her second-floor office in the West Wing of the White House — a location, on the "policy" side of the White House, never before occupied by a First Lady. But Gephardt also warned her that the House could not offer "a ready-made majority" on any key issue. And he added, "As many problems as we have in the House, they have more problems in the Senate."

Gephardt made the same case privately to the President that day. He told the President the health care reform package had to be "backed by the full force of his political and moral leadership"; the leadership in Congress needed the President to be out front driving the plan and process in order to foster party unity and break the policy deadlock.

The next day, when Hillary Clinton came to the Hill to meet with key senators, Mitchell met with her and Magaziner in his office before assembling the others. He told her that he agreed with Gephardt's assessment; it would be extremely difficult to win more than fifty-one votes in the Senate, and also warned her about the danger of letting time slip away. "I told her," the Senate leader said, "that if you wait until next year, the second year of the Congress, especially if you wait until the summer, the rules in the Senate are such that you dramatically enhance the leverage of the opposition." In August, September, and October of that second year, he said, the "potency" of delaying tactics grows with every passing day.

Mitchell's words would prove to be devastatingly prophetic.

On the evening of February 17, exactly four weeks after his inauguration, President Clinton went back up to Capitol Hill to deliver his first address to a joint session of Congress. It was a vital test — the introduction of his budget and economic plan and his prime-time debut as President before a huge television audience. Elements of the plan had been leaked to the press, but this was Clinton's chance to explain the overall design to the public and to a somewhat skeptical Congress. In an effort to begin preparing public opinion, Clinton had made a short address to the nation from the Oval Office two nights earlier.

It had not gone well. He had seemed awkward and out of place behind the big desk, and his rhetoric had been stilted and inflated. But two nights later, facing the even more daunting challenge of a live assemblage of fellow politicians in the House chamber and a bigger national TV audience, Clinton was in peak form. The text was strong, but what really impressed people was the young President's facility in improvising, playing off an unexpected bit of derisive laughter from the Republicans, or a shouted word of encouragement from his fellow Democrats. On this critical occasion, Clinton showed that he knew what he wanted to do — and that he was ready to take on anyone in the battle.

While his focus was on the economy, the budget, and taxes, Clinton also used the speech to make the policy link between health care reform and deficit reduction. "All of our efforts to strengthen the economy will fail unless we also take this year — not next year, not five years from now, but this year — bold steps to reform our health care system. Reducing health care costs can liberate literally hundreds of billions of dollars for new investment and growth and jobs, reducing not only our deficit but expanding investment in America."

That passage was a consolation prize the President gave to Hillary and Magaziner, when they failed to persuade him to describe their project as an integral part of the first-year budget plan. The First Lady and Magaziner had tried to wedge their way into the February 17 speech during the two weeks when its contents were being argued in meeting after meeting at the White House. But they had no specific plan ready to offer, and Clinton's economic advisers wanted the focus of this speech to be clearly on deficit reduction. So Hillary's pleas were rejected.

President Clinton had decided, under pressure, to reverse the political priorities of Candidate Clinton. When he ran for President, his main theme — sounded even more often than the promise of health care reform — was that he would find a way to get the economy growing and provide more jobs. The budget deficit was not his focus; he had left that to Paul Tsongas in the primaries and to Ross Perot in the general election. But when his economic team had met with the

President-elect in Little Rock, Lloyd Bentsen, Bob Rubin, and others urged Clinton to reexamine his priorities. To unlock private investment, they said, Clinton had to persuade the bond markets and their signal-setter, Federal Reserve Board Chairman Alan Greenspan, that he was dead serious about reducing the deficits, which his predecessor George Bush had projected to run at a staggering three hundred billion dollars a year.

The debate in the Clinton White House was fierce, because the change of direction meant that Clinton would have to abandon the middle-class tax cut he had promised during the campaign and scale down or postpone much of the social spending Democratic constituencies were anxious to restore after the twelve "lean years" of a Republican White House. But Clinton ultimately came down on the side of the budget cutters. Reducing the deficit was declared the first objective of the new administration.

His speech contained other bad news for the health care reformers. Clinton's budget cutters on his economic policy team were eyeing Medicare and Medicaid savings as a way of reducing the deficit by fifty to sixty billion dollars. Hillary Clinton and Magaziner were opposed; they wanted to preserve at least some of that money to help finance their reform. But the speech showed the economic team had won. Clinton proposed sixty billion three hundred million dollars in Medicare and Medicaid savings over the next five years. In the end, Congress slashed fifty-six billion three hundred million dollars from those health accounts — the greatest portion in the President's deficit-reduction plan.

The initial positive response to the President's speech bred false optimism within the White House. Stephanopoulos and other White House advisers with Capitol Hill experience argued for a one-two punch: First, win a great budget victory in April or May; then follow up immediately with the introduction of the health care plan.

But Chris Jennings, a White House aide who had been making the rounds on Capitol Hill for Ira, did not agree. Jennings had learned the intricacies of congressional health care politics while working for Arkansas's Senator David Pryor, the chairman of the Aging Committee and a member of the Finance Committee. When Clinton began his race, Jennings joined the campaign. Passionately devoted to the health care cause, Jennings began lining up congressional support for Clinton's initiative even before the inauguration. He felt strongly that public opinion had created "the last best chance" for at least twenty years to enact major reform. So on February 22 he alerted the First Lady to the danger signals emanating from Capitol Hill over the rumored White House consideration of a two-bill strategy:

> In discussions earlier today with the leadership of the House, including Gephardt, Rostenkowski, Dingell, Ford, Waxman and others, as well as John Hilley of Senator Mitchell's office, great concerns have been raised about the possibility of NOT folding in health care in the budget reconciliation process. Without exception, these members stated or implied there was NO chance the comprehensive health reform initiative can pass the Congress on a separate legislative track. . . . The consensus of the leadership of the committee chairmen (no women chairs) of both the Senate and the House is that there's nowhere near sufficient support for going to the well twice for difficult votes on health care and cuts.

Two weeks later, Magaziner raised the timing issue once again, with additional arguments, including one James Carville had made in a meeting the previous week. "I am not a congressional strategist," Magaziner acknowledged in a memo to the President, "but the more time we allow for the defenders of the status quo to organize, the more they will be able to marshal opposition to your plan and the better their chances of killing it."

He continued: Reaction to the President's February 17 speech and to the First Lady's early proselytizing visits to Capitol Hill had convinced the interest groups the Clintons were dead serious — and might prevail.

"Interest groups are coming to us," Magaziner told the President, "offering things that they typically would not have offered. They're running scared." Delay would eliminate "the fear that has caused their cooperation," discourage the supporters in Congress, and, most important, give the Republicans "the opportunity to mount their own initiative, which is bound to be less comprehensive and less serious, and probably would be more acceptable to conservative health care providers. . . . Interest groups may then decide to mobilize in opposition and in an election year . . . passage becomes less likely. Then you have to start over with a Congress that's going to be less friendly."

Coming from a man who was scorned by many congressional Democrats — and by many in the White House — as a political naif, that memo is a remarkably prescient forecast of what in fact happened.

It also made a larger point: Without health care reform, the economic plan was unlikely to produce the intended political results. "The fact that health care costs are growing two to three times as fast as wages means that over 100 percent of the increase in workers' wages that we are predicting would be eaten up by increased health care costs," Magaziner told the President. "Therefore people won't feel the living standard improvements. . . . If you don't do health care and slow down growth of costs, then even if we get the economic kick we're looking for, it may not be felt by people."

That is what happened. During the first two years of Clinton's presidency, economic growth accelerated and millions of new jobs were added. But with health care costs still rising rapidly, real wages for most American workers continued to decline. The results were felt at the polls in November 1994, when Democrats lost their congressional majorities.

The President accepted the logic of Magaziner's argument, which was reinforced by Ted Kennedy and the House chairmen. They endorsed the Mitchell-Gephardt view that the President would have only one roll call on which he could ask Democrats to put aside their reservations and give him, the new Democratic President, and his program a chance — and Clinton had better get as much from that vote as he could.

Looking toward 1996, the year the new President would try to get reelected, Clinton's outside political strategists had also weighed in on the health care team's behalf. Carville, Begala, and Grunwald all argued that they would rather Clinton run having given people health care than a budget package. In his presidential campaign he had promised health care reform, not deficit reduction.

Important counterarguments were made inside the White House.

The budget and economic legislation was difficult enough in itself; loading health care reform on top might sink everything. Howard Paster, the head of congressional relations, argued strongly against adding this huge reform to the budget package on those grounds. In addition, some of the Republicans the White House counted on for bipartisan support said they would have no choice but to oppose it if the administration "tried to stuff it down our throats" in an omnibus reconciliation bill without giving them any chance to reshape it. Bob Dole, the Senate minority leader, had told Clinton at their first White House meeting of 1993 that the Republicans had decided they would unanimously oppose his budget — no matter how the President framed it. If Clinton wanted Dole as his partner on a bipartisan health care bill — as he certainly did — then it would have to be a separate piece of legislation.

Nor was it certain the health care plan would be ready in time to be stitched into the budget bill. Ultimately, however, what really stopped Clinton from pursuing this strategy was a roadblock named Robert C. Byrd.

The Clintons pushed that reconciliation strategy as hard as they could, until they ran into the immovable object of Senator Byrd. "Everybody went to see him on this," a top official recalled. "Jay Rockefeller probably prostrated himself. I mean, everybody tried, and he would not budge. At that point we had to regroup."

As chairman of the powerful Senate Appropriations Committee and a recognized guardian of Senate procedure, the West Virginia senator believed the health care plan didn't belong in the streamlined budget bill process. The "Byrd rule" against adding anything to a budget reconciliation bill that is not directly related to deficit reduction was inviolate. The Byrd rule was developed by that master of Senate rules as a procedural safeguard against maneuvers to include extraneous matters in the budget reconciliation bill and ramrod them into law under the procedures for accelerated action provided for that particular legislation. As George Mitchell observed, in quiet understatement, "Senator Byrd was opposed to it on the grounds that it went outside the spirit of the rules."

Byrd had no ulterior motive for thwarting the strategem. Having grown up in poverty in the West Virginia coal fields, as an infant adopted by an aunt and uncle after his mother died of influenza, Byrd knew how important the guarantee of health care would be to his constituents. But he was a man possessed by history and his own views of the Constitution, a senator out of the past: a man dressed meticulously in three-piece suits, given to theatrical gestures and homely aphorisms. By then Byrd was seventy-five years old and had been in the Senate for a third of a century. He was courtly, graying, proud, but there were signs of his age in the way his hands trembled as he spoke. There was nothing frail in his passionate defenses of the institutions of the Senate, however. He had written a four-volume study of the Senate, and he lectured his Senate colleagues on its essential qualities. "I said that what made this the premier upper body in the world is not just its role in treaty making and in impeachments but the fact that all measures are open to amendment and to lengthy debate. As one who believes in the institution very strongly, and who believes the framers were correct in creating a body of this nature, I would have to oppose such a maneuver."

Mitchell pleaded with him. Rockefeller tried. "The effort was to get me to turn my cheek, look the other way, not make a fight on that" — enforcing the Byrd rule against extraneous matters — Byrd explained months later.

In a last effort, the President called Byrd and asked him to relent. "Mr. President," Byrd replied, "I cannot go along with putting this into the reconciliation bill. I believe the Senate was created to deliberate. This is such a complex bill, little understood. People have a right to be informed. Woodrow Wilson said the informing function of this body is superior even to its legislative function." Byrd reminded the President that under Senate rules the reconciliation bill could be debated for only twenty hours before it came to an up-or-down vote. The conference report of the final version, ironed out by negotiators for the House and Senate, would receive only ten hours of debate.

That may have sounded wonderful to Clinton, but to Byrd it would have been "a prostitution of the process" to put on the reconciliation bill "a very complex, very expensive, very little understood piece of legislation."

He would not have it.

The precedents of history and the principles of the Constitution were on Byrd's side. The American government was designed to make large-scale policy change difficult. The Senate in particular was intended to be a place where innovation was subjected to critical scrutiny. But in the past three decades, as the national consensus had eroded, the Senate had more and more often become the place where a President's policies on everything from Vietnam to energy conservation were stymied and his nominees for the cabinet and Supreme Court were turned down. A determined minority could — and did — use the Senate rules to thwart even measures that most of the public and the lawmakers favored. Clinton knew that and so did Bob Byrd. But the new President was getting his first lesson in the justly celebrated stubbornness of Senator Byrd when it came to the Senate rules. Many other newcomers had been through the experience. That didn't make it any easier to take.

With the advantage of hindsight, President Clinton told us in 1995, Byrd's veto of the reconciliation bill strategy should have been the signal for a fundamental shift of strategy on Clinton's part. "This is entirely my mistake," he said, "no one else's. I probably made a mistake in not then going for a multiyear strategy, and not trying to say we've got to try to do it in 'ninety-four."

In our experience as reporters, there have been few moments when a President has sat in the Oval Office and said, flat out and without a trace of rationalization or self-pity, "I made a blunder." But the next sentence was even more striking: "I set the Congress up for failure," Clinton said. He set himself up for failure, too, he said, but Congress "had to stand with it" sooner — in 1994 — "and I didn't, and I feel badly about that. We had an opportunity, and our leaders thought we might make it. But I think that our system probably cannot absorb this much reform with this much involved that quickly.

"What we should have said," he thought, after the showdown with Byrd, "is 'This might take three years.' "

Did he really think, looking back on it, that he had had the political freedom to ask the public for that much time? "I don't think I did," he said, "because I had made it such a big issue. But in retrospect, I think it would have been better to go before the American people and just say: 'Listen, I know you're frustrated about this and we need to do it, but better to take another year and do it right.' I might have been able to sell that to the American people and it might have made a difference in the way the American people viewed the Democrats in the 'ninety-four election."

The President's comments made it clear he had two regrets: the loss of his keystone program and the consequent Democratic loss of Congress. It was, as he knew better than anyone, a classic lose-lose proposition. And he blamed no one but himself.

These thoughts, however, occurred to the President only afterward. At the time, he was impatient to press forward. Because of his determination, Magaziner was driving the task force members at a brutal pace. It started in total confusion. Roger Berry, a young congressional staffer who had explored local health purchasing cooperatives for his boss, a Florida Democrat named Harry Johnston, was flattered and excited to be invited onto the task force by Gephardt's chief health policy aide, Andrea (Andie) King. Barely three years after his Harvard graduation, Berry found himself and scores of others in the Indian Treaty Room of the Old Executive Office Building, with Magaziner, Judy Feder — who had been exiled to the Department of Health and Human Services and was now working for Secretary Donna Shalala — and Walter Zelman, the California health care expert now working for Magaziner, trying to get the work organized.

"People were talking, picking up pizza, parading through," Berry recalled. Within a few days, "it was growing like an amoeba, and people were being assigned every which way to every group." Initially, Berry was placed in the technology group — a subject he knew nothing about — but finagled his way into the health care cooperatives cluster, led by Zelman.

In short order, he found Zelman had been changed from "a functioning human being with good ideas" into someone "really beaten down by the chaos. He was overwhelmed." So were many others. "There were businessmen over there who couldn't comprehend how we could do any sort of work in this kind of environment," Berry remembered. As more and more people were added to the task force, the workload — primarily producing background and decision papers for the "tollgates" that rolled around every couple of weeks — became harder and harder to organize.

Simply getting clearance into the Old Executive Office Building could take an hour, so numerous were the temporary workers assigned to the building. Meetings were held in rooms too small for the number of people invited. Latecomers stood in the doorways, or the halls, straining to hear the discussion.

"Everybody took their responsibilities very, very seriously," said Vivek Varma, another recent college graduate who was placed on the task force by his boss, Oklahoma Democratic Representative Mike Synar. "You were really just a research rat, but if you had a memo for the group to look at the next day, you stayed up all night and you did it."

When a tollgate was reached, Magaziner would schedule meetings for the various groups starting at 7 A.M. on Friday and continuing straight through the weekend. "If you're here in group twenty-three," Varma found, "you'll probably give your presentation somewhere between ten-thirty and eleven on Saturday night. I mean, it was really intense."

Inside this cauldron of endless activity, even senior officials who strongly disapproved of the sprawling process acknowledged that, as one put it, "there was a tremendous amount of interesting discussion and dialogue." At the same time, the sheer size and sense of reexamining — and reinventing — positions meant that more and more critical time passed. "We spent the first two months reinventing the wheel," recalled that same official, who came to the task force out of a long congressional and health policy background. "I can only say what I would have done," this person said, "and that is move much more quickly with the plan that we had and start working immediately with Congress. We could have done that in February; we had the basic outline of the plan then. I think the First Lady definitely wanted to lay out as much structure as she could. With the general outline of the plan done, I would have taken a smaller piece and negotiated the final structure with the congressional committees. Have them involved in the decision-making process right from the start."

No matter how many people became involved in this continually expanding process, in the end, as always, decisions were made by a few people. Numbers were the key. When all the policy planners had their say, the hard question that always had to be answered was, How much will this cost?

It was in Ira Magaziner's office that those critical calculations were made. The group that assembled there consisted of six or seven people from the White House staff and the cabinet offices. Their sessions were, if possible, even more intense. One of those policy makers recalled,

> We'd meet every night until two or three in the morning sometimes. Basically, we were taking the policies this group of six hundred had developed and analyzing the numbers on them. That's where policy was really made, in Ira's office. It was grueling, exhausting. Every night it was always, "God, we gotta get this done tonight." It drove some of the policy people who had different opinions berserk, but that's how the decisions were made. We were dealing with very technical questions about insurance rates and so on, testing out policy hypotheses with numbers. They really did crystallize, in very crisp terms, the policy choices we were facing, with some of their implications. Then we'd have a day or two to go through these huge cost projection simulations. Then the next night we'd start meeting at seven, eight, nine o'clock. We'd go on for two, three, five hours. Night after night after night, and that was always after a full workday. I'd begin at eight and leave at midnight or early in the morning.

To what purpose was all this effort? that official was asked. The answer was oddly ambiguous, if not an open admission of irrelevance: "Once you've gone down that road, and you've built up this massive superstructure, it's hard to disengage."

If that was a view from the top of the task force, the view from the bottom was even less reassuring. In the end, when their work was completed, there would be thank-you notes from the First Lady and an invitation to listen to post-launching pep talks from the President and Hillary Clinton. But along the way, as young Roger Berry said, "you felt like you were delivering a ton of words to a black hole and somehow, in the end, they were going to decide what they were going to do anyway. So there was a lot of that frustration. It was just too big, too crazy, too diffuse."

At least once a week, and frequently more often, Hillary Clinton was on the road, meeting with health care providers and ordinary citizens. One week it was inner-city residents in Philadelphia; another, members of a Montana Indian tribe. Magaziner was also in constant motion. Frequently joined by the First Lady, he met often with influential members of Congress and interest-group leaders. Initially, the reaction was mostly favorable. Even Representative Robert S. Walker of Pennsylvania, the chief deputy to Minority Whip Newt Gingrich and a hard-edged conservative, told *Congressional Quarterly*'s Alissa Rubin in May that Hillary Clinton "is very good at having a dialogue on an issue."

But privately, many were skeptical about the seriousness of these missionary visits. Representative Fred Grandy of Iowa, a moderate Republican Ways and Means Committee member who had pushed the Bush White House for a serious health proposal, said:

> Ira would come up and share with us what he was thinking, but I always got the impression that he was playing three-dimensional chess in his head. He knows where all the pieces are, but he can't quite tell you, because he couldn't describe it in a way that you would ever understand. Anything you would suggest, he essentially never said no. I mean, he gave a great meeting. And then right behind him was the First Lady, who was also very deft at that kind of big-tent theory. But of course once the details came out, we realized that while they had no problem collecting our input, they never intended to use it.

Those Republican suspicions were heightened by the Clintons' decision that staff members who worked for GOP senators and representatives would not be permitted to join the task force. "The Phil Gramms of the world will want to try to torpedo us," one staff person said. Senator Dave Durenberger of Minnesota, who had devoted years to the issue, said that "Republicans were really frozen out of the process. By May, when Hillary knew she wasn't going to have a bill for a long time, she started coming up here and doing that PR thing so at least she could say Republicans are being consulted. The reality is we may have been consulted, but we weren't involved."

But still Magaziner hoped he could enlist at least one Republican, Rhode Island's Senator John Chafee, a moderate who, as head of the Senate Republican task force, had signed up almost half the GOP senators, including Bob Dole, for a phased-in universal coverage plan that would require every individual to buy a policy.

When Hillary Clinton met with Republican and Democratic senators behind closed doors on April 30, Chafee impressed many in both parties with his candor. As Bob Dole sat in the corner, and other senators gathered before her, the First Lady implored them to tell her what she was doing wrong. Then, in a sly dig, she remarked that she had no trouble meeting with Democratic senators; but, for some reason, she couldn't seem to get together with Republicans as she wished. What am I doing wrong, she asked, so I can make myself better?

Among those present, it was common knowledge that Dole's staff had told Republicans they were *not* to meet with the First Lady. One of the senators in the room remembered, "John Chafee, with his Yankee inability to be anything but honest, got up and said to the First Lady, 'Well, to be really frank with you, we just haven't wanted to meet with you until we've got our own plan in order.' "

As Chafee said that, Dole glowered in the corner.

Later at a private meeting, Hillary Clinton asked Chafee if he would like to work out a joint proposal. No, he replied, it would be better for "you to get your bill, and we will get ours. Then we will sit down." Chafee promised to speak positively of the Clinton effort — and he kept his word.

Whatever his reservations about the Clinton proposal, and he had many, Chafee believed a major bill would pass the Congress within a year. The odds for passage were about sixty-forty, he thought. It wouldn't be as sweeping as the Clinton version, and it was likely that the final legislation would more resemble his bill than the Clintons'. He understood that even if a final bill bore more Republican than Democratic principles, the public would treat it as a Clinton victory.

"And rightfully so in many ways," Chafee would say privately, "because the President and Mrs. Clinton have fought for this, and it'll be a big plus for them."

There would be credit enough to go around, he would add, and it need not be a negative for Republicans. Most Republicans he worked with — especially Dave Durenberger of Minnesota, Jack Danforth of Missouri, Bob Packwood and Mark Hatfield of Oregon, Bill Cohen of Maine, Jim Jeffords of Vermont — all strongly believed in reform.

Magaziner told associates that he felt he had an "in" with Chafee because they were both Rhode Islanders. On this, as on other human relations, he was mistaken. Chafee said of Magaziner, "I cannot say that I really know him," and Christy Ferguson, the staff aide on whom Chafee heavily relied, took a dim view of Magaziner and the whole task force operation. She found Magaziner "very naive" in his theory of managed competition and anything but open-minded. "Anybody who was a Republican, regardless of what they'd done in the past, was evil," she complained. "Either evil or didn't care. Wasn't morally correct."

Sheila Burke, Bob Dole's top assistant, sat in on all the meetings Hillary Clinton and Magaziner had with the Republican leadership. "She is stunning," Burke said of the First Lady. "He's a disaster. She is a worthy opponent and a worthy proponent and I think she would be a wonderful colleague working through these issues. I have been enormously impressed by her.

"Ira, on the other hand," she said, "may be extraordinarily bright and very thoughtful in his own right, but I think people left feeling uncomfortable."

That problem was recognized inside the task force. "Ira was an outsider," a White House colleague said, "and he didn't know exactly how he could relate. He didn't speak the language" the legislators used. He tried to cover up by prefacing his comments to lawmakers with the self-effacing statement, "I don't know much about the political process, but let me tell you about policy." The lawmakers, of course, knew that policy and process were two sides of the same coin. And it did not help that Magaziner repeatedly addressed members of Congress as "you guys." Congressional staff members complained to the White House congressional liaison team that this did not show sufficient respect for their chairmen, but the habit was hard for him to break. "He just didn't get it," another White House colleague said.

In February, as the task force began work, Magaziner sent the President a warning that eleven hundred decisions would be required to shape the final plan. Starting in March, Magaziner began to walk the President through some of the simpler pieces of the puzzle, giving him a forty-five-minute briefing and decision-memo exercise on the American Indian health service, for example, or the many possible definitions of full-time, part-time, seasonal, and contract employees — and how each category should be handled under the plan.

Magaziner and the First Lady had developed a comfortable division of labor. As she told Dana Priest of the *Washington Post* at the time, "We understand each other. He is an extraordinary analyst. I'm sometimes a better translator, and we have a great working relationship."

By the end of March, a more formal process began. Cabinet members, National Economic Council Chairman Bob Rubin, Council of Economic Advisers head Laura D'Andrea Tyson, and the White House political and policy team joined in debating major decisions.

Rubin and Tyson were a study in contrasts. Rubin, educated at Yale and at Harvard Law School, was fifty-four, and had made a fortune on Wall Street as co-chairman of Goldman Sachs and Co. He was one of the biggest Democratic fund-raisers in that Republican precinct, but, even more striking, a man who used his access and influence to press elected officials to push harder on programs for the cities and especially the inhabitants of their blighted neighborhoods. Soft-spoken and conciliatory in manner, he let people figure out how much wisdom his head contained — which Clinton was quick to do.

Tyson, on the other hand, was more controversial. Critics complained she had been chosen for her gender, not because she was best for the job. Slim, youthful, and soft-spoken, she was a microeconomist who came to the administration from the Berkeley campus of the University of California without prior Washington experience. She had a reputation for advocating government promotion of American industry — a sharp contrast to Rubin's free-trade philosophy. Tyson quickly made her mark inside the White House as an outspoken adviser, but also as one who knew how to marshal her facts and arguments.

Tyson and Rubin came to the table with many questions about the issues that needed to be decided: How comprehensive should the benefits be? Are short-term price controls needed? How long a phase-in to universal coverage? How many health plan choices do you give consumers? Above all, how do you pay for covering additional millions? The controversies were sharp, the disagreements vehement. "And we started running into trouble," Magaziner said, in a masterpiece of understatement.

Trouble came on two fronts, directly linked. The process was already behind schedule, and the centerpiece of that effort, the First Lady, was absent for a critical month that spring.

On March 20, Hugh Rodham, Hillary's father, suffered a stroke. The First Lady left immediately to be by his side at a hospital in Little Rock. For the next weeks, until he died on April 7, she spent most of her time in Little Rock. When she returned, the experience had strengthened her determination.

"Nobody in my family had ever been really sick until my father, in his early seventies, had to have a bypass," she said later. "So we didn't have a lot of experience with hospitals."

In Little Rock, she had noticed that when the doctors came in to order a new drug to help her father, nobody asked, How much does that cost? Toward the end, when nothing had worked, the family made the decision to take Mr. Rodham off life support. But he did not die — something his daughter thought very characteristic of him.

As long as he was alive, the doctors told the First Lady, they had to give her father feeding tubes. Then, within forty-eight hours, they would have to transfer him to a nursing home. There he would no longer be covered under Medicare. The Clintons would face the cost of paying for the twenty-four-hour nursing care he would need.

Hugh Rodham did not live long enough to be transferred from the hospital. But confronting the reality of what uninsured long-term care could cost even well-off families like the Rodhams and the Clintons was a stark reminder of the kinds of problems people faced daily. The experience, someone close to her said, upped her moral commitment even more than it was.

Her days in the hospital with her father taught painful lessons. While there, she had conversations with other patients' families. "It made me realize what a totally devastating experience health care problems are for people and how everybody suffers in silence on their own," she said. "People think it's somehow their fault that they can't afford prescription drugs, that they can't afford to get their parents into a good nursing home. And you know, these are systemic problems. And we are being so shortsighted in not resolving them to our benefit; we are turning our back on all these solutions."

"So," she said, "I came back even more convinced that this was not only the economically and politically smart thing for us to take on, but it was the right thing to do. I find it very hard to accept members of Congress, who are well insured, looking me in the eye, telling me people don't need what *they* have. So I think," she also reflected, "if anything, my father's experience really reinforced what this is truly about; that it wasn't some policy-wonk abstract discussion."

Whatever the experience added to Hillary Clinton's sense of mission, her absence was a serious problem. Magaziner had come to depend on her to run interference for him with the cabinet departments. The President was preoccupied with the budget battle on Capitol Hill and most of his staff members had little time for any other subject. Magaziner continued his usual heavy schedule of meetings, but without Hillary, few decisions could be made. Watching from Capitol Hill, Jay Rockefeller noticed the difference. "When Hillary's father died," he told us, "the whole thing came to a halt. There was nobody to step in. She has a very small staff and it's very hard for her to advance her project except by her own work. Nobody else was going to do it."

7

Loose Lips and Missed Deadlines

WHEN HILLARY CLINTON RETURNED to Washington, a conflict surfaced that had been building for weeks. Hillary and Magaziner wanted to finish work on their plan and get it to Congress. The rest of the White House staff wanted nothing to distract from the battle of the budget. In addition, the President's economic advisers were deeply skeptical about the outlines of the health care reform plan — no one more so than Treasury Secretary Lloyd M. Bentsen Jr., the most experienced legislator in the cabinet.

Of all Clinton's senior advisers, the Texan could best claim that he understood how to work The System. In truth, Bentsen was The System: a consummate legislator with a sure sense of the intricacies of controversial issues and the skills necessary to reach political consensus on them. He was tall and courtly, a fastidious dresser who wore splendidly tailored suits and who spoke in carefully chosen words, and his formal manner and position as a pillar of the establishment contributed to the lore that had grown up around him.

Few, if any, could maneuver so well through the tricky shoals of the Senate. Bentsen had served there for twenty-two years, and before that in the House of Representatives. Bentsen knew the pressures that bore on the senators, forcing them to deal often with irreconcilable demands, constantly pitting personal ambition and political principle against economic and political realities. That was the price for their public service. Bentsen understood what made

them give, and what made them take — and, if possible, how to
reach them to strike a deal. During his years as chairman of the
Senate Finance Committee, Bentsen had repeatedly shown that in
Washington he was a key man to see. More often than not, Bentsen
delivered.

Lloyd Bentsen was a proud man, proud of the career he had
forged, proud of the service he had rendered in The System. Hints
of these emotions would emerge during tours he gave visitors of his
grand Treasury office, where an oil portrait of Alexander Hamilton
hung over the fireplace. Bentsen would point out a "power wall"
of pictures showing him dealing with every major Democratic figure since Harry Truman. Bentsen didn't boast when he explained
the circumstances behind these pictures. His pride spoke for itself.

His moment of national fame came near the end of his Senate career, when he was chosen as the Democratic vice presidential nominee on a ticket headed by Governor Michael Dukakis of
Massachusetts. That ticket, it was hoped, would follow the successful example of linking a Massachusetts presidential nominee, John
Kennedy, with a Texan, Lyndon Johnson. It was not to be, but
Bentsen emerged from that disastrous 1988 Democratic defeat with
his stature enhanced. He provided the most memorable moment
of a lackluster campaign when, in a nationally telecast vice presidential debate, he left his young opponent, Senator Dan Quayle of
Indiana, speechless, with a classic putdown: "Senator, I knew Jack
Kennedy. Jack Kennedy was a friend of mine. Senator, you're no Jack
Kennedy." Bentsen instantly became a prospective presidential candidate in 1992; but changing political conditions and his age worked
against his presidential ambitions.

Bentsen was pleased to accept Bill Clinton's offer of the Treasury
post, and had genuine affection for the young President. Clinton reciprocated, treating Bentsen as something of a father figure. Still,
Lloyd Bentsen was increasingly frustrated. He felt ignored by the
health care planners. His advice was not often sought and less often
taken. He joined the other two top economic policy makers — Bob
Rubin and Laura Tyson — in expressing reservations about the
scope of the plan and the speed with which it would be implemented.

Bentsen's style, as described by a longtime friend and colleague, was "courtly, not confrontational. He would say that the hundred-day deadline was 'very ambitious,' not 'crazy.' " The Clintons were slow to pick up the signals, but others in their meetings knew what they meant.

Tyson was more outspoken. It was an irony noted by several of the insiders that the women in the room — Tyson, Shalala, and Rivlin — seemed to have more gumption about challenging the President, the First Lady, and Magaziner than their male colleagues in Treasury and OMB.

It might be better, Tyson argued at these early meetings, to encourage people to buy their own long-term care insurance than to set up "a new entitlement, which could be very, very expensive over time." As a way to save money, others suggested that Medicare patients be required to join managed care programs to qualify for a proposed prescription drug benefit.

While these arguments raged, the Clinton budget and economic plan began bogging down in Congress. As a political strategem, Clinton decided to give the congressional Democrats something their constituents would like — a spoonful of sugar, as it were, to make the bitter medicine of the budget go down. He called it his economic stimulus package — $30 billion of old-fashioned public works spending (later cut by half) designed to create half a million new jobs in an economy where job growth had just about stopped. In hopes of getting fast action, Clinton decided to separate it from the big budget reconciliation bill that would come along later. It was a fatal miscalculation, because that left it open to filibuster. The bill went through the House in March but hit a roadblock in the Senate. Republicans claimed it was pork barrel spending, a sop to urban constituencies who were not going to like some of the President's planned long-term budget cuts. The forty-four Republican senators held together and blocked four separate attempts by the Democrats to cut off their filibuster. When the White House offered a belated compromise, the Republicans rejected it. Clinton was angry at the Republicans and angry at his own political and legislative advisers for not warning him of the ambush.

*   *   *

As the debate intensified, an unpleasant but inevitable fact of Washington life began to torment the administration: leaks. Every administration had encountered them, but the Clinton group found them particularly pernicious and destructive.

Early on, a blanket of secrecy had been imposed on the task force operations. Magaziner objected, in writing, to the secrecy order, but was overruled by George Stephanopoulos and others on the White House communications team. Their fear was that stories about proposed changes — changes that might never be approved by the President — would alarm people and divert attention from the budget battle.

Magaziner had a more conspiratorial interpretation of the secrecy edict. The communications guys, he thought, wanted to keep him from becoming too visible a figure.

Hillary Clinton signed off on the decision — with no compunctions. She felt she had been burned badly by the press during the 1992 campaign and complained in an April 1993 speech that "the bane of all people in political life . . . is the unfair, unjust, inaccurate reporting that goes on from coast to coast."

But in fact the secrecy policy was the first of many mistakes and failings that ultimately deprived the public of essential information on which to form judgments.

Instead the administration let itself be subjected to a variety of leaks — the inevitable byproduct of unwarranted secrecy. Some were simply misleading or out-of-date. Others were plainly destructive.

On April 13, Health and Human Services Secretary Shalala told *USA Today*'s editorial board that a value-added tax was one of the ideas under consideration. Three days later Vice President Gore tried to fudge the leak with a TV statement that it "was not likely to occur in the near term." In fact, it was one of three ways to finance reform Clinton had been presented in an April confidential briefing memo.

A more serious incident erupted when Magaziner showed the President and others charts detailing possible methods of implementing reform, highlighting their impact on national spending. The first chart presented three different options for designing the benefit package, with the richest costing $50 billion, and with projected costs rising by an additional $100 billion as a result of higher prices and more people retiring and receiving health benefits. A second chart showed potential savings to be achieved under the three plans, while the third estimated the net effect of reforms.

Someone not only leaked the first chart to the *New York Times*, but altered it. An explanatory footnote on the chart stating that this was the gross national investment *without* savings was blanked out to make it appear, inaccurately, that the Clinton plan called for $150 billion in new taxes. The deleted footnote, which was printed on the chart in unmistakable uppercase letters, specifically stated that those figures were "before any calculation of savings."

The *New York Times* story ran on May 3. That was the Monday after Clinton's original hundred-day deadline for drafting the plan expired, so there were negative television reports on Clinton's failure to present his plan to Congress as promised. But the *Times* story was worse:

HEALTH-CARE COSTS
MAY BE INCREASED
$100 BILLION A YEAR

———

FIGURES BEGIN TO EMERGE

———

U.S. Financial Experts Estimate
Spending on 3 Proposals
Clinton Is Considering

The White House spent days trying to clear up that distortion and never did repair all the damage.

Toward the end of the battle, when the cost of secretiveness was obvious, Hillary Clinton told us that if the secrecy policy ever had been justified during the task force days, it should have been relieved by what she called an "off-the-record, bring-people-along strategy" of keeping a cadre of reporters informed of the work and goals of the task force.

That did not happen. No substantive policy interviews were permitted with the First Lady, Magaziner, or with members of the task force. Dana Priest, who was covering the task force for the *Washington Post*, recalled in 1995 how frustrating that policy had been. "They really tried to shut down the flow of information," she said. "They wouldn't let documents go out of the room. They numbered each copy of certain memos. They wouldn't even let the staff have phone numbers of other staff members, because they didn't want us to be phoning in to people." Much of her reporting involved canvassing "people who knew people who were working on the project . . . and those people were ultimately helpful. But I don't think it was necessary. They hurt themselves a lot, because the idea formed that they were creating 'a secret plan.' "

As critical stories about the "secret process" proliferated, both Clintons came to understand that the secrecy policy had been a serious misjudgment. That was a mistake, the First Lady later acknowledged to some people, and she accepted responsibility for it, saying she didn't understand it at the time.

"It created a negative reaction," the President said, blaming that decision for the start of Hillary's bad press. "In retrospect, I think that was a mistake, because it was the most inclusive legislative process in modern history. There was nobody shut out." That is an overstatement. A great many frontline officials from health-delivery organizations — hospital administrators, nursing supervisors, medical school professors — were brought into the discussions, along with staff people from Congress and the executive branch, but Republican staff members and most of the Washington lobbyists were excluded. Still, the process was more inclusive than the secrecy order let people know.

The secrecy policy did create a cloud of public suspicion, and the press by its actions probably deepened the problem. Faced with a policy debate of great complexity, many news organizations essentially threw up their hands and said, "We can't cope with this." Others tried hard, but were thwarted by the conventions of the news business and the meanderings of the protracted policy process.

It was a story of direct, and vital, importance to the lives of every American and to the functioning of the American economy.

But because of its immense complexity, it was a story that required detailed, persistent, imaginative coverage for people to understand how it affected them, their families, and their country. For the print press, which should have had more time to prepare longer in-depth articles, it was, at its best, a challenging assignment to help the public understand the stakes involved and to sort out fact from propaganda in the political battle for public opinion. With notable exceptions, too often the print press failed to meet that challenge; coverage was desultory, inconsistent, or focused on the political points being scored by opposing sides in the health wars. For television, by nature a fragmentary medium for conveying information, with increasing emphasis on entertainment as news and "sound bites" featuring conflict, charge, and countercharge as news high-lights, this story was nearly impossible to report. Compounding all these inherent problems was the way the Clinton plan had been formulated. The policy of secrecy made a bad situation infinitely worse.

Magaziner knew without being reminded that his original hundred-day deadline had expired. That was gone, but there were only a half dozen key decisions on cost, comprehensiveness, and financing left to make. And, despite the press problems, as far as he and the First Lady were concerned, "the understanding was that we're going to come on like gangbusters in May and really do this thing quickly."

By the middle of that month, however, as tensions over the President's budget rose, the stakes in the internal battle grew even higher. The budget reconciliation bill came out of the Ways and Means Committee on a straight party-line vote; audible grumbling from conservative Democrats made it clear the end-of-the-month floor vote would be very close. In the end, it passed 219 to 213 — a 6-vote margin garnered only after Clinton, Gore, and the cabinet members had twisted arms and made last-minute deals. "People were on edge," Magaziner recalled. "They were upset. And there were a number of people, for whom the deficit-reduction package was the most important thing, saying put off health care till the fall."

Amid this argument about timing, Bob Rubin, the chairman of the White House National Economic Council, suggested that they stage four internal health-policy debates in the Roosevelt Room, a spacious White House conference room, so the President could hear the differing views. The first, on May 20, focused on the comprehensiveness of the benefits provided and the length of time before everyone got them. Atul Gawande made the case for the "robust" version the task force was developing; Len Nichols, an economist on leave from Wellesley College to work for Panetta and Rivlin, argued for the more modest package that would have been preferred by the key members of the economic team. Ken Thorpe, the North Carolina economist who had gone from the campaign and transition team to work for Donna Shalala, gave the President the relevant budget numbers for both plans. It was a spirited, serious discussion, staged before a large audience of White House aides, who applauded at the end. It worked well as an educational device for the staff; the President and First Lady were pleased.

As usual, Clinton dazzled his audience with his command of the technicalities. His explanation of why he preferred the more complicated option of capping health insurance premiums to setting a ceiling on payroll taxes left some of the non-experts in the room floundering. But he also gave full weight to politics. If the plan offered only the benefits Nichols had described, starting with catastrophic-illness coverage now and gradually expanding from there, "Jay Rockefeller will dump on us," the President said. When Tyson argued that the 1996 election would turn on the economy and jobs, and expressed concern that health care taxes might lead to unemployment, the President disputed her history. "FDR's job programs did not get us out of the Depression," he said. "What reelected Roosevelt in 1936 was the passage of Social Security. That was the tangible expression of his concern; this can be ours." The political consultants endorsed his stand. Mandy Grunwald argued for boldness and high speed. "I have a bias," she said. "I'm wondering what's going to happen in 'ninety-six. The long transition doesn't warm my heart very much." To no one's surprise, Clinton said he favored the more comprehensive approach that jibed with his campaign rhetoric, but the economic team took heart from his suggestion that drug benefits and long-term care for Medicare recipients might be phased in more slowly, to reduce the costs. At the end of the session, both Bill and Hillary Clinton asked everyone present to keep the meeting private so they could use that same format again.

The very next weekend accounts of that session appeared in the *Washington Post* and the *New York Times*. The Clintons found the *Times*'s version seriously misleading. The President was furious. Flushed with anger, he said, "If we can't do this this way, we'll throw everybody out of the room." The next three debates were indefinitely postponed.

Much more than temper was at stake; this incident, and others, made the Clintons and Magaziner feel they were being subjected to intentional acts of disloyalty. Someone with a great deal of access was deliberately trying to sabotage the program. The fingers of suspicion pointed at Shalala and Thorpe, in part because they had lost control of the drafting to Magaziner and his team, and in part because they were old Washington hands, well known to the health care reporters who felt shut out of the task force deliberations. The inner circle drew all the closer, further sowing suspicion and distrust.

The longer health care was delayed, the chancier its prospects became. But Clinton was preoccupied. Everywhere the new President looked, it seemed, he was in deep political trouble. There were controversies over the firing of the White House travel office staff; over a $200 presidential haircut on Air Force One; over the abandonment of the Lani Guinier appointment as assistant attorney general for civil rights.

Clinton's standing in the polls plummeted, and with it, prospects for getting his budget and economic plan approved on Capitol Hill. Senators were threatening to jump ship unless he abandoned his proposal for a new energy tax. Gephardt and Mitchell were warning that the votes might not be there. On Monday afternoon, May 24, Magaziner and the First Lady joined the President in the White House residential quarters. Magaziner started to walk him through the arguments on a payroll tax versus an employer mandate as the main way to pay for reform. "But I could tell he wasn't focused on it," Magaziner recalled. "Usually he gets excited about policy issues, but you could tell his heart wasn't in listening to us." Soon the President steered the discussion to his preoccupation — the budget. He suggested that Hillary and Ira "keep working on multiple alternatives" until he could get back to thinking about health care. "And essentially," Magaziner said, "that was the last health care meeting I had with the President until August sixth."

Chief of Staff Mack McLarty and George Stephanopoulos, two of the President's most trusted aides, reinforced the decision. "Just hunker down," Magaziner was told. Work on the plan, if you want, "but don't pass out anything." Congressional leaders gave similar advice to the White House. Their view was, as Magaziner said, that raising questions about how to reform and finance health care then "could only muddy the water. We ought to just cool it on health care." Magaziner thought he should at least tell the key congressional players where things stood. He went to Capitol Hill with some memos. Speaker Foley, fearing a leak, immediately called the President and said it should not happen again.

On Monday, May 31, the task force officially disbanded.

In mid-June, after the President made concessions he had refused to make during House consideration, the budget measure squeaked through the Senate Finance Committee by an eleven-to-nine vote. One concession was particularly painful and would have major repercussions on later House consideration of the health care plan. Clinton had called for a broad energy tax, based on a unit of measurement called the British Thermal Unit, or BTU. The BTU tax was hard for many House Democrats to swallow, since it would raise costs for every driver and every homeowner. But Clinton said he would fight for it to the end, and it was included in the bill the House passed. But when Senator David Boren, an Oklahoma Democrat and member of the Finance Committee, said dropping the BTU tax was the price of his cooperation, Clinton caved. Forever after, House Democrats were afraid of being "BTU-ed" again.

On June 25, Gore broke the tie and cast the vote that gained Senate approval, fifty to forty-nine. House liberals were up in arms about the BTU flip-flop. The House-Senate conference on the budget would be a mess. And still ahead were final votes on whatever the conferees were able to put together. Clinton was holding on to his agenda by his fingertips, and health care reform was being shunted off until another day.

Ira Magaziner's assignment had turned into the job from hell. "Almost every day since I got here last January," he remarked, "I felt like I was one wave away from drowning."

He felt trapped. The entire strategy had been built around getting the plan to Congress in the first half of the year, and then passing it before the end of 1993. As the clock relentlessly ticked away their lost opportunities, Magaziner understood that continued slippage would further imperil chances for passage. Yet, intellectually, he thought that he "would have made the same decision" the President made if he had been responsible for overall administration strategy. That was, First pass the budget. "I think Hillary felt the same frustration," he would say. "The right decisions are being made, but we see health reform slipping away."

For Magaziner, the period from May to September of 1993 — the period of waiting, of dodging questions, of seeing the timetable fall farther and farther behind — "was, without question, the worst time in my life."

One night, Magaziner woke up shaking, remembering what first felt like a dream but in fact was a memory. He had taken his family to Hawaii on vacation and while he was taking pictures of others on the beach, his son, not yet three years old, ventured unnoticed down to the water. "I looked over and there was a wave coming over him that was taking him out to sea, and I started to run and I tripped. I remember looking up and thinking, 'Oh, my God, there's my son going out and I can't do anything.'"

His wife rescued their son in Hawaii, but who was going to rescue the health bill? "I woke up having the same feeling: I see it slipping away and I can't do anything."

Hillary Clinton saw the same thing, but seemed more stoic in her attitude. "She would just say, in a frustrated way," Magaziner recalled, " 'There's nothing we can do.' "

Looking back on this period, watching the rest of the White House struggle to save the President's budget while their own operation slowed and almost stopped, some of the task force officials felt they were isolated "in a Siberian outpost." As one official said, "They were focused on their thing, we were focused on our thing." Another sardonically referred to their operation as "Planet Ira." And this was a White House that, as Lyndon Johnson might have said, could not walk and chew gum at the same time.

The President's preoccupation with the budget fights pushed health care off to the side, but it did not stop other administration officials from fighting serious policy battles over the shape of the program. Although the President had promoted a hybrid plan in the campaign, relying both on market forces and direct controls to restrain health spending, his advisers were split on which approach to emphasize. At a June 7 meeting to update other White House officials, Magaziner remarked that "there are two religions on cost control. Some believe only in competition, and some believe competition won't work, that you need a budget. We think cost control is so important that we want to do both. Also, that way both religions will be able to claim victory."

That policy compromise made many people uneasy. Alain Enthoven and Paul Ellwood, two of the leaders of the Jackson Hole Group, which designed the managed competition concept, withdrew their support. Enthoven and Ellwood had close ties to some of the moderate and conservative Democrats in Congress and to parts of the health care industry. Treasury Secretary Lloyd Bentsen knew this defection spelled trouble.

June slid into July. In response to demands from Shalala and Bentsen, HHS and Treasury specialists were allowed to review the Magaziner draft plan. At one level, Magaziner could sympathize with the frustrations of those who had been excluded for so long. Later he would say their unease over secrecy was both profound and understandable. "I mean, if I'm Lloyd Bentsen sitting over there, and I know I'm going to be asked to testify as the lead person in Congress on this, and I'm sitting here in June and July and I'm not getting any information, and I've got some of my own people saying that we don't know about these numbers, I'm going to be unhappy."

In early July, with the First Lady away on a presidential trip to Japan, Magaziner got her permission by phone to schedule a meeting with Shalala and the economic team. On July 15, Boorstin reported the senior White House staff was opposed. Magaziner argued his case for moving ahead on health care to Stephanopoulos, McLarty, and Gergen. He was overruled. The budget battle was at too sensitive a stage to take any risks, they said. He tried lobbying them individually over the next few days; he made no headway. On July 22, he sent the three of them a memo warning that unless they made health policy decisions by mid-August they might never get a bill passed:

> The American public wants health care reform and expects President Bill Clinton to do it. Early this year, polls found overwhelming support and a confidence that the President could "pull it off." This feeling intensified after the State of the Union speech. The "stop and start and stop again" nature of the health care decision process, the pernicious leaks and the constantly changing deadlines — early May, late May, late June, late July, September — have seriously slowed our momentum, undermining our credibility with Congress, interest groups, the media and the American people.

Magaziner went on to detail the damage delay was doing with each of those groups:

> In the absence of action from us, we are having to fight daily to persuade the media not to write the "what went wrong" stories: Too complex or secretive a process devised by Magaziner, a plan being watered down, a feud between the First Lady and the economic team, a program where $100 billion of new taxes can't be sold to the President and he can't make decisions, etc.
>
> Interest groups who are offering support and a willingness to compromise on health decisions are now backing away. Congressional leaders eager to support health reform are questioning whether we are serious and are getting nervous that we will leave them high and dry. The business community already angered by the economic package grows increasingly worried about reputed huge taxes in health care reform.

Then Magaziner addressed a gnawing problem: The President had thought he was being smart when he gave the First Lady and Magaziner authority to set up a separate operation, not part of the regular White House or departmental bureaucracy. But others on Clinton's staff and in the departments regarded the Hillary enterprise as an alien force. Rumors had spread in the White House that Hillary and her team were waiting impatiently to displace the President's top advisers — the people who had been leading the budget fight — by moving health care to the top of the agenda:

> You questioned last Thursday night whether there was somehow a "separate White House" waiting to "move in" to do health care after reconciliation. On the contrary, we have been trying since February to capture the attention of the rest of the President's senior White House staff to prepare for this initiative, which has always, since early in the transition, been viewed as next in line after the budget.

Once again Magaziner emphasized that reform was a tough challenge but one that they could meet. The key, he said, was "a sustained effort from the President and from all of you." Then he warned,

> The President and First Lady are "way out front" on the health care issue. It's hard to imagine a retreat from it without severe adverse consequences for this administration. Even worse than backing off, however, would be to do the job in a "half-assed" way, to have the health care initiative crash shortly after launch. If we don't release [the plan] and go all-out beginning in September, we will fail at health care reform. If we have a half-hearted release of principles, with a couple of speeches, and then postpone serious consideration of our bill until January, we risk being beaten so badly that it will be embarrassing. A Republican bill will contest the single-payer bill and we will be viewed as bumblers who are irrelevant.

Magaziner may be faulted for many things, but not for underestimating the risks in the situation.

Capitol Hill was no happier with Magaziner than the cabinet secretaries and others on the White House staff were. Early discussions with key committee staff had gone well — at least from Magaziner's perspective — but now those staff members "were saying to us, 'If you really want us to get this done by December, you've got to start giving us paper and numbers pretty soon.' And I was saying to them, 'We're getting there. We're getting close.' But then we had to go from the end of May until September saying to them, 'We can't give you paper.' And they were thinking, 'What the hell is this? Either he's bullshitting us and he's really hiding the ball; or else they don't know what they're going to do. And how the hell do they expect us to get something done by December if they don't know what the hell they're going to do?' "

While Magaziner was being hammered by congressional staff for more information, congressional leaders were telling him to keep his file drawers locked. Leak of a Treasury document suggesting that wine, beer, and booze might be taxed — along with cigarettes — brought a direct protest to the President from none less than Mitchell, Foley, and Gephardt. That leak caused the California delegation to rise in protest. So did the House delegation from North Carolina, crucial to administration calculations for passing the budget. "In North Carolina," Magaziner recalled, "they were ready to hang me in effigy."

Internally, the same cross-pressures were operating. One day in July, Marina Weiss, Bentsen's health aide, complained to Magaziner that Bentsen was being kept in the dark. The same day, Roger Altman, on leave as Bentsen's deputy to manage the White House drive for passage of the budget, admonished Magaziner that "it will kill us if one of those things [the health care reform cost estimates] leaks."

An incident involving Hillary Clinton dramatizes just how sensitive, and concerned, the political players were becoming. When the First Lady arrived for a meeting in Speaker Foley's Capitol office, she brought some summary decision papers with her. "What are you planning to do with those?" the Speaker asked the First Lady. "Mr. Speaker," Hillary Clinton replied, "they're for the members."

Foley, normally the calmest and most gentlemanly of major Washington figures, immediately responded in alarm: "You pick them up right now and take them back to the White House."

* * *

If all these problems were not enough, the reformers faced another, and potentially fatal, one. They were losing their public relations battle.

Public attitudes always loomed large in their minds. Just days after the task force was formed back in January, the pollsters briefed the newly assembled health team. Harvard's Bob Blendon repeated the message derived from his postelection survey: A huge gap about the nature of America's health care problem separated the man in the street from the policy experts. The experts blamed excessive usage of a badly out-of-date delivery system. The public blamed greedy doctors and hospitals.

Stan Greenberg, the Clinton campaign's top pollster, added a different warning. Public expectations, he reported, "exceed those in any other field." More than half the population wanted a major overhaul of the system, and thought that should be accomplished in six months. But, as Jay Rockefeller had warned Clinton during the campaign, their motive was not altruism. To the public, costs were the greatest concern. If savings were achieved, people wanted them used either to reduce their bills or to expand their benefits. Making coverage universal was a much lower priority. And they didn't want government taking over the system.

Celinda Lake, Greenberg's former partner, underlined that last point. The phrase "managed competition" was a loser for Clinton, she said bluntly. People believe government is a lousy manager but a great regulator. She flashed another red light: The quality issue, she said, is the Willie Horton of this battle. At the moment, people believe that the more you can afford to buy, the better your care. People didn't like that; but, she said, raising another warning, watch out if they decide the Clinton plan threatens the quality of their health care.

On May 4, Arnold Bennett, media director for Families USA, sent Bob Boorstin a cautionary memo. Though Families USA was relatively small compared with the major business interest groups, it played a significant part in the struggle. It was exactly the kind of group that the Clinton planners counted on to deliver for them: an aggressive lobbying organization that grew out of the civil rights and anti-Vietnam protest movements of the 1960s. Families USA had its origins in 1981 as a foundation created by a $40 million grant from Philippe Villers, an engineer and liberal activist who founded Computervision, a high-technology company. Families USA advised Clinton while he was a presidential candidate and now wanted to rally the progressive ranks of the old Democratic coalition to pass the plan.

That cause was Arnold Bennett's livelihood. A political activist, Democratic consultant, and documentary filmmaker in his mid-fifties, Bennett spoke often of the "peace of mind" that reform would provide. By the time Bennett sent Boorstin his warning memo, he and his partner, Ron Pollack, were already ginning up publicity praising the administration initiative. With his memo Bennett sent a *Wall Street Journal* story that he said was bad news. The article, Bennett wrote, "is unfortunately not the only report that conveys the notion the Clinton health reform will help the uninsured at the expense of the middle class, and that new taxes on *us* are needed to insure *them.*"

"This stuff can kill us," he warned Boorstin, who was quickly becoming his partner in activism. "We should never define universality as getting protection to the uninsured," Bennett reminded Boorstin. "It's guaranteeing that *you'll never lose* your family's health protection."

Bennett, who had spent much time studying the Canadian system, gave additional advice in his memo. Any new taxes should be explained as providing subsidies for small business and protection for workers who might lose their insurance when laid off. "I've field-tested this on a couple of reporters," he said, "and I think it works." For emphasis, he added: "I think this is absolutely critical. If the reason new taxes are needed is to insure the uninsured, then we have given our imprimatur to the notion that the poor are the winners and the middle class is footing the bill."

Here was the heart of the problem: The public wanted reform, and for most Americans, that meant relief from the costs of medical care. People were not willing to take on many additional burdens just to support those without insurance. This point was raised often in internal debates, but in the end the public came to see the Clinton reform as threatening the security of the middle class, not benefiting it. In the battle for the American mind, failure to win this point would be disastrous.

Another problem made it more difficult to reassure people about how reform would work. John Rother of AARP expressed that worry best. He had seen how clever lobbyists had exploited public anxiety about the much simpler Medicare catastrophic-insurance bill in the late 1980s and whipped up such a storm among retirees that the measure was repealed before it ever took effect. "As a veteran of Medicare catastrophic," he said in the summer of 1993, more than two months before the formal launching of the Clinton plan, "I've got to worry about the complexity of this [plan] and the ability of people to feel comfortable with something that is so complicated. If you're explaining it, people's eyes glaze over. If you're attacking it, you need only that one rhetorical salvo."

The very terms the public was beginning to hear — terms that have been used and defined previously in this book — added to the growing sense of its complexity, if not incomprehensibleness: alliances, mandates, managed competition, cooperatives. They sounded heavy, bureaucratic, authoritarian. They were neither simple nor reassuring.

Magaziner himself was beginning to fret about the lack of an effective political support team. Shortly before Bennett's memo that spring, he sent one of his own to Hillary Clinton. He urged her to "recruit some more seasoned people to lead the political side" of the fight. He recommended two people, both hard-nosed New York lawyers, that he knew stood well with the First Lady: Susan Thomases, who had managed scheduling in the campaign, and Harold Ickes, who had run the Democratic convention for Clinton.

Neither was available then, but out of that memo came the decision to set up a War Room, similar to the Little Rock campaign headquarters, and to pull Jeff Eller from the White House communications office to run it. But the new War Room was barely established in early June when it was reassigned to Roger Altman, the number two man at Treasury, as the command post for the battle to rescue the President's increasingly embattled budget. Once again, the budget fight had pushed health care offstage.

* * *

By mid-July, David Gergen was urging that the plan not be introduced until 1994 — but Hillary Clinton and Magaziner thought
that was a death sentence. Magaziner had taken time to read the
history of the Carter administration, "when they basically put off
health care and put it off, and then eventually it died of its own
weight."

Among White House political strategists, the belief was that the
legislation had to be introduced in September to have any chance
of winning passage before the 1994 midterm congressional elections. From the beginning, everyone realized those elections would
be a critical test for the Clinton presidency and a demonstration of
whether a Democratic President and a Democratic Congress could
in fact combine to create real change. As Atul Gawande had written
Candidate Clinton so long ago, passage of reform legislation before
those elections would be his crowning achievement, on a par with
Roosevelt and Social Security nearly sixty years earlier, and "could
restore a Democratic lock on the middle class."

Now, in the summer of '93, health care wasn't the concern of the
President's political aides. They feared his presidency could be ended
for all practical purposes if Congress rejected his budget. With yet
another moment of high irony, success or failure in that budget fight
came down to the behavior of one man — Bob Kerrey of Nebraska,
the very person who had first raised the health care issue as a candidate the year before and who was crushed in that campaign by Bill
Clinton.

On the afternoon of August 6, with everyone in the White House
holding their collective breath over whether Kerrey would cast the
final Senate vote needed to pass the budget approved just a day before by the House, the First Lady slipped a health care meeting onto
her besieged husband's packed schedule.

Starting at 5:15 P.M. that Friday, the President spent two full hours
trying to get refocused. It did not work. In Magaziner's eyes, Clinton
looked "as exhausted as I've ever seen him," distractedly trying to
follow the plans Hillary and Magaziner had worked out.

Later that night, at 8:30, the President finally found relief, although it came after a battering. A disgruntled Kerrey looked into the
TV cameras and told his former rival: "I could not, and should not,

cast the vote that brings down your presidency." The budget victory was not without pain, and political damage, however. Before providing Clinton the vote that created a tie in the Senate, Kerrey added: "My head aches with the conclusion that I will vote yes for a bill that challenges America too little . . . how I wish this evening that I could trust you." With Vice President Gore casting the tie-breaking fifty-first vote, Clinton's budget passed.

His presidency was saved, but by the slimmest possible margin of victory. It was a clear and dramatic warning about the growing difficulties of passing anything in a bitterly divided Congress. Seldom in all of American history had a President's major legislative proposal been decided by so narrow a margin. Not a single Republican member of the House of Representatives had voted for this new President's budget. When it came before the Senate, not a single Republican voted for it. The one-vote margin of victory sent congressional historians scrambling for other significant matters that had been decided so closely. There were few examples: the single Senate vote that kept President Andrew Johnson from being convicted on impeachment charges in the venomous post–Civil War Reconstruction period was one. The lone House vote that enabled the extension of the military draft to pass just weeks before Pearl Harbor was the only other comparable action. These analogies provided powerful evidence of the new divisions — gridlock, as it was inexactly termed — that threatened to bring The System to a standstill during Bill Clinton's first term. The rising polarization also pointed to another dismal portent: If a President's budget proposal produced such deadlock, what were the prospects of passing the immensely more difficult and controversial health care reform plan?

Nonetheless, the very next day after the budget vote, Magaziner began rounding up the Cabinet and economic team: Now the President was ready to focus; high-level decisions were needed before he began his vacation.

In meetings of senior advisers the following Monday and Tuesday, acrimony reigned. The cabinet members and senior White House officials were exhausted after the budget battles and resented being summoned back, with sorely needed vacations barely begun, to address the immensely complicated plan. Many hadn't focused on it in months, and many had serious doubts about it. They wanted answers and time to think, but they feared the President, the First Lady, and Magaziner would make decisions without them. Some of them suspected the decisions had already been made. The debates about how best to improve coverage while containing costs were tense. Nothing was resolved. On Tuesday night, Magaziner briefed the President, outlining five "scenarios" that he said spanned the range of views among the advisers.

On Wednesday, just before he was due to go on vacation, the President joined the counselors. Clinton was in a cantankerous mood. Moreover, he was reluctant to be swayed by the same administration officials whose advice in the budget fight he had found faulty. After listening to some of the economic advisers' complaints about the implausibility of the "overoptimistic" scenarios Magaziner and his staff had drawn up, he jumped in, griping that even the most ambitious plan would not do enough. Even if Magaziner's prescription was followed, he groused, costs were still projected to increase to 17 percent of the whole economy — up from 14 or 15 at that time. The inflation had to be controlled better, he told the assemblage, and he was convinced there was a helluva lot of waste in the system.

"I've seen it myself," he fumed. "I've heard stories from other governors, from people inside hospitals," the President insisted. "The salaries of doctors and other health care professionals had gone up six times as fast as everyone else's for fifteen years, with no productivity gains. You people say we're tightening down too much. Then tell me why do other countries get by spending just nine percent of their gross domestic product? How can you complain we're being tough by trying to hold it to seventeen percent? Give me a break! We have to do better than that." The President was angry.

But Bentsen, Shalala, and the economists were not convinced. They thought the cost containment measures should be less stringent than Magaziner had proposed. Shalala questioned the steepness of the Medicare cuts; Bentsen aired concerns about the size of the benefits package and the tightness of the caps that would be placed on insurance premiums. Defending Magaziner, Hillary Clinton said that health care alliances had just started in Florida and California, but already were showing significant savings. She talked about the

Mayo Clinic and Minnesota and about the new plan in Washington state. The projections looked quite reasonable to her.

But the questions multiplied. Robert Reich, the Labor secretary and a longtime friend of both the President and Magaziner, expressed skepticism about the effects of all these changes on employment. He wanted time for his own experts to do some projections. Laura Tyson was particularly outspoken — despite her shaky status as one who had not made it into the inner circle of presidential advisers. She worried that "if you put tremendous pressure in a very short period of time, the system could break down." The health providers who would be asked to deal with new patients and new procedures while cutting their costs were the very ones who would have to cooperate in order for the transition to a new system to work. It just looked too risky.

"I was concerned," Tyson recalled, "that by making it so ambitious, we might actually cause it to fail — not politically, but in the real world."

Magaziner tried to quash the doubts by reiterating the view, which he knew Clinton shared, that harsh competition from the Japanese had forced American car makers to eliminate waste. The same would be true in health care. Real competition that the alliances would force on the hospitals, the insurers, and the entire medical system would quickly compel them to shape up and eliminate waste, he said.

Never happy when his advisers were in disagreement, Clinton decided not to make any decisions. After he finished venting his anger and frustration, he told Magaziner to work on it further. They would try again after his vacation.

Again, Magaziner was devastated. When Congress returned after Labor Day, he would still have no plan to give them.

By then, the September calendar of presidential events had been set. It carefully allocated the President's time among three major initiatives due to be launched that month. First was the plan to "reinvent government," the ambitious effort formulated by Vice President Gore that was supposed to modernize federal personnel and procurement policies and reduce the size of the bureaucracy. Second was the formal opening of the congressional battle to ratify the controversial North American Free Trade Agreement (NAFTA) linking the economies of the U.S., Mexico, and Canada. Finally, and placed last on that crowded month's schedule, was health care reform.

The September 22 date for Clinton's health care speech to Congress had already been announced; it could not be postponed. If we don't define the issue, consultants Grunwald and Greenberg argued, our opponents will, and we'll never recover.

Despite the fact that major questions remained unsettled, Clinton's schedule called for him to give an outline of his plan to the National Governors' Association meeting in Tulsa August 16. The date had been set months ahead of time, and Clinton had told leaders of the association he wanted to talk to them about health care reform. On the appointed morning, they gathered around the huge four-sided, square table they always used for their plenary sessions, seated in order of their states' admission to the Union. Behind each governor sat his or her top staff aides, and another thousand spectators — lobbyists, reporters, family members — filled the room, eager to hear what Clinton had to say.

The governors were of vital importance to Bill Clinton. Under the scheme he was contemplating, states would have huge responsibilities for organizing the regional purchasing cooperatives, or alliances, as they were now being called. Besides, these were his old buddies. He cared more about their reaction to his ideas than he did about the views of most members of Congress.

But before they heard from Clinton. the governors heard from John Motley, vice president and top Washington lobbyist of the National Federation of Independent Business — the biggest small-business organization. As Clinton listened in a nearby "holding room," Motley attacked the "untried, untested" approach Clinton was preparing. The administration plan to require all businesses to provide insurance for employees was like "tying small businesses to a sled and pushing them down a mountain, hoping they'll remain upright," Motley charged. Thousands of them would go bankrupt, he warned, threatening a national recession.

It was a bold, bare-knuckles assault, a declaration of war, as it were, coming even before the administration plan was formally

introduced. Clinton was taken aback. He huddled with the First
Lady and other advisers and hurriedly rewrote his speech.

He began his rambling remarks with a bath in nostalgia. "I miss
you," he told the governors. "I miss this," he added, meaning the
informal and candid exchanges of views among the state executives.
The President confessed to his erstwhile gubernatorial colleagues
that he had had a bellyfull of "the kind of rhetoric and air-filling
bull" that he heard so often in the nation's capital. "I treasure the
kind of partnership that I have had with so many of you," he went on,
proceeding to salute the teamwork he and Republicans like Lamar
Alexander of Tennessee and Mike Castle of Delaware had achieved,
working for education reform and welfare reform, on behalf of their
fellow governors.

Reflecting on the rigors of the just-completed budget fight, the
one in which he won not a single vote from any Republican member
of Congress, he embraced the principle of political bipartisanship. "I
never want to go through another six months where we have to get all
of our votes within one party," the President said. As for health care,
it must be done "on a bipartisan basis," he said. "I don't much care
who gets the credit for this health care reform as long as we do it."

But, obviously nettled by Motley's attack, the President answered
the lobbyist by name. He promised the governors that the mandate
requiring employers to pay a portion of their workers' insurance
expenses would be phased in over time and its economic burden
eased by granting subsidies to small firms. "It just defies common
sense to say that we can't maintain the world's finest health care system," the President declared, "stop all this cost shifting, bring our
costs back at some competitive level, cover everybody — and create
jobs."

Clearly, the President was prepared to fight. Then he and the First
Lady left for Martha's Vineyard to begin their first real vacation in
four years. He had just a month to go before unveiling his health plan
to the American people.

In early September, the President made the final decisions. On three
vital matters, he ruled for Magaziner — and against the combined
judgment of most of his economic advisers and cabinet officials.

Bentsen and Shalala, joined by the members of the economic team, argued against the proposed price ceilings on insurance premiums. Those so-called premium caps would be viewed, correctly, as proxies for price controls — and Congress despised price controls.

They argued that the alliances were too regulatory, the overall plan too bureaucratic. And they said the Medicare cuts were too extreme and would cause severe problems, both in urban states like New York and rural ones like South Dakota. These, Bentsen knew well, were potential time bombs for the Senate Finance Committee, where Democratic senators from those states, Pat Moynihan and Tom Daschle, were expected to carry the ball for the President.

The President heeded their advice on only one point. He improved the benefits for poor children so none would receive less from his plan than they did from Medicaid. But on the three major objections, he overruled them.

Afterward, Shalala and Bentsen complained to associates that Magaziner had stacked the deck against them in the briefing papers he had prepared for the President. Magaziner of course denied this. But Bentsen realized after these meetings that the Clintons were putting Magaziner's judgments ahead of his. He could do nothing about that. But he damned well wasn't going to be embarrassed. As the final preparations were being made, the Treasury secretary put in a protest call directly to Hillary Clinton. If he was to be the leadoff witness at the Senate Finance Committee, he told the First Lady, he wanted all the background paper he would need to defend the plan. He got it — but it came very late.

Donna Shalala was no less concerned than Bentsen. The task force process had been as bad in her judgment as she thought it would be when she and Alice Rivlin tried to talk the Clintons out of doing the program that way. The whole thing was crazy, she thought. All those people slaving away for all those months, and here they were, up against the deadline, trying frantically to write a plan — and the Clintons still seemed to be in thrall to Magaziner. Bentsen, Panetta, Rubin, Tyson, Shalala, Rivlin — all of them were expressing the gravest reservations in a debate that Shalala thought had "bonded" them against Magaziner — and the "shocking" fact was that none of it seemed to register with the Clintons.

In those final meetings, Laura Tyson was again particularly outspoken, acting as one of the administration's tougher guardians of the free marketplace. She posed many questions about Magaziner's optimistic estimates of how much "waste" could be wrung from the system, and how fast new benefits could be provided. The disagreements the President heard in those meetings had been building for a long time. A sense had been growing among members of the economic team — fed by reports from the people they had detailed to work with Magaziner — that if Magaziner was not actually fudging the numbers, he was squeezing them very hard to fit with his precast conclusions.

As early as February, for example, James R. Ukockis, a Treasury career official, sent a memo to two of Bentsen's deputies, complaining that Magaziner "became impatient" when the "scoreable savings in a short time period" from Medicare cutbacks came up far less than what he wanted, and "was not interested in a balanced evaluation" of options on price controls. "The process is being driven by a narrow focus on the need for budgetary savings. . . . It is used to justify risking major dislocations in the health care system."

Another official, detailed to the task force from the Office of Management and Budget, said, "I think all of us thought there's something wrong here. These [savings] numbers are too big. The principals were happy because you are, after all, giving them what they're asking for. But you know deeper and deeper in the back of your mind just how tenuous these estimates really are."

A third official, working for Tyson and Rubin, said, "Lots of the economists were worried that, regardless of what the numbers said, this was a real deficit-buster. You could not tell that to Ira, because you would get excluded. So what you did if you were me, you actually produced the numbers, and then you told your bosses that you thought it was stupid and they had to deal with it."

A fourth official raised the same challenges to the realism of the "incredibly tight premium caps," or price controls on insurance policies that Magaziner was proposing, and said he worried that Magaziner was shielding the President from these problems.

Tyson did bring many of these doubts to the table for the last decision meetings, but the President was not ready to second-guess Magaziner at this point. Neither was Hillary Clinton, whose strength was not numbers-crunching. In August, the President had allowed the naysayers in his administration to delay the final decisions on health care. Now he had to decide, and Tyson for one was not surprised that he went with the man who seemed to have all the answers.

It was not that Clinton was being manipulated. In the budget battle inside the White House in the first month of the administration, Clinton heard everyone out, Tyson said, because "he did not come in knowing precisely what he wanted to do." On health, by contrast, he had figured out during the campaign the approach he would take. "Health care was different," Tyson said, "because you had the structure to begin with. You were talking about how you were going to decorate this room."

When the arguments were over, some of the advisers wrote private memos to the President or to Hillary expressing their disagreements and misgivings. Bentsen's ran to thirty-eight pages, single spaced. Treasury staffers were involved in drafting various sections, but no one saw the whole memo, before or after he placed it in the First Lady's hands. Her only reaction was to ask that Bentsen's staff help Ira with drafting the bill.

8

The Moral Imperative

ALL THROUGH THE PROCESS, the First Lady and Magaziner were making political decisions along with their policy judgments. But their negotiations with interest groups went no more smoothly or predictably than the detailed drafting work within the task force.

The case of Gerald W. (Jerry) McEntee and his union, the American Federation of State, County and Municipal Employees (AFSCME), illustrates the vagaries of the negotiating game. AFSCME was the first of the major unions to endorse Clinton for the nomination and, as a political powerhouse, was accorded great access during the campaign. Like other labor leaders, McEntee, in his late forties, had historically favored the Canadian approach, but he was more than ready to accept the outlines of Clinton's plan — as long as it dealt with the runaway inflation that was putting employers in the position of saying, "You've got to take [a] zero to two percent [raise] in wages or else your benefits are going to be cut."

No sooner was the celebration of Clinton's presidential victory over than McEntee was horrified to read in a *Wall Street Journal* interview, the first with the President-elect, that Clinton was considering ending the deductibility of employers' health care costs and taxing workers on the value of those benefits. McEntee immediately called the President, warning of the "bells and whistles" his comments had set off. Clinton offered reassurances, and that problem, at least, never reappeared.

But there were other disputes. At one meeting with the First Lady, McEntee questioned the provision in the bill that allowed large private-sector employers — those with more than five thousand workers — to stay outside the alliances and negotiate their own health insurance deals. "If that's okay for them," he asked, "why shouldn't my workers have the same privilege?" The First Lady replied, "You can't expect the public to believe that this is a good plan for everybody and then tell them, 'By the way, we're exempting the people who work for government.'"

"Well," said McEntee, "Magaziner has agreed to let the postal workers stay outside." Hillary Clinton asked Magaziner if that was true. When he confirmed it, she expressed her irritation that the commitment had been made to the employees of that autonomous government corporation but she insisted that public workers must use the system she was proposing.

At that point, McEntee reminded her that "we have a lot of friends on Capitol Hill," where the AFSCME political action committee (PAC) was a major resource for Democratic candidates.

Acknowledging reality, she said, "If you can work it out up there, go ahead."

AFSCME came through for the administration as few other organizations did, but McEntee was privately critical of the way the White House dealt with his union and other interest groups. "Of course, everybody was trying to get as much as they could," he said later, "but the administration didn't come to closure with anybody. It was just impossible to do all of these things all of these groups wanted. If they had called in a lot of the groups and said, 'Hey, this is the end of the road. There's no more talk. This is the best we can do,' it would have been okay. But instead, they said, 'Hey, even when we send it up to the Hill, we'll still have time to talk.'"

So a dynamic was created in which major groups were given certain guarantees and then allowed or even encouraged to bargain for more. Senior citizen groups, for example, would be crucial supporters. Retirees were promised immediate prescription drug benefits and a first step toward extensive long-term care benefits. More important, they were exempted from the basic thrust of the Clinton plan, which would move most working Americans quickly into managed care programs while the Medicare population would be allowed to continue in expensive, fee-for-service medicine.

Big business was a second potential ally, so the auto companies and other old-line manufacturing firms were promised a government takeover of the insurance costs of their early retirees, a feature that could save some companies millions of dollars.

And small business, potentially the biggest stumbling block to reform, was wooed with the promise of subsidies for the costs of insuring their employees. Inside the task force, the policy makers pointed out that it would be far cheaper and more efficient and more equitable to give subsidies to low-wage workers than to small firms, which might or might not need help. But, politically, it made sense to throw a bone to small business — not that it did any good in the end.

The negotiating process was far from a success. Enemies were not appeased, and allies were too often not fully enlisted. And Hillary found the whole process distasteful.

After Labor Day, the First Lady tried to move the debate back to its basics and to reinvest it with the moral imperative those who worked with her insist was always uppermost in her mind. "This has been an extraordinary process," she said in an address at George Washington University on September 10. "It has involved literally thousands of people, not only those here in Washington but throughout the country. . . . I have sat and talked with men and women who have worked for a living for years and years, often for the same company, and yet cannot find their way into the insurance market. I have talked with physicians who treat our most vulnerable populations and who tell me repeatedly that a sensible health care policy would not only be humane and moral but economically significant, because we could prevent problems before they deteriorated."

This was Hillary Clinton at her best: a determined policy maker convinced of her cause who clearly had made great effort to master a highly complex issue and was now prepared to make that case public in ways that everyone could understand.

"You all know the stories that are legion," she told the university audience, who packed a ballroom to capacity, "that have brought us to this point. And what I hope we will do as a nation in the next months is not just to continue talking and wringing our hands, sharing the anecdotes . . . but to roll up our sleeves and together solve the problems posed by a country that spends more money on health care than any other in the world, yet does not provide quality, affordable health care easily accessible to all of its citizens." She had been gratified by congressional support, she said, adding, in remarks that later would have a bitter aftertaste: "In my consultations that have gone on repeatedly since last February on the Hill, I have found an extraordinary range of interest and support from both Democrats and Republicans . . . who have moved beyond rhetoric on this issue, who have been willing to get into the very difficult, detailed analysis necessary for us to make the right choices."

That consultation was not over. It was intensifying. But once again, the old self-destructive problem of leaks arose at a critical moment.

In early September, after two all-nighters. Magaziner and his staff completed a rough draft of the plan embodying the final decisions Clinton had made on the alliances, the Medicare cutbacks, and the insurance price controls. The next day, Magaziner and the First Lady went to the Capitol to brief members of Congress and their staffs. When they reached Pete Stark and the Ways and Means Health Subcommittee, he threw one of his celebrated tantrums. He demanded the document Magaziner brought be left with him. Then, the California congressman addressed the First Lady directly and even insultingly.

As Jay Rockefeller retold the story of that scene at the time — obviously having just heard the First Lady's version — it went like this: "Stark says, cold as steel: 'Some of us would like to be helpful, but until we get the information which has not been coming to us, because we have not been given access to this process, it's very hard for us to come out in support of this plan.' And she says, 'Pete, you will have a copy of the plan tonight.' And he did."

In the ways of Washington, that supposedly secret copy of the plan spread like wildfire. From the closed-door session with Stark and his aides, it made its way rapidly to the American Hospital Association. From there, it flew over fax machines to favorite reporters throughout the capital. "I didn't know Xerox machines could work that fast," said John Rother of AARP. "This is yet another way to try to pull the rug."

On September 11, four days after the draft plan was finished, both the *New York Times* and the *Washington Post* ran stories describing and analyzing it. The day after that, Magaziner held a press briefing, attempting to answer the myriad questions and criticisms that the leaked document had unleashed. Cost and savings projections in their plan "are solid and we stand firmly behind them," Magaziner asserted. He added, "The vast majority of Americans will pay less for the same or better health benefits." Magaziner was at special pains to deny the *Times*'s report of a hospital tax. That idea had been dropped in May, he said. He also tried to ease fears that Medicare would be slashed to the bone, arguing that it would continue to increase "at roughly twice the rate of inflation over the decade," and that Medicare recipients would receive new prescription drug and long-term care benefits from the plan.

It was a skillful, but necessarily defensive, cleanup job, and it did not fully minimize new doubts sowed about the plan just days before Clinton was to make it public.

John Rother was worried. "It instantly changes the nature of what people like me do, from trying to communicate the big picture to focusing in on the most arcane details," he said a few days later, describing how he was now forced to put out brushfires from misleading leaks. "The more this focuses on the details and on the process and the less it focuses on the goals, the worse off we are."

Even Rockefeller, whose enthusiasm for health care sometimes clouded his political judgment, expressed concerns. "I think the managed competition thing is brilliant," he said on the eve of the plan's introduction. "It's a price club. It's something the American people are going to be able to understand very easily. I think Adam Smith would be pleased. I think my great-grandfather [industrialist John D. Rockefeller] would be pleased."

On the other hand, he said, because "we've never done managed competition before, Bill and Hillary Clinton decided we've got to introduce a backup, and we call that a national budget. That is displeasing. That is unnerving. That provides great fodder for Republicans, who are able to then really talk about government bureaucracy and top-down control."

Pressure did not ease even after the final policy decisions were made and announced in the President's September 22 speech to the joint session of Congress. Despite the difficulties with the wrong speech in the TelePrompTer, that televised address in which the President introduced his plan and held up the Health Security card was a huge lift for all those who had labored over the plan. The first wave of reactions — in the polls and in the comments from congressional leaders of both parties — was so favorable that a mood of euphoria enveloped the White House. Clinton seemed to have found a way to bring health care to everyone, slow medical cost inflation for business and government and, in the process, chart out a new private-public cooperation with few direct taxes. In outline, it looked wonderful; too good to be true, the skeptics said.

But it was not yet a bill that was ready for introduction. During much of October and November, Magaziner again found himself pulling more of what he called "double all-nighters" — forty-eight-hour work binges, forcing him to sleep on his government-issue office couch. Interest group representatives and members of Congress besieged him, all demanding last-minute adjustments. Heavy pressure came from inside the government — particularly from career bureaucrats — worried about parts of the bill that would ease government regulation.

"The drafters came over from the departments and the bill grew by about four hundred pages," Magaziner would later complain. "By the time the Labor people, and the HHS [Health and Human Services] people, and the Treasury people looked over all the sections, there were more penalties — more this, that, and the other thing."

At the same time, Magaziner was under pressure from the people who were writing the actual legislation to stop the changes and let them finish their work. They were career professionals in the Congressional Office of Legislative Counsel, recruited for the task by House Majority Leader Dick Gephardt. "By then," Magaziner remembered, "the drafters weren't even talking to me, because they were so angry. Finally, I just decided to let it go. I had put in a huge memo about regulatory stuff in the bill I wanted to strip out, but finally we just let it go."

As Hillary Clinton constantly said, their idea was that the bill was designed to be rewritten. She understood that many of its "movable parts" could be changed. The two bedrock principles that could not be compromised were universal coverage and cost containment. They must remain intact.

When it was all over, Ira Magaziner said he had found the experience brutal — "somewhere between awful and terrible." The start-and-stop schedule, dictated by outside political events, the imperative of secrecy, the knowledge, as he said, that he was "pissing off everybody," wore on him. A workaholic, he regularly put in eighteen-hour days and awoke before the alarm went off, worrying, Did we get this right? Did we do this right?

The cost in human terms was driven home to him on Thanksgiving, when he was playing a board game with his five-year-old daughter, Sarah. "You know," she told her father, "this is the first time you've played with me since Bush was President."

Still, he was inordinately proud of the process he had invented, not only because of the plan it produced but because it prepared him for any question anyone might ask. Or so he thought. Visitors to his office were directed to survey the shelves, where thirty-five black binders — very thick books of options and analysis — represented the ammunition in his bunker for the congressional battles ahead. "These are going to be very important," he said, "because when somebody says, 'Well, I'm not so sure about the malpractice thing. Did you think of this? Did you think of that?,' chances are we're going to have an analysis that says, 'Here's what we thought about that and here's why we didn't do it. Or, if you want to go in that direction, here's what we'd have to look at.' "

At the end of the drafting process, Magaziner was pleased. "I think we've put out a bill that is *live* on arrival," he said, "even though nobody — myself included — agrees with everything in it. The leadership and all the committee chairs feel it's a vehicle they can use and work with. We've been able to divide some of the opposition, even though it's going to be a tremendously rough road ahead. And probably most important of all, we've got a detailed health bill out there that is serious enough in its import so that the eventual bill that comes out has a decent chance of working."

He recalled, with pride, a very early conversation with Clinton about his taking on the assignment. "The first thing I said to the President when I accepted this job was, 'You know, you're still going to be President when this thing is implemented. It can't just be something that passes Congress; it's got to be something that works.'"

Even some of Magaziner's critics conceded that he and his task force had accomplished an extraordinary job. Bob Reischauer, the Congressional Budget Office director who had tried to caution Magaziner to proceed more slowly, was nonetheless impressed with the task force product. "It is a remarkable achievement," he said. "It has all the pieces, and they are connected. When you're thinking of reforming the health care system, there's a million questions you might ask And within that one thousand three hundred sixty-four pages, you can find the answer to almost any question."

Bruce Fried, the organizer of the Blueberry Donut Group and no fan of Magaziner, said, "There were good things that came out of it, a lot of thoughtful development. But I do not think it was necessary. The time it has taken to go through this process was a terrible waste of capital, of opportunity. The plan the transition team had put together was more than sufficient for the President to have met his obligation and to have given the Congress enough direction to move ahead."

Others were far more critical. The general congressional reaction to Magaziner was captured in Dan Rostenkowski's comment to Hillary Clinton: "I wish he had some dirt under his fingernails." Jim McDermott, the congressman/psychiatrist who led the single-payer advocates in the House, said Magaziner "has been almost Rasputin-like in the view of most of us. He has kept all the knowledge to himself. He's the only one who has been at all the meetings. He's the one who has all the books. He is viewed as having way more power in this situation than he ought to have, if the President were smart."

McDermott said Pete Stark "can't control his reaction to Magaziner's 'arrogance.' " And McDermott himself had similar problems, saying sarcastically of the Rhodes scholar: "I didn't go to Rhodes University. I don't even know where it is. But I got elected to Congress, and you never ran, and you don't know shit about nothing."

Nor was such criticism limited to Congress; similar snide comments came from within the task force itself. One of the task force file boxes forced open by the lawsuit against the First Lady and Magaziner contained a revealing doctored version of a "Far Side" cartoon by Gary Larson. In its rewritten version, two courtiers are saying to an obviously deranged despot: "Sorry, your highness, but you're really not the dictator of TOLLGATE, a small European republic. In fact, there is no TOLLGATE. The hordes of admirers, the military parades, this office — we faked it all as an experiment in human psychology. In fact, your highness, your real name is IRAS-CIBLE MAGAZINER, you're from RHODE ISLAND, and it's time to go home. ROSTY."

David S. Abernethy, staff director of the Ways and Means Health Subcommittee, said Magaziner "was arrogant enough that basically whatever advice was proffered by anyone who did understand the government or was an expert in health care policy was ignored." The Magaziner task force, he thought, "wasted an incredible amount of time which we need desperately. They just screwed us." Members of Congress were rightly resentful, he said, because "that son-of-a-bitch Magaziner has so boxed us in by making their plan look cheap." He complained that the savings and cost controls assumed by the administration plan "are beyond anything that any professional health policy person has ever felt was achievable. I have been doing this all my life and I just marveled at the chutzpah of the administration coming out with these numbers. It begs the straight-face test to think you're going to cover thirty-eight-and-a-half million new people and not spend any more except a little tobacco tax. They just went out and told the American people, 'Don't worry. This will be very easy.' "

Abernethy was not alone. Three days before the President was to introduce the plan, Pat Moynihan, the chairman of the Senate Finance Committee, had gone on NBC-TV's *Meet the Press* and called the projected Medicare and Medicaid savings and the $91 billion in deficit reductions a "fantasy."

In the end, one great question arises about the task force process: Was it worth it?

One can understand Bill and Hillary Clinton's wish to construct their own program. They knew that in the previous Congress, both Gephardt and Mitchell had been unable to forge a solid consensus among Democrats in their respective chambers on a bill that was simply to be used to draw a veto from President Bush. There was no reason for the Clintons to assume that leaving the design job to Congress would produce agreement.

Critics like Bruce Fried would later charge that Hillary and Ira should have stopped with the principles the President enunciated and not tried to write a bill. But on this charge, they can be acquitted. With few exceptions, the committee and subcommittee chairmen who would handle the bill wanted legislative language. "Rostenkowski," the First Lady later recalled, "came in to see me and said, 'If you don't give me legislative language, nobody will think you've really done your job. That gets the process started.' "

The charge made by Jim McDermott and others on Capitol Hill that it was all an elaborate facade for educating Magaziner and the First Lady is also false. By the end of 1992, Magaziner had invested a huge amount of time in attempting to master health care. One can argue that his conclusions were wrong, or that he was too rigid in adhering to them. But he cannot be called a policy innocent. Hillary Clinton had done less on health care and needed more time to get up to speed, but Sheila Burke's comment about Hillary being "a worthy opponent and a worthy proponent" — coming from a prominent Republican staffer capable of high partisanship — indicates how well the First Lady had mastered her brief.

As for the President, he was, as usual, better informed than anyone outside his close circle expected. He brought to this issue the same intense scrutiny that he focused on any domestic issue that interested him. "Much has been written about how much Mrs. Clinton knew, and she knew a lot, but actually the President, I think, was the most knowledgeable person of all," Senate Majority Leader Mitchell said.

"More than any other public official, he achieved a grasp of the issues involved, of the details involved; he really knew the subject well."

A third charge — that the task force process delayed the introduction of the plan in Congress — is also a red herring. What kept the President from sending it forward was, first, Senator Byrd's refusal to incorporate it into the budget reconciliation bill and, second, the delay from February to August while Clinton was pushing the budget through Congress over unanimous Republican opposition. Had the Republicans been less partisan or the Democrats more unified behind their new President, the health plan would have reached Congress in the spring. But the budget was never safe until Al Gore cast the final tie-breaking vote. It was fear of upsetting the budget applecart — a well-justified fear — that delayed the health care plan so long.

Still, even to many on the task force, the detail of the plan suggested a process that had run amok. Even before they knew that it was going to produce a nearly fourteen-hundred-page bill, some White House officials had begun to speculate that Ira Magaziner and Hillary Clinton had lost sight of reality. They had been caught up in a sophisticated version of "I dare you," egging each other on to answer every conceivable question. But the First Lady and Magaziner had a ready rationale for their work. As she put it, "Whatever the President came out with, I wanted to feel was totally defensible." So she spent "countless hours studying, reading, talking, quizzing."

Clinton himself had invested significant time in 1992 in framing his basic approach. No one would have condemned him for abandoning it, but he had persuaded himself that he knew what needed to be done. It was Bill Clinton's approach that determined the basic structure of the plan that emerged from eight months of extraordinarily hard work. And it was a complex design, including new structures — the alliances — for which no working models existed.

What can be questioned about the task force process was not so much its workings as its location in the White House, not so much the time it took as the definition of the assignment.

Clearly, any serious proposal would have to confront the intricacies of an existing medical system with multiple parts and complex interactions — a system that was *already* 40 percent government financed but that had powerful private sector participants as well in the insurance companies, the hospitals, the doctors and other providers, and the parts of business that were paying much of the bill.

No one seeking to address such a system comprehensively could hope to come up with a simple solution. The Clinton administration cannot be faulted for the complexity of its plan. But the absence of a few simple, structural principles, readily grasped by the public, was a crippling defect — and one that could have been anticipated.

The Clintons had studied the failure of the Medicare catastrophic bill in the late 1980s, but they apparently did not grasp the point made by Professor Arnold Rosoff of the University of Pennsylvania's Wharton School of Business in his analysis of that legislative fiasco. Rosoff said that successful management of information flow is the sine qua non of health legislation. That requires simplifying the essentials of the proposal for the public. The Clinton plan was difficult to explain even to legislators with long experience in the field. It also required working with the press to increase public understanding of the problem, and the Clintons mistakenly decided to try to keep the press at bay.

A useful model for the Clintons would have been Ronald Reagan's tax reform, which produced a sweeping revision of the Internal Revenue code in 1986. Nothing has more arcane byways than the tax code. But the basic proposition of the Reagan plan was simplicity itself: Eliminate a lot of special-interest loopholes and you can reduce rates for everybody, an idea that could be expressed in a single sentence and could be grasped by everyone.

Another aspect of the Reagan tax reform worthy of emulation was that it was initially shaped far from the White House. When Reagan promised, before the 1984 election, that a major tax reform would be high on his second-term agenda if he were reelected, the assignment of drafting it was given to the Treasury Department. Then-Secretary Donald E. Regan told the professional staff of his department, the career people, Write the best policy you can come up with and don't worry about the politics; that's not your responsibility.

After the election, the technicians' work was made public in a document that came to be called "Treasury I." It was shocking in its boldness. Few sacred cows were spared. Political wiseacres said that it would be "dead on arrival" on Capitol Hill. President Reagan kept his distance from it. The technicians who prepared it — the Ira Magaziners, if you will — were anonymous careerists, who were never allowed out of the back rooms to mingle with lawmakers. Nobody hated them, because nobody knew who they were.

"Treasury I" was turned over to James A. Baker III, who had just become Treasury secretary in a job swap with Regan for the White House chief of staff position, and to Baker's deputy, Richard Darman. Together, they took the temperature of the legislators in both parties on the House Ways and Means and Senate Finance Committees. Then they rewrote "Treasury I" into a still tough, but politically tuned, reform proposal. That was the plan Reagan sent to Capitol Hill, with his good wishes but also with the admonition that he would not promise to sign or veto anything until he saw what its final form was at the end of its journey through Congress.

In contrast, Clinton decided to take the drafting of the plan directly into the White House. There, he turned over the project to his wife and to his close friend. With that arrangement, he gave himself no leeway at all. Whatever emerged would clearly bear his personal stamp. He could profess flexibility as much as he wished, but he could not remove his fingerprints from the detailed design that his personally chosen and high-visibility agents had created.

Within the administration, the selection of the First Lady had other consequences. As much as she said she wanted open debate, her presence — and her status — clearly made it harder for administration critics of the plan to make their case. One cabinet official who had great experience in this area — and grave misgivings about the ambitiousness and complexity of the plan — said softly, "You make your point once to the President's wife, and if it is not accepted, you don't press it." Jim McDermott, noting the deference paid the First Lady by congressional colleagues who he knew believed her to be wrong, remembered thinking, "It shows you the way politics really is, that no one's going to tell the President's wife: 'Ma'am, you don't have any clothes on.' Nobody's going to say that."

The other way in which the Clinton process deviated from the Reagan model was the blending of political and policy judgments. The technicians at Treasury who fashioned "Treasury I" were told,

"Forget politics. Give us good policy." They did — and then the political dealing was turned over to two consummate deal makers, Jim Baker and Dick Darman.

The Clintons and Magaziner never made a similar separation of functions. Most of the decisions were driven by policy considerations. But some critical decisions were politically driven and constituency-oriented. Major concessions were made in hopes of enlisting support from senior citizens' groups, big business, and organized labor. An effort was made to blunt the opposition of the small-business lobby.

Observers like Harvard's Bob Blendon said there was too much policy bias in the Clinton-Magaziner approach. "They thought it was a policy problem with some political elements," he said. In fact, "it was a political problem with some policy elements." From his viewpoint, the starting point for discussion should have been, What coalition will get us 218 votes in the House and 51 votes in the Senate, and what kind of plan will it take to hold that coalition?

That is the approach Baker and Darman and Regan used to pass tax reform. But whether or not Blendon was right, the approach the Clintons and Magaziner used was neither clear and principled in policy terms nor a successful political coalition-building tool. Before it went to Capitol Hill, Leon Panetta asked skeptically, "Who's going to be *for* this?" Shalala worried that the administration was "building a negative coalition." Mike Lux, who worked on health care in the public liaison office of the White House, warned in a May memo, "I'm beginning to grow a little concerned that in our health-care decision-making, we may end up with a reform package that excites no one but our opposition." AFSCME's Jerry McEntee said at the time, "They never closed the deal." His point was that when the Clinton-Magaziner team offered benefits to this group or that, they did not effectively say, "Now, you've got to support the whole plan." Dan Rostenkowski had the same complaint, lamenting that "they gave away all this stuff and didn't get any commitments in return."

The First Lady adamantly insists that she did — and that she was later betrayed. Every interest group she thought she had signed up went back to Congress and tried to get more. Many of them continued to hedge on supporting the plan, while they pursued their own goals. All of them — including AFSCME — felt free to work on their own agendas. And they could claim, as McEntee did, that Hillary had opened the door for them to do exactly that.

Whether she knew it or not, Hillary Clinton had not closed the deal. The President was committed; few others really were. And time was already growing desperately short.

BOOK THREE
The Debate

9

Hillary on
the Hill

HILLARY CLINTON HAD THE SPOTLIGHT, and she knew
how to use it. After the frustrating delays and setbacks, she immediately moved to make the most of a public now clearly focused
on health reform after the President's widely praised congressional
speech.

For weeks, political advisers and schedulers for the President and
the First Lady had been planning for this moment. Bill and Hillary
Clinton's schedules were crammed with daily events — "Health
Care A-Go-Go," White House aides privately referred to them —
around the country, all calculated to attract maximum media coverage, particularly television. Regional town hall meetings in
Pennsylvania; a Tampa seniors conference beamed by satellite to fifteen hundred locations; a United Nations event featuring the First
Lady, timed to follow the President's long-scheduled address to the
United Nations General Assembly; a national presidential "teach-in"
carried live over ABC-TV; network interviews; morning and evening
talk show interviews — all these were packed into the schedule in
those hectic few days immediately following the address. While the
Clintons were employing the "bully pulpit" of the White House to
win public support, cabinet officers were dispatched around the nation — to New York and Ohio, Kentucky and Tennessee, New Mexico
and Oregon.

These first frantic days were only the prelude to the most exten-
sively covered and highly praised of all the Clinton efforts, Hillary

Clinton's appearances before five congressional committees. They began six days after the President's September 22 speech and just before the Clintons were scheduled to fly together to California for more appearances — the final push, or so it was thought, shortly before delivering their plan in legislative form to Congress, where the effort would be brought to a successful conclusion.

Hillary on the Hill became one of those events charged with political symbolism, and unforeseen consequences. It was dramatic. It was triumphant. But its very success also triggered new and intense activity among opponents who saw in this formidable First Lady a foe whose defeat would require their most determined efforts. It also stirred new and largely unexpressed concerns about the role and power of this young woman, neither elected nor confirmed to a public position, especially one so consequential, at a time when feminism remained a controversial issue in American life.

Until Hillary Rodham Clinton traveled to Capitol Hill to begin those three days of televised hearings, only two other First Ladies had ever testified before Congress. Both times they dealt with far narrower issues. No First Lady had assumed the leading role Hillary Clinton played in developing and delivering major national legislation.

Those earlier precedents were much on the minds of the First Lady and her devoted staff as she prepared for her full emergence into the public spotlight. "This is as big as it comes," one of her aides told Maureen Dowd of the *New York Times*. "This is Eleanor Roosevelt time."

Eleanor Roosevelt was, of course, the first to appear before Congress. But myths notwithstanding, Eleanor Roosevelt testified only twice: during the Depression, about the plight of migrant workers, and during World War II, about slum-housing conditions in the District of Columbia. The other First Lady was Rosalyn Carter, who testified about mental health efforts in the late 1970s. Hillary Clinton's appearances before five congressional committees — three in the House, two in the Senate — far eclipsed any public role her predecessors had played.

Mindful of that history, and eager to do all he could to make her Hill appearances both symbolic and successful, Ted Kennedy thought of having her appear in the grand Senate Caucus Room, where his brothers had announced their presidential candidacies. He instructed his staff to do research into other historic events there. They reported back that hearings on the sinking of the *Titanic* had been held in the Caucus Room. Uh-oh, Kennedy thought, that's not one we want to advertise. This could be another *Titanic* — a huge ship with a big prow that can't turn easily when it's heading straight toward a massive immovable object.

For all her confident public demeanor, privately Hillary Clinton displayed her anxiety as she prepared to go to Capitol Hill. During a "prep" session with her staff at the White House the night before, she almost "jumped down the throat" of one staffer who tried to make a couple of suggestions to her. The next morning, as she was about to leave for the Hill, her staff saw her again, and she was, understandably, "very nervous." But she displayed none of these emotions when she strode through the crush of reporters into the bright lights that sharply illuminated the hearing room for the TV cameras. She was cool and poised as she sat alone, without notes, expressing herself clearly and convincingly hour after hour, easily fielding all questions. The few critical remarks directed at her were deflected with an earnest reply or self-deprecating humor. Introducing herself in her opening words as "a mother, a wife, a daughter, a sister, a woman," she also consciously appealed to all women, seeking to undercut the tensions that exist between America's homemakers and its career women. It was a bravura performance.

Most members of Congress, in that male-dominated bastion of political power, were almost obsequious — many women thought patronizing — in their praise. "I think in the very near future the President will be known as your husband. Who's that fella? That's Hillary's husband," gushed Dan Rostenkowski when she testified before his House Ways and Means Committee. Her testimony, Rosty added effusively, had fundamentally altered the terms of the debate. No longer was the question whether America *would* have health reform, he said, "but what type of reform we *should* have." John Lewis, a Democratic member of Congress from Georgia who as a young black civil rights marcher had been clubbed nearly to death by seg-regationists, added his praise: "I really believe when historians pick up their pens and write about this period, they will say that you were largely responsible for health care reform in America." A first-year congresswoman from California, Democrat Lynn Schenk, passed on a message from her mother: "She said to tell you that not since Eleanor Roosevelt has she admired a woman in public life — and my mother is not a woman who admires easily."

The praise was bipartisan. In the Senate, Jim Jeffords of Vermont, a Republican moderate with a strong independent streak, publicly endorsed the Clinton approach after she testified, telling her, "I am pleased to be the first. I am absolutely confident I will not be the last." His words were echoed by another Republican moderate, Jack Danforth of Missouri. "We will pass a law next year," Danforth flatly predicted after the First Lady's appearance.

In her appearances, Hillary Clinton did not miss any opportunity to win her audience's favor. Whereas Bill Clinton was notoriously late, Hillary Clinton arrived before the appointed time. The mem-bers of Congress spoke of her competence and respect for their well-regulated procedures. She also showed she knew how to play to their highly developed egos with ingratiating flattery. More than once, she deferred to a congressional questioner, saying modestly, "as you have pointed out," or praising the politician's mastery of a subject "which you know better than I." To John Dingell, it was an appeal to family pride. The Congress, she told the chairman of the House Energy and Commerce Committee, has "yet to fulfill your father's dream" of universal health insurance. Though that bill of half a century before was uniformly described in books as the Wagner-Murray-Dingell bill, when she referred to it before Chairman Dingell, it became the Dingell-Wagner-Murray bill.

The most celebrated moment of her triumphal round of Hill ap-pearances came when the First Lady neatly, and surgically, put down one of her, and her husband's, most caustic critics, the conservative Republican Dick Armey of Texas.

Armey was the chief lieutenant for Newt Gingrich's combative House Republicans, noted for his "go for the jugular" style of politi-cal exchange. Not long before the First Lady came to the Hill, Armey had compared the Clintons' ideas to those of Dr. Jack Kevorkian, the so-called suicide doctor who helped terminally ill patients die. Armey denounced the Clinton plan as a "Kevorkian prescription for the jobs of American men and women." Months earlier, Armey had said publicly of Hillary Clinton, "Her thoughts sound a lot like Karl Marx. She hangs around with a lot of Marxists. All her friends are Marxists."

Now, when Armey's turn came to question the First Lady, he began with an attempt at graciousness. "Mrs. Clinton," he said, "let me also express my appreciation to you for the work you've done and your willingness to come before this committee today, and tell you what a joy it is to see you here."

"Thank you," the First Lady said, smiling brightly.

"I listened to the chairman's opening statement," Armey continued, beginning to apply the stiletto, "and while I don't share the chairman's joy on our holding hearings on a government-run health care system, I do share his intention to make the debate, the legislative process, as exciting as possible."

Nodding calmly, and continuing to smile, the First Lady answered, with wry double meaning, "I'm sure you will do that, Mr. Armey." Laughter filled the hearing room.

"We'll do the best we can," said a flustered Armey.

The First Lady continued to smile disarmingly. Then she quietly replied, "You and Dr. Kevorkian." This time, the laughter in the room was loud, sustained, and punctuated with strong applause.

Armey appeared stunned. He leaned forward, his face flushed, and said grimly, "I have been told about your charm and wit, and let me say" — he was interrupted by more laughter — "the reports of your charm are overstated and the reports on your wit are understated."

The First Lady, unruffled, still smiling, but in a thinly veiled tone, replied, "Thank you. Thank you very much."

It was this kind of performance that won Hillary Clinton rave notices. As Tamar Lewin wrote in the *New York Times*, virtually overnight Hillary became "feminism's first mainstream icon: a powerful, smart woman with mass-market appeal."

By the end of her first day on the Hill, the elevation of Hillary to icon had occurred. Standing in a deserted Ways and Means hearing room, in a scene captured best by Maureen Dowd, a male staff member stared at two blue-and-gold china cups from which the First Lady had drunk tea that day. "This one has a better lipstick print on it," he said, examining a cup. "Maybe I'll auction it off."

For the First Lady's staff, the praise showered on her after that first day of testimony was vindication of all their efforts — and of their faith in her ability to come through under immense pressure.

Bob Boorstin and other staffers sat behind her as she testified. Once again, Boorstin thought he was witnessing history, a generational culture shift only hinted at in the actions of Eleanor Roosevelt. Hillary was magnificent, he thought. She could pander with the best of the pols. He gloried privately in the way she spoke familiarly about Chicago to Rosty and was even more impressed when she casually remarked that she knew Representative Bill Brewster, an Oklahoma Democrat, was a pharmacist. This was an amazing moment, Boorstin thought. "She absolutely knocked them over and all we, the loyal staff, could do was to sit there and exchange invisible high fives." When the day was over, Boorstin walked down Capitol Hill in the bright sunshine shaking his head in wonder.

But not all the reaction was complimentary. From William J. Bennett, the conservative former Education secretary and drug czar in the Reagan-Bush administrations, came a little-noted attack on both the Clinton proposal and on his fellow Republicans for failing to take on the President and the First Lady. "In the midst of the largest power grab by the government in recent history," grumbled Bennett as he spoke to reporters on the day Hillary Clinton finished her appearances, "most Republicans are either nowhere to be seen, fawning approvingly, or asking questions about the fine print. Here is a monumental assault on the private sector, on individual liberty, and those sworn to its defense are largely silent."

Characteristically, Newt Gingrich was not reluctant to take on the First Lady. It was just good manners that kept Republicans from attacking her, Gingrich said to reporters, adding, "If Ira Magaziner had tried to defend that same plan, he would have been destroyed." Gingrich went on to promise an attack on the high costs and Big Government inefficiencies and crafted a sound bite for the press:

"The bureaucracy that can't get the right speech in the TelePrompTer can't get the right CAT scan to the doctor either."

At that point Gingrich's steadfast determination to oppose the Clinton reform was unknown to the public. He was biding his time, convinced that history and the political tides were on his side. Many Republicans feared that the administration effort had irresistible momentum. Not Newt Gingrich. "I never worried about it," he told us much later. He was convinced at that moment and became even more certain with the passage of time that the Clintons' plan was "doomed." He was also convinced, though he never said so publicly then, that his tactics of "coagulation" ("clot everybody away from Clinton on health reform," he had instructed his House Republicans) would prevail. The Clintons adapted the tactics of failure. "They were going against the entire tide of Western history. I mean centralized, command bureaucracies are dying. This is the end of that era, not the beginning of it."

But little attention was paid to Gingrich's views in the fall of 1993. And he preferred it that way. While the public spotlight was strongly focused on the Clintons and their plan, Gingrich quietly, deliberately continued to form his opposition ranks. He conducted private strategy sessions with Republican pollsters and members of Congress, assessing the Clinton plan and probing for its weaknesses, all the while waiting for the chance to spring the trap he privately promised his troops would kill the reform effort. But this was not that moment; for now, the Clintons were riding the crest.

As the President and the First Lady boarded Air Force One, Sunday, October 3, to fly to California, they were sustained by a chorus of applause for their efforts in the ten days since the speech to Congress. Picking up a copy of that Sunday morning's influential *New York Times* "Week in Review" editorial section, they read words that politicians would kill for: "Hillary Rodham Clinton dazzled five Congressional committees last week, advocating health care legislation in the most impressive testimony on as complete a program as anyone could remember, and raising hopes that an issue that had stymied Congress for 50 years was now near solution."

Ira Magaziner was aboard the presidential flight. Even though he was exhausted and feeling ill from the cumulative pressures and around-the-clock working schedules of the previous weeks, Magaziner was experiencing the happiest days since he began his labors. Things are going well, he thought, so well in fact that they might just be able to pull this off. For the first time, the reformers would have the full attention and talents of the President. Their schedule called for them to have four or five weeks of the President's time. Within the next two weeks, by mid-October, they intended to submit the legislation to Congress.

There were new concerns, to be sure. Magaziner had learned only a couple of days before, while Hillary was on the Hill, of a private report from representatives of the U.S. Chamber of Commerce who had come to see him and said "all hell was breaking loose" around the country as the National Federation of Independent Business (NFIB), the potent small-business lobby, was planning an all-out opposition campaign. At the same time, Magaziner shared with the First Lady more disturbing information: that NFIB, the Health Insurance Association of America (HIAA), and other groups were meeting privately to plot joint opposition strategy. They reportedly wanted to "blow the Clinton train up."

This was most troubling news, and it came from someone who attended that first meeting of the No Name Coalition. Magaziner was disturbed, but not alarmed; he did not yet appreciate the full power of the opposition that was forming. Besides, he reflected, the tide is now running our way. They had the public's attention. They had the combined talents of a committed President and First Lady. With such a team, they would continue to dominate the national news with more and more events carefully planned to promote the cause.

But those plans were swiftly shattered. En route to California on Air Force One, the President received word of a foreign disaster. In far-off Somalia, on the horn of Africa, U.S. Army Rangers had been pinned down by warlord clan factions for sixteen hours after a botched raid on the suspected clan leader's headquarters. Eighteen Americans had been killed, and nearly eighty wounded. Bodies of American soldiers had been dragged through the streets before taunting mobs. An injured helicopter pilot had been captured and was being held hostage.

The President had a crisis on his hands. Immediately, he began

altering his schedule. While he was still airborne, his California trip
was cut short, so that he was able to make only a brief appearance at
the first event, a senior citizen rally. Magaziner had a sinking feeling.

Once in California, the President grappled with the situation in
Somalia, a situation inflamed by brutal television scenes showing
those dead Americans and the wreckage of their failed military mission. Immediately Clinton returned to Washington and scrapped
the next week's health care events. He dispatched seventeen hundred more army troops to Somalia and ordered an additional thirty-
six hundred Marines to be stationed offshore. Days later, while the
President's and the nation's attention were still focused on Somalia,
another international crisis erupted. This time it was in Haiti. In a
humiliating rebuff, sending a worldwide signal of U.S. weakness and
irresolution, Haitian thugs stopped American and Canadian engi-
neers from landing at Port-au-Prince to aid rebuilding projects that
were part of a United Nations agreement. Within days, heated national debate raged over a Clinton decision to deploy U.S. warships
carrying lightly armed troops off Haiti to enforce U.N. sanctions.
Then Russia teetered on anarchy as Boris Yeltsin's regime appeared
to be in danger of being toppled. And by the time that crisis had
eased, the impending votes in Congress on approving NAFTA were
commanding the White House's full political attention. Faced with
all these unexpected crises, all but one presidential health care event
scheduled for October was canceled.

"We lost him," Ira Magaziner said. And October, the month
planned to mark the rebirth of the stalled reform, instead became
what foes later privately described as the October of Opposition.

To Bill McInturff, polling for Republicans and for major private-
sector opponents, October 3, when the Clintons flew to California,
was *the* critical date. McInturff's daily "tracking" polls after
Clinton's speech were highly favorable for the President and his plan,
as were Stan Greenberg's polls for the President. Support was rising; then the disaster of Somalia struck, powerfully affecting both
Clinton's standing and the prospects for health reform. "That poor
soldier gets dragged dead through the streets of Mogadishu, on October third," McInturff said, "and what did October become? Somalia,
Haiti, Russia!"

It was a classic example, McInturff thought: Presidents don't control the agenda. "If Clinton had had his four weeks, that health reform outcome could have looked very different," he said later.

The Clintons didn't need a pollster to tell them that the momentum gained from the President's September 22 speech and Hillary's follow-up week of congressional testimony had been lost. It was all too obvious that this disastrous month of repeated crises had so diverted them that they were in danger of losing their war after it had barely begun. When four weeks later they attempted to reignite public enthusiasm and political support, they chose Statuary Hall in the Capitol as their new launching pad for what turned out to be one of the most contrived media events ever staged in that tradition-steeped chamber.

There, on October 27, in the old chamber where the House of Representatives had met for half a century, from 1807 to 1857, where Congress in the last summer of the Civil War had authorized each state to place marble and bronze statues and busts of citizens "illustrious for their historic renown," and where the great figures of the past, peering down on all who entered, stirred memories of epic achievements, the Clintons would yet again relaunch their faltering health effort. That setting alone guaranteed extensive press coverage.

It was a perfect stage for the Clintons, who excelled at these ceremonial events, another opportunity for them to regain lost public support for their plan. The hook was the formal presentation of their plan to Congress. Televised scenes of the President and the First Lady, flanked by Democratic and Republican leaders of Congress posed against a backdrop of historic leaders — Adams, Calhoun, Clay, Lee among the many — would almost certainly be a political plus. So, at least, the White House political strategy team calculated.

Both the President and the First Lady spoke. They stressed their hope for bipartisan action. They had no "pride of authorship," each of them emphasized. They were eager to engage in a broad debate about the need for reform and the best way to achieve it. They had only one "bottom line": to provide comprehensive coverage for all Americans. The President, again, was emotional. As he finished his remarks, he pounded on his lectern and warned about the costs of doing nothing.

Their performances were polished and rhetorically effective; but this time the old magic did not work. For one thing, as was immediately pointed out in press commentary, this ceremony took place under false pretenses. Though it was billed as the moment when the Clintons would deliver their revamped Health Security Act into the hands of Congress, the legislation was still not drafted, a fact that led Danny Rostenkowski, standing among the leaders, to dismiss the event as "theater." Once again, the Clintons had missed their own deadline. But a more ominous sign of deep political trouble surfaced at the ceremony. And it came from a most unlikely source.

Among the Republicans invited to join congressional Democrats in making brief remarks was House Minority Leader Bob Michel of Illinois. In personality and style, Michel was unlike Newt Gingrich, the man he knew would succeed him as Republican leader in the next Congress. Where Gingrich was combative, confrontational, Michel hardly ever sounded strident or rigidly ideological — and rarely if ever would he use a ceremonial occasion like this to deliver a partisan message.

But this time Michel stunned people with the forcefulness and boldness of an unsparing attack on the very premise of the Clinton plan. Speaking in his flat midwestern voice from the same lectern just used by the Clintons, Michel sounded the battle cry of all-out Republican opposition. His words were unequivocal in their political meaning. He and other Republicans had "substantive and profound policy differences" with the Clinton approach, he said. This coming debate was about much more than health care, he continued; it was about the role of government in our society. It was about the threat of expanding bureaucracies, taxes, mandates, maintaining the time-honored private doctor-patient relationships. Then adopting the code language used by all the opposition groups, Michel said the test for America in this battle was whether the nation's health care system could retain the private-sector character that had made it great or whether Americans would "embark on an uncharted course of government-run medicine."

Even those who had not closely followed the debate immediately understood what this laying down of the gauntlet by a moderate like Bob Michel meant. It was as clear a signal as possible that House Republicans were now willing to mount a strong public attack on the Clinton plan. It was also clear that this could not have happened unless Republicans believed public support was rapidly eroding.

Although he did not realize the significance, the President already had sent another House Republican into the opposition camp. During one of the barnstorming trips he took after his televised address to Congress, Clinton had offered a ride on Air Force One to a Republican congressman from Florida, Representative Michael Bilirakis. Bilirakis told Clinton he would like to make this reform a bipartisan effort. Clinton, always eager to appear sympathetic to anyone he's with, said that nothing would gladden his heart more than making this entirely bipartisan. Bilirakis came away from the talk believing that Clinton was very flexible on the timetable for achieving universal coverage. In short order, he collected 103 signatures, mostly Republican, on a letter to the President suggesting that "access" to health insurance be increased over an unspecified number of years, partly by reforming insurance practices and partly by expanding the number of community health centers serving the needs of the uninsured. His answer from the White House was a blunt reiteration of the President's commitment to guarantee health care for all within five years. Rebuffed on that front, he approached J. Roy (Doc) Rowland, the Democratic physician from Georgia who had his own reservations about government health programs as well as stacks of complaints from medical colleagues about Medicaid and Medicare, with the idea of crafting an alternative. In due course that alternative bill would become a major stumbling block to getting the Clinton plan out of the House Energy and Commerce Committee, on which they both served.

It wasn't just Bilirakis who was turned away. Public doubts about the provisions, or even the existence, of the Clinton plan had been growing dramatically. Immediately after the Clinton speech, public approval of the Clinton plan topped disapproval by thirty-two points in a *Washington Post*-ABC News poll. Three weeks later the margin was only twelve points. The battle had barely begun, but the administration already had lost vital ground by surrendering the initiative to opponents of the proposal.

While six out of ten in that latest poll still said they thought the Clinton plan might be better than the status quo, there were danger signs that the proposal was being viewed as a welfare program — not something that would benefit the middle class. The majority of those polled said the plan would do more harm than good to retirees, the middle class, people with insurance, and people like themselves. Conversely, the beneficiaries were seen as young people, poor people, and people without insurance. Three out of four said the plan would hurt small business. Majorities of 56 to 72 percent said they felt "big concern" over the possibility it would add to bureaucracy, damage the quality of medical care, boost costs, limit the choice of doctors and hospitals, raise taxes, and cost jobs.

When the *Washington Post* reconvened its Blue Ash, Ohio, focus group, three weeks after its members had gathered to watch the President's speech, their doubts clearly had grown. "Everybody talks about the plan," said machinery operator Frank Duvall. "I haven't seen any plan. I don't know of anybody that can hand me a paper and say, 'This is the plan.' " The focus group reflected the poll's increase in fears that the Clinton plan would cost them money. "When have you ever seen the government involved in anything that wasn't more red tape?" asked Tracy Hedleten, who had just lost her job at a savings and loan. "I just can't believe that they can do it any more efficiently than competitive business people. I just can't buy that."

"Right now," said Carol Templeton, the Mary Kay cosmetics manager, "he has opened a can of worms. I thought that something was going to really come through and really put security in what he said. Instead, he has frightened everybody."

10

The Interests

HUGO BLACK, a great liberal voice on the Supreme Court during the New Deal era, once warned against what he called a
dangerous threat to democracy and effective government — the increasing power of the special-interest lobby. "Contrary to tradition,
against the public morals, and hostile to good government," Justice Black said, in words bristling with indignation, "the lobby has
reached such a position of power that it threatens government itself.
Its size, its power, its capacity for evil, its greed, trickery, deception
and fraud condemn it to the death it deserves."

From the vantage point of a vastly more sophisticated, and cynical, America in the 1990s, Black's warning seems quaint, even naive. Lobbies have not died; over the decades they have steadily
expanded their reach and power. Washington has become not just
the center of government but the headquarters of literally thousands
of associations, coalitions, and interest groups, with their attendant lawyers, lobbyists, pollsters, researchers, and propagandists,
representing virtually every cause or claim imaginable. The influence industry has become one of the principal mainstays of
the local economy; the constitutional right of individuals to "peti-
tion their government" has become a very big business, measured
in billions upon billions of dollars. Even more, it has assumed a
leading role in the functioning of the government and its political system. By the nineties, the collective power of the lobbies had
increased to such an extent that it seemed to drive and dominate The
System.

Health care reform may well be the most expensive lobbying battle in history. Estimates of the total amount spent range from $100

million at the low end of the scale to $300 million. Close to $50 million of campaign contributions came from groups with major stakes in the battle.

For more than a quarter century, campaign reform has focused on reducing the role of special-interest contributions. After the health care battle, we heard the explanations that attributed the defeat to the financial advantage its opponents possessed. But the people who were fighting for the Clinton plan knew otherwise. In the midst of the battle. Representative Mike Synar, an Oklahoma Democrat who had long been a leader in campaign finance reform, said, "On this one [health care], there's so much money in play that it's a wash. It's an absolute wash."

When the war was over and the opponents had won, Representative Dick Gephardt of Missouri, majority leader and commander of the Clinton forces, said, "It's not money. It's votes. The common view is that all of these interests came in and intimidated people by either giving them money or not giving them money. I think money had little to do with the outcome. It's the political work they do at home."

In this fight, the interests demonstrated their ability to move far beyond traditional techniques of "buying" political access. They showed — at least on the opponents' side — that for the first time, they had learned to use all the tools of modern politics and political communications for their special-interest objectives. Like the officials they were trying to influence, these groups showed they could manipulate public opinion and mobilize Main Street supporters to deliver at the ballot box. As we will see, seasoned political operatives ran some of the lobbying campaigns. The same organizational and propaganda techniques that were employed in the campaigns of Ronald Reagan and George Bush were used to kill the Clinton bill. The interest groups for which they worked were almost indistinguishable from presidential campaign organizations in the scope of their fund-raising, the scale of their field organizing, the sophistication of their advertising and public relations skills, and the speed of their electronic communications. But unlike the political parties, which represent broad coalitions of voters who agree on at least a general approach to government, these groups represented narrow interests with very specific economic goals. Together, their combined financial resources and the influence they exerted on legislators exceeded those of the Democratic and Republican parties. And like those parties, they pursued their goals continually, learning from one fight how better to wage the next one.

The success they achieved in 1993–94 emboldened them to use these same techniques, not to thwart a President's initiative, but to advance their own objectives in a new Congress their resources helped to elect. Their operations illuminate how The System operates today — and explain why so many citizens believe that government no longer represents them.

More broadly, the health care reform fight shows that our mental picture of the lobbying process is badly out-of-date. As Walter Lippmann once observed, we are all captives of the pictures in our heads. We think the world we know is the world that exists, and the world that will be. When it comes to the power of special-interest groups, the health care reform struggle requires us to redraw the pictures in our heads and see the new world as it really is.

What happened was nothing less than a war, a war without quarter, waged until one side had thoroughly defeated the other. Bill McInturff, one of those who played a key strategic role on the winning side, likened what had happened to World War II. What McInturff — who polled for the insurance industry and the Republican National Committee and helped formulate strategy for Newt Gingrich and his troops — meant was that the Clinton forces were occupying fixed, static positions like the French in 1940 inside their Maginot Line; there, they were easily bypassed and cut off by Hitler's panzers, leading to France's quick defeat. "They didn't understand what was going on," McInturff said. "They didn't see it." Unbeknownst to the administration, the opponents had used the time between May, when the Clinton people were supposed to have introduced their plan, and September, to prepare for a political assault the likes of which had never been seen.

The groups that mobilized to fight the Clinton plan included not just those with the most direct economic stake in the outcome, like the Health Insurance Association of America (HIAA), the Healthcare Leadership Council, the Business Roundtable, and the National

Federation of Independent Business (NFIB), but such seemingly disinterested organizations as Pat Robertson's Christian Coalition, which became one of the groups meeting privately at the conservative lobbying group Citizens for a Sound Economy with the No Name Coalition. Christian Coalition newspaper ads — featuring a picture of a friendly family doctor preparing to give a child an immunization shot — warned, "Don't let a government bureaucrat in this picture." The Clinton plan, it said, spelled rationing, mandatory abortion options, less choice of doctors, and maybe a million lost jobs.

This opposition coalition was further cemented by private meetings its members held with congressional opponents of reform. Soon after the Clinton bill was introduced, William R. (Billy) Pitts, the top assistant to House Minority Leader Bob Michel, began Monday morning meetings in his office with the Republican staff directors and counsels of the key committees. Meeting with them each week were lobbyists working to kill the bill: grocery manufacturers, wholesalers, firms like Pepsico and Burger King with large numbers of franchises hiring part-timers without insurance. They exchanged intelligence, targeted legislators for special attention. Nothing was left to chance.

Long after the battle was won, Deborah Steelman, a Bush administration official who became a major player among the lobbyists opposing reform, enumerated the extraordinary set of circumstances that combined to make victory possible. "It was just a lineup of the stars you don't get in politics very often," she said.

Steelman gave that explanation while sitting in her corner law office in a pin-striped vested pantsuit and fashionable laced-up boots before a "power wall" anchored by a framed picture of a cocky, hands-on-hips cowboy. She told us all the major elements of the Republican coalition combined in opposition to reform: the social conservatives, the deficit hawks, and the business groups. They operated with total unity. Their opposition was strongly assisted by the *Wall Street Journal* editorial page, whose blasts at the Clinton plan were echoed by Rush Limbaugh, by every small business, and by the combined political power of the conservative Christian churches.

Steelman's point is easily documented — and she spoke from personal experience, having worked with McInturff and others. When

Clinton came to power, she took after his plan like predator after prey. A pillow on her office couch spelled out her target. "Red Meat," the graceful needlepoint read.

In the aftermath, Bill Clinton would wonder how he had failed to appreciate the extent of this opposition and the tactics that would be employed against him. Assessing the defeat, the President told us he understood from the beginning "that we were going to be at a disadvantage. I always knew that the stakes for me were high and the prospect of victory not good. Any time you try to change something that's big and complicated, the people who are against it have a better argument because they can be simple and straight. That's number one. Number two, any time you've got something that touches people where they live — and health care is profoundly important to everybody — it's easier for people to be frightened than it is for people to live on their hopes."

Despite these doubts, the President still had believed his side would prevail "because I thought the need to do something was so self-evident." But his greatest frustration in defeat echoed the case made by McInturff. The many interest groups who in the beginning enthusiastically favored reform never coalesced. Ranks of proponents fragmented while those of foes hardened. "So the opponents more and more moved to a position of total opposition," the President said later, "whereas the supporters were always thinking about how they could get a better deal. That was very frustrating."

Two groups that were part of the No Name Coalition and sent people to Billy Pitts's meetings played an especially critical role in the defeat of the Clinton plan. They were the Health Insurance Association of America (HIAA) and the National Federation of Independent Business (NFIB). Both of them understood that this battle would require far more than a standard lobbying effort. Both were prepared to engage in living rooms and communities across the country. The operations of both demonstrate vividly what the lobbies *really* did in this fight.

Eleven days after Bill Clinton's inauguration, HIAA hired A. Willis Gradison Jr., a sixty-four-year-old Republican representative from Cincinnati, to become its new president. Bill Gradison had made an enviable record in his nine terms in the House, rising to positions of influence on both the Ways and Means Committee (and its Health Subcommittee) and on the Budget Committee. A slim, soft-spoken Yale College and Harvard Business School graduate with a scholarly bent and a laid-back personality that made him a natural mediator, Gradison was a classic moderate conservative, increasingly rare on the Republican side of the House. In 1992 he was decisively defeated by a right-wing opponent in a Republican caucus election for a minor leadership post. That rejection in the House Republican Conference led Gradison to decide that he might be better rewarded and more influential in shaping health legislation from outside Congress. He brought with him Charles N. (Chip) Kahn III, who had been the Republican minority's top health policy counsel on Ways and Means and earlier had held a similar staff position in the Senate. Kahn, a New Orleans native whose sharp wit won him affection as well as respect among his congressional and lobbying colleagues, became HIAA's executive vice president.

HIAA was an organization in turmoil when Bill Gradison became its president. It represented some 270 of the private firms that sold health policies to businesses, groups, and individuals. Most were small or medium-size, and their clientele represented only a third of Americans with health insurance. Before Gradison arrived, five of HIAA's largest insurers — Prudential, Cigna, Travelers, Metropolitan Life, and Aetna — had severed their ties to the group.

These large firms were already moving beyond writing insurance policies to organizing their own managed care networks. They saw their strategic interests in the debate diverging from those of the smaller firms, which made up most of HIAA's membership. As members of the Big Five, the chances were good that they would be in the select group of insurers chosen to compete under the new Clinton plan. With their marketing strength and their provider networks, as the "big guys," they would profit at the expense of the rest. By the autumn of 1993, operating as the Alliance for Managed Competition, the Big Five were running ads that drew praise from Senator Harris Wofford. "We may differ on important details," the ads said, "but we agree on this — the time for reform is now. And let's make it bipartisan."

Out of the upheaval caused by this organizational split, HIAA took two steps that shaped its approach. First, in a December 3, 1992, policy statement, HIAA endorsed the goal of universal coverage and the employer mandate as a way of financing it. Then it hired Gradison.

Both its new policy stance — which the *New York Times* characterized as "an industry offer to cooperate" with the Clinton administration — and its new association president made HIAA seem like an organization that would go along with some kinds of reform. But there were reasons to be suspicious of appearances. According to former HIAA president Carl J. Schramm, until the upheaval in its leadership and the defection of the Big Five insurers, HIAA had adamantly defended underwriting practices that "routinely redlined" small firms with elderly or accident-prone workforces and thus barred coverage of millions of people with previously identified medical problems. In October 1993, Schramm told a Harvard School of Public Health audience that "much of the behavior of the nation's insurance companies is absolutely reprehensible. Understandable, but reprehensible." J. Brian Smith, a Republican campaign consultant who had been hired by HIAA in 1989 to consult on reform, said in a 1993 memo that "in twenty years of working with corporations and trade groups, I have yet to encounter an industry as politically moribund as the health insurance industry. . . . What you have here is an industry group that stubbornly refused to accept what was happening across the country on the health reform issue, kept its head in the sand, and only now is getting involved in the issue in a clearly negative way."

Now Gradison was saying it was a new era and a different HIAA. He radiated reasonableness — and that was the reputation he brought with him from Capitol Hill. As McInturff, the HIAA pollster, said, "Bill Gradison's an unlikely wartime consigliere. It's not his style." But however reasonable, Gradison understood that if the Clinton reform became law as proposed, many of his member firms would go out of business.

Discussions between Gradison and the Clintons got off to a rocky start — and then went downhill. During the task force months, Gradison's two meetings with Magaziner left an indelible mark. "In the first meeting," Gradison said, "he said to me, 'Bill, I'm not a politician but our pollsters at the White House tell us that it will help sell our plan if we identify as enemies the pharmaceutical industry, the physicians, and the health insurers.' " Magaziner later claimed that he meant it as a joke, but Gradison left the session convinced the Clintons had "a plan to demonize the industry."

Gradison used that first meeting to "indicate our strong support for most elements in their plan — but our strong disagreement on three points." These differences were not trivial. One was over whether all insurance companies could continue to operate in a marketplace — or only those certified by the new alliances. The administration wanted a certification process, in part to make the choice more manageable for consumers and in part as a way of monitoring the cost and quality of insurance. Gradison's member companies wanted to keep their present customers and compete for more. They emphatically didn't want any alliance bureaucrats barring them from the marketplace.

Cost controls, or "premium caps," for insurance policies was the second issue. The administration had decided that a "backup" was needed, in case the managed care theorists overestimated the capacity of a restructured marketplace to limit costs through competition. Magaziner knew that big business and the politicians wanted some guarantees against continued soaring medical costs. But for the insurers, having bureaucrats dictate the price of their product was their worst nightmare. It raised the specter of a new government program that could slash profits and expose them to unpredictable losses if their costs outran their premiums.

The third issue — a bit more recondite but still vital — was what Gradison called "pure community rating." Existing insurance companies made their money by their underwriting skill; they gauged the likely medical liabilities of an individual or group and priced the protection they provided accordingly. Managed competition called for blending those individual rates into a community rate, raising costs for healthier people a bit in order to lower rates for the more vulnerable. Insurers no longer could "cherry-pick" the best or least expensive customers, leaving others with poorer health or major physical problems facing exorbitant rates, or unable to purchase any coverage. For Gradison's members, community rating was another way of dictating their prices — and potentially putting them out of business.

The issues Gradison raised with Magaziner in their first meeting were irreconcilable with the Clinton reform ideas. But everything in Gradison's experience motivated him to seek a negotiated compromise. In the end, he expected to sit down with his former chairman, Dan Rostenkowski, and work out the best deal he could get. In the meantime, he wanted to make his case to the administration, while the plan was still being formulated, to salvage the most he could.

To that end, he wrote a letter to the First Lady on May 28, 1993, restating HIAA's support for universal coverage and saying, "We stand ready to help you." But he complained of three recent occasions on which Hillary had attacked the health insurance industry for "price-gouging, cost-shifting and unconscionable profiteering" and other crimes. Gradison said, "The facts about our industry don't support the quotes we have been reading," and requested a meeting with her. He didn't get it.

What made this impasse, and the feud that emerged from it, all the more inexplicable was the fact that during all of 1993 and 1994, the chairman of HIAA, the very person who had guided its new policy direction and hired Gradison as its new president, was a loyal Democrat and Clinton supporter. G. David Hurd, then the chairman and chief executive officer of the Iowa-based Principal Financial Group, made contributions to Clinton's campaign, signed ads for Clinton's election, and appeared with Clinton in 1992 events designed to undercut Republican claims that Bill Clinton was some kind of radical.

When Gradison's talks with Magaziner went nowhere, Hurd approached his friend and fellow Iowan, Senator Tom Harkin. Though Harkin was one of the presidential primary candidates Clinton had defeated, he nevertheless became an enthusiastic supporter of Clinton's candidacy and a backer of his policies as President. Hurd asked Harkin to speak to Hillary Clinton about meeting with him. Harkin tried and failed. Indeed, when the President scheduled a meeting with Iowans, and Harkin proposed that Hurd be included, "someore in the political section of the White House axed that because of his position as the head of HIAA. I told them that he had been a Clinton supporter and contributor," the senator said. "We had a number of phone calls [with the White House about Hurd], but they didn't want him there, because 'HIAA has been taking us on.' I thought if he got in there, he was in a position to calm things down, but they didn't see it that way."

The final rupture, Gradison and his aide Chip Kahn say, was over an attack memo the White House distributed for Democratic members of Congress to use during their August 1993 recess in order to counter an HIAA advertising campaign. Among other things, Democrats were urged to tell constituents, "We're going to crack down on profiteers who make a killing off the current system. The Clinton plan will . . . insist that the insurance companies . . . charge fair prices." Hurd was so incensed when he received a copy that he angrily scribbled fifty notations in the margins citing its inaccuracies. McInturff recalled meeting with Hurd then. "This is awful," he remembers the HIAA chairman saying. "They're just killing us with crap that isn't even true." Gradison lashed back publicly. Instead of a negotiation, a war had begun.

Though both Gradison and Kahn privately expressed dismay at the turn of events, in truth HIAA's differences with the Clinton plan may well have been too large to be bridged at any meeting with the First Lady. Gradison was playing a double game. While he wanted to diminish public support for a Clinton plan that could adversely affect the insurance industry, he also was eager to appear accommodating, so that he would be able to make adjustments in the reform bill he believed would ultimately pass. Even before discussions with the administration turned negative, HIAA was preparing to fight the Clinton plan. In early 1993, two California consultants, Ben Goddard and Rick Claussen, had been placed on retainer for a public relations and ad campaign. Their firm had made a reputation in a California referendum battle the previous November by *defeating* a state employer mandate plan contained in Proposition 166 and supported by the California Medical Association.

HIAA also retained two able Washington pollsters, Democrat Bill Hamilton and Republican McInturff, to monitor public opinion. And it hired a matched pair of outside lobbyists, Republican Nicholas E. Calio (formerly top congressional liaison for the Bush White House) and Democrat Lawrence F. O'Brien III, to handle part of the congressional liaison task. Judy Norrell, a Democratic activist with the political advantage of coming from the President's home state of Arkansas, was later added to the team.

In the spring of 1993, when Clinton originally planned to submit his reform plan, HIAA began a three-and-a-half-million-dollar advertising campaign. Aired mainly on CNN, the ads promoted HIAA's approach to reform and offered more information to anyone calling an 800 number. Those who responded received a primer on what was wholesome and what was dangerous, as judged by HIAA's lights.

The ads, using man-in-the-street cameos, were modestly effective, but drew little media comment. Hamilton and McInturff conducted more focus groups in St. Louis, Charlotte, and Atlanta and found certain phrases resonated well with the public. Among them were "They choose, you lose" and "There's got to be a better way."

Because the public distrusted the insurance industry — HIAA's own polls showed people trusted their own agent but not the industry as a whole — a front group was needed. In the California referendum fight, Goddard and Claussen had formed a coalition of allied groups; that concept was expanded into the national Coalition for Health Insurance Choices. Some of the partners were obvious — the organizations of insurance agents, for example — but because HIAA had endorsed the employer mandate, groups like NFIB, representing small business, which were fighting the mandate, did not want to co-sponsor the ads.

The decision to launch a major television campaign was not an easy one for Bill Gradison. As an inside player in The System for nearly two decades, he was nervous about HIAA's assuming a high-profile role challenging important aspects of the emerging Clinton plan. "Bill was not enthusiastic about television," Chip Kahn recalled. "His attitude always was, 'Well, let me tell you ten reasons why we shouldn't.' "

But the member-company CEOs who formed the HIAA strategy committee were eager to take on the fight. And, as it turned out,

Gradison unknowingly supplied the right metaphor. In speech after speech Gradison would say, "This issue will be settled at the kitchen tables in homes all across America."

After his initial reluctance, Gradison was persuaded to begin running a series of ads set at a young middle-class couple's kitchen table. Early in September, before the President's address to Congress, he said, "Our concern is that if questions like the ones we're raising aren't raised now, and if, as a result, the President has the field to himself, and the poll ratings show a great acceptance, there might be a bandwagon psychology by the members of Congress, and we'd never realistically have a chance."

But HIAA was in a quandary. If they went blatantly negative, Gradison would not be welcome at congressional bargaining tables, where he would have the chance to minimize the bite reform would take out of industry profits. So they tempered their opposition with supportive-sounding comments about the need for some reform before their critical punch line: "There's got to be a better way." In the end they knew the negative would reign.

For this new round of ads, Goddard-Claussen hired two actors, a man and a woman, to play the part of the middle-class couple. The first script identified them merely as "He" and "She." In a second script, the first names of the actors, Harry Johnson and Louise Caire Clark, were substituted. When the script was distributed to the press, reporters wrote about the "Harry and Louise" ads. The ad campaign focused on one of those themes voters had responded positively to in McInturff's polling: distrust of bureaucrats. "The government may force us to pick from a few health care plans designed by government bureaucrats," the announcer says. Louise: "Having choices we don't like is no choice at all." Harry: "They choose." Louise: "We lose." An American advertising classic was born.

McInturff's polling identified critical elements that would prove decisive not only for HIAA's position but for the fate of the entire battle. "In a lot of those early focus groups," he recalled, "people wanted health care to pass. They wanted Clinton to get credit." But the discussions also showed that "people don't believe the federal government can get anything done." Therefore, he concluded, HIAA might prevail if it could sell the notion "that this plan is a bad idea because, ultimately, they're trying to tell you that government's going to deliver this service."

Playing on, and intensifying, public distrust of government became the strategic aim of *all* reform opponents. As Gradison conceded in an interview when the first Harry and Louise ads began, "One can legitimately say that what we're trying to do is plant seeds of doubt. I would not question that characterization."

Long before the battle began, negative public attitudes toward government had been growing stronger year after year. By the 1990s deepening distrust of Washington had generated such pervasive anger and cynicism that candidates and their consultants found running *against* government an increasingly successful tactic. Historically, a healthy skepticism about politics and politicians had blended with strong pride in the Constitution, the organs of government, and their leaders. The White House, the Supreme Court, and the Capitol were temples of democracy. Now, The System, and all within it, had been transformed into the enemy.

These attitudes were both understandable and paradoxical. Reasons for the spreading distrust were self-evident: the sense of hurt and betrayal over the assassinations of John and Robert Kennedy and Martin Luther King Jr. and the ruin of the reputations of Lyndon Johnson and Richard Nixon — all in the span of eleven years; the disillusionment fostered by the lies and coverups during Vietnam and Watergate; the suspicion spawned by conspiracy theories involving the Central Intelligence Agency and J. Edgar Hoover's Federal Bureau of Investigation; the hostility to government regulators and tax collectors; and, from 1980 onward, the growing dismay at the refusal of the national government to live within its means and avoid unprecedented deficit spending.

Presidents of both parties had been elected by running "against Washington." In 1980, Ronald Reagan memorably argued that "government is not the solution to our problems; government is the problem." In 1992, Bill Clinton decried "the brain-dead politics of Washington." The press played a significant part in fanning these negative feelings. By highlighting political indiscretions, often minor, as major scandals, by unremittingly portraying Congress as corrupt, and by rarely exploring or explaining the successes of The System, newspapers and television added to the cynicism.

And successes there were. In those years of growing negativism, government actions brought about the greatest expansions of basic civil rights in the nation's history; a measurably cleaner, safer environment; a significant improvement in the health and well-being of senior citizens; and countless breakthroughs in science and technology that helped fuel the growth of an economy that was the envy of the world. That same government also trained and equipped the most powerful military forces in the world and led an international alliance that thwarted expansionary international communism, won the Cold War, and ushered in the peaceful liberation of the Soviet Union and Eastern Europe. With such a record of success, America was the model for all other societies to emulate.

Yet these achievements were eclipsed in the public mind by harshly critical attitudes about The System, and these feelings made it infinitely more difficult to win broad support for any new governmental action, especially one as huge and important as the entire health care system.

Operating in such a negative climate, opponents of activist government thrived. Interest groups opposed to change were spectacularly successful in making government appear to be the enemy. Their ability to exploit — and to heighten — those negative attitudes about government was critical to their success.

In McInturff's view, HIAA had a chance for success even though "ten million dollars [initially budgeted for its TV ad campaign] is not going to change public opinion." But if it could "attach itself to the very powerful wave" of pervasive skepticism about government, it could prevail. He convinced all his clients to talk constantly about "government health care," not "national health insurance."

"Just that word change made a powerful difference," he said.

Initially, Chip Kahn had been almost as skeptical as Gradison about the advertising approach. "I thought the President would define the issues," he said after the fight was over:

This is a legislative process. I teach health policy, and the first thing I always say is that nothing major ever happens unless the President sets the theme, provides the moral suasion. I didn't think the final plan would be as ambitious as he was talking about in his rhetoric. But I thought he would prevail with something. He had a pretty big margin in Congress and you had Republicans who just didn't have any credibility on this issue.

I assumed that what we needed to do was design a strategy that got us to the table and enabled us to make the plan as inoffensive as possible — that allowed our part of the industry to remain competitive in the marketplace. I thought we could prevail with persuasion and normal lobbying.

But, in time, Kahn came to think that Clinton "didn't have any understanding of the congressional process at all. If it had been a normal congressional approach, then Harry and Louise and everything else would have been absurd. The different ingredient here was the way the White House played it. They made it into a campaign — an election model." And because of that, Kahn said, "the campaign strategy that I was being forced into [by HIAA's member companies and the California consulting firm] — which I had resisted" turned out to be a shrewd move. "I thought it was like spitting into the wind. But I realized by August it was quite different. The fact is, we *did* define the issue."

McInturff was amazed at the reaction to the commercials. "I think all of that [ad] is very innocuous by today's political standards," he said. "I mean, if you can't withstand having a couple sitting in the kitchen saying 'Isn't there a better way to do this?,' believe me, you couldn't pass anything."

By moving early, aggressively, and publicly, HIAA became a major player in the debate. Thanks to Harry and Louise and the attention Gradison was drawing through his press conferences and TV appearances, HIAA was perceived as the spearhead of the attack on the Clinton plan. On the morning of September 22, just hours before Clinton's televised speech to Congress beginning the battle, Dave Hurd, speaking for HIAA, was interviewed on TV along with former Ohio Governor Richard F. (Dick) Celeste, who had just taken over the task of supervising the Democratic National Committee's effort.

Harkin had arranged for Hurd to meet Celeste later that same day to consider a Hurd proposal to reopen communications between the White House and the insurance group. As an inducement, Hurd unilaterally offered to end the Harry and Louise ads. In return, as Chip Kahn put it, "we hoped they would stop bashing the industry and talk to us in a real way, not in an Ira Magaziner way, where he turns his hearing aid off as soon as you walk in the room."

The offer to cancel the ads was confirmed in a phone call from Gradison to his personal friend, Celeste, before Clinton's speech. Once again, the administration made no response, so Harry and Louise returned to the air. "We ran the ads and all hell broke loose," Kahn said.

A trivial incident revealed the depth of White House anxiety. A woman working for the Democratic National Committee in California contacted the actress playing Louise and asked her to recant the views expressed in the ad, promising that if she did so she would be invited to the White House. If she did not, the threat was made, big-name Hollywood Democrats would see that she never got another part. It was also intimated that the producers of the commercials would never get another Democratic contract. Louise complained about the pressure to Goddard-Claussen; Gradison protested to presidential counselor David Gergen; and the Democratic National Committee's Dick Celeste quickly called to say that it was an unauthorized approach, an unfortunate example of a "rogue operation." It wouldn't happen again. But it underscored the intensity of the fight and the lengths to which each side was prepared to go to win it.

Inside the White House, the ads were viewed as so damaging that on November 1 the First Lady weighed in with a scathing attack. In a speech before the American Academy of Pediatricians convention in Washington, she accused the insurance industry of greed and of deliberately lying to the public about the reform plan in order to protect its profits. She specifically denounced the Harry and Louise ads' claim that the Clinton plan "limits choice." Insurance companies, she said angrily, "like being able to exclude people from coverage because the more they can exclude, the more money they can make." She also said, "They have the gall to run TV ads that there is a better way, the very industry that has brought us to the brink of bankruptcy because of the way they have financed health care."

Rarely, if ever, has a First Lady publicly attacked any American industry or industry group — and certainly never in such strong language and such a furious manner. Her assault made front-page newspaper stories and network TV news shows and called more attention to HIAA's role and message. The *New York Times* coverage was typical. Underneath its page-one masthead, a two-column headline read,

HILLARY CLINTON ACCUSES INSURERS OF LYING ABOUT HEALTH PROPOSAL

Says Industry Ads Mislead Public to Guard Profits

It had another consequence: It made the First Lady's highly public policy role all the more controversial. From then on, it was all-out war.

HIAA described Hillary Clinton's tongue-lashing as "Carville tactics," making the assumption it had come from James Carville, the "Ragin' Cajun" consultant to the Clinton presidential campaign. Carville had once worked for Billy Tauzin, a conservative Democratic congressman from Louisiana who would in 1995, after Republicans won control of Congress, defect to the Republican party. Tauzin had told his friend Gradison to expect a tough counterattack. In fact, Carville was not masterminding the White House public relations. The First Lady was calling her own shots. How she decided to strike back at the insurance industry is revealing both of her temperament and her political judgment. It was, as one member of her staff recalled, "completely, totally unplanned, unscripted. Total spontaneity." While being driven to the pediatricians' convention, the First Lady and a key aide, Melanne Verveer, were talking about how angry the Harry and Louise ads made them. Hillary had been advised by White House political people to "be quiet and go out and sell the Pablum," as one staffer put it. The conflict playing out then over the upcoming NAFTA vote, in which big business and the White House were allies, made it untimely to raise the temperature of the health care debate. But the First Lady marched right to the podium and, without notes or text, delivered her attack.

Nor was that the end of her public condemnation. Months later she told another audience that she wanted to answer Harry and Louise with ads based on the real-life letters in her file, but "we can't afford to keep up with the health insurance companies who have [used] all your premiums to buy television."

In March of 1994, the Clintons did indeed answer Harry and Louise. In a White House video that drew huge laughs at the annual dinner of the Gridiron Club, an organization of Washington newspaper reporters, Harry and Louise were played by Bill and Hillary themselves. Mocking the shock expressed by the HIAA characters, Hillary/Louise keeps finding hidden provisions on page 3764 or 27,655 of the Clinton health plan. "Even if we do all this," she says in alarm, "on page 27,655, it says that eventually we are all gonna die."

"Under the Clinton health plan?" the stunned President/Harry asks. "You mean after Bill and Hillary put all those new bureaucrats and taxes on us? We're still all going to die?"

"Even Leon Panetta," Hillary/Louise replies.

But the joke would soon sour. The video — "paid for by the Coalition to Scare Your Pants Off" — was released to the TV networks, giving HIAA even more publicity. Gradison was both surprised and delighted at the attention. "What they did was to give our advertising a much larger audience than it would have had with the amount of money we had available," he said. Nor was he alone in that view. Kathleen Hall Jamieson, the dean of the Annenberg School of Communication at the University of Pennsylvania and an authority on political advertising, said that "by attacking Harry and Louise, the White House invited the press to focus attention on the campaign and to feature them as key players in the reform debate." In Jamieson's view, the HIAA ads were given more prominence than their audience size deserved. But by making news, and becoming part of the media-political debate in Washington, the Harry and Louise ads highlighted the insurance lobby's efforts against health reform. Before long Gradison proudly began showing visitors to his downtown Washington office campaign-style buttons reading "Friends of Harry and Louise."

Harry and Louise also gave an immense boost to Gradison's fund-raising. "The tone of the criticism unbuttoned pocketbooks of members in ways that we had been unable to do ourselves," he said. In the space of a few weeks, the budget for the campaign expanded fivefold from $4 million to $20 million — with $14.5 million of it already pledged to the health battle.

But that was just the beginning. In the end, HIAA raised and spent about $30 million more than its normal annual operating budget of $20 million — a grand total of almost $50 million. One company alone, according to McInturff, gave $5 million to the lobbying effort. "I never had to worry about money," Chip Kahn said, in classic understatement.

Nor did any of the other interests arrayed against reform. In terms of numbers of people hired, amounts of money spent, and the use of television advertising to shape a public-policy issue, the battle was unprecedented. Whether it was $100 million or $300 million made little difference. The difficulty in determining the full amount spent reflects the subterranean — and secretive — way in which money now flows through The System to influence events and manipulate public opinion.

Lobbying disclosure laws are weak, and record-keeping often poor. The most authoritative study, *Well-Heeled: Inside Lobbying for Health Care Reform*, by the Center for Public Integrity, an independent liberal public-interest organization in Washington, came up with the $100 million overall figure after a full year of examining all available public records. But that study did not include the costs of polling and advertising as well as the vast sums spent on the grassroots campaigns that many companies and associations ran during the battle. Whatever the ultimate cost, it greatly exceeded the combined amount all candidates spent running for President of the United States in 1992, a year that marked a record for campaign spending. The old connection between money and politics was nakedly exposed and given historic new dimensions. During 1993 and in the first quarter of 1994, special-interest organizations representing health care concerns gave $25 million to members of Congress, according to Federal Election Commission records. As time for action neared on House and Senate bills in 1994, as much as $4 million a month was being spent by the interests. While unions and a few other liberal groups put their funds into the treasuries of the bill's backers, their lobbying efforts were feeble and ill-coordinated when compared to those on the other side. The President, he told us later, had been highly frustrated by this failure. And not just in retrospect either; he felt that frustration throughout the entire battle. One day in 1993, he responded heatedly when Magaziner and Mike Lux, another White House aide, showed him a long list of pro-reform groups who far outnumbered those against his health plan. "It doesn't matter," the President said emotionally. "It's an intensity issue. And these ten groups over there against us are going to be as intense as hell about it. And they'll beat the eleven hundred over here" unless the pro-reform groups demonstrated similar vigor.

Which was exactly the case with groups like HIAA and their Harry and Louise ad campaign.

The money HIAA accumulated for the fight paid for not only Harry and Louise but also a grassroots campaign that dwarfed anything the interest group had ever done. That effort produced more than four hundred fifty thousand contacts with Congress — phone calls, visits, or letters — almost a thousand to *every* member of the House and Senate.

HIAA hired field operatives in six states whose senators and/or House delegations were expected to be crucial: Kansas, Louisiana, New York, North Dakota, Oklahoma, and Texas. Early in the campaign, the operation nearly crashed. A prospective field organizer, who was turned down for the job, leaked a copy of HIAA's organizing manual to Families USA, the consumer group supporting the Clinton plan. In a press conference, Families USA denounced the "deceitful and unethical" role of HIAA as the financial and organizational muscle behind the Coalition for Health Insurance Choices. But its exposé attracted little attention; HIAA's grassroots campaign continued.

The muscle and manpower for the field operation came from the member companies and their network of employees, managers, and agents. They were particularly populous in the South and the Midwest, which were expected to become crucial swing areas in the congressional battle.

Representative Mike Kopetski, an Oregon Democrat and a supporter of the plan on the House Ways and Means Committee, said, "The insurance industry is in every state and they're organized. It's your agent, you know, it's the guy down the street. It's the man and the woman beside you in church and on civic boards; they're really into the community. So they're very powerful."

And they enlisted powerful allies. The field directors' mission was to identify "grass tops," or "high-level influencers," as the jargon goes, especially people with "a good connect" to a targeted member of Congress. These people may have worked on someone's campaign, been a golf buddy, a friend of the family, or even, as one HIAA operative put it, "the wife's best friend's son's old dog's new owner." The point was to find people who were authentic — not paid Washington lobbyists — who had access to the congressman. And then plug that person in, using faxes, phone calls, and E-mail, when a critical vote was coming up in Washington. "Without the computer systems and phones to organize and track what we had, we couldn't have done what we did," HIAA's Peggy Tighe said. But it was the grassroots organizing that put the right people on the other end of the phone calls and faxes.

The process of engineering grassroots opinion has produced a whole new breed of Washington operatives — some of whom have made fortunes from their work. Perhaps the star of the trade is Jack Bonner, who in this battle was working mainly for the big insurers, the Alliance for Managed Competition. "What a great thing to go up against," Bonner said, reflecting on the battle. "Mandatory health care alliances, I *have* to join it? It's horrible! In America you don't use the word 'mandatory.' It's pejorative. If they hadn't used it, we would have. So that one was truly a walk in the park. Premium caps were a trickier proposition, because no one's thrilled with the increase of insurance premiums over the years. We said, 'Look, price controls don't work. Let me give you a few reminders of it from history.' "

Located on the eighth floor of a downtown Washington high-rise, Bonner and his staff of professional phone callers had been helping businesses look like populists for an entire decade. Packed in little cubicles below four clocks marking the time zones, they rounded up "real people," the ones outside the Beltway, and funneled them into the political arena for congressional and other public appearances. And many of Bonner's aides, among them former Hill staffers and temporarily unemployed political operatives, know quite a bit about their targets on Capitol Hill.

There's nothing spontaneous about this kind of operation, and Bonner concedes that "there's a big debate over what's grass roots and what's Astroturf" — the synthetic substitute:

> In my own mind, the difference between grass roots and Astroturf is quality. Does the person who's communicating to the member know both sides of the issue, can they explain in a way that makes sense to the member why they, as a farmer or businessperson, care about the issue in a way that rings true?
>
> If they can do that, the fact that they were informed about that issue by the insurance industry or from reading the *Washington Post* or getting it off of a box of Rice Krispies while they're having cereal in the morning is irrelevant. If they understand both sides, how they are informed is irrelevant.

Grass roots or Astroturf, Bonner has learned to deliver a quality product to his corporate clients — for a fee. And he was not alone in demonstrating his skill.

The National Federation of Independent Business (NFIB) and John Motley, its chief lobbyist, played a role in the battle that was even greater than that of HIAA's. In Motley's twenty-four years with NFIB, waging countless high-stakes political battles, health reform became far and away the biggest single issue with which he and his group had ever been involved. While that battle was still being fought, Motley said, "We've blown the budget to hell. We continue to do what's necessary." If the dollar amounts were extraordinary, the lobbying methods NFIB perfected became models for future business efforts to affect The System — a point powerfully proven by the results of the 1994 midterm elections.

Martial language came naturally to Motley. From his corner office overlooking the Washington Mall, he gazed upon the imposing structure that formed his constant target: the U.S. Capitol, and all those within who possessed the life or death power over legislation Motley sought to influence.

Motley fought on two fronts: first, by mounting a grassroots campaign in the home districts of members of Congress. He compared that to "the bombardment before the invasion." Then, after the congressional members had been "softened up" by pressure from their constituents, he "sent in the ground troops," as he put it, in the form of his lobbyists.

The congressional members knew that when Motley, or one of his agents, came to call, they spoke with the powerful authority of hundreds of thousands of mobilized and vocal small businesses across America backed by a $60 million annual budget. After all, Motley boasted, he modeled his lobbying operation on the White House itself — and commanded far more manpower and money inside and outside Washington. While the White House had four full-time people assigned to political liaison work in the House of Representatives, Motley had six. "I believe in visibility, I believe in coverage, I believe in good information," he said, "and I also believe in aggressiveness. I want all six of my House lobbyists up there, with me, looking at the members as they vote so *they* know that *we* know how they voted on each issue."

Motley prided himself on this pugnacious, bare-knuckles approach. Swiveling around in his desk chair, he enjoyed showing visitors a framed photograph of himself speaking at the National Governors' Association from a podium bearing the official seal of the President of the United States. Nearby on the same wall, in another frame, was a front-page *Wall Street Journal* article, "Motley's Crew," illustrated with an artist's sketch of Motley and describing him as one of the most effective generals among Washington's special-interest lobbyists. The characterization was deserved.

By the spring of 1993, while the Clinton task force was still laboring to produce its recommendations, NFIB already had started mobilizing its forces to kill the key element in the President's plan — the "employer mandate" that would require all businesses to provide health insurance for their employees.

This requirement was poison to the more than six hundred thousand small businesses — representing everything from dry cleaners and home builders to hardware stores — that make up NFIB. Not long after the inauguration, Motley met with Hillary Clinton and Ira Magaziner and emerged after more than an hour of conversation "completely convinced that they had already made up their minds that an employer mandate was going to be the primary financing mechanism of the final pathway to universal coverage."

As a result of that initial meeting, NFIB made a coldly calculated decision to reject an invitation from the First Lady to testify before the task force. It was, Motley admitted, a way to get the press to report that the task force hearings were a charade because the Clinton administration already had made a decision to require employers to provide insurance for their workers.

After Motley's refusal to testify, Vice President Al Gore noted NFIB's absence at the hearing, giving the organization what Motley considered to be valuable public attention in the media. From that point, Motley and NFIB began mobilizing behind the scenes. At the same time, NFIB tried another path to change the Clinton approach — personally lobbying the President himself.

That June, Motley and NFIB's president, Jack Faris, a small businessman from Tennessee, met with Clinton in the Oval Office. They had two goals: to make sure the President understood their position and to invite Clinton to speak to their organization's fiftieth-anniversary meeting just five days later. Faris, a lean, hard-charging Republican party man brimming with self-assurance, displayed an extraordinary arrogance in dealing with the President. Faris told the President he knew from the President's public schedule that Clinton would be in Washington that next week. We're the largest small-business organization in America, he told Clinton, and "we need you to show up."

When do you want me to come? the President asked.

"When you show up — Monday or Tuesday," Faris said, "but, quite frankly, we prefer Tuesday morning at nine o'clock." This was said on a Thursday, weeks after the President's schedule had been set.

The President turned to David Gergen, his counselor, and asked, "Can I do that?" To which Gergen replied, "Mr. President, we can probably work that out."

"Well, I'll come by then," the President told Faris agreeably.

Then Faris made what he himself concedes was at least a breach of protocol, if not an outright gesture of disrespect, in dealing with a President. "Maybe I shouldn't have done this," he said, "but I just eyeballed him and said, 'Now, in Arkansas and in Tennessee when a man says he's going to be somewhere, his word's his bond. So, Mr. President, before I go telling my members that you're going to show up, are you going to show up? Will you be there?' He looked at me and he said, 'You can bet on it. You can book it. I'll be there.' "

Not content, Faris made another insulting remark: "Well, this Tennessean accepts that Arkansan statement." Then he left the room. "I found out later," Faris said, "you're not supposed to do that. The President's never supposed to guarantee he'll be anywhere, and I should not have put him on the spot. But he did show up, he did come."

When Clinton arrived at NFIB's meeting, Faris was introduced first; the President had to follow *him* to the head table. If the President was angry at this treatment, he didn't show it when he addressed the group, stressing again his belief that health reform would aid the entire American economy and telling them his plan contained provisions to give small businesses a tax break to help them provide employee benefits. The audience reaction was tepid.

Clinton remained accessible to Faris and saw him twice more. In another Oval Office meeting, Faris told Clinton that "the employer mandate is absolutely repulsive to small-business owners in America, and to every one of the members that we have in Hope, Arkansas. We want to have meaningful health reform without it." Clinton assured him, Faris says, that he and his administration wanted to work cooperatively with the small-business group to achieve reform. The President repeated that openhanded gesture when they talked briefly a third time. Throughout the debate, the administration kept trying to win small-business support.

Meanwhile, Motley, their chief lobbyist, never paused in his behind-the-scenes campaign to kill "Clintoncare." When in the late spring of 1993, Motley began meeting privately with groups of business leaders who thought their interests would be adversely affected by reform, he immediately encountered a problem. While the groups were opposed to the Clinton plan as they saw it emerging, "nobody," as Motley put it, "wanted to go out that early and cross a new President of the United States."

In those early months, said Jack Faris, "we were the only organization in this town that was absolutely opposed to the employer mandate. All the polls were saying Americans are for the President's plan. The polls were saying they want the employer mandate. The polls were saying they want universal coverage."

But NFIB was determined to do everything possible to prevent enactment of a law that would require its members to provide insurance for employees. Sixty percent of all the small businesses NFIB represents employ fewer than ten people. Of those firms, only a fourth provided any insurance for their employees. Faris argued that "it's just absolutely too expensive," and that NFIB's job is to deal with all legislation "that impacts the profits of their business." Everything else was secondary.

Faris knew his people. Their psychology was his own. Pete Stark, the liberal Democrat from California, could dismiss the NFIB members as "greedy, inconsiderate folks, without any social conscience." But Faris thought they were battling for their lives.

"They say three things kill them," Faris said of his members. "Government interfering with me trying to do my business. Government regulation that keeps me down. And government trying to control more of what I do." As for their motivation, he added, "They sure don't start a business to buy insurance for their people. They go into business for freedom."

In the private strategy meetings on how to stop the Clinton plan, some wanted to kill the employer mandate the old-fashioned way, in the back rooms of Capitol Hill. But, Motley remembers, just like Gradison and Kahn at HIAA, there came a time when "we realized that battle is not going to be a typical inside-the-Beltway battle." A light went on, Motley said. "This battle is going to be waged across the country with the American people."

Unlike many legislative processes in which lobbyists can make their case quietly to members of Congress or their aides without attracting much public notice, health care had been a public issue since the presidential campaign. People around the country were very aware that the President and his wife aimed to alter the system dramatically and were anxious because the changes would affect them personally. The way to win the battle, Motley thought, was to build *public* opposition to reform. Make it seem a spontaneous groundswell of opposition was forming. Then Congress, which initially feared going against what was seen as a popular reform, would respond to this new evidence of negative public feelings. So NFIB began making its case to its members directly, developing groups of activists and having them attend local meetings where their members of Congress appeared.

Not only was NFIB's political operation, in Motley's words, "the largest single focused grassroots lobbying campaign we have ever done," but one that "used virtually every resource at our command." It became a model for the way the highest-stakes lobbying wars would be fought and won in the 1990s. NFIB's entire staff worked against Clintoncare: the twenty-four people in its federal government–relations section, the eighteen in its public-affairs office, the ten lobbyists working the House and Senate under Motley.

From its Washington headquarters, NFIB dispatched a constant stream of "Fax Alerts" and "Action Alerts" to its tens of thousands of small-business owners. The sheer magnitude of the effort was extraordinary — and, as it turned out, extraordinarily effective. More than two million pieces of mail were sent to small-business owners. These contained critical dollars-and-cents analyses of the Clinton plan for its members to use in pressuring Congress. Every eight weeks every one of NFIB's six hundred thousand members was polled on attitudes about the health plan. Results of those polls streamed into congressional offices in big, specially designed packets. Detailed studies making the case against reform as powerfully as possible were regularly distributed to both congressional staff and members of Congress themselves. To command extra attention, the background congressional papers NFIB deemed most important were printed on hot pink or yellow paper.

Always focusing on the world beyond Washington, NFIB conducted numerous seminars in states that would be critical when the time came for Congress to vote. Its operation in Montana provides a classic example of power and pressure. There Motley's organization targeted Montana's Democratic senator, Max Baucus, who would be, by Motley's calculations, "absolutely key in the Finance Committee."

Motley's warriors planned the Montana campaign as thoroughly as the army had fought and crushed the Indians there more than a century before. Studying the economic statistics of Montana, Motley's strategists found there were only a hundred firms with more than a hundred employees in the entire state. Thus, Montana's entire economy was based on its small businesses. To prepare the ground for his assault on Baucus — a senator whose initial public comments had been favorable to the Clinton plan — Motley's crew papered the state with a number of special anti-reform mailings. They were a prelude to statewide meetings NFIB arranged.

There was nothing subtle about their tactics. "We wanted to remind him that [in 1990] he voted *against* an employer mandate on the Pepper-Rockefeller Commission," the last congressional group to deal with the issue, Motley explained. "In fact, *we* had been very active in getting him to [cast that] vote." When Baucus had faced reelection in 1990, his reward was a letter from NFIB praising his support of small business.

Now, in 1994, NFIB staged three public forums in Montana. The first was in Helena, the second in Billings, the last in Missoula. "We really went hog-wild to turn out people," Motley said. "In the first two, we turned out over seven hundred business people. Now that's extremely unusual in the state of Montana. In the meantime, we did innumerable newspaper and local television interviews. We were in the news all day long there."

The effort was spectacularly successful. By the time NFIB's operatives left, Senator Baucus had sent a letter to Montana small-business owners pledging to vote against any bill that he felt hurt small business. When the employer mandate came up in the Senate Finance Committee, he was one of five Democrats who joined nine Republicans in killing it. "We thought we were very successful," said Motley with uncharacteristic understatement.

NFIB applied the same tactics in other areas — in Louisiana, Washington, Georgia, Oregon, Pennsylvania, Florida. While traditionally most lobbying groups prefer to keep their efforts hidden, and emphatically do not want the press to call attention to their work,

NFIB took the opposite approach. "We have never structured a campaign in the past which was as press-focused or press-conscious as this one was," Motley says. "This is the first one that I can remember in my twenty-four years that we actually did things to *get* coverage by the press."

Working the press meant planting questions, planting interviewees, and using the powerful talk radio show networks to generate more opposition. "We needed to make sure that our members knew what the consequences were," Motley said, "to make sure that when called upon, they would respond."

Hillary Clinton was the fall guy in one press stunt, stage-managed by NFIB, when she made informal private visits to both the House and Senate small-business committees shortly after her triumphal tour of the major committees on the Hill.

Congressmen opposed to the Clinton plan seized upon a remark the First Lady made to the House Small Business Committee: "I can't be expected to go out and save every undercapitalized business in America." A number of congressional members friendly to NFIB immediately called Motley's lobbyists with that quote. "We passed that on to the *Wall Street Journal* and to a number of other people because of the arrogance of her remark and what many people think is a punitive attitude toward business," said Mike Roush, Senate lobbyist for NFIB.

That wasn't the end of NFIB's bout with the First Lady. The next week she was scheduled to talk to members of the Senate Small Business Committee. "So I thought it would be a fun idea if somebody from the committee would be willing to give her a letter saying they opposed the employer mandate, particularly the mandate on small business," Roush recalled. The lobbyist huddled with members of South Dakota Republican Senator Larry Pressler's staff. Between them, they drafted a letter and got all but one of the Republican senators on the committee to sign it. "I had written it pretty hard-core," Roush said, "but Senator Dole, I am told, made a modification so it wasn't like 'we will never, ever, under any circumstances,' support this."

Because Senator Pressler presented the letter to the First Lady, the manipulating hand of NFIB was hidden. "It had an effect for a couple of days," Roush said. "She was like pissed and we were like gleeful. We zinged them on this. We got that coup. And it was played in the papers. And more than just being cute, it was a way to get senators early on the record against the mandate."

NFIB then promoted the anti-employer mandate position adopted by those senators in its press releases — without acknowledging its role in the drafting of that position.

For NFIB, even more than most of the lobbying groups, this battle was part of a larger plan. And as Debbie Steelman, the Bush administration veteran and health care operative, remarked, these plans "fitted like tongue-in-groove with Republican strategy."

The fit was symbolized by one man that NFIB brought onto its staff, Marc Nuttle. Nuttle had held senior positions at the Republican National Committee and in many statewide campaigns and had earned a reputation for his grassroots organizing skill.

His job was to make a reality of a point Jack Faris made in all his speeches to NFIB members. "If you run a business, you better get involved in politics, or politics will run your business. If you don't get involved politically now, you'll have to spend seven days a week later getting involved because you won't have a business."

Faris initially asked Nuttle to assess NFIB's operations and its political potential. Faris vividly remembers Nuttle telling him, "The potential that NFIB has for the free-market economy in America is incredible. It could be more powerful than either political party."

Nuttle was then hired to head NFIB's new political affairs department. His charge was to erect a new structure to motivate and train small-business owners across America to run for office or help others like them to run. "We'll give you the tools if you want to help somebody," Faris said. "If somebody on the ground floor helps somebody get elected to office, they become the best lobbyists in the world."

Long before the health care battle was won, NFIB began formulating a far more ambitious political goal: to have the power, through similar grassroots operations, to determine the presidential and congressional elections, so that America's elected officials would be guaranteed to be supportive of its goals. This was what Jack Faris began describing privately as NFIB's "endgame."

When he first spelled out his plan to us in 1994, he seemed to be indulging in breathtaking hyperbole:

> Our goal for the year 2000 for the election of the President of the United States is to have candidates from both parties who are sold out for small business and free enterprise. That's our goal. In the Senate our goal is to have at least sixty members that either own small businesses or who have proven by their voting records they understand what's good for small business. We want two hundred fifty votes in the House of Representatives either to be small-business owners and/or those who supported small-business owners. That's our goal. And we don't care whether they're D's or R's [Democrats or Republicans].

Much more than "tomorrow the world" bombast was behind this boast. When the Republicans captured Congress in 1994, Marc Nuttle's recruiting and training had helped assure that more than half the new members came out of a small-business background; NFIB's dream of exercising greater power over The System came even more quickly than its leaders had hoped. And as the new Congress rapidly rewrote government laws and regulations affecting business, NFIB members saw the return on their investment.

But all that was to come. For now, all that John Motley was thinking about was that damned health care bill.

11

The Void

WHILE ALL THE OPPONENTS MOBILIZED, Clinton's Capitol Hill allies took their consolation wherever they could find it. Jay Rockefeller gleaned some hope from the strange ceremony in Statuary Hall. Once again, he was filled with apprehension as he watched the President begin his remarks, and once again he was relieved by the time the President finished. "He did get seriously diverted by Somalia and Haiti," Rockefeller said, sitting in his Capitol Hill office that night. "But you saw him in those last five minutes of his speech in Statuary Hall. I mean, he was absolutely on fire. He brought the place down. That's the Clinton I want out during the spring and during the summer fighting for reform."

Wishes were one thing, realities another, and Rockefeller was acutely aware of the differences. He was, frankly, deeply disturbed about the direction — or lack of direction — taken in the crucial weeks since the great speech back in September. "It's classic Clinton style," he said, "a fabulous launching and then a vapid follow-through."

Day after day Rockefeller had become more concerned about the void the Clintons had allowed to occur, a void that was being filled daily by the battering given their plan through the Harry and Louise ads and the grassroots opposition efforts of the small-business lobby. The problems went much deeper than the foreign-policy crises that diverted the President. There was, Rockefeller thought, "an enormous planning vacuum" at the White House. So upset was Rockefeller that he erupted at a private White House meeting called by Hillary Clinton. In front of the First Lady, members of her and the President's staffs, and friendly invited members of Congress, Rockefeller strongly criticized the continued drift and lack of an effective plan to sell their bill. "I let her have it," he said, "which was very strange for me to do. But I felt I had to. Sometimes you just have to run down your capital. And I let her have it pretty good. She said absolutely not one word."

Part of the problem was Hillary herself. Paradoxically, her very success as a salesperson was becoming a negative. She was so visible that she detracted from the President, who in the end would have to be the principal force out waging and winning the battle. The problem was one Rockefeller had discussed with the First Lady many months earlier. Much as he valued her leadership on this issue, he said, her highly public role was going to make it difficult for the President.

Increasingly, the public saw the First Lady, not the President, as having power and mastery over this issue. And in this fight, as in all with great national stakes, the full force and commitment of the President was needed — and, in Rockefeller's mind, especially the singular kind of passion that Bill Clinton at his best could bring to the debate.

"Hillary Clinton's kind of like a moving museum of art," Rockefeller observed. "Everybody wants to touch her, they have to see her. It's like the *Mona Lisa* exhibition. You file by but you haven't been to the museum unless you've seen that picture." Rockefeller appreciated the great talents the First Lady brought to the fight. But there was a price. "Everybody wants her, and she says yes to everybody. And she needs to. That's her value. So she's always gone. Or, she's putting out fires or seeing the eleven hundred groups that she's seen. And it's very hard for her to pull back and look and say, 'How do we get a plan to win this, how do we get a good bill?' "

Hillary couldn't wage and win the war alone, though; she was too involved as the public point person. Ira Magaziner, in Rockefeller's judgment, shouldn't do it; he was part of the problem, not a strategic political thinker. To win, they needed — and quickly — someone else to run the political operation.

Rockefeller had a candidate, one he had already mentioned to the First Lady. That was Harold Ickes, the New York lawyer and veteran Democratic operative who had run the New York nominating convention for the Clintons and had earned their respect and confidence. They desperately needed an Ickes to take charge, Rockefeller told the First Lady shortly after the meeting where he expressed his frustration to her in front of their allies. Several days later, he phoned the First Lady. "Can I press my point about Harold Ickes again?" he said. This time, the answer was yes. I want him, the First Lady replied. We've got to get him, and we will, after he finishes working on the New York mayoral campaign of David Dinkins. That is very good news, Rockefeller said.

Toward the end of October, Ira Magaziner received a note, typed on a White House notepad, from Chief of Staff Mack McLarty. "The President asked me to forward this to you," McLarty wrote Magaziner. Attached, and stamped across the top with the words "THE PRESIDENT HAS SEEN," was a copy of a *Rolling Stone* article, "Freddy Krueger Does D.C.," by Alan Cranston, the former senior Democratic senator from California, about Bob Dole. The subtitle was: "Meet Bob Dole, Nightmare on Capitol Hill."

The President marked its penultimate paragraph in brackets:

> In either case, it's never been clear exactly why Dole wants to be president, except as an exercise in partisan warfare and personal advancement. Dole has never put forth a clear view of what he wants to do for the country in all the time he has previously run for president. Ironically, Dole never seems to have come up with "the vision thing" any more than did his detested rival, Bush. What is clear, is that Dole still spells big trouble in the Senate for Clinton. The good news, one might say, is that Dole isn't president. The bad news is that nobody's told him.

Clinton, Magaziner understood, sent him that memo as a political intelligence advisory. Clearly, the President was beginning to focus on the politics of the 1994 midterm congressional elections, the 1996 presidential prospects of rivals like Bob Dole, and the part health care would play in both of them. So, increasingly, were the Republicans.

* * *

Nearly a full month later, on November 20, the President's bill was finally presented to Congress. It was the last day of the 1993 session. Immediately, the legislation came under criticism from opponents who saw in its length and language proof that their claims were correct: This was government-run health care. Not all the criticism came from the Republicans.

Some of the supporters were also dismayed. John Breaux, the senatorial charmer from Louisiana, who was one of Bill Clinton's closest allies on the Democratic Leadership Council before he became President and who still talked regularly with both of the Clintons, had been concerned from the beginning about the way the plan was put together. He had argued about the lack of savvy political advice in the making of the policy. "That," Breaux thought, "was a fatal mistake." Technically, the plan may have been fine. Politically, it was not feasible. No one was raising that political alarm, Breaux thought. No one was saying, "Hey, wait a minute. This is just not going to sell, because you're going to get hit by the NFIB and you're going to get hit by the insurance companies."

Breaux offered another homely, but apt, analogy between the plan and the process that finally brought it to the Hill: "I've compared it to the making of Louisiana gumbo. You put everything in the pot at the same time. You stir it up and hope it comes out tasting really good. The problem is you can't put things in the same pot that are mutually inconsistent — makes it taste really bad."

Even within the administration the bill drew harsh criticism, further fracturing a White House already badly divided into two camps. On one side was the West Wing, or President's aides, who were most concerned about economic issues — the budget, deficit reduction, NAFTA, and planning for welfare reform. On the other was the Health Care Team, which was viewed strictly as an operation of the First Lady. The two ran on parallel tracks. These divisions had existed from the beginning of Clinton's presidency. As we have seen, his cabinet officers and economic policy planners, backed by the professional policy experts in the bureaucracy and large numbers of congressional Democrats, waged a strong fight against what they considered this ill-advised, ill-timed, and ill-drawn health plan — Hillary's stepchild, some thought — that was diverting them from more important public business.

Even some within the health team viewed the final bill with serious misgivings. "The plan itself is disastrously complex," Bob Boorstin said. days after it was presented to Congress. "We did a count of the number of new councils or commissions or bodies that this thing sets up. It's in the nineties. I mean, that's a joke."

The more Boorstin thought about the bill, the worse it seemed. "We came up with such a big, fat, ugly bill that was such an easy target," he said months later. "We created a target the size of Philadelphia. I mean, Harry and Louise were good ads, but come on, they weren't that difficult to create. Somewhere, somebody — George [Stephanopoulos] or somebody — should have come in and said, 'We cannot send this fucker up to the Hill.' George or Mandy [Grunwald] or Stan [Greenberg] or myself or somebody should have gone to Ira and Hillary and said, 'This isn't a working document.' "

Before the bill was sent to the Hill, Boorstin had completed a section-by-section analysis. At one point, it said that if a health plan was oversubscribed, people would be "assigned on a random basis." He cut out those three words: "a random basis." He also cut out "entitlement" wherever it appeared. He cut out "capitating," a favorite term among health care economists. He cut out "random" wherever it stood alone.

Boorstin said reading it through made it clear that "the plan itself is over-bureaucratized." It raised all the old doubts about Democrats and Big Government. To Boorstin, there were two explanations. "One is, this is what happens when bureaucrats write a plan," he said. "Two is, you actually do need somebody or something to control certain things, to set standards."

A third explanation arose, one Boorstin hoped was the real answer. Maybe many of the cumbersome provisions and bureaucratic-sounding new structures were included as strategic devices. They would be so controversial that they would be bargained away by the White House, still leaving a major health reform that would win passage.

*   *   *

The complexity of the Clinton plan baffled the press and confounded its efforts to explain the proposal to the public. The *Washington Post*'s Dana Priest said that covering the story, she was constantly aware that while she and other reporters were giving people "an endless stream of detail, they can absorb information only in small chunks. This was just too big a ball of wax to try to dissect. It was the plan itself — and their conceit that they could change such a large part of the economy all at one time" that made the reporting challenge so difficult.

When the Clintons went out to sell the plan, she said, "they had to generalize about it, which led to sugarcoating, which forced us into truth-squading and saying 'This isn't right.' So then the public wondered, 'What is right?' "

Karen Tumulty, who covered the story for the *Los Angeles Times* before moving to *Time* magazine, said she felt "swamped by the immensity of the policy stuff and the political dimensions. It was so complicated, it had so many moving parts, and it affected different people and different regions in so many different ways, it just overwhelmed you." Asked how well the administration had explained the plan, Tumulty said, "They were awful. The plan was virtually unexplainable, and at first, they were just arrogant. They refused to confront hard questions. Then as it started to get in trouble, they realized it was out there and they couldn't move off it, and they became defensive. When you questioned something, they lectured you on your inability to grasp their grand vision. Pretty soon, it was all being lost in confusion and fear."

What she and others were describing was quantified in a March report from the Times Mirror Center for the People & the Press, in conjunction with the Kaiser Family Foundation and the *Columbia Journalism Review*. Their study of the coverage from September through November of the previous year demonstrated "the difficulties faced by the American news media in telling a complex story in a way that is understandable to the American people." A survey commissioned for the report found that "the public has become increasingly frustrated with the media and less informed on the basic facts of the proposal as the focus of the reform story has shifted from the impact of the Clinton proposals on ordinary citizens to questions of policy and political infighting."

Examining almost two thousand print and broadcast stories in national and regional media, the report found that the *politics* of the battle was reported twice as often as the *impact* of the plan on consumers. There was little evidence of editorial bias and the coverage was judged to be quite balanced, with Hillary getting notably better press than her husband. But television cut back coverage significantly after the big splash of the presidential speech and the First Lady's congressional testimony. As a result, the public actually lost sight of some of the plan's significant features.

For example, by December, 10 percent fewer people knew that the Clinton plan would cover everyone and would guarantee coverage if workers quit or lost their jobs than knew those facts in September. The percentage of the public rating press coverage of the story as excellent or good fell from 72 percent in September to 54 percent in January, with a commensurate increase in the percentage rating it only fair or poor.

The print media stayed with the story longer than television and devoted more attention to discussion and analysis of the plan, while television emphasized such obvious media events as speeches and hearings. But both largely ignored such important topics as portability of coverage, long-term care, mental health services, and rural health facilities.

The report found that as information declined, so did support for reform, and it attributed most of this to the efforts of the plan's opponents, but also noted the "broader critical trend" in coverage of Clinton and his plan.

It was certainly not the responsibility of the media to "sell" the nation on the reform. But by failing to explain it clearly, the media made it easier for the critics to undermine public support.

On a Friday night early in December, Jay Rockefeller, talking again in his office, was even more disturbed than he had been at the end of October. "When does this come out?" he asked us, referring to the book where his words would appear. "Oh, the hell with it," he said, without waiting for a reply. "I'm in a state of rage, befuddled, all the rest of it. I'm furious right now at the White House for several reasons. There is still no organization on health care. There's nothing out there. And the health care polling numbers are heading southward as it gets more complicated and gets picked apart."

The vacuum he had complained about to Hillary Clinton still existed. The White House was simply not fighting back. There wasn't any effective political operation to win the battle. "Lots of good people are sitting around talking about how health reform's going to happen, arguing over the details, but nothing's happening in the American public except HIAA's out there bombing with nobody responding."

An inept political operation was only part of the problem. This critical White House failure was compounded by an unintentional blow inflicted by the President on himself. As he came to realize much later and to acknowledge openly to us, the President failed to appreciate the magnitude of the tasks he had created for himself by taking on so many ambitious policy battles. Yet he had crippled his policy efforts by severely cutting back on the number of people who worked for him. Economy, leanness, efficiency — these had been his campaign hallmarks. He was a New Democrat, one who cut government rolls, not added to them. And he had promised, as had many leaders before him, often to their regret, "to do more with less" once he got to the White House. As a result Clinton had slashed his staff, thus significantly increasing the pressures on the fewer staffers remaining.

Again, he accepted full responsibility; it was another presidential lesson painfully learned. "I had cut back the staff of the White House as I said I would," he told us, "and we'd roughly doubled the workload of the White House because I was taking on all these major initiatives, one right after the other. We didn't have the resources to do it, and we should have."

But understanding the consequences of this version of a penny-wise pound-foolish political philosophy would come much later. Now, in December 1993, Jay Rockefeller was venting his continuing frustrations about the faltering campaign. "We need somebody to come in and take it over," Rockefeller repeated, and Harold Ickes was agonizing privately about whether to take the position. Rockefeller said he had just spoken to him and that he felt "burned out" from his campaign in New York, concerned about his ability to take on such a key Washington insider job without much experience in the capital, and also worried about how he would deal with Ira Magaziner. Ickes raised the question with Rockefeller of whether Magaziner would be willing to report to him or how they would work out their respective responsibilities.

To Rockefeller that meant still more delay. "Why don't they see they need a general?" the senator asked rhetorically. He produced a calendar that he had recently gone over with the Senate majority leader, George Mitchell. It showed dates carefully marked out for the first six months of 1994. June was absolutely the last target date to get a bill ready for Senate debate and passage. "There's not that much time," he said. "There's no more time for screwing around." He repeated himself: "There's no more time for screwing around. So I'm very frustrated with the White House." Besides, he added, it was clear that though the White House wasn't moving aggressively, there was increasing evidence that the Republicans were.

In fact, the Republicans were moving even more aggressively than Rockefeller or other Democrats knew.

On December 2, just a few days before that conversation in Rockefeller's office, William Kristol, a leading conservative operative whose opinions carried great weight, had privately circulated to Republicans in Congress what came to be a celebrated strategy document. Barely forty, Kristol had carved out a remarkable role for himself as a staff man who could marshal support from elected officials simply by the power of his ideas.

It helped that he was the son of two icons of the neoconservative movement — writer-editor Irving Kristol and his wife, historian Gertrude Himmelfarb. Bill Kristol had zoomed through Harvard College in three years and had his Harvard doctorate in government at twenty-six. After teaching at the University of Pennsylvania and the Kennedy School of Government at Harvard, he went to Washington to work for another intellectual, William Bennett, the Reagan administration Education secretary. There was some surprise when Kristol became chief of staff to Vice President Dan Quayle, but he escaped the ridicule often rained on his boss. In the press, he was never blamed for Quayle's gaffes, and often credited for Quayle's successful speeches.

Operating now from a conservative think tank, the Project for the Republican Future, Kristol wrote that congressional Republicans should work to "kill" — not amend — the Clinton plan. His reasons were Machiavellian. Clinton's health plan presented a clear danger to the Republican future; its passage would (as Democrats had earlier advised Clinton) give the Democrats a lock on the crucial middle-class vote. "It will re-legitimize middle-class dependence for 'security' on government spending and regulation," Kristol wrote. "It will revive the reputation of the party that spends and regulates, the Democrats, as the generous protector of middle-class interests. And it will at the same time strike a punishing blow against Republican claims to defend the middle class by restraining government."

Nearly a full year before Republicans would unite behind the "Contract With America," Kristol provided the rationale and the steel for them to achieve their aims of winning control of Congress and becoming America's majority party. Killing health care would serve both ends. The timing of Kristol's memo dovetailed with a growing private consensus among Republicans that all-out opposition to the Clinton plan was in their best political interest. Newt Gingrich had long held this view, and was meeting regularly with House Republicans, interest-group representatives, and pollsters like Bill McInturff to plot the strategy that would enable them to win the war. But until Kristol's memo surfaced, most opponents still preferred behind-the-scenes warfare, largely shielded from public view. The boldness of Kristol's strategy signaled a new turn in the battle: Now it was not only politically acceptable to criticize the Clinton plan on policy grounds; it was politically advantageous. By the end of 1993, blocking reform posed little risk as the public was becoming increasingly fearful of what it had heard about the Clinton plan.

As Senator Bob Bennett, the Utah Republican, told us, Clinton's proposal, the "incredibly bloated, complex, unresponsive, incomprehensible health plan, came to symbolize everything people hated about government." The symbolism of Big Government and the rising "fear in the postwar world that you, the middle class, were going to be hurt," began to mean trouble for the Democrats as "the fear was directed at Clinton. The forty-six-year-old rocket scientist at Lockheed with two kids in college votes. He asks, 'What happens if I get caught in downsizing? I'm going to lose my coverage *because* of Clinton.' There was more fury against the thing than there ever had been driving for it, and it just took on a life of its own."

Something else happened those early December days that would prove fateful. That was the disclosure, little noted at the time, of the existence of certain files dealing with an investment Bill and Hillary Clinton had made long ago in a private Arkansas land development called Whitewater. Those files, it was reported, had been secretly removed by presidential aides from the White House office of Vincent Foster, a close friend of Bill and Hillary from Arkansas, after Foster's suicide the previous summer.

12

Beyond the Beltway

D R. CHRISTINE KLASEN strode briskly across the driveway, her stethoscope bouncing against the front of her white medical coat, past lines of people forming outside the doors of the sprawling century-old white hospital atop a hill. She moved quickly through even more people packed inside the waiting room of Los Angeles County General Hospital, one of the largest such public institutions in the United States and, in terms of what it represents, one of the most illuminating, and disturbing.

A mass of humanity occupied virtually every inch of the room. Demographically, they formed a rainbow of the American experience: Latinos, mainly from Mexico but also from Central and South America; Asians, spanning the rim from Cambodia and Thailand to China and Korea; African-Americans; a sprinkling of whites. Most were poorly dressed; many were unable to speak English. People stood in lines, two-deep against the walls of the waiting room. Every seat was taken by men, women, and children. Mothers nursed babies. Others, both the old and young, sat in wheelchairs or stood on crutches. Long lines formed at windows where hospital aides took names and gave times and dates for appointments. So great was the backlog for medical appointments, patients would have to wait months for them. It was mid-October 1993, a warm, hazy southern California day, and just weeks after the President had launched his battle.

* * *

Far beyond the Washington Beltway, in the public and private hospitals, clinics, and community and migrant health centers throughout the Los Angeles area, where we interviewed frontline people like Chris Klasen for a week that October, everyone had a huge stake in the successful enactment of reform. There, institutions dealt most intimately with the severe problems afflicting the American health system and would be among the biggest losers if Congress failed to pass legislation extending coverage to most Americans — undocumented workers being a big exception to those included under the Clinton plan. All of the providers closely followed the debate just beginning in Washington; all knew that what happened a continent away in the capital would directly affect them and the patients they treated. But the disconnect between the policy and political deliberations of Washington and the often harsh conditions encountered daily on the front lines could not have been more stunning, often shocking, especially when those most in need received the worst treatment, often at exorbitant cost. Sometimes, they received no treatment at all. "Poor people's medicine," one of the Los Angeles practitioners bitterly called it, and so it was, with all the problems and inequities that that term implies.

Nor was there any doubt in these health care workers' minds that the United States faced a health care "crisis" of confounding complexity. Probably nowhere in the nation were these problems more evident than in the sprawling Los Angeles metropolitan area, where boiling racial and ethnic conflicts were commonplace, where pervasive violence that sent more and more victims to emergency rooms contributed to soaring hospital costs, and where the gap separating America's most affluent haves from its most desperate have-nots was most nakedly exposed.

With its ten million residents, Los Angeles County, which includes the City of Los Angeles, is the largest local governmental entity in the nation.

By the time of the 1992 presidential election, while Bill Clinton was formulating the ideas that would result in his plan, leaders of L.A. County were trying to alert the public and the political players in The System to the growing health care crisis. They sent a special bipartisan task force report, which reported alarming statistics, to the L.A. County Board of Supervisors. One in three persons under the age of sixty-five in L.A. County, or nearly three million people, had no insurance; one in six depended on Medi-Cal, the California name for Medicaid, the national program for the poor; one in seven lived in poverty; one in seven received welfare payments from the Aid to Families with Dependent Children (AFDC) program; one in twenty over the age of sixty-four had no Medicare coverage.

Other figures documented worsening problems there and, by extension, throughout the nation. In recent years, the report found, the county's population had increased by 19 percent, the number in poverty had risen by a third, and the uninsured by more than 100 percent.

Compounding these problems was the failure of The System and its political leaders, and ultimately the public they lead and serve, to provide basic services essential to the well-being of all citizens — and to acknowledge, candidly, the price the taxpaying public must be willing to bear to maintain those services. The System was not serving the people as it should. In California, the tax-cutting wave of previous years had severely limited county property tax revenues, making the county increasingly dependent on state revenues. The state's budgets, in turn, were slashed, in part because of a dramatic erosion in federal money, forcing cutbacks in funding for *all* public services.

California's fiscal situation in the 1990s was more extreme than the nation's generally, but the same lack of adequate public funds affected state and local budgets everywhere; and everywhere, inadequate funding hit public health services with special severity. A vivid example of how greatly local services were impacted by the lack of funds was buried in that special bipartisan L.A. County health report. Between 1980 and 1992, the proportion of the county's general funds allocated to its Department of Health Services, the nation's largest, had declined from 18 to 8 percent.

The worst was yet to come. After the Clinton plan died ignominiously and Republicans won control of Congress, the new Republican majorities set out to balance the federal budget, cut taxes, and drastically shrink the federal government in large part by shifting responsibility from Washington to the states, counties, and cities already battling severe fiscal constraints. Major public facilities like L.A. County General Hospital, where Chris Klasen worked amid increasingly difficult conditions, would pay the heaviest price.

When the debate on the Clinton plan began that fall of 1993, L.A. County's public health system was already experiencing terminal problems. A prime example was its countywide hospital trauma system, created in 1983 when new centers were established within existing hospitals to care for victims of injuries requiring emergency care. By 1986, the L.A. County trauma system was regarded as the best in the world. But within a year, the system started to fall apart, collapsing under the rapidly increasing weight of the uninsured. About 50 percent of the people who went to the trauma centers for treatment did not have health insurance. By mid-October of 1993, when we did our Los Angeles interviews, half of those trauma centers had been forced to close, leaving huge gaps in the L.A. County network. "Those holes mean that more than a million and a half people in L.A. don't have trauma service at all," said David Langness, head of the Hospital Council of Southern California, which represents all the hospitals in southern California and is the largest and oldest such council in the nation. "A good example is at the airport. There's no trauma center near the airport. The impact of this huge number of uninsured people — not all of them poor, but all of them uninsured — has jeopardized the health care infrastructure for everyone."

California's recession of the late 1980s and early 1990s, the most severe since the Depression, had placed heavy burdens on the public- and private health care system. Cuts in federal defense spending after the end of the Cold War caused unemployment and more uninsured workers. Dave Langness told us:

What we've seen in all hospitals is a declining rate of income and therefore profitability, and therefore solvency. We closed forty hospitals in southern California in the last five years, and that's out of a total of two hundred seventy-five.

We closed fourteen trauma centers in southern California and over twenty emergency rooms. So the impact on hospitals is immense. That's why hospitals, of all interest groups, have been most supportive of health care reform. I don't want to be a cynic, but it's probably because they're in the worst shape — much worse shape than doctors, insurance companies, pharmaceuticals. Hospitals are losing money hand over fist.

At that time, nearly 60 percent of the hospitals in southern California were operating in the red, and those in the black were averaging only a 1 percent profit margin, in sharp contrast to just ten years before, when 80 percent of California hospitals were in the black, enjoying an average annual profit margin of 22 percent. Aside from the recession, forcing more people to lose jobs and insurance, two additional factors powerfully contributed to this downturn in health care fortunes. The first was the immigration that poured into southern California throughout the late 1980s and early 1990s. Mythology about a tide of illegal immigrants flooding southern California aside, most of this Pacific Rim/Mexican Border immigration was legal. The second factor was what Langness described as "an enormous retrenchment in the insurance industry, cutting people from insurance, and ensuring that if you have a preexisting condition or major illness, especially AIDS, which has hit southern California hard, you are not going to be covered."

So, he said, by that fall of 1993, the rolls of the uninsured had quadrupled.

And who were these uninsured? They were everybody, and their demographic profile did not match the public stereotype. Most were white, young, and male. About 75 percent of them were either employed or in college. Typically, they came from middle- or lower-middle-class backgrounds. And there were many Latino working mothers.

From the beginning, local officials and community leaders in places like L.A. County argued that only the adoption of comprehensive reform providing universal access to health care would address these problems. They looked to the federal level of The System for legislation to set uniform standards, and warned that shifting costs from federal to state and local jurisdictions would exacerbate already massive problems. While their greatest concern was the increasing strain on underfinanced public facilities, they were aware that the burden fell on private facilities as well.

Only ten miles by freeway from L.A. County General stands Cedars-Sinai Medical Center on Beverly Boulevard. "The hospital of the stars," Cedars-Sinai is often called, and so it is. There in its air-conditioned marble corridors and comfortably appointed waiting rooms, you might glimpse the famous Hollywood faces of those who come for the most advanced medical treatment. Of Cedars it is said you can buy a mink coat at the gift shop and enjoy one of the largest private art collections in the world. In its new eighteen-hundred-vehicle parking garage directly adjoining the towering medical complex, you can gawk at the latest-model Bentleys and Rollses and Mercedes-Benzes and Jaguars.

Cedars is a major private hospital, the largest voluntary, not-for-profit such institution west of the Mississippi, that represents the best of medical care, not only in the United States, but in the world. Prior to 1993, with an operating budget of $520 million a year, Cedars employed six thousand people, twenty-two hundred of them physicians, and admitted forty thousand patients a year while handling fifty-five thousand visits annually to its emergency rooms. One percent of all the internists in the United States were on its staff. It was the dominant provider of health care services in the Los Angeles marketplace, covering an area from Santa Monica in the west to downtown Los Angeles, north into the near San Fernando Valley, the bedroom community of Los Angeles, and south to the Los Angeles airport. Twenty-five percent of all the inpatient hospital admissions in that area came to Cedars for the broadest range of treatment, everything from psychiatric care and rehabilitation to organ transplants.

It was also a major academic medical center, with a full-time, highly specialized faculty that not only carried out a range of clinical services, but also provided educational functions for the medical center. Backed by some $19 million a year of research money, 40 percent from the federal government's NIH (the U.S. National Institutes of

Health, based in Bethesda, Maryland) and the remainder from private donations, Cedars operated an active research program.

With such an abundance of riches, and the backing of wealthy benefactors enabling it to provide the best care assisted by the latest medical technology, a great private medical center such as Cedars-Sinai would seem to have been in the most enviable position. Yet for all the stark differences between Cedars and L.A. County General, Cedars, too, grappled with many of the same severe problems.

By mid-October of 1993, Cedars's revenues were down 12 to 15 percent from projections a year before. Even greater declines were expected. "Over sixty percent of the hospitals in the state of California are losing money now," Thomas M. Priselac, its energetic executive vice president (soon to be president and chief executive officer) told us. "We were one of the few that was making money, but as a result of the kind of drop we're experiencing, if we don't adjust our expenses, we're going to be in a financially losing situation."

The reasons for that condition were as complex, and as simple, as those of America's health care crisis. Public and private hospitals as dissimilar as L.A. County and Cedars-Sinai, serving different segments of American life, faced common problems: Their costs were spiraling, while the demands on them were increasing.

Hospital care accounted for two-fifths of all health care costs, with Medicare paying a fifth of *all* hospital bills. Those costs continued to explode. Changing demographics were partly to blame. As the number of older Americans increased, costs rose as well; 27 percent of Medicare dollars, for example, were expended during the last year of a patient's life. Part of the problem came from technology. Dramatic advances in new life-extending medical equipment and procedures were accompanied by the higher costs of these wondrous new technologies. A CAT scan, though routine, could be priced as high as $1000. But the greatest cause of soaring costs lay in the extraordinarily expensive — and lucrative — trillion-dollar national health delivery system. It was riddled with waste, duplication of services, and overspecialization of practitioners. Between 20 and 30 percent of spending was unnecessary and of no benefit to patients. On a typical day that fall, when the reform battle began, four out of ten American hospital beds were empty and forty cents out of every premium dollar went to insurance administration. Excessive specialization characterized the system. While half of the doctors in other industrialized countries provided primary care to patients, in the United States fewer than a third practiced general medicine.

Cedars-Sinai offered a case study. "One of the greatest challenges that health reform puts before all hospitals and their medical staffs," Tom Priselac said, "is that it basically forces hospitals and physicians to come together in ways they've never had to."

Even as Priselac spoke, and before any congressional committees began to deliberate on the reform plan, dynamic change was already reshaping the southern California system. New mergers and alliances were forming. Hospital administrators like Priselac shared the view that any hospital not in an alliance within a year would probably be forced out of business. Historically in Los Angeles, Priselac noted, physicians were on medical staffs at multiple hospitals. "For organizations like ourselves," Priselac said, "we have had to ask physicians to dedicate themselves to one facility over another. In our case, that means asking physicians to hook their star with ours. There's no question that physicians, the hospital, and the public will be better off for it, because what we're all facing now is that doctors and hospitals don't have the same incentives. Other than those who are in managed care, physicians are still largely paid on a fee-for-service basis. There is not the incentive to try to match up the use of resources with the requirements of the patient in the most effective way."

He gave a riveting example. Cedars's patients for a hip replacement routinely needed seven days for recovery. But some needed eleven days and some took as long as fourteen days. If they were Medicare patients, the hospital received the same amount of money whether the patient stayed for seven or fourteen days.

Then there were medical supplies. Traditionally, hospitals have competed to make themselves as attractive as possible to many different physicians, each of whom could choose from among a number of hospitals where they sent their patients. Priselac explained:

As a result, until very recently we have stocked and supplied hip implant products from seven different vendors. With the emergence of managed care and the need to ask what is necessary for this patient, a couple of things change. On the supply side, we've sat down with our division of orthopedics and said, "This is costing us a lot money. If it costs us money, it costs your patient money, and it costs you money because it's money we're spending unnecessarily. It's money that could be put into other programs and services you might otherwise need."

So now we've standardized our hip vendor and we've saved the hospital five hundred thousand dollars. That's one example in one service, and it gets multiplied around the institution.

Faced with these crises, people like Tom Priselac looked hopefully, if guardedly, to the Clinton plan as a way out of the system's difficulties. Looming over them was the certainty that public hospitals and clinics would be forced to close for lack of funds, placing pressure on private ones to meet new needs. Priselac knew that even such a favored private medical institution as Cedars would be severely impacted. "Clearly, we can't afford to continue the way we are," he said. "It costs too much for the employers in the county, and there are too many people not getting adequate care."

At L.A. County General, Chris Klasen confronted more grimly immediate problems but expressed a similar thought. "When is America going to wake up to the fact that we need a national health care program?" she said.

I've just personally been involved with so many families that have had devastating illness or have been wiped out. So when this health reform movement started politically during the campaign I wasn't surprised, I was happy. I think Clinton's plan is great. It's a cradle-to-grave concept of absolute health security. But the next question you have to ask is, What does that include? It may not include saving the life of a one-pound preemie at a cost of seven hundred fifty thousand dollars, or it may not include a cardiovascular resuscitation to an eighty-year-old woman so she can live three more months in the nursing home. Is the Clinton plan workable? Hey, it's got to be better than what we have.

She said that to us while she moved purposefully through the mass of people inside L.A. County's waiting room and walked briskly toward a corridor leading to the trauma emergency rooms. Everyone entering that corridor has to pass through metal detectors manned by security guards. "They don't allow family members in," Dr. Klasen said in matter-of-fact tone as she continued walking. "What's happened is gang members came in with the trauma patients and there were problems. Shootings, threatening the staff members. Stuff like that. So they're very tight with the security now."

She continued down the corridor past photographs showing nineteenth- and early twentieth-century scenes of a very different L.A. County General in a very different America: a sea of white faces, bearded young doctors, nurses in heavily starched uniforms, uncrowded hospital rooms, sparsely filled emergency rooms.

Just a few months before, Dr. Richard May, a friend and colleague of Dr. Klasen, was one of three doctors shot while treating trauma patients in the emergency room. He was the most seriously injured. He was shot in the head by a skid row man with a long history of dysfunctional behavior who had waited hours to be attended, and just "wigged out." "The staff here is working like a factory as best they can, but there are so many people and there are no more trauma units because the private hospitals have pretty much gotten out of the trauma business [with Cedars a notable exception]," Klasen said. "So if you're in trauma, you're brought here into County, or maybe one or two other places. So you wait and you wait and you wait. This guy couldn't take any more of the waiting. He just pulled a gun. Bang, bang, bang. The doctors were like the frontline people. So that changed the way the county started securing its facilities."

Unlike many physicians who train at a place like L.A. County and then move to more lucrative private practice, Chris Klasen chose to make her career at a huge public hospital where one in every two hundred of all the children born in the United States is delivered, and where one in every fifteen doctors in the nation has done some training. She always wanted to deliver care to indigent patients, she said, and in this society that means the county hospital. We take all comers, she said proudly. Nineteen years ago, she had visited county hospitals across the country, among them Tulane in New Orleans and Bellevue in New York, and found L.A. County the best. She had been there ever since.

The changes she saw in those years were dramatic; they reflect the changes in American society in general and the delivery of American medicine in particular. "This is a place that's very good at crisis intervention," she said:

> Somebody pulls a gun and shoots you through the chest, you want to be in L.A. County. You don't want to be in any of the other private hospitals in Los Angeles, because these doctors here are like that. [She snapped her fingers.] They know how to take care of business fast. You work long enough in the emergency room at a big county hospital and you see some of the worst trauma you'll ever dream about, because L.A. is full of gangs. They come in all blown up, and the doctors fix 'em up, patch 'em up, send 'em back out there on the streets. Then they come back to you. If you've been around long enough, you'll see the same kid again. So you pour all of your energy and effort into trying to help this kid and their family in a compressed period of time, the time you see them here in the hospital.

She stopped outside the doors of an emergency room, permitting a view through a window at medical personnel bent over patients lying on operating tables. After a brief period of silence, she stepped aside and, with her back against the corridor wall, spoke with renewed intensity:

> It's crazy, you know. We spend a tremendous amount of money in this country on curative care, but we spend very little money in this country on preventive care. And this is what this whole county hospital is about. The crisis. When that person comes to you with a blood pressure of ninety over sixty, we're great at being able to save their life and take care of them so they walk out of the hospital. But we don't change one iota of what that person is about. We can spend thousands of dollars on chemotherapy and surgery for the woman with extensive invasive

cervical carcinoma, but we don't have the money to give that person routine Pap smears — or education about routine Pap smears.

So much could be prevented if our priorities would shift, she said. A few years before, a measles epidemic swept southern California, and several children died. "Now this is totally unacceptable in this most industrialized society in the world," she said indignantly. "But, again, that's our priority. Our country has to make some very harsh choices about rationing care. And it's going to cost. The more we want to do, the higher the price tag is going to be. Americans have to know that."

Julie Delgado lives the health care crisis. She is a clinical social worker at the Hudson Comprehensive Health Center, located near L.A. County General and also part of the University of Southern California Medical Center.

Early each morning when she arrives for work at the clinic, Delgado encounters the same scene: long lines of people forming outside the doors, inside the small waiting room, and on through the corridors of the two-story structure. Sick people, old people, grandmothers with small children, mothers breastfeeding infants, all wait, hour after hour.

The scene is even more dismaying than at L.A. County General. At Hudson, people spill over from the few chairs to the corridors, where they sit on the floor, backs against the wall, forcing patients and staff to step around or over them. It is like being on the teeming streets of Calcutta. In the world's greatest democracy, this shameful scene can be replicated in countless other underfunded clinics dealing with increasing numbers of the poor and the ill. At Hudson, the backlog for appointments is great; that fall of 1993, appointments were booked four months in advance.

People who come there are, Julie Delgado says, "the throwaway people" — who cannot speak English, who do not vote, who have no voice in The System. They are people who, like the majority of Delgado's clients, are basically "homeless people from skid row, mostly gay and bisexual men of color. If you have absolutely no money, you're going to end up here. Most of my clients have active substance problems, and the big drug is crack cocaine."

Public clinics like Hudson, where the needs are the greatest, are the very ones to see their services cut first under budgetary pressures. This cruel paradox is a reminder that The System works best for those best able to influence it — a point made by nearly everyone in Los Angeles we interviewed that mid-October of 1993. But even groups possessing the greatest political influence are affected by the failure to treat people in poorest health. "You have to have a uniform standard of care for everybody," Julie Delgado says. "The American population has to come to terms with that because not to come to terms with it puts themselves at risk. These people bring infectious disease. If you're sitting on a bus and the guy next to you has TB, all you care about is he's got TB."

At the Hospital Council of Southern California, David Langness reinforced her point. People who have health insurance, he said, pick up costs for people who are here illegally and for small-business owners who don't cover their employees. "We're all in this together, you know," he said. "When you go to a restaurant and eat with your family, the chances are the cook and all the restaurant help are probably not legal. They're the people who cook our food, mow our lawns, wash our cars at the carwash. We're coming into contact with them every day. I use the tried-and-true public health argument: If those people are sick and don't have health insurance, you're going to get it and you're going to pay for it. Germs are equal-opportunity employers."

Langness offered another textbook example of how The System treats those with the least political power. For more than a decade, California had suffered from governors who viewed health care, especially for the poor in Los Angeles, as far down on their priority list. In the eighties, Governor Deukmejian cut an average of about $50 million out of the state budget for health care every year of his term, Langness told us. The present governor, Pete Wilson, was better, but not much. Through those years, the county had lost revenue from the state each year. The county used to get matching funds; it no longer did. It used to get block grants; they had been cut. It used to get a large subsidy from the state to care for the poor. "L.A. County

has half — actually the figure is forty-seven percent — of the total Medicare enrollment and Medicaid enrollment in California,"
Langness said. "So we've got about half the poor people in this
state in this county. And the governors know that number one, L.A.
County didn't vote for them, and number two, the folks who took
advantage of that health care aren't going to vote for them no matter
what they do. And, in fact, probably aren't going to vote."

The inequities were more fundamental than inadequate facilities
and services for the most needy. Throughout the entire debate,
every player in The System, whether for or against reform, enjoyed
the best, and in many ways the least expensive, insurance. All of
them, including those who publicly inveighed against the evils of
"government-run health care," had *their* insurance premiums subsidized by their employer, the federal government — and their insurance was not available to other Americans. We saw the starkness
of this inequity every time we visited a public health clinic, hospital,
or migrant center in Los Angeles.

   Of many examples, two stand out. The first involves a Mexican-
American man who worked in a factory where none of the employees
had insurance. When a worker became ill on the job, or suffered an
injury, the factory employers took him or her to a storefront doctor in the inner city for treatment. Cash payment was required. It's
what experts call the "gray," or illegal, area of medicine; it's black-
market medicine. No forms are filled out, no records kept. In the case
of the Mexican-American factory worker, each time he had to have
medical treatment — he was vomiting from inhaling dust at the factory — he was taken to the inner-city doctor and charged $200. Af-
ter a cursory exam, he was given painkillers and sent back to work.
That was standard procedure for all workers at his factory.

   The second example involves an illegal immigrant couple from
Guatemala. Both worked in low-paying jobs in the Los Angeles gar-
ment industry, earning from $7 to $10 a day. They had been in the
United States five years and had three small children. Neither had
health insurance, nor did any other employees where they worked.
What happened to each of them would try the patience of Job.

   In a small inner-city building where community workers assisted undocumented workers, she sat in a back office, a sheaf of papers clutched tightly in her hands; she kept ruffling the papers throughout the interview. She was visibly nervous, lowering her eyes and seeming afraid to talk. Though she was only thirty-four, she looked much older. Her face was creased with lines, her long black hair already flecked with gray. She wore a long, plain brown cotton garment, more a smock than a dress, and spoke in a low, hesitant tone. With prompting from the interviewer, and gentle urging from a migrant center volunteer who translated her Spanish, she began describing the serious health problem she had experienced.

Two years before, in 1991, she came down with a severe case of measles in the epidemic to which Dr. Chris Klasen had referred. Despite her extremely high fever, her husband didn't take her to the hospital. He was not able to pay. After three days of suffering, during which her condition worsened, her husband no longer could put off an emergency room visit. A friend drove them to L.A. County General. "When I got there," she said, "they realized that I was in really bad shape. My tongue was completely dried out and there wasn't a drop of moisture left in me."

She was speaking more rapidly now, daring to look up, and leaning forward intently, still nervously ruffling those papers.

"We got there about seven o'clock that night," she went on. "It took them about four hours to get around to taking my temperature. They asked to see my ID. My husband told them I didn't have my ID with me. They asked if I had medical insurance and I told them I didn't. They only started to treat me after my husband grabbed a nurse and said, 'This woman is *really* sick. She's in terrible shape.' Once that happened, they made me fill out forms to apply for Medi-Cal. So I filled out the forms but I knew I wasn't going to qualify. I was not in the country legally."

Here, she stopped and looked at the migrant community center worker, silently seeking his approval for having made this confession. Go on, he said, gently. It's all right.

"Well, they injected me with some stuff and then they gave me some pills that I had to take. A little while later I got a bill from the hospital for three hundred dollars for those pills. Given the amount of money I make, I could never pay that bill."

She received repeated notices for non-payment, and finally a collection notice, which she was unable to pay. Because of her illness, and the time it took to recover, she lost her job — a blow at any time, but nowhere approaching the gravity of the ordeal she and her husband next experienced. It was this situation that led her to agree, after the repeated urgings of the migrant worker counselor, to tell her story.

A year later, her husband developed acute appendicitis, she said.

He kept getting worse day after day, but we had no money and couldn't do anything about it. Finally he got to the point where he was hurting so bad, obviously his appendix had burst, and he said, "Look, rather than take me to some hospital where they're going to charge thousands of dollars, just let me die here." And I ran screaming out of the apartment; I had no idea what to do. Finally I found some woman that I knew and she said, "Call the police. Maybe they'll help you." And the police sent an ambulance. They took him to [L.A. County] General Hospital and left him in the ambulance for two hours. I thought he was dying in my arms because he was in terrible shape and they said that there wasn't a bed free to operate on him. So they took him to the Good Samaritan Hospital. They asked us if we had medical insurance. They asked us if we qualified for any government programs, if we had jobs, if we had a bank account.

Now, her words poured forth. The more she talked, the more emotional she became. "I was just yelling and screaming and crying in the waiting room because I knew my husband was dying," she said, "and I finally convinced some nurse to talk to some doctor and she swore to the doctor that we would pay if it took us the rest of our lives. We would pay it off, but don't let my husband die. They finally did the operation, and we've got a bill here for nineteen thousand dollars that we're now paying off, like five to ten dollars a month."

By then she was sobbing uncontrollably, her body shaking and heaving. She handed over the bill, and the paperwork, that she had been clutching in her hands. They were from the Hospital of the Good Samaritan, Los Angeles, California, marked for inpatient services, account number 00666114-211. The period for services covered

six days: 7/18/92 to 7/23/92. As of the latest date on the statement, 10/5/93, it showed a balance due of $18,995.39. Noted on
the monthly bill was a statement that said "pay this amount." The
payment due: $10.

At that rate, it would take them two hundred years to pay their
debt. "They told my husband that if he didn't pay this bill he would
go to jail," she said, "and we don't know any other way to deal with
it. But he has to or he's going to go to jail. He's all worried what's
going to happen. We'll never have that much money and I don't know
what to do."

Their experience showed the human face of the crisis. Whether
or not their $19,000 bill for an appendectomy was justified, it was
being carried on that private hospital's books as a loss and will trans-
late into higher bills for other patients. In the end, everybody in the
system pays.

The hardworking couple, whose potential for a good life was
wrecked because they can't pay a hospital emergency bill, happen to
be illegal aliens. But the same kind of hopeless situation applies to
many American citizens who, like them, become desperately ill and
either have no insurance or woefully inadequate coverage.

After the interview, we told Tom Priselac of Cedars-Sinai about
that woman's situation. "Unfortunately," he said, shaking his head,
"that's all too common."

Whatever their differences, and no matter whether they were from
the public or private health care sectors, the frontline people we met
that October were in broad agreement that *some* reform would become law within a year. As Tom Priselac said, "A year from now I
think we will be coming to the final strokes of finishing a legislative
package that will ultimately be passed by Congress."

His view was widely held then. But so were doubts about whether
the reform adopted would be broad enough to meet America's challenges. Many doubted Congress would follow the President's lead.
Several spoke almost wistfully about a federally financed single-
payer system as being the most equitable, theoretically at least, and
regretted that political realities prevented it from passing.

Chris Klasen was one of the most pessimistic. She feared that "the American people are not ready to hear how much medical care costs. They're not ready to make some of these hard decisions and hard choices." But she had a more immediate and personal reason for doubts.

The night before we talked, she had had a discussion with a friend, a small-business owner in Los Angeles. Klasen strongly argued the case for reform, and warned of the consequences if it failed.

"Well, I have eighteen employees," her friend said. "I can't afford to give health insurance to them. And the plan Clinton is talking about sets up health alliances. What's going to happen to those people whose jobs will be lost when these alliances force them out of business? What's going to happen to the insurance companies and their families when the government forces them out of business? What about *their* health care?"

"Dennis," Klasen replied, "it might come down to what you like least. There's no good way to do this. The question is, What's worse? There are two bads, and which is the worst of the bads?"

"I don't care if somebody's unemployed," the small businessman said. "I just don't want to be that somebody."

His answer infuriated Klasen; but it also made her more pessimistic. "And this guy lives in a two-hundred-sixty-thousand-dollar house," she said. "I just wanted to go — Pow! I don't know what it's going to take. You've got to confront the American people. If that means a change in the law, it's going to take that. It has to come to a crisis before the American people act. Just like it had to come to a goddamn crisis before they'd get security in the hospital [after her doctor friend had been shot]. Somebody had to get their head blown in."

13

Waves of Whitewater

UNTIL LATE 1993, Bill Clinton's presidency had been a high-wire act. One near-disaster had followed another: The embarrassing early stumbles over top appointees. The White House Travel Office fiasco. The "two-hundred-dollar" haircut. The hairbreadth escape from a disastrous budget defeat. The repeated diversion of health reform. The constant policy dissension within the top ranks of his administration. The foreign-policy crises over Somalia, Bosnia, Haiti, Russia. But now, early in December of 1993, with Congress in recess, Clinton's star was rising.

The controversial North American Free Trade Agreement (NAFTA) had passed with strong bipartisan support. So had an even more bitterly polarizing piece of legislation behind which Clinton had placed the prestige of his office — the Brady bill, fiercely opposed by the National Rifle Association, requiring a waiting period before the purchase of a handgun for police to check criminal records.

Clinton's own poll ratings, after sinking to historic lows for a first-year President, had soared to 60 percent, surpassing even Ronald Reagan's standing after a year in office. In Washington, the White House was wreathed in greenery and glistening with decorations for the traditional Christmas parties hosted by the President and the First Lady. And Clinton, with typical energy and fascination with policy, threw himself into a round of intense meetings to set priorities for his critical second year.

For eleven days, from December 10 to 20, he huddled in the Cabinet Room for four hours each morning and three each afternoon going over each department's budget and debating plans and strategies with the department heads. When the discussion turned to health reform, each time the President delivered the same message: He was going to assert himself more aggressively. He was going to drive the process hard and work with congressional leaders to speed the legislative schedule. He wanted a bipartisan health reform solution. If there's a better way, he said again and again, tell me. Let's do it. Anybody who's got a better idea, put it on the table. Let's discuss it.

Hillary Clinton was also planning for the critical battles to come. Her popularity was then even higher than his, with approval numbers in the 65 to 70 percent range. That was a problem, one of the top White House operatives, Steve Ricchetti, chief congressional liaison for the Senate, warned her. "Right now," he said, "you are too strong in this process. They are going to come after you. It's politically imperative for them to take a pound of flesh out of you. One way or another, that's going to happen." Ricchetti offered other advice. Go around the country, he urged. Feel the warmth of the people. You've been successful; you can be proud of this year. So enjoy the festiveness of the holiday season. We'll come back in January and refocus attention. Then you'll be in a strong position to make the case to pass health reform.

Despite all the false starts and setbacks for health reform, Ricchetti himself was in an optimistic mood when he went home to Ohio for the holidays. From his contacts in the Senate, he believed that if the administration moved swiftly and surely, it could seal a deal that would win sixty and perhaps sixty-two votes — more than enough to forestall a filibuster.

Then the political world changed again, with crushing impact.

On the night of December 19, CNN broadcast excerpts from allegations in an article to be released the next day by the *American Spectator*, a right-wing publication that had been attacking the Clintons incessantly throughout the year. "Living with the Clintons: Bill's Arkansas Bodyguards Tell the Story the Press Missed," by David Brock, was a lurid exposé of supposed extramarital affairs Bill Clinton had while serving as Arkansas governor. It was based upon charges made by four Arkansas state troopers, two of them anonymous. CNN's report gave those charges a national airing.

Two days later, on December 21, a front-page article in the *Los Angeles Times* added further fuel, with the charge by two of the troopers — immediately denied by the White House — "that Clinton, as president, sought to discourage them from speaking out by offering them federal jobs."

On Christmas Eve, a *New York Times* article damaged the credibility of the two troopers when it disclosed they had been involved in a fraudulent $100,000 insurance claim from a 1990 auto incident; their allegations about Clinton were never proven, but "Troopergate" had been born. It stirred old stories about Clinton's infidelities and focused new press attention on Clinton's actions in Arkansas, especially his and the First Lady's involvement in the late 1970s in a real estate development deal called Whitewater.

From his Ohio home that Christmas, Steve Ricchetti followed the press reports with dismay and disgust. How could this be happening now? he thought. They were obscene, even the timing of them obscene. But if these stories continued, he said to himself, they would diminish the political capital the President and First Lady would have available when Congress returned in January, threatening again to erode legislative prospects.

The First Lady reacted no less emotionally. After all the frustrations and batterings from political foes during the previous months, that period from late November to Christmas had been the best of times for her as well as for her husband. "We thought we had a real window," she recalled. "I said to Bill after NAFTA passed and his ratings were so high, 'Well, I wonder what's in their arsenal now.' We soon found out. We had Troopergate. We had Whitewater as an issue, and in the immortal words of Rush Limbaugh, 'Whitewater's about health care.' We had to deal with this whole onslaught. We were under siege again."

Harold Ickes arrived in the White House two days after the New Year of 1994 and set up shop in his West Wing basement office. As deputy White House chief of staff, his charter was broad and his power great. A longtime friend and confidant of both Bill and Hillary Clinton, a connection that began years back when they had all been involved in the antiwar movement, Ickes was chosen to be the political director of the health care reform battle in its critical final phase, as Jay Rockefeller had long urged. Ickes seemed just the commander they needed to win this war.

The Clintons over many years had come to rely on Ickes's judgment and candid, no-nonsense advice. They dined often with him when they went to New York, where Ickes practiced law. Tough, crisp, direct, a slender man with thinning hair, a lean, long face, cleft chin. and an intent manner that gave his blue eyes a hard, cold, piercing look, Ickes had the political savvy and experience lacking inside the Clinton White House.

At fifty-four, Harold Ickes had spent most of his adult life in progressive political causes. In the civil rights movement in the 1960s, he was beaten so severely during voter registration protests in Louisiana that he lost a kidney. In 1968, when dissent against the Vietnam War swept campuses, Ickes, then just four years out of college himself, became co-manager of Eugene McCarthy's antiwar presidential campaign. After that came presidential campaign service for some of the brightest names in the Democratic Party: Edmund Muskie, Morris K. Udall, Ted Kennedy, Walter Mondale, Jesse Jackson. In 1992, he managed Clinton's New York presidential primary campaign, that summer ran his nominating convention, and later served on his presidential transition committee.

Unlike many of the Clinton people, Ickes was no stranger to Washington. By birth and personal connections, he was part of the Democratic Establishment. His father, Harold Ickes Sr., was a progressive muckraking journalist and crusading Chicago lawyer with a legendary temper — the "Old Curmudgeon," he was called — who was one of the original Bull Moosers for Theodore Roosevelt's third party effort in 1912. He became FDR's first secretary of the Interior, and one of the New Deal's leading lights. One of the first things the son did after moving into his new White House office was to hang a photograph of his father laying the cornerstone at the Interior Department in the mid-1930s. A scrawled inscription read: "To Harold — Stop making mudpies. Franklin Roosevelt."

Though Ickes grew up in Washington, graduating from the prestigious Sidwell Friends School, he had never felt a part of the capital and had never worked there as an adult. His mother was embittered by her experience in Washington after his famous father's death. Ickes was only twelve when his father died at the age of seventy-seven in 1952, but he saw through his mother's eyes how people ignored her after her powerful husband was gone.

The son shared his mother's distrust of the fickleness of Washington. After his high school graduation, he left Washington never to return as a resident. Literally and figuratively, Harold Ickes had turned his back on Washington, and, for a long period, a traditional career path. For three years after high school, he was a wanderer, restlessly exploring other avenues of American life, a journey that led him to Western rodeos, roping calves and herding cattle, and then into the emotional causes that shaped his future life and his attitudes about government and politics. He didn't graduate from college, at Stanford, until seven years after high school; another seven years elapsed before, at age thirty-two, he earned his law degree from Columbia University.

Like Ira Magaziner, whom he in no other way resembled, Ickes was acutely aware of his lack of Washington expertise. He worried about it, worried, too, whether he was up to taking on such a difficult role in leading the President's health care reform fight, especially a battle that had already received so many serious setbacks and for which he had no policy or legislative background.

After anguishing over whether to remain in New York or help the President and the First Lady win a reform that he, like them, believed fundamental, Ickes accepted their offer and prepared to take hold and reenergize the sinking health care effort. Instead, from virtually the first moment, he found himself diverted by the most serious political problem yet to hit the Clinton administration.

By that first week in January 1994, a familiar capital phenomenon was occurring. There was blood in the water, and the sharks were circling. Now the press focus switched from Troopergate to Whitewater. With the scent of scandal in the air, the question being raised in story after story, in print, radio, and over TV, was whether that long-ago Arkansas development deal represented a genuine scandal that could topple yet another President.

In a time of deepening public cynicism about The System, Whitewater struck with stunning force.

The story wasn't new.

It began in 1978, when Bill and Hillary Clinton, together with another Arkansas couple, Jim and Susan McDougal, purchased 230 acres along the White River in northern Arkansas. Clinton had met McDougal in the final and unsuccessful reelection campaign of Senator J. William Fulbright. In 1979, after Clinton was elected governor of Arkansas, the Whitewater Development Corporation was formed, and the White River property deeded to the corporation. Three years later McDougal acquired Woodruff Savings and Loan of McCrory, Arkansas, changed its name to Madison Guaranty, and moved its principal office to Little Rock.

In the spring of 1984, the Federal Home Loan Bank Board issued a critical report on Madison stating, "Substantial profits from the service corporation on the sale of real estate owned have been improperly recognized. Such profits were recognized as a result of contract sales and submarket interest rates. Correcting entries will adversely affect net worth and result in an insolvent position." The next year, 1985, Hillary Clinton and the Rose Law Firm in Little Rock, where she was a partner, represented Madison before the Arkansas Securities Department concerning Madison's recapitalization plan. That same spring Jim McDougal held a fundraiser to help retire Clinton's 1984 gubernatorial campaign debt; questions were later raised about whether those funds might have been improperly diverted from Madison to the Clinton campaign. Finally, three years later, on March 2, 1989, federal regulators closed Madison with estimated losses of $60 million. That November Jim McDougal was indicted on bank fraud. He was acquitted in 1990.

All this formed the background for the first national attention to what came to be called Whitewater. On March 8, 1992, an article by Jeff Gerth in the *New York Times* revealed the involvement of both Clintons in Madison and in Whitewater. That story, coming in the midst of the 1992 presidential campaign, led to the release of a report from the Clinton campaign claiming that the Clintons were "passive investors" who invested and lost nearly $69,000 on Whitewater. That first national Whitewater story did not lead to other revelations; the matter quickly dropped off the public screen. But it had a direct effect with major consequences: It prompted a Resolution Trust Corporation investigation of Whitewater by the RTC's Kansas City office. By September of 1992, as the presidential contest was reaching its final phase, the inquiry led to a criminal referral from the Kansas City RTC office to the U.S. Attorney in Little Rock. The referral, about a Madison check-writing scheme, mentioned the Clintons as witnesses. It made no allegations about them, and attracted no public notice.

There the matter slumbered as Clinton became President and advanced the ambitious agenda of his first year. Months later, a tragic event dramatically heightened interest in the Clintons, the White House Arkansas connections, and Whitewater.

Late in the afternoon of July 20, the body of Vincent Foster, deputy White House counsel and boyhood friend of Bill Clinton and former Little Rock law partner of Hillary Clinton, was found in an old, isolated Civil War fort on federal parkland overlooking the Potomac in nearby Virginia. He had been shot in the temple. A pistol was clutched in his right hand. Discovery of his body came only hours after Foster had left his White House office, seemingly in good spirits, and immediately after having been congratulated by colleagues for successfully shepherding two widely praised presidential nominations through the difficult confirmation process — the new Supreme Court justice, Ruth Bader Ginsburg, and the FBI's new director, Louis J. Freeh, who was sworn in that very day by the President in a sunlit Rose Garden ceremony.

Vince Foster's death, ruled a suicide after extensive official investigation showed he had been deeply depressed and was seeking medical help, sparked lurid conspiracy theories. All subsequent negative criminal investigatory findings notwithstanding, these conspiracy theories deepened from that day forward as the Foster suicide — murder, the rumormongers claimed, even directly alleging complicity by the Clintons — became a staple on conservative radio talk shows and in publications nationwide. These intensified when it was disclosed months later in December 1993 in an article in the conservative *Washington Times* that certain files, including some dealing with the Clintons' Whitewater investment, had been removed from Foster's White House office the night of his death after Bernard Nussbaum, Foster's boss and White House counsel, accompanied by Patsy Thomasson, an Arkansan and director of the White House Office of Administration, and Maggie Williams, Hillary Clinton's chief of staff, entered Foster's office.

At that point, Foster and Whitewater were joined, as salacious gossip from Troopergate was widely aired.

Though the public was unaware of it, the Whitewater investigation had been quietly proceeding for months, posing potential damage to the Clinton administration. Between August and September of Clinton's first year in the White House, nine additional criminal referrals relating to Madison Guaranty were compiled by the RTC's Kansas City office. None alleged criminality on the part of the Clintons. At the end of September, all nine were forwarded to RTC headquarters in Washington for review. At that point, high administration officials were drawn into the inquiry, primarily because Roger Altman, since 1993 deputy secretary of the Treasury, had months before been named interim chief executive officer of RTC and was thus responsible for overseeing RTC's actions.

Private briefings began between Treasury and RTC officials — and, inevitably, leaks began spouting from within the bureaucracy to congressional opponents of Clinton. By early October, Clinton himself had been informed by his close aide and longtime Arkansas political associate, Bruce Lindsay, about the criminal referrals. Days later, the nine criminal referrals were sent to the Justice Department for consideration, prompting meetings between Clinton White House aides and Treasury staff over how to deal with potential "press inquiries."

Within a month, House Republicans, sensing an issue that could embarrass and possibly seriously wound the Clinton administration — another Watergate, GOP political strategists began saying privately — seized the opportunity to turn the tables on Democrats who had long investigated Reagan and Bush administration officials.

When in early December Republican requests for congressional hearings on the failure of Madison Guaranty were turned down by Democratic congressional leaders and committee heads, the Republicans upped the ante. They demanded access to Madison documents from federal regulators. Then, they began publicly calling for a special prosecutor to investigate Whitewater. On December 15, four days before the surfacing of Troopergate, Jeff Gerth of the *New York Times* reexamined the Whitewater case, setting the stage for other stories to come.

All this took place against a backdrop of a generation conditioned to expect the worst from public officials, and a press with a penchant to turn any hints of wrongdoing into a full-fledged scandal, tagging them all with the soubriquet "*-gate.*" From Watergate, a genuine and extensive criminal conspiracy that led to a score of criminal convictions of White House aides and impeachment proceedings against a President, had flowed a succession of supposed scandals in administration after administration. Most were minor. Even the meaning of their names was quickly forgotten — Billygate, Peanutgate, Koreagate — still, they came, one after the other, and not only from the more sensational tabloid journals, but from the mainstream press as well. In Clinton's first year, these multiplied rapidly: Nannygate. Travelgate. Troopergate. Finally, perhaps inevitably, came Whitewatergate.

These all created static on the screen of national attention. At the very least, they distracted the public from policy battles the President was trying to wage and carried a potential danger of eroding his authority to lead — a precious commodity already in short supply because of the narrowness of his presidential victory and the doubts about his character sown in his campaign.

In Whitewater, the "scandal," if there was one, was exceedingly murky. The land and financial dealings long antedated Clinton's race for the presidency; some even went back fourteen years before he came to Washington. In the Whitewater investigations conducted from 1992 through 1995 by special prosecutors and congressional committees, no illegal actions were ever even alleged on the part of Bill and Hillary Clinton. Some serious questions were raised about the handling of Whitewater papers, especially in the frantic hours and days following the suicide of Vince Foster. White House counsel Bernard Nussbaum infuriated Justice Department officials by throwing up a protective screen around the office where Foster had worked as his deputy handling some aspects of the Whitewater inquiry. A dozen White House aides were subpoenaed and sworn in as witnesses at congressional hearings, creating an indelible portrait of official complicity in *something*. But the Clintons were never shown to have come near to the lawbreaking and obstruction of justice that destroyed Richard Nixon's presidency. Nonetheless, in a time of pervasive cynicism, the saga of Whitewater made it harder than ever for The System to work. And it burst with sufficient force to threaten another presidency.

It was into this atmosphere of suspicion and distrust that Harold Ickes entered the White House. For his first two weeks on the job, when he should have been focusing on health reform, Ickes spent nearly all his time coordinating the White House response to the torrent of Whitewater stories and the rising clamor for Clinton's attorney general, Janet Reno, to appoint a special prosecutor to investigate the complex, nearly incomprehensible, situation.

By the end of those first two weeks in January, Whitewater had taken on a life of its own. It dominated the news to such an extent that the *Washington Post*'s "National Weekly Edition" devoted its full first page to a bold headline "**WHITEWATER**," with a subhead "More Questions Than Answers." Beneath was a color photo of the waving, smiling First Couple superimposed over a fragment of daily headlines culled from such recent mainstream daily publications as the *Post*, the *Times*, and the *Wall Street Journal*. All of them suggested sinister dealings involving the President and the First Lady: "Ever-Growing Paper Trail: Whitewater Records Go from Nothing to Volumes" . . . "Janet Reno's Shameful Delay . . . How Bad Is It?" . . . "On Arkansas Sex, Not Inhaling, and Whitewater" . . . "A Special Counsel for Whitewater."

Along with the daily flood of new stories came an inevitable political reaction as Republicans linked Whitewater with health reform, raising doubts that the public could trust Clinton in either case.

Ickes understood perfectly how serious a problem Whitewater

represented for the President, and for the fragile prospects for health reform passage. Already, opponents had succeeded in sowing doubts about the Clinton plan, and especially about the Big Government dangers they said it contained. "It's going to come down to public faith in the President and the First Lady," Ickes said, looking weary and drawn in his basement White House office, some weeks after beginning his job. "That is why Whitewater and these related problems hold real danger for this effort, because it erodes the public confidence in him and her.

"Our research shows this is very, very personal. People don't give — to use the vernacular — a fuck about the national interest when they think about health reform. They want to know: How is this going to affect me, my children, my parents? You can talk national interest until you're blue in the face, but they want to know: Is it going to help me or hurt me? That's why trust in the Clintons is going to be a critical element in carrying the day on this."

The President had one last chance to draw public attention back to health reform before the congressional process wrestled with the actual legislative proposals, and once more Clinton's political consultants and White House strategists concentrated on a nationally televised speech — the President's State of the Union address before a joint session of Congress on January 25. This time, the President faced an even greater test of political salesmanship.

Four days after Ickes began his job, Stan Greenberg gave him an update on his latest polling data at the White House. His message was not reassuring. Voters believed health reform less important for the Clinton legislative agenda in 1994 than eliminating the deficit, cutting government spending, and combating crime. While public support for the Clinton plan was holding at 52 percent, the pollster said, the negatives were up sharply. Significantly, the public responded more negatively when asked whether the Clinton reform would help or hurt their families. Even more alarmingly, Greenberg reported, Clinton's job approval on health care had dropped 7 percent, to 50 percent approval. That was an all-time low in Greenberg's data. "We've had a collapse in seniors' support," he told him, "with more opposing now than favoring our plan."

The four factors Greenberg found most critical in the debate underscored how seriously public confidence in both the President and the First Lady had eroded in recent weeks. First on Greenberg's critical list was "trust in POTUS." Second was "trust in HRC." Ranked behind them in importance was how to define the health battle for the public, then how to reassure people about how the reform would affect them.

In a city of anonymous bureaucrats and aides, Lawrence O'Donnell Jr. stood out. As chief of staff of the powerful Senate Finance Committee, chaired by Senator Daniel Patrick Moynihan, O'Donnell was one of those players who made The System work. Moynihan and his committee would be crucial in the health battle, and O'Donnell, his top aide, then forty-two, wielded considerable behind-the-scenes influence on his own.

While The System celebrated the skills of the insider, O'Donnell gloried in being the outrageous outsider. He rode a Harley-Davidson motorcycle to work, was married to the actress Kathryn Harrold, and commuted to their New York City apartment on weekends; they also maintained a home in Los Angeles. Little about him bespoke the traditional path to power; he had not worked in Washington before 1992. After graduating in 1976 with an economics degree from Harvard, where he had been on the staff of the humor magazine *The Harvard Lampoon*, O'Donnell wrote scripts for TV pilots and articles for publications including *Vanity Fair, People*, and *Spy*.

In 1983, while still in his twenties, his book *Deadly Force* was published. It was later made into a CBS movie, for which O'Donnell wrote the screenplay. His defiant attitude, his long association with the celebrity worlds of New York, Hollywood, and the Hamptons, even his manner of speaking, set him apart from the normal world of Washington. He spoke with a torrent of words laced with pungent and often profane observations about other political players, and he had a habit during animated conversation of tossing his head back and running his hands nervously through his long, prematurely graying hair.

O'Donnell was more than flamboyant. On the Hill, and in the

White House, he was intensely controversial. Many thought him arrogant and destructive. "Prince Lawrence," he was called derisively. "He has an ego bigger than the Capitol Dome," one top official said. "Contemptuous" was a term often applied to O'Donnell; but no one doubted his influence, his shrewdness, or his toughness. He was devoted to Pat Moynihan, whom he had met through Moynihan's daughter Maura, and became active in the senator's 1988 reelection campaign. O'Donnell's roots were in Boston. His father had been a Boston cop who worked his way through law school and became a prominent defense lawyer. Through close observation of his father's cases, O'Donnell came to understand that the people his father defended did not necessarily have to be innocent and to appreciate the complexity of the law — and to recognize the ability, often even the correctness, of people on the other side. To O'Donnell, that essential cast of mind, that "critical gene," as he put it, sadly didn't make it into the health care deliberations inside the Clinton White House.

O'Donnell distrusted the Clinton planners, especially Magaziner. He thought them politically naive and impractical. They struck him as being on a religious crusade. If you spoke to them realistically, he found, they reacted as if you were an atheist, or were plotting against them. Nonetheless, O'Donnell held forth for two hours telling stories and explaining Senate personalities at a White House luncheon for Finance Committee staff the first week in January 1994. O'Donnell told the Clinton team the fate of reform would not be decided by technocrats like them; instead the final deal would be pure politics.

Sometime next June, he said, Pat Moynihan and Bob Dole will decide what they can live with, and Dole will show Moynihan the list of votes that he can produce for passage. Then they'll all come to the Oval Office and lay out the deal with the President. It will probably be something like the bill Chafee has proposed. Magaziner might be the only person in the room who understands that the deal doesn't quite achieve guaranteed, can't-take-it-away universal coverage for every American. But, O'Donnell said, we'll show you how this legislation will reduce the numbers of uninsured from, say, thirty-seven to seventeen or so million people. We'll fudge the remaining figures. Then you'll have a presidential moment enabling them all to claim success.

"Oh, he'll veto that," O'Donnell remembers Magaziner saying afterward while they talked alone in a White House hallway.

"He would?" an astonished O'Donnell replied.

"Oh, yes, absolutely," he says Magaziner insisted. That bill doesn't have enough money to pay for universal coverage; it wouldn't get by CBO [Congressional Budget Office].

"I immediately got myself out of the conversation," O'Donnell said, with typical contempt, "because I knew I was talking to a child in terms of understanding strategic legislative action. And I hoped I was talking to someone who would not be in the room for that presidential moment."

Magaziner did pass on his conversation with O'Donnell to the President, but Clinton discounted O'Donnell's judgment. There were more important players who would carry greater weight.

Three weeks later, O'Donnell sat in the front row of the House chamber as Clinton gave his State of the Union address. In the most dramatic moment of the speech, a moment that became engraved in the public mind, Clinton unequivocally laid down the gauntlet, promising to fight to the end. "If you send me legislation that does not guarantee every American private health insurance that can never be taken away," the President said, his voice rising, "you will force me to take this pen" — he waved it theatrically — "veto the legislation, and we'll come right back here and start all over again."

Listening, O'Donnell froze. He couldn't believe what he was hearing. He had a sudden, horrible, sinking feeling that what he had said to Magaziner twenty days earlier had provoked a chain of counsel to the President that locked him into this intractable veto pledge. A tragic mistake, he thought. It was almost always a mistake for any politician to draw a line in the sand at such an early stage in a delicate, complex political negotiation — especially something as controversial as health reform. Oh, my God, O'Donnell said to himself. This veto threat could kill health reform on the Hill.

Stan Greenberg's Dayton, Ohio, "dial group" had similar misgivings about Clinton's State of the Union address. Fearful of more bad news leaking to the press, Greenberg distributed a confidential memo to only seven in the White House, carefully numbering each memo and listing the names and numbers of each person who received it: 1. President Bill Clinton. 2. Vice President Al Gore. 3. Hillary Rodham Clinton. 4. Mack McLarty. 5. George Stephanopoulos. 6. David Gergen. 7. Harold Ickes. For Memo copy No. 8, he listed his own name.

Clinton's lengthy discussion of foreign affairs sparked the least interest: "Incredibly flat," Greenberg wrote of voter reactions. The biggest moment in the speech came when voters responded over- whelmingly to a passage about crime, when the President said those who commit repeated, violent crimes should be told that when they commit a third violent crime, they will be put away, and put away for good. "Three strikes, and you are out," he said. The President's health reform section did not draw as strong a response as those on crime and welfare, where he promised to "revolutionize our welfare system" and "reward work over welfare." His welfare prescription was filled with tough rhetoric: Teenagers who had a child out of wedlock would be denied checks to set up separate households; ab- sent parents who failed to pay their child support would have their wages garnisheed, be pursued across state lines by authorities, and, if necessary, be forced to work to meet their obligations.

Some members of Greenberg's focus group were chosen to reflect the attitudes of Perot voters, who were likely to be decisive in the next presidential election. Perot voters "began very skeptically on health care," the pollster noted. "While Clinton voters jumped up on al- most any mention of health care, Perot voters moved up reluctantly. They responded, not to the general discussion, but to the specific charge that insurance companies are calling the shots, to the need for a comprehensive package, and to the commitment not to squeeze seniors."

The reaction was anything but positive, and the President's melo- dramatic waving of his "veto pen" had not accomplished what his political strategists hoped.

Clinton made that unequivocal pledge on the advice of his com- bative political consultants and amid mixed signals from Democratic leadership in Congress. Speaker Foley, who learned of it during a White House meeting just the night before the President's speech, recalled that he "wasn't too happy about it. I don't like deadlines.

I don't like that kind of categorical threat.' It was dangerous, he thought. Presidents should not lock themselves into irrevocable positions on important and controversial legislation. "You don't need that," he said. "You can always say what you hope to accomplish without saying, 'I will take this pen and veto it.' "

But Dick Gephardt, the number two House Democrat, reflected the view of many Democrats who supported reform, but "wanted to be assured that if they took the lead on reform he'd stick with them and would ultimately veto a bill that didn't do X, Y, and Z." The First Lady and her team supported the Gephardt plea that the President give a strong message to rally his wavering supporters. They knew what formidable opposition he was now facing, and they wanted him to signal in the strongest possible way his determination to fight. Clinton had to counter the feeling on Capitol Hill that he wasn't a fighter, that he was a trimmer who would cave under pressure, that he would let down those who stuck their necks out for him. The President thought he had ended that problem when he battled majorities in his own party to pass NAFTA and took on the National Rifle Association over the Brady bill. But, he was told, House Democrats still remembered him "making them walk the plank on the BTU [energy] tax" in his budget bill and then capitulating quickly to Senate opposition.

When the time came for the speech tryout in the White House family theater, the consensus of his aides and advisers was that the veto threat made good political sense. "We thought if we did this, we could energize our own supporters, increase the chance that the Republicans would submit a good bill, and that we could then engage in a real serious dialogue," the President told us later. In his mind, as always, was the memory of how other Presidents had tried and failed in this very battle. As he told us, "There was a reason this had never happened before. There was a reason that Truman proposed these things twice and got murdered. There was a reason that Richard Nixon had this proposal and it didn't get out of committee when he had a Democratic Congress. There was a reason that none of this stuff ever happened — because the forces against change were more powerful."

He thought he could send them a message that he would not

quit without a victory. That it didn't work out was no surprise to the dissenters, inside and outside the White House. Walter Zelman, Magaziner's top health aide, saw it as a political blunder, because "it boxed us in" and meant "we couldn't shift gears." Billy Pitts, a top aide to House GOP leader Bob Michel, thought it signified a lack of trust among Democrats in both their congressional leaders and in their President.

In time, the President himself came to regret making that dramatic gesture. "I shouldn't have issued the veto threat as it turns out," he told us.

The barrage of Whitewater stories continued, creating a siege mentality at the White House and emboldening foes of health reform, who became more and more aggressive in criticizing the Clinton plan — and the Clintons.

Republicans openly embraced the latest advice of the conservative strategist William Kristol: Oppose any Clinton health reform "sight unseen." Now, at every opportunity, they also publicly adopted Kristol's phrase: "There is no health care crisis."

Bob Dole used this language in the nationally televised Republican response to the President's State of the Union address that January 25. "Our country has health care problems, but not a health care crisis," Dole said. "But we will have a crisis if we take the President's medicine — a massive overdose of government control. . . . Clearly, the President is asking you to trust the government more than you trust your doctor and yourselves with your lives and the lives of your loved ones. More cost, less choice, more taxes, less quality, more government control and less control for you and your family — that's what the President's government-run plan is likely to give you." Even if you discount for partisan rhetoric, it was a notably tough message from the man Pat Moynihan counted on as his negotiating partner in putting together a compromise bill in the Senate Finance Committee.

During his talk, Dole employed a Rube Goldberg–like chart to hammer home his points: It's government-run health care. If adopted, it would result in a greater intervention into the private economy and people's lives than all the New Deal and Great Society programs put together. It would abolish most current health care insurance. It would force the vast majority of people to leave their doctors and join health maintenance organizations (HMOs). And, almost certainly, it would lead to rationing.

The chart, first used by Senator Arlen Specter of Pennsylvania, depicted a bewildering array of new government agencies and programs. Incomprehensible arrows and boxes bore labels of government bureaucratic acronyms run amok: PWBA, NGFSFHP, NQMP, CHBI, NLPP, NHDAC, PTAC, RAAC. Included were other confusing terms emanating from the Clinton plan that the public was attempting to understand: National Health Board (NHB), Regional Health Alliance (RHA), Corporate Health Alliance (CHA), FFS Provider Plan, HMO Provider Plan, PPO Provider Plan. Sprinkled throughout the chart were other words designed to trigger negative public reactions: taxes, regulation, drug-pricing scheme.

It was all negative, and all brilliantly effective. From then on, that chart became a centerpiece in Capitol Hill debates. It further frightened a public already suspicious of government and increasingly distrustful of the President and the First Lady who had designed this new government program.

Fear drove the debate from the beginning, as Republican Senator Bob Bennett of Utah said, first helping, then hurting Clinton. "Gradually," Bennett said, "that fear was directed at Clinton: 'Wait a minute, *I'm* going to lose my coverage because of Clinton.' The combination of the fear and loathing of Big Government — and the Clinton health plan was the symbol of Big Government — meant there was more fury against his plan than there ever had been driving for it. It just took on a life of its own, and it was incredible to watch."

It didn't "just happen," of course. Political calculations and elaborate anti-reform campaign planning by the special interests drove the debate. So did a critically influential — and intensely controversial — pair of articles that appeared about this time by a then-obscure young woman in New York named Elizabeth (Betsy) McCaughey, on the staff of the conservative Manhattan Institute. McCaughey's articles, first on the *Wall Street Journal*'s conservative editorial page and then in the liberal *New Republic*, were presented as an exhaustive scholarly analysis of the Clinton health plan.

She painted a devastating, and fearsome, account of the impact

of the Clinton plan — a plan, she wrote, that offered "No Exit" to
the patient trapped in a giant, repressive, new governmental bureaucracy. As she portrayed the Clinton plan, it would mean that a
doctor could be paid only by the plan, not by the patient. Fee-for-
service medicine would be doomed. No longer would Americans be
able to choose their own doctor. And, among other dire aspects of
the plan McCaughey claimed to have discovered, another dangerous Big Brother would be created, threatening individual privacy
rights of patients by requiring doctors to report their clinical encounters to a "national data bank containing the medical histories of all
Americans."

No other articles more infuriated the White House for what it,
and other independent experts, regarded as patent falsehoods and
distortions of the Clinton plan. Michael Kinsley, in a caustic, detailed critique, dismissed her writing as a "screed." James Fallows,
examining her claims in *The Atlantic*, denounced them as "simply
false." At Yale, Theodore Marmor, professor of public policy, was
quoted as saying his fellow health experts, whether left, right, or
center politically, considered the McCaughey articles risible. And
Mickey Kaus, in perhaps the strongest and most devastating critique
based on analyzing McCaughey's nine thousand words and the tens
of thousands more words of controversy that followed, concluded in
a *New Republic* article, "She got some things right. But she got a
lot wrong. In the process, she completely distorted the debate on the
biggest public policy issue of 1994." Notwithstanding such criticism,
the articles became highly influential, especially in conservative circles. Speaker Gingrich, for one, told us those articles were "the first
decisive break point" in support for the Clinton plan. "They never
recovered from her analysis. From that point on, it was all downhill." The controversy did not hurt McCaughey. On the contrary, it
served as a springboard for her. Though she had no prior experience
as a political candidate, she was elected the Republican lieutenant
governor of New York in the great conservative sweep of 1994 after
health reform had died. Her articles stand as a classic example of
what Senator Bennett meant when he remarked that fear drove the
debate.

Sowing distrust of the Clinton plan meshed with the efforts to use

Whitewater to undermine trust in the Clintons themselves in a growing wave of stories in conservative publications and radio talk shows.
"When the Whitewater stuff began coming out, that's when the real
rabid conservatives began saying, 'We found the crack, we found the
crack. Now is the time to force that crack open as wide as we can make
it,' " said Christy Ferguson, Republican Senator John Chafee's key
health care staff member, and someone who had worked for years
to pass a Republican reform bill. "That's when the no-health-care-
reform stuff started. People were saying, 'We're going to win. This
is a major thing. This is another Watergate.' "

The pounding affected not only the President's credibility. Now,
increasingly, the First Lady was the target of negative stories. Even
on the day of the State of the Union address, Harvard's Bob Blendon
was warning that any damage to Hillary Clinton could deliver a fatal blow to health reform. "She has the credibility the rest of them
don't have," he said then. Two days later, in a private conversation,
AARP's John Rother expressed similar fears. "Whitewater seems to
go much more to Hillary than to Bill," he said. "If there's one person you can't afford to lose, it's Hillary. The thought that she would
be touched by this and in any way brought down from where she is
would be a really huge setback."

Already Hillary's credibility was eroding; the worst was soon
to come. Within weeks, stories surfaced about her stunningly successful 1978–79 commodities trading in Arkansas when her husband was the state's attorney general. These stories suggested she
had received favored treatment. Her trading in cattle futures, arranged at the time through a close friend, Jim Blair, an attorney for
Tyson Food Inc. — the single most powerful economic interest in
Arkansas — was remarkably profitable. From a modest investment
of $1000 in October 1978, she realized net gains of $26,541 that
year — and profits of $5300 on the first day of trading alone. She
earned an additional $72,996 for seven months of trading the next
year. Then she got out of the commodities market.

As with the Whitewater stories, no wrongdoing by Hillary Clinton
was ever proved. But that didn't matter; politically, the damage
was done. The disclosures about her high-rolling market ventures
gravely undercut her criticisms about the speculative orgy of the

eighties. She had cashed in big during what liberals liked to call "a decade of greed" — a point critics immediately, and repeatedly, made. Her moral authority had been diminished. The woman who had used her White House platform to condemn "profiteering" by insurance companies and pharmaceutical companies had turned a nice profit herself. It was an almost unbelievable turn of events for someone who only a few months before was hailed as a new Icon, a First Lady so popular and powerful that members of Congress fawned, as one remarked cynically then, "to touch the hem of Hillary Clinton."

Early in February, another sleazy story dealt another blow to the President. A former Arkansas state employee named Paula Corbin Jones announced, during a Washington news session arranged by the Conservative Political Action Conference, that she was filing a lawsuit against the President. She claimed he had sent state troopers to bring her to a Little Rock hotel room, where the then governor propositioned her for sex. In the suit filed those many years later, she charged that Clinton had sexually harassed her and violated her civil rights while he was governor and therefore her boss. No President had ever been the subject of such demeaning legal action. Once again, the allegations were unproven, but the damage was incalculable, raising further suspicions about the character of the President.

Private and public polls tracked a steady drop — a "nosedive," Ira Magaziner called it — in support for the reform and in trust for the President and the First Lady. From a seventeen-point spread in favor of the Clinton plan at the end of December, surveys at the end of March showed, for the first time, more people polled opposed the reform than favored it. And Hillary's personal standing plummeted even more than her husband's.

Political enemies, fate, even the elements, seemed to conspire against the effort: Harold Ickes, barely on the job and diverted totally to Whitewater damage control, slipped on the ice going to a Georgetown dinner party and broke three ribs. He sat through the dinner, then in mounting pain was driven to the hospital by another guest and administration colleague, Donna Shalala. In a final note of exquisite irony, at first the hospital demanded cash payment in advance of emergency treatment because Ickes's government insurance was not yet in effect. As Jay Rockefeller said after learning of the accident, "It's a perfect metaphor for where we are."

With his gift for expression, Jim McDermott perfectly described the poisonous atmosphere of Whitewater enveloping Washington in late winter and early spring of 1994. "It's like when you go into Los Angeles and notice this gray layer over the horizon," the congressman from the state of Washington said. "At first you don't see it, then you do. It's subliminal. It saps the energy. It's like a political smog that's settled. Whether the Santa Ana winds will come and blow it away, I don't know. But I do know you can't help noticing it and being affected by it."

Now Whitewater was everywhere, and affecting everyone. It seeped into conversations, leaped out in daily headlines, blared from television sets, boomed on radio talk show commentary, and became the subject of increasingly venomous conspiracy theories — about Vince Foster, the Clintons, the Rose Law Firm — in broadcasts, in publications, in full-page newspaper ads. In one week in mid-March, at the peak of the press frenzy, the nation's seven largest newspapers published ninety-two Whitewater stories. During that one month, the three TV networks aired one hundred twenty-six Whitewater stories. By comparison, from the first of the year to the end of March, the three networks aired one hundred seven stories on Bosnia, fifty-six on the Middle East, and forty-two on the health care debate. More Whitewater newspaper stories were published in major papers than on the combined total of health care, welfare, and crime legislation.

Republicans had seized on Whitewater even more aggressively, directly linking it and health reform.

How they combined these issues to maximum political effect — and how they used The System to get their message across to the public — can be seen in a letter that Lamar Smith of Texas sent each of his House Republican colleagues and all their administrative assistants and press secretaries toward the end of March. As chairman of the House Republican "Theme Team," Smith was part of Newt Gingrich's network, and by March, Gingrich was openly trying to derail the Clinton plan by any means available. In a speech that month he warned that "the Democratic leadership will try to ram through a secret Clinton plan because they can't pass an open Clinton plan." Smith urged his colleagues to focus on one theme in their speeches, columns for the press, and media and constituent contacts for the next week. The theme: "Whitewater and Health Care." As Smith wrote, "Whitewater and health care. The Clinton administration and the Democratic leadership cannot get past the first one, so Congress cannot get to the second. Whitewater raises fundamental questions as to how equipped Congress is to oversee a nationalized health care system. . . . The Democrats cannot get past Whitewater and to health care until they admit that full disclosure congressional hearings lie in front of them."

Included in the congressman's four-page letter were quotes to be used by all GOP colleagues day after day. Each linked Whitewater and health care. The first "quote of the day" read "Small business owners must look at the first family with a mixture of envy and anger. Envy at how they may have avoided paying many taxes over the years, and anger at their decision to sock it to the middle class." Among many other suggested "attack" quotes aimed to hit "a government-owned, government-run, taxpayer-insured health program" was a typical comment from Mac Collins, a Republican from Georgia: "The Whitewater development was a small business. Whitewater failed, probably due to undercapitalization. That reminds me of the First Lady's comments when she was asked about the effects of the President's health care plan on small business, and I quote: 'I cannot be responsible for every undercapitalized small business.' " Another quote that expressed the common theme came from Wisconsin's Toby Roth: "The cancer of the Whitewater/Madison scandal, Mr. Speaker, is robbing the presidency of what little integrity it has left."

From Rush Limbaugh, the conservative talk show host with an audience of millions, came an almost daily assault. "I think Whitewater is about health care," he said. "Most people think that health care is a good idea, but they haven't read the plan. They're taking the President's word for it. Now. . . if people are going to base their support for the plan on whether they can take his word, I think it's fair to examine whether or not he keeps his word. This is not about getting rid of the President. This is about people who would like to stop health care in a legitimate democratic sense, trying to compete for the minds and hearts of the American people on the basis that maybe what the President's saying isn't true."

The lowest moment came when Limbaugh went on the air to broadcast a wild rumor he had received in a fax from a conservative newsletter published in California: that Vince Foster had been murdered in a Washington apartment owned by Hillary Clinton. Then, Foster's body was moved to the park in Virginia. Airing of that outrageously irresponsible rumor — totally false — caused the stock and bond markets to plunge sharply. Limbaugh defended his broadcast by saying, "That's what it said in the fax."

By then, Attorney General Janet Reno had bowed to critics and appointed a special prosecutor. Increasingly nervous Democrats on Capitol Hill, drawing farther away from a weakened President and First Lady, realized after weeks of acrimonious public debate that they would be unable to forestall Whitewater congressional hearings. They were scheduled to begin in mid-June — around the time congressional leaders hoped health care reform bills would have cleared committees and headed to the floor for final debate and votes on passage.

In his Senate office one night during this period, Harris Wofford found himself trying to remember what it was like during the Watergate days leading to Nixon's impeachment proceedings. There was a feeding frenzy then, too, he recalled, but that had been such a genuinely big scandal. Compared to that, this was nothing, he said. Now, he thought, the press on Clinton and Whitewater was the worst he'd known in his lifetime. He said,

> In a profound sense, this is going to be a real test of whether the better angels of our nature among all the key players — the legislators, the White House, the President — prevail, or whether we yield to various temptations. That's going to be the test for all of us. Passing health care is going to require all of us to compromise. But there's a temptation in what Rush Limbaugh represents and what a huge amount of people fear: that the government can't do anything right. It's fear and hostility. It's something that Phil Gramm knows how to tap. My

hope is that as we get toward an election, people are going to want to show that they're constructive and not destroyers. I may be proved wrong. The destroyers sometimes win.

Nowhere were the destructive effects of these suspicions and accusations more insidious than inside the White House. From the highest office to the lowest staff position, everyone was affected. Spirits were drained, morale diminished, attention diverted from other issues. The staff itself became divided.

Inside the Delivery Room, where the mostly anonymous staff continued to work long hours, Whitewater was demoralizing. "A lot of us at our level knew that we needed a Harold Ickes type, and we were looking forward internally to that kind of leadership inside the White House," said Jason Solomon, one of the young aides working there on communications strategy. "Then just when he gets here, he, Mrs. Clinton — everyone — had to deal with Whitewater all the time. It made us feel, What are we doing, how could this happen? Mrs. Clinton was a huge weapon for us in scheduling public events, then for a long period of time we couldn't get her out there. Because of Whitewater, you know." No one was immune. The senior staff, including Ickes, found themselves having to hire lawyers to answer questions about meetings they might have attended when Whitewater was discussed, even in passing. "You feel trapped," said George Stephanopoulos. "You know that until this cycle is broken, nothing we say is going to matter. Nobody's going to hear anything we say, no matter what. Every story is seen through the Whitewater prism."

The President tried to maintain a sunny public demeanor, but in private his emotions were not always in check. At night, in the White House family quarters, the President and the First Lady constantly discussed the Whitewater developments. "We talked about it all the time," the President later told us. "We thought it was just crazy. Here we are trying to do something that needs to be done. It's the opportunity of a generation, and every day there's three times as much coverage on this deal where we lost forty-eight thousand dollars that neither one of us had anything to do with until that whole thing came a cropper."

Clinton understood the immense political damage that White-water was causing him; and that knowledge only added to his great frustration:

> There's no question that during that time the people who didn't want anything to happen [on health reform] had time to get organized, raise money, mass their forces, develop their strategy. They saw us getting weaker and weaker under this Whitewater thing. It was maddening to me, frankly. I agreed to the Special Counsel even though I thought it was wrong, since no President had ever been subject to one before, for something unrelated to his service as President or to his campaign for President. I agreed to one in no small measure because I thought it was the only way that the press would permit me to be President and fight for health care and fight for the things I believed in.

As the weeks passed, and the Whitewater attacks multiplied, his frustrations rose. Like others who had seen past actions resurrected in embarrassing fashion, he began to sound very defensive: "For three months there I thought I was lost in the funhouse," he said. "I didn't know what had happened to my country. I just thought it was bizarre. I had to fight hard to keep my mind and my spirit in the right frame so that I could focus on what I was trying to do for the people. In that period I was more bewildered than anything else at the prospect that we would squander this historic opportunity to solve a major problem on something that didn't amount to a hill of beans."

He did not always succeed in maintaining his spirits. During that period, some senators got calls late at night from the President and listened as he expressed his frustration and rage. "It was the most gushing outpouring of rage, humiliation, frustration, I've ever heard," one of those the President phoned said shortly after their conversation. He sought their advice, wondered aloud how this could be happening, anguished about what they should do about it. Not only were they fighting a welter of rumors, he complained, they also had to figure out how to raise as much as a million dollars for legal bills for their defense. (Those legal bills continued to mount throughout 1995 and into 1996 as more hearings and investigations were held.)

"They've become paranoid," a cabinet officer who admired the Clintons said. "They think people are out to get them — this right-wing conspiracy stuff. They feel sorry for themselves. They talk about it all the time: 'There really is a conspiracy out there to get us. We don't have a chance. People don't understand how much good we've done. Our message isn't getting out because these people are beating us up.' "

Heavy as the toll was on the President, it was worse on the First Lady. Her staff, always protective of her, became even more so. "They adopted this bunker mentality," a senior White House staffer said. "It's the only thing you can call it. They basically run a flying wedge for her and keep away anything bad that she doesn't want to hear about. They've managed to build wall after wall around the First Lady, at least around her own operation, quite stupidly in my opinion. They are totally preoccupied with Whitewater, completely spooked about it. There is something rather Greek in the whole way it's been mishandled."

It was much more than a case of a zealous staff protecting an admired superior. The First Lady herself set the tone. Against the advice of many inside the White House and on Capitol Hill, she was adamant about not agreeing to the appointment of a special prosecutor, or turning over Whitewater documents, or releasing their tax returns from 1978 and 1979, or explaining her case to the public through a press she now distrusted even more than before. At one meeting, which quickly became a legend inside the White House, the First Lady launched into a tirade as soon as people began assembling in the room. She was so intense that people didn't get to sit down for the first twenty minutes. She angrily accused the White House staff members present of mishandling Whitewater, of treating it as serious when it was nothing, a deliberate right-wing diversion. They were making things worse for the President and her, she said furiously.

The longer she remained silent, the more she seemed to stonewall, the greater the suspicion she had something to hide. When, far too late, the Clinton tax returns were made public, more embarrassments occurred. Instead of the previously claimed loss of $69,000 on their Whitewater investment, they acknowledged they had lost nearly $21,000 less. The difference, the President explained, was because he had remembered a loan to his mother only while reading the galleys of her memoirs. Instead of Hillary having sustained losses in a second commodity-trading account, it turned out she hadn't. Instead of having stopped trading because she was about to give birth to her daughter, Chelsea, she hadn't.

The more the wagons were circled, the tighter the group around the First Lady grew. Once, in this period, a White House operative who criticized the First Lady's staff for failing to keep others there informed about her Whitewater defense plans was angrily attacked by Maggie Williams, Hillary's devoted chief of staff. "Maggie was ranting and raving for about ten minutes," this person said, "about how her only job was to protect Hillary — Hillary, Hillary, Hillary. And I said at the end: 'Maggie, the two words you didn't mention were "The President." ' It's stunning, isn't it?"

Understandably, as the daily assaults continued and grew more personal, the toll on the First Lady and her staff intensified. Melanne Verveer, one of her closest aides, regularly received transcripts of broadcasts about the First Lady, articles, and ads in publications like the *American Spectator* that offered bumper stickers and posters maligning the First Lady: "Heil Hillary," one read. Another showed her as a witch on a broom. Some of them, with sadistic appeal, used the President and the First Lady as targets, with their faces in the center of the bull's-eye. "She's probably the biggest fund-raiser the radical Right has ever had, between their direct mail and the other kind of stuff they are churning out," Verveer said.

Even the direct accusation that she had been involved in the murder of Vince Foster was broadcast on Jerry Falwell's Christian television broadcasts. "There's been a collective demonization, a portrayal of her that's completely off the mark, completely unjust," Verveer said. "It became very dispiriting to come to work, dispiriting on a lot of levels. One was that I knew these people. Hillary was the kind of person who would get up every day and say 'Do the best you can for other people.' But it got to the point after seeing herself described in ways that were totally unrecognizable where she was asking herself, 'What kind of person am I? Why is this happening?' It had terrible, corrosive impact."

Another White House staff member was struck by the sense of an unfolding tragedy that affected not only the politics of reform but also the First Lady's personality:

> Hillary is simultaneously incredibly rational, extraordinarily intelligent — everybody knows that — and yet blind as a bat to what people think of her and how to handle people. She's changed in one sense. She's a much sadder person than she was when she started this job. That's the only word I can use to describe her. I think the combination of the attacks on him and her and the death of her father, the disappearance of her private life, all in little more than a year, have made her a much more sober and sad person — much less believing, less idealistic, less sure that she can do certain things. As a result, as she's gotten more sad, she's become sharper at times. She's always had a very caustic edge to her. Well, it's gotten even sharper, that edge. It's razor-sharp now. When she loses it around a group of us, she gets dismissive. She gives you the look of death — basically like you're an idiot, you know.

An admirer on Capitol Hill was struck in this period by how the public Hillary seemed unaffected by the daily battering she was taking in the press and on the talk shows. She's got this pride that won't let her show her pain, this person said, describing a visit the First Lady made to a gathering of Democratic members of Congress. You would have thought it was the day after the election, he added. She was smiling, serious, poised, sharp.

In private sometimes, a different Hillary was displayed. "When you close the door and you're alone with her," said a friend, "she goes into this reflexive yawning that she cannot stop because she's past exhaustion. She's killed herself for this plan for the American people because she believes in it."

When the White House was not worrying about Whitewater, it worried about Bob Reischauer and his independent Congressional Budget Office (CBO).

As CBO director, Reischauer was supposed to provide objective, apolitical assessments of legislation's impact on the federal budget. He had a fixed four-year term that could not be changed — and he could not be removed — without a majority vote of both houses of Congress. Favorable analysis from CBO was critical for any measure; with health care, potentially the largest domestic governmental initiative ever, and already the most controversial and sweeping undertaking in a lifetime, a positive CBO finding could be decisive. A negative one could be fatal.

For months, relentless pressure had been building on Reischauer and his office about the analysis they would make of the Clinton plan. From Reischauer's perspective, he had two principal tasks. One was to render a careful estimate of the cost, a process called "scoring" by those inside the Beltway. To that end, he was determined to examine the impact of reform not only on the federal budget but on overall national health expenditures. The second was to decide how to treat these new creatures — the alliances. Should they be regarded as governmental agencies? If so, the premiums they collected from employers and individuals would be taxes, and the money they forwarded to insurers and health providers, government expenditures. Or were they private agencies? In that case, those billions would never show up on the federal budget.

This was the heart of the controversy. Fanning the flames on one side were Republicans. They wanted to portray the Clinton plan as a Big Government enterprise, and include everything as taxes and spending in the budget. On the other side were administration supporters, strongly arguing that the alliances were nongovernmental. Private expenditures by private companies would be mandated by the government, they insisted, but they were not government funds. "If I work for X company and they buy my health insurance, is that a government expenditure?" asked one top Democratic congressional aide. "No! No more than the fact that they pay minimum wages as required by the government or that they hire people required by OSHA. Those are not government expenditures."

In meetings with Clinton planners, Reischauer suggested a way to avoid the problem. They could accurately describe the new alliances in a budget appendix as something new, something never tried before, and promise a full accounting of them but not regard them as part of the budget.

The politics became intense, personal, and abusive. As Reischauer and his team of budget analysts — twenty in a larger working group, eight in a smaller one — wrestled with these questions about this vast new plan, he began receiving pointed inquiries.

Some Republicans, adopting a first-strike tactic, leaked word — incorrect though it was — that Reischauer had decided to declare the alliances nongovernmental activities, thereby proving that CBO was in the pocket of the President. Then, as work intensified during the Christmas season and beyond, Reischauer began receiving phone calls. Many were nasty; not a few were threatening.

As time for his final report neared, Reischauer was subjected to the most intense and unpleasant pressure of his life, all amid the most complex and difficult analytical work he had ever done. "I received numerous phone calls," Reischauer said some weeks later, "from people of great fame and with common household names telling me what they thought the right answer to this question was and questioning why I would have the audacity to decide otherwise. I also got probably a quarter as many phone calls from the other side who said they were sure we had caved in to the administration, and that our institution was going to be marked for its entire life because of this."

Some who called accused him of trying to destroy a President. Others angrily warned him that if health reform died because of an unfavorable CBO verdict, children would suffer, and some would die. That's going to be on your conscience, he was told. Not all were so accusatory. A number of "very important people" called to say simply "Do what you think is right. We'll take our lumps if we have to." One such was Pat Moynihan. Another was Dan Rostenkowski. A third was Jim McDermott. "You have the shittiest job in America," McDermott said one afternoon. "I'll fight for you in the inner circles of Ways and Means and support you in anything you need." Reischauer laughed. "Does that include professional help?" he said to McDermott, the psychiatrist/politician.

For Reischauer, the worst moment came at nine o'clock on a Sunday morning, shortly before his report was to be released. At highest levels, word had begun to circulate about the judgment he would render. The phone rang. His wife answered. It was Ted Kennedy.

Kennedy was furious, and let Reischauer know it. For nearly half an hour, Kennedy assailed Reischauer, bellowing his outrage:

Reischauer was going to bring down the Clinton administration. Here was a President with a once-in-a-lifetime opportunity to do something as historic as health reform, and you, a minor staff official, are taking it upon yourself to thwart the will of the American people. The American people elected President Clinton because they wanted to have national health insurance, and now when the President is delivering on that promise, you block him. You aren't elected. Who are you to say the President didn't fulfill his promise? Who are you to say this isn't private insurance? Who are you to say whether this is on budget or off budget? What right do you have to do that?

Reischauer was shaken. He had never experienced such a tongue-lashing. That it came from Ted Kennedy was particularly upsetting, especially given the long and close ties between the Reischauer and Kennedy families forged over many years through Harvard, Cambridge, and political connections: His father, Edwin O. Reischauer, the Harvard Asian scholar, had served in the Kennedy administration as ambassador to Japan.

Kennedy's reaction was not some spur-of-the-moment eruption. He and his top aides were sincerely convinced that Reischauer was about to exceed his authority — "flat-out dishonesty and flat-out lawlessness," one of them raged — and, furthermore, was flat-out wrong.

As time for the decision neared, Reischauer summoned his executives to a meeting at seven o'clock at night in his office. Panic had set in at the White House. There were suggestions that CBO put off its report. Either that, or analyze the Republican alternatives as well as the Clinton plan.

Reischauer spelled it out for his executive staff. This is such a controversial issue, he said, unlike anything before, with such high political overtones that there almost certainly will be institutional repercussions. The political environment was so highly charged, he told them, that there was a good chance CBO could see its budget eliminated or slashed to a point where none present would be interested in working there. He wanted to make sure they understood the stakes; and be certain, also, that they fully discussed the most controversial part of their report and came to a decision about it: the chapter in their projected seventy-seven-page report that described the proposed health alliances as governmental activities financed with government funds.

For an hour and a half that night the CBO executives discussed the issue. Then Reischauer gave each a piece of paper. "I want you to vote yes or no," he said.

Every person voted yes. There were no dissenters. They voted to include the chapter in the report even if it destroyed their agency and their jobs.

This triumph of principle over politics was never reported; their deliberations, and their vote, remained private. But theirs was an example, almost completely misunderstood amid all the assaults on government and its employees, of one part of The System — the largely anonymous and detached policy analysts — performing in the interests of the other part, the political side. Reischauer and his professional staff understood that their mission was not to advance any particular policy but to provide the policy makers with the most reliable data that would enable them to perform their jobs. It was a signal example of how The System should work in the best public interest by not allowing itself to be politicized by narrow or ideological interests. Reischauer himself typified that tradition when he told us, in his usual understated manner:

> Personally, I'm a tremendous believer that we need health care reform of almost any kind. I would take almost any of the plans being debated rather than the system we now have. But I'm hired to do a certain job. I've been in this town long enough to realize there are no absolute truths. You know, I'm a principled person, I hope. And the people here are too. You've got a funny kind of esprit de corps that builds up in this place. Sort of a pox on all your houses. We're going to tell it the way it is no matter what happens. Lightning strikes and thunder rumbles. Then we get the pleasure of performing our jobs. Really, it's an institutional kind of personality. CBO is of no use at all unless we shoot straight. If we deviate one little bit because of politics or pressure, everything we do becomes suspect because virtually everything we do is controversial. We don't get everything right. There's no question about that. We don't have the resources or we don't have the intelligence. But we try. And

people in this political environment often find that very hard to believe.

In the end, CBO emerged with its credibility and reputation intact. Despite all the fears of the administration and its allies, it is important to note that Reischauer's analysis confirmed the larger claims of the Clinton plan. Although it would be initially more costly, by the year 2004, reforms would actually lower national health care costs by 7 percent. The Reischauer report did not, as feared, destroy the Clinton health reform at that most critical moment. Despite all the forces arrayed against it, health reform still had a faint heartbeat.

Mike Deaver, the public relations mastermind who staged Ronald Reagan's presidential media performances, was one of many private consultants interviewed by the Health Care Reform Project, the Democratic coalition that was seeking to hire experts to help win the war for the Clinton plan.

Each consultant was asked the same two-part question: Do you think that Republicans will support health reform, and what should we be doing to make that happen? Deaver's reply differed from all the others'. "The only way you're going to get any Republican in Congress to vote for this is to go after their voters," he said. "In the end, the dynamic is such that the Republican leadership will make sure that if Republican voters aren't telling Republican senators and congressmen that they want health care reform, you're doomed."

To Deaver, grassroots political pressure had to be the engine that drove the issue, and it had to be focused on Republicans, especially in the critical House Energy and Commerce and Ways and Means Committees. It was sound advice, and rejected.

The Democratic congressional leadership locked itself into an impossible dilemma: They sought to win enough Democratic votes to pass something as sweeping and controversial as Clinton's reform plan without trying to get Republicans who, on an issue like NAFTA, had demonstrated bipartisanship by breaking ranks to support the Democratic President.

Jay Rockefeller knew they needed to focus on Republicans and he knew that such targeting would cost money. So he invited the First Lady and about eighty other people into the breathtaking living room of his mansion in Rock Creek Park early one Saturday in December. It was his version of a "bonds for Israel fund-raiser." He served heart-shaped scones. "At one point, when the door was closed, he went around the room asking people what they might contribute," consultant Bob Chlopak remembered. Jerry McEntee of AFSCME opened one of the drawers in a piece of furniture. He pretended to look for money. "I don't see anything in here, Jay," he said. "Where are you hiding all those bills?" They joked about having Rockefeller sell one of the masterpiece paintings in his home to provide money for the cause.

The gathering was full of "all these people who do good work but have no money," McEntee remembered. "So we came up with the first one hundred thousand dollars for the Health Care Reform Project."

Their business supporters — Chrysler, Southern California Edison, and others who did have big bucks — "didn't show up," Rockefeller said, "and I wanted them there because I wanted them to go after Republican congressmen and senators."

"By that time," Reform Project president Bob Chlopak remembered, "Harry and Louise had done their first run, and I think people were, for the first time, feeling like we had to do more. There was a sense that our separate efforts aren't enough. We're falling behind." Chlopak, a twenty-year veteran of many business, media, advertising, and political campaigns and a former Democratic Capitol Hill aide, knew it was time to act.

Within that gorgeous mansion, with rooms equal in splendor to the White House, there was a real sense of hope, power, and potential. The First Lady gave a rousing speech, with a message she would repeat over and over again: You've got to be out there. All of you. You've got to be heard. You've got to be unified.

Majority Leader Dick Gephardt also spoke. He implored them to be tough, aggressive, and to confront their opponents. The consultants were anxious to take his advice but could not agree what message to use.

That failure to invent a slogan to generate public support was a huge problem for the pro-reform forces. From the beginning, the Republicans had one: government-run health care, and all the evils that implied. Or, as opponents said repeatedly in ads and speeches: If you like the compassion of the IRS or the efficiency of the post office, you'll love how they run your health care.

Focus groups conducted for the Health Care Reform Project identified one theme with the potential to counter that Republican message: Give every American health care coverage as good as what we already give our members of Congress. Here, they believed, was a rallying cry that could mobilize voters, could force Congress, Republicans and Democrats alike, to pass real reform. AARP's John Rother, who with Jay Rockefeller had been instrumental in organizing the coalition of thirty pro-reform organizations, said, "This is the message that really gets people going, a good populist line that produces the response you want, whether you're liberal or conservative. It reinforces the employer mandate. It actually reinforces the health alliance since the federal health program is structured similarly."

When Harold Ickes invited the key members of the Reform Project's management committee for a night meeting at the White House early in February about political strategy and message, Bob Chlopak took the idea with him.

The night before the meeting, Chlopak had called consultant Mandy Grunwald, who, with pollster Stan Greenberg, formed part of a team White House staffers privately called "Standy." Stan, the short one, would deliver the polling data, then Mandy, the tall one, whom even admirers of her talents described as abrasive and overbearing, would ruthlessly batter dissenters to win her points.

Chlopak and Grunwald had known each other for years; at one point Grunwald had been a partner of Chlopak. During their phone call, for nearly an hour Chlopak discussed the results of his group's grassroots research. He stressed the power of the message: giving the people as good health insurance as members of Congress gave themselves. Not once during that phone conversation, Chlopak says, did Grunwald give a clue that she disagreed with that approach, or was opposed to Chlopak's suggesting it.

The next night a blizzard struck Washington. Chlopak needed four-wheel-drive to travel the few blocks from his office to the White House. Ellen Globocar, the political director of the union AFSCME, another in the small group invited to the meeting, trudged through the snowstorm in boots to get there on time.

Seated around a conference table in the Old Executive Office Building, facing Ickes and Grunwald and a few others, Chlopak made his presentation, referring to research data in a large looseleaf book. The best pro-reform message, he said, one they had just started using in their ads, was about giving the people what Congress already had. He elaborated, citing polling and focus group responses.

Ellen Globocar observed Grunwald fidgeting impatiently while Chlopak made his case. She said then, "Mandy started going kind of crazy."

To Chlopak's astonishment, and fury, Grunwald tore into his idea. "She goes on a forty-minute rampage," he recalled, "about how this was the wrong message. *They* had the answers. This is what *we* should be doing. *They* didn't want to complicate things by raising the issue of what health insurance Congress got. The congressional leaders didn't want that." What they should do, Globocar remembers Grunwald saying, is bash the insurance companies. That's what works.

The Reform Project people continued to argue their case, to no avail. The meeting ended abruptly. "Ohhh, that snowy night," Globocar said later:

It was so sad. We wanted to let the White House know what we were doing and thinking. Ickes was relatively new. So, finally, we thought, aha, a new health care person. We're going to bond with Harold. Everybody had told me Harold was fabulous. He was a political guy. He'll ride herd. There won't be all this undercutting with everybody going off doing their own thing. When it was over, we all went out and got drunk. Bob was really upset with Mandy. He was very angry at her. I was just depressed, because nothing we had done, nothing the White House had done, had worked. We felt we had something that could change the debate. Not only could people understand it, it would energize our activists. Every time we tried it out, people said: "That's it! That's the message!"

It seemed to us the Project was over. Nobody would let us use the message that we knew worked. We were tired of bashing insurance companies; we didn't see where it took you. You can bash them and bash them and bash them, and so what? It was like they had taken away our best weapon, but we're still supposed to be loyal soldiers and go out and play. We've got slingshots and the other guys have got nuclear bombs. I was tired of trying to win a fight where the other side is not fighting fair and we can't use our best argument.

The next day Bob Chlopak saw Ickes at a larger White House meeting. When it was over, Ickes approached Chlopak. Even though they really didn't know each other, Ickes said, he had heard great things about Chlopak; they needed to work together. Ickes was concerned that Chlopak had seemed "really pissed off last night." "I was," Chlopak replied, "but not in the least with you." He then told Ickes about his lengthy phone conversation with Grunwald. "I was set up," he said. "All she wanted to do was try and embarrass me and the coalition in front of you. That's what that was all about. And I won't take that from anybody, much less somebody I've known for a long time. That's why I was pissed off."

After that, the Reform Project management committee met and decided that for health reform to pass they needed to maintain a relationship with the White House. So they continued bashing insurance companies in their next wave of advertising. Months later, the old message about giving the people coverage the Congress had was finally tried. It had a powerful impact, but it was too late.

The problems the Reform Project had with the White House and with consultants like Mandy Grunwald were characteristic of the chaos and backbiting that crippled all of the efforts to sell the President's plan. Early in the summer of 1993, when the goal was still to pass a bill in that session of Congress, David Wilhelm, the youthful chairman of the Democratic National Committee (DNC), was told by the President to gear up a grassroots effort. Wilhelm first tried to set up a tax-exempt "educational" foundation, separate from but allied to the DNC. When word of that plan leaked, critics said it would allow power brokers with their own agendas to curry favor with Clinton by secretly financing his pet project. Wilhelm backed off and said the DNC would run the program itself — and disclose the names of all donors.

The plan at that point emphasized grassroots organizational work so that, as Wilhelm said, "party supporters in every state, every congressional district, conceivably every county in this country, would be organizing, engaging in the debate, taking on the special interests, and we would see that they had the information to do that."

It was a grandiose notion. Wilhelm hired Celia Fischer, a veteran Pennsylvania political operative, as director for the project, and she began hiring field workers to recruit and train this volunteer army. Within a few weeks, two dozen were on the payroll, but two things quickly became obvious. The battle over this legislation would not be won or lost in 1993; it would go well into 1994. And the DNC did not have the money to support this sustained a drive. Originally, Wilhelm thought he might reach a budget of $6 or $7 million — maybe even $10 million. But, he said, "Business people, business interests, wealthy individuals had virtually no interest in contributing money for the health care campaign. It was like pulling teeth." What made it worse was that the AFL-CIO unions, to demonstrate their displeasure with Clinton after he got Congress to pass NAFTA over their bitter opposition, cut off their regular contributions to the DNC for a period of almost six months.

At the same time, Wilhelm found himself being undercut by Grunwald, Begala, and the consultants. Wilhelm was no match for them. The party chairman was a political prodigy at thirty-six — an Ohioan who had moved from organizing for liberal causes to a political consulting firm whose most notable success prior to 1992 was the election of Richard M. Daley as mayor of Chicago. Clinton hired Wilhelm principally for his know-how in Illinois — a state vital in both the presidential primaries and the general election — liked him, and named him "manager" of the election campaign. Boyish, trusting, and easy to get along with, Wilhelm knew better than to compete for power with the likes of George Stephanopoulos, James Carville. Paul Begala, Mandy Grunwald, or Stan Greenberg, and he made a useful contribution to the victory by troubleshooting ticklish situations out in the states and dealing with a variety of Democratic leaders.

Sent off to the DNC, he lost the regular access to Clinton that the consultants enjoyed and he had little support of his own on Capitol Hill or in the state Democratic organizations. So when the consultants began arguing to the President and the First Lady that they should junk Wilhelm's grassroots efforts and instead use the money for a media campaign, his squawks of protest were barely heard.

Wilhelm needed an ally with some muscle, and he suggested to the Clintons that they recruit an old friend of his from Ohio, former two-term Governor Dick Celeste, to be the part-time chairman of the DNC's health care campaign. Celeste, who had a private business in Columbus, came down for a meeting with Hillary and Magaziner; a phone call from the President persuaded him.

With Celeste's arrival, things only got worse. He learned after the fact that he was replacing Celia Fischer and cooled his heels at the DNC until a place was found for her at the Peace Corps. In his first week on the job, Mandy Grunwald brought him a TV spot she wanted the DNC to put on the air. "I looked at it and said, 'No, we shouldn't do that commercial until we have a media plan.' I guess nobody had ever said no to Mandy Grunwald, and this was a sort of audacious thing to do." Also foolhardy, as he learned.

Celeste tried to schedule an appointment with Magaziner. He finally got in at ten o'clock one night. He asked, naively, "To what extent am I going to be part of the process of focusing decisions for the President?" He was told that if political advice was needed, the consultants would take care of that. Wilhelm pleaded with him to help on fund-raising, which Celeste did not want to do.

Instead. Celeste went to see the President and Mack McLarty with a proposal for a $4 million campaign, from January through August of 1994, half for field organization and half for media, to be targeted on forty key congressional districts. Celeste said it should be separate from the DNC, so he could be free to put pressure on wavering

Democratic members of Congress as well as Republicans, without having them complain that the party headquarters was beating up on them. The President and McLarty said they liked the idea. But it never happened.

"There was no buy-in by Grunwald, by the core consultant team, who could move into any meeting, who could say we're operating on behalf of the President and the First Lady," Celeste said. And, he added, "there was internal friction between the First Lady's people, who had worked heroically on this, and the senior White House staff who didn't feel any ownership of the thing."

Grunwald came up with her own plan for a $10 million national media campaign, and persuaded Ickes that was the way to go. Celeste said it was an unrealistic budget; they would do well to raise half that amount, and it was unlikely that $5 million worth of ads, spread across the country, would shift any votes in Congress.

In all this time, nothing was done to launch any kind of support campaign. The field staff that had been hired in 1993 had been laid off and no new organizational or media efforts were going forward. In March, Celeste left Washington for a couple of weeks to take care of his own affairs, and while he was away, he received a call from an aide informing him that in the briefing materials prepared for a presidential strategy meeting with outside support groups, "the DNC's health care campaign isn't even mentioned anymore."

When Celeste returned to Washington, he went to see Hillary and told her he was accomplishing nothing — and quit. The consultants had won the battle, but the enemies were winning the war.

One more blow was struck. At the end of February, the President invited a small group to the White House for a dinner. Among the guests was Senate Majority Leader George Mitchell of Maine, who was given the honor of being seated next to the President. During dinner, they had a lively conversation. Then, during a lull, Mitchell told the President he would like to see him alone for five minutes after dinner. Sure, an obviously intrigued, and surprised, Clinton replied.

When all the other guests had left, Clinton turned to Mitchell.

Let's talk over here, he said, leading the senator to a room across the hallway. There, Mitchell dropped his bombshell. He had decided to leave the Senate after the congressional session ended the next fall. His reasons were personal; it was time to move on. Clinton was stunned.

But George Mitchell was often surprising. In public, Mitchell appeared understated, reflecting his judicial background. But his calm demeanor masked a steely character. He approached each new task with painstaking determination. When he started trying cases in Maine. he seldom lost. Then he lost a case on appeal. After reading the transcript of his arguments, Mitchell was dumbfounded. My God, he thought, the reporter must have got this wrong. Mitchell prided himself on being clear and concise. This transcript read like someone who could hardly speak the English language. After that, Mitchell began a practice that continued throughout his service as a federal judge and then as a U.S. senator. Before going to bed, he would think about what he had done during the day and how he could have done it better. He would concentrate particularly on how he had answered questions and how he could have phrased his responses more effectively. Now, he was clear and direct as he explained himself to an astonished and dismayed President Bill Clinton.

Mitchell and Clinton talked for nearly an hour, the President stressing how much he relied on the majority leader, how much they'd already been able to accomplish in a tough political period, how much more they could accomplish in the future, how difficult it would be if Mitchell weren't there. Finally, the President asked Mitchell if he would postpone his decision so they could discuss the matter in greater detail. The senator politely declined. He had decided, he said, and felt it was right. He was going to do it.

The President asked Mitchell to come down to the Oval Office with him. There, still alone, they continued their conversation. When Mitchell stood up to leave, Clinton insisted on walking with him to his car, parked inside the White House grounds. The senator's driver was startled when he saw the President approaching. Willie, Mitchell joked, the President wanted to come and say hello to you. Then they drove off into the night.

After Mitchell left, the President went up to the White House family quarters and gave the First Lady the bad news.

"George says he's not going to run for reelection," the President said, "but he's going to sleep on it overnight."

No less stunned than the President had been, she said, "I sure wish you could talk him out of it."

Around midnight, Mitchell's phone rang. It was the President, who continued their earlier conversation. He had been so surprised by Mitchell's news, he said, that he hadn't thought fast enough to make other points. Now he made them. But Mitchell's decision was firm. He was going to leave the Senate.

When the news was announced on March 4, a principal reason for Mitchell's decision was that he wanted to devote his full energies in the closing months of that Congress to passing a historic health reform bill. It would be the capstone of Mitchell's career, a cause for which he had long fought. So important was the reform to Mitchell, it was widely said, that he, a former federal judge, had even given up a Supreme Court seat to lead the health care battle. This was true. After Mitchell announced he would not seek reelection, it was immediately leaked that Clinton had offered him the Supreme Court seat made vacant by the retirement of Justice Harry Blackmun. Naturally, this account heightened a tale of a public servant who believed so strongly that America needed health reform that he was willing to sacrifice a lifetime seat on the nation's highest court, and perhaps even a special place in history, for it was possible he could have become Chief Justice.

Mitchell's ardor for the cause was probably a factor in his decision to forgo the court and fight for reform in his final months in the Senate, but clearly other considerations contributed to his decision to leave public life. Two weeks after his stunning announcement, in a long conversation in the Senate majority leader's office in the Capitol, Mitchell expressed what increasing numbers of major players in The System were feeling. He spoke of the rising level of hostility and negativism, at its worst unfairly damaging or even ruining political careers and personal reputations. He spoke also of the "complete loss of privacy to a point where's there's no aspect of your life that is not regarded as fair game for discussion." He spoke of the growing frustration of talented people of goodwill in both parties at the difficulty of getting things done.

There had been a dramatic increase in the tactics of political obstruction, Mitchell observed. For most of our history, the political rules worked because there was a voluntary, implicit sense of comity, of self-restraint that kept The System from tearing itself apart over intensely controversial issues. He gave an example:

> For much of this century into the late 1970s, in the Senate there was on average fewer than one filibuster a year. There were many entire Congresses, of two-year periods, where there were no filibusters. By common consent, they were reserved for matters of grave national interest. They were unrelated to political parties; the civil-rights filibusters of the past are an example. But increasingly it has become a regular party tactic to the point where in the most recent preceding Congress to this one we filed motions to end filibusters forty-eight times. This week we filed our forty-ninth and fiftieth in this Congress — and we still have six months to go. We're now on our third filibuster this week. Twenty or thirty years ago, ten years could pass before you had three filibusters. Now we have three in a week, on almost every bill, for reasons as trivial as a senator's travel schedule. The result is, it is extremely hard to get anything done.

He didn't want to be misunderstood, the majority leader said, nor sound as if he were complaining. Taking the long view, no matter how cynical the public was about politicians and public service, American democracy and The System that implemented it had in recent years led to higher ethical standards, not lower, in public life, as well as a substantial broadening of our concepts of individual liberty and human and civil rights. But, he added, "There clearly are other trends which I think are negative."

One was the deliberate denigrating of the Congress as part of an overall political strategy. The most virulent bashing has come from Republican members, Mitchell said, and "not surprisingly, that's had an effect on the country." Now, "there is just an intensity of hostility to the institution, a much higher level of hostility." Compounding these tendencies was the echo chamber effect of the mass media on The System. "No one has fully or accurately documented the effect of television on society or human life in ways that cause changes that could never have been foreseen," Mitchell said. "You can see it in politics. We've always had negative campaigns, but we've never had negative campaigns in the context of a medium so powerful, so pervasive, as television. That's one of the major contributing factors in the decline of public respect for all institutions in our society and especially public institutions. Political campaigns now are largely waged in terms of negative ten-second spots, so the public not surprisingly believes we're all a bunch of bums since we spend most of our money telling them we're all a bunch of bums."

The media amplify and magnify these negative feelings, he believed, not out of some ideological conspiracy, but from a highly competitive battle for news:

> Newspapers don't compete just with newspapers. Newspapers compete with radio stations, they compete with television stations, mostly for profit. There is now a news machine operating in our society that requires constant feeding. It's like one of those big old boilers on the ships you used to see in the movies. You had to keep shoveling coal into those boilers around the clock; now, you've got to be shoveling news in all the time. It's incredible. Everybody's operating under deadlines. This has — and I don't mean to sound personally critical of anybody — exacerbated controversy where it exists and created it where it doesn't exist. Increasingly, the standard of what is news in our society has become what is controversial. The absence of controversy means it has no newsworthy content. That's created a situation where people stoke controversy. I know that's the case.

He gave an example that greatly upset him. In the last two years, he said, Congress passed two major acts dealing with post-secondary education and the federal government's role in it. "If you can find me an article on page thirty-two of the *Washington Post* about those bills, I'll frame it," he said. "It's as though they didn't exist. Clearly, the television news wouldn't touch it. There was no controversy. There were differences of opinion, but they weren't associated with scandal. It's a striking thing: Major social acts, in an area very important to our country's future, are largely viewed as non-news because they're not controversial."

As we have seen, it was widely believed that Mitchell's decision not to seek reelection and to relinquish his majority leader's post would free him to devote greater effort to win health reform, quite possibly guaranteeing victory. Surely George Mitchell, one of the most respected and effective majority leaders ever, was the man who could see this fight through successfully.

Whatever they said in public, two people thought otherwise. The President knew Mitchell's departure was an immense, perhaps irreparable, setback. So did the First Lady. It was, she said months later, "a big, big blow to us."

14

The Playmaker Fails

IN THE POTBOILERS about the pressures of Washington, plots revolve around the figure of a powerful — corrupt or noble — President, and the President's influential aides — trusted or treacherous — with a malevolent intelligence operative, a terrorist, and a sultry, manipulative mistress thrown in for spice. Rarely is the Congress depicted as the center of dramatic action and character. Even less often is the congressional process explored as the focus of high drama, of monumental decisions and pressures. But in The System, Congress is at the center of almost everything.

It holds the power of the purse. It alone is granted authority to raise armies, to declare war, to levy taxes, to write laws that change lives and regulate private business. Congress can totally thwart the legislative and political goals of a President — or, if it is so disposed, advance them. Congress with its thirty thousand employees is a world unto itself, ruled by its own power struggles, passions, and personality clashes. Some take place out in the open of committee hearings or floor debates. Many more are known only to those who slip into the numerous "hideaway" Capitol offices behind unmarked doors or who attend the closed caucuses and weekend retreats where both parties plot their strategies.

It was in that universe of public debate and subterranean maneuver that the Clinton plan now struggled for survival.

* * *

The Clintons had an explicit congressional strategy. Their political and policy advisers agreed to it on September 2, 1993, after Magaziner described it in a slide briefing. "The winning congressional majority for health care reform depends on holding almost all liberal and moderate Democrats, winning a significant number of conservative Democrats, and attracting eight to ten moderate Republicans in the Senate . . . and fifteen to twenty in the House."

Theoretically there were two ways to get there: Start from the center, writing a bill that would appeal to conservative Democrats and moderate Republicans, and tell the liberals that was the best they could get. Or start from the left and move as far to the center as needed to reach a majority. The White House was divided on which path seemed most promising. Mack McLarty, the chief of staff, was a centrist by instinct, and he found an ally in presidential counselor David Gergen. In notes to the President, the veteran of Republican White House staffs made the case for the middle-road strategy. He gave Clinton an analysis of major social legislative initiatives going back half a century. Social Security in the 1930s, civil rights and Medicare in the 1960s, the Social Security rescue operation and the Medicare catastrophic bill in the 1980s all became law after a supermajority of the Senate voted in the affirmative.

Those all passed with Republican support, Gergen pointed out. They represented the powerful consensus of the center, the middle ground where the successful battles of The System were fought and won. A bipartisan solution is good public policy and good practical politics, Gergen told the President, and he agreed with the prevailing White House view that the President could not count on support from House Republicans. You couldn't have a good-faith conversation with the Republican Right, he thought, especially with "this Ayatollah," Newt Gingrich, who operated as leader of an increasing "tyranny of the Right," and who was uninterested in negotiating with the White House. But Gergen felt the same wariness toward Democratic liberals, who often seemed more interested in making polemical points than in uniting to win the battle.

Gergen and McLarty had allies on Capitol Hill. Moderate Democratic senators like Louisiana's John Breaux argued that the middle was the place to be. So did his allies in the Democratic Leadership Council. So did Pat Moynihan, the chairman of the Senate Finance Committee, who was convinced they would *need* sixty votes to break a Republican filibuster, so they had better enlist the help of Republican moderates from the beginning.

But that was not the unanimous view of the Senate Democratic leaders and assuredly not the way the House Democratic leadership saw it. Although Ted Kennedy and George Mitchell agreed that ultimately Republican votes would be needed, they disagreed with Moynihan about needing a supermajority before bringing a bill to a vote. Mitchell and Kennedy argued that if the Democrats could put together fifty-one votes for the Clinton plan — a simple majority — Republicans would risk a terrible public backlash if they then mounted a filibuster. The majority leader and the veteran battler for universal coverage were so convinced that the voters would cheer their effort that they were confident Republicans would jump aboard the bandwagon, not destroy it. Conversely, they said, telling Bob Dole and other Republicans in advance that you wanted their support before bringing a bill to a vote would give the opposition a veto power it should not, and need not, have.

The House Democratic leaders were even more emphatic in rejecting the centrist approach. Unite the Democrats, they said, and deal with the Republicans later — or, if they are as recalcitrant as we expect, don't deal with them at all.

Ira Magaziner weighed in on the side of the "start left, go center" camp. In a September memo to the Clintons, he reminded them that the center-right was not ready to sign up with Clinton. Instead, Republicans like John Chafee of Rhode Island and moderate Democrats like Breaux and Representative Jim Cooper of Tennessee had told the White House they were going to introduce their own bills.

What settled the argument was not the Magaziner memo but the adamant view of Hillary Clinton. People close to her said she believed it would be ridiculous and disastrous for the President to present a bill that was immediately repudiated by the most ardent reformers. The idea of a Democratic President introducing a bill that is immediately denounced by every union, by ninety of his single-payer government-financed stalwarts in the House, and by a lot of citizen groups around the country struck her as foolish. That was out of the question. They had to convince this base that they were doing the best they could politically before any compromise could be reached. To start with something they regarded as a slap in the face would leave them dead in the water. She believed that passionately.

She was not unwilling to compromise. Indeed, the First Lady told everyone what features in the plan could be negotiated away; she and Magaziner had discussed them and, as usual, his memo spelled them out in numbing detail.

He presented his colleagues with a list of fourteen "main event" issues and a sampling of the hundreds of "side show issues" subject to negotiation. The multiplicity of issues, he said, offered Clinton a strategic advantage. Bargaining with "virtually every member we convert [to support of the Clinton plan] will involve policy changes which the member can claim to have won. There are so many issues embedded in the bill which are so important to the over fifteen hundred health care interest groups and their constituencies that we can make hundreds of these modifications without hurting the integrity of the bill in order to gain votes," he said.

Showing off, Magaziner told the Clintons what he thought they might get in the end under the "most optimistic" scenario, and what they could salvage under less favorable circumstances. Whatever they thought of his predictions, the Clintons also had a separate memo from Howard Paster, the former labor lobbyist now head of the White House congressional team, endorsing the fundamental strategy decision. "Ira is correct in the premise that we need to solidify our support on the left before we move right," Paster wrote. "The distrust of our motives among single-payer supporters and others means that a rush to the right will leave us without the means of finding a majority in the Congress." Paster also thought it was essential to get the financial and organizational backing from the unions to offset the public relations campaign he assumed some business interests would mount against the bill.

Further support came from an analysis of House members written by Chris Jennings and Steve Edelstein of the task force staff. They said that consultations with the House leadership turned up "seventy-nine members who they are confident will support the reform bill. To reach our goal of two hundred eighteen from there will require the targeting of roughly two hundred fifty members." Most of them would come from committees with health care jurisdiction and from such liberal-leaning groups as the Black Caucus, the Hispanic Caucus, the Women's Caucus, and the rural health care task force. To win, however, they would have to reach into the middle ground and enlist some of the thirty-six Republicans who were not as rigidly conservative as most of their colleagues. "This group [the Republicans] may well provide the margin of victory," the memo said, but they would be the last to come aboard.

They did not know, of course, that Newt Gingrich was determined there would be no Republican support for the only kind of reform Clinton would offer. "Any time they want to write a bill which is incremental, free market, and within our values, we'll help 'em write it," he told trusted colleagues at the time — and later repeated to us. "But once you get outside of this box, we have no interest in helping you."

He meant more than not helping. He meant doing everything possible to derail the Clinton plan. Philosophically, Gingrich found all the justification he needed in the belief that "these folks were committed to a government-controlled, left-wing vision of America." He saw no prospect of compromise. "There is no fix," he said. "This is a choice," of one kind of America or another.

Politically, he had no interest in compromise. His pollsters and advisers were telling him that stopping the Clinton plan was the necessary prelude to defeating the Democrats in the 1994 midterm election. As we have already seen, as early as 1991 Gingrich had concluded that thwarting Democrats on health care was the key to halting and then rolling back decades of Democratic efforts to build an encompassing social safety net — a net that he believed was strangling the American economy, trapping millions of supposed beneficiaries in red tape and regulation, and making them more dependent on government and the Democratic Party that provided the government-supplied benefits.

There would be no compromise — at beginning or end — with Gingrich and his forces. And he was not alone. In the Senate, former House colleagues of his — senators like Trent Lott of Mississippi,

Phil Gramm of Texas, Dan Coats of Indiana, and Robert C. Smith of New Hampshire — shared his determination to sink the Clinton plan and replace the Democrats in power. In time, their pressure would erode the support John Chafee had developed for a Republican alternative not that dissimilar to what Clinton was proposing. And in time, they would influence Bob Dole to abandon Chafee and other would-be Republican reformers and instead join them in routing the President.

None of that was foreseen — or perhaps foreseeable — in the White House strategy meetings in late 1993. What Paster and Magaziner and others clearly did understand was that they needed a consensus Democratic position by the spring of 1994 in order to negotiate with Senate Republicans and secure the sixty-one votes to break a possible filibuster, permitting the President to get a bill he could sign.

As early as April 1993, there had been discussion of writing the health bill in an ad hoc supercommittee in the House. Such a panel could be created out of senior members of the three major committees with principal jurisdiction on health, with some members drawn from other committees that had at least a tangential claim on the subject. There was precedent for the Speaker and the majority leader doing that when overlapping jurisdictions might delay action on some issue. Hillary Clinton pressed Speaker Tom Foley at a meeting also attended by Mitchell, Gephardt, Magaziner, Stephanopoulos, and Paster to appoint a supercommittee. The talk did not go far. Foley told the First Lady that would create problems with the committee chairmen who had jurisdiction. The System didn't work that way, he told her. Gephardt felt strongly that "in order to pass this, you needed the support of lots of people in the Congress. And the surest way to drive them off is to say, 'Your opinion doesn't count, because we've got some smart people that are going to go in a room and play Congress.' There's always this desire to reduce the number, to get a committee that will be like Solomon and will walk in a room and figure this thing out, and then everyone else will kneel down and say, 'This is the right answer.' It doesn't work that way. People all want to be involved. The least you can do is go through the committee process."

Once the supercommittee idea was discarded, there were only two places to write a bill that could pass the House. Ways and Means was one; Energy and Commerce the other. The third committee with jurisdiction — Education and Labor — was a liberal bastion; over the years, the big unions that were major bankrollers of Democratic congressional candidates, including the National Education Association and the American Federation of Teachers, had packed that committee with people of unquestioned loyalty. "Ed and Labor" was certain to report both the administration bill and the single-payer plan favored by many of the unions. But Ed and Labor was well to the left of the House. It had no jurisdiction over financing provisions and only a marginal claim on Medicare and Medicaid, the major existing health care programs. It was not likely to provide legislation the leadership could take to the House floor. Its involvement was only a way of ensuring constituencies of the left they would have a voice at the table for the final dealing.

John Dingell wanted to be the point man for the House effort. He had been waiting a lifetime for this moment, and he was determined not to waste the opportunity. If anyone could carry the day on reform, it was John Dingell. He was as powerful a politician as The System knew, the real playmaker of Congress. Every year since he had come to Congress in 1955, Dingell had introduced H.R. 16, his national health insurance bill. The bill carried the number of the Michigan congressional district he inherited from his father, John D. Dingell Sr., a New Dealer who had been the earliest House advocate of universal health care.

H.R. 16 was more than an act of filial devotion. It was also a serious philosophical and political commitment from a man who was at the height of his legislative powers and wanted nothing more than to achieve this reform as his claim on history. In 1965, when the House passed the Medicare bill, expanding Social Security to provide health care for retirees, House Speaker John W. McCormack of Massachusetts — a friend of the elder Dingell — invited the son to preside. Now he wanted to complete his father's work. Since becoming chairman of the Energy and Commerce Committee in 1981, Dingell had steadily enlarged its jurisdiction.

By 1993, it originated 40 percent of all the legislation that reached the House floor. He had shaped its Democratic membership to accommodate regional and industry interests — but in a fashion that furthered the prospects for having his way on issues. A succession of House Speakers had listened closely to Dingell's preferences for Energy and Commerce vacancies; he had even been able to encourage Republicans he thought "reasonable" to join the minority side.

It was a big committee. With twenty-seven Democrats and seventeen Republicans, it encompassed one-tenth of the House. Its subcommittee chairmen, notably Representative Henry A. Waxman, a Los Angeles Democrat who headed the health panel, were power centers in their own right. Energy and Commerce, because of its size, its diversity, and the strength of its leadership, was regarded as *the* committee that almost always prevailed on the floor. The administration counted heavily on Dingell to deliver a version of the President's bill that would pass the House.

Dingell had no doubts about his mission. His Sixteenth Congressional District, centered on Dearborn and the "Downriver" industrial towns outside Detroit, is dominated by the auto industry, its suppliers, and its workers. The Dingells, father and son, had their political base in the union halls, where the first- and second-generation immigrants from Europe and migrants from the rural South congregated. But the younger Dingell also looked after the interests of the auto companies who employed those workers — especially on the environmental and other regulatory issues over which he held jurisdiction. His politically savvy wife, Debbie, worked in the Washington office of General Motors. The rising cost of health insurance — it had passed $1000 per car — was of major concern to the auto firms, especially since their Japanese and European competitors carried no such heavy burden.

Thus Dingell, unlike many other legislators, faced few cross-pressures at home. That freed him to be an honest broker among his committee members, to "take whatever steps we can to provide them cover," as he put it. "That is what a chairman has to do — to make the job [of voting for legislation] as easy and comfortable as he can for his members."

Dingell personally favored a single-payer, government-run insurance program. But from his first meeting with Clinton, he made it clear that he would push for the President's proposal. "You won't go as far as I would like to go," Dingell recalled telling the President-elect, "but you'll take us a helluva lot farther than we've ever been able to get on our own. And I'll be with you."

His relationship with Hillary Clinton got off on the wrong foot but ripened into a close partnership. When Hillary was making her initial rounds of the key committee chairmen, she walked into Dingell's office, accompanied by two aides. His walls were lined with heads of deer that Dingell, an avid hunter, had felled. When the conversation turned to the financing of health benefits for the uninsured, the First Lady incautiously suggested that in addition to raising tobacco taxes, guns and ammunition might be appropriate targets for higher levies. Dingell took off his glasses, furrowed his brow, and said, "Mrs. Clinton, with all respect, you're going to have enough problems with this bill. Speaking as a member of the NRA's [National Rifle Association's] board of governors, where most of them are Shiites and I am the exception, I would recommend that you probably not take on that fight."

Dingell thought the time was right for health reform. Like the auto companies, much of business would welcome a plan that offered relief from ever-rising costs. He also believed that nurses, hospitals, and even some doctors would back the President's approach. But Dingell also knew that this would be "the toughest job of legislation I've ever faced." The twenty-seven Democrats on his committee had been assembled when national health care was little more than a gleam in the eye of the chairman. Many were allied with Dingell on other issues, but they had ideological or constituency problems with the Clinton plan. Without Republican votes, Dingell would be hard-pressed to win twenty-three of the twenty-seven Democrats needed to report out a bill. Privately, he suggested Clinton might have to settle for a "good start" on his plan in this Congress, then hope for a bigger victory and clearer mandate in 1996 to enact the rest. But Dingell was determined to get as much as he could.

*   *   *

One Democrat who could cause Dingell trouble was Jim Cooper of Tennessee. Cooper was only a year old when Dingell came to Congress and was a very junior member — fifteenth in seniority — of Energy and Commerce. But Cooper had his own sense of political dynasty. "Great expectations" had surrounded Jim Cooper from the time of his youth. His father, the late Prentice Cooper, had been the three-term governor of Tennessee during World War II. The son went to Groton, Franklin D. Roosevelt's prep school, whizzed through the University of North Carolina at Chapel Hill in three years, went to Oxford as a Rhodes scholar, and then to Harvard Law School.

In 1982, when redistricting created an open House seat in a sprawling district that included his hometown of Shelbyville, Jim Cooper left his law practice to run. His Republican opponent was Cissy Baker, the personable daughter of then Senate Majority Leader Howard H. Baker Jr. Cooper borrowed $600,000 to finance his campaign, beat her two to one, and, at twenty-eight, became the youngest member of the House.

Like his father, Cooper had strong conservative instincts on fiscal matters, although he supported liberals on issues like tobacco and guns and flag-burning; these stands in his conservative, rural district took political courage. Because many of his uncles and cousins were physicians, Cooper had a lively interest in medical care and joined the Health Subcommittee of Energy and Commerce as quickly as he could.

In 1990, through Atul Gawande, the Harvard Medical School student who later advised Clinton, Cooper became familiar with the work of the Jackson Hole group and its managed competition program. Few others in the political world were then even aware of this approach, which appealed to his conservative, market-oriented instincts, and in 1992 he introduced a bill embodying the unfamiliar principles of managed competition.

It had no requirement that employers pay for most of their employees' insurance, nor did it provide direct controls on insurance premiums. In the eyes of insurers and small business these were big pluses. But Cooper's plan would tax the so-called Cadillac plans, which provided more generous benefits — anathema to unions, which had negotiated them. And, unlike the President's plan, it set no deadline for insuring all Americans.

On the face of it, Cooper was no match for Dingell. He was a junior member with no favors to hand out and no plausible threats to deliver. Physically and politically, "Big John" was intimidating — a chairman who could play hardball and had no reluctance to use his political muscle. Cooper was thin, soft-spoken, formal, and aloof, a bit like the headmaster of a good boys' school — not someone who would serve as an obvious rallying point.

But appearances were misleading. Cooper was as stubborn and unrelenting in his way as Dingell was in his. The Cooper family tradition prided itself in its determination. When his grandfather William Prentice Cooper married Argentine Shofner, the fifth generation of her family in Tennessee, he planned to move her to his home county in Kentucky. Her father objected. A long dispute was resolved only when great-grandfather Jacob Morton Shofner met his son-in-law's demand to build the young couple an exact duplicate in Shelbyville of the fine stone house Cooper had built for his bride in Kentucky.

The dispute that polarized the Energy and Commerce Committee represented much more than personal differences between two stubborn antagonists. In miniature, it symbolized the civil war within the Democratic Party. Dingell was one of the lions of the New Deal generation — Democrats forged in the Great Depression and World War II, whose loyalties lay in the working-class communities in and around the big cities. They saw government as the ultimate protector against the vagaries of the marketplace and the tyrants in the world. Dingell preferred the government to provide health insurance for everyone, paid for by an additional Social Security tax. Still he was ready to compromise in order to cover everyone under Clinton's complicated plan. Without the guarantee of universal coverage, something Cooper's version of the Jackson Hole plan would not do, John Dingell thought a health bill would be a fraud.

Cooper, a full generation younger, was emblematic of the "New Democrats." He was highly educated, somewhat snooty, untouched by personal experience with economic privation, thoroughly comfortable in the worlds of business, finance, and the professions, and almost as skeptical of governmental bureaucracy as his Republican neighbors. Cooper and his friends in the House Conservative Democratic Forum were convinced that the Democratic Party must become more business-friendly if it were to survive. He proudly called himself a "Yellow Pages Democrat," attuned to Main Street concerns. While Dingell was a hero in his union halls, Cooper was despised by the leaders of organized labor as a turncoat who opposed their stands not just on health care but on striker replacement, minimum wage, and family-leave bills.

In the 1992 campaign, Clinton had been clever enough to hold both these wings of the party together: Cooper's brother was one of Clinton's first backers in Tennessee; Dingell's district voted for Clinton in the Michigan presidential primary and in the general election. The Clinton health plan derived from the same intellectual roots and was fashioned by the same hands as Cooper's. But the concessions Clinton made to the single-payer block — the promise of price controls, the insistence on employer mandates and a complex system of subsidies — made it tolerable to Dingell, unacceptable to Cooper.

Cooper seemed more aware of these larger differences than Dingell. Early on, the Tennessean remarked of his chairman, "He comes from a different tradition than I do. I just think that my tradition is more likely to be the future of the party. It is a battle between Old Democrats and New Democrats. Big government doesn't work. Great Society doesn't work. New Deal doesn't even work. We've got to have a new way for government to work cost-effectively." All these sharp ideological and generational differences were creating new fault lines in The System.

The Clinton legislative strategy required that the John Dingells and Jim Coopers of the world finally be brought together to support the same bill. Early in the game, while the task force was still meeting, the White House began wooing Cooper. In mid-May of 1993, after discussions with Magaziner, he was invited to sit down with the First Lady to explore their differences. The first conversation was indecisive, so he went back on June 15 "to give formal notice that we were going to have to be off the reservation unless they changed their plan," Cooper said. "It was not a happy meeting. I have always thought that the best way to be someone's friend is to tell them the truth, and the second-best answer in the world is no. Maybe I was too up-front, but I wanted them to know that we were worried, that we could not support their plan, and that we would have to introduce our bill."

According to Magaziner's notes of the meeting, Cooper not only expressed his concerns about Clinton's policy direction, but argued that the administration was being pushed to the left by the liberal single-payer block in the House. He also said that his delay in reintroducing his own plan was making him look weak to his Tennessee constituents, confirming the strong White House suspicion that Cooper had a political agenda of his own.

Cooper was running for the Senate in Tennessee and raising money from the hospitals and insurance companies. The White House took umbrage at a newsletter Cooper sent his supporters that spring, saying doctors were dismayed about the direction of the Clinton plan. Hillary Clinton described it to friends as "attacking me personally when we hadn't even presented the legislation." They say she complained he was using her as a tool to raise money and suspected Cooper was in league with the for-profit hospitals, who, she is said to have argued, basically wanted to gobble up all their competitors and monopolize the hospital industry, leaving a few Catholic and community hospitals and academic health centers to take care of all those that can't pay the bill. If so, those who were basically funding Jim Cooper's campaign were, some around her thought, being very shrewd and very cynical about what they were accomplishing.

The First Lady thought Cooper was being foolish and was in danger of destroying himself with the black voters and unions in Memphis whose support he would need to win.

Mutual mistrust notwithstanding, the conversations between Cooper and the White House continued. A week after the contentious June meeting with Hillary Clinton, Magaziner made a point of attending a Cooper fund-raiser in Washington and found he was able to talk to him with less strain. At Cooper's request, Magaziner stepped up his meetings with conservative House Democrats. In August, Cooper tipped off Magaziner that he had heard that House

Republicans were preparing a memo asserting they would oppose requiring employers to provide insurance for their employees. Cooper said he was inclined to do the same thing himself. That would be a mistake, Magaziner said, because it would come back to haunt Cooper if he later agreed to a compromise including the employer mandate. If Cooper was going to be as recalcitrant as the Republicans on this, an irritated Magaziner said, "you might just as well go ahead and introduce your own bill." You want to fight, we'll fight you.

But early in September, when the Clintons returned from vacation, Cooper went back to the White House with Senator John Breaux of Louisiana, who had agreed to co-sponsor his bill in the Senate. Cooper and Breaux acceded to the Clintons' request to delay introducing their bill until after the President's televised September 22 speech launching the administration effort. In a follow-up session with Magaziner, Cooper gave him a draft copy of his bill. They agreed that neither side would be so critical of the other's work as to preclude future negotiations. Cooper also hinted, according to Magaziner, that he might eventually support an employer mandate and universal coverage — the key elements of Clinton reform — but he would have to be "dragged" to it after trying to do something for small business.

For his part, Jim Cooper was convinced the White House would have to bend and accept his position. "Some people in the White House got bad advice, thinking that we had nowhere to go, that we'd have to cave in, or that they somehow could cut a deal with enough Republicans on their own where we'd be left out in the cold," Cooper said.

He thought he could show them they were wrong, for he had found a significant partner for his version of managed care in former television actor Fred Grandy, of *Gilligan's Island* fame, the Republican representative from Iowa.

On October 6, just two weeks after Clinton's speech, Cooper and Grandy introduced the updated version of Cooper's 1992 bill, along with forty-four co-sponsors, twenty-six of them Democrats and eighteen of them Republicans. Cooper and Grandy were two very junior members of the House without national reputations, without significant power positions, but word had circulated that they were picking up a great deal of support. The television cameras formed a solid wall as they stood before the microphones at the biggest media event either of them had ever staged. The committee hearing room they had borrowed was jammed with reporters, lobbyists, and staff members of the sponsoring congressmen — all eager to get the details of what seemed likely to be the main House alternative to the Clinton plan. Cooper and Grandy estimated the cost of their bill at $40 billion. It did not include an employer mandate. It would end the employers' unlimited right to deduct the cost of health insurance they bought for their workers, but it would continue to keep those benefits tax-exempt to the workers themselves. Like the Clinton proposal, their plan would keep costs down by encouraging competition among health care providers. They estimated that three out of five of the uninsured would be covered immediately. The rest would be covered as savings materialized from the expected slowdown in medical inflation. "Our bill is squarely in the middle" of the available alternatives, Cooper said.

There was good reason to pay attention to the Cooper-Grandy bill and see it as a threat to Clinton: An actual piece of legislation was available for inspection, while the Clinton plan was still being converted into bill form. The two men had also stockpiled names of other potential sponsors, planning to make them public in matched sets of Democrats and Republicans, to give an impression of growing momentum.

Second, as Cooper said, "it was a bipartisan proposal, and there haven't been a handful of proposals since Truman's time that have ever gotten real bipartisan support." It was also an advantage that their plan looked, at least on the surface, as if it were less vulnerable to attack as heavy-handed government. Cooper's favorite description of it was "Clinton Lite." Like Newt Gingrich, he believed that the Clintons had come up "with a policy that was not in tune with the country. They said they were for bipartisanship, and they ended up producing a proposal which we predicted — I think accurately — would not really have bipartisan support."

Another factor made players take this bill seriously. Important White House officials liked Cooper's approach better than the First Lady's and Magaziner's. From September through the following summer. Chief of Staff Mack McLarty, presidential counselor David Gergen, and members of the economic team were urging Cooper, Breaux, and their allies to "hang in there." They believed, as did Cooper, that in the end a deal would have to be struck for a bipartisan bill. "We have some very powerful friends in the White House," Cooper reported, accurately, at the time.

But the Cooper-Grandy bill had as many detractors as it had supporters. Jay Rockefeller was particularly scornful. "Jim Cooper is a real fraud," he said. "A real fraud. I hope he doesn't make it to this place [the Senate]." Cooper's plan, Rockefeller complained, has "no [cost] discipline, no [employer] mandate, no budget or premium caps or anything of that sort. That is pure sham," he raged. "It has no substance to it."

Hillary Clinton was even more indignant — and personal. One of the First Lady's aides described a meeting in her West Wing office, with seven or eight people, where she "kind of got this evil look and said, 'We've got to do something about this Cooper bill. We've got to kill it before it goes any further.' [Delivery Room manager Jeff] Eller suggested that he fly down to Tennessee and plant some stories. We put a couple people on the radio down there to beat up on the plan. And by the end of it, we had elevated Cooper into this huge thing. It was a massive error."

The President tried diplomacy. He invited Cooper to go jogging with him. He invited him for golf. They talked, but Cooper was not moved. "Universal coverage as defined by some people at the White House," Cooper said, "is the mother of all entitlements. We can fix ten thousand problems in a bipartisan way. But if you hold out unrealistic expectations of peace of mind and security for all, as what I call the Hare Krishna group does, those promises will never be achieved. I think we can move small mountains, maybe not whole mountain ranges, in this bill. We can do as much as anyone since Roosevelt if we get bipartisanship."

Cooper was less perceptive in reading the minds of his Republican allies. Like the Clinton people, he thought many Republicans were searching for something to support. "They introduced their own Republican bill [the Michel bill] and so they need a little face-saving to come our way," he said before Congress adjourned in 1993. "But I think they will acknowledge that the Republican bill's basically a hodgepodge, not real reform." Based on private conversations with them, Cooper thought he would get help from some key House Republicans closer to Bob Michel than to Newt Gingrich. "They're warming up to me," he said.

He was wrong. In time, Cooper conceded he was much too sanguine about the Republicans' readiness to rally behind his bill. At that time, however, he believed it, and it stiffened his stand in dealing with Dingell and the other Democratic leaders of his committee.

In fact, you could hardly call the conversations he had "dealings." Cooper continued to talk with Gephardt — a carryover of the negotiations the majority leader had conducted the previous year — and with Pete Stark, the fiery Californian whom Gephardt had chosen to represent the liberals in those abortive negotiations. Cooper brought Paul Starr, one of the designers of the managed competition approach, to Waxman; that session was not productive. As for Dingell, relations were distant at best. "The only thing Dingell said directly to me was to ask, 'Are you going to play delaying games?' " Cooper said as the effort to draft a bill began. "That's never been my purpose. All I want is fair debate and final votes."

Cooper could not get anywhere with John Dingell, but as 1993 turned into 1994, he was scoring lots of points in the business community. NFIB liked his approach from the start for an obvious reason: It included no employer mandate. But big business — represented by the National Association of Manufacturers (NAM), the Chamber of Commerce, and the Business Roundtable — was not a natural ally for Cooper. Magaziner had high hopes of getting their backing, or at least of gaining their neutrality, because some major companies that already provided benefits actually wanted their smaller competitors to be required to provide insurance. Big business did not like the part of the Cooper proposal that would end the deductibility to the employer of the cost of the so-called Cadillac plans for generous benefits. So the White House pressed its case.

In 1993, Magaziner met nine times with National Association of Manufacturers president Jerry Jasinowski, his board, and his top members, starting barely a month after the task force was formed. Memos of those meetings show NAM shifting from a generally supportive posture on mandates and even temporary price controls to a more cautious, skeptical stance, as Jasinowksi learned more of the scope of the alliances, the size of the basic benefits package, and the skimpiness of proposals to limit business liabilities in cases brought by dissatisfied consumers for recovery of medical costs and "pain and suffering" awards. Magaziner explains the overall legislative strategy of starting left and moving to the center, in order to secure early endorsements from labor, seniors, single-payers, and consumer groups. That, he acknowledges, means that Jasinowski cannot endorse the plan without running into a buzz saw from his own members. But Magaziner's line, repeatedly, is that many of these concerns can be worked out on Capitol Hill, where the plan is likely to be revised in the direction that NAM wishes.

When the plan was leaked in September, Jasinowski said, "There's a lot to like in President Clinton's health reform plan, but it needs substantial improvement before it will win support of manufacturers." He avoided any mention of mandates but later wrote Magaziner, raising "our strongest criticisms of the plan with you privately: The bulk of my members are open but undecided about the plan at this point and require a great deal of education and selling."

Clearly Jasinowski intended this as a signal that NAM had substantial reservations about the direction Clinton was going. Magaziner, not for the first time, seemed to miss the message. So he was shocked to get a phone call from the President at the crack of dawn on October 21, saying he had thought all these discussions with NAM were generally constructive. So what was this in the paper? Clinton was referring to a *Washington Post* story on a NAM board of directors statement saying the President's plan is "too ambitious by half" and needs to be scaled back "dramatically."

The specific objections were exactly those Jasinowski had outlined — too many benefits, too much regulation — but the rhetoric had sharpened. "There is, to be frank, profound skepticism that your [Clinton] plan will successfully reduce the growth of health care costs," the NAM statement said.

Magaziner called Jasinowski: "What the hell is this?" Jasinowski said he felt terrible he had not reviewed the press release, but the spirit expressed was in keeping with their earlier discussions. Some of the board members who opposed the Clinton plan wanted to make sure that Ira wasn't "just rope-a-doping" NAM into seeming to be supportive. They strongly wanted to describe the things they wanted changed. Jasinowski said the supportive language on other parts of the plan was also strong. "Bullshit," Ira exclaimed. "This isn't a case of the press misreporting. You put out a press release like this, and it says one thing."

Jasinowski wrote a letter of apology to the President that day, but the differences were, indeed, unbridgeable. By February 5, when the NAM board was to meet again, Jasinowski told Bob Rubin, who was scheduled to make the administration pitch, there was no point in coming. That day, the NAM board passed a resolution declaring its opposition.

The biggest struggle took place over the Business Roundtable, perhaps the most prestigious of all business groups, numbering more than two hundred top corporate chiefs. As early as 1986 the Roundtable had identified health care costs as a major threat to its member companies' bottom line. Health costs were also a central component of any successful strategy to deal with its number one public-policy goal: curbing the federal deficit. John Ong, longtime CEO of B. F. Goodrich and the Roundtable's 1993–94 chairman, felt that what Clinton said during the campaign and at the "economic summit" in Little Rock during the transition "was really music to our ears." His colleagues were saying, "Hey, the guy's a Democrat and none of us know him. But, by God, he makes sense." In February 1993, leaders of the Roundtable, including Robert Winters, chairman of Prudential Insurance Co., the head of the Roundtable's health task force, met with the President, the Vice President, McLarty, Rubin, and Panetta — but not the First Lady — for a discussion of both economic and health policy. It was not until May, when Hillary Clinton addressed the Business Council, a separate, smaller elite management group, that Ong and Winters had a half-hour conversation with her. This led to a June session in the White House with her and Magaziner.

By that time, the Roundtable executives were getting nervous. Ong said he had scrutinized the list of the task force members when it became public. "About five hundred people, and I didn't know a single one of them. They were all from inside the bureaucracy."

The June meeting added to their disquiet. Magaziner did the briefing, but Ong said, "It was not very definitive — sort of, we're thinking about this, we're thinking about that." Much more revealing was an incident toward the close of the session. Ong recalled Ralph Johnson, CEO of Johnson & Johnson, saying to Hillary Clinton, "You've said that these regional alliances that you're thinking about aren't regulatory bodies, but as I hear what Mr. Magaziner says, they're going to collect premiums from employers, they're going to negotiate with providers, they're going to set standards for employer participants in their alliances, they're going to cap rates. They sound like regulatory agencies to me."

"And she slammed the table like that," Ong said. "I was looking her right in the face, and with daggers coming out of the eyes, she said, 'I said they were purchasing cooperatives, and that's what they're going to be!' And it registered with me that there was maybe less than open-mindedness in this process."

There was more to this revealing moment than an argument about definitions. Ong and his colleagues believed Hillary Clinton and Magaziner were playing a sophisticated double game. In the original Jackson Hole version of managed competition, the purchasing cooperatives were little more than buyers' clubs, or what Jim Cooper liked to call farmers' markets. The CEOs believed that the Clintons had renamed them "alliances" for a reason. They wanted to give them additional regulatory powers — in part to assure that costs would be controlled and in part to satisfy the single-payers and others on the left that this was a system that would achieve the goals they wanted — or, in time, be easily converted to that kind of government-run system. When Johnson and Ong called them on it, Hillary Clinton blew up. Standing on the sidewalk on Pennsylvania Avenue outside the White House after the meeting, the six Roundtable participants agreed they were worried about the direction the Clinton people were taking — "a very public-sector, command-and-control kind of approach."

Months later the First Lady did her best to disabuse them of their suspicions. Speaking in September to the Roundtable's private policy committee meeting at the Willard Hotel, Ong recalled, "She basically took our February policy statement and said, 'You're for this. I'm for this. You're for that. I'm for that.'"

But when the Clinton plan appeared, Winters's task force voted overwhelmingly to recommend opposition. The regulatory functions of the proposed alliances that Johnson had listed were, as Ong said, "something the business community could not stomach." The Clinton plan relied too much on "price controls that never worked."

In mid-January, members of the Roundtable policy committee — a somewhat larger group than Winters's task force — endorsed their opposition in a pair of conference calls that also disclosed a real split in the organization. The majority wanted to reject the administration approach; the minority, including the big three auto companies and Bethlehem Steel, which would benefit directly from the early-retiree provision, said, in Ong's words, "Let's work with them. Let's cooperate and see if we can't get some compromises."

A leak to the White House in early December of a letter from H. Bruce Atwater Jr., chairman of General Mills, a staunch critic of the Clinton plan, to a fellow Roundtable executive had alerted the Clinton team to the fight that was developing and to an effort to swing the Roundtable behind the Cooper bill. Immediately, Bentsen, Rubin, Altman, Magaziner, and McLarty began phoning friends in the Roundtable and urging them to stay neutral or postpone any decision. The talks convinced them of two things. A number of the executives had little knowledge of what was in the Cooper bill. But they knew what they didn't like about the Clinton plan — and those objections had to be taken seriously.

Some of the more supportive executives, from the airlines and auto industry, Kodak, Xerox, and TRW, were invited to the White House to spell out the changes they would like. Business was afraid of being "steamrollered," in what they then expected would be a rush to put a bill on Clinton's desk. A public statement by the White

House endorsing some of the pro-business changes would set those fears to rest. It would pave the way for a favorable Roundtable vote at the early February meeting.

That made sense, Magaziner and Altman thought. They wanted to send a positive signal; it was time to appear conciliatory. Others in the White House disagreed. Even if concessions were made, there was no assurance of Roundtable support. The congressional leadership said the concessions should be negotiated with *them* — not with the administration, and the decision went that way. As a result, the Clinton allies in the Roundtable were told, as Jasinowski had been, that their comfort would have to come from Capitol Hill. It left Magaziner with a feeling of frustration. "Labor is saying, 'Don't compromise. You've already screwed us on NAFTA.' The committee chairs are saying, 'Let us do the deals, not you.' And you're just left impotent to do anything about it."

Still, the administration and its supporters continued to press. Bob Rubin and John Dingell did a "good cop, bad cop" tattoo on John Ong, who described Dingell's message as saying. "Look, I've always been willing to work with the business community. But you're becoming the enemy, and if you position yourself that way, you leave me no recourse. I've got to fight you. There's going to be a confrontation." Rubin's approach was one of "reasoning together." Basically, he said, Look, this is crazy. We share the same objectives. All of us here [in the White House] don't love every part of this approach. But if you guys come out against it, you are going to disarm the administration moderates and get the backs up of the others.

On February 1, the day before the crucial Roundtable meeting, Hillary Clinton invited a half-dozen of its sympathetic members to a White House meeting. They were joined by the President. Both Clintons urged the business leaders not to choose among the plans. That night, several of the other Roundtable big shots, including Ong and Winters, were invited to Rostenkowski's office. At first, Ong said, Rostenkowski was his usual self, gruffly tempting them to negotiate with him. "We all know him and have worked with him before," Ong said, "and he said, 'We ought to work these things out. I understand you guys, but you have to understand me. I may not like everything in this, but goddamn it, they put these goddamn things together and they throw 'em on my desk — some of it's a bunch of shit — and then they expect me to do something with it.' " But Ong noticed that as White House officials arrived to join the discussions — first Stephanopoulos, then Ickes, then Pat Griffin — Rostenkowski became "more and more forceful in stating the administration's position and saying to us, 'What's wrong with you guys? Why can't you get with the action?' "

Despite the pressure, the Roundtable endorsed the Cooper plan as the best "starting point" for congressional action. They expressed concern that the Clinton approach would "create additional unfunded, off-budget entitlement programs [and] impose government regulation of the health care industry and what are in effect price controls." Not long after, AARP's John Rother reported to the White House that a Prudential lobbyist had told him, "We can't stand the Cooper bill. We just used that as a way to derail Clinton."

Harold Ickes had been right. It came down to a question of trust more than a question of issues. As business saw it, the Clintons were trying to have it both ways. Privately they promised to accommodate them. Publicly they denounced them. P. Roy Vagelos, the chairman and chief executive of Merck & Co., who had been host to Clinton for the main health care speech of the 1992 campaign, was disgusted by his dealings with this White House. He told the *Wall Street Journal*, "We would love to work with them. We've tried repeatedly to get with them. Unfortunately, we're always left with the feeling if we're not supportive of what they want, we'll be excluded. So you're either a supporter or an enemy." John Ong said that other pharmaceutical and insurance executives told their colleagues, "You can't deal with these guys. You can't trust them. Look what happened to me. I thought I could trust them, and now I'm a profiteer and I'm taking food from the mouths of widows and orphans and all this kind of stuff."

They also thought they had been conned by Hillary Clinton and Magaziner. "They told us we were going to have a voice and we really didn't," Ong said. "Whatever inputs we had a chance to make apparently were ignored."

The day after the Roundtable meeting, at a congressional hearing, the Chamber of Commerce of the United States changed its position and came out against the Clinton plan. The circumstances suggested a last-minute flip-flop, but there was more to it than that. In a prepared statement that arrived the day before the hearing, Robert Patricelli, a benefits expert who was chairman of the Chamber's health committee, placed on the record support for an employer mandate — as long as the cost was reduced to 50 percent of the most minimal plan. (The Clinton proposal called for business to pay 80 percent of the basic premium.)

That testimony was withdrawn. The lame excuse was that it was a staff-written document that had not received necessary clearances. Instead, Patricelli testified that the Clinton plan had so many flaws it could not serve as the basis for sound legislation. "If employer mandates become the vehicle for those who favor the trappings of a government-dominated system, we will not accept those mandates," he said.

Behind the change of direction was an intensive grassroots campaign, waged against the Chamber's national leadership by congressional Republicans and the No Name Coalition. They used the *Wall Street Journal* editorial page, radio talk shows, and the communications network of the NFIB and other small-business groups to pressure Chamber executives to take a much more antagonistic stand. At Gingrich's urging, prominent House Republicans boycotted a Chamber awards dinner and urged their local Chambers to protest the national policy. Chamber officials reported threats from congressional Republicans to "take a walk" on other issues if the Chamber backed Clinton. In the end, the Chamber bucked. After delivering the revised testimony, Patricelli resigned from his post along with the executive who had been steering Chamber policy on the issue.

What the White House had expected to be a major pillar of support for reform — the big-business community — had been eliminated. Speaking specifically of the Roundtable, Dingell said much later. "When the administration failed to get them, there was a big shift in sentiment inside my committee. That was a defining event."

Jay Rockefeller called a news conference to denounce the business shift, saying "There's a special place in hell waiting for Bob Winters," the chairman of Prudential and head of the Roundtable health care policy panel.

On February 5, Hillary Clinton took up the cudgels herself in a Philadelphia speech. She ripped into the insurance and drug industries in particular for being "rife with fraud, waste, and abuse." While the United States has the finest doctors and hospitals in the world, she said, "we have the stupidest financing system in the world. The insurance companies are in charge and basically pick and choose whom they cover. We are basically taking the billions and billions of dollars we spend on financing health care and dropping it in a black hole as far as I'm concerned."

The White House could rail at its big-business critics as much as it chose, but the damage had been done. Administration aide Chris Jennings said immediately after the meeting that it was a "strategic blunder" for the White House to have involved the President and the First Lady in lobbying the Roundtable. "No one would have made that news unless we attempted to dissuade them at that level," he said. "We were dressed down by many people in the House leadership for doing that. Rostenkowski was just livid with us. He said, 'That's a non-news story that the Roundtable and the Chamber aren't with you. They're never with you on any major reform piece of legislation. They're always against it until the end. You should expect it. Why are you even playing around with them?' " The veteran lawmaker gave them a lesson on the way The System works — or should work. He told the newcomers that the process would have its highs and lows "but you don't knee-jerk react to everything that goes on out there. These crises," he said, referring to the contretemps with Reischauer over the CBO scoring of the Clinton plan and with the Chamber and the Business Roundtable, "were created right in this [Oval] office. They were nothing. The press wouldn't even have picked up on it if it wasn't generated here at the White House."

A labor leader supporting reform blamed the fiasco on Clinton's "eagerness to appease big business," linking it to the President's early emphasis on budget-cutting and to his support of the NAFTA free-trade agreement with Mexico and Canada. The failure reflected something even more characteristic of Clinton — his desire to placate people, his eagerness to have everyone on his side. In this fight, that was seeking the impossible. And in the end, the administration lost all the major business organizations.

In the postmortems, the White House and the business executives were far apart in their explanations of what had happened. When Hillary Clinton spoke of the reasons that business turned against the plan, she told a tale of cowardice and betrayal. In her mind, she could prove to the General Electrics and Fords that in bottom-line dollars these companies would be helped by the Clinton plan. Not only did it propose government subsidies for costs of early retirees but it forced small business to shoulder its part of the load and provided government help for the uninsured. That, the First Lady contended, would eliminate providers' need to charge the big firms more to make up for the cost of those without coverage.

It should have made sense to the CEOs, she thought, but four things undercut that logic. The first was simple ideology. These men were largely conservative Republicans, and whatever their heads told them, their hearts were uncomfortable signing off on a plan that came from a Democratic White House and represented an expansion — the biggest in decades — in the welfare state. Second, she believed, was the subversive activity of the employee benefits bureaucracy within these big corporations. Their work would be severely reduced, if not eliminated, by the introduction of standard benefits and the elimination of special underwriting deals. So, she believed, they set to work to undermine their bosses' confidence in the promise of the Clinton plan. Third, she said, the insurance company and pharmaceutical executives who sat on the board of directors of the big manufacturing companies and met with them as fellow CEOs filled them with horror stories about the dangers of government medicine. Finally, Cooper and his allies in the Jackson Hole group, who had great entree to the executive suites, lobbied hard against the Clinton plan, arguing it was a regulatory approach — a view that obviously resonated with regulation-averse businessmen.

The "scare tactics," as the First Lady called them, could be refuted point by point, when she was talking to the executives at White House dinners and at meetings. But inside their own tight little world, these men fed off what she regarded as a mixture of antigovernment prejudices and simple misinformation, which she had no way to counter.

Executives involved in the debate told a very different story. From

their perspective, the Clintons were latecomers to a battle they, the
CEOs, had been waging for years — the fight to control their companies' health care costs. For much of the 1980s, it had been a losing
struggle, but lately — out of sheer business necessity — their firms
had developed strategies that were beginning to pay off: a transfer of
costs to employees or retirees; tougher bargaining with insurers and
providers; a shift to managed care programs with more predictable
costs; an emphasis on exercise regimens, anti-smoking drives, and
other "wellness" programs.

Now, just when they were beginning to bring their health care
bills down closer to the overall inflation rate, along came the Clintons
with their elaborate scheme that would standardize benefits, bring
new governmental and quasi-governmental regulation, and set a
"ceiling" on employer contributions that, for big firms dealing with
strong unions, would in effect become a floor.

Most of all, the CEOs said, control of this big cost element would
be shifted from their hands to government's — the same government running huge deficits and threatening early bankruptcy of its
Medicare trust fund.

There was something else, they said privately. Many executives
had now had firsthand dealings with Bill Clinton, and the "trust
factor" that Harold Ickes had said would be crucial was not there.
Many had worked with Clinton in the NAFTA fight. They admired
his courage in taking on the unions and the majority of his own congressional party. But they had also seen Clinton's seeming need to
comfort everyone he met by appearing to agree with his or her position. So they discounted his assurances that he would stick to his
own plan and not let it become a stepping-stone to a single-payer,
government-run system.

Clinton's concessions to single-payers were a warning sign to
business. The provision allowing any state the option of setting up a
single-payer system within its borders, for example, was a clear threat
to multistate employers who wanted to negotiate with their own insurer for a package covering *all* their workers. "In the end," said one
executive, "most of us decided that in a showdown, Clinton would appease the left wing of his own party and leave us holding the bag."

* * *

All of these lost battles made John Dingell's task look more difficult as he began his roundup of votes on Energy and Commerce.
And the problem looked worse when he took the temperature of
the committee Republicans. One day in March of 1994, Dingell
plopped himself down next to Carlos Moorhead of California on
the House floor, and said, "I want to talk with you about working out a health bill." He reminded Moorhead, the senior Republican on his committee, of past occasions when they had written
bills together. "I think we ought to try and see what we can do,"
Dingell said.

Back in his office, a few days later, Dingell quoted what he said
was Moorhead's response: "John, there's no way you're going to get
a single vote on this [Republican] side of the aisle. You will not only
not get a vote here, but we've been instructed that if we participate
in that undertaking at all, those of us who do will lose our seniority
and will not be ranking minority members within the Republican
Party."

When we asked Moorhead about Dingell's account of their conversation, he gave what reporters call a non-denial denial. "That
doesn't sound like anything that happened," he began. "We had
not been instructed not to participate in any discussions. The problem was that John was not his own man on that bill. He had to
carry water for the Clintons. He was tied to the administration. I
told him that if he were divorced from the administration, we could
work together. But he couldn't get out of that rut. And I wasn't
willing to participate until they gave up their socialistic medicine
approach."*

In fact, as he was later to confirm to us, Gingrich had decided to
try to kill the Clintons' health bill "the day she [the First Lady] decided they were going to go for a grand solution." But that time, in
the spring of 1994, his decision was well camouflaged. Supposedly,
signals for the Republican health strategy were being called by

---

*If Moorhead thought he had carte blanche to negotiate, he was wrong. A year later, after the
Republican takeover, Gingrich showed what he thought of the Californian's acuity by passing
over him, the senior Republican on the committee, and instead naming Thomas J. Bliley Jr. of
Virginia as the new chairman of Energy and Commerce. Later in 1995, Moorhead announced
he would retire from Congress at the end of his term.

J. Dennis (Denny) Hastert of Illinois, a member of Energy and Commerce. Minority Leader Bob Michel had charged Hastert with coordinating the GOP health reform — a decision that initially made Gingrich "very angry."

Denny Hastert insisted to us that he'd been given no orders to stop reform. Hastert, a beefy former high school history teacher and coach representing a solidly GOP suburban district west of Chicago, was the kind of laid-back conservative Bob Michel felt more comfortable with than the Newt Gingrich–style of firebrand. When Michel chose Hastert as head of the House GOP health task force, the White House mistakenly took comfort; it meant, they thought, that Michel was not ceding control of the issue to Gingrich. Rather he was keeping a "reasonable" person in charge.

Hastert was reasonable — but also deeply skeptical. Back home, he told town meetings that the Clinton plan offered "the efficiency of the post office and the compassion of the IRS" — a line widely, and privately, circulated to opponents in Congress by members of the No Name Coalition. Hastert thought the Harry and Louise ads "really raised questions out there, legitimate questions."

On one hand, Hastert would say, "we just got done putting together a telecommunications bill, a huge piece of legislation affecting maybe one-sixth of the economy, and we did it on a bipartisan basis." On the other hand, he would say that health care was a lot more personal issue than telecommunications, and it looked to him as if the Democrats "want to get two hundred twenty or two hundred thirty votes on their side, and roll us — not have to deal with us." Hastert was suspicious of compromises being bandied about in the House. In the end, he suspected a House-Senate conference committee would produce something like the original Clinton bill — and force Republicans to vote on it, just a month before the election. But he insisted that his hands were not tied. "Absolutely not," he said in March. "I sat down with Newt Gingrich and said, 'We need to work toward a consensus. We don't want our people picked off for some plan. But if we come together and open up some discussion, that's what we're looking for. We understand that we can't pass a Republican bill. It has to be unbundled and put back together on a bipartisan basis. That's been our bottom line. I can tell you from the license Gingrich has given me to go talk to people — and Bob Michel's given me the same license — that's exactly our position."

John Dingell did not believe a word of that. He was convinced the Republicans would fight him and Clinton to the end. But some Republicans wanted to believe they could play a more constructive role. One of them was a forty-one-year-old Michigan congressman, Fred Upton, whom Dingell had encouraged to join Energy and Commerce. Upton was a grandson of the founder of the Whirlpool Corporation, and his district included Kalamazoo, home of pharmaceutical giant Upjohn. Before he came to Congress, he had served as the assistant to Reagan administration budget director David Stockman. Despite this, Upton was anything but a rigid conservative.

In March of 1994, Upton met with about thirty union leaders from his district. To his dismay, one of them handed him a memorial card from the funeral mass for his sister, who had died two weeks earlier without health insurance.

Talking to us the next day, Upton still seemed preoccupied by the card. "If she had had health care, maybe she would be alive today," he said, staring at the card with the name Bonnie Sweet on it. "I told him [the brother] the story about a guy who used to head my local Chamber of Commerce. After he left that job, he took another, where there was no health insurance. He had a minor heart attack and survived. When he had a second episode, he argued with his wife — really fought her — not to call 911, because they didn't have health insurance and they couldn't afford it. Probably could have saved him, really, but he didn't want her to call. She finally did, but it was too late.

"I want reform," Upton continued, and told of a recent conversation with an executive of a middle-sized manufacturing firm in his district who said his company was going to have to end medical benefits for retirees in the near future. "He wasn't that far from retirement age himself, but he said, 'We have no choice. The costs are just eating us up.'"

Upton had "gotten hostile mail from some folks back home, who want to do nothing," but had replied that if nothing changed, health care costs would undermine family, business, and government budgets alike. Even as he said that, Upton was, as he said, "coming to the swift conclusion that we're not going to see any meaningful reform this year."

Earlier, he had been much more optimistic. He and his wife had both been to the White House and had come away impressed. He had met with Magaziner, and his wife had joined congressional spouses for a briefing by Hillary Clinton. Upton was more attracted to Cooper's bill than to the administration plan, but he did not co-sponsor the Cooper bill, in part because "the word is out that Dingell is fairly hostile to those folks that are co-sponsoring Cooper," and Upton wanted to preserve his own relationship with the chairman.

On the same day he was handed Bonnie Sweet's memorial card, he had two other experiences that deepened his pessimism about any agreement on reform. At noon, he attended a "Tuesday lunch bunch" meeting of thirty Republican moderates with Pat Griffin, who in January 1994 had succeeded Howard Paster as the chief White House congressional lobbyist. For Griffin, health care was not an abstract issue. He had come to the President's service after many years of working with Congress, first as an aide to Senator Robert Byrd and for the last seven years as a lobbyist with several health care clients. Though he had not been a Clinton intimate in the presidential campaign, the prospect of helping pass reform led him to accept Clinton's offer. Like Paster before him, he now found himself the target of people who were dissatisfied with the way the administration was handling the issue. Why, these Republicans asked, had Griffin waited until now, two months into the session, to meet with them? "You in the White House have got to get out of that campaign mode," Upton told Griffin. "You're going to get in trouble. This is gridlock coming from your end."

Griffin told the group something Upton did not want to believe: "They had gotten a signal from Republican leaders not to deal with — don't even talk to — our Republicans. And they honored that pledge." Walking back to the Rayburn House Office Building after a roll call vote later that day, Upton heard John Dingell confirm that the message from the GOP was "in no uncertain terms not to talk to any of the Republicans on the committee." There would be no bipartisan deals on this one.

* * *

Stymied on the Republican side of the aisle, Dingell turned back to his Democrats — and once again found himself facing that aggravating opponent, Jim Cooper. When we asked Cooper early in the Energy and Commerce proceedings if he thought Dingell was "trying to thwart you or to beat your brains out or to try to find some way to accommodate you," he said, "I'm not sure. I'm scared. He knows the members of the committee and I think he knows our strength. We've got the four to six Democrats it would take to be a negative player. What we're looking for now is to be a positive force."

Cooper was unaware that Dingell believed he was not seriously interested in compromise and should be disciplined. The chairman decided the best way to bring Cooper to heel was to create trouble for him in Tennessee. Dingell had no problem enlisting some of his trade union friends, for they also had little use for Cooper. The March issue of the United Paperworkers International Union newspaper had a front-page headline "Jim Cooper, Grand-Standing on Health Care, Forgets His Constituents." Inside, other headlines said "Cooper's Constituents Live with the Crisis He Wants America to Dodge." Another featured "the $30,000 Party," a Cooper fundraiser at the "lavish Nashville home" of Clayton McWhorter, the head of Healthtrust, Inc., a for-profit hospital chain. "It is no coincidence that Cooper's well-funded Senate campaign is built around a proposal that protects the exorbitant profits of the rapidly growing companies which helped create our current health care crisis," the story said. Reprints of the four-page Paperworkers' special report turned up all over Tennessee.

At a union-sponsored rally in Chattanooga, a copy of the "phony" Cooper-Grandy bill was ceremonially burned. Unless Cooper changed his tune, threatened Jim Neeley, the president of the Tennessee AFL-CIO, labor would either "sit out" the Senate election or possibly endorse Republican candidate Fred Thompson.

The most damaging blow fell at a civil rights meeting in Memphis. AFSCME (the American Federation of State, County and Municipal Employees) distributed a flyer that claimed "Cooper's plan would punish African Americans more than others" and "is an injustice to our community." Cooper, the flyer said, has joined forces with the "health care profiteers" to offer "a fatal dose of phony reform." Ellen

Globocar, AFSCME's political director, justified the tactics: "Cooper probably did more damage to Bill Clinton's program than anybody. We took him on as a full-time project. We had a guy hanging on to him. We would get calls from the DNC [Democratic National Committee], and the DNC would say, 'Why are we beating up on him?' And we'd say, 'Maybe it's because he was trying to kill the President's health care proposal.' "

After several weeks of pressure, Globocar's boss, AFSCME president Jerry McEntee, set up a meeting with Cooper in the office of Senator Jim Sasser, the Democrat who would be defending the other Tennessee seat in November. Sasser wanted a cease-fire to the civil war that was damaging the entire Democratic ticket. The meeting was loud and contentious. Finally, Cooper said he might relent. He would give Dingell a vote for *his* bill, if Dingell would agree to clear the *Cooper* bill as well. That was exactly what Dingell wanted. Two days later, Cooper called McEntee. He couldn't switch his vote, Cooper said, but would try to get another opponent to go along with the deal. McEntee called Dingell. The chairman was blunt: "He's a liar." The pressure resumed.

This was a risky tactic to use on someone almost certain to be the Democratic candidate for a shaky Senate seat, but labor was doing exactly what Dingell wanted. "He's getting his ass burned at home," Dingell remarked with satisfaction. "And I'm somewhat comfortable with his distress."

By late March, John Dingell was a thoroughly frustrated man. He scaled back his "chairman's mark," or negotiating position, several times in private negotiations with other committee Democrats, but little headway was made. On March 21, he let his staff leak an eight-page revised draft that included a big concession to small business. It would exempt firms with fewer than ten employees from the employer mandate and reduce basic benefits. Further, it would be optional for companies and individuals to buy their health insurance through the alliances that would be created in each state. The goal of covering all Americans would be preserved by requiring a 1 or 2 percent payroll tax to pay for insurance for workers in firms that refused to pay for their policies.

Dingell realized that the members of Congress — and public opinion — were moving away from him and the realization of his father's dream. About that time, a *Los Angeles Times* poll showed that crime had replaced health care at the top of the voters' agenda. Only a third of those polled would be upset if Congress postponed passage of a universal coverage bill. "The members are listening to what their people back home are saying," Dingell remarked just before the Easter recess.

By that point, Dingell was fighting a two-front war. While he vainly struggled to find the votes for some version of the Clinton plan, he became aware that a conservative alternative that made him livid was developing a dangerous amount of support. It was the bill concocted by J. Roy (Doc) Rowland, the conservative Democratic physician-legislator from Georgia, and Michael Bilirakis, the Florida Republican who had received what he thought was a green light from President Clinton, during their conversation aboard Air Force One back in September.

Rowland-Bilirakis was a minimalist bill. Its insurance reforms would allow people even with serious health problems to buy protection. It permitted small employers to form voluntary purchasing groups. It limited malpractice suits, increased penalties for fraud, standardized claim forms, and promised to expand community health centers for indigent families. But it included no way to pay for these changes and promised no additional coverage of the uninsured.

The lobbyists who met regularly with Billy Pitts, Minority Leader Michel's top aide, were mobilizing support for the Rowland-Bilirakis bill. Pitts enlisted Alan Kranowitz of the National Association of Wholesalers and Debbie Steelman, the former Bush administration health aide turned lobbyist, to help the two sponsors improve the drafting of their bill and expand its circle of supporters. By May they had seventy co-sponsors, half from each party. For those who didn't want to vote for employer mandates, Rowland-Bilirakis was beginning to be seen as an attractive option. It helped that the two sponsors were likable, trusted by their colleagues, and that their aims seemed refreshingly modest compared to the Clinton plan. "We said from the first press conference where we outlined the bill that we did not intend for it to be the cure-all for everything," Bilirakis said. "We decided it should be a foundation. It would start helping people now, and it would start saving money now. And it would lead to further access."

Denny Hastert reported growing support for Rowland-Bilirakis at the Republican leadership meetings in Bob Michel's office. For a brief period, there was talk that a majority might be assembled in Energy and Commerce to report that kind of bill. Debbie Steelman, for one, thought it might happen, "but we missed the window because of Jim Cooper. He wouldn't ever come along. He had his own bill and his own deal."

It is the ultimate irony of this story that Cooper ended up frustrating both sides. He refused to compromise his differences with the Clinton administration. Until the very end, when it was too late, he refused to join forces with the Rowland-Bilirakis group. He thought his policy approach was right. And he thought it would emerge from the Senate. "I stole all their clothes," he bragged in March of 1994 to reporters at the *Washington Post*, "because most of the business groups in America have already if not endorsed, come close to endorsing, our approach. Where is [Republicans'] support going to come from? These folks got caught unprepared."

Cooper was oblivious to the deliberate opposition activity that was going on around — and through — him. While he stood fast, events passed him by.

In one of our interviews during this period, Dingell, a masterful legislative technician, explained the limitations of his role in The System. "My job," he said, "is to try to make The System work. A lot of times I've pushed things that are far different than what I would have done had I had the sole responsibility for making the decision. But I do it, simply because somebody's got to do that or The System breaks down in its entirety."

For his kind of brokering to work, Dingell said, there has to be a public consensus. "We're the servants of the people," he said. "Politicians poll their constituents all the time; they know what the people want. And when the people don't make their views clear, this place doesn't function."

On health reform, Dingell said, there was agreement on some points, but not on "the critical elements: Who pays? How much do they pay? And who's going to get what? These are not yet subject to consensus. And may not be. I never met anybody who wanted to spend money on somebody else."

And without that kind of consensus?

"It's going to be very hard. It has been very hard and it will be very hard."

When the House came back from the Easter recess in April 1994, Dingell resumed his meetings with individual committee members. By this time, he had taken personal charge of the rescue effort. As is customary, the bill had first been referred to Waxman's Health Subcommittee. Anticipating trouble, Dingell set a deadline for subcommittee action. When Waxman was unable to get a majority to report anything that resembled the administration proposal, Dingell reclaimed the bill. "Henry [Waxman] took this thing very, very personally," Dingell said afterward. "He was quite outraged about it. But I told him, 'We only have so much time to do this. If you can't do it in the subcommittee, I have to take over and try to do it in full committee. This is not to denigrate you. It's just something I've got to do.' Henry finally understood."

Having bumped Waxman aside, Dingell felt even more pressure not to fail. One staff member described him as "a man possessed," and warned visitors that the fabled Dingell temper was even shorter than usual. "Big John" prowled the House floor, seeking bits of intelligence that might help his cause. He ignored protocol and called on wavering freshman members in their own offices. One of them, Californian Lynn Schenk, said, "My staff doesn't get impressed by a lot of folks. But Chairman Dingell walks in and everybody snaps to, saluting. We lowered our eyes as he passed."

In Schenk's cramped third-floor office, Dingell made himself comfortable on the government-issue couch. His staff had been communicating with Schenk's aides. He knew the biotech industries in Schenk's district had problems with the Clinton proposal. "What can I do to help bring you along to where you and I both want you to be?" he asked. Often, thereafter, he would quietly slip into the chair next to hers on the House floor, and their conversation would continue. He would appear. She would talk. He would listen patiently; then, another day, he would reappear, often without warning.

"He listened to what I was worried about," Schenk said. "He listened to the reasons I was worried about it. He didn't say anything in response at first."

Later Schenk figured out why: "He was gathering information so that by the time the meeting [where he actually asked for her vote] took place, he was prepared to say, 'Well, on your concern about biotech, I think we can do this. On your concern about small business, here's what we're thinking about doing.' It wasn't like a contract negotiation, where you sit down at the table: All right, here are my list of ultimatums and here are yours. It was much more collegial than that."

In April, Schenk and key staff met with Henry Waxman in Dingell's office for what seemed a final negotiation. By that point Schenk said, "My heart wasn't beating quite as fast and the lump wasn't quite as big in my throat." Agreeing to eliminate government regulation of prices for newly discovered drugs wasn't a tough concession for Dingell. It eased the way for Schenk and another freshman, Marjorie Margolies-Mezvinsky of suburban Philadelphia, to claim credit with their biotech companies and still support the bill.

With other members Dingell had little more success than Waxman had. He was *still* short one vote. After it was over, he said, "We tried hard to get Tauzin. We tried hard to get Cooper, although Cooper isolated himself by the games he played with Republicans." Nothing worked. Dingell asked Mike Synar of Oklahoma to try his luck. Synar took Cooper, whose family was living in Tennessee, to a four-hour dinner at the Red Sage, a favorite politicians' hangout in Washington. "I just couldn't get him to budge," Synar said afterward. "Pride of authorship is not what's driving him. He really is convinced that he owns the Senate Finance Committee, and so he doesn't have to deal over here." Cooper had told Synar that his co-sponsor, Senator John Breaux, was convinced that only two Democrats on Finance — Majority Leader George Mitchell of Maine and Senator Tom Daschle of South Dakota, Mitchell's protégé and 1995 successor as leader of the Senate Democrats — would hold out for the Clinton plan. The others would gravitate to some hybrid of the Cooper-Breaux bill and John Chafee's Republican plan requiring all individuals to buy their own insurance, the so-called individual mandate.

Over the third of four tequilas they drank that night, Synar said, he tried his only other ploy. Cooper was risking his Senate race by his obduracy on health care, Synar argued. "I explained to him that he had problems with labor, problems with blacks, problems with regular Democrats down there, that the race was close and that the enthusiasm of those supporters would be critical. He looks at me and says, 'I need not remind you that Al Gore never mentioned the name Walter Mondale when he ran for the Senate in 1984.' " Gore won that race, and Mondale was crushed by Ronald Reagan, "so he is absolutely convinced that moving to the right of Clinton is the politically expedient thing to do. Besides, he said, 'I am sufficiently far ahead, they [the Republicans] can't catch me.' So it just doesn't play."

Both of them were wrong. Synar was defeated later that year in a September Democratic primary runoff in Oklahoma, and Cooper went down in November in Tennessee.* But neither of them foresaw their peril that night.

With concessions to the biotech interests and other backroom deals, Dingell could count twenty-two of the twenty-three votes he needed to report a bill. But he was running out of bodies. His search came down to one man — Jim Slattery of Kansas.

Dingell thought he would get Slattery. He told other Democrats that Slattery was someone he had always respected "as a man of real substance and ability. Slattery grunts and strains a lot when you give him a hard question, but he usually comes through and he usually stands like a rock. I've always thought he was a real man. But he's disproved that thesis." The problem was that Slattery was running for governor of Kansas in 1994. In a conservative state that happened to be the home of Senate Minority Leader Robert J. Dole, a key player on health care, Slattery had a limited capacity for brave gestures. With his gubernatorial campaign intensifying and the spotlight on

---

*Synar's death, in January 1996 of a brain tumor at age forty-five, removed one of the brightest young Democrats from public life.

him as the swing vote on Energy and Commerce, Slattery turned out to be "just a scared politician thinking only about the election." Dingell invited Slattery to tell him "what we need to do to get him," and instead of answering with specifics, Slattery "slithered all over the lot." At least that's what Dingell thought.

Slattery drew heat from both sides. Speaker Foley talked to him a couple of times, and gave up. "Instead of needing a little push, as Dingell said, I thought that, if anything, my discussion and dialogue with him was hardening his views," the Speaker said. "The more he had to defend it, the more his position became firmer. So I told John, 'I'm not doing any good here.'"

Then the President weighed in. He joined Slattery in Kansas at a health care meeting with small-business owners. Still no commitment. During the Easter recess, the Health Care Reform Project of organizations supporting the Clinton plan ran ads in Slattery's district. One focused on the small-business issue. An upholsterer who bought insurance for his employees was shown complaining that "other companies cut corners by not covering their workers and that gives them an advantage." Another ad was the one that Mandy Grunwald had managed to kill during that bitter White House meeting on the snowy night four months earlier. Alarmed by the steady slippage in public support for the Clinton plan, Bob Chlopak of the Health Care Reform Project had decided to go ahead and make the case that the American people should have as good health insurance as members of Congress gave themselves. The ad said members of Congress "get it [health insurance]. They pay thirty percent — our taxes pay the rest. Not a bad deal. Tell Congressman Slattery you want health insurance at work, just like his deal. Nothing less." Phone banks and direct-mail pieces backed up the ads, and the calls to Slattery's office urged him to support the Clinton plan.

AFSCME's Ellen Globocar worked hard at influencing Slattery. Her operatives began following Slattery wherever he went in Kansas, always wearing costumes from the Wizard of Oz. "We had these characters who followed Slattery around," Globocar recalled. "One of my staff people was there dressed as the Scarecrow. That was supposed to be Slattery. So he came up to her at a campaign rally and asked, 'I don't understand. Why am I the Scarecrow?' She didn't want to tell him it was because he didn't have a brain. . . . But we never got him. Of course, he was running for bigger office, and there was too much power from the other side."

Much of the counterpressure came from Hallmark Card and Pepsico, two of the biggest employers in Kansas. Dingell said, "Slattery told us that he was called in by those two firms and told that if he voted with us on this, he would get no money whatsoever." Hallmark and Pepsico already had health plans for their own employees, but both firms were big franchisers, and they did not want the thousands of small card shops and pizza and taco parlors to be required to provide insurance for their employees. So Dingell made exceptions in the bill to assist very small businesses; but Slattery was not satisfied.

Slattery maintained that he had reasons for objecting. As a budgeteer, he was worried about what he considered the shakiness of the cost estimates for the Clinton plan. As a representative of a state with thousands of small businesses, he feared that the imposition of insurance costs would cause many who were "struggling and hanging on by their fingernails, just to close the door, say 'Thank you very much. Here are my keys.'"

Furthermore, he thought it was unrealistic to design "a uniform health care package to fit everybody in America." Hallmark, he said, offered very good benefits to its employees, but kept its costs down by putting heavy emphasis on exercise and antismoking programs and "teaching personal responsibility as part of the corporate culture. Now, for the federal government to come in and say, in effect, 'You can't continue to do what you've done — and done successfully. You're now going to have to provide this package of benefits to everybody under these conditions. Whether you like it or not, whether the employees like it or not, whether it costs more or less is immaterial. You're going to have to do this.'"

At that point, the famous Dingell temper exploded. "You can make an argument for the employees of the small-business franchises," he stormed, "but it's pretty goddamn hard to tell anybody that you ought to be deeply concerned about the travail of a major U.S. corporation listed on the New York Stock Exchange. The bonuses of the heads of those corporations alone would pay for the damned health care for their employees."

What made Dingell's efforts futile was the power wielded by the National Federation of Independent Business (NFIB). This was not a battle of Washington lobbyists. It was not a deal that could be negotiated quietly between a chairman and a committee member. It was not a chit that could be cashed by the Speaker. As John Motley had recognized early in the game, this was a war that would be won in the field, district by district, state by state. That's where NFIB had the Clinton forces vastly outgunned. It put out an "emergency alert" to its eight thousand Kansas members to inform Slattery that "an employer mandate of any type would be devastating" to their bottom lines.

Ron Wyden of Oregon, one of Dingell's and Gephardt's House loyalists, observed that "the opposition's done a very good job, a magnificent job of roiling the waters and frightening people. They have conveyed a sense that the President is going to tear up the sidewalks, cause bedlam, have everyone who's now covered to have their policies canceled and go to a Rube Goldberg contraption called an alliance and start over."

Wyden did not know the half of it. Michael Weisskopf of the *Washington Post* reported from Kansas on the grassroots lobbying campaign against Slattery. The treasurer of Slattery's election campaign, Mike Van Dyke, was also the congressional district coordinator for the health care campaign of the National Association of Life Underwriters (NALU), with 140,000 members nationwide. Many of these agents also sold health insurance policies, using that as a foot in the door for more lucrative life insurance underwriting. Van Dyke was not just a key supporter of Slattery; he had been Slattery's teammate on their high school football team and such a close friend that Slattery was godfather to Van Dyke's daughter. "In Jim's case, he knows I have an interest personally but that I'll tell him the good, the bad, and the ugly," Van Dyke told Weisskopf.

NALU organized teams of grassroots lobbyists in the districts of all Energy and Commerce members. Van Dyke had three other insurance agents and two business clients (also supporters of Slattery's campaign) working with him. They and their friends were spreading the word to their clients — using the leverage they gained, as Weisskopf noted, "as financial adviser to Main Street businesses," as the people in most small towns who "sit on school boards, work for civic groups, head up charity drives, run for public office and bankroll politicians."

Slattery well understood their power. "When you go to the town hall meeting or the Rotary Club," he told Weisskopf, "they're the ones who understand health care. When agents tell people what a proposal will do, they listen." Now they were telling everyone that the Clinton plan — with its mandatory alliances — would put them out of business and force people to deal with an anonymous bureaucrat on the other end of an 800 line.

NFIB had been pressuring Slattery since January. Its attention was reflected in the weekly memos that NFIB's House lobbyist, Mark Isakowitz, sent to Jack Faris, the group's president. For example:

February 12: Rep. Jim Slattery, who could be the tie-breaking vote in the Health Subcommittee on the mandate, met with Hillary Clinton. Prior to the meeting, his staff had told us he had decided to oppose the mandate. After the Hillary meeting, his staff said he was still open to compromise on the mandate. Our latest anti-mandate Action Alert just went out in his district.

March 4: Kim heard from a good source that Rep. Jim Slattery of KS would offer a compromise 50 percent employer mandate in the Commerce Cmte. Eight GAC members are going to see him on Monday. [GAC stands for Guardian Advisory Council, an informal board of directors of NFIB activists in each state.]

March 11: Eight Kansas GAC members met with Rep. Jim Slattery in Topeka on Monday. He is a key swing vote on Commerce, and he told our members he believes there should be some employer mandate in the bill. He is running for governor so there might be some additional grassroots we can do here.

March 25: Rep. Jim Slattery appears to be the major deal maker with Chairman Dingell on this [compromise] plan. Today, an Action Alert to ALL Kansas NFIB members is going out specifically on Slattery. We are going statewide with the alert because he is running for governor and has to be sensitive to concerns outside his district. Kim and I met with Slattery on Tuesday.

April 8: The day before Clinton arrived in Topeka to campaign for health care reform with Rep. Slattery, a group of business owners (including an NFIB member) unveiled the ad to appear in the next day's Topeka paper announcing the coalition of more than 1 million employers opposing the mandate.

April 15: Chairman John Dingell continues to negotiate with the people we have been targeting but does not yet have a majority on the Commerce Committee. There are signs our grassroots are working. Slattery has retreated some on the mandate, is said to have proposed this week a way to get to universal coverage without the mandate; he had told our members in March this was impossible.

April 22: Rep. Jim Slattery announced his opposition to the employer mandate on Thursday, saying he was against it and that he wouldn't vote for it even to just move the process forward in the Commerce Committee. As you know, this is a complete reversal. We got some credit for it in *The Washington Post* today.

It was true. On April 21, the same day he held a final four-hour meeting in his office with executives of Hallmark and Pepsico, Slattery informed Dingell (and also Vice President Gore) that he would oppose any bill including an employer mandate. No matter how restricted it might be, he said, it could ultimately be extended to include small firms. A fallback plan that he had once seemed ready to endorse — parallel to Dingell's compromise of a 1 percent payroll tax for the smallest firms — was also unacceptable, Slattery said.

Dingell's last resort was the two-track strategy. He approached Cooper with an offer for a straight vote swap. Dingell would provide enough votes to report the Cooper-Grandy bill and commit to see that it could be offered as a floor amendment to whatever measure the Democratic leadership finally framed. In return, Cooper would give Dingell the votes to report out the administration bill. At a meeting in Gephardt's office in late May, Cooper said no. "I don't think a procedural fix gets us very far toward a solution," he told reporters later. "We need to negotiate on the substance of the plan."

Synar said Cooper told him he didn't trust Dingell's assurances that he would "protect" Cooper's bill from hostile amendments and efforts to deny it a floor vote. "He doesn't trust John," Synar said. "He said, 'Give John Dingell [control of the] procedure, and he'll screw you every time.' "

The frustration was getting to Dingell. Talking in his office after another futile bargaining session with Cooper, he said, "I don't want to tell you I have iron control. I've been tempted to pound holes in the wall like everybody else. There are some sons of bitches around here that would be punished for what they've done if I had my way. But I'm a patient man. I've been waiting thirty-eight years for this. So you know I've lived with frustration."

The targets of his wrath were the Democrats he could not get. But the real source of his frustration was the opposition being orchestrated by Newt Gingrich, the Republicans, and their business allies. Tom Bliley, the congressman from Richmond whose corporate constituents were dominated by the makers of Marlboro cigarettes and who was the ranking Republican on the Health Subcommittee of Energy and Commerce, was feeling as smug as Dingell was downcast.

"As we've gone home and had town meetings with our people, they say to me, 'Congressman, I have insurance. Why should I have to give that up to go into something else? I'm satisfied with what I have,' " Bliley said. "And of course, the insurance industry association has done a bang-up job with Harry and Louise. People say, 'I don't like this thing because it looks to me like I'm going to be paying more and I'm going to be getting less in order to provide for my neighbor who doesn't have it. Why should I have to do that?' "

Every time he went home, Bliley saw how effectively NFIB and its partner, the National Restaurant Association, were spreading the world. "You hear it everywhere you go," he said. "Any place you go for dinner. The guy who runs the service that takes care of my yard. The Delegate [state representative] from my district who's in the nursery business. Anyone who uses casual labor, it's a killer for him. It's just everywhere you turn."

Bliley was supporting the minimalist Rowland-Bilirakis bill, as were more and more members of the committee. When Dingell was asked if he could settle for that being reported out of his committee, he said wearily, "Well, I don't think I'm going to settle for it, but I'm going to have to settle for some damn thing. I really think the only sensible approach is the single-payer plan, and I'm well below that line already. I can accept the Clinton plan because it does the things I think are important. I can accept our somewhat abbreviated version of it. But when I sink much below this, then I get to the area where I don't find it very acceptable."

On June 28, John Dingell, the Playmaker of Congress, one of the most powerful legislators in decades, threw up his hands and admitted failure. He was unwilling to make any more compromises. In a formal letter to Speaker Foley, Dingell said he was at an impasse. "At this point, it would be counterproductive to convene the committee, call up legislation and consume an enormous amount of time and resources without any assurance of success." He took a final swipe at Cooper and Slattery, blasted the Republicans for partisanship, and warned against the Rowland-Bilirakis compromise as a measure that would "perpetuate or worsen the inequities and inefficiencies of the current system."

By the time Dingell gave up, his pal Billy Ford had reported two health care bills — the Clinton plan and a single-payer plan — out of the House Education and Labor Committee he chaired. But Education and Labor was a liberal bastion, unrepresentative of the political makeup of the House. As Jim Cooper said, "When Energy and Commerce deadlocks, that is a powerful signal, because Dingell and Waxman are the two ablest chairmen in modern history. If they can't get a bill out, then there is a major problem." For once, Bill Clinton was in total agreement with Cooper. "When Dingell doesn't get anything out," he told us, "it begins to look like maybe there's no bill."

15

Make a Deal

THEY WERE A MISMATCHED PAIR, touchy, unpredictable, brilliant, explosive: Pat Moynihan, the intellectual gadfly from New York who became chairman of the Senate Finance Committee in 1993 after Lloyd Bentsen's Treasury secretary appointment, and Bob Dole, the acerbic lawyer from Kansas who led the Senate Republicans. For all their differences, Democrats and Republicans knew that if the Senate were to produce a health care reform bill, Moynihan and Dole would have to create it. In Clinton's first year as President, they had emerged from two bitter clashes with a victory apiece. In the spring of 1993, Dole had stopped the Clinton administration's economic stimulus package — a measure to jumpstart the slowly recovering economy and produce a quick wave of jobs in the cities where Moynihan's heart lay. Dole won by organizing a successful Republican filibuster. Then in the summer, Moynihan outmaneuvered Dole on the main budget bill, guiding it to passage by a single vote.

In the fall, Moynihan and Dole joined forces to win Senate approval of NAFTA, the giant free-trade agreement with Canada and Mexico, a cause in which both fervently believed. That is what professionals in The System do. They fight. They win or lose. They join forces when their interests and inclinations dictate. No one knew whether health care reform would bring them together or provide another test of strength.

Moynihan and Dole were not at all alike, yet in a pressure cooker System where true friendships are rare and the clash of egos and ambitions constant, no two men understood or appreciated each other's abilities more.

On the surface, their mutual admiration seemed astounding. Pat Moynihan, the Democrat, believer in government, puckish, quixotic, with his arched eyebrows and droll way of speaking, the product of the mean streets of New York's Hell's Kitchen, was perhaps the best upholder of the liberal tradition — not the liberalism of the New Left, with its confrontational tactics and racial, ethnic, and gender manifestos, but of the old Franklin Roosevelt New Deal tradition, which believed government had a practical role and a moral responsibility to alleviate the social and economic problems of all Americans. Bob Dole, the Republican, believer in limited government, dark, scowling, his internal anger always so close to the surface that even his bursts of rapier humor were laced with acid, the product of the rolling prairies of small-town Kansas, was perhaps the truest exemplar of the old conservative tradition — not the radical brand masquerading as conservatism, which increasingly dominated his party in the nineties, but the Republicanism of Theodore Roosevelt and Dwight Eisenhower, which preached individual responsibility while seeking to expand opportunities.

They were legislators, these two, who believed in getting things done within The System. They could make deals. They had made one in 1983, when they were fellow members of a presidential commission that saved the Social Security system from threatened bankruptcy. Now they might do another deal if it served their interests and if circumstances permitted. In 1993, when the battle was beginning, they had talked privately about the final outcome and laughingly discussed the timing of "the Moynihan-Dole bill" that could emerge in the spring of 1994 as the final compromise between all health care reform versions. In his conversations with the President, the First Lady, and other strategists, Moynihan often referred to his dealings with Dole and to his belief that, in the end, they together would produce a bill.

But two factors, riven with ironies and political paradoxes, greatly complicated their relationship. Dole, the conservative Republican, believed there was need for major reform. But as Senate Republican leader, he knew that many of his colleagues were deeply skeptical of the Clinton approach and he didn't want to become a general deserted by his own army. Most important, he wanted to do nothing that would damage his 1996 presidential ambitions in a party moving farther and farther to the right. Thus, the tough, almost hostile tone of his response to Clinton's 1994 State of the Union address.

Moynihan, the liberal Democrat, had a long record of fighting for innovative social reform, but this time he was a most reluctant crusader. He wanted to prove he could deliver as the new chairman of Finance, demonstrate he was a major player and not the political dilettante his critics described. But he did not believe that health reform was the most important battle and was never totally committed, emotionally or intellectually, to winning that war.

Their committee, Finance, which Dole had chaired for most of the 1980s and where he remained a powerful force, had principal jurisdiction of the Clinton plan. But to avoid hard feelings, Majority Leader George Mitchell, another Finance member, had also given the bill to the Labor and Human Resources Committee, headed by Ted Kennedy, the Massachusetts liberal who had made health care his personal crusade for three decades.

Thirty years of waiting had made Kennedy only more impatient. He knew he could get a bill out of his committee that included the essential elements of the President's proposal. In the past his committee had pressed for major health care reforms only to see them stymied without debate for lack of Senate support. Now, Kennedy was on fire. Time, he believed, was the great enemy of reform. Throughout Clinton's first year Kennedy kept warning the Clintons that "delay is going to kill us." He had his staff study the polls on Ronald Reagan's first year in office. They showed what he feared: By September of 1981, Reagan's approval ratings were down to the critical 50 percent. He passed that message to the White House; still they delayed. As did Hillary Clinton, he chafed at the repeated postponements in submitting the plan.

When Kennedy finally got a draft of the bill, on the last day of the 1993 session, he wanted his committee to meet during the holiday recess and be ready to bring something to the floor on the first day in

January. Mitchell cautioned against starting a "race" with Moynihan and Finance. Reluctantly, Kennedy agreed to wait.

He quietly invited Democratic senators — no Republicans yet — to meetings with staff members, where they went through the bill, section by section, and discussed tactics for passage. They would begin at eight o'clock each morning and work for two hours before the Senate began its normal schedule. A month later, in February, top committee aides began the same private process with Republican senators and their staffs. It was a determined, serious effort, "exhilarating and promising," as one senator described it. By May, the full committee was engaged in an exhaustive effort to secure a bill.

Kennedy was relentless. In 1972, three years after Chappaquiddick, he had published a book called *In Critical Condition*, about the need for health reform, and to many of his colleagues and staff assistants it seemed that passing a bill for universal coverage was still Kennedy's path to redemption — the political legacy he wanted most to leave. Though he was viewed by his critics as a caricature of a big-spending, Big Government liberal, Kennedy the legislator was far more pragmatic than the public understood. "We make progress on all the great issues only when it's bipartisan," Kennedy would say. The civil rights laws and the measures that forced an end to the Vietnam War showed that "the major historical efforts in this institution have been bipartisan. That's true for health care reform. Everyone understands that this is an issue of such magnitude, of such proportion, that if progress can be made it has to be made with Republicans."

To Kennedy, the perfect example of bipartisanship was passage of another highly controversial and intensely lobbied bill, the Clean Air Act. That's when, Kennedy recalled, George Mitchell and John Chafee sat down in a room with other Democratic and Republican senators and conducted "a continuing seminar" on the issue. That quiet process was successful. It was the political model he had in mind.

While he negotiated inside the Senate, he raged at the liberal interest groups — labor, senior citizens, health advocacy organizations — imploring them to get into the fight. The unions, which Lane

Kirkland had told the President would be his "storm troopers on health reform," had, Kennedy said, "burned out and lost interest" after their defeat in the battle to stop NAFTA. "They are not energized," he complained. "They are divided, they are confused, they are uncertain where they're going." So he would call them in, time and again, and tell them to stop quibbling. Get behind the plan.

"When the heat is really turned up and the American people are focusing on it," said David Nexon, Kennedy's top health aide, "we're going to have the votes for universal coverage with shared responsibility, with reasonable cost containment, because that's what the public wants."

And that's what Kennedy's committee would offer. The seventeen senators on Labor and Human Resources — ten Democrats, seven Republicans — represented a much more liberal cast than Moynihan's Finance Committee. Even the centrist John Chafee categorized the Kennedy committee's ideological composition as "Murderer's Row of the left wing." Though its Republicans included such strongly conservative members as Strom Thurmond of South Carolina, Thad Cochran of Mississippi, and Dan Coats of Indiana, none of whom could be expected to support any Democratic measure, it also had such pro-reform Republicans as Dave Durenberger of Minnesota and Jim Jeffords of Vermont and the centrist Nancy Kassebaum of Kansas. Unlike those on the Finance Committee, Labor Committee Democrats could be counted on to give their chairman their votes.

There was serious disagreement, however. On the left, Paul Wellstone of Minnesota and Howard Metzenbaum of Ohio expressed concerns that the bill would slide too far to the right. In the center, such Democrats as Chris Dodd of Connecticut, who represented a state dominated by major insurance company headquarters, and Barbara Mikulski of Maryland, a blunt, short woman from a working-class district of Baltimore, had misgivings. They worried Labor's bill was too complicated, too costly, too bureaucratic. "I don't know about all this smart stuff," Mikulski would argue. "I just know what works and what doesn't. I'm telling ya, people don't like this." Also seeking a more centrist approach were such Democrats as Jeff Bingaman of New Mexico and Harris Wofford of Pennsylvania. But in the end, Kennedy knew, none of these Democrats would be likely to break ranks or defect from their party and President.

Because of his own ideology and the makeup of his committee, Kennedy did not accept Moynihan's view that broad Republican support had to be assured before any reform bill could be brought to the floor. Kennedy wanted a bipartisan bill and thought eventually Republicans would come aboard, but disagreed with Moynihan that they had to start their process by securing a supermajority before bringing a bill to a vote.

If you want eighty votes in the end, Kennedy said, citing the overwhelming number that would demonstrate strong bipartisan support to the public and opposing lobbyists and represent far more than needed to kill any filibuster, first line up a simple majority of fifty-one senators. He did not believe the Republicans would prevail on a filibuster that would require sixty votes to override. As he pointed out several times in meetings with the President and Pat Moynihan, they had beaten filibusters mounted by Minority Leader Dole and Republicans twice in Clinton's first year, once on a bill creating a National Service Corps, another on an education reform bill. Each time, the majority Democrats were able to win enough Republicans to give them more than the sixty votes needed to defeat a filibuster.

Kennedy's point was that the only way to get the desired eighty votes to signal the strongest political support for reform was "to push Dole to the mat." Conversely, Kennedy was certain "the one way you won't get eighty votes is to give Dole the power of deciding what's going to happen."

His views collided directly with Moynihan's. Nick Littlefield, a longtime Kennedy confidant and the staff director and chief counsel of the Labor Committee, spelled out the differences:

> You've got the chairman of the Finance Committee saying we're not going to do a bill unless we make a deal with Bob Dole. Once you tell your political opposition and chief rival that we're not going to do this unless we and you can make a deal, you have essentially given the ball game away to the other side. It's an impossible situation. You've given all power to the opposition, the people who are dead set on defeating

you — defeating you substantively, and defeating you politically. And that reverberates over to the House, where the House says if the bill is not going to happen in the Senate unless Bob Dole signs on and Bob Dole is moving away from this faster than ever, why should the House act?

George Mitchell, the majority leader, agreed with Kennedy, but he could not impose that view on others. So the fundamental strategy question was never resolved. On June 9, Kennedy reported a strong version of the Clinton plan from his committee by a vote of eleven to six, with Jim Jeffords of Vermont the only Republican to endorse it. And Pat Moynihan continued to search for a deal with Dole.

Of all the players the Clintons dealt with, none proved more frustrating than Pat Moynihan. Relations began badly and never got better. Deprecating, even insulting, remarks about the chairman leaked repeatedly from within the Clinton camp. They began even before Clinton was inaugurated, and not long after he took office someone in the Clinton team told Joe Klein of *Newsweek*, "We'll roll right over him [Moynihan] if we have to." When Clinton read this quote, he erupted in the Oval Office, denouncing anyone serving him who could have made so stupid a comment about a politician whose support they badly needed. But the snide comments, attributed to White House aides, continued to appear in Washington columns.

Moynihan, too, made one damaging public remark after another about the Clinton reform, and sometimes even about the Clintons themselves. On *Meet the Press*, on September 19, 1993, three days before Clinton even gave his launch speech to Congress, Moynihan dismissed the economic calculations in the Clinton plan as "fantasy numbers." On that same program, Moynihan, joining with Republican critics, struck at the very heart of reform by saying there was "no health care crisis." When Whitewater broke, it was Moynihan, once again on *Meet the Press*, who alone among the Democrats said he thought the Clintons should urge the appointment of a special prosecutor.

These wounding words from each side intensified the strains between the chairman and the White House. Not that the Clinton White House, especially the First Lady and the President, failed to appreciate Moynihan's importance. They tried hard to gain his support. Moynihan was one of the first people Hillary Clinton called on after being named to head the reform battle. She was frustrated to find they were not on the same track, especially after the senator said in that first meeting in January 1993 that he didn't understand health care (something he also privately told us), didn't think it was something they needed to address, and thought it a waste of her time.

Not a very good beginning, the First Lady concluded. It never got better. She didn't understand all the reasons for their differences, but, as a political pragmatist, she did understand some of his motives. Moynihan was primarily interested in passing the budget. He didn't want to do anything that would lessen the belief that he could chair his committee as effectively as Lloyd Bentsen. He was totally committed to passing NAFTA and to dealing with trade arrangements between the United States and its major western partners. The First Lady was best able to spark Moynihan's interest in health care reform by asking him, How are we going to do welfare reform without health care reform?

The explanation for their problems went deeper than a disagreement on legislative priorities. It was embedded in the complex personality of Pat Moynihan. As his wife, Liz, a formidable force herself, told Todd Purdum of the *New York Times*, "They [the Clintons] definitely don't get him."

By the time he became Finance Committee chairman, Daniel Patrick Moynihan could claim to have been right more often on the great social and foreign-policy questions facing America than most leading players in The System. It was Moynihan, years before, who drew outraged attacks from liberal friends for his carefully documented warnings about the disintegration of the black family. It was Moynihan who said that the soaring rate of out-of-wedlock births was contributing to the growing pathology of an increasingly violent urban America. No one had been more prescient about the toll of supply-side economics during the Reagan years, recognizing that

Reagan "consciously and deliberately brought about" higher deficits to force congressional domestic cuts — only cuts were never made, causing deficits to balloon even higher. This historic condition, Moynihan would say, overlay everything in Washington in the 1990s. The tragedy was that Bill Clinton, an activist President, came to Washington pushing for an extraordinarily ambitious and expensive domestic reform at a time when we have no money. "The truth is, we're broke," the senator would add, "and that affects everything you try to do."

When he chaired the Senate Intelligence Committee in the Reagan years, Moynihan was among the first to spot the duplicity of CIA director William J. Casey, later exposed during the Iran-Contra scandal. He was right, too, and largely ignored, for his careful documentation of the false economic assumptions the CIA had made in the 1950s about the strength of the Soviet economy, which misled American policy makers and contributed to the wasteful Cold War expenditure of billions of dollars.

On health care, Moynihan harbored deep private doubts about what Clinton was proposing. For him, welfare reform, not health care, was of most urgent importance. To prove his point, Moynihan would hand over the latest charts showing the continuing rise in the U.S. illegitimacy rate — it had tripled in one generation — as further proof of his contention about the true crisis facing the American family.

He believed that America had succeeded in providing a health care system that satisfied most people. He also believed those satisfied citizens weren't interested in having less in order to give others more. Privately he would say the 15 percent who don't have health care "are not deprived. They are cared for, you know." Then he would add: "We do have universal health care in the country, actually." He meant that no one needing emergency care in America is denied it, even if those with insurance end up paying hospital costs for those without. Moynihan doubted whether it was a good idea to elevate this issue into the great national challenge Clinton presented to the country, and he feared that the Clinton plan had "the making of a huge corporate state enterprise — which I don't think we're very good at." Voicing his deep-seated skepticism about government planning, he said that it made as much sense to overhaul the whole health care system as it would for Washington to start up its own automobile company.

He wouldn't say so aloud, but clearly he thought the Clintons naive in their approach, especially when they claimed that their reforms would produce great savings that would enable coverage to be expanded. In the privacy of his office, Moynihan cited the latest studies to make his point about the soaring rates of Medicaid costs, an especially critical problem in New York. "Here I have it, sir," he said, handing over charts and statistical analyses. "Data. Documents for you. Medicaid doubled in the eight years of the Reagan administration, then doubled again in the four years of the Bush administration." Adopting his professorial role, Moynihan arched his eyebrows, peered owlishly over his spectacles, and asked genially, "Assuming geometric progression, sir, what day is the day on which we reach the point where Medicaid doubles in one day?" A pregnant pause, then with the delight of the scholar who has discovered a vital truth, he answered his own quiz: "December twenty-ninth, 1996." He tapped the charts and pointed at that day a month after the 1996 presidential election.

The Clintons could not ignore "Baumol's Disease," Moynihan would say, citing the scholarly work of New York University's William J. Baumol on the inevitable escalation of costs in labor-intensive social programs.

So taken with Baumol's diagnosis was Moynihan that he invited Hillary Rodham Clinton to a private luncheon with the scholar at the Moynihans' top-floor Pennsylvania Avenue apartment with its panoramic views of the museums, galleries, the Capitol, and the Supreme Court. Moynihan watched as Baumol told the First Lady that he was all for her attempt. But, Baumol warned, "the one thing you mustn't say is you're going to stop the rise in costs."

Baumol had spent decades documenting his case that there is no way to stop the spiraling of costs in certain service sectors, particularly those the government subsidizes. He made his case to Hillary, and Moynihan thought the First Lady looked as if she had been kicked under the table. She disagreed with Baumol; they would control costs.

After that luncheon, as a way of showing how seriously she took Moynihan's advice, she invited Baumol to visit her at the White House. There, she urged the scholar to write articles showing how they could do health care reform without triggering the "cost disease" Baumol had warned against. But nothing seemed to matter, White House people would say later, recalling the times she spent with Baumol. They would come back to Senator Moynihan with memos from Professor Baumol and say, Senator, Professor Baumol has looked at this. He thinks a public utility model might work. He thinks this approach might work. Moynihan remained unconvinced.

Despite these fundamental disagreements, the Clintons and Moynihan tried to keep the relationship from degenerating into the personal enmity that produces bitter political feuds. Both the First Lady and the President went to great lengths privately to court the New York senator. As one of the President's top White House strategists later said,

We tried everything with Pat. We had Liz [Moynihan] and Pat and Hillary and Bill dinners. We had Liz and Pat and Hillary and Bill movies. The President went to Mcynihan's December 1993 fund-raiser in New York and practically prostrated himself But there was one perceived insult after another. And nothing made up for it. We even let him claim he'd picked the first Supreme Court justice [Ruth Bader Ginsburg of New York] and ran the confirmation process out of his office. Nothing could defuse it. And Lawrence [O'Donnell] had minimal respect for anyone at the White House. I think he kept working Pat up.

There was truth in that last point about O'Donnell. Referring to the times when the Clintons would invite the Moynihans to dinner or a movie or a special White House ceremony. or just a private lunch for Hillary and Liz, O'Donnell would say the Clintons obviously didn't understand Moynihan. Flattery wasn't what moved Pat Moynihan. Nor was he the kind of man who responded to praise by reacting like "a clapping seal." Being listered to, taken seriously — engaged, not necessarily agreed with — was what mattered most to Pat Moynihan. With good reason, he regarded himself as a national leader whose long career in public service had put him in the forefront of the widest range of issues — everything from critical domestic- and foreign-policy questions to the construction of major federal office buildings, even the details of their architecture. Then O'Donnell said, in words that vividly expressed the underlying contempt for the Clinton operation, "Nobody working for Hillary Clinton, as far as I can tell, gets politics one whit better than Ira Magaziner does. They don't get politics. That's Whitewater, that's everything. They have a War Room for everything. They don't understand it's not a fucking War Room. War Room is: I win. War ends when a person surrenders. Nobody here surrenders ever. You don't fucking win. And you do not have an election against us where there's a vote cast where we have to leave. We are here forever, and we don't fucking surrender."

O'Donnell was far less restrained in expressing his views than Moynihan, but there were times when Moynihan himself would surprise people with an unmistakably disparaging reference to the Clintons. During a private discussion Moynihan had with AFL-CIO leaders in Washington, Douglas Dority, president of the Food and Commercial Workers' Union, was telling Moynihan and his fellow union presidents about how hard it was to get health care for poultry workers. "Well, if you're into poultry processing, maybe you'll get something done by those folks," Moynihan said, in an unmistakable reference to the Clintons' connections with Tyson Foods and other big Arkansas poultry interests. One of the participants was so stunned he wrote a memo for his files immediately after the incident. "It was just a gratuitous slam at the Clintons," he told us, "and I was surprised he did it in such a public way."

When the meeting ended, John Sweeney of the Service Employees' International Union (SEIU)* turned to another trade union president and said, "Now you know what we're up against." And another person present said, "The whole tone was that the chairman just wasn't trying."

Nevertheless, the President continued to court the senator, some-

---

*In 1995, after Lane Kirkland was forced out as AFL-CIO president, Sweeney was elected his successor.

times with amusing consequences. The day after his 1994 State of the Union address containing his threat to veto any bill that did not provide universal coverage, Clinton made a confession to the ever-colorful and blunt House Ways and Means chairman, Dan Rostenkowski. Rosty had long counseled the President to try to make a deal with the Senate. You'll have an easier time in the Senate than in the House, Rosty told Clinton, after a White House leadership meeting that day. There's no chance of a deal of any kind with the Gingriches and the Armeys, Rosty said. Besides, if you try to deal with the House, the House will lead you to water, but then they'll take away the bucket. Furthermore, Rosty continued, Pat Moynihan "tells me he can get it done a hell of a lot quicker than we can. And if he can do that, fine." Then Rosty offered Clinton a personal critique of Moynihan: "Bill, goddamn it, Moynihan is a great guy. He wouldn't step on a fly if he could avoid it, and he's got good basic instincts. But somebody blows a little smoke up his poop and he goes off."

At that point, Clinton remarked, "Danny, you know, I've got to call Moynihan every day."

"What?" Rosty replied. "You never call me every day." The President realized, Rosty recalled, he had stuck his foot right in his mouth. "Mr. President, don't you like the sound of my voice?" Rosty said jokingly. As he left, he said to Clinton: "You know, I'm expecting a call from you."

The next day Rosty's phone rang. "This is your call," the voice said. It was the President. Shortly after, at a Democratic leadership retreat in Maryland, Clinton walked across the room to Rosty, and said, "This is in lieu of a call to you." The next day, Rosty returned to his home district in Chicago. The phone rang. "The President can't call you today," said Vice President Al Gore. "I'm calling you."

The President continued to reach out to Pat Moynihan. Among his colleagues, Moynihan, however frustrating, was a beloved figure — his personal handwritten notes, written with a green felt-tipped pen, were legendary. John Chafee, the Republican from Rhode Island who was deeply committed to health care reform, said of the chairman, "I'm a big fan of Pat's. I love the lectures you get. Did you hear the old story about the difference between Moynihan and [New York's other senator, Republican Al] D'Amato? You write Moynihan about a passport and you get a history of the passport office. You write D'Amato about a passport and you get the passport."

But with health care reform, the problem was, as Chafee observed, "Pat was never wild about this." And a leading Senate Democrat summed it up this way: "If we were at the goal line when the bill was introduced, we were probably three hundred yards behind when we began the process on the Finance Committee because it took so long for the White House to get the bill up here. Then you take the chairman, who can't stand the President, who doesn't like health reform, who has a very, very poor relationship with the majority leader [George Mitchell], and you put him in charge of it, and it goes downhill from there."

While the battle for reform was being fought publicly in Washington in 1993 and 1994, Senate Minority Leader Bob Dole was waging his own internal war between, as it was so often said, sometimes even mockingly by Dole himself, "the good Bob Dole and the bad Bob Dole."

The picture of Bob Dole that emerges is of a conflicted man — part calculating politician, part national leader — who zigs and zags as the policy debate itself twists and turns. His conversation, recorded in interviews and recalled by peers and colleagues in their private meetings with him, reflects this overriding ambivalence. "If it were Bob Dole and Pat Moynihan," he remarked in one conversation, "we could get a bill that would satisfy most everybody — everybody but the far right and the far left, that is." Typically, he added another conditional, defensive-sounding remark: "Even people on the far right and the far left get sick and need health care. And there are probably a lot of good conservative people out there without health care. And there are things that we can do to make it better."

A man of quick wit and self-deprecating humor, capable of gestures of kindness and generosity, Bob Dole also had a strong reserve that kept people from feeling they really knew him. More than one colleague would say Dole has very few friends up here. But Dole was capable of displaying great emotion in public, even to the point

of being overcome when something touched him deeply. Once, paying tribute to George Bush, a man who had badly defeated if not
humiliated him, Dole stopped suddenly and wept.

Dole also possessed what colleagues invariably referred to privately as his "dark side." He carries a lot around, a fellow senator who
admires him said, "this darker thing, this bitterness at life's lot." He,
like others, speculated that this stemmed from Dole's World War II
wounds. During a German attack in Italy, where he was an infantry
platoon leader, a shell tore into Dole's right shoulder, fracturing his
collarbone, the scapula behind the collarbone, and the upper bone
in his arm. A shell fragment also tore into his vertebrae, affecting
his spinal cord. He found himself in a military hospital, encased in
a cast from his chin to his hips, paralyzed.

The next four years were agony. At times it appeared he would
not live; for a year he couldn't feed himself or walk. Then began the
long painful process of rehabilitation in veterans' hospitals. To de-
fray the costs of a private neurosurgeon who performed seven operations on Dole, townspeople in Russell, Kansas, contributed nickels,
dimes, quarters, dollars into a fund that began with a cigar box
on a soda fountain counter. Bob Dole emerged with his right arm
shattered and without full use of his right hand. From then on,
he always held a fountain pen in his hand to avoid the pain of a
handshake.

That Dole at times was consumed by bitterness was known to all
of his Senate colleagues; it could emerge in a flash, causing his face to
darken in a saturnine scowl, his words erupting, lashing and caustic.
Then it would pass.

No one doubted his commitment to health care reform. As one
colleague put it, you can't go through the pain and agony he's
been through without wanting real reform. During the Reagan-Bush
years, Dole took the lead in urging other Republicans to fashion a
major initiative. As one of the leading Republican business lobbyists
put it, having worked closely with Dole over the years, "Bob Dole's
been a squish on health care for years and years and years. If you
go through Medicaid and Medicare for the last ten years, Bob Dole's
fingerprints are all over them, those programs. Bob's always been on
the side of improving them."

He also made the case to the Reagan and Bush White Houses that Republicans needed to develop their own approach — especially on an issue on which the public thought the Democrats had shown much more concern. He was rebuffed. "We thought [Bush's failure to respond] was a mistake at the time," said Sheila Burke, Dole's chief of staff, who participated in those discussions with people like John Sununu, Bush's chief of staff, "and I think we were proven right. It *was* a mistake." Dole shared that view. He understood it was a difficult issue for Republicans, raising all the ideological red flags about new taxes, government intervention, government control, personal rights and responsibilities. But when Clinton took office and moved health care squarely to the center of the national agenda, Dole's basic instinct was to work for reform, thereby demonstrating, as he would say, "We're a major party, we're a responsible party, and we've got something to offer."

Burke herself was an important player. She came to Dole's service in 1977 with a background as a professional nurse, who had trained at the University of San Francisco and engaged in clinical work, including at a "psych detox unit," which Dole would teasingly say perfectly prepared her for the Senate. She also had studied at Harvard's Kennedy School of Government. Dole was seeking someone knowledgeable on health care issues to work for the Republican side of the Senate Finance Committee. He heard through the grapevine about Burke, then working in New York, and hired her even though she was a Democrat, had never met Dole before their first interview, and knew nothing about Kansas — or Washington. It was a superb choice. Sixteen years later she was far more than a congressional health specialist; she was a consummate political player, deeply involved in the shaping of all overall strategy and policy for Senate Republicans. Lawrence O'Donnell was not exaggerating when he said in the spring of 1994, "The most powerful woman in American government is someone no one's ever heard of before named Sheila Burke."

Trim, blond, blue-eyed, and athletic-looking, Sheila Burke was a classic congressional aide — competent, loyal, forthright, and possessed of the fabled "passion for anonymity." During all her years on the Hill. she had studiously and successfully worked to keep her own name and views out of the public discussions, and especially out of the press. How far she had moved from being a single-issue staffer to overall political operative could be learned from the sign she posted on her inner office door in the Capitol: "Until you've been in politics you've never really been alive," it read. "It's rough and sometimes it's dirty and it's always hard work and tedious details. But it's the only sport for grownups. All other games are for kids."

Even as her responsibilities increased, she kept a close eye on her own specialty. She was highly critical of the Magaziner task force process and the bill it produced — "far more complicated, far more regulatory, than anybody ever thought it would be." She had numerous reservations about that plan, but not about the need for reform. She was certain there would be serious consequences for the nation if the effort failed. "If we are unable to grapple with it now," she said early in the battle, "it will get no more simple. It will get no less complex, no less difficult, to make those decisions long-term. And in the process you will begin to bankrupt states and institutions. That will pressure us to make decisions that are very shortsighted, do the easy thing, and all that crap. It will be a lost opportunity."

Burke saw health care reform as a critical test of The System and of the country's character. "We have the best health care system in the world and it is self-destructing internally because of our abuse of it. There's no excuse for this in a country like ours. There's no excuse for someone going without prenatal services. There's no excuse for people going without immunizations."

But Sheila Burke's was far from the only voice Bob Dole was heeding. The cold calculus of presidential ambition also drove him. In 1976 he was the GOP's vice presidential nominee. He lost. Twice, in 1980 and 1988, he had tried for his party's presidential nomination. Each time he failed. Now he was embarking on his last attempt against a sitting Democratic president who had made health care reform his major domestic goal. And he was leading a Senate Republican party that was increasingly fissured, increasingly tugged to the right.

* * *

The Republican membership of Finance reflected those divisions. Bob Packwood of Oregon, the ranking Republican, had served as chairman in the mid-eighties and was a skilled negotiator. Still boyish at sixty-one, Packwood had gradually acquired power and influence — and the trust of his colleagues — by handling major tax legislation, notably the great reform bill of 1986. He was responsive to the business interests of his state, but liberal on social issues and clearly a potential reform ally. But Packwood was operating under a huge dark cloud: investigations by the Senate Ethics Committee and the Justice Department of charges of sexual harassment, brought against him by former Senate staff aides and women who had worked in his past campaigns. He was resisting turning over his personal diaries to investigators but his tenure in the Senate was in doubt and his influence greatly diminished.

Dole sat next to Packwood in Finance. On his other side was Senator William V. Roth of Delaware, a hard-shell conservative with an ill-fitting toupee, whose only passion in life appeared to be cutting tax rates and streamlining bureaucracy. Roth was a probable opponent of any major reform bill, but he was not a senator who would carry others with him.

Then came three Republicans who were among the most knowledgeable on health issues and by all odds the likeliest to join in writing a bipartisan bill: John C. Danforth of Missouri, the lawyer-preacher who, in his usual independent fashion, had announced his plans to retire at the end of the current Congress; John Chafee, Dole's choice to head the Republican health care task force and the principal sponsor of a bill that could serve as a fallback to the Clinton plan; and Dave Durenberger of Minnesota, who, like Packwood, combined a superior mind and grasp of the issues with an erratic personality that got him into trouble. Durenberger's ethics problem involved his accounting for reimbursed expenses on an apartment he used as his Minnesota residence after his divorce. He, too, had announced he would not run again in 1994.

At the far end of the row sat three more conservative Republicans. With Bill Roth, they would be the hardest to convince on reform. Charles E. Grassley of Iowa and Malcolm Wallop of Wyoming were opposed, not only to the Clinton plan, but to Chafee's propo-

sal or anything else that smacked to them of "government medicine." Orrin G. Hatch of Utah had signed on to the Chafee plan, but
his colleagues knew that his cautious instincts and his home state's
aversion to new federal regulations could easily push Hatch into
opposition.

All these were senior senators, Finance being perhaps the most
highly prized of Senate committee assignments. The real tugs to
the right came from those elected more recently: assertive conservatives who provided ever-stronger challenges to the consensual politics Dole preferred. Their voices were heard loud and clear when the
Senate Republicans caucused privately in Annapolis on the weekend
of March 4 and 5.

Chafee, who organized the retreat and whose bill nominally had
more support than any other from the Senate GCP, tried to disabuse
reporters in advance that he was likely to emerge with solid party
backing. "I can tell you now there won't be unanimity," he said.
"I'm a realist." Dole conceded that the idea of an individual mandate — the auto insurance model, requiring every person to obtain
insurance, which was at the heart of the Chafee bill — was "an area
of disagreement now. Mandates are going to be hard to sustain in all
these plans," he said.

Going into Annapolis, Dole and Chafee still held the view that
public opinion and political prudence required Republicans to come
up with an alternative. The erosion of public support for the Clinton
plan was viewed as an opportunity for the Republicans to steal
Clinton's thunder, not to block any change. "I don't think anyone in
our party does not want health care reform," Dole said as the meeting
began.

Dole had been burned by the public reaction to his response to
Clinton's State of the Union address five weeks earlier. He adopted
the Bill Kristol line that there was no health care crisis, thus no need
for major legislation. Dole's office was flooded with indignant calls
from people with family members facing illness and unpaid bills. "It
was stupid," Sheila Burke said of that Republican no-crisis strategy.
"Unfortunately, it underscored everyone's worst expectations about
Republicans — that they don't care about these issues, that they're
negative, that they're removed from reality."

Conservatives attending the Annapolis retreat strongly disagreed. A week before the meeting, they began leaking complaints to friendly reporters that Chafee had stacked the meeting with liberal pollsters and health policy consultants. Senator Dan Coats of Indiana, Dan Quayle's successor, said that all mandates were out of the question as far as he was concerned. Senator Trent Lott of Mississippi said, "Republicans have to make clear we are not signing on to any of this government control and mandate stuff." Coats and Lott were typical of the younger GOP senators, many of whom had, like them, come to the Senate from the more fiercely ideological House, where they had been allies of the Gingrich conservatives. Lott had been House minority whip, the same job Gingrich now held, and he shared the Georgian's impatience with those who accepted minority status as the permanent fate of congressional Republicans. As a skillful inside player, over the next few months Lott organized die-hard Republican resistance to any health care reform measure — just as his friend Gingrich did on the House side.

At Dole's invitation, Gingrich came to the Annapolis meeting. House Democrats were offering no reform compromise, Gingrich told them, implicitly warning that any Republican concessions would be met with more Democratic demands. Another House alumnus who attended was even more vocal, both in public and in private. Phil Gramm of Texas, an unannounced but certain challenger to Dole's 1996 presidential nomination ambitions, was more forceful in opposing the Dole-Chafee strategy — and in driving a wedge between those two would-be reformers.

Gramm inveighed against *any* Republican compromise on health reform. He wanted *no* health care bill, not a Chafee bill — "socialism with a smile," he called it scornfully in the presence of Chafee and other Republican senators — not a Dole bill, not any bill. Gramm was determined "to make sure that we don't go wobbly." In the phrase he began using repeatedly, he declared that health care reform would pass "only over my cold dead political body." Gramm's opposition was directed not only against health reform. As every Republican knew, it was targeted squarely on Bob Dole's leadership.

That Annapolis session was chaotic. The original list of speakers was expanded to include business lobbyists and consultants suggested by the conservatives. On the second day, when Chafee had hoped to get his colleagues to begin listing areas of agreement, he and the others found themselves listening to speeches of opposition from Paul Coverdell of Georgia, a freshman senator and former insurance executive, and from other conservatives. As the assault continued, with Gramm taking more time than anyone else, staff members who had hoped to come away with guidance on drafting a consensus bill noticed that Chafee and the other moderates became more and more silent. It was left to Don Nickles, a conservative from Oklahoma who was sponsoring the Heritage Foundation plan, based on the existing program for federal employees, to challenge the Gramm view that the best outcome was no bill at all. As for Dole, he was "quiet, quiet, quiet," one of the staffers said. "I think what he was doing was counting votes." By the time the hour arrived for the buses to leave, taking the Republicans back to Washington, only two of the seven "building blocks" that Chafee hoped to discuss had been aired — and no agreement had been reached on those.

So Annapolis turned out to be a crucial step, not in forming a Republican alternative to the Clinton plan but in demonstrating to Dole how dangerous it would be for him to be part of any compromise. Gramm told us with undisguised satisfaction that "Annapolis convinced Republicans, especially those who were in the middle, that this was not a battle that was going to end with a whimper. I'm not saying that in terms of logic and facts I won the debate at Annapolis. I don't claim that. But I think we left Annapolis with people convinced that we were going to be in a real war and that if they got in the line of fire, they were going to get hit."

After Annapolis, more and more conservative senators openly questioned Dole's seeming willingness to compromise and get a health bill. As one conservative GOP senator remarked of Dole, "There's an undercurrent of resentment among the Republicans about him; you know, he's the leader, leaders are supposed to lead; so what's he going to do on this issue?" The more time passed,

the greater the number of Republican senators who were adamantly opposed to passage of any Democratic-sponsored health care
reform bill.

John Chafee would say Dole was "riding two horses: He's the minority leader and he's a candidate. Boy, he's got these tugs from the
right, and he's responding to them." Publicly and privately, Dole
dithered. "If it's a bad bill, we probably don't want a bill," he would
muse. "We'll take it to the voters." Then, almost in the same breath,
he would express another kind of uncertainty: "I don't know how it
plays out in 'ninety-six. If we don't get a bill this year, obviously it'll
be a big big issue in 'ninety-six."

But before long, he went into reverse. By March 21, when the
full Finance Committee held a retreat in Leesburg, Virginia, to canvass members on the issue, Dole was talking of a "voluntary" approach that would eliminate any form of mandate for now. Like the
Rowland-Bilirakis bill in the House, it would give up on the goal of
covering everyone until some indefinite time in the future. "If a voluntary approach doesn't work," Dole said on *Meet the Press*, "we
could come back and maybe have to do some of this mandatory stuff
in five or six years." Privately, such Democrats as Jay Rockefeller
began saying that Dole seemed to be swinging to the Gingrich view
that no bill at all was the best politics for Republicans in 1994.

Six weeks later, the Democrats held their own retreat in Williamsburg. It was the eve of the Finance Committee "markup," the final
legislative process when members begin hammering out language
and provisions in a bill they hope to bring to a committee vote. By
the time they gathered that April 15, it was clear to everyone that
Finance was in big trouble. Democrats were at least as divided
as Republicans, and Moynihan's doubts about the effort were well
known.

Clustered to the left and right of Moynihan politically were ten
Democrats. Max Baucus of Montana was next in seniority. He had
survived two House elections and three Senate contests in a closely
balanced two-party state by paying sharp attention to Montana issues and carefully constructing a record that was neither too liberal
nor too conservative. His vote would be hard to win.

Next was David L. Boren of Oklahoma, an even harder case. Boren, as intellectually bright as Moynihan, was a political reformer when it came to issues like campaign finance but as conservative as his state when it came to taxes. Like the President a Rhodes scholar, and governor of his state when he was only thirty-three, Boren was no fan of Bill Clinton, who was occupying an office to which Boren himself might have aspired. He had challenged the President and backed him down on the energy tax portion of his first budget and was unlikely to do him any favors on this bill — especially since he was about to leave the Senate after seventeen years to become president of the University of Oklahoma.

Bill Bradley of New Jersey, the former New York Knicks basketball star, was yet another Rhodes scholar. Bradley was much more of a loyalist Democrat, and while health care reform had never been his legislative interest, he was a serious legislator and would want to put his stamp on the bill.

Then came five Democrats who would — if this were a baseball team — constitute the heart of the President's batting order on Finance. George Mitchell sat next to Bradley. Then came David H. Pryor of Arkansas, a home-state ally of Clinton and a man whose work on the problems of the aging had given him a solid grasp of the issues. After him was Donald W. Riegle Jr. of Michigan, a liberal-labor Democrat committed to reform but vulnerable enough after various mini-scandals that he was not seeking reelection in 1994. Jay Rockefeller sat next to Riegle. Then came Thomas A. Daschle of South Dakota, groomed by Mitchell to be his successor as majority leader and Mitchell's loyal ally on this bill.

At the end of the bench were two Democrats who would be at the center of any deal. Louisiana senator Johnny Breaux was co-sponsoring Jim Cooper's bill but plainly shopping for a compromise that the White House and the great majority of his colleagues would accept. Savvy and skeptical of all ideologues and intellectuals, he was convinced his down-home wisdom and ready wit could solve problems that defied the "experts' " analysis. The other Democrat was young (just forty-five years old) Kent Conrad of North Dakota, as serious as Breaux was playful, but a vital swing vote. Conrad came to the Senate in the 1986 election as a prairie populist with a streak of fiscal conservatism so strong he promised his voters that if the federal budget was not balanced in six years, he would not run again. It wasn't. He didn't. Just before Election Day, the other Democratic senator from his state died, and Conrad was persuaded (without enormous difficulty) to seek election for the balance of that term, thus technically keeping his pledge while staying in the Senate. Like Bradley and Baucus, he was clearly a potential "yes" vote — but not a certainty.

George Mitchell decided to use the Williamsburg retreat to prod Moynihan into action — or to position himself to replace him as the playmaker for the President's bill. For weeks, Mitchell had been carrying a single index card bearing one typewritten sentence. It was from the Chafee plan, signed by twenty-three Republican senators. Mitchell would take the card from his pocket and slowly read aloud: "Subtitle F, Section 1501, Universal Coverage Requirement." That's the heading in the thing, he would say, glancing over his glasses, then continuing to read aloud: "Effective January first, 2005, each individual who is a citizen or a lawful permanent resident of the United States shall be covered under a qualified health plan or an equivalent health care plan."

The majority leader would pause again, letting the meaning of those simple words sink in, then, lest the point be lost, say, "There it is. A Republican bill which provides for universal coverage and a mandate to achieve it."

However long the odds against passage of any reform were becoming, that bill, and that language, made Mitchell believe a bipartisan deal could still be struck. As he said, "This represents the basis for a compromise because it includes the one thing that the President says is necessary — universal coverage — and the means to achieve it, a mandate."

Like Pat Moynihan and Bob Dole, George Mitchell was a legislator. He prided himself on his mastery of the political art of what he called "pick-up sticks" — the laborious process of building consensus on a complicated issue among intensely competing interests and personalities.

Although he would not say so publicly, Mitchell had little patience for Moynihan's evident reluctance to make an all-out effort for the

Clinton plan. Mitchell had been on the Finance Committee, and its Health Subcommittee, for almost fourteen years. "In the Senate, there are a number of us who have worked on health care in a nonpartisan way until now," Mitchell said. "We want to get a bill passed." He talked about the "pride of 1986," when the Republicans controlled the Senate and Minnesota's Republican Durenberger was chairman of the Health Subcommittee and Mitchell the ranking Democrat. "We never once had a partisan disagreement," Mitchell remembered. Two other Republicans, Packwood and Chafee, worked as cooperatively with Mitchell, then in the minority, as had Durenberger.

"Here's my view, my experience," Mitchell would say. "If you take a group of people who begin a process with the goal of getting the job done, you can figure out how to get the job done. If you begin a process where people have the goal of preventing something from happening, they can think of ninety-three reasons why it can't be done. It's an attitude. While it's clear that House Republicans and large numbers of Republicans in the Senate begin with that latter attitude, there are still plenty in the Senate who genuinely want to get something done."

In advance of the Williamsburg meeting, Mitchell went to the White House and asked Magaziner for options that would "get the job done" from the President's point of view and still be more palatable politically to conservative Democrats and moderate Republicans.

In Williamsburg, without any show of deference to Moynihan, Mitchell offered the options as his own. They included changes that Magaziner had long previously outlined to the President and Hillary Clinton as concessions that likely would be demanded — and could safely be made without compromising their goals. One would drop the size of companies that could self-insure outside the alliances from five thousand workers to one thousand. Another would reduce the employer share of the insurance premium from 80 percent to 50 percent. Others would change the subsidy plan and alter the basic benefits to provide additional assurance of budgetary savings.

Clinton joined the group for a brief pep talk and made it clear he was comfortable with the variations Mitchell had outlined.

Magaziner and Judy Feder stayed throughout the meeting and provided further reinforcement.

It was a bold attempt on Mitchell's part to light a fire under Moynihan. If that was the goal, it did not accomplish much.

The central problem confronting Finance when it held its first closed-door session on April 19 still was how to finance the program the President wanted. "It is about who pays," said James Mongan, who was in a superb position to make that judgment. For twenty-five years, first as a Finance Committee staffer when the Nixon insurance proposal was debated in 1974, then as the White House staff person six years later when Carter's proposal was debated, and finally as a principal planner and coordinator of Finance's Williamsburg retreat, Mongan had seen one promising reform after another crash in the Congress. All those attempted reforms called for achieving universal coverage. All died for the same reason. Who pays? And the heart of that problem was this: Achieving universal coverage would require subsidizing millions of American families either totally without insurance or lacking the resources to pay for adequate insurance. That meant The System would be forced to deal with a subject it desperately tried to avoid. Taxes. Republicans were dead set against tax increases — and, by large majorities, against requiring employers to pay for reform. The public favored giving the bill to employers and continued to show strong support for the *concept* of universal coverage. That support rapidly eroded if people thought they would be required to pay more taxes themselves. It also shrank if the survey raised the possibility that employer mandates could result in the loss of jobs.

By the time Finance met, these antitax, antigovernment attitudes had hardened. As Mongan assessed the situation, "Politicians of both parties from the courthouse to the White House have convinced Americans and American business that they are staggering under an oppressive burden of taxation that saps most productive effort. Although there is little evidence from other countries to support this belief, it is widely and deeply held. This economic, social, and political climate fosters a self-centeredness, a focus more on the individual's own needs than the community's needs."

Backers of reform had no choice but to contest those attitudes. They had to tell somebody they were going to pay more — most likely employers. "It's very clear," Mitchell told reporters after that first session, "that you can't have universal coverage without some kind of mandate." John Chafee agreed: "I don't know how the dickens you do it without a mandate."

A Gallup poll released the day the committee met gave superficial support to the concept of a mandate. Fifty-four percent of those surveyed said employers should pay all or most of the costs, with another 35 percent favoring a fifty-fifty split between employers and workers. But that was the only good news for reformers. Only 43 percent favored the Clinton plan, while 47 percent opposed it. Sixty-three percent said the level of government involvement contemplated was too much, and by a two-to-one margin thought quality of care would decline and they would be worse off. Hardly a ringing mandate for action.

A month later, as the desultory committee process continued, opposition to mandates of any form had grown stronger. Dole went on *Meet the Press* to say "individual mandates aren't going to pass. I see about three votes for individual mandates on the Finance Committee." Mitchell, appearing on the same program, still held out hope for a blend of individual and employer mandates, but even his optimism was fading. In mid-May, while conservative Democrat David Boren endorsed the Chafee bill with its individual mandates, Bob Packwood deserted the cause, saying he had supported mandates in the past but would do so no longer because NFIB and its ally, the National Restaurant Association, "have done a first-rate job of lobbying against the mandates." Bill Kristol issued another memo, warning Republicans against the Chafee bill. Two days later, at the weekly luncheon of Democratic senators, John Breaux floated the "John Dingell compromise," offering a plan that would exempt very small firms from the employer mandate. As in the House, it did not prove to be the icebreaker Dingell and Breaux had hoped.

On the following Sunday's *Meet the Press*, Jay Rockefeller said publicly what more and more Democrats were saying privately: "Bob Dole is really a major problem here. He wants to be President in 'ninety-six. All those running against him are running on his right, so therefore he has to protect his right flank, so therefore I don't think he's going to be for health reform." What Rockefeller was saying, of course, was that the Moynihan strategy of striking a deal with Dole was doomed.

But Dole continued to send private signals that he wanted some kind of deal. To John Chafee, laboring diligently to produce an acceptable Republican compromise, Dole kept urging, "Keep going, keep going, keep going." To Vice President Al Gore, Dole sent a private message about his willingness to compromise: "Al, tell the President not to be so rough on us. When we introduced our bill we didn't say one word about their health care plan. We're not trying to sell this as a partisan plan. We're trying to reach out to Democrats. It's a good plan." He told the vice president to inform the President that "maybe we could still put something together."

Moynihan's and Dole's two top aides, Lawrence O'Donnell and Sheila Burke, respectively, kept in contact about the possibility. O'Donnell and Burke also talked to Christy Ferguson, Chafee's health aide.

At one point that spring Ferguson was startled to hear O'Donnell, who so reflected Moynihan's thinking, say out of the blue, "What is it like to be a pariah in your own party?" At that point, Ferguson thought, it must be finally dawning on Pat Moynihan that he was being depicted as a renegade in Democratic politics for failing to support his President more forcefully.

Throughout these weeks, Moynihan was taking testimony in public hearings. One fine May morning, as the senators, their staffs, the reporters, the lobbyists, the witnesses, the spectators all began filing out of the room, Dole approached Moynihan, and unobtrusively slipped him a handwritten note. Just as unobtrusively, Moynihan put it in his pocket. Then he left the room through the doors behind the high mahogany bench where the senators sat.

Once out of public view, Moynihan withdrew Dole's note. "Is it time for the Moynihan-Dole bill?" he read.

This was the moment, Moynihan felt, the moment he had been certain would come, when he and Dole would quietly get together, make a deal, and the bill would pass. He handed the note to Lawrence O'Donnell. A piece of history, O'Donnell thought as he read it, a talisman to be framed alongside a photograph of the bill-signing ceremony with the President and a beaming Moynihan and Dole.

Ten minutes later, Moynihan, thinking similar thoughts, asked O'Donnell, "Do you have my note?" He took it back. With his eye on history, as always, Pat Moynihan wanted to keep it.

Dole knew he would need something to carry into any bargaining session. No longer would the Chafee-Dole plan suffice. Clearly, there was not enough Republican support for any kind of mandate to allow Dole to use that bill as a vehicle. Late in May, Sheila Burke fashioned the outline of an alternative plan for a stripped-down standard benefits package that firms would be urged — but not required — to offer workers. It would be combined with the insurance and malpractice reforms embodied in almost all the bills. There was no timetable for insuring everyone and no provision for additional federal subsidies to the uninsured — unless and until savings were achieved in Medicare and Medicaid. In essence, it was closer to the Rowland-Bilirakis bill than to anything Chafee or Dole, let alone the Clinton administration, had originally supported.

Even as Dole moved toward compromise, pressure from the Republican Right increased. On May 31 six prominent conservative activists — Reagan political operative Richard Viguerie, Phyllis Schlafly of the Eagle Forum, L. Brent Bozell of the Conservative Victory Committee, Sandra Butler of United Seniors Association, Burt Y. Pines of the National Center for Public Policy Research, Morton C. Blackwell of the Leadership Institute Press — sent Dole and Gingrich an open letter warning that any "willingness to compromise on behalf of big government" would make it "almost impossible" for Dole and Gingrich to find conservative grassroots support in 1996. Compromise on the Clinton plan, they warned, "would be the death knell of the Republican Party." Viguerie added a separate warning: "Any Republican who wants to be seriously considered on the ticket . . . should not be on the wrong side of this issue." Gingrich, understanding that Dole was the real target of the threat, quickly said, "I agree with the spirit of the letter and I oppose any health reforms that call for new taxes, mandates of any kind or price controls." Sheila Burke, noting that the letter writers "obviously have influence," said Dole would "take it seriously."

While all this was happening, Pat Griffin, in charge of White House liaison with Congress, was trying to maintain an optimistic stance. Inwardly, he had a sinking feeling. He was standing on the outdoor deck of a home in northwest Washington, seeking a shady spot to escape the suffocating capital heat, and chatting about prospects for health reform. It was a Sunday afternoon during the weekend after the 1994 Memorial Day holiday. Around him were other members of the White House staff, attending a private party in honor of one of their group about to be married.

Griffin was deeply involved in the issue. It was, Griffin thought, a chance to affect history. He was convinced from the beginning that this was "a Hill deal" — meaning that Congress, not the White House, would make the final decisions. And he had been convinced that a bill would pass. He just couldn't believe, as he put it, that "these guys are going to walk home without a bill."

But now, on this first weekend in June, Griffin was forced to face doubts he did not voice. Health care reform, he feared, had slipped through their fingers. "I thought it was over," he said later, "when we didn't get it out of the Finance Committee by Memorial Day."

Inside the White House, gloom spread, though on June 9 there was a brief moment of cheering news when Ted Kennedy's committee reported out a bill that called for all Americans to be covered by insurance by New Year's Day 1998. But elsewhere, the portents were discouraging. Senator Dianne Feinstein, the California Democrat facing a tough fight for reelection, quietly pulled her name off the Senate version of the Clinton plan; she had been an original cosponsor. In liberal Vermont, one of the President's staunchest allies, Governor Howard Dean, himself a physician, gave up hope of enacting a state reform plan designed to mesh with the Clinton proposal. It died in a conflict between the Vermont state House of Representatives and the Senate. Those who thought it too ambitious and those who wanted to go further could not resolve their differences any more than in Washington. "The opponents of reform were much more motivated than the supporters," Governor Dean told the *New York Times*, reflecting another national reality in the battle.

In Florida, on the same day that Kennedy's committee voted, Governor Lawton Chiles, another Clinton ally, saw his health care reform killed in a special session of the legislature. The principal Florida Senate committee divided four-four and refused to send the bill to the floor. It was a reminder to the President, if one were needed, that missing by a single vote was as damaging as missing by a mile.

The next day Magaziner attempted to mobilize the White House for its final fight. In an extraordinarily candid — and bleak — assessment, Magaziner drafted a five-page confidential memo for the small group of critical players: The President, the vice president, the First Lady, White House Chief of Staff McLarty, and Clinton's advisers Ickes, Stephanopoulos, and Griffin. It was headed, simply, WHERE DO WE GO FROM HERE? Magaziner intended it, he said later, "to sound the panic alarm." It did:

> We have been losing the public battle on health care for some time now. The public wants universal coverage and the various other goals the President has outlined but has become increasingly confused, apprehensive and skeptical about the Administration's ability to achieve those goals without upsetting or even destroying what they have today. Many Republicans now believe that they can fight the President on health care and "bring him to his knees" without negative public consequence. They believe that they can successfully argue that they want health reform which is prudent, as opposed to his "radical, bureaucratic government takeover of the health care system which will destroy American health care."

In a less charged political environment, Magaziner wrote, making a deal on health care reform would be possible. He listed eight Senate Republicans — Chafee, Jeffords, Durenberger, Packwood, Danforth, Kassebaum, Mark Hatfield of Oregon, and William Cohen of Maine — as possibly joining fifty-two Democrats to provide the filibuster-defeating sixty votes for universal coverage. But that good faith, bipartisan political climate no longer existed. "In the political world we are now in," Magaziner wrote them, "there is a deadly chain whose links threaten any deal short of presidential surrender."

He added:

The Republican right and many mainstream Republican interest groups want to defeat the President on health care. They
pressure Senator Dole so he can't move. He now smells blood
and also wants to defeat the President. He convinces the moderate Republicans who otherwise would support universal coverage to hold back, beat the President and build reform out of
a Republican/conservative Democrat bill which will fragment
the Democratic Party. . . . Because the ultimate anchors of this
chain, the conservative Republicans, want outright capitula-
tion, the threshold keeps moving away from us whenever we
probe what it would take to get a deal.

Magaziner's advice was to approach Chafee, Durenberger, and
Danforth to see if they were willing to "break the chain and bargain
in good faith for a real universal coverage bill in the Finance Committee." He urged that they be called immediately by the President
and invited to meet with him individually in the Oval Office to discuss bipartisan strategy. At the same time, the President should also
ask Pat Moynihan and Bob Packwood, the man who twenty years
earlier had introduced President Nixon's comprehensive national insurance plan, to meet him in the Oval Office "to see if Packwood is
interested in serious discussion." If that didn't work, then "there is
no quick deal to be cut and we must fight."

The peril for the President, Magaziner warned, was to slip into
a deal, which meant Clinton would have to repudiate his own plan
and accept one that did not achieve universal coverage. Both from
a policy and political standpoint, the consequences would be enormous. Magaziner, who often displayed a tin ear for the nuances of
politics, made a prescient observation about what fate might befall
the President and his party: "He will not be able to claim victory for
health reform. The summer will be filled with who lost health care
and White House ineptness stories possibly fueled by sources in our
own Administration. The President will be accused of lacking back-
bone by many Democratic constituencies and the media. We will face
a summer of Whitewater hearings and health care failure, which will
guarantee retaliation against Democrats this November."

All the more reason, he urged, for them to make a fresh start.
They should acknowledge publicly that their bill was flawed, that

they had heard the American people and others with "good ideas on how to improve our original approach." Then they should offer a new joint bill under the leadership of George Mitchell that would have "less government, less bureaucracy, but still guarantee universal coverage."

It was a desperate last-ditch effort to salvage reform, but the situation called for desperate measures.

Everyone understood the effort was sinking. Moynihan's response was to give the White House an unneeded demonstration of how far it had fallen. On June 9, knowing that it had no Republican support and significant Democratic opposition, he introduced his variant of the Clinton plan. It had an employer mandate for all firms with more than twenty workers and would extend it to those smaller firms unless they voluntarily covered virtually all their employees within five years. It trimmed the benefits package somewhat to assuage Moynihan's own well-publicized doubts about the financing of the Clinton plan but still called for extensive new taxes: $1.76 on a pack of cigarettes, a 50 percent excise tax on handgun ammunition, and a 1 percent payroll tax on big companies that self-insured. In a New York fillip, the senator proposed to tax health insurance premiums and dedicate the proceeds to teaching hospitals and academic health centers — of which New York had many.

Some administration loyalists, like Rockefeller, thought the move was at best an ill-timed effort to demonstrate to a stubborn White House how little support such an approach could command. But John Breaux, the deal maker, argued that it would not impede the search for a compromise.

It looked increasingly doubtful, however, that Dole would be part of any deal. At a Republican meeting in Boston on June 11, he promised to "filibuster and kill" any bill with an employer mandate. He sounded as if he would rather have an issue than any legislation. "In my view," Dole said, "we've reached a point where I'm prepared to say, Okay, let's have a referendum on this in 1994. Let's let the voters decide. If they want the Clinton plan, then they'll vote for their candidates. If they want something else, they will vote

for Republicans. If that happened, we would end up with probably three hundred House members and seventy-five Republican
senators."

That did not sound like a man looking for a deal.

With Moynihan and Dole giving no clear signal that they would lead
the search for consensus, centrist senators on and off Finance decided
it was time for a try of their own. The initial group included Finance
Republicans Chafee, Durenberger, Packwood, and Danforth and Finance Democrats Breaux, Baucus, Boren, Bradley, and Conrad. Joining from outside the committee were Republicans Nancy Kassebaum
of Kansas, Bill Cohen of Maine, Jim Jeffords of Vermont, Christopher
"Kit" Bond of Missouri, Mark Hatfield of Oregon, and Democrats
Joseph Lieberman of Connecticut, Bob Kerrey of Nebraska, and
Dianne Feinstein of California.

The genesis for this "rump group," as they were originally called
in the White House and on Capitol Hill, was the increasing frustration felt by those dedicated to bipartisan reform — not only the
senators, but even more so their staffs. The closer the deadline for
action on Senate legislation approached, the greater the pressures
grew. With them, inevitably, came divisive rumors about Democratic
Senator X cutting a private deal with Republican Senator Y. Clouds
of distrust hung over the process. Charges of betrayal were privately
bandied about.

By late spring, these suspicions threatened to destroy the already
slim prospects for agreement. To restore trust, members of Republican and Democratic Senate staffs met privately around Memorial
Day to exchange accurate information and spike rumors. The reasoning was simple. "If you can't get the staffs to bond and trust each
other, you're never going to get the senators to bond and trust each
other," explained Chafee's top health aide, Christy Ferguson, who
took a leading role in organizing that first private meeting of Republican and Democratic staff members, and who herself was working
brutally long hours from early morning to late at night seven days a
week.

The initial staff meetings were useful; but the pressures on their
senators did not abate. Nor did rumors of more private deals and

more defections. To alleviate those problems, Ferguson went to her boss. "I think you need to call these guys in," she told Chafee, referring to the principal moderate Republican senators. "You need to tell 'em you're not cutting any deals without 'em, and they need to tell you that they're not going to cut any deals without you."

Chafee did. Invited to a meeting in his fifth-floor Dirksen Senate Office Building early in June were Republican senators Chafee believed he could count on to help pass health care reform: Durenberger, Danforth, Bond, Cohen, Jeffords, Hatfield, Packwood, Kassebaum. The meeting was short; Chafee was direct. He couldn't negotiate a health bill by himself, he told them. "I'm not going anywhere without at least all of you, and hopefully more," he said. He needed a commitment. They had to stand together. They agreed; they were blood brothers. Danforth, the ordained Episcopal minister, even made that analogy explicit. Addressing them solemnly during this first meeting, Danforth articulated what he called their "blood oath." "All right," Danforth said, "now we're going to have a blood oath, and everybody here is going to live with it all the way through this process." He meant, he explained, they would pledge to stick together on whatever points of agreement they reached, and hold that unified position all the way through to a final Senate vote. Danforth repeated that oath before every subsequent meeting, including those later attended by Democrats. They all agreed at their first meeting that it was time to start talking privately with like-minded Democrats. And, as Ferguson remembered, "They all agreed that we had played around with Dole too long, that Dole was gone."

From that point, an expanding number of Democratic senators began attending.

As those senators were beginning to exchange ideas, Moynihan and Packwood met Clinton at the White House on June 14. Packwood was blunt — almost unbelievably so in the eyes of some who attended that meeting. "He just laid it on the line," one participant said. "Without reservation, all the way through, at all points, he said exactly what he thought. I have never been in a meeting with a President when someone else showed so little sign of being intimidated by the presidential presence." The votes aren't there for health

reform — not for mandates, not for universal coverage, not for alliances — Packwood told the President, and the Republicans to my
right are very happy to take this to the polls in November. They think
they will win.

After an hour, Moynihan and Packwood faced the crowd of reporters and TV cameras encircling them in front of the White House.
Moynihan was diplomatic, but also candid. Reading from notes he
had just taken in the Oval Office, he said he and Packwood had
agreed "that there is not now a majority for any health care reform
plan in the Senate Finance Committee." He softened the blow by
holding out hope: "We will continue to work on a bipartisan basis to
provide legislation that covers everyone."

A reporter called out: "Is the President's plan dead as he presented
it?" "Not at all," Moynihan replied amiably. "This is a large piece
of legislation and some of the principles are absolutely essential and
others are negotiable and he knows that."

Packwood was not so politic. "At the moment all plans are dead,"
he said, addressing the cameras, then adding, "There's not a majority
for any single plan."

A faint glimmer of hope remained. "It is very clear," Packwood
told the reporters, "that we are all wanting to go in the same direction, but there is a strong, large feeling on the Republican side
against any compulsion that absolutely forces people to do things
they don't want to do." Packwood suggested that a proposal from
Breaux for a "trigger mechanism," something that would require
Congress to reconsider mandates if lesser reforms did not achieve
near-universal coverage in a few years, might be worth exploring. It
was a way of deferring the hard decisions — something politicians
always find convenient. "It is not universal coverage," Packwood
conceded.

The next day, the President began individual Oval Office explora-
tory meetings with Senate Republican moderates. The visitors —
Chafee, Durenberger, Danforth — left impressed by Clinton's detailed knowledge of the compromises under discussion and his eagerness to have them find some way to move the process forward. But
there were no magic bullets. Clinton complained to Durenberger,
"Every time I start in the middle, Bob Dole moves the middle to

the right" — a comment the senator did not even try to refute. Instead, he urged Clinton to be even more open-minded about what he would accept. "Mr. President," Durenberger said, "with all due respect, forget the plan. We're beyond the plan. You can chuck my plan, chuck your plan, chuck all the plans. Let's figure out what is health reform and how we're going to get it done."

Of all those involved in the debate, Durenberger was most attuned to the changes in the health care marketplace and most insistent that any plan recognize the realities of that private-sector world. His great frustration was that "nobody understands medical markets," most notably Hillary Clinton and Ira Magaziner. "They talked about managed competition," Durenberger said, but then added a whole complex scheme of regulations and controls that worked against the efficient operations of a marketplace. When he confronted the First Lady with this contradiction, he said, her response was, "To tell our Democratic friends we're going to get universal coverage within five years, and to satisfy the Congressional Budget Office on costs, we have to have employer mandates and global budgets and cost controls and all these other things."

For Durenberger, "the moment of truth" about the unworkability of the Clinton plan had come early, when the big businesses that were already providing insurance for their workers turned against the administration proposal. Durenberger saw this, not as duplicity or selfishness on the executives' part, but rather as a hard-headed judgment that the Clinton proposals would interfere with — not assist — the forces of change in the marketplace.

Those changes clearly were accelerating even as Congress wrestled with the reform plan. In 1991, the majority of people insured through their jobs — 53 percent, actually — were in traditional, fee-for-service medicine. Three years later, only 35 percent were covered that way. The rest were in some form of managed care, most of it run by for-profit companies. At least three-fourths of the doctors and an even higher percentage of hospitals signed contracts in 1994 to reduce their fees for patients enrolled in managed care and to accept some degree of second-guessing of their diagnosis and treatment plans by those administering the program.

As a result of this revolution, the inflation rate in health care was drastically cut in those years. Formerly autonomous hospitals and doctors rushed to form their own "networks" of integrated providers rather than wait to be swallowed up by the expanding HMOs invading their territories. Business reveled in the new competitive atmosphere. A survey of large firms — clearly those in the best bargaining position — showed that the increase in premiums fell from 14 percent in 1991 to 6 percent in 1994. During the Finance Committee deliberations, a front-page story in *USA Today* cited another employer survey pegging the rate for the first three months of 1994 at just over 3 percent, the smallest increase in any quarter since 1973. In mid-June, the San Francisco Bay Area Business Group on Health, a voluntary alliance, reported that it had negotiated new HMO contracts for its eleven big employers with annual premium *reductions* of 5 to 10 percent.

Scholars warned that these might well be one-time savings and that demographic forces and technology changes would continue to drive up costs. Even now, it was not all rosy. Complaints multiplied about people being denied referrals for treatment by specialists in some HMOs. Certain cost-cutting devices — like the imposition of a standard twenty-four-hour limit on the hospital stay after the birth of a baby — showed little consideration for the patients or their families. And the number of uninsured continued to rise, in part because companies were saving money by dumping their retirees from their coverage.

Still, the marketplace changes reduced pressures for rapid or large-scale reforms. In May, the *New York Times* surveyed a cross-section of big-business executives; now they were as opposed as their small-business counterparts. More than two-thirds of the big-firm bosses said the Clinton plan would increase their health costs, provide fewer benefits than existing policies, and make the overall U.S. health care system worse. Durenberger and others like him continued to work, but they knew they were swimming against the tide.

The Senate environment was also increasingly hostile to bipartisanship. Something new — and destructive — was at work.

For all its internal differences, personal and political, and its courtly, stuffy manner of operating that made it easy to caricature as "the Cave of the Winds," the Senate had been relatively free of the narrow partisanship that animated the House of Representatives. But no longer.

It was true that in the clash over health care reform, some senators acted out assigned roles — or roles others suspected them of playing. Jay Rockefeller thus was regarded by other Democrats as the foot soldier for the First Lady; Tom Daschle of South Dakota as the foot soldier for Senate Majority Leader Mitchell; Mitchell as the foot soldier for the President's bill; Bob Bennett of Utah as the foot soldier for Minority Leader Dole, assigned to take the political temperature of fellow Republican senators and report his findings to Dole. Still these roles were enacted in the more traditional Senate manner.

But now, increasingly, the Senate was being torn by the same ideological warfare that had developed over decades when House Republicans were members of the permanent minority. "You were almost always completely ineffective as a Republican during the six years I served in the House," reflected Bill Cohen of Maine:

> You were treated with contempt by Democrats, with the back of the hand. If you do that over a long enough period of time, you're going to build some real animus. That's what exists over there. That's why you've got a Newt Gingrich who can rally these kinds of forces. And that's filtering into the Senate. It's not the same place. There are no Scoop Jacksons or Abe Ribicoffs or Howard Bakers or Ed Muskies, people with a real sense of the institution. What you're seeing is more and more people coming from the outside, either governorships or state legislatures or from the House. And they're much more partisan. There's no sense of quote The Club. The Club doesn't exist anymore. It's hard to have coalitions today; it's every person for him- or herself. That's something new in the last ten years and it has gotten progressively worse. Then add to the disintegration of spirit that used to animate the Senate the enormous amount of money that's poured into the process — and more important even than money are talk radio shows, television, C-SPAN.

There used to be a certain mystique about public officials, said Cohen, who rose to national prominence as a principled freshman

House Republican who voted for articles of impeachment against Richard Nixon in 1974 and was one of the pro-reform Senate moderates. You entrusted the machinery of government to those people. Maybe you liked them, maybe not. But at least you deferred to them initially. "That's gone," he said. The ideological talk radio shows — the Rush Limbaughs, the G. Gordon Liddys — contributed to the poisonous atmosphere, Cohen said. But so did the politicians, "everybody who runs *against* the institution contributes to it. When we're throwing stones at ourselves, you can expect that the public's going to continue to escalate the stone throwing."

Cohen's was not an isolated view; it was expressed again and again during the debate, and by Republicans as well as Democrats who saw the struggle become intensely polarized and ideologically driven.* The stakes were rising. The System was in danger of coming apart.

Clinton's vulnerability contributed to the stridency of the GOP positions against any bill. Buoyed by polls showing stronger public doubts, Republicans were far less fearful of voter retribution for opposing what had been perceived as public desire for action. "What's our hurry?" Dole heard other Republicans say privately. "This thing is going to go down the tubes, the polls look better for us, people are upset, and Clinton's down to forty-two or thirty-six percent support on health care, depending on what poll you read."

Many Republicans other than Newt Gingrich began to see a tantalizing prospect of winning control of Congress by opposing the Clinton health plan as a quintessential example of Big Government Democratic liberalism run wild. In this volatile atmosphere moderates found themselves subjected to heavy ideological pressure and attack. The knives were flashing, and drawing blood.

Typical was an article about Dole in the right-wing *American Spectator* that spring. The sine qua non of Dole's presidential prospects among Republicans, wrote the conservative Grover G. Norquist (father of a "no new taxes" pledge for Republican candidates in 1994 and 1996), "will be Dole's ability to block any government-run health-care system." Then, conspiratorially referring to Dick

---

*In January 1996, Cohen, expected to win easily in his Senate reelection campaign, surprised his colleagues by giving up his Senate seat.

Darman, an influential Bush White House aide whom conservatives regarded as the manipulative figure who had pushed Bush to the left, Norquist wrote, "But senators note that Dole must come to grips with his own 'Darman problem': A key staffer, Sheila Burke, has been maneuvering the Republicans into a compromise on health."

By June, Sheila Burke found herself experiencing abuse of a kind she had never before known, all as a consequence of "the Right being ginned up." The True Believer mentality was at work, she thought. "They support nobody who doesn't totally agree with them," Burke said then. "It's not about governing, which is what we do." She paused, and repeated for emphasis: "It's not about governing. That's not how they think.

"It makes it very hard," she said. "The sharp lines get drawn and Bill Kristol sends out a memo a week. And the [Republican] staff meetings are pretty rancorous. You have two or three people who are trying to stop anything from happening, who disrupt those who attempt to sit down and work through what are reasonable alternatives, their view being, If you move at all, you lose it all. If you have to make any move toward the center, you have given up ground."

Christy Ferguson, Chafee's health policy expert, also was forced to conclude that "the rabid conservatives were out to get all of the 'liberal staff.' They went out to get Sheila in a big way; they went out to get me in a smaller way because I'm not as visible. They were planting stories in the newspapers, Evans & Novak, the *Washington Times*, the *Wall Street Journal*. They had a continuous campaign about Sheila, making her Rasputin to Dole, and went after me to make it seem I was even more liberal than Chafee was."

On June 7, during the Senate Finance Committee deliberations on the reform bill, the *Washington Times* weighed in with more of the same. "Some GOP colleagues and their staff view Mr. Dole's chief of staff and health care guru, Sheila Burke, as a liberal Democrat," the paper said, adding, " 'Our No. 1's No. 1 is a liberal Democrat,' said a critical GOP Senate aide, referring to Ms. Burke. 'The general's general is a member of the enemy camp.' "

"It's an indirect way of getting at Dole by the right wing," Burke said in a conversation that June:

It's terribly frustrating. It's gotten very personal, which is an experience I've not had in the seventeen years I've been here, and I find it quite distasteful. It makes me very angry. It's as if you can't debate substance. You've got to talk about personalities. This kind of personal attack is hard to take. It makes me stop and think, Maybe it's time for me to get out.

I look at Dole potentially running in 'ninety-six and I think, Here's somebody I have enormous faith in and I'm committed to. Do I want to become a problem for him? Do I want to become a target? And I don't. That's not what I'm about. Do I want my kids or my neighbors to read that kind of crap in the paper? No. I'm not in public policy for that. That's not why I came. I'm used to working in a bipartisan environment on most issues where reasonable people can do the reasonable thing. It has become so politicized. I suspect it will get more so. They really believe if they can frighten off the individual, they can change the outcome of the issue — which I think is not the case. But it certainly makes you stop and think. The extremes seem to be reigning at the moment and some of this stuff will wreak havoc with The System as we know it.

They were certainly wreaking havoc with health care reform.

It was not just the internal forces that were pulling Dole, Packwood, and others on the Finance Committee away from any compromise legislation. The lobbying groups were pounding hard. The Republican National Committee launched a half-million-dollar assault on the Clinton plan, targeting states with members on Finance and Ways and Means. Citizens for a Sound Economy announced a quarter-million-dollar effort focused on two Finance Committee Democrats who were actively seeking a compromise plan, John Breaux and Bill Bradley. "Mandated universal coverage," the CSE ads maintained, equaled "government-controlled health care . . . a big bureaucracy, tax increases, loss of jobs, waiting lines, limiting your right to choose doctors, rationed medical care." Empower America, run by Jack Kemp and William J. Bennett, chimed in with radio ads decrying the Clinton plan.

In the third week of June, HIAA's "Harry and Louise" campaign returned for another month's run, this time targeting provisions in the Clinton plan that would impose backup controls on health care spending and require "community-rating" or standard premiums for all those insured. The first, Louise tells Harry, would cause "rationing, the way I read it. You know, long waits for health care and some services not even available." The second would cause thousands of people to drop their insurance, a new character, Harry's kid brother from New York, warns. In a print ad that ran only in Washington and was obviously intended to appear conciliatory to the playmakers of the capital, HIAA emphasized its support for universal coverage. It read: "If we all cooperate, if everyone is in the system, universal health care coverage and insurance reform can work for America."

The cynicism of sending one message to the country and a different message to the capital was remarkable, even by the standards of this fight.

Pro-reform groups fought back, but were badly outspent. In mid-June, the Democratic National Committee, for example, announced a one-week, $150,000 ad campaign, ostensibly designed to produce phone calls to Congress demanding "the real thing" in reform. But the DNC bought time only on Washington, D.C., stations — not in the grass roots, where it counted.

Hillary Clinton was frustrated by the one-sidedness of the battle. On June 19, she and her husband assembled the top White House staff members and gave them a pep talk, recommitting themselves to fight for coverage for every American. The next day, she called in about a hundred representatives of labor, senior citizen, and consumer and supportive elements of the health care providers and read them the riot act. The Indian Treaty Room in the Old Executive Office Building was jammed when the First Lady began an extemporaneous update. Time was running out, she warned. Stop focusing on your own concerns, and focus on the universal-coverage goal. Pounding the lectern in front of her, she blamed her allies for "taking it for granted that Congress will pass a bill" and "asking for this and that" to be included. Keep on seeking your "parochial victories," she warned, "and you'll end up with no bill being passed — or a bill so weak the President will veto it." The opposition had been much more forceful, much more focused, thus much more effective, she told them. The proponents of reform had been all over the map. They were not unified; they were not "on message." They had to get back on track.

Now, as she became more impassioned, you could hear a pin drop in the room. To some, their heads bent over notebooks recording her words, it seemed as if the podium was shaking from the intensity of her remarks. Don't worry about all the other issues, the First Lady concluded. Concentrate on universal coverage, because if this bill doesn't contain a guarantee that all Americans will have coverage, and a mechanism to provide it, the President will veto that bill.

She was preaching to the choir, of course. Most of the people in the room had signed a letter to the President earlier that week urging him to "veto any legislation that falls short of universal coverage." One of them, John Rother of AARP, said it was a "call to Jesus" speech, and that it was needed.

Rother had been feeling deep frustration, at times so overwhelming that he did not even want to talk about where the battle stood for fear of exposing his emotions. He was not alone. By late June, virtually everyone involved felt the same way. They were, as Rother remarked, figuratively pulling out their hair and venting the same complaints to each other: There were too many different plans, too many different congressional committees to deal with, too much public confusion about the impact of the Clinton plan on people's lives. That complex blueprint, he thought, had almost become like the Bible: you could find anything you wanted in it to support your point of view. The American people had become disenfranchised from the debate, Rother was forced to conclude to himself. All the hopes of generating pro-reform grassroots pressure on Congress from beyond the Beltway had come to naught.

Talking with Rother during those weeks was like talking to a man battling the most serious doubts.

> In my public role, I have to be out there saying, "Okay, we can do this. If we just write one more letter, go to one more meeting, we can put this through." I have to constantly pump myself up. But I really feel terrible about what's happened.
>
>   This is an indictment of our country's ability to take on serious issues. Here's a debate as central to the future as any-

thing we can think of, and yet we're not able to deal with it in a straightforward way. As recently as last year, I had hopes that we could get the public involved. Maybe that's proof that I'm a policy wonk and I'm hopelessly out of it, but I did feel that on this issue which affects people directly, one that they're emotionally involved in and have strong views on, that we'd have this great national debate. Instead, we've had a lot of fear-mongering. We've had people take positions that they know are intellectually unsustainable. But they take them with a straight face and use the issue for other purposes. If we get through this with something that really works, it'll be a — I won't say "miracle" — it'll really be beating the odds. If this comes out with something good at the end, it won't be because of The System we have. It'll be in spite of it.

The more he thought, the gloomier he became. "The System is breaking down structurally," he said. "The press doesn't write about it because it's not an event. It's not conflict between two people."

Still, in public, and in group meetings with pro-reform groups, Rother struggled to appear hopeful. He wanted to believe, as he said, that "there's still a role for the good old pragmatic American who doesn't want government but is prepared to admit that in some things there needs to a governmental role." He took comfort in reminding himself that legislative battles were "like football games: a lot of action can happen after the game's two-minute warning sounds. You could still come back and snatch victory from defeat."

A day after the Hillary pep talk, the President chose an unusual venue — a meeting of the Business Roundtable, which long since had come out against key elements of his plan — to defend the correctness of his insistence on universal coverage and to lash out against his critics. "This town," he said, "is still too partisan, too negative, too obsessed with process and conflict instead of results and progress, too interested in blame and too little interested in responsibility." The Roundtable response was a letter warning the administration and Congress not to make concessions to small business that would impose additional burdens on big business.

*   *   *

In all this time, Moynihan was seeking a formula that might attract bipartisan support in the Finance Committee. But he no longer had the franchise to himself. The group of backbenchers who had begun exchanging ideas informally had shaken down into a "rump," or "mainstream," group meeting regularly to draft its own compromise. With Chafee in the lead, Republicans Danforth and Durenberger (but no longer Packwood) and Democrats Bradley, Breaux, Boren, and Conrad were readying their own compromise.

Dole's response was to collar Packwood and set their staffs to drafting an alternative that would be more modest and would appeal to conservative Republicans off the Finance Committee. It was widely — and correctly — seen as an effort to impede the mainstream group's operations.

Another defection came from Baucus, the Montana Democrat who had been a target of particularly intense NFIB pressure, who walked away from the group after the first meeting, claiming it was not giving adequate attention to cost-containment measures. His action led one of the Democrats to quip sardonically to the group that "Baucus is caucusing" and a Republican to mutter aloud that "on the first tough decision day, Max walks."

On June 29, as Moynihan prepared for the first votes on his own draft, Dole stole a march and released details of a Republican plan that had no employer or individual mandates, no premium caps or price controls. Like the plan the Bush administration offered in election year 1992, it would rely on insurance reforms and limited public subsidies for low-income individuals to buy private policies, with no deadline for insuring everyone. Bob Packwood, now fully aligned with Dole, said their plan, unlike the President's, meant "no mandates, no taxes, no bureaucracy." It was endorsed by forty of the forty-four Republican senators — all but Chafee, Durenberger, and Danforth, from the bipartisan rump group, and Jim Jeffords of Vermont, who had co-sponsored the Clinton plan and Kennedy's variant. With forty votes, Dole could almost certainly sustain a filibuster, if necessary.

The major business lobbies fighting the Clinton plan swung behind the Dole-Packwood bill in the Senate, as they had done behind the Rowland-Bilirakis bill in the House. Incremental reform was all they would support. The Republican National Committee, happy to have something to be for, launched ads saying that this was the way — the only way — to bipartisan agreement.

Dole had solved his most pressing personal problem. As Senate Republican leader and as prospective presidential contender, he could not afford to be part of a small group of GOP senators who joined the Democrats on a compromise bill that would escape a Senate filibuster. Now, he had surrounded himself with all but a handful of his fellow Republicans. Clinton, Moynihan, and Mitchell would have to come to him. His loyal aide, Sheila Burke, thought Dole was "where he needs to be now." But Burke couldn't help but reflect that "it would be sad at the end of this process to have done absolutely nothing, because we will never be at this point again."

Moynihan finally brought out his long-awaited proposal in the last week of June. It started with insurance reforms and then set a complex set of deadlines — sooner for large firms, later for smaller — which, if not met, would trigger an employer mandate for those companies. To finance subsidies for small firms and low-income families, it included taxes on cigarettes, health insurance premiums, guns and ammunition, as well as on payrolls of companies that self-insured. It omitted direct controls on premiums.

No sooner was the plan advanced than it began to be dismembered. The triggered mandates disappeared on a fourteen-to-six roll call, with the moderates joining the conservative Republicans in opposition. Other sections that the White House hoped to preserve followed it into the discard pile. Two days before the Fourth of July, numb with fatigue and frustration, the committee, with what the *Baltimore Sun*'s Karen Hosler accurately described as "a melancholy air," voted out a bill that failed to meet the President's bottom-line goal of guaranteeing universal coverage. The bill did not require a mandate for employers to provide insurance. It did not make clear how it would raise money for the subsidies it promised to the poor to help them afford insurance. It scaled back a proposed increase in cigarette taxes by $1 a pack. While it set a goal of covering 95 percent of the population by the year 2002, it did not provide any teeth to enforce that goal; instead, it fell back on the old political standby of directing a commission to report to Congress if the goal had not been reached by that time. It even struck one of Pat Moynihan's "most cherished provisions" from the bill, a tax on ammunition for handguns that would make the cost of obtaining particularly lethal ammunition prohibitive, thus helping reduce the personal suffering and soaring costs of emergency treatment of gunshot wounds. His idea would eventually prevail, Moynihan told Adam Clymer of the *New York Times*, but added, wearily, "I think this might take about three hundred ninety years and about two hundred thousand children's lives."

The vote was twelve to eight. As an indication of how sharply divided, and disappointed, committee members were, even Jay Rockefeller voted against it.

Words were not a measure of Rockefeller's emotions then; a mere glance at his stricken face expressed volumes about what he was really feeling. Among Republicans, Chafee, Durenberger, and Danforth voted for it. Most significantly, Bob Dole did not. Herblock, with his genius for capturing a moment, caricatured Dole as the undertaker for health reform in his *Washington Post* cartoon.

In announcing his committee's action, Moynihan professed pride in what had been achieved. "I am pleased to bring this forth today," he said, after enumerating the bill's provisions, "and I look forward to seeing this legislation continue us on the historic path undertaken by Franklin Delano Roosevelt in 1935."

He added a scholarly postscript that was pure Moynihan: "In this situation, we must remember the central principle of medicine: *Primum, non nocere* — First, do no harm."

Eloquent words notwithstanding, the experience had been torturous for the Finance Committee and especially for its chairman. Just the afternoon before, while the committee was recording vote after vote on critical provisions in the bill, and striking many of them down, Moynihan was encountered walking alone in the subway tunnel from the Capitol grounds toward his office. He was pensive.

"I told the President a few days ago that on a bad day we'd get five votes on the employer mandate and on a good day we'd get six," he said. After pausing for half a second, he added, "And today we got six. The question that needs to be asked when this is over is, Why was this such a hard message to get through?"

His private frustration was reflected inside the White House. Two days before, reacting to what he felt to be the wreckage taking place in the Finance Committee, Ira Magaziner wrote another, even more critical advisory; its distribution was limited to only three people: The President, the First Lady, and Harold Ickes. Magaziner's health team, he told them, had been analyzing what was coming out of Finance and had concluded "it contains serious policy and political flaws." Not wishing to slow down the committee deliberations, Magaziner said, "I am not voicing the concerns in this memo to anyone." But while the White House may want publicly to agree to passage of the Finance bill, "we should not support its elements. The proposal will alienate our base Democratic supporters and will potentially hurt many middle-class Americans. Personally, I believe that the whole approach is so seriously flawed that the nation would be better off with a minimal reform which accomplished insurance reforms and expanded Medicaid or public health."

He recommended that the President privately urge George Mitchell to propose a blend of the Moynihan and Kennedy committee bills by using the Finance compromise as its base but adding guarantees to "achieve real universal coverage and control cost growth." Neither he nor the President could accept that the game was really over.

The President shared Magaziner's frustrations over the emerging bill and over Pat Moynihan. At a White House leadership meeting before the July Fourth congressional recess, the President launched into an emotional critique of the committee and its chairman. There were no numbers behind what they were doing, he raged, waving his arms in the air. There was no policy behind what they were doing. They were just cobbling things together. At one point, he said, "This thing's slipping away from us." Moynihan had failed them.

In time, Clinton took a more benign view of the chairman. Speaking of Moynihan a year later in the summer of 1995, the President told us he understood that Moynihan thought the whole project was doomed from the beginning:

> I think he believed that it was too big and too complicated and that Congress was not capable of dealing with it within the time frame allocated to it, especially since we didn't get an earlier start because it took so long on the budget and on NAFTA. He just simply thought that something of that magnitude could not be done correctly within that time frame, especially given the political composition of the Congress and the committee with which he had to deal. I think he honestly believed it was an error to try. And I think he was honest about it in his heart.

The President also said he understood Moynihan's conviction that Clinton and the Democratic Congress *could* come together on a welfare reform bill. The senator and the President were in broad agreement on that issue. In retrospect, Clinton said he could see Moynihan's point that passing a welfare reform bill in that congressional session "would broaden the political support for our administration and make it possible that we could get more done on health care over the next two years. . . . He honestly believed that the responsible choice was to take up welfare reform and get it done," the President told us, "because we could do it and we could do it in a bipartisan way."

In his retrospective musings, Clinton also told us that he regretted that his dealings with Dole on health care had been "too indirect." However remote the chances of enlisting Dole's support, he should have made a more personal, direct appeal to the Republican leader. Looking back, he told us that the best opportunity was in the fall of 1993, while Dole was still nominally supporting the Chafee bill for universal coverage through an individual mandate. If ever there was a chance for him to reach an understanding with Dole, Clinton said, that was it. "It should have been right then, or the day after they presented their bill," the President said, "where I should have tried to have a direct understanding with Dole."

Whether it would have resulted in a different ending is highly doubtful. The remark of a prominent Republican moderate senator, made privately early that summer of 1994, was probably more accurate. "I think Dole is a slave to the right wing," this senator said. "The nature of the Republicans in the Senate has changed and he's changed with them. He's just become a puppet of the right wing in the Senate; he's doing whatever they want him to do."

But the person who was most frustrated by his dealings with Dole was of course Pat Moynihan. The White House had always been skeptical of a Dole-Moynihan agreement. "Never, never, never, never," said one leading White House operative when asked if he thought a Moynihan-Dole deal was ever possible. But Dole continued to tantalize Moynihan. Even after the Finance Committee had voted and two days after Congress returned from its Fourth of July recess, Dole told Gloria Borger of *U.S. News & World Report,* "I don't think it's one hundred percent impossible now" for a deal still to be struck. Who knows what will happen on the Senate floor when time for debate on a health bill arrives? he asked rhetorically. But Dole also said then, "I don't think the Democrats want a Dole or Moynihan-Dole bill."

Privately and separately, Moynihan and Dole reluctantly concluded the time for a deal had passed. It was too late politically for Dole with his presidential ambitions, too late for Moynihan caught in a crosscurrent of competing political forces for a reform that had no bipartisan support.

The famous note Dole slipped Moynihan in May asking if it wasn't time for the Moynihan-Dole bill never produced a face-to-face meeting between the two senators. No meeting. No deal. With that lost opportunity went one of the best chances for health care reform.

16

The Baron Falls

PETE STARK COULDN'T WAIT to get started on the big reform bill. He felt none of Moynihan's ambivalence about the project, nor, as it turned out, did he have Dole's flexibility of principle. It mattered not a damn to the chairman of the Ways and Means Health Subcommittee whether those senators thought they could write or pass a bill. Pete Stark had as little regard for their competence as he did for the fools at the White House. He and the staff director of his subcommittee, David Abernethy, had written more health legislation than Ira Magaziner had ever read about. Their view of the Clinton plan and its principal drafter was contemptuous. When Magaziner and congressional liaison Howard Paster visited Stark for the first time, two weeks after the inauguration, Stark upbraided Magaziner for planning to meet with the designers of managed competition, who included insurance executives, at Jackson Hole. These were the advocates who urged forming networks of hospitals and doctors called health maintenance organizations (HMOs), which provide all services for a flat fee for those who enroll. Its entire purpose, he said, was to save the insurance companies.

Although he lived across the bay from Stanford University at Palo Alto, the intellectual home of managed competition, the essentially private system largely relying on market forces of supply and demand, Stark came from a different world. His East Bay district, south of Oakland, had none of the chic of San Francisco nor the intellectual and social peaks of Palo Alto. It was a rough-and-tumble blue-collar area of diverse ethnic groups, solidly Democratic, though Stark, who was sixty-two in 1993, was no proletarian himself. A graduate of MIT, with a business degree from the University of California at Berkeley, he was a banker by profession. But the Vietnam War had shaped his politics. As a protest, he put a giant peace symbol atop his bank and placed the same logo on the checks. In the 1972 Democratic primary, he beat the incumbent Democratic congressman, who had supported Johnson's and Nixon's Vietnam policies, and came to Washington to launch a long career.

With his banking background, Stark sought a Ways and Means assignment; by 1985 he was chairman of its Health Subcommittee. That meant he was a central figure in the Medicare catastrophic-insurance fiasco, but it did not quench his ambition to expand Medicare to more and more of the population. As he told Alissa J. Rubin of *Congressional Quarterly*, "I've been running the Medicare system, or our committee has, for the past nine years. We're its board of directors. I understand all its foibles, which are many, but I also know it has a ninety percent acceptance rate among its constituents, the seniors. . . . It's working."

In a densely populated, fast-growing area like the East Bay, the idea of requiring every individual and small business to buy insurance through a single government-chartered "alliance" seemed cumbersome and bureaucratic. Stark did not like the idea that these alliances would be established and run by appointees of Pete Wilson, the Republican California governor. He had a better idea. As quoted by Representative Jim McDermott, the Washington state psychiatrist and single-payer advocate, Stark said, "Never mind all that alliance bullshit. Let's just put them in Medicare. We know how to run that." The idea was to use an expanded Medicare to insure the uninsured. Have the federal government set a standard benefits package. Workers who were insured through their jobs would continue to be covered that way, with the employer paying 80 percent of the bill. Small firms and individuals without insurance would simply be brought into Medicare, with the premiums again falling mainly on the employer.

The most notable things about Pete Stark — as Ira Magaziner quickly learned — were his temper and his tongue. In the House, where people generally learned to curb their anger when it might cost them colleagues' votes, Stark was the exception. Democrats and Republicans alike knew he could turn on them at any moment. With blazing eyes, and biting tones, he would tear into anyone who seemed dense, recalcitrant, or just an obstacle. In such moments, he had something of the look of Thomas Hart Benton's portrait of John Brown — his youthful face contorted by the moral rage that consumed him. Jay Rockefeller saw that expression often during the work of the Pepper-Rockefeller Commission in the 1980s. During one verbal battle Stark said, "I'm going to take out an advertisement in every single West Virginia newspaper calling you the son-of-a-bitch you are."

The Clinton administration did everything it could to appease Stark, including finding a place on the Health and Human Services Department payroll for his third wife, Deborah, thirty-five years his junior. Still he was unrelenting. As Howard Paster confessed in a memo to Mack McLarty in December 1993, "I despair of making progress with Pete Stark."

At his first meeting with Magaziner, Stark argued long and hard that Clinton should abandon the proposal he made during the campaign and instead push to expand Medicare, step by step, until every eligible citizen was covered by the year 2000. Pay for it with a fifty-cents-an-hour payroll tax, he said. Call it a substitute for a minimum wage increase; the employers can't object to that. And by all means keep the Medicare price controls on what doctors and hospitals can charge. That's the only way to discipline spending.

When Magaziner pointed out that this was about 180 degrees removed from Clinton's thinking, Stark said, "Then just send us some general principles. We'll write the legislation." Clearly, he wanted to draft his own plan.

The Clintons and all the others in the House and Senate leadership, including the committee chairmen, were telling Magaziner the opposite: They wanted detailed legislative language. When he met again with Stark in early April 1993, there was an explosion. Chris Jennings, a liaison to Congress, said in an April 4 memo,

> As you know, last Wednesday, Ira was the recipient of a classic Pete Stark personal attack. In the meeting, Congressman Stark, among many extraordinarily negative comments,

stated that he had no desire in meeting with Ira until after decisions and a paper were available to review. Following the meeting, most of the members, embarrassed by the treatment Ira received, expressly stated that they disagreed with Congressman Stark and requested that we set up meetings separately with them, even if the subcommittee chairman would not attend. Hours later, Chairman Rostenkowski called to apologize on behalf of the entire committee for Congressman Stark's behavior.

A week later, Magaziner returned. This time the discussion was more peaceable. But Stark was clearly going his own way.

And so he did. The idea of expanding Medicare — conceptually much simpler than the Clinton plan — became the centerpiece of the bill Stark asked his subcommittee to start considering on March 13. Rostenkowski had sponsored a similar plan in the previous Congress but it never got out of committee. Stark liked the idea, not just because Medicare was his primary interest, but because the cost controls in Medicare — imposed directly on participating doctors and hospitals — would likely survive even if conservatives in Congress killed the backup cost-control features Clinton proposed for private medical providers. Thanks largely to Pete Stark's aggressive sponsorship, Medicare C, as it was called, became the House version of the Clinton plan.

Temperamentally, David Abernethy, the chief Health staffer on the Ways and Means Committee, was Stark's opposite — slow, steady, unflappable — but a great policy resource for both Stark and Dan Rostenkowski, the chairman of the full committee. Before coming to Capitol Hill, Abernethy had run the Haight-Ashbury Medical Clinic in San Francisco and been deputy health commissioner of New York state. He shared Stark's belief that the scheme Magaziner had devised was crazy. In April of 1993, while the task force was still trying to complete the Clinton plan, Abernethy wrote a speech for Rostenkowski that disparaged the idea of alliances and national health boards. "Some of the proposals I've seen," Rostenkowski said, addressing a medical association, "include elaborate linkages between several different institutions, none of which exist here or anywhere else at the moment. These plans are the domestic equivalent of Star Wars, where the plan was that a series of nonexistent technologies would be developed and linked to one another so that they would work flawlessly." The comparison to President Reagan's scheme for a space-based, laser-and-computer-operated defense against nuclear missiles was cruel, but one Stark strongly endorsed.

With Abernethy beside him, Stark assembled the Democrats on his subcommittee around the table in Room 1309 of the Longworth House Office Building in early March and walked them through what he had in mind. Stark and Abernethy sat at the head; the others chose places on the sides. They were a diverse crew. On one side, McDermott and John Lewis, the former civil rights hero from Atlanta, were ardent single-payers. They had recently been to the White House to tell both Clintons they should not be so preoccupied in negotiating with moderates that they lost the single-payers. At the other end of the spectrum was young Mike Andrews from Texas, often absent from these early discussions because he was fighting a losing battle for the nomination to fill Lloyd Bentsen's old Senate seat. Andrews was an original co-sponsor of the Cooper-Grandy bipartisan managed competition bill; he showed no give in the administration's direction.

The other three were in the middle of the party. One was a born legislative deal maker, Benjamin L. Cardin of Baltimore, who was close to Majority Leader Dick Gephardt. When he was Speaker of the Maryland house of delegates, Cardin pushed through that state's notably successful hospital cost-containment plan. He wanted to be sure the plan did not become so "nationalized" that innovative states like his own would lose the gains they had made. Mostly, he wanted the Democrats to pass health reform.

Sander M. (Sandy) Levin of suburban Detroit was another professional politician. His brother, Carl, was the junior senator from Michigan; Sandy had been a Democratic Party chairman and a candidate for governor before starting his House career. But in 1994, Levin was worried. Redistricting had pushed him farther into the Republican suburbs and farther from the safe Democratic base of Detroit. In 1992, George Bush nearly carried the district; Levin himself won by a close margin. As McDermott observed during subcommittee considerations, "Sandy doesn't want to be on record anywhere voting for anything that looks like a tax. He knows that some place down the road he's going to have to vote for one, but he wants it to be some convoluted thing where you can vote yes and no and maybe on the same issue. He is hoping for a miracle."

Gerald D. Kleczka of Milwaukee had none of Levin's election worries but was inclined to fuss about details. A ten-year House veteran but a newcomer to Ways and Means in this Congress, he would raise questions about things some colleagues thought secondary but Kleczka believed would upset his blue-collar constituents.

With little prospect of support from the four subcommittee Republicans — Willliam M. Thomas of California, Nancy L. Johnson of Connecticut, Jim McCrery of Louisiana, and Grandy — Stark had to figure out how to get six of the seven Democrats to report a bill by a six-to-five margin. Andrews was probably beyond reach. McDermott and Lewis should be easy because Medicare C involved a big increase in the number of people — maybe as many as fifty-five million — who would be insured through the government, potentially a large step toward a single-payer scheme. Winning support of the other subcommittee Democrats would be more difficult.

On Tuesday, March 15, in Room 1314 of the Longworth House Office Building, at a meeting of the full subcommittee, Fred Grandy of Iowa offered the first amendment to the legislation Stark and Abernethy had drafted. With a disarming smile, Grandy said, "This is an amendment I would describe as technical in nature. It would strike the employer mandate." Laughter filled the room. Turning serious, the former TV actor said the mandate issue was "the fundamental dividing line" between two approaches to reform. The bill he and Cooper had written would require employers to offer — but not pay for — health insurance. It would increase access without disrupting the economy, he said. The approach Clinton favored, which the Stark bill embodied, would cost between six hundred thousand and one million two hundred thousand jobs, he said.

From the Democratic side of the horseshoe table, Mike Andrews asked to second the amendment. One-size-fits-all legislation would cost too many jobs, he said.

Stark pounced. If the mandate is removed, he said, it would draw a veto from the President "who has correctly and courageously insisted on universal coverage by a time certain." This amendment leaves open the question of how and when we reach that goal. Forty million are uninsured; one hundred and fifty million live in fear their insurance will be canceled by their employer.

Back and forth the debate went, Republicans decrying "the mother of all entitlements," Democrats saying the GOP was trying to drive "a dagger in the heart of the deal." Only Sandy Levin seemed uncertain which side he was on. "I'm in favor of changing the mandate to leave more time for adjustment," he said. But without an employer mandate, the only financing provision would be a tax increase — and that would be worse.

At 11:06 A.M., the first roll call was held. All four Republicans voted aye on the Grandy amendment, as did Mike Andrews. The other five Democrats joined Stark in voting no. Six-to-five. Finally, the process was under way.

That first-vote pattern persisted on most of the subsequent amendments. One Republican proviso passed: imposing a limit of $350,000 on pain and suffering awards in medical malpractice cases. Not coincidentally, that happened to be the cap Maryland had established during Cardin's term as Speaker. Now, he switched sides to make it the norm for the nation.

As the final subcommittee votes were taken, the question became whether the same six-to-five margin that saved the employer mandate would survive in the bill Stark would send to the full committee. Stark himself never wavered. As Jim McDermott remarked, "He's like Johnny One-Note. He knows how to blow that note real good and that is all he's got. But that one note [Medicare] works."

On March 23, when the showdown came, Stark prevailed. He forced his subcommittee members to take a stand for or against him. By then, a lot of deal making had transpired. A proposal to boost cigarette taxes $1.25 a pack was out, then in. It was pressed hard by Mike Andrews, with the fervent backing of the specialists at the

M. D. Anderson Cancer Center of the University of Texas in his district. To appease Levin, the employer mandate was delayed: until 1996 for firms with more than one hundred workers; until 1998 for smaller companies. But funds to subsidize small business and insure the uninsured were still skimpy. Stark wanted an eight-tenths of a percent payroll tax. Levin, especially, was unhappy with that. As John Lewis, Stark's fellow liberal, remarked, "He really was very worried about anything that smelled of t-a-x." On the evening of March 22, Levin and Stark confronted each other behind closed doors. "I made it clear that I would not vote for it with a general payroll tax in it," Levin said. "I wasn't going to vote for a bill I could not defend. I made that clear to the White House. They wanted to get a bill, to keep the momentum going. No matter how much I wanted the momentum, I wanted to make it very clear that it wasn't a single-payer bill." When they parted that night, Levin said, "it was very, very much up in the air."

Every time Stark thought he had six votes secured, one of them slipped away. Then Kleczka threw another curve. He turned on Andrews, who had pressed to get the cigarette tax raised — an issue that clearly was going to cause problems in the full committee — and said, "You're loading up this wagon with all of your shit and you're not prepared to pull it." If Andrews didn't vote to report the bill, Kleczka told the group, he wouldn't either.

Stark's temper — always close to the surface — erupted. As the saintly John Lewis put it, "The chairman said a few choice words. He just said he had had enough of it." Stark stormed out, with others hotly pursuing, pleading with him not to capitulate. "I said something sort of strange," Lewis said. "I don't know where it came from, but I said, 'This reminds me of what A. Philip Randolph said during the March on Washington back in 1963: "We've come this far together. Let's stay together." ' "

While Lewis invoked the idealism of the civil rights movement, Andrews phoned Rostenkowski to warn him of the blowup. "We've got a real problem here," Andrews told Rosty. "Pete's acting like he is fifteen." Rosty's response was, "He's nine." But Stark's tantrum had an effect. Andrews and McDermott — the most conservative and most liberal of the Democrats on the issue — huddled and agreed it would be bad for everyone if the bill died in subcommittee. Stark was persuaded to return. Tempers cooled. Within hours, they voted — again by a six-to-five margin as on their first roll call — to send the bill to the full committee.

Before he could turn to health care reform, Rostenkowski had important business to conduct.

On March 15, he faced a renomination challenge to the North Side Chicago House seat he had held since 1958. Rosty was thirty years old when he entered Congress, and already was a political veteran bearing a long political legacy: He had served six years in the Illinois legislature and was a second-generation ward heeler, a loyal lieutenant in the organization led by Mayor Richard J. Daley. Rosty's father was the Thirty-second Ward Democratic committeeman; he controlled a number of city jobs that enabled him to perform countless favors for his neighbors in the Polish and Ukrainian-American neighborhood around Milwaukee Avenue — as long as they reciprocated with their votes. It was politics of the most basic kind: He took care of rezonings and property assessments; he found jobs for out-of-work nephews and nieces; he "straightened out" problems with police and building inspectors. His son inherited both his father's position as ward committeeman (and held on to it long after he had become chairman of Ways and Means in Washington) and his way of thinking. With such a background, Rosty became a superb deal maker, almost unrivaled at putting together majorities for his bills. But he was also too willing to accept favors from people seeking his help. Contributions flowed into his campaign fund from every interest group that had business before Ways and Means; the total from 1981, when he became chairman, through 1994, was an astonishing $5,514,861. Most of that time, he had only token opposition in his reelection campaigns. The money multiplied.

By 1992, the last year that members of Congress could legally convert unspent campaign funds to personal use, his account had reached more than $1 million. Instead of retiring and taking the money, Rosty stayed and ruled his committee. He liked Ronald Reagan, having teamed with the President to pass the historic Tax Reform Act of 1986. George Bush was an old pal; they had served

together in the 1960s when Bush was a junior Republican member
of Ways and Means. When Bush took his oath in 1989, he singled out
Rosty for a salute on the inaugural platform. Despite these close ties
to Republican Presidents, Rosty wanted to work with a Democrat.
In 1992, he thought he would have that opportunity.

Danny Rostenkowski's personal saga was almost an American fa-
ble. He was a product of the school of hard knocks: no law degree, no
profession of any kind except politics. His grammar was suspect; his
language not what the nuns would approve. But Rosty had outgrown
his own limitations. He had learned that his bulk and his scowl lent
force to his words. His willingness to accept colleagues, constituents,
lobbyists, and tycoons on their own terms — neither kowtowing nor
condescending to them — earned him their respect. He was at ease
both with Presidents and, helped by an able staff, with the toughest of
policy problems. He was a workhorse and, on issues that intimidated
politicians with less self-assurance, a warrior.

But Rosty was also a symbol of a kind of government that increasingly drew public suspicion. He was a backroom operator who
gloried in making private deals and who scorned the reformist
clamor for more and more changes in lobbying and campaign finance
rules. In an era of blow-dried, TV-conscious candidates, he was a
symbol of the old order; his very girth and homeliness made him an
anachronism. Worse, his personal conduct raised eyebrows.

If he passed up the big money by postponing his retirement, he
was hardly immune to favors. Although he lived in a small apartment
in Washington, Rosty enjoyed the restaurant and golfing circuit. Phil
Kuntz of *Congressional Quarterly* vividly captured his lifestyle in a
June 1993 article:

> After a frenetic day of politicking and legislating on Capitol
> Hill, Rep. Dan Rostenkowski likes a nice dinner out with
> his pals.
>
> On a typical night, the chairman of the Ways and Means
> Committee will gather with a group of colleagues, aides and
> lobbyists at Morton's of Chicago, a Georgetown steakhouse
> where the best cuts go for $28.95. They sit at one of
> Rostenkowski's favorite tables, near the brass plaque that
> says "Rosty's Rotunda," next to the flaming grill. They order

drinks, most likely a Gordon's Gin on the rocks for the chairman, maybe two. After the waiter rolls up a display cart of the day's choice steaks, the barrel-chested chairman orders his Pittsburgh-style — charred on the outside, rare inside. With dinner, a bottle of Châteauneuf-du-Pape.

And then Rostenkowski, one of Washington's great raconteurs, holds forth with stories about his life in politics — about how he helped throw a fully clothed presidential aide into the White House pool in Lyndon Johnson's day; about witnessing the investiture of the first Polish pope; about the time George Bush sat alone with the chairman just days after being inaugurated and said with boyish amazement, "Well, Danny, I made it."

When the bill comes, Rostenkowski may allow one of the lobbyists to pay it or he may grab it himself, as he did recently when he growled in mock anger at a lobbyist who reached for the bill, "F —— you! I'm paying the check."

But even when Rostenkowski picks up the tab, it seems unlikely that the money will come from his own pocket. Maybe he'll charge his campaign for the dinner. Maybe he'll expense it to his political action committee (PAC).

When it comes to paying for life's many expenses, Dan Rostenkowski's personal, political and official worlds have become inextricably merged. So, after 34 years in Congress, the chairman has found that he can tap a host of generous sources to subsidize his lifestyle: lobbyists and others seeking influence over his committee, contributors to his huge cache of campaign funds and the taxpayers.

Danny Rostenkowski's lifestyle had attracted the attention not only of journalists but of federal prosecutors. An investigation of the House post office — long a place where senior members of Congress found patronage jobs for their friends — had turned up allegations that the chairman had converted stamps purchased with his office allowance into cash. Examining those records, the FBI and the IRS also turned up leads suggesting possible misuse of other official accounts — for such things as office rental and leased cars. Leaks suggested that Rosty may have helped himself and his friends to large amounts of money for questionable purposes. There was talk of an imminent indictment in 1992, but one of the first acts of the Clinton administration was to remove all the Republican-appointed U.S. attorneys, including the man in Washington directing the Rosty investigation. Conservative columnists cried dirty tricks, but in short order it became clear that the new U.S. attorney, a Democrat, was pursuing the chairman's trail. As 1994 began, a federal indictment hung over Rosty's head.

Those legal problems emboldened his congressional reelection challengers, and no fewer than five of them filed against him in the March 15 primary. Two weeks before the voting, President Clinton went to Chicago to praise Rosty for his "vital" role on the budget and NAFTA fights of 1993 and the approaching health care reform showdown. New federal aid projects were announced almost every day leading up to the election. With all that — and a huge financial advantage — Rosty was able to win only 50 percent of the vote; luckily for him, the opposition splintered the other half. He survived.

Now that Stark's bill had been sent to Rosty's Ways and Means, Rosty began doing what he always did — finding out where his committee stood. Like Dingell, he had no illusions about getting Republican help. To provide a majority in his thirty-eight-member committee, Rosty needed twenty of the twenty-four Democrats.

Rosty gathered them around the big green felt-top table in his expansive office, just a few steps off the House floor. The seven Democrats who had been through the subcommittee battle were reasonably expert, but Rostenkowski had David Abernethy begin to introduce the others to the issue, listening closely to their comments and questions to gauge where his problems lay.

Mike Andrews had watched him before and was struck by the difference between Rosty's approach and Stark's. "Stark has been in the trenches on Medicare for years," he said, "and he has strong policy feelings. With Rosty, the overriding factor is getting the job done. And if he sees it's necessary to move in a certain direction to get it done, he moves in that direction. He counts the votes in his head all the time. With each one of us now, he's trying to see whether he can work with you, or get around you, or beat you. And he's got good staff to tell him where he is and to help him on the details."

Rosty also had help on the committee from Robert T. Matsui, an eighth-termer from Sacramento, whose wife was on the White House staff. Matsui had led the President's fight for ratification of NAFTA and was equally committed to passing health care reform — even though he had no formal leadership role. While the bill was still in subcommittee, Matsui began inviting seven or eight of his committee colleagues to weekly meetings in his office. The group included loyalists like Ben Cardin and Mike Kopetski of Oregon and four or five others who would go along, providing significant problems for their own insurance or tobacco constituents could be solved. Rosty was kept apprised of the sessions — and welcomed the help.

Rosty felt encouraged. "People are nervous," he said privately. "They want to be able to go home and explain it to their constituents. But there's an optimistic atmosphere in the caucuses. They're the best attended I've ever had. Except for maybe one member of this committee, every Democrat's been in this room." He was hopeful enough about finding at least twenty votes on the Democratic side that he was stiff-arming the Republicans. "My bottom line with them is, 'Can you support an employer mandate?' Most of them say no. And I say, 'Why should I negotiate with you when I know ultimately that the day that it's going to be most important for passage, you're not there?' "

While he counted heads, Rosty also began the negotiations and maneuvers he thought necessary to form a winning coalition. His approach was quite different from Dingell's. The Energy and Commerce chairman liked to work behind the scenes, encouraging allies to mobilize forces or, in the case of someone like Jim Cooper, to harass an opponent. Rosty was more direct. He liked being in the limelight. His oratory was not polished, but his meaning was clear.

Thus, at the end of April, as the full committee caucuses were beginning, Rosty went to the Harvard School of Public Health and warned in a speech that something more than a few cigarette taxes would be needed to finance health insurance for every American.

The speech illustrated his technique.

First, he stuck his chest out and declared unequivocally, "We will report a bill that provides universal coverage." This is not just cheerleading. This is a message to all the interests with a stake that

it's going to happen, with or without them. So they better get down
to serious negotiation.

The following sentences amplified that message:

> In my view, that will lead us to a decision to require employers
> to provide — and partially pay for — health insurance for
> their workers. [*The mandate is not going to be killed, and you
> better understand that.*] . . . We will do what we can to mod-
> erate the impact on smaller employers. We hear their com-
> plaints and understand their problems. [*NFIB, we know you're
> there.*] They won't be totally happy with the solution we ulti-
> mately embrace. [*But don't think you can push us around.*]
> They may temporarily feel some pain, but they will adjust, sur-
> vive and thrive — because that's what American business does
> best. [*We've heard these cries of doom before; you're talking to
> somebody who wasn't born yesterday.*] If they're smart, they
> will realize that it is now time for them to help us help them. It
> is time for the business community to stop opposing mandates
> and start seriously discussing how best to make them work.
> They are the experts and we can use their help. But if they fail
> to participate in the debate, they forfeit their right to complain
> about the result. [*No translation needed.*]

But the big news in the speech was the chairman's declaration that
"we'll need a substantial amount of new revenue — tens of billions
of dollars a year" to pay for universal coverage. "It is hard to see how
we can raise the needed money by simply amassing a large enough
collection of cats and dogs." It will take "a broad tax increase that
has some impact on virtually every American."

The *T* word was anathema to the Clinton administration, which
had been pummeled for raising top-bracket tax rates in the 1993
budget. The whole rationale for the employer mandate had been to
avoid payroll taxes. Obviously Senate Republicans were not going to
welcome the idea. So why did Rosty do it?

In part, it was a signal to the tobacco-state Democrats in the
House, particularly Ways and Means member L. F. Payne of Virginia,
that the plan would not be financed entirely by their constituents.
Rosty had argued with the President that with the tax increase
Clinton was seeking — seventy-five cents a pack on cigarettes, even

more proportionally on smokeless tobacco — "you might just as well say, 'Close it up. Get out of town.' " Rosty told Clinton, "If you think for one minute, Mr. President, that I'm going to put some people out of business, that's not the job I envision the chairman of the committee having. I want to nick 'em. I don't want to kill 'em." In order to win votes for approval of NAFTA in the fall of 1993, he had promised the tobacco-state members he wouldn't hurt them on health reform. He was going to keep his word. Besides, he told Clinton, the more you talk about taking it all out of tobacco, the harder it is "for me to go someplace else to find the money."

The second reason was to test the wind on a tax increase. That was part of the chairman's job, he thought, to be the first to stick his head over the parapet and see how much fire he drew. Sitting at the committee table a week later, with just one staffer in attendance, Rosty told us that his members "talk with me privately and I think they like the idea that I've given them some cover." Even more privately, he conceded that this was a no-lose proposition. If the political climate allowed for some taxes, they could provide all the benefits the President and Hillary hoped for. If not, the benefits would have to be scaled back, but the relief that members felt at not having to vote for new taxes would make it easier to get a more modest bill approved.

And third, there was substance. "I think we've got to have revenue," Rosty said privately. "My people tell me, 'Boss, the rosy scenarios that are written, particularly in the cost-containment area, are just not going to happen that way.' "

These were the same doubts that Treasury and Office of Management and Budget officials had expressed about the Magaziner estimates of savings. "I have a helluva lot more faith in what my staff is telling me," Rosty said, "than I have in the pundits down there at the White House that are whispering in Hillary's ear that it's going to be easy if we get the whole bill."

The day after Rostenkowski's Harvard speech, Clinton, somewhat shaken, called him to ask what the chairman was doing. "I'm not trying to undercut you," Rosty said. "I'm just trying to protect my reputation as well." Rostenkowski had warned the Clintons against meddling in his committee's drafting of the bill and had called the President to complain when Treasury officials Lloyd Bentsen and

Roger Altman publicly offered to drop the alliances from the Clinton plan. Rosty knew the alliances were doomed, but he wanted to get concessions in return. During all the time that the bill was working its way through Ways and Means, the White House was passive. "It's basically in their court at this point," Harold Ickes told reporters as the Ways and Means markups began. "It's going to be very messy at times, and at times the whole thing will dissolve before it reemerges. We are confident it can be pulled back together in the end."

Rosty was very fond of Hillary, who made a point of reminding him that he was now "her" congressman because his district stretched into the western suburbs of Chicago, where she grew up. During his primary fight, she called to say she was "on standby" anytime he wanted her to fly out and help. She ended many of their phone conversations, "I love you, Danny." Bill Clinton was less easy for Rosty to embrace — or sometimes even to understand. After one White House session where the President was quizzing him about how he planned to handle specific provisions in the bill, Rosty confessed to his staff that he was uncomfortable trying to match Clinton in detailed knowledge of the bill.

Some Ways and Means staffers marveled that Rosty could compartmentalize his life as he did. He would go downtown to meet with his lawyers and discuss the grand jury proceedings, which were drawing inexorably closer to the moment when indictments would be drawn, then return to Capitol Hill and resume his negotiations on the bill. Rosty's most significant deal was with Bill Gradison to take Harry and Louise and the health insurance industry to the sidelines while Ways and Means did its work.

Those negotiations began with a speech Rosty made to HIAA leaders in February 1994, suggesting it was time to stop the cannonading and start talking. After his speech, Rosty brought Gradison to a White House meeting with Ickes, Stephanopoulos, and Magaziner, but no permanent truce was arranged.

Chip Kahn, Gradison's deputy, got better results when he began discussions with David Abernethy, the Ways and Means Committee staffer. Kahn told Abernethy that the Medicare C plan that was at the heart of the Stark bill would be a death knell for the small-

and medium-sized insurers who made up HIAA. They began discussing modifications that might ease the pain, allowing more leeway for firms to market policies selectively, for example, providing more flexibility on community rating and the ban on barring people with preexisting medical conditions.

"It really wasn't much of a deal," Kahn said later. "Basically, we got them to moderate their plan. And we said we wouldn't run any advertising during the committee markup."

As always, Gradison was looking ahead to a final negotiation that would set the terms under which his member companies would have to compete. "Bill felt that if he could negotiate this with Rosty and show good faith," Kahn said, "then later he would have a beachhead to go beyond Ways and Means, which clearly was going to go too far to the left, and approach the [House Democratic] leadership with Rosty" to negotiate a better deal.

But the indictment guillotine was almost ready to fall. "These were the last days in the bunker," Kahn said. "We had a symbolic meeting between the two of them and Rosty just looked pitiful. It wasn't the Rosty I remembered."

When the Rostenkowski-Gradison deal became public, interest groups on the left were furious. Cathy Hurwit, a lobbyist for Citizen Action, told the *Washington Post,* "It's a backroom deal that doesn't have any visible benefits for the people who are uninsured or inadequately insured." But for Rosty, neutralizing HIAA's opposition and shutting down its ads, even temporarily, would make it easier for some of his members to report out the bill. And he had no compunction about negotiating with the insurers — or anyone else with a stake in the outcome. "I've got to live with the insurance people," he exclaimed. "I mean, they've got votes on this deal." To be exact, they had four: Democrats from Hartford; Springfield, Massachusetts; Omaha; and Indianapolis, all from districts with powerful insurance companies.

Rosty repeated the advice he gave Hillary Clinton earlier in his office: "I said, 'Hillary, don't insult anyone, because the very people who will walk away from you first, the very people that become a little bit belligerent about this, are the people ultimately that you're going to be negotiating with, because they're going to be bringing votes to you.' She didn't take my advice until I called her a couple of times."

Rosty had a code and applied it here: He would help those who helped him get his bill passed. Recalling how many times Gradison told him that HIAA wanted reform, supporting mandates and universal coverage, but had problems that must be resolved, Rosty would remark, "I'm going to find out from them whether or not they're cheerleaders." His tone was not sarcastic, but it wasn't trusting. "If they're not cheerleaders, you know I don't put things in a bill so people will get what they want and then not support the damn thing. If I'm going to do things that are going to be painful to me, I want support. Otherwise, I'll just take those things out."

This was more than talk. As he watched Rosty wheel and deal, Speaker Tom Foley recalled a favorite line of the chairman's: "In Chicago, if they push you once and get away with it, the next time they walk up your back." Foley mused privately about the character of the man he was counting on to get a bill out of Ways and Means: "He's not all that he seems," he said of Rosty. "In some ways he's a much more sentimental and softer guy. But with the lobbying groups, if they start to cross him, he wants them to know that there is a penalty that might have to be paid. For that reason, few people want to cross him."

The week of May 23, after news of the Rostenkowski-Gradison deal had leaked, Rosty scheduled the first public markup sessions of the full committee. It was not known that he was close to making similar deals with other key constituencies. To regain big-business support for employer mandates on smaller firms, he had been negotiating with IBM chairman Louis Gerstner. And he had opened talks with pharmaceutical executives, hoping to neutralize some of their opposition by exploiting industry divisions between the generic and the proprietary drug makers. He was absolutely open-eyed about Stark. "Stark knows more about the bill than anybody," he said privately at the time. "But Stark has tunnel vision. Nothing's gonna change his view about a provision or an industry, and he becomes nasty when you disagree with him. But I'm negotiating with these people, and they're depending on me to control Stark."

Rosty wanted to close those negotiations, so he announced that the first two days of open committee sessions would be devoted to general discussion, with voting to begin after the Memorial Day recess. He would have his proposal ready then. If you wanted the chairman on your side, you'd better make your deals now.

But Rostenkowski was not to remain chairman. On May 31, a federal grand jury in Washington indicted him on seventeen counts of conspiring to defraud the government. The indictment said his various kickback and embezzlement schemes had cost the Treasury at least a half million dollars. The day before the indictment, he rejected a plea bargain agreement that would have required him to plead guilty to one minor count, serve six months in jail, and resign from the House. Instead, he asserted his innocence and vowed to mount a vigorous defense. Under House rules, he was required to step aside as chairman until the charges were resolved, but he remained a member of the House and of the Ways and Means Committee.

The loss of Rosty came just as John Dingell was about to admit defeat on writing a bill in Energy and Commerce. It coincided with one of the many cyclical downturns in the tortuous negotiations with Pat Moynihan and the Senate Finance Committee. For the Clintons, Rosty's fall was in some respects the worst blow of all. For all the differences in their ages and backgrounds, Danny Rostenkowski had become a kind of protective big brother for the President and the First Lady. He didn't hesitate to tell them when they were blundering, as they did all too often from his point of view. But he demanded nothing of them except that they let him do his job without much interference. And they knew that he had no purpose other than to pass the best bill he could get — passing it, not just in committee, but in the entire House of Representatives. Rosty could be replaced as chairman, but no one else would or could assume the role he had played.

News of Rosty's indictment reached Sam Gibbons in Paris, where he had gone with a large delegation of colleagues to celebrate the golden anniversary of the Normandy landings in World War II. It was an emotional occasion for Gibbons. As a twenty-five-year-old infantryman, he had parachuted behind enemy lines eight hours before the first landing ships reached Omaha Beach.

The anniversary was the occasion for a family outing with his wife and his grandchildren at a borrowed home on the coast where he had fought. But the fax announcing Rosty's indictment reached him at a hotel in Paris, during a day of trade talks. While still in France, he took his first steps to assert control, phoning Janice Mays, the committee chief of staff, and directing her to continue work on refining the Stark bill as the starting point for committee deliberations.

Gibbons had traveled a long road to reach this point. After the war, he had gotten his law degree and by 1952 was in the Florida legislature. He moved on to Congress in 1962 and, as a Southern liberal, was given the honor of being House floor manager of Lyndon Johnson's bill to create Head Start, the preschool program for children. He was chosen, Johnson told him, because "you can talk southern and vote northern." On Ways and Means, his specialty was trade legislation, and he persevered in his free-trade position even as many others in the party became more protectionist.

If Rosty was known for his gravel-voiced camaraderie and his bear hugs, Gibbons was notable for his perpetually red face — and a prickly personality that seemed to go with it. He would not tear into people as Pete Stark did, but he would turn away from them. And the more isolated his position became as a white, liberal Southern Democrat, the more of a loner he seemed on the committee. His personal relationship with Rostenkowski was correct, not cordial. And others were hard put to say who were his buddies, but the isolation did not hurt him at home. Tampa was a blue-collar city with significant minority and student populations. The Republican Party, ascendant in so much of Florida, had trouble getting a handhold there. Secure as Gibbons was in his district, he was far less certain of his role as acting chairman of Ways and Means.

A few weeks before Rosty was indicted, his friend Tom Downey, a New Yorker who had served as a member of Ways and Means until his 1992 defeat, mused on the difference between the two men: "Rosty is the franchise player," Downey said. "He built the committee over the years. Except for the most senior members, all the Democrats on Ways and Means are there because the chairman picked them. Their loyalty to him is very high. He is the best deal maker in the

Congress and he is fearless in dealing with others in the House, in negotiating with the Senate and even in telling the President what he can and cannot have. Sam [Gibbons] is a good guy and a bright guy, but you're bringing him in cold and asking him to pitch the seventh game of the World Series."

Gibbons rejected that view. Before Rosty's indictment, he had been sitting in on Stark's subcommittee markups and was "thoroughly familiar with the bill." The caucuses Rostenkowski had been conducting gave him a good sense of the memberships' positions. "I think I know where people are and I think I could pull it together," he said as news of Rosty's impending indictment began to circulate shortly before he left for France. As for himself, Gibbons said he was flexible. He had been a longtime backer of the single-payer plan, but he found out "it wouldn't fly. I was the second or third person to co-sponsor the President's bill," he said.

And should Rosty be forced to step down? "It would mean a ten- or fifteen-minute delay," Gibbons said. "I don't think it's any big problem. I'm ready to go."

What Gibbons could not claim was Rosty's unique position. The members simply did not owe Gibbons, as they did Rosty. Rosty had a speech he gave every time the Ways and Means Committee was approaching a major issue: "I look around this room with a very penetrating eye, and I say, 'There are very few members on this committee that I have not used my influence to put on this committee. And there are very few of you who have not whispered in this ear that when the tough vote comes, I'll be there. Now the tough votes are going to come. I want you to know I remember who you are and what you whispered in my ear. Now, it's our responsibility to get that thing out there on the floor.' "

It was Rosty's version of the Knute Rockne locker-room speech, and no matter how often he used it, it did not lose its force because the history was real — and it was that loyalty that made the Ways and Means Committee the powerhouse it had been.

Sam Gibbons did not have that kind of influence, but it didn't inhibit him. "I had already determined before I went over there [to France] that I thought it was imperative to move as rapidly as I could on health care," he said. Back in Washington, he quickly lined up support from Foley and Gephardt to quell talk of a possible challenge from another senior Ways and Means member, Charles B. Rangel of Harlem. Instead of rebelling, Ways and Means members pledged to work with their new leader. Gibbons expressed his hopes that Rostenkowski would remain engaged in the effort, but added in a television interview, "He understands as well as I do that there can only be one chairman at a time." Gibbons fired the committee's press spokesman, a Rosty intimate, but kept the key policy staffers. He met with Stark, and the two of them decided that Medicare C, with the employer mandate, would be the plan they would try to drive through the committee. Rostenkowski had been considering that, but was not sure he could find twenty votes for it. Gibbons was determined to show he could.

One of the first side effects of the transition was to kill the Rostenkowski-Gradison deal on the Harry and Louise commercials. Gibbons had not been part of the talks and did not feel bound by them. And he listened to Stark and the other committee liberals who thought Rosty had conceded too much to get the ads off the air. "As soon as Stark and Gibbons got their hands on [the deal]," said HIAA's Chip Kahn, "they threw it out the window, so we went back on the air. We almost had to. We weren't going to be pushed around."

It was war, after all.

Sam Gibbons was eager to get moving so he gave the Republicans a seventy-two-hour deadline for submitting proposed amendments to the bill. Two of the three days fell on the weekend, and the result was a remarkable scene described by the *Washington Post*'s Dana Priest. The understaffed GOP members put out an emergency call to business lobbyists for help in drafting amendments, and on Saturday morning the Ways and Means Committee room was filled with lobbyists representing everyone from the Alzheimer's Association to drug maker Upjohn. Many were on their way to the golf course or the beach, so they came in shorts and sneakers, carrying briefcases with their proposed amendments. They were disconcerted to find a *Post* reporter in their midst, but that did not stop them from doing their work. The result was a public reminder that those with access and influence were utterly uninhibited in steering members of Congress where the interest groups wanted them to go.

Gibbons, too, had work to do: to find his majority. "I had to establish that I could get twenty votes," he said, "or I'd get whipsawed all over the place." One of the shifting members was Peter Hoagland of Omaha, who had told Gibbons that he could not support a bill based on Medicare C.

Hoagland had reason to be nervous. He had been reelected to his third term in 1992 with only 51 percent of the vote. He had nine major insurance companies in Omaha, employing twenty thousand people. Already he had given the opposition more issues than they needed.

Peter Hoagland was literally the man in the middle. During the Memorial Day break he held a long meeting with retailers and other small-business people opposed to the employer mandate. The next morning, a delegation from AARP came seeking assurance that the long-term care and prescription benefits promised by President Clinton would remain in the bill. At lunch with executives of the big insurers in his district, he was urged to be sure that they could stay in business, with no price controls on their policies and with federal rules that preempted what they found to be increasingly restrictive state regulations. Then came the union folks, led by the state AFL-CIO president, demanding support for employer mandates and protection against taxation of the health benefits already negotiated in their contracts. "You know," Hoagland told the labor delegation, "I used to think the fault lines in politics ran between the Republicans and the Democrats or the liberals and conservatives. Now," he said, drawing an imaginary line from his navel to the top of his nose, "the fault line runs right through yours truly."

With no way to avoid offending some constituency, Hoagland sought instead to find a path he thought was intellectually honest. The product of a fifth-generation Omaha Republican business family, he had switched parties because of Richard Nixon and Watergate. All of his campaigns were tough. "As hard as we have to work to get here," he said during the markup, "and as tedious as the fundraising and the parades and all the other aspects of this job are, if you're not free to vote your conscience on policy, then the job's really not worth it."

He put his best staffer, Roger Blauwet, to work full-time on health care and spent hours on the issue himself, even visiting Jackson Hole for a personal briefing from the managed competition advocates. He concluded that an employer mandate was necessary but that some relief had to be granted to small businesses and even to some large restaurant and retail chains, where the costs of insurance could be two or three times the additional profit each employee produced.

On June 13, when Fred Grandy offered the amendment to strike the mandate, Hoagland said it was "one of the most difficult issues" he had ever faced. He voted to keep the mandate in the bill, his vote providing the margin of victory on a twenty-to-eighteen roll call. He did so having just read an *Omaha World-Herald* poll that showed him trailing his November opponent, Republican Jon Christensen, by eleven points. And Christensen himself had flown to Washington and taken a front-row spectator's seat from which he could look directly at Hoagland as the roll was called. Christensen immediately went to a phone and called the biggest talk show in Omaha to denounce Hoagland as a "Clinton yes-man" who had just voted to "put hundreds of people out of work."

But having cast that vote, Hoagland still was unhappy with the overall bill. He thought that a plan "that could result in over half of all Americans being in Medicare is just the wrong thing to do, when we could just as easily put together a system that would leave most of those decisions in the private sector."

He thought Rostenkowski had been "really simpatico" to his concerns and those of other moderate Democrats. The old chairman was working with HIAA and "would have found a way that people like me could support it on the floor." Gibbons, he thought, was "more from the Franklin Roosevelt school of old-style liberalism." Like so many others, he found Stark a pain. Stark's view was that the insurance companies *should* be put out of business. "That angers me. It's nuts. But he is so convinced he's right, he has no regard for the feelings of the rest of us."

Gibbons was well aware of Hoagland's views on the bill and knew that his vote to keep the mandates in place did not augur support for the overall measure. So he had to look elsewhere.

His gaze focused on L. F. Payne, a forty-nine-year-old Virginian who had gained a seat on Ways and Means in 1993. Payne's district was in the heart of Virginia's tobacco country, and tobacco taxes clearly were his price for playing. But he was not a one-dimensional politician. An army veteran and real estate developer, he had won a special election to the House in 1988 by striking a moderate posture that let him get votes from the conservative, rural counties and from the blacks who made up one-quarter of the population. In 1992, Charlottesville, the home of the University of Virginia and its teaching hospital, was added to the district — giving him yet another constituency.

Gibbons sat down to try to negotiate a deal with Payne. The Virginian did not find it easy to do what his tobacco growers wanted. Only half-kidding, he told Republican Bill Thomas, whose California district was a center of truck farming, "Frankly, I wish I represented artichokes instead of tobacco. I've got to do my job for my people, but it's damn tough."

In fact, Payne had more than one goal in mind. As far back as 1992, he had joined Jim Cooper in backing a managed competition bill, and he opposed insurance premium controls and employer mandates. But his district included more than just the five thousand tobacco growers. He also had a hundred thousand constituents who had no health insurance and fourteen of seventeen counties that were officially designated as "medically underserved" areas. Payne put two staff people on the Magaziner task force, mainly to work on rural health center programs.

But tobacco was uppermost. An early visit with the Clintons convinced him that they were intent on raising much of their needed revenue from tobacco taxes. When the task force floated the possibility of a $2-a-pack levy, he and twenty-nine other tobacco-state Democrats wrote the President a letter saying they could not possibly support a bill that included such a tax. When the Clinton proposal emerged at seventy-five cents, the same message was delivered in another letter.

Privately, Payne and his allies had given the same clear warning to Rostenkowski and to Gephardt. Assuming solid Republican opposition and a certain number of conservative Democratic defections, those thirty tobacco votes would almost certainly be needed to pass anything in the House. Rostenkowski got the message and had begun bargaining with Payne, expressing personal sympathy for the Virginian's effort to save the cigarette industry. They had reached no figure before Rosty was indicted, although there were indications that they might have settled at sixty cents.

Gibbons had not been part of those talks, but the very day after he took up his duties as acting chairman, Payne led a delegation in to discuss tobacco taxes. "We felt we had some leverage," Payne said, "but there were lots of people on the committee who felt the tax should be at least as high as the President had asked and maybe as high as the dollar twenty-five the subcommittee had set. Gibbons had a lot of pressures on him."

The two men negotiated the deal directly, settling on forty-five cents with a slow phase-in to reach that figure. "He [Gibbons] convinced me that was as low as he could get it," Payne said. He wanted to lock in that ceiling early in the markup, in order to avoid a series of amendments that would propose popular benefits to be financed by higher cigarette taxes. Gibbons wanted it done early, too, so Payne would be part of his twenty-person majority against other unwanted amendments. A way to do it turned up on June 15.

One of the other Democrats who was having real problems with the legislation was William J. Jefferson of New Orleans. Like others in the Congressional Black Caucus, Jefferson ardently supported the goal of universal care. "In my state," he said, "almost a million people don't have coverage. They go to the charity hospital when they get really sick, but it's not a substitute for a preventive care system."

Health care was one of the reasons Jefferson wanted to get onto the Ways and Means Committee. From the moment he was elected in 1990, he campaigned for that assignment and, he said, "I never stopped the campaign." His first step was to win election from the twenty-nine freshman Democrats as the whip for their class — the person who did the head counts of their views before every major vote. That got him into the meetings that Majority Whip David Bonior of Michigan, the number three man in the leadership, held every week the House was in session. Bonior became an unofficial coach for Jefferson's effort to win support from others in the leadership for a Ways and Means assignment.

The key, of course, was Rostenkowski's attitude. Jefferson did not approach the chairman directly but instead made a point of becoming a gym buddy of Rosty's closest pal, fellow Chicagoan and Ways and Means member Martin A. Russo. Russo was a real jock, a multisport man who led the Democrats in the annual grudge-match baseball game against the Republicans. One day in the winter of 1991, after a basketball game with Jefferson, Russo asked him if he played any baseball. Jefferson said he had played some infield. "I got just one question to ask you," he said to first baseman Russo. "What's the assist record around here?" "I'm gonna love you," Russo said. And he smoothed the way with Rosty for Jefferson to put in his bid. That is how in January 1993, second-termer Jefferson got the assignment he prized.

Now that he was there and health care was on the agenda, he had a problem. His district included all but a small slice of New Orleans, and people in the tourist trade — especially the small businesses that operated in the French Quarter — were up in arms about the employer mandate. "Those people selling books and videos and maps and I don't know what, they have two or three people working for them, making a thousand dollars a month, and when the government gets through they have eight hundred dollars, and when they pay the rent or whatever, they can't pay the one hundred fifty dollars for the health coverage," Jefferson said. "And the hotel, motel, restaurant people, they're bigger, but they also have a real problem. So I told the chairman I had a problem with the mandate."

He also had a problem with the cigarette tax — not for the reason Payne did, but because "most of the folks who smoke or chew tobacco are the least well educated and poorest folks in the country. These taxes would be regressive." This was, of course, a favorite argument of the tobacco lobbyists, whose PACs had put $16,800 into Jefferson's two campaigns.

When the full committee met, Jefferson said, "L.F. [Payne] and I talked and we realized that we were the two people who could vote in the end to send the bill out of committee, but who were unwilling, at that point, to vote. We were the ones who were left out there un-committed. So we talked about the tobacco part and the marginal low-wage employer part, and how we would pay for it." The staff suggested that it could be done by delaying the start of long-term care, and so it all came together as the Jefferson amendment.

When they brought the idea to Gibbons, he welcomed it with open arms. He knew that he was likely to lose the two most conservative Democrats on the committee, Mike Andrews and Oklahoma's Bill K. Brewster, and he could not count on Hoagland. There was no margin for error.

On June 15, Jefferson was recognized by Gibbons to offer what fellow Democrat Mike Kopetski, a blithe spirit, called the "Elmer's Glue" amendment. One part would roll the cigarette tax back to forty-five cents. Another part would halve the cost of the mandate to firms with fewer than twenty-five employees. A third section would provide a smaller break to companies with twenty-five to forty-nine workers; and a fourth, aimed at the insurance industry and its friends on the committee, would cut in half the tax employers who bought their policies directly from insurers, rather than going through the new purchasing alliances, would have to pay on their premiums. To make up for the $36 billion in lost revenue, the Jefferson amendment would postpone the start of long-term care for the elderly by three years.

When word of the deal began to leak, the senior citizen lobby was up in arms. AARP's John Rother said, "It's just amazing, even to someone who's fairly cynical, that people would make a conscious decision to screw the elderly and the disabled in order to help to-bacco." Gibbons had briefed the Democrats in their caucus on what was in store, but it quickly became apparent that he hadn't nailed down the necessary votes. McDermott and Lewis both denounced the tobacco tax rollback, and McDermott went further, saying that the delay in long-term care made him inclined to oppose the whole measure.

Sensing an opportunity to split the shaky twenty-vote Demo-cratic coalition, Bill Thomas of California, a wily Republican, asked for a separate vote on each part of the Jefferson amendment. As he did so, Thomas taunted the Democrats with the reminder that the night before, Senate Finance Committee Chairman Daniel Patrick Moynihan of New York and the committee's ranking Republican, Bob Packwood of Oregon, had informed President Clinton that their Senate panel was deadlocked on the employer mandate issue and was seeking other ways to finance expanded coverage. Thomas told the Ways and Means Democrats that there was no point sending a mandate requirement to "the black hole of the Senate."

Thomas was playing a complex game. He was the House sponsor of the Chafee plan, using an individual mandate to reach the goal of universal coverage. That meant he was a target of suspicion from Gingrich and others in the GOP leadership who wanted to sink health reform, not rewrite it. Early in the process, while the Stark subcommittee was still at work, Thomas was offering amendments designed to draw Democratic support, because, as he said, "helping to frame a bipartisan approach is the only way we're going to go forward." At that point, he spoke privately of conceding a political victory to Clinton: "He's the President. He initiated the health care discussion, and it will be a victory for him, no matter what, no matter if I wrote one hundred percent of the bill he signed."

But by June, when the full committee took up its work, Thomas said that Republicans had cooled on the Chafee approach but had no alternative to offer. "There isn't a coherent plan coming out of our leadership," he conceded privately. "We don't have a ready vehicle we can rally around." Now, he said, "the business of the opposition is to oppose." Thomas had no compunctions — none — about trying to blow up the Democratic strategy.

His tactic of demanding a separate vote on each part of the Jefferson amendment threw Gibbons into a panic, and he abruptly banged the gavel to adjourn the committee. If McDermott and Lewis broke ranks on the tobacco tax rollback, then Payne and Jefferson might bolt on the mandate provisions and the whole bill could unravel. And the news from the Senate made the risk even greater. For months, House Democratic leaders had promised the members that they would not be asked to vote for politically risky provisions — like the mandate — that had no chance of surviving in the Senate. "We don't want to get BTU-ed again," said Bob Matsui of California, the Clinton loyalist.

When the committee adjourned after the Thomas motion, Gibbons gathered the Democrats in his office and considered his options. The Democrats were angry at Thomas's tactic, and they spent some time venting their frustration. Gibbons, who has a short fuse himself, said that when the committee resumed the next day, maybe he'd just rule Thomas out of order and put the Jefferson amendment to a vote. The House parliamentarian was summoned and asked if that ruling would be sustained. Normally, he said, a motion to divide a multipart amendment was in order, but if they put all the provisions into one long paragraph, Gibbons might have a plausible case. Even then, he said, it might not stand scrutiny if Republicans brought the issue to the House floor. The caucus ended when bells called the members for a vote. Gibbons said he'd reassemble them the next morning, before the committee went into public session.

An hour or so later, as the House worked into the evening, two of the junior committee Democrats, Ben Cardin and Mike Kopetski, huddled and quickly discovered that neither of them was comfortable with what Gibbons had in mind. Kopetski said, "The Republicans probably already know what the parliamentarian has told us. There are very few secrets on the Hill. Thomas might go to the Ethics Committee and say, 'Here's a chairman directly and knowingly violating House rules.' "

Speaker Foley was on the floor. On the spur of the moment, Kopetski decided he ought to share his disquiet with the Speaker. As always, Foley said he was reluctant to interfere or tell a committee chairman how to manage his committee. But he agreed with Kopetski that appearing to finagle the rules could cause all kinds of problems. He made the same point directly to Gibbons later in the evening. Others were having the same thoughts. "Some of us," said Indiana's Andrew Jacobs, "said, 'Brier Patch City, Br'er Rabbit.' They want nothing more than an issue like that." Dan Rostenkowski was even more blunt Asked what he thought of simply slam-dunking Thomas with a ruling from the chair, he said, "Jesus Christ, that makes me look like a cream puff."

But what was the alternative? Cardin and Kopetski came up with the idea of negotiating a set of votes where those opposed to a particular provision would pass rather than vote no. At the morning caucus, they struggled for hours trying to figure out how that would have to be orchestrated to be sure that Gibbons never lost his majority. Finally, Jim McDermott broke in. He thought all the political maneuvering was ridiculous. He had convinced himself that single-payer, taxpayer-financed health care was the only way to go. He also thought any variation of the Clinton plan was politically doomed. But he cut through the dithering with the comment, "If all of us stay together on this — just vote no every time Thomas tries to pick off one section of the amendment — then it becomes process, not substance. I'm willing to do it, if everybody else is willing to do it."

He was proposing what seemed to be a far-out idea: that the Democrats walk back into the big Ways and Means Committee room, jammed with lobbyists who would note every vote, and, with C-SPAN cameras beaming the roll call into living rooms around the country, vote against their principles on mandates, tobacco, and long-term care. Just tell the people who were sure to question their votes — whether the American Cancer Society, the National Federation of Independent Business, or the American Association of Retired Persons — that this was a test of party loyalty, so principle be damned.

Most times, that appeal would have fallen on deaf ears. The markup process was just beginning, but already there had been several blowups, and feelings were raw. Half-joking, Kopetski confided, "We're at the point where people should be frisked for guns and knives before being allowed in the room."

But that morning, the *Washington Post*'s Dana Priest reported on an interview she had had the previous day with Fred Grandy, the Iowa Republican who was working toward some kind of bipartisan compromise. Grandy told her he had received new "marching orders" from Newt Gingrich not to try to improve the bill through amendments. "It's disappointing," Grandy said, "but we have a leadership that preempts policy with partisanship."

The challenge implicit in Grandy's words inflamed the Ways and Means Democratic caucus. Barbara Kennelly of Hartford said, "The Grandy quote changed things. We suspected that was the strategy, but to read it in the *Washington Post* — well, if they've got their agenda, we better stand together for ours!"

In the altered atmosphere, McDermott's offer was instantly seconded by Mike Andrews of Houston, one of the most conservative Democrats and the prime proponent of higher tobacco taxes. Andy Jacobs joined in. A bandwagon mentality developed and the quarrelsome Democrats pledged, if not their "lives, fortunes and sacred honor," at least their votes at the public session — with firm assurance from Gibbons that the issues could be revisited, individually, before the markup was ended.

To everyone, that was the turning point for the committee. "It really helped rally the Democrats together," Gibbons said soon afterward. Mike Kopetski was elated. "We knew by that morning that the Republicans had broken out the champagne the night before. They thought they had us, that this was the end of health care. But it was a classic tactical error of immense proportion. It gave us something the public could understand — to say this was not a vote on substance, it was a process vote, a vote to break gridlock. In just a few hours, we rallied and became a cohesive unit."

Why did Grandy give the Democrats what Kopetski in his excitement called "a gift of magnanimous proportions"? Grandy, a moderate Republican, had just lost a hotly contested challenge to his state's conservative GOP governor, Terry Branstad, falling short by a 52-to-48 percent margin. He had given up running for reelection to the House in order to make the gubernatorial bid, so his Capitol Hill career was coming to a close. As Kopetski remarked, "I'm sure because the Republican Party in his state rejected him, he wasn't feeling a lot of solidarity with the Republicans."

Thus, the same kind of state political ambitions that made it impossible for John Dingell to recruit Jim Cooper and Jim Slattery into a majority coalition on Energy and Commerce helped Sam Gibbons put together a Democratic majority on Ways and Means. But there was more to Grandy's comment than that. Rural hospitals in his district were in trouble, in part because of cutbacks in Medicare reimbursements, and as early as 1989, he had started searching for solutions. In short order, he discovered the truth of the comment he had heard Senator Alan Simpson, the Wyoming Republican, make:

"Health care is like bear meat. The more you chew it, the bigger it gets." Along with a handful of others, Grandy tried to get the Bush White House to frame a proposal, but was rebuffed. So he hooked up with Jim Cooper on their bipartisan plan.

When Grandy saw the Clinton proposal, he thought, "He's trying to do too much for too many too fast." But at the time the Cooper-Grandy bill was introduced, his private judgment was that "a little less than one-quarter of the Republicans would ever commit to something like that. There are probably more than half our members of Congress who are looking for a good reason to vote no on everything." In November of 1993, as the fight was just beginning, Grandy remarked privately, "A lot of our people say, 'Tactically, why should we even get involved? The President's going to try and lift this thing. He's going to fail. He'll get a hernia. It'll crack the entire Democratic Party and we'll walk in in 1996.' "

That happened — but in 1994, not 1996.

Now, still behind the scenes, Newt Gingrich redoubled his efforts to bring down the Democrats and shift control of Congress to his Republicans. Privately, Gingrich lined up more and more Republicans behind his strategy of killing the bill, and he had a strong ally in Bill McInturff, the pollster for HIAA and the Republican National Committee. In meetings in Gingrich's office, McInturff used the analogy of *The Bridge on the River Kwai.* He cited the hapless British colonel who makes a deal with the enemy to save his bridge — and then winds up dead because he dealt with the enemy.

> My concern in May was that we had a Republican group — mostly senators — who had spent ten to twenty years of their careers trying to do the right thing, trying to find a fairly rational health care plan for this country. I said, essentially, "Hey, what do you want? Do you want a Republican majority in the Congress or do you want health care policy?" We had a group of Republicans who would have picked health care policy.
>
> Our most important problem, from the political side, was not letting those people defect and pass a health care plan that I personally wouldn't have wanted and that would really have eroded our party's ability to be in the majority. That was our

major problem in that May-to-July period: holding our people in place, especially in the Senate, so that *our* people didn't hand Clinton a victory he no longer deserved.

Muscling Grandy back into line was part of that process. But even McInturff did not believe then that they could stop Clinton cold. "When Newt asked me in May what I thought the likely outcome would be," McInturff remembered, "I said that Bill Clinton's not going to get the package he wants, but he's going to get *something*. The Democrats are not going to be so dumb as to let nothing happen and go home. That's just so idiotic it couldn't possibly happen in my lifetime. Never in a million years."

Even after Grandy's comment to Dana Priest, voting to lower the tobacco tax was a wrenching experience for some of the Democrats. Six years earlier, Mike Andrews, at the behest of Houston's M. D. Anderson Cancer Center, had brought top leaders of Congress and leading lung cancer specialists and activists together for a weekend conference "where one of the top things on the agenda we set was raising tobacco taxes. It has been an important passion for me," he said. Still, Andrews did not personalize his battle with Payne over tobacco taxes. "I have a lot of respect for L.F. We are friends," Andrews said. "He's fighting for his constituents, using all the leverage that he's got at his disposal."

When Andrews had the leverage, at the subcommittee level, he pushed the tax up to $1.25, knowing it was not likely to stay there. Now, Payne had outmaneuvered him. "I don't fault him for it," Andrews said, "nor do I take it particularly personally. But he traded a lot to get that lower tax. He voted for the bill."

The vote was even harder for Andy Jacobs of Indianapolis. "I watched for a year as my dad died from that poison," he said, explaining his passion against smoking. "Eventually there will be another vote" on tobacco taxes, "but on this occasion, we did what we had to do. And we walked out with probably the same feeling that Democrats had in Franklin Roosevelt's days. For that brief shining moment, there was camaraderie. And I must say, it was tasty. And it probably can't last."

He was right about that. All through June, Gibbons was bailing as fast as he could just to keep the ship afloat. He had not counted on Jacobs's vote in reporting the bill because the Hoosier was a born maverick who survived in his conservative Indianapolis district by the irregularity of his support for liberal initiatives. But Jacobs came to Gibbons with a proposition that the chairman found irresistible. Jacobs had an influential constituent named Patrick Rooney, who was the president of Golden Rule Insurance Company, a major health underwriter. (Ironically, it was that very company that John Dingell targeted for an investigation when he decided to send a warning shot across the health insurance industry's bow.)

Rooney was probably the country's most assiduous promoter of a proposal for medical IRAs. The idea was that individuals would set aside a certain sum of money for their health care costs, with or without help from their employers. They would be encouraged to use a portion of it to buy insurance against catastrophic medical costs and the rest to pay their ordinary bills. Whatever was left at the end of the year, they could keep tax-free. The hope was that that approach would provide an incentive, lacking in the present system, to buy insurance and medical services as wisely as possible — and thereby reduce health care inflation.

The idea was popular with conservatives — Senator Phil Gramm of Texas made it the centerpiece of his alternative to the Clinton proposal, as did Newt Gingrich, whose political action committee was a major beneficiary of contributions by Rooney. Liberals like Stark regarded it as a cop-out. When Jacobs brought the idea to Gibbons with the promise that if medical IRAs were included as an option he would vote for the bill, Gibbons did not hesitate for a second. "Andy's that kind," Gibbons said. "You don't need to ask him a question. He'll just literally respond."

But even with that "extra" vote in his pocket, Gibbons couldn't relax. He had never felt the kind of pressure from the press and his party leaders that he was encountering on this bill. In public sessions, he tried to keep his composure, but in the closed-door caucuses he frequently exploded. Mike Andrews was a target, because once again, he had made it clear that he would not support the approach embodied in Stark's Medicare C. A week after the great coming-together on the Jefferson amendment, Andrews suggested an amendment in the Democratic caucus affecting the backup price controls the Clintons wanted in the bill. Another member had broached the idea but withdrew it when the first comments were chilly. When Andrews brought it up again, Gibbons erupted. Red-faced and stammering, he turned on Andrews, who was sitting just a few feet down from the chairman's seat at the head of the table. "I don't need your advice," he shouted. "You're nothing but a troublemaker. You're causing disruption. You're a lame duck. You're not going to vote for this bill whatever we do. Don't waste my time." Rostenkowski, who had tried not to dispute his successor, said, "Wait a minute. This is the guy who saved us by agreeing to vote for the Jefferson amendment. What are you doing to him?"

If Gibbons was a trial on occasion, Stark was a constant bully, trying to ride down any opposition to a plan that still bore his stamp more than anyone else's. He was particularly overbearing toward the two women on the committee, Barbara Bailey Kennelly of Hartford, a Democrat, and the Republican from the same state, Nancy Johnson. Johnson was one of the moderate Republicans who, like Fred Grandy and Fred Upton, had begun three years earlier to try to break through the Bush White House's passivity on health care. She had put in three years of hard work on the House Republican health task force between 1991 and 1994 and, perhaps naively, believed there could be and should be bipartisan legislation. Johnson, a former teacher, had a love for detail and a capacity for understanding the complexity of the health care system that few of her colleagues could match. She sometimes tried people's patience by her penchant for explaining more than they cared to hear. But during one public subcommittee markup session, when Johnson was disputing a point with McDermott, members were stunned to hear Stark break in to dismiss her in the most patronizing way possible. Referring to the fact that Johnson's husband is an obstetrician, Stark said, "The gentle lady got her degree from pillow talk and the gentleman from Washington got his degree from going to medical school. You guys can debate it all day long if you choose."

Stark, by the testimony of several members, was even tougher behind closed doors with Kennelly, who had learned her way around politics from her father, John M. Bailey, the near-legendary Connecticut and national Democratic Party chairman who helped engineer John F. Kennedy's nomination and election. Kennelly, from Hartford, and her next-door neighbor, Richard Neal from Springfield, Massachusetts, thought they needed to get some concessions for the insurance companies in their districts before they could vote for the bill. What they wanted was, in fact, almost exactly what Rostenkowski had negotiated with Bill Gradison while he was still chairman — changes in the bill that would allow firms as small as a hundred to self-insure with commercial insurance carriers, rather than going through the alliances, and would allow modest variations in community rating of all applicants. Those concessions had been dumped by Gibbons, but now he found, as Rosty had before him, that without them, he might not get his twenty votes.

Neal and Kennelly had agreed to support each other and, as might be expected of two real pros, they had done their homework and lined up the votes for restoring the terms that Rosty had accepted. But Stark was not party to the deal, and he chose to go after Kennelly in very personal terms, describing her as a lap dog of the insurance companies — and worse. Kennelly kept her cool, contenting herself with pointing out that if politics were her motive, she would vote against the bill and save herself a lot of grief with her home city's biggest employers. But Stark continued to berate her. Others were once again appalled by Stark's behavior. "Pete went crazy over it," Ben Cardin said. "It was the chairman's role to call a halt to that," Kopetski said, "and it just kept going on and on. Stark saw a power vacuum there and rushed in to grab it. Sam had to turn to somebody. He wasn't going to turn to Rosty, so he turned to Stark, and Stark tried to intimidate everyone else."

Kopetski found the process so grueling that a month later, he still had a twitch over his right eye. During the worst times, he had taken up the role of class clown, just to break the tension. Jake Pickle, the Lyndon Johnson crony from Austin who would retire at the end of this Congress, could get his colleagues laughing with one of his stories of the wild characters in Texas politics. Kopetski used what he called "the Snickers ploy." He would come to each caucus with a box of miniature candy bars. "When somebody said something nice or contributed to the process, I would just quietly walk over and put a little Snickers on the table in front of them."

On June 30, the decks were cleared for a final vote sending the bill out of committee. Gibbons rechecked to be sure he would prevail, then gaveled the meeting to order. All fourteen Republicans voted no, as expected. So did Andrews, Brewster, and Hoagland. Andy Jacobs kept his word to Gibbons and voted yes. But Jim McDermott, the single-payer advocate, surprised the chairman and voted no, making the final count twenty to eighteen to approve the bill. From the beginning, he had been skeptical that anything meaningful could pass in this Congress and dubious that the Clinton approach was worth much. "Clinton is running up against two things," McDermott remarked privately even before he saw the administration plan. "He can't get any new money and he can't convince people that government can run this program." He also sensed early that Clinton could be pressured: "There's no bottom line to this guy." And he had the same view of Foley, Gephardt, and Bonior — the Big Three of House Democrats. "Our leadership is pretty fluid in the House. It's hard to find anybody there who has a firm belief about how it [health care reform] ought to be. They just want two hundred eighteen votes."

Almost half that number were single-payers, and McDermott calculated that by voting no in committee on reporting the Stark-Gibbons bill, he could extract more concessions from Gephardt. He said that committee amendments meant too much out-of-pocket spending for families, too much variation in insurance rates from one individual to the next, and too much difficulty for states that might want to set up their own single-payer systems.

The narrowness of the twenty-to-eighteen margin was a clear sign that the battle was far from over. But Hillary Clinton was exhilarated and sent Gibbons a case of beer as a thank you.

At last, things seemed to be moving the reformers' way. A week earlier, the House Education and Labor Committee had reported out a slightly modified version of the Clinton bill and, in a bow to its most liberal members, also sent a single-payer bill forward "without recommendation." The White House hailed the action as bringing "us one step closer to achieving our goal of universal coverage." But few Democrats disputed the judgment of a Republican committee member, Wisconsin's Steve Gunderson, that "there isn't a chance in hell that this plan can pass the Congress of the United States." If anything was going to make it, it would be some variation of the Ways and Means bill. And Barbara Kennelly was realistic when she said, "We'll have to have a lot of intense caucuses to get people to feel comfortable about this."

Partisanship had grown more intense during the lengthy mark-ups, and the Republicans were more committed than ever to blocking the legislation. Bill Thomas, who had begun by hoping for a bipartisan compromise, explained why the dynamic had worked against it. "We could have dealt with health care as health care [as a policy problem] if there were a Republican in the White House," he said. "Then, it would be the Democrats looking at the substance of it, and we would be trying to defend the President's positions. They would want to get something done but realize they had to do it within the area the President had laid out or he'd veto it."

But with a Democrat in the White House, Thomas said, "it was a closed family fight" among the Democrats. The White House let Stark and Gibbons go their own way during the markup. Gibbons politely turned aside the administration's offer to help. Pat Griffin, the chief White House lobbyist, checked with Gibbons frequently, but "we never had to call on the President to twist any arms," Gibbons said. Mike Andrews was struck by the "passivity" of the White House during this period. Clinton called him before the critical committee votes and, to Andrews's surprise, kept the conversation going on Texas politics — commiserating with Andrews on his loss in the Senate primary, telling him "he knew how it felt to lose," and asking about the November prospects of primary winner Richard Fischer. Nothing about health care. "I asked, 'Is there anything else, Mr. President?' And he said no."

Would the outcome have been different had Rostenkowski not been indicted? Some thought so. The former chairman said he would have used Stark's bill as the starting point, just as Gibbons did, but would not have stopped there. Kopetski said, "He would have made changes here and there to be positioned better on the floor. If Rosty was chairman, I think we could have had twenty-three votes, and if we had twenty-three, we would have had twenty-four, because I think the holdout — Mike Andrews or Bill Brewster — would have wanted to help the process go along." Rosty himself was not so certain. When the markup was over, he said privately that he had promises from McDermott and Andrews to report out the bill. Both of them voted against Gibbons. But Rosty said he had never been able to secure such a pledge from Brewster. As far as Hoagland was concerned, he said, "I would have given him a pass." He had told the embattled Omaha congressman, "Peter, you shouldn't be on this committee — not because I don't want you here or I don't think you're courageous. But you can't get reelected and take the heat that's generated in this committee. You should be on Public Works, giving things away."

What griped Rosty, he said after it was over, was that Gibbons jettisoned the deals he had made with the industry groups, thereby forcing individual members like Payne and Jefferson, Kennelly and Neal, to fight to line up enough votes to make it possible for them to report out the bill. While the members were satisfied, the outside groups escaped the commitment Rostenkowski had demanded to support the overall legislation. "They got almost everything back in the bill, those outside interests did, and they don't owe us a goddamn thing," Rosty said privately. "And they're not going to volunteer. They're not going to walk in and say, 'Well, you've been a good guy and we're gonna be there.' Baloney! They're gonna say, 'Up yours! Goodbye.' And that's what irritates me more than anything else."

Bob Matsui also believed that if Rosty had remained, "Gradison would have ended up supporting this. And he probably would have gotten either the doctors or the hospitals." From watching him in the past, Matsui thought he knew exactly how Rosty would have operated. "The interest groups would've come in late at night — seven or eight o'clock. He would've sat them in his office and said, 'If we do these things, will you endorse the bill?' He would intimidate them. And if they wouldn't, he'd say, 'Well, this train is moving and if you're not on board, then we probably won't be able to help you.'"

The main point, several of the members said, is that Rosty never would have reported a bill that had no chance on the floor. "Any bill he would have reported would achieve that," Matsui said, "because he would always be looking at the floor, at how you get to two hundred eighteen votes. These people forgot that." That was a harsh verdict, but events would prove it to be true.

17

To the Rescue

GEORGE MITCHELL LOOKED DIRECTLY at Ira Magaziner. With them, surrounded by aides, were the President, the First Lady, Speaker Foley, and House Majority Leader Gephardt. Choosing his words carefully, Mitchell told Magaziner, "I'm going to need a supreme effort from you and your people. We're going to have to come up with a bill I can propose that doesn't have an employer mandate and still gets us close to universal coverage."

Dead silence greeted Mitchell's words; later, some present remembered that "everybody sort of held their breath." Then they began to speak at once.

Do you really think it's that bad? the President asked Mitchell.

Yes, he said, nodding slightly.

Everyone understood the meaning of Mitchell's remarks: If reform had any chance, they had to make a new start — and immediately, given the inexorable political calendar that was working against them and the implacable opposition to the Clinton plan that was eroding political and public support. As the full Senate prepared to deliberate over reform legislation, they needed, desperately, a reborn bill. And a bill, with powerful irony, that did not even bear the name of the person most responsible for thrusting this issue to the forefront of the national political agenda, the President of the United States.

It was in that context that George Mitchell delivered his disturbing message. All of them knew, as one said, that "this thing is moving away from us."

They had assembled in the Map Room for this critical strategy session on Friday morning, July 1, just before the Fourth of July congressional recess and the Senate Finance Committee's final action.

The room was the famous basement chamber where FDR, sometimes joined by Churchill, had charted the daily progress of World
War II; now, over the mantelpiece, hung a map of Europe, its bright
colors marking the disposition of Allied and Nazi forces in the spring
of 1945. It was the last situational map FDR saw before leaving the
White House for Warm Springs, Georgia, where he died of a stroke.
Hillary Clinton had gotten it from a naval officer, had it framed, and
proudly showed it to visitors. But it was not that war that was now
on their minds.

The First Lady and Magaziner disagreed with Mitchell on what
kind of bill was needed. You could do a single-payer bill based on the
Canadian model, in which government paid the bills for all citizens
and guaranteed coverage for everyone, they told Mitchell.

That's not what he had in mind, Mitchell replied.

Dick Gephardt tried to persuade Mitchell to keep working for a
universal coverage/employer mandate bill. He reiterated the points
he had made minutes before. If the Senate can muster the votes to
give Clinton what he wants, "I can get a universal-coverage bill with
an employer mandate," Gephardt told them, outlining the tactics to
carry them through the remaining days of summer and into the fall
of 1994 before the crucial congressional elections. "I'll build it off
the Ways and Means bill. I've canvassed my people. I can get enough
votes for it."

Gephardt, the inveterate cheerleader, conceded, "It's not going to
be the easiest thing I've ever done in my life, but we can get it done."
To others in the room, it seemed apparent that the more Gephardt
talked, the clearer the difficulties became: House Democrats were
afraid of being "BTU-ed," Gephardt said. Having been burned in
1993 on the energy tax portion of the Clinton budget, they were not
about to take another potentially destructive plunge on this even
more controversial issue. Besides, Gephardt conceded, it would take
weeks to write a universal-coverage bill. Though his words were not
entirely explicit, their import undercut his own professed optimism:
Support on the House side of the Hill was tepid, especially for a bill
that would rely on government financing in the current viscerally
antigovernment political environment.

In any case, Mitchell had made up his mind. "Look," he said, "I'm

telling you what I'd like to propose and I need to engage people now
to get them there." Mitchell thought he might be able to get a bill
passed by the Senate that provided health insurance for 95 percent
of the population with a "hard trigger" — a legal requirement that
the government step in and guarantee coverage if the 95 percent goal
were not reached by a certain date.

Magaziner said later, expressing the political peril then facing the
White House, "We didn't feel we could go with something labeled
'the Clinton Bill' because by then the label, 'the Clinton Bill,' was
poison. We even talked about putting something out that was virtually the same bill but not labeling it 'the Clinton Bill.' We needed a
new vehicle."

From the President down, none of these players doubted that
need or the urgency of this moment. They were not agreed, however,
on the best vehicle for their new beginning. The President, the First
Lady, and Magaziner thought supporting the more liberal bill that
had recently passed Ted Kennedy's Labor and Human Resources
Committee was the best alternative. Back that kind of bill, they argued, and we'll re-ignite enthusiasm among our pro-reform groups
and reengage the public in the debate.

Mitchell disagreed. The best approach was to reach out to moderates during July, form a consensus, and bring the new compromise bill to the Senate floor for a vote. Then they could proceed
to a conference with members of the House on the final version of
the bill.

He made two compelling points against the Clintons' continuing
desire to get a universal-coverage bill: You won't be able to turn public opinion around that fast. Furthermore, you should not count on
the public influencing their congressional members by pressing for
reform when they meet with constituents over the holiday recess, as
some in the White House had then urged. Members only meet with
a small sample of the public when they go home, Mitchell pointed
out. "They may have a town hall meeting, but the town hall meetings
are all going to be packed by the insurance industry and the NFIB
anyway," he said. "You're not going to be able to change these people. You won't be able to turn the public debate in the way you hope
unless we can engage the moderates."

As always, Mitchell's analysis was impressive. "The truth is persuasive, as it always is," Magaziner remembered thinking. "I must say that by the end of the meeting, I wasn't so sure anymore. I felt he may be right. I didn't want to feel that he was right, but listening to him I felt he might be."

After more discussion, the President and the congressional leaders were in agreement. They would rally behind what would become a new, stripped-down, compromise Mitchell bill, eventually covering 95 percent of Americans, and mount the last, most intense, effort to win their war. Whatever reservations they felt, and there were many, as Magaziner recalled, "they had to go with it. It was our only chance."

George Mitchell, riding to the rescue, had carried the day.

Mitchell was not the only senator attempting to rescue reform. In the Capitol Building, one of the most extraordinary, and most revealing, efforts in this entire tale was unfolding day by day behind a door that bore no name, only a small plate reading S-201. It was the "hideaway" office suite of Senator John Chafee, the Rhode Island Republican moderate.

There, in a windowless room, with Oriental rugs on the walls, old photos of Chafee with former Presidents stacked against the walls, what was now known as the Mainstream Coalition — Republican and Democratic senators and their staffs — met almost daily around a conference table under a large chandelier, often for hour after grueling hour. They were trying to hammer out an acceptable bipartisan compromise.

Cynics will doubt the sincerity of their commitment, but the words and actions of the senators who met in Chafee's hideaway that summer are persuasive evidence of their convictions. They believed a small bipartisan group of committed senators could form a critical political mass. Even in the highly polarized Washington of 1994, even after the failure of the bipartisan rump group on the Finance Committee, they thought they could make a difference. They could become the bridge, the swing votes enabling passage of reform.

Their coalition was forged out of necessity, based on their belief that the United States badly needed to reform its health system.

The quiet person who led them was the perfect symbol of what they represented politically.

The very background of John Chafee bespoke the old tradition of the mainstream Republican Party of the past, and of a political center that was becoming rare in American life. White, Episcopalian, a New Englander — Yale undergraduate, Harvard law — Chafee was of the generation that came to maturity in the Great Depression and fought valorously in World War II. He was a marine platoon leader for three years in the South Pacific who returned for two more years of service in the Korean War. He entered public service and was for six years governor of Rhode Island; then, under Richard Nixon, secretary of the Navy. He was elected to the Senate in 1976.

Chafee was seventy-one years old, having celebrated that milestone exactly one month after Clinton launched the battle with his September 1993 speech to Congress. Like Dole, Chafee did not show his age. His figure was trim, his hair still brown, and he moved in a modest, unobtrusive manner that reflected his temperament. He was no political bomb thrower like the hard-right figures who were dominating his party. But he knew who he was and once convinced of a position would defend it tenaciously. Years before, Chafee became acquainted with a postal worker in Rhode Island whose son was disabled. The family's insurance was dropped, their bills mounted. Eventually, the son died at the age of seven. Spurred by this tragedy, Chafee championed the disabled, studied the health coverage issue, and became committed to reform. It was Chafee who had urged Dole to appoint a Republican task force in the summer of 1990, and Chafee who was determined to do all he could to achieve needed change.

Out of those initial meetings in the Bush years came regular strategy sessions with GOP senators. Chafee led them with quiet firmness, and such persistent attention to schedule and detail — including ringing a bell to bring them to order — that Republicans began referring to him as the Captain. By 1991, two years before Clinton was inaugurated, these efforts had produced a Chafee bill, which became the model for the Republican plan signed by twenty-three Republican senators in the fall of 1993. It set a goal of covering all citizens by the year 2000 and a requirement that all Americans buy insurance.

Chafee's efforts won him unusual bipartisan praise. "John Chafee is as good a man as I've ever met in my life," Democrat Jay Rockefeller remarked privately one night, "but he also chairs the Republican Conference, or has. He can be very partisan. But he wants health care desperately."

To Chafee, the legislative battle in 1993 and 1994 ranked as the most significant since he had come to Congress. "It is the biggest by far," he would say, "because it affects every single person in the United States from the urban baby needing prenatal care to the one-hundred-five-year-old man. And it affects problems in our society that aren't directly associated with health care — unwed mothers, the violence from handguns, the drug problem, illegal immigration, all these ramifications."

He never lost that conviction, and as the pressures and problems of the 1994 fight intensified month after month, Chafee never allowed his doubts to overcome his desire to pass a bill. By late March, he was saying privately, "I don't think Republicans want to be caught in the position of killing health care." He even found reason for solace amid the battering Clinton and the Democrats were taking from Whitewater (though privately he thought Whitewater vastly overblown as a scandal). "All this has made our plan far more attractive for Democrats" who would be seeking a compromise, he said during one of many conversations in his office. When Clinton appeared to have weathered the worst of Whitewater, Chafee employed a Napoleonic analogy as grounds for optimism about attracting the President and Democrats to the Mainstream compromise: "Now that they're on their way back, in the winter snows from Moscow, when they get to the Polish border this is looking pretty good."

Still, John Chafee was a realist, and he appreciated better than anyone the difficulties of forming bipartisan agreement after all the months of failure. By the Fourth of July recess, just as Mitchell was beginning his effort for a new compromise reform bill, the Mainstream Coalition was huddling daily in Chafee's hideaway.

Given the political and economic pressures each senator was under, and especially considering their egos and personalities, their unity of purpose and determination to reach agreement on a bi-partisan reform was astounding. And conflicting personalities they did have, as members of the group remarked privately of each other. Danforth was the preacher, the moralist in politics who didn't care much for the details. Breaux was the dealer — "make a deal, make a deal, make a deal" was his constant refrain — so eager to close the connection, those in the group would say, he would trade his mother for the right deal. Bradley was the dodger, as befits the former great pro basketball player, "who moves from one spot to another as fast as he can." Durenberger, respected for his knowledge of the arcane nature of health care, was nonetheless thought of at times as a mum-bler. Boren, "to the right of Atilla the Hun," as one of the Republicans said of the Oklahoman, was a politician with a foot in ten corners simultaneously, but informed, serious. Conrad, one of the youngest and most earnest, "who listened and listened and listened," was re-garded at first by some as "wishy-washy"; but, in time, he demon-strated a strong independent streak that won him favor. Kerrey was thought of as hot, quixotic, stubborn. "He's a killer, you know," one of them said, referring to Kerrey's training as a navy SEAL, but Kerrey also won their respect for his steadfast determination to achieve real bipartisan legislation.

As centrists, they operated without the financial and ideological backing of the Right — or the Left. Because they had no constituency groups behind them, they had to depend upon no one but them-selves — and did. "It was a wonderful process to be involved in be-cause you can see that it is possible for a group of members to come to a conclusion on controversial issues," said Ferguson, the Chafee aide who organized and attended all their meetings. "It doesn't hap-pen very often unless you're in a crisis mode — and, of course, we were."

Chafee conducted their laborious search for consensus in typical painstaking fashion. He called them to order by tapping a glass three times with a spoon — ding, ding, ding — a process he repeated more sharply when the conversation bogged down, to bring them back to business. The clock was ticking away their time, but the Captain was in command.

* * *

The motives that prompted the Mainstream Coalition to assemble, the ideological composition of its members, the power — or lack thereof — they represented politically, all sharply illuminated the state of The System.

No one understood those larger points better than Dave Durenberger, whom all in that group recognized to be the Senate's preeminent expert on the workings of America's medical market-places and on the complex set of questions that made reform so devilish a political issue.

Durenberger had been in the Senate for sixteen years and he, like the rest of the Republicans, had seen it change markedly, nowhere more strikingly than within his own party. His career had not been without its difficult phases, including charges of dishonorable con-duct. The past few years had been particularly tough: In 1990 he was formally denounced by his Senate colleagues for unethical fi-nancial dealings; in 1992 he faced a civil suit from a former law cli-ent; and, finally, in 1993 a federal grand jury indicted him on two felony counts for billing the Senate for rent at a Minneapolis con-dominium he owned. But these troubles did not keep Durenberger from being a player, nor lose him the respect colleagues had for his expertise. He, Danforth, Chafee, Cohen, and Jeffords were in the rapidly dwindling ranks of Republican moderates in a party that had undergone a dramatic shift to the right — and a Senate that would almost certainly be more strongly conservative with the an-nounced departure of Durenberger himself and Danforth after this session.

When people like Chafee, Durenberger, and Danforth came to the Senate in the 1970s, they represented the Republican center. At that time, a number of Republicans occupied a more liberal, or left, position. Among them were such men as Jacob K. Javits of New York, Lowell Weicker of Connecticut, Clifford Case of New Jersey, Edward W. Brooke of Massachusetts, and Charles McC. Mathias Jr. of Maryland. Now, as Danforth would say when the Mainstream group began meeting, there were no Republicans to his left, no real GOP liberals in the entire Senate.

Not only had there been a sharp ideological shift; the style of the Senate Republicans had changed notably as power rapidly flowed

from the old Midwest and Northeast GOP bases into the dominant ranks of Republicans from the South and West. Now the Republican Senate increasingly displayed the combative, in-your-face
style of the Newt Gingrich House. "Those of us from the Midwest
and the Northeast are not as familiar with that particular style,"
Durenberger dryly remarked that summer of 1994. "Part of the reason for the nastiness we're all now experiencing comes from that
shift to the southern-western Republicans. They do have a different
attitude."

Durenberger's analysis of the political condition facing moderates
was perceptive:

> We are suffering currently from what is leadership in the Re-
> publican Party. What is it? Is it going to be known by what
> you're against or what you're for? It's so much easier to say
> you're *against* employer mandates and you're *against* large
> government and you're *against* taxes. Then what are you *for?*
> Clinton is *for* universal coverage. Nobody knows what the hell
> that means. And Dole is *for* whatever the people are at the mo-
> ment. Dole's problem is basically the Mondale problem: You
> can't get to be President unless you go through that damn
> convention, and if you go through that damn convention you
> probably won't be President. That's the bad news. And the
> good news is that the Democrats have the same problem we
> have. It's a helluva problem when the parties have moved so
> far from the middle there's no room left for real leadership.

Like Bill Cohen and other Republican moderates, Chafee had
begun worrying about the increasing partisanship. Not that partisanship was absent in the past, Chafee would say, but this was different. "There's a new breed of pit terrier around here," he said
that summer. "What they want to do is get a hold of the calf of
somebody's leg and hang on. There is a spirit of meanness out
there."

Moderates in both parties shared his view. It explains why they
were willing to try to put aside party labels to achieve something they
all believed, with greater and lesser degrees of passion, was genuinely
needed. Those who stuck to the bitter end knew, as Danforth had

warned them, that their stands would cause them problems within their parties.

They all knew something else: They had little time in which to act. "As every day goes by, the politics of this argue to do nothing," Durenberger said as their meetings began. "It's a lot easier to do nothing and blame somebody else than it is to do something." It would be a political tragedy, Durenberger thought, if this year ended without health reform, for the next two years would be consumed by presidential politics, making the prospects for real reform even less likely.

This view animated the Mainstream meetings, which Dole disparagingly began referring to privately as the "Midstream" meetings. Nor was Dole alone in disparaging them. Bill Kristol weighed in with another of his famous memos urging all-out opposition to health reform. "The Chafee-led rump group runs the serious risk of snatching defeat out of the jaws of victory," he privately advised Republicans. "We're going to defeat Clinton on health care, win seats in November, and pass our own health bill next year."

Ted Kennedy realized his bill would not be the final version, so he and his aides went all-out to work with George Mitchell to draft a compromise bill that could attract the support of Chafee's Mainstream Coalition.

In public Kennedy was positive. In private his doubts emerged. "Oh, he's devastated," said someone who visited Kennedy regularly at that time. To anyone who asked, Kennedy and his people would say, Look, we've already accomplished something that hasn't happened in nearly a century of debating this issue. Four of five congressional committees have reported out bills. Besides, Kennedy would frequently say, this issue has taken hold among Americans. When he first began introducing reform bills in the 1970s, most people viewed insurance as somebody else's problem. Now everyone feels vulnerable. They know they're one pink slip away from losing their coverage.

Furthermore, Kennedy would say, echoing the White House political line, the issue still works in favor of Clinton and the Democrats. The Republicans, they would say, are overplaying their hand and being seen as obstructionists, and some White House advisers still clung to that belief. But Kennedy knew otherwise. A private conversation with Jay Rockefeller early that summer more accurately reflected Kennedy's reading of political realities. He was now convinced, Kennedy told Rockefeller, that Republicans were committed to blocking health care reform so they could recapture the White House in 1996. If Clinton doesn't win health care, he can't be reelected. That's the Republican strategy, Kennedy said; that's how they plan on winning. Which was exactly Newt Gingrich's plan from the beginning, though his maneuvers to kill reform were still largely hidden from the public.

Nevertheless, Kennedy did not give up the fight. Immediately after the Fourth of July recess, and continuing throughout that dispiriting summer, Kennedy held meetings with pro-reform groups night after night in his Labor Committee hearing room. Among those who crowded into the room, often more than a hundred strong, were leaders of public-interest groups; the nursing, hospital, physician organizations; the labor unions and some business representatives; the seniors; the disabled and children's rights groups. Each night, either at the beginning or end of their meetings, Kennedy addressed them extemporaneously.

They were pep rallies, emotional "win-one-for-the-Gipper" performances. To those present, it wasn't so much what Kennedy said, but how he said it that they remembered. "There's something about his voice and his ability with the language that communicates more emotion than anybody else," said AARP's John Rother, who regularly attended. "He can really charge people up in a way that no one else can. You're conscious of the history, you're conscious of commitment. It's not like he's conveying information. It's more like 'This is something we have to do. People are counting on us. This is our moment in history.' "

Bob Bennett, the canny Republican from Utah who was providing intelligence on Republican health care thinking in the Senate for Minority Leader Dole, knew, after a conversation early that summer with Richard G. Lugar, his GOP colleague from Indiana, that a political sea change was occurring.

Lugar, the respected centrist who was seeking another Senate term that fall, and in 1996 would try to win the GOP presidential nomination, had just returned from a series of town hall meetings with his Indiana constituents. Back in Washington, he heard Bennett and other Republicans discussing strategy, including the perceived need to offer a "placeholder," a Republican alternative bill to counter the Clinton plan.

By then, Republicans like Bennett knew the political dynamic in the Senate had changed dramatically. The Clinton plan was dead. Mitchell would do anything, even accept a minimal compromise bill sponsored by Bob Dole and Bob Packwood in order to pass a Senate bill and bring it to a conference with the House. If that happened, Bennett and other Republicans feared, they might be placed in an intolerable political position. To block the Clinton reform, they could be forced to filibuster, thus reinforcing the public feeling that selfishness motivated Republicans.

After listening to Bennett, Lugar said, "I'll tell you what *my* voters want. They don't want us to do *anything* on health care."

Bennett was startled. What a change that represents, he thought. His mind went back to Clinton's speech to Congress in September 1993. He remembered how convinced Republicans were then that they *had* to offer an alternative if they were to be seen as politically responsible. Now here's *Dick Lugar*, Bennett thought, not Phil Gramm, not any of the bomb throwers, saying he thinks a Republican bill is a really dumb idea.

That was the moment, Bennett said later, when he realized the country beyond the Washington Beltway had begun to change dramatically. "The rest of us soon began to get those vibes from the country," he said. "Pretty soon it was respectable in the Republican [Senate political strategy] conference to say, No bill. Once that scenario became a likely scenario in our minds, the whole thing shifted to: We can't let anything pass. We can't let the Democrats get to conference with *anything*."

Here was the final turning point in all-out Republican opposition. Bennett recalled, "All the co-sponsors of Dole-Packwood were prepared to vote against Dole-Packwood, including Dole and Packwood! I remember Sheila [Burke] saying to Dole in my presence as we were bringing up something with respect to Dole-Packwood, and some senator (it may even have been me) saying to Dole, 'I can't vote for that.' Sheila said to Dole, 'And neither can you!' "

The reversal was of course not made public. But from then on, unified Republican opposition drove the battle and it greatly affected how the Chafee Senate moderates dealt with the challenge of rescuing reform that summer.

In the House, the problems were nearly as great. When Speaker Foley and Majority Leader Gephardt sat down to take stock that summer, the picture was grim. A bruising and frustrating session of Congress was ending. Despite all the strife of 1993, major legislative victories had been won during Clinton's first year. Besides the President's budget and economic plan, lowering the deficit for the first time in years, NAFTA had been approved. Congress had also passed the Brady bill to impose a waiting period on handgun purchases, family leave legislation, a bill easing voter registration, a liberalization of the Hatch Act, controlling political activities by government employees and a measure creating a National Service Corps so young people could work in local communities and earn money for college tuition. No Democratic President since Lyndon Johnson thirty years before could boast of as strong a record of accomplishment.

But 1994 was very different. A string of special-election losses had signaled a weakening of public support for congressional Democrats and an increasingly aggressive Republican minority had stymied bill after bill. Among the casualties of what newspapers called "a return to gridlock" were campaign finance, lobbying and congressional organization reforms, welfare reform, a major telecommunications bill, a striker-replacement bill important to labor, and two big environmental measures — the Clean Water Act revisions and a new approach to Superfund toxic waste cleanups.

When the House returned from the July Fourth recess, Foley and Gephardt struggled not only with health care, but with the high-priority crime bill and a measure approving the General Agreement on Tariffs and Trade (GATT), which had also been designated "must-pass" legislation by the President.

Though the link was not then made public, the GATT agreement had a fateful connection with the outcome of the health care battle.

During that Fourth of July holiday weekend, presidential adviser George Stephanopoulos talked by phone with Moynihan's top aide, Lawrence O'Donnell. O'Donnell listened as Stephanopoulos articulated what he called a "lose-win" strategy for the President. Lose on health care in this Congress, Stephanopoulos told him, but win by taking the issue to the voters that fall and charge Republicans with blocking reform. O'Donnell countered with what he called a "lose-lose-lose" scenario: *lose* health reform in this Congress, *lose* GATT in the Senate because of Republican opposition, then *lose* the Senate in the fall election. GATT posed a major peril for Clinton and the Democrats, O'Donnell warned. Republicans on the Senate Finance Committee were beginning to send strong private signals to him, and to Moynihan, that if Democrats alienated them by pushing health care, they would retaliate by defeating GATT. From then on, that private Republican threat to oppose GATT loomed over the fate of health care reform — so much so that Moynihan expressed his alarm to us in a private conversation early that July. "The consequences of health care going down are as nothing to the consequences of the GATT going down," Moynihan told us. "You have to have GATT; that means leadership of the Free World."

Serious though that threat was, it was only one of the major legislative concerns confronting Foley and Gephardt as they grappled to set their agenda in the little time left before the critical fall elections. The result was that health care — despite its supposed priority — again had to fight for breathing space. Foley, approaching the end of his third decade in the House and his fifth year as Speaker, seemed even glummer than usual. A serious, sober, taciturn man who began each day with a session of weight lifting, Foley appeared to associates to be bending under the burdens of managing the House for a President of unlimited policy ambition in a time of limited financial resources and sharply heightened partisanship.

Speaking privately, Foley admitted that he thought the Clintons had bitten off more than they could chew. Health care reform, he said, is "a bigger task than I think was maybe fully appreciated by the President and First Lady when they undertook it. Of course, he had made it an issue in the campaign, but the political mandate of the election was ambiguous."

In fact, Foley believed that Clinton had carried Foley's eastern Washington district only because Ross Perot was on the ballot. The President's 43 percent national plurality suggested a caution, Foley thought, not a breakneck push for major change. "I remember saying to people [during the presidential transition] that I hoped that we wouldn't absolutely commit to getting this finished [in one Congress], that it would be a multiyear process."

Before he became Speaker, Foley had served as chairman of the Agriculture Committee, as majority whip, and as majority leader. He prided himself on understanding the moods and the rhythms of the House — and he tried to serve as a tutor to the Clintons. But often, he found himself bringing them advice they did not welcome. When they proposed a single supercommittee to process the bill, Foley told them it would be "unwieldy"; it would cause more problems than it would solve. When the Clintons wanted to make health care reform part of the 1993 budget reconciliation bill and put it on a fast track, it was "unrealistic," Foley told them. When they wanted it passed as a separate bill by the end of 1993 — "a kind of Christmas present" to the nation, as Hillary put it — that was "not really feasible," Foley told her.

Foley thought the basic problem, which the Clintons did not want to acknowledge, was that there was no consensus to support a plan as ambitious as they had offered — not in the country, not in the Democratic Party, not in the House. Foley did not like being a naysayer, but he thought they were "pushing it faster than our ability to develop a political consensus."

Still, there was no question that Foley would try to deliver the best bill that the House would support, using Dick Gephardt to manage the complex legislative process.

Gephardt's unusual capacity for building political alliances and his endless patience for the kind of backroom conversations that are required to engineer voluntary agreements within a House made up of autonomous, self-centered politicians gave them some hope. He had run for the Democratic presidential nomination in 1988 and was a competitor in the race with Michael Dukakis until his money ran out. That experience gave him a broader political horizon than most House members possessed and deepened his appreciation of the importance of presidential leadership. Like many others in the battle, Gephardt had personal reasons for wanting to see all Americans protected against medical risks. His son, Matt, had survived juvenile cancer, diagnosed when he was just a two-year-old, thanks to the excellent care Gephardt and his wife were able to obtain and to pay for with his law firm's health insurance policy. When he spoke of others he met in the hospital corridor who were not so lucky, his voice became husky. "I'll never forget the nights I spent, sitting at Matt's bedside, talking to the parents of his roommate — a young child with a severe cancer, and a family that couldn't afford health insurance," Gephardt said in a speech at the National Press Club. "Every time they brought him to the hospital for treatment, they had to scrape together about three hundred dollars — borrowed from friends, from family, sometimes from people they hardly knew.

"It was bad enough that they had to live with the pain of their child's illness. They also had to live with the indignity, the injustice of having to borrow and beg just to give him decent care. As long as I live, I'll never forget the words that father spoke to me, after one long and painful night we spent together at the hospital. He said: 'I know my son's sickness might be stronger than he is. I know he probably will die. And I can figure out how to live with that. But what I can't live with is the thought that he might die not because of the disease God gave him — but because of the dollars I couldn't give him.' "

Characteristically, Gephardt took an upbeat view of the prospects for reform. He had, after all, been an Eagle Scout. He did not dwell on the narrowness of Clinton's victory, as Foley did, but instead rejoiced that "for the first time in my experience in the Congress, we have a President who is entirely committed to leading on health care. I have always believed that is a necessary condition for getting anything done."

After his futile experience in 1991 and 1992 trying to negotiate an agreement between Pete Stark and Jim Cooper on a Democratic bill, Gephardt knew better than anyone else the depth of the differences within his party. But he pronounced himself "very encouraged" by the experience and told both Clintons that "while it wasn't definitive, it moved the ball down the field" and set the stage for action.

Unlike Foley, Gephardt thought the Clintons had come up with a workable design. He was skeptical of the alliances from the beginning, believing that they "got in the way" of the changes already taking place in the marketplace, and was not sorry to see them discarded. While he knew from the start that the notion of requiring all employers to pay for their workers' insurance was something that would make many members of Congress "turn pale," it was preferable to raising taxes — and the only way to get to universal coverage.

Through all the rigors of the 1993 budget battle and the fight over NAFTA — an issue on which Gephardt voted against the President's position — he remained optimistic about reform. He monitored the developments in the three House committees closely, gave regular pep talks at Democratic caucuses, and urged the Clintons to keep working on the issue, even when things appeared to be bogging down on Capitol Hill. If reform could be rescued, Dick Gephardt was an eager volunteer.

First, Gephardt had to decide which bill to take to the House floor. No contest. The Education and Labor Committee bill was a beefed-up version of the Clinton plan, with more benefits in a shorter time than even the optimists on the Magaziner task force thought affordable. The only bill (other than the government-financed single-payer plan, which Gephardt and Foley both regarded as unpassable) that had a plausible financing provision was the Stark-Gibbons bill passed by Ways and Means. That would have to be it.

Gephardt detailed his top health aide, Andie King, to work through the fine print of the bill with staff specialists from other committees with responsibility for health care legislation while he organized the sales job on Democratic colleagues and outside interest groups. His aim was to win the 218 votes needed for passage.

Gephardt found it the most intense work of his life, "more intense by a factor of ten than anything I've ever been involved with," he said. "We'd have early morning meetings, late morning meetings, afternoon meetings, and night meetings. I personally called every undecided Southern conservative at least twice. Had half-hour or forty-five-minute conversations with them on the phone or in the office, going over in great detail what their problems were. Others did the same."

It was an all-hands effort. Sam Gibbons came up with the idea of using the Ways and Means Committee room as Information Central. He invited all his colleagues to send their legislative assistants, press secretaries, and "letter-answerers," as he called the correspondents, to three-hour briefings on the bill. Three sessions were held, with as many as three hundred staff members attending. Then in the Capitol office off the House floor he had taken over from Rostenkowski, he set up a phone-bank operation to answer questions from members, staffs, and constituents trying to understand how the bill would work. "There's so much public misinformation," he exclaimed privately. "Some of it is so inaccurate that it is pitiful. Some of it is so inaccurate that it's almost criminal."

Loyalists like Ben Cardin and John Lewis who had worked on the bill named themselves the Green Berets and conducted small group meetings to bring the waverers into line. Hillary Clinton joined some of them, bringing computer printouts that showed the number of uninsured in each congressional district.

Two members of the leadership, David Bonior of Michigan, a foe of abortion, and Vic Fazio of California, an abortion rights supporter, were charged with trying to negotiate an abortion compromise. That would be no easy task. Thirty-five Democrats were on record as opposing any measure that *included* abortion services. Twice that number vowed to oppose a bill that *omitted* abortion coverage.

All of the discussions were held under the shadow of the Senate maneuvering, where the White House and George Mitchell were trying desperately to put together their new rescue bill. Gephardt's task was made immensely more difficult by the House Democrats' fear of "being BTU-ed" again.

While Gephardt was trying to line up the votes, Foley tried to quell a vicious battle over committee jurisdiction. Nothing in the congressional saga — not even Stark's sniping or Moynihan's ambivalence — revealed the mentality of long-entrenched Capitol Hill barons in more unflattering terms than the no-holds-barred jurisdictional battle fought out of public view in the late summer of 1994.

The President's most important policy initiative was hanging by a thread; a historic commitment of the Democratic Party was facing imminent defeat; an election disaster was looming. And for almost an entire month, committee chairmen and staffers on Ways and Means, Energy and Commerce, and Education and Labor used every weapon they could find to stake out the widest possible jurisdictions for themselves to maintain *future* control of a program that might not even pass.

Foley always found arbitrating disputes about which committee and which chairman had principal jurisdiction over a major issue to be one of the least attractive parts of the Speaker's job. The debates were "Talmudic" in their intensity. "These committee staffs were arguing over the meaning of every word and its possible ramifications," he told us. "I had this simplistic notion that we could do a bill and that everybody would go back to their previous jurisdictions. But that turned out to be impossible to sell, so it became necessary to write a new guideline, a kind of constitutional covenant spelling out who possessed what committee jurisdictional oversight. It wasn't just the principals," he said, meaning the committee and subcommittee chairmen. "The mandarins of the committee staffs would take the document back to their cubicles and immediately agreements fell apart."

Disagreements among the committee staffs became so intractable that the Speaker had to call in the warring parties three different times and pound the table. "And the committee chairmen would all dutifully promise cooperation and then they would go back to their committees where they and their staffs would [rewrite the bill to ensure their own primacy over the issue], and the promises would be broken," he said.

At the Speaker's invitation, Dan Rostenkowski sat in on the leadership discussions with the Democratic committee chairmen. Rosty was disgusted by them. At one point, he told his colleagues, "If we go out that door and the Fourth Estate finds out that we are arguing about jurisdiction, as opposed to molding together a legislative product, we'll be the laughing stock." Looking straight at Foley, he declared, "You'd better goddamn well assume your responsibility." But when Foley ruled, at one point, that Ways and Means would have to share more of its health jurisdiction with other committees, Rostenkowski led the complainers. No one could shame anyone into cooperation.

On July 19, the President addressed the summer meeting of the National Governors Association in Boston. As always when appearing before his former colleagues, Clinton said what he really thought — not what he was scripted to say. The night before, he had been in Maine for a Democratic fund-raiser with George Mitchell, who continued his secret attempt to draft an alternative to the Clinton plan that Mitchell hoped would provide coverage for 95 percent of all Americans without requiring employers to pay the greatest share of their employees' insurance.

After the President's formal speech, Governor Ben Nelson of Nebraska, a conservative Democrat, asked Clinton to reassure the governors about the impact of his health care reform plan on the plans the states were already initiating. Suddenly, startled reporters and White House aides heard the President say that his bottom-line demand for universal coverage could be satisfied by a "phased-in, deliberate effort" to expand the ranks of the insured from the current 85 percent to "somewhere in the ballpark of ninety-five percent upwards." As if that were not enough, Clinton also said that he was "open to any solution" on how to pay for more coverage and that "there may be some other way than an employer mandate to do this."

Pandemonium. Donna Shalala, the Health and Human Services secretary, was at the session. She knew nothing of that White House strategy session a month before, where the President, the First Lady, and the congressional leaders had agreed with Mitchell to work secretly for just that kind of bill. After the President's remarks, Shalala ran to Mark Gearan, the White House communications director, and Carol Rasco, the domestic policy adviser, and said, "Did you hear what he just said!" Even before Clinton left the Boston Sheraton, Mack McLarty, Harold Ickes, and press secretary Dee Dee Myers moved among the White House reporters, trying to convince them that no signals had been changed. Clinton himself was persuaded by his staff to tell reporters that "I think you have to have a universal-coverage goal" even if "you cannot physically get to one hundred percent coverage."

The chaos spread from Boston. John Rother had been watching Clinton's speech on C-SPAN in his Washington office. Immediately he put in a call to Harold Ickes. "What gives?" he demanded. "Tell any reporters who call you that this is no change," Ickes replied. Rother tried the line on inquiring reporters; he wasn't surprised that it was met with universal skepticism. "This is fucking unbelievable," Rother said to himself. "Here's a President who I believe is the smartest one we've had since Thomas Jefferson, and he doesn't know beans about negotiating. Ronald Reagan could teach him how to negotiate. You come in strong, you maintain your moral position, and you cut your deal at the end. You don't give it away in public with nothing coming back."

When Clinton returned to Washington that afternoon, the White House scrambled even harder to erase the impression of compromise Clinton's words left. It did not make matters better when Republicans and conservative Democrats immediately went on television to hail the "new tone" of accommodation they professed to hear. Ever helpful, Moynihan said, "The President seems to be responding to a situation much like the Finance Committee did. I think this is good news." But the liberals were not having it. Pete Stark said, "If there is a bill without universal coverage, I would leave and a lot of liberal members would say no." Jim McDermott said, "He just put in jeopardy all the single-payer votes."

The next day, Hillary Clinton and Vice President Gore both denied there had been any backing down. A statement was issued in the President's name in which he actually apologized: "I'm sorry that after all my skills and efforts at communicating, the point I really made yesterday somehow didn't get through." His point, he said, was that anything less than universal coverage was likely to make matters worse.

Clinton had misspoken but he had not misstated the new policy goal he was secretly trying to achieve through the Mitchell rescue bill.

To loyalists on Capitol Hill like Bob Matsui of California, Clinton's House floor leader on NAFTA, that Boston incident was just the latest evidence of a persistent problem with this President. "The trouble is," Matsui said privately a couple days after the Boston speech, "he can't seem to keep his mouth closed. He keeps talking about these things and the message gets confused and ambiguous."

The President had done NAFTA just right, Matsui said. "He didn't really speak on NAFTA until two months before the vote, but when he did, he came booming out, with all the former Presidents at his side. He created drama, and then for the next two months, it was just a drumbeat."

But on health care, Matsui said, Clinton had been speaking so long and so often, "there's not much more he can tell us now."

The strain of the administration's false starts and repeated mistakes was beginning to tell. John Rother went to see Foley and Gephardt the day after the Boston speech and told them they seemed remarkably calm. "It's the eye of the hurricane," Gephardt replied, without disclosing the private strategy the congressional leaders had agreed upon with the President. Rother asked where things stood, and Foley said, "We feel like we've got one hundred eighty votes — solid." But, the Speaker fretted, "if we move to the right, we start losing votes on the left, and if we move to the left, we start losing votes on the right."

Two days after the Boston speech, the Democratic congressional leaders went to the White House and attempted a sleight of hand that they hoped would clear the stage for a final push on Capitol Hill. After their meeting with the President, Mitchell, Foley, and Gephardt briefed the reporters, declaring the Clinton health care proposal officially dead. A new policy would soon be forthcoming from the leaders of the House and Senate, they said solemnly, facing the mass of cameras and microphones on the south lawn of the White House. With straight faces, the three congressional leaders said they had just broken the news to the President that they were moving away from his bill in favor of one that would be "less bureaucratic and provide for a longer phase-in period" en route to universal coverage — failing to say, of course, they had already told the President and his team about their decision three weeks before at the private White House Map Room meeting.

* * *

It was midnight Friday, July 22, and Ira Magaziner was at his home in Rhode Island where he was celebrating his son's birthday. He had just gone to sleep. The phone rang. It was the President, calling from the White House.

Clinton was worried. He wanted Magaziner to come to the White House immediately, not realizing that the White House operator had reached him at his home in Rhode Island.

The President was alone; Hillary was in Oregon, launching a bus caravan for health care.

Magaziner told the President he couldn't come over then because he was in Rhode Island. But the President felt the need to talk anyway, and did so.

Clinton was deeply concerned. The Mitchell bill was about to be unveiled in the Senate. You know, the President mused aloud, if we wind up with nothing, how bad is that going to be?

You know the answer to that, Magaziner replied. It's going to be pretty bad politically and also substantively.

Yeah, I know, Clinton said.

The President knew he and his party would take a heavy political hit if no bill emerged. But they might have to pay that price rather than accept something that did more harm than good.

Magaziner agreed.

The President gave him an order: "I want you to tell me when that line is crossed."

Now they were down to their last stand: trying to win back the public. They had one final chance to ignite the kind of political support that had brought them to the White House: a bus trek across America to generate their own grassroots message to Congress *for* reform. Brutal as their battle had been so far, they could never have foreseen that the worst was yet to come.

18

The Phony Express

B Y THAT SUMMER, the First Lady thought she was prepared for anything. Every day for months, she had been demonized on right-wing talk radio shows, in print, and in national advertising campaigns. But nothing equaled what she experienced on the West Coast in late July, where she went to launch buses carrying volunteers to Washington to pressure Congress. It was the hatred on the faces in the crowds that so disturbed her.

They called their bus caravan the "Health Security Express," and the people they enlisted to travel on it "Reform Riders," a play on "Freedom Riders," the civil rights protesters who endured the bloody bus tours through a segregated Deep South in the early sixties. The Reform Riders had been chosen with the help of database files kept by the White House, Families USA, and HealthRIGHT, an organization created by former aides to Claude Pepper in 1992.

That earlier bus caravan had made history; the public, revolted by the violence against the Freedom Riders, touched by their courage and their appeal to the American conscience, had rallied behind the protesters, paving the way for the historic civil rights legislation Congress passed that decade. The Clinton bus caravan of the nineties, carrying people who were ill and their doctors, nurses, families, and friends, hoped to achieve the same end through the same tactics: to demonstrate to Congress through mass public pressure that the people demanded action on reform now. But what had had powerful political effect in the sixties was no longer operative in the nineties.

The public had long since wearied of, and grown cynical about, the politics of mass protest — the chanting demonstrators, the sign-waving citizens encamped before a statehouse, or the U.S. Capitol, or the White House, all playing their parts for the TV cameras. In his 1992 presidential campaign, Clinton had capitalized on his outsider, common-folks appeal on campaign trips by bus that allowed him to mingle with the citizens of Main Street and rural America. By the summer of 1994, only two years later, the very idea of another carefully staged political bus trip inspired either indifference or greater cynicism from a public and a press already deeply suspicious of media manipulation. The first rally, in Portland, Oregon, was an ominous foretaste of what was to come.

As the buses prepared to leave Portland on their route east, after a send-off that included an emotional speech by the First Lady, a rock band, appearances by a Hollywood actress, and a sixteen-year-old cancer patient, and a barrage of balloons loosed into the skies, people at the rally spotted a plane flying overhead. It towed a banner that read "Beware the Phony Express."

Even before that moment, troubling signs were visible. "Signs and banners of protesters almost equaled those of Clinton supporters," reported Patrick O'Neill in the *Portland Oregonian*. Furthermore, as Hillary Clinton learned that day, the protesters were more than a match for the supporters of reform when it came to raw emotional intensity. When the first buses reached the highway, they found a broken-down bus wreathed in red tape symbolizing governmental bureaucracy and hitched to a tow truck labeled "This is Clinton Health Care."

For the First Lady, the most alarming sign of hatred came the next day in Seattle, on Saturday morning, July 23, hours after her husband had made his emotional midnight phone call to Ira Magaziner. For days before she arrived in Seattle, anti-Hillary rhetoric had filled the talk shows. People were urged to demonstrate against her, against the President, and against "Clintoncare," the shorthand now used everywhere by opponents of their plan.

Hillary Clinton was accustomed to heckling; what she encountered as she spoke at that outdoor rally went far beyond. Standing at the front of the crowd were hundreds of angry men. "They were men in their twenties, thirties, forties," she said not long after. "I had not seen faces like that since the segregation battles of the sixties. They had such hatred on their faces. I mean, I've often been protested against by pro-life people, and I respect them. Usually, it's a couple of men who are in charge of a large group of women and children. This was different. Qualitatively different. Those faces, that's what scared me, that's what really bothered me."

When the loud jeers and catcalls came, some of the nurses tried to talk to the protesters. They were answered with furious expressions of rage — and not about health care alone. Exhibiting a deeper level of resentment, those protesters shouted that Bill and Hillary Clinton were going to destroy their way of life. They were going to ban guns, extend abortion rights, protect gays, socialize medicine.

After the First Lady finished speaking, she and her party got into their limousine. They had traveled only a short distance when their car was surrounded by protesters. "There must have been literally hundreds of them on either side," said the First Lady's aide, Melanne Verveer, who was in the car with Hillary. "I have never seen such frightening faces."

Later, the First Lady learned that there were concealed weapons at the rally. Two guns and a knife had been confiscated by her Secret Service agents working that Seattle crowd.

"I don't think the Washington press corps understands the depth of what's going on out there, and the way a lot of unbalanced, alienated, mean-spirited people are being given a license to be very disruptive," the First Lady told us in a White House conversation after her West Coast trip. "There isn't any counterbalance to this incredible twenty-four-hour-a-day hate that is being spewed out."

While Hillary was encountering that unsettling scene on the West Coast, readers of the *New York Times* were given a glimpse of an even more disturbing story that weekend: the revelation of Newt Gingrich's ultimate political goal. Until then Gingrich, uncharacteristically for so voluble and volatile a politician, had kept his strategic hand hidden, ceding the public spotlight to others. But in an interview with Gingrich, David E. Rosenbaum reported in the *Times* that Gingrich had united House Republicans against passage of health reform and hoped "to use the issue as a springboard to win Republican control of the House." He quoted Gingrich as saying that Clinton had won "an accidental election for President" and that Republicans believe "the health issue is their lever for prying control of the House away from the Democrats." The health issue, Gingrich told the reporter, "goes to the core of the difference between Democrats and Republicans." Gingrich predicted Republicans would pick up thirty-four House seats in the November elections, and if that happened, six disaffected Democrats would switch parties to give Republicans control of the House. Rosenbaum discounted that prediction. "Most neutral observers think a thirty-four switch is unlikely," he wrote. A gain of fifteen or twenty-five Republican seats was more realistic, leaving Republicans far short of their majority.

The story attracted little attention. It ran on page twenty-two, on Sunday morning, July 24, at the height of the summer vacation season. People had other things on their minds than Newt Gingrich and the possible future composition of the House of Representatives — or that Reform Rider bus caravan just beginning to wend its way across America.

Every one of the caravan routes — which set out from Portland, Dallas, Independence, and Boston — became an expedition into enemy territory; and at nearly each planned stop on the schedule, the enemy was there: better prepared, better armed, better mobilized. As the reformers traveled, they found their way marked by more angry protesters, by more planes buzzing overhead with their "Phony Express" banners trailing behind them, by more rusty buses covered with red tape and anti-reform placards. They were riding not to glory but to disaster. The longer they traveled, the greater the signs of opposition they encountered. Some of it was frightening; implicit threats of violence hung over the caravan, forcing local reform groups and the caravan organizers to cancel scheduled stops.

Only two days out, as they headed into Idaho, tour organizers "were so concerned about protesters in Boise that they canceled their appearance at the planned health care rally on the steps of the state capitol," Abigail Trafford reported from the scene in the *Washington Post*. When they rolled through Twin Falls, Idaho, they were further disheartened to find themselves greeted by nearly as many reform opponents as supporters — and, again, the opponents were far more vociferous.

Five days into their tour, moving across the Nebraska prairie, the Reform Riders ran into a nasty exchange with protesters in front of the North Platte Holiday Inn, where they planned to stay overnight.

"Most of you don't like Bill and Hillary and wouldn't support motherhood and apple pie if they were for it," said Tom Brownell, a Nebraskan, to shouting opponents who met them as their bus arrived.

"That's the truth," a fellow Nebraskan, Roger Carper, answered. "Bill and Hillary are immoral homosexual communists. I don't want them running health care."

That night, network newscasts reported more dismal scenes from the field. "The administration's bus caravan for health care kept on trucking today," network anchor Connie Chung began her lead-in on the *CBS Evening News*, "but the engines are groaning and flak is getting heavier with every step."

Correspondent Linda Douglass has that side of the story, Chung said, as the network switched to Douglass, reporting from Dallas. "It was another rough day for the health-reform bus crusade," the correspondent proclaimed. "Protesters gleefully towed a lame bus to the kickoff site in Dallas, while the original kickoff event at a church was canceled — too closely linked to the White House, said church leaders. Today's buses were met by fierce protesters — well-organized conservatives, anti-abortion activists, Ross Perot supporters — many afraid of what they've heard about the Clinton health reform."

None of this was coincidental. Nothing better displayed both the muscle and the tactical planning of the opponents than the crushing of this forlorn bus caravan that summer. It was the crowning success of the No Name Coalition and especially of the conservative political interest group, Citizens for a Sound Economy (CSE), in whose Washington, D.C., offices the No Name Coalition met.

By that summer, Citizens for a Sound Economy and the other groups allied with it had perfected their grassroots operations and their ability to manipulate the media to stir public fears.* They produced local newspaper ads and radio commercials targeting senators in politically conservative states — Georgia, Louisiana, Texas, Oklahoma, Montana among them — and House members as well. They sponsored scores of town hall meetings and forums, contacted hundreds of radio talk shows regularly, and made a stream of spokespeople available to attack the Clinton plan.

Their material poured out of Washington. Bumper stickers: "Government-Run Heath Care Makes Me Sick!" Posters: "Do you enjoy the *compassion* of the I.R.S. and the *service* of the Post Office . . . if so, you'll love Government-Run Health Care!" Campaign buttons: "Gov't Run Health Care" in the center of a bull's-eye with a line slashed through it. T-shirts: On the front, above a rippling American flag, the words "Government-Run Health Care?" Below the flag: "Not in My Country!" On the back: "Top Ten Reasons Why Government-Run Health Care Is a BAD Idea," followed by a list beginning "Having the government pick your doctor because he is the *cheapest.*"

They even passed out beach balls and Frisbees imprinted with their slogans to people attending holiday weekend picnics and state fairs and sent anti-reform material to high school debate teams nationwide. At one event, a beaming Newt Gingrich was photographed holding a beach ball with an anti-Clintoncare message.

Their most popular item was designed immediately after Clinton had displayed the red, white, and blue Health Security card before the nation — the card the President promised in his September 22, 1993, speech would guarantee all Americans health coverage that could never be taken away.

The Citizens for a Sound Economy version was a caricature of

---

*Citizens for a Sound Economy is one of the conservative groups, which include think tanks, magazines and newspapers, backed financially by Richard Mellon Scaife, an heir to the Pennsylvania Mellon bank and oil fortune, whom Newt Gingrich praised after the 1994 congressional elections as among those who "really created modern conservatism." Other New Right and ultraconservative groups funded by Scaife through grants and gifts totaling $400,000 a week, or more than $200 million over 20 years, include the Heritage Foundation, the Cato Institute, and the *American Spectator* magazine, a leading force in pushing the Whitewater/Vince Foster conspiracy theories. Scaife's powerful role in financing right-wing political efforts was best documented in a page one *Wall Street Journal* article by Phil Kuntz on October 12, 1995.

the Clinton card. Also red, white, and blue, it bore the message
"Health Insecurity" above a doctor's staff with a jagged line through
it. Underneath, alongside a made-up recipient's health number, it
said, "U Will Suffer." On the back this message was printed:

> This Card Entitles You to Endure Government-Run Health
> Care.
>> 1. The government will limit your choice of doctors.
>> 2. You will wait in line for health care.
>> 3. The government will decide what insurance you buy.
>> 4. The government will undermine development of new
>> drugs and treatment.
>> 5. You will pay *more* for *less* care.

All these efforts were the result of long, careful — and quiet —
advance planning. By the time the ill-fated bus caravan took to
the highways, Citizens for a Sound Economy operatives, working
closely — and secretly — with Newt Gingrich's Capitol Hill office
and with Republican senators, had mapped out plans to derail the
Reform Riders wherever they went. The first step was to obtain the
routes the buses would take; that was easy, because the Health Security Express planners issued public calls for volunteers to meet their
buses and help plan rallies en route to Washington.

For the opponents, lying in wait like a guerrilla army, these
routes were, as one said, "a dream come true." Texas, Oklahoma,
Louisiana, Nebraska — this was *their* turf, and they marshaled *their*
forces to overwhelm the overmatched reformers. "We let all our
members know, tens of thousands of them," said Elizabeth Sauer,
Citizens for a Sound Economy's mobilization director, "and gave
them the routes. We had built up a great activist base for the last year
that we could call upon to say, 'Hey, this is it. This is the time. Make
your sign; let's go!' "

Their armies sprang to life. They prepared to meet the buses with
protest rallies of their own, working with the Christian Coalition and
other conservative and antitax groups.

And protest rallies were not the whole story. This was a battle
to win media coverage, to influence reporting so that it appeared
the American people, on farms and on Main Street, were ardently

opposed to this Big Government plan. NFIB made small-business owners available to the press in every one of the thirty-six states and all the state capitals through which the bus caravan passed. NFIB's idea was to allow these members to express *"their* real-life opinions" and especially their opposition to an employer mandate. To that end, CSE media director Brent Bahler, a former aide to Bob Dole, mounted an aggressive, and effective, press campaign. He timed protests to coincide with local TV deadlines as the buses arrived. He arranged for a "middle-class truth squad" to be planted at the rallies and to offer opinions by its members to local reporters. He supervised the mailing of radio scripts to five hundred media outlets along the routes. The scripts urged listeners to demonstrate against the caravan, calling it "a media stunt pushing government-controlled health care," and a forerunner of "big bureaucracies, more regulations and a huge price tag. Who pays for it? The middle class . . . like we always do." Listeners were urged to "get on the phone" with their senator and "make him understand [the Phony Express] doesn't speak for you."

The goal, as Elizabeth Sauer articulated it, even before their assault was launched that summer, was to "hit from all sides" and "beat them at every level."

So they did. To ensure the greatest media exposure, and the most concentrated political attack, Citizens for a Sound Economy operatives talked daily with the Rush Limbaugh show and with their Republican allies on Capitol Hill. On the day the first buses left Portland, the House Republican Theme Team, operating under Newt Gingrich's guiding hand, ridiculed the bus tour, leading the *Wall Street Journal* to report the next day that "House Republicans label the Clinton bus 'The Phony Express' " — the very name Citizens for a Sound Economy had chosen secretly weeks before.

To ensure that everyone was "on message," a goal the Clinton side seldom achieved, Lamar Smith, chairman of the Republican Theme Team, advised all House GOP members on July 22, "We will keep you informed of the week's themes via your fax machines, electronic mail [and personal aides]. Members are encouraged to come to the floor and join us. Prepared speeches are always available and themes are posted in the Republican cloakroom."

He singled out a speech by Porter Goss of Florida as an example of what GOP members should be saying about the bus tour. "Contrary to what the White House war room and political consultants might believe, government is not like a campaign. Every time you run into trouble, you cannot just climb aboard a bus and run over the truth."

To older stalwarts of The System, this latest example of a negative media political war was an insult, an affront to the real players who were charged with forging policy and making hard public choices. While the bus caravan lumbered on its three-thousand-mile journey that summer, Robert C. Byrd arose on the Senate floor to deliver one of his famous orations in defense of the institution he believed to be the premier governing body in the world. His theme was the outrage of abusing The System through improper procedure. The year before, when the Clintons had wanted Congress to pass their health plan under the streamlined reconciliation legislative process, Byrd had blocked them. The senators would not have had proper time for deliberation, he felt. Now, as he addressed the health reform issue in the context of the daily assault on the bus tour and the increasing wave of negative ads against the Clinton plan, he worried that the much-awaited Senate debate had been reduced to irresponsible sloganeering before it even began.

"It is critically important that we turn down the noise and cool off the rhetoric on this far-reaching issue," Byrd told his colleagues. "The interest groups are swarming, and the pulling and tugging on each senator is enough to sever arms and legs from the corporeal whole — and all of this before we even have seen a bill which we will be voting on."

With quavering voice, the West Virginia Democrat, a former Senate majority leader, railed against this latest example of "the oversimplification and gross politicization" of a hot issue. He protested that the American people were ill served "by these chaotic orgies that occur whenever there is a lot at stake in Washington," bemoaned the lack of a climate "for cool, reasoned study and debate, which is as rare in this town as any of the rarest endangered species." "How can anyone," he solemnly asked, reaching back to antiquity for his analogy, "fail to be influenced by the cacophony of noise and shrill rhetoric on this issue? One would have to take up residence in a cave like Timon of Athens and then wear earplugs to avoid the din."

The old senator was right, of course. Right, too, philosophically in his penultimate message to the Senate: "This Senate is being looked to for leadership by the nation on a matter about which people care very deeply. They will watch and judge and rightfully hold us accountable for whatever we enact in the way of health reform. There is no ducking this one. There is no finessing it. This health care legislation will have ramifications for years in every facet of our national life. Too timid a proposal could be hurtful to our people, while too broad a proposal could devastate our economy. Now is the time for thoughtful analysis and calm, reasoned thinking."

But in a larger sense Byrd was wrong. His precious rational Senate no longer existed. They could not close the chamber doors and tune out the rhetoric. Media manipulation was part of The System. The cameras were already in the room, and they, the senators, posed and postured before them. In the media skirmishes of the nineties, sound and fury, not sober reflection, won the war.

As Bob Bennett, the Republican from Utah, watched the bus caravan unfold through news reports and private advisories from political field operatives, he became convinced the tour was providing a symbol for the failure of the entire Clinton campaign. In the Senate cloakroom, Bennett and Republican colleagues swapped stories about how outnumbered the Clinton reformers were, how small were the crowds of supporters they were drawing. When Bill Clinton campaigned in Seattle in 1992, Senator Slade Gorton told Bennett, he drew something like seventy-five thousand people. When Hillary was there with this bus tour just a few days earlier, she drew something like twelve hundred people.

"We had an ongoing report of towns where the bus tour didn't stop because they had been told in advance that the picketers outnumbered the supporters," Bennett recalled. "They were told to just keep rolling through; it would be embarrassing for them if they stopped."

When the buses were about to enter Salt Lake City, his state capital, Bennett planned to go on the air to oppose them. On advice of his press aides, he decided not to. "Don't do it, senator," he was advised. "It will give them more attention than they'll get if you say nothing." So the buses came and went through Salt Lake, Bennett said, "and I don't think twenty people turned out to greet them."

In Washington, the planners of the bus tour were glum. The purpose of the caravan was to remind wavering members of Congress that America's middle class, not just those people without insurance, backed reform. The Reform Riders were chosen from the ranks of the middle class whose personal stories could enlist support from others like them. From the beginning, though, they suffered from lack of funds and the broad public support they needed to persuade an increasingly doubtful Congress they enjoyed significant backing. No business organization supported them. For sponsorship, and for funds, they relied on liberal groups like Families USA, HealthRIGHT, and the unions — hardly the heart of America's middle class.

Now another hope was dashed: that their tour would attract favorable press coverage, thereby signaling members of Congress that the public was rallying behind health reform. Instead, the actions of their opponents attracted most attention.

As the bus tour ran into daily obstacles, leading to more negative daily stories, planners in Washington raged about the coverage. "This is not a traveling road show," said Greg Marchildon of Families USA while perched on a Formica conference table in their makeshift D.C. political "boiler room" late that July. "Last night's CBS piece was an atrocity, the most unbalanced piece of television news I've ever seen in my life. These are real people, with real problems, on these buses. This is all about trying to put real faces behind the mysterious poll data we keep hearing about: that eighty percent of Americans want guaranteed health care, that seventy-five percent want their employers to kick in for health insurance. If Congress doesn't take action, these problems are not going to get solved. It's time for Congress to shut up and get it done."

But no amount of railing or frustrated political rhetoric could alter the reality of what the Reform Rider caravan experienced. "We are trying to get Congress to respond to the American people," said

Families USA's Arnold Bennett above the din of the bus tour activities he directed from his Washington headquarters. Unbeknownst to most reporters covering the tour, Bennett said, nurses on the caravan were collecting letters and postcards written by constituents and urging their representatives to support health care reform. "But the problem is," Bennett complained, "it just doesn't get in the papers." Besides, in this war, relying on postcards and letters for victory was like employing slings and arrows against howitzers and rockets.

The great media event of the caravan, the one planned to generate a new burst of public support for reform, took place in Harry Truman's hometown of Independence, Missouri. There, on July 30, the President, the First Lady, the Vice President, and Mrs. Gore would make speeches. After their appearances, the last of the bus caravans would depart, to the accompaniment of hoped-for favorable media coverage, scheduled to arrive at the Capitol at the same time as the buses from all the other cities.

Both the date and the place provided another example of how symbolism drives substance in the media battle for public notice. Exactly twenty-nine years before, in 1965, Lyndon Johnson had flown to Independence on Air Force One to sign the bill enacting Medicare into law, seated next to Harry Truman, who had fought for such national health coverage long before. With appropriate ceremony, LBJ presented the old Missourian with the pen he had just used.

The Clintons and the other officials participating at the Independence event in 1994 did their best to live up to this history. They spoke ardently. They reminded people of their campaign promise to "put people first." They held ailing children's hands. They appealed to the nation's conscience.

It didn't work. Everyone appeared distracted, and so was the nation. By then, other events had intruded. The day before, trade talks with Japan had collapsed. Negotiations with the Bosnian Serbs were failing. A doctor had been shot to death at an abortion clinic in Pensacola, Florida. National newscasts were focusing on these and other matters: on peace prospects in the Middle East, on people starving in Rwanda, on horrifying scenes of "ethnic cleansing" in the

Balkans, and, most of all, on the nationally televised murder case of O. J. Simpson.

Against this backdrop, and in the enervating summer heat, senses were dulled, especially to hearing more "health care horror stories." The public had tuned out. The Reform Riders resumed their trek to Washington, but by now little public attention was being paid to them.

Two days later, Jerry McEntee of the American Federation of State, County and Municipal Employees accompanied the President on Air Force One to a bus stop rally in Liberty State Park, New Jersey. He was struck by Clinton's physical appearance and by his state of mind. "He was absolutely exhausted," McEntee said of the President. "In about twenty minutes he must have yawned fifteen times." But even as he yawned, Clinton still wanted to talk. The President expressed deep disappointment. The press wasn't helpful, Clinton complained; it didn't cover the issues adequately. Neither were some members of his own party helpful, especially in the Senate; they seemed to have forgotten their political affiliation. As for the Republicans, well, obviously, the President said, their House and Senate leaders had no interest in cooperating. Look, he went on, Dole was in New Hampshire a month after I was sworn in; it doesn't take a rocket scientist to know where he's going. Still, Clinton's fatigue and frustration notwithstanding, McEntee was struck by the passion with which the President spoke, both privately and then, shortly, in public. Standing in the shadow of the Statue of Liberty, pounding the lectern so hard that he knocked the presidential seal to the ground, Clinton denounced the "name-calling" and "demagoguery" employed by opponents. "Don't let the fearmongers, don't let the dividers, don't let the people who disseminate false information frighten the United States Congress into walking away from the opportunity of a lifetime," the President implored. But even as he spoke, the assault on the bus caravans converging toward Washington continued. The day before, in Louisville, the Midwest caravan had experienced more bitter heckling from protesters who once again were far better organized than badly outnumbered reformers. When the Reform Rider bus pulled into a parking lot of the First Unitarian Church that Sunday, the first four passengers to disembark in wheelchairs were greeted by masses of protesters waving right-to-life signs and chanting "Go back to Russia!" The riders encountered more fierce protesters the next day as their bus moved east toward Richmond, Virginia, at about the same time the President was hoarsely trying to rally public support while framed against the backdrop of the Statue of Liberty.

On August 3, McEntee heard Clinton give another emotional address — "one of the greatest speeches I ever heard him make" — in the White House Rose Garden, where he and the First Lady greeted six hundred of the Reform Riders after their buses finally arrived in Washington, timed to coincide with the day Mitchell introduced his health reform "rescue" in the Senate.

It was an emotional occasion. The Clintons listened intently as some of the riders told their personal stories. One of them, Daniel Lumley, who made the long bus trip from Oregon, told how he had lost an arm and a leg in a motorcycle accident after college, and described the difficulties he had endured since as one of those Americans without health insurance. Even more emotional was the moment when John Cox of Athens, Texas, explained how his wife, Jan, had died of stomach cancer while he was on the bus caravan to Washington.

Cox, a former newspaper editor and manager of a Christian radio station, was unemployed and without health insurance when his wife was diagnosed in 1991. When the Coxes heard about the bus caravan, his wife told him, "John, get on it. Take a message . . . tell every person you can," Cox explained to the hushed audience on the White House lawn. "We buried her on Monday and I'm here today to tell Congress right is right," he said. "Unless we can assure universal health coverage to all Americans, then life, liberty, and the pursuit of happiness for some is just a dream."

He ended with an emotional plea. "Let us tell the Senate," he said his voice rising, "let us tell the congressmen: 'Do it now!' "

The First Lady wept. The President was visibly shaken.

"Congress has to decide whether it's going to listen to the insurance companies or to Jan Cox's last wish," the President said, when he spoke to the bus riders.

In her speech, the First Lady decried the Washington lobbyists and special-interest groups. "They are being paid to stop our progress and stop your journey," she said. "You are the American Association for Ordinary Hardworking Citizens." *That* story led the evening network news.

Bruce Fried, the lobbyist founder of the Blueberry Donut Group two years before, attended the event that day. As he heard Cox speak, conflicting emotions washed over him in the summer heat. For a moment he was moved. He was glad to be reminded that there was something more profound at stake than who would win the White House in 1996. This fight was still about whether the country would attend to its own human needs.

But how the hell did we get here? he thought, when he paused to think of the policy options left. The health care battle was hanging by a thread. If they got the votes to pass anything, it would be something people thought was the lowest common denominator six months ago.

The caravan made its last stop the next day. Around noon, under a blazing Washington sun, several hundred people began descending from buses parked near the Capitol steps. Some were lowered from the buses in wheelchairs. They brought with them thousands of letters collected during their two-week tour that urged Congress to act immediately.

Their final rally began. David Bonior, the Democratic House majority whip, tried to stir passions. Standing on the west steps of the Capitol, he offered a political play on words: "We had hoped to work together with Republicans, but instead they keep on *doling* out misinformation . . . and *doling* out mistruths . . . and *doling* out falsehoods . . . and *doling* out scare words like 'Big Government' and 'socialized medicine.' " A union president, Owen Bieber of the United Auto Workers, offered more of the same: "Bob Dole and Newt Gingrich are leading a cynical campaign to mislead the American people. Bob Dole and Newt Gingrich couldn't care less about the thirty-nine million without health care insurance. They don't give a damn."

One of the bus riders, Karen Divinity of New Orleans, a Medicaid mother whose daughter suffered from diabetes, asthma, and epilepsy, broke down in tears as she told her story, adding, through her sobs, a plea to her senators: "Please Senators Breaux and Johnston, pass health reform. Do it for my sake!"

Peter Yarrow, the folk singer who had stirred countless protest rallies during the civil rights and Vietnam War demonstrations of the sixties and seventies, stepped forward and strummed a familiar anthem on his guitar. To Woody Guthrie's *This Land Is Your Land*, he added verses for the occasion:

> *This has been a war, my friend,*
> *But now it's got to end.*
> *We're going to pass this law*
> *You and me . . . you and me!*

His words rang out in the stifling summer air. Nearby, a small crowd of the curious — tourists and passersby — watched. The turnout was sparse; the steps of the Capitol, where they assembled, were barely covered by people. Soon it was over. They slowly filed back to their buses. It was not the sixties. This was the nineties, as if anyone watching needed to be reminded of the difference.

19

Summer of
Discontent

GEORGE MITCHELL ENTERED the Labor Committee
room shortly after five-thirty in the afternoon and for the next
two hours, behind closed doors to a standing room audience of pro-
reform leaders, gave what many present described as an astonishing
presentation of the politics and possibilities of reform. It was not an
academic exercise for the Senate majority leader. By this last Friday
of July, in a summer of discontent for American politics in general,
for Democrats in particular, and for the reformers most of all, this
was the make-or-break moment. Even as they assembled, the ill-
fated Reform Rider caravan was experiencing its difficulties on its
nationwide journey to the capital, the President and the First Lady
were preparing to fly to Independence, Missouri, the next morning for their hapless attempt to re-ignite public enthusiasm, and
Republicans, sensing the kill, were on the attack everywhere.

In the hearing room, as Mitchell began speaking, the mood
was one of disbelief. No one knew better than these leaders — the
unions, the consumer groups, the seniors, the nursing and hospital
groups — how precarious their position was. They turned out in record numbers, though, for good reason: This was the moment when
the majority leader would unveil the outline of the rescue bill that
he would introduce to the Senate the next week simultaneously with
the measure in the House that Majority Leader Dick Gephardt had
adapted from the Ways and Means Committee bill.

Mitchell spoke without notes for about five minutes, defending his compromise bill as "a voluntary system which builds upon the private insurance market" and which would abolish Medicaid, rolling its recipients into the private sector. His compromise was much less bureaucratic and government-driven than the Clinton plan. It put off any requirement that employers provide employees health insurance until early in the next century. It made a major concession to small business by exempting any employer with twenty-five or fewer employees from providing coverage; that included the great majority of all small businesses in America. It aimed at guaranteeing insurance for 95 percent of Americans by the year 2000, leaving the rest of the distance to universal coverage for later.

Then, relaxed and in obvious good humor, Mitchell told the supporters he would stay as long as they wanted in order to answer any questions For nearly two hours, calmly and confidently, displaying a sure grasp of the issues and a convincing sense of how they could be resolved politically, he fielded every conceivable question — from mandates and cost containment to taxation and benefits to malpractice reforms and burdens on providers. It was an extraordinary performance, and, long after, when reform itself had died, people there recalled it as one of the few bright moments in a terribly dark affair. "I don't know George Mitchell," a union leader who attended said, "but to see him sit there and deal so directly and forthrightly with issue after issue and answer any question anybody wanted was amazingly impressive."

His confidence was contagious. By the time their meeting adjourned, Mitchell had made believers of cynics. Not only did they see a slight chance of saving something; they just might win their war after all.

When August began, the hope among congressional and White House strategists was that both Senate and House leaders would rally their Democratic majorities behind two pending measures. The first was final action on a crime bill already passed by both houses and seemingly agreed to in a Senate-House conference. This seemed an easy matter. At a time when the specter of crime led all public concerns in the polls, this bill appeared to have widespread public and bipartisan political support. It provided more money for prisons and police, added strong new provisions for punishing criminals (including "three strikes and you're out"), expanded the list of banned assault weapons, and added funds for crime prevention programs. Ideologically, the bill represented a move to the right by liberal Democratic majorities. The bill bore the fingerprints of many, from Ted Kennedy on the left to Phil Gramm on the right; seemingly, all political arguments had been resolved by this summer. The Senate had passed its version nine months before, in November 1993. The House passed its crime bill the following April. Now, more than three months later, all that remained was final approval of the already agreed upon joint House-Senate conference report. Once it was approved, or so the Democrats thought, they would pass the respective health bills cobbled together desperately in July by Mitchell and Gephardt. Then they would take their summer break and head home well positioned to defend their record before voters in the November elections.

George Mitchell had his moment, a capstone of his career, it was said in the press, when he stood before a tangle of microphones and wires sprouting from a lectern positioned directly beneath a Stuart painting of George Washington in the Capitol. A horde of reporters jostled each other amid TV cameras, Democratic staff members, and reform supporters who came to cheer Mitchell on. It was Tuesday morning, August 2, and in typically measured manner, the majority leader described with pride the essence of his reform bill: over the next six years, thirty million more Americans would be insured. He would formally introduce his bill in the Senate the next day, Mitchell announced, with debate to begin on August 9.

At the White House, in an orchestrated response, the President hailed the Mitchell bill and stressed the significance of this moment. "During the course of this historic floor debate," the President said, "there will be those who say that reaching universal coverage is not necessary. To those people I say, 'Let the debate begin.' Those of us who are fighting for universal coverage are fighting for middle-class Americans."

Not surprisingly, the First Lady was even stronger. She was on the Hill when Mitchell stood before the microphones and, at a separate gathering of supporters, she characterized opponents as ideologues who "believe in a Darwinian world where the fit get whatever they can grab for themselves and the rest are left to nature's mercies." Health care was a "moral challenge." She dismissed the opposition as "a small minority with loud, squeaky voices that are driving this debate."

Bob Dole disagreed in a statement he gave the press that day at the Capitol. To him, the Mitchell bill was warmed-over Clinton, "very similar in that it prescribes more government, more taxes, and more entitlements." But for once, the reformers had the upper hand in the media. In a lead editorial the next morning, the *Washington Post* praised the Mitchell bill as a "substantial improvement in the U.S. health care system." The paper added: "The question isn't whether he should have made the plan more ambitious in some respects. It's whether even this plan can survive. The answer lies mainly with the moderates of both parties, but the Republicans particularly. Do they vote for this, or do they cave in the face of pressure within their own party and continue to backpedal?"

Positive press coverage continued that day, August 3, as both the Mitchell and Gephardt bills were formally introduced. To maintain the public-relations edge and to set the stage for the congressional debate, the President greeted the Reform Riders at the White House; then he scheduled a prime-time TV news conference for the next night, where he continued to court public support by employing a favorite Ronald Reagan tactic: He singled out two of the Reform Riders, invited to his news conference, as the kind of people who would be helped. The President hoped the coming debate would "grip the imagination of ordinary citizens" and create a climate for passage of a bill "that works, that solves the human problem."

Democratic congressional leaders reinforced his point, and further heightened public expectation that, finally, the time for reform had arrived. Hours before the President's news conference, Speaker Tom Foley held his own Capitol press briefing. All members of Congress had been told to postpone their August vacations until after health reform bills came to a vote, he said, speaking for himself and George Mitchell. Foley said gravely, underscoring the importance of the moment, that the House would set aside five full days, beginning Monday, August 15, to debate and then vote on reform legislation. Thus, by the end of that week, every member of the House would be on record as either supporting or opposing reform.

Among the many questions about prospects for passage, Foley was asked one about the pending crime bill. The Speaker expressed confidence. The joint Senate-House conference on the crime bill would be concluded and the conference report adopted, he said with assurance. When asked how important the crime bill was to the Democratic Party in the crucial November elections, now only three months away, the Speaker replied: "It is high priority, and we intend to pass it."

One-two, crime and health: Quick successes, then on to the elections.

For a brief moment, everything seemed to be falling into place. Gephardt introduced his bill, based on the Ways and Means measure. It promised to give every American health insurance by 1999, either through private plans financed largely by employers (the employer mandate) or through a vast expansion of Medicare to include millions of workers and the poor.

On August 9, the American Association of Retired Persons (AARP) formally endorsed both the Mitchell bill and the more liberal Gephardt measure. It ended an embarrassing situation for AARP's John Rother. Even though he had been working ceaselessly as head of the Health Reform Project to build support for the Clinton plan, his own organization had held back. AARP had been badly burned by the failure of the Medicare catastrophic-insurance legislation five years earlier. It endorsed that bill early, saw it become law, and then watched rival organizations of senior citizens lead the battle to have it repealed. This time, its directors wanted to err on the side of caution.

The early failure of AARP to endorse the President's bill had been a source of intense frustration at the White House, particularly to the First Lady. Rother tried to explain that AARP was not an organization that committed easily to such a major national fight. He said its board of directors and its officials around the country had been subjected to unprecedented pressure from the anti-reform groups, and those pressures were increasing.

Rother had never experienced anything like it. He could not keep up with the rumors. It was amazing, he thought, where people got their information — from talk shows, from opposition ads, from all the anti-reform literature flooding the country. "I guess," he said wearily, conceding defeat in the battle for public information, "none of us has gotten through to them on the larger issues."

It went beyond misinformation, though, Rother felt. This wasn't a case where people agreed to disagree, as is normal in The System. A lot of the phone calls, a lot of the opposition, had been fueled "by a kind of hatred that [went] well beyond health care."

Rother himself had been the target of anonymous hate calls to his home, and members of his board received calls demanding his resignation. Goodness knows there had been bitter battles in Johnson's, Nixon's, and Reagan's time, Rother said, "but not like this, and not with these tactics, this kind of stoking up of hatred. It's profoundly discouraging, not just for health reform, but for what it says about the country, what it says about our institutions. I thought we were better than that. Win or lose, let's have a debate, let's vote, let's decide. It doesn't feel like we're going to deal with it that way."

But Rother had kept working on his board of directors. At one board meeting that summer, Rother began his presentation by citing a Paul Conrad cartoon in the *Los Angeles Times*. It showed a U.S. senator in 1935 railing against Social Security, against taxes on small business, against Big Government and bureaucracy. We've had the same argument over and over again for sixty years in this country and we still haven't resolved it, Rother told his board. You'd think after Social Security, the GI Bill, Medicare, at least some of these issues would be resolved. But they haven't been. Now we have another chance.

AARP summoned up its courage and endorsed the Democratic proposals.

Meantime, the proponents finally began coordinating their message. At seven-thirty each evening, White House, congressional, and outside reform allies convened in the vice president's splendid office in the Capitol building to plan their strategy for the next day.

At one of their early meetings, an old idea resurfaced: have Democratic senators take to the floor and hold up *their* health care benefits cards. They would remind the American people this is what the taxpayers have provided every member of Congress: guaranteed, comprehensive, highly affordable insurance, offering a range of private choices, covering preexisting conditions, with 75 percent of it paid for by the taxpayers. This was the theme that had been proposed six months before — and rejected at that memorable White House meeting during a February blizzard. Now, at this last moment, it was suggested again and this time endorsed. C-SPAN viewers heard: "Congress has mandated its employer — the taxpayers of the United States — to pay approximately three-quarters of their health insurance. If it's good enough for Congress, it should be good enough for the American people. Demand that Congress give the American people as good a plan as they have."

To drive home the point, they introduced a bill providing that members of Congress be disqualified from participating in the Federal Employee Health Benefits program if "the Congress has failed to enact legislation that extends health insurance to all Americans and reduces inflation in health care costs."

For perhaps the only time in the entire debate, Democrats momentarily regained the initiative. It didn't last.

Newt Gingrich struck. For more than a year, he had marshaled his forces and coordinated the Republican attack strategy with the congressional Theme Team and the economic allies in the grassroots campaign. Now the time had come to spring his "ambush" — and he did so with an audacity that stunned the Democrats. He attacked not the Democratic health bill being introduced in the House, but the least expected target, the crime bill.

Although most Republicans had voted for the separate versions of the bill when it passed the House and Senate months before, Gingrich decided the compromise crime bill already hammered out in the House-Senate conference committee offered a great target of opportunity. For months he had planned, as he boasted to us, to "ambush the jeep" carrying health care. Now, he established a road block around the crime bill. His intent was to bring Congress to a halt, strand the health effort, send the lawmakers home, and deny Democrats the opportunity to record a vote on health reform before the fall elections.

As was often the case, divisions among the Democrats created the opportunity for Gingrich. Rural Democrats, sensitive to pressures from the National Rifle Association (NRA), had joined most Republicans in opposing the gun-control features of the crime bill. But Clinton had rallied public opinion and most Democrats on closely contested votes, defeating amendments that would have stripped gun control from the legislation. But while the bill was in conference between the House and Senate, the Congressional Black Caucus joined by some white liberals mounted a last-ditch effort to modify the tougher death penalty provisions. Claiming that African-Americans were singled out disproportionately for capital punishment, they fought to allow appeals to cite statistics of "disproportionate" application to blacks. It was, in effect, an argument on the "quotas" issue in an emotion-laden Death Row setting.

The White House tried to find a formula to appease the liberals, but ultimately gave up and let the death penalty forces prevail in the conference. To soften the blow, it persuaded the conferees to increase spending on some inner-city social programs designed to keep youngsters out of the criminal justice system.

On Gingrich's signal, House Republicans launched a superbly coordinated assault on those programs. In speech after speech, they stigmatized the crime bill as loaded down with "old-fashioned pork barrel programs." They wanted the bill redrawn, the Democratic social-welfare crime prevention "pork" removed, and an anticrime measure with even stronger penalties passed. All the elements that had been employed so successfully month after month in the health battle — the grassroots lobbies, the fax alerts, the carefully coordinated messages — came into play. Their most effective weapon was fear of Big Government. Now that theme was used to defeat the crime bill and block a vote on health reform.

Notwithstanding that many conservative hands fashioned the crime bill, now it was depicted as an example of liberal Big Government run amok: It was a $30 billion boondoggle for the "compassion and welfare industry." It was a bill that would trample states' rights and create such do-good, liberal "crime prevention" programs as midnight basketball leagues for inner-city youths, arts-and-crafts centers, gender-sensitivity training sessions for federal judges. While the Republicans and the talk shows focused on the "pork barrel" social spending, the NRA stirred up a flood of letters, faxes, and phone calls to Capitol Hill on the gun-control provisions. It was a devastating one-two punch.

The intensity of the attack took both White House and Democratic congressional leaders aback. They were slow to realize that delay of the crime bill would mean yet further, and potentially fatal, postponement of action on health.

From the beginning, virtually every administration political strategist from the President and First Lady down took comfort in the belief that Republicans would pay a fearful political price if they delayed or filibustered a health bill in the final weeks of Congress. They did not consider the possibility that Republicans could defeat reform by blocking the bill that *preceded* health care on the calendar.

Gingrich had outsmarted them.

The Founders of The System created its many checks and balances to make it difficult for political power to be abused and for unwise acts to be hastily passed into law. But they also feared the destructive effects of factions that could thwart progress and subvert the will of the majority. Free elections were intended as one remedy. The rise of the political parties provided a way for the political majority to set the legislative agenda and force action on critical issues. For most of the past sixty years, the American people had entrusted that power to the Democratic Party.

And since January 20, 1993, President Clinton, the first Democratic President to work with a Democratic Congress in more than a decade, had placed his political fate in the hands of his party's congressional leadership. Now that leadership in the legislative body closest to the people, the House of Representatives, sought to exercise its power on the most basic of procedures for the majority, setting the calendar for floor action. On August 11, Foley and Gephardt decided to bring the crime bill before the full House for debate and then a vote. It was four days before members were supposed to begin debating health reform, and a week, which now seemed like a month, after Gephardt had introduced the health bill. It was a fateful moment.

Democrats knew the procedural vote to begin debate on the crime bill would be close, but they expected to prevail. Behind closed doors, where the Democratic whips were caucusing to bring their troops into line, Gephardt was warned that his attempt might fail. He exploded, then uttered what proved to be a bitterly prophetic remark. "If we can't even call up the crime bill for a vote, dammit, we might as well give Republicans [control of] this place," Gephardt said angrily. "We sure as hell can't run it."

To his consternation, the Democrats couldn't. The procedural motion was rejected by the House. It wasn't even close. They lost by fifteen votes, two hundred twenty-five to two hundred ten, a defeat made more bitter by the way it was fashioned. Eleven moderate Republicans defected and voted with the Democratic majority. Under normal political calculus, that would have guaranteed victory. Not this time. Fifty-eight Democrats bolted *their* party and joined the opposition. Most of those Democrats were rural representatives who had been targeted heavily by NRA lobbyists fighting gun-control provisions in the bill. But ten of the defecting Democrats were members of the Congressional Black Caucus who had failed to achieve restrictions *they* wanted on the death penalty. For wholly different reasons, the liberal and conservative wings of the Democratic Party handed Gingrich a victory he could not have achieved on his own.

Pleading for votes that August 11, Speaker Tom Foley closed his speech with a rare emotional appeal to his colleagues. "Let us not be a helpless giant!" he cried. Yet that is what they had become. The Democratic leadership had lost control of the House floor. Their party's congressional and presidential power was unraveling dramatically.

The night after that crushing defeat, the two top White House aides, Leon Panetta and Harold Ickes, went to Foley's Capitol office. They were joined by Gephardt and other Democratic House leaders. After huddling behind closed doors, they moved across the Capitol to Majority Leader Mitchell's office on the Senate side. When they emerged after four hours, their faces were grim, and they did not even attempt to disguise the enormous loss they had suffered. Health care would be delayed indefinitely, they announced. Congress would postpone its August vacation in order to permit Democrats to reopen negotiations on the crime bill with dissident members of their own party — and the few Republicans whose votes would be crucial for passage.

Once again, health care would have to wait. And wait. And wait some more.

Delay and obstruction also tied up the Senate, and there, too, the majority Democrats showed they could not stand together.

No sooner had Mitchell introduced his bill than Democrats heard it derided — as "a budgetary disaster," as "an immense taxing and spending bill," as a bill that "promotes and subsidizes abortion," as one that would "force hospitals to close," as another example of how Democratic "health scare bills have frightened middle-class Americans." Phil Gramm of Texas repeated the cry he had been sounding for more than nine months: He would filibuster any "government takeover of the health care system"; health reform would pass only over his "cold, dead political body." His conservative colleague Malcolm Wallop of Wyoming expressed the view of those whose distrust of the federal government is deepest: "Make no mistake, this government does not seek to serve, but to control. Americans are frightened of it. We will let it control us at our peril."

Democrats were equally apocalyptic. If this effort failed, it would be "another generation" before reform could be achieved, Claiborne Pell of Rhode Island said. Herbert Kohl of Wisconsin warned of other consequences. If they fail to pass reform, "the people's judgment will be severe," he said. "This debate then is about more than health care. This is about whether we can govern."

But the opposition was unrelenting. After forty hours of Republican speeches spread over six days of Senate sessions, on Monday, August 15, Mitchell made an extraordinary threat. He would keep the Senate in nonstop, round-the-clock session until Republicans agreed to start voting, he declared. That would mean, the normally mild-mannered majority leader said, the Senate would "remain in contentious session" until health care was resolved.

Through it all, Mainstream Coalition members kept slipping into John Chafee's hideaway in search of a bipartisan solution. They faced even greater problems than before in writing a bill they could defend as economically sound. Once more, it came down to a judgment by the Congressional Budget Office (CBO).

By then, the seventeen analysts in Bob Reischauer's CBO shop were swamped. As Dick Gephardt later admitted, "None of us foresaw that you were going to have eight competing plans trying to work through the Senate and House. CBO was just not capable of giving us the estimates you need."

From Reischauer's point of view, there was a problem, all right — but not the one Gephardt described. It lay with the members of Congress, not the CBO. Reischauer was no Congress-basher. As an academic, he had a rare appreciation for the pressures operating on political people. He thought it "amazing" that some of the legislators and their staffs could hack even partway through the jungle of questions involved in redesigning the entire health care system — especially when they had such limited time and faced such political pressures. Privately, the CBO director said too many of the plans "weren't viable." In some cases, they weren't even plans. He said, "It's absurd to think that a group of twenty people [like the Mainstream group] could do something like this [in the time at hand]." It would have been far wiser, he thought, for congressional leaders to "create a special committee" with adequate staffing to wrestle with "the major domestic policy change of the last hundred years. But in this Congress, the leadership is so weak and the power centers so diffuse, they couldn't do this."

Now, with all these different individuals and groups — Mitchell, Gephardt, the Mainstream, Cooper-Grandy, Rowland-Bilirakis, and the rest — constantly revising their bills, Reischauer and the CBO were struggling with "all the inconsistencies and missing pieces":

> We'd do one of these six- or seven-page cost estimates and give
> it back to them, and invariably they were two hundred billion

dollars in the hole over a ten-year period, which they didn't want to be. It's like chump change — like one or two percent of government health spending over this period — really a tiny amount. But it had an electric impact. They would agonize and give us options on how to bring this together, and then they'd have to try and sell them to the interest groups. Often they were standing up there saying, "We're waiting for CBO numbers." And my staff is telling me, "Call your friends in the press and tell 'em we worked all Sunday night and gave them the goddamn numbers. They're in their back pocket. It's just that they don't like the numbers."

For the Mainstream group, time constraints and political pressures compounded these problems. Reischauer compared those Mainstream meetings that August to an Indian sweat lodge: twenty senators talking past each other and fifty staff people lining the walls in hundred-degree temperatures with everybody trying to drink water so they wouldn't die of dehydration. Each senator had a different question and a different demand on a different issue. This one was interested in subsidies, that one in tobacco taxes, another in cost control. After laboring for hours, the staff would sort out the various proposals, often staying up until three in the morning to write summaries on areas of agreement before resuming meetings at ten. More than one of those staff members burst into tears from the stress.

Everyone felt the strain, and for good reason. At one closed-door Mainstream session, Reischauer's chief aide, Linda Bilheimer, was pressed aggressively by senators for answers to a complex set of alternatives. You haven't told me the specifics of what you have in mind, she said.

Damn it, she was told, we don't care about these details. That's your problem. Just tell us what the cost is.

Recalling that difficult moment, Reischauer said, "It got very ugly. Linda, who is tough as nails, came back almost in tears. She threw her stuff down on the desk and said, 'You don't pay me enough to go through what I've just gone through.' "

They were dealing, in a very short period of time, with the heart of the difficulties: How much would this cost? How would the costs be allocated? How many benefits would it provide? What guarantees are there that the costs will not explode? How can we be sure the estimates are solid? Is there a better way to do it?

These were not academic exercises. They represented, as Reischauer put it, "the guts of it, the real nitty-gritty." Hundreds of billions of dollars, to say nothing of lives across the country, were at stake. A wrong decision on any question could mean nightmarish problems down the road.

The external pressures grew even more intense. The day after Mitchell made his threat to keep the Senate in nonstop session, disrupting long-planned vacations and crucial fence-mending expeditions at home before the fall elections, the final round of Harry and Louise TV ads began airing nationally. At the same time, the final outpouring of faxes, phone calls, and letters mounted by the small-business lobby flooded Washington offices. ("We will soon do another Action Alert to NFIB Guardian members in key Senate target states, and caller-connect telemarketing is also starting with more than 2000 calls going to each senator over a ten-day period," a small-business lobbyist advised his group's president, Jack Faris, in one of a stream of daily memos.) Republican senators were meeting daily, coordinating filibuster tactics. So were the business groups that worked closely behind the scenes with them. ("The purpose of this meeting is twofold: 1. Confirm that all of our organizations find both Democratic leadership bills . . . to be unacceptable, and 2. Discuss specific, well-targeted and effective collaborative efforts that will support our individual activities," read an internal memo summoning top lobbyists of ten major business groups, among them NFIB, the National Association of Manufacturers, the U.S. Chamber of Commerce, to a private strategy meeting at the City Club in Washington that second week in August.) Polls showed the President's popularity had sunk to its lowest point ever. The peril of Whitewater loomed again. Under strong pressure from conservative GOP senators like North Carolina's Lauch Faircloth and Georgia's Paul Coverdell, special prosecutor Robert Fiske, a Republican accused of going easy on the Clintons, was replaced by a more conservative one, Kenneth Starr. Seven days had passed since the crime bill was defeated in the House, and nothing was going right for the White House.

It was at this moment that Clinton reached out to Bob Kerrey, the Medal of Honor winner who lost a leg in Vietnam, the Democratic presidential candidate who first advanced health care as a major issue in the early skirmishes in 1992, and the man who cast the difficult deciding vote a year earlier to save Clinton's endangered budget and his presidency. The President asked him to the White House for a private session, hoping to probe what was going on in the Mainstream group and to gain support for the Mitchell bill. He knew that Kerrey had moved a long way from his position in the 1992 campaign, when the Nebraskan was advocating a variant of the single-payer plan. But he was not prepared for what Kerrey did just twenty-four hours after the White House called. Operating as always with a starchy, stubborn spirit of independence, Kerrey, to the dismay of the White House and George Mitchell, delivered a Senate speech opposing the Mitchell plan.

It was a major blow, and it had major consequences. No sooner had Kerrey taken his stand than the White House called, canceling his invitation to meet with the President. As Kerrey told us in his office minutes after his meeting with Clinton was called off, this was another demonstration that "they consider any statement in opposition to be destructive. They confuse their enemies with their friends, and it may produce the tragedy of not enacting legislation."

Kerrey still wanted reform, he insisted. Brushing past the practical questions, as he often did, Kerrey said he wanted the President and Congress to raise their sights. "At its most fundamental level," he said, "it's not just life and death. It's who we are. The most difficult questions in health care are not economic. They're moral and ethical." Kerrey intended his Senate speech to prod everyone into facing those issues. As he said, "sometimes the most effective way to get something done is to be an uncompromising bastard."

It was against this corrosive background that the Democrats gathered for their private leadership luncheon on Thursday, August 18. Though the initial remarks by senators were polite, they clearly contained strong criticism of the Mitchell bill. Then Tom Daschle called on Kerrey.

Kerrey was blunt. Eighty percent of the people in his state of Nebraska wanted them to do nothing, he said. They were frightened by what they heard about the Clinton plan. He told them why he thought the majority leader's strategy of seeking to pass health reform by the minimum fifty-one votes, far short of the sixty needed to defeat a filibuster, was misguided. He also said that Mitchell's bill itself was seriously flawed. If they kept on this way, Kerrey said forcefully, they were going to lose the Senate. He repeated himself, even more strongly: *They were going to lose the Senate!* Their best hope lay in working with Chafee's Mainstream group. He finished what he had to say, got up, and walked toward the door.

Ted Kennedy was seated farther down the table and clearly didn't like what he had heard. His face got red. Isn't somebody else going to get a chance to speak? he said, in a booming voice. Then he launched into a full-scale attack on the views expressed by Kerrey. His voice rising, "in full roar," as a fascinated Lawrence O'Donnell described it minutes later, Kennedy mocked the Mainstream Coalition efforts, derided what Kerrey had said, and became more and more emotional. It was, O'Donnell characterized it, "a wall-shaking, unprecedented" moment.

Suddenly, Bob Kerrey, who was just about through the door, wheeled around and stalked back into the room while Kennedy was still speaking. He stormed back to a point directly across the table from Kennedy, and confronted him in a tough, loud voice. The Mainstream group doesn't have to meet, he shouted. It can stop right now. We can vote right now on Mitchell, and *it will go down!* Again, he repeated himself: *It will go down!* Kennedy, stung, roared back. God, O'Donnell thought, it's like two Irish pugs, two Boston Southies, of differing generations and backgrounds, brawling on the street corner.

Dead silence. Finally, after what seemed an interminable moment of tension, the soft drawl of Wendell Ford of Kentucky broke the silence. "Well, George," Ford said quietly, addressing Majority Leader Mitchell, a smile creasing his face, "that's about the best exchange I've heard."

Another explosion of emotion, this time the laughter of relief, in which Ted Kennedy joined.

The tension was broken, but the division remained. When his turn came to speak, Dennis DeConcini of Arizona, who had already announced his plans to retire from Congress after that session, backed Kerrey. DeConcini, too, warned they were going to lose the Senate if they continued on their course. If I were running again, DeConcini told his colleagues, I would give a speech saying I was against it, and I would vote against it. John Kerry of Massachusetts, like Bob Kerrey a decorated Vietnam veteran, gave a careful, solemn warning that they were following the wrong course. He, too, favored a filibuster-proof sixty-vote strategy before committing themselves to a vote. The time was approaching, he said, when they had to make a fateful decision.

John Glenn of Ohio, usually laid-back, phlegmatic, mild in manner and speech, felt he had the answer: "Charge!" Glenn, the first American to orbit the Earth and a valorous marine combat fighter pilot in World War II and Korea, took Bob Kerrey on. He didn't agree with Kerrey, he said. I'd rather lose the Senate fighting for something we know is right, Glenn continued, to an outbreak of applause from his colleagues. If we're not going to be victorious, I'd rather go down with flags flying. Jesus, O'Donnell thought, the only two guys in this room who can really talk about flags flying are on opposite sides. Kerrey, representing the other divide of the combat generations, and the new rifts in the Democratic Party, listened stonily; then, as more applause sounded, he turned and walked out of the room.

The debate among the Democrats continued. Chris Dodd of Connecticut, Ted Kennedy's close friend, said this was one of the great moments of our political life; it was no time to turn back, or be paralyzed by a tactical debate. Russ Feingold of Wisconsin endorsed that view. If we try to pacify the Right, he said, we'll fail. No matter what compromise we come up with, the Right will say it's Big Government. They'll keep beating us with that no matter what we do. More discussion. Then, finally, George Mitchell took control. Calmly, deliberately, he moved the discussion back to far less emotional issues — to cost containment, to the rendering of the latest Congressional Budget Office assessment of his new plan, to the strategy they should follow.

It was over, but not forgotten. Nor were those divisions healed.

Something elemental had surfaced. More than one person in that room had a foreboding that the Democratic Party itself was splintering. Lawrence O'Donnell, usually assured and assertive, was awestruck. "We, the Democrats, are coming apart in a more dramatic and high-speed way than I could have possibly imagined," he said.

The tensions had been building for years. In the 1960s, the Democrats had divided over Vietnam, with large parts of the party supporting Lyndon Johnson and the decision to intervene, while others — younger, wealthier, better educated — went into opposition. The battles had been replayed in the 1970s and 1980s, this time on domestic policy, with the new generation pushing for approaches that would appeal to suburban and middle-class voters, while the traditionalists counseled loyalty to the workers and their unions, the minorities and the causes of the New Deal.

Clinton had tried to bridge the gap and had done so successfully in the 1992 campaign. His own generational and political roots were with the New Democrats, as he called them, the revisionists. But at the outset of his presidency, he accepted the counsel of the congressional Democratic leaders, the Mitchells, the Foleys, and the Gephardts, that his best hope for passing his programs was to rally the traditional party constituencies and interest groups and count on them to deliver their allies on Capitol Hill.

Dan Rostenkowski, that symbol of the Old Guard, had put it in blunt terms one day while talking with the President in the White House family quarters, at a time when it seemed the Democrats still had an excellent chance to enact their health care reform. The conversation switched to the welfare proposals being discussed in Congress. You know, Clinton told Rosty, the Republican welfare bill isn't all bad. Yeah, Rosty replied, but they won't vote for it. What do you mean? the President asked. It's *their* bill. To which the old Chicago pol answered: They'll take you up to the water, then they'll pull the bucket away. Whatever you want, they'll do something different. "I says," as Rosty remembered their conversation later, "how do you negotiate with Republicans that want you to go to the right and keep Democrats that are on the left? I mean, you better stay in your party here, pal."

The President *had* stuck with his party. But now the question became, Is there any longer a Democratic Party worthy of the name and capable of governing? George Stephanopoulos looked at the severe party divisions on the crime bill, and concluded mournfully, "There is no Democratic Party, there are five Democratic parties."

Now those divisions were plaguing health reform. A shift of seismic proportions was under way, but few but Newt Gingrich could then see its full dimensions.

Late the next afternoon, August 19, the Mainstream Coalition produced its alternative proposal. It was immediately denounced by both Left and Right. The Health Care Reform Project said it "prescribes little more than a dose of cold water" to the country's mammoth health ailments, falling far short of providing every American guaranteed affordable coverage and the comprehensive benefits the Congress enjoyed, and leaving "millions of hardworking, low- and moderate-income Americans without coverage because the subsidies won't materialize under the fail-safe mechanism." The view from the right was of total dismissal. With a mere glance at the proposed bill, Phil Gramm predicted, "We are not going to pass a health bill before we recess."

The bill deserved a better reception. As Paul Starr, the Princeton sociologist who was one of the early architects of the Clinton plan and one of the most respected analysts of health reform, said, "For all its flaws, the bill would have been a historic advance." As Starr analyzed it, the Chafee plan was the only centrist reform that significantly broadened coverage and was fiscally defensible. It would have extended coverage to 91 or 92 percent of the population by imposing a cigarette tax, a tax on high-cost health plans, and cuts in Medicare. The problem with the Mainstream plan, Starr correctly said, was not about policy, but politics: "It was too big for conservatives, too little for liberals."

Yet even in that third week in August, some continued to cling to the hope that a compromise still could be struck. As Jay Rockefeller said on *CBS This Morning* after the Mainstream announced its compromise, "John Chafee and George Mitchell will now negotiate, and where they can't agree, then we'll vote in the Senate. . . . I'll win

some, John'll win some. But the point is that he's put us on the path
to a negotiated settlement."

That was Rockefeller's public stance. Privately, he gave us a
different analysis. "The gods are angry," he said.

Bill Clinton and Ira Magaziner, at the top of the chain, were not
among the optimists. Neither was Jason Solomon, near the bottom.

One night that August, the phone rang in the Washington apartment of Dave Durenberger, the Republican from Minnesota who was
one of the moving forces in the Mainstream Coalition. It was after ten
o'clock at night; the President was on the line. Clinton unburdened
himself. He was stewing in frustration about the sandbagging of
the crime bill and the plight of health reform. All these delays; all
these new issues being raised. "It's like acid in your stomach," he
said. Durenberger said he sympathized, but there was nothing he
could do.

Magaziner felt the same frustrations. August 19, the day the
Mainstream group presented its bill to Mitchell and Dole, was a day
Magaziner would always remember. "It was the day," he said, "when
I knew this thing was going down."

Everything about that day was painful for him to recall. He had
been sick most of the summer with walking pneumonia and still
had not completely recovered. Despite his feeling ill, he had for days
pulled his old trick of working around the clock with little sleep. That
morning he became dizzy, tripped on a step at the White House, and
fell, bruising his ribs. He went home early in the afternoon. A few
hours later he received a call from a White House aide on Capitol Hill.
The Mainstream group had come forth with a proposal that moved
further to the right and further from the White House position than
they had been hoping. Until then, Magaziner believed they had a
chance to pass a version of the Mitchell bill that would put them on
the path to universal coverage with decent cost containment, a bill
that could be strengthened in the House. The phone call was the final
blow.

He left his house, where he stayed alone when his family was in
Rhode Island, went to a grocery store, and bought the ingredients
for a huge pot of spaghetti, which he cooked and ate, and then went

to bed. He had a hard time sleeping. His mind played over the long battle scenes he was now certain were over. The next morning, he met with the First Lady. "Hillary has a certain look when her frustration has reached the peak," he said, and she had it then. But she did not admit defeat; she turned the conversation back to how they could still rescue reform. "So we basically started out to see what we could do to turn it around," Magaziner said, "but in my heart I knew it was over."

After his meeting with Hillary, Magaziner drafted a strategy memo for the President and the First Lady. They had three choices, he counseled, none good: They could count on Mitchell's striking a deal with the Mainstream group that labor, seniors, and other re-form supporters "can stomach," and hope for a stronger bill in the House. They could urge Congress to go home without voting on a bill and vow to continue the fight next year. Or they could propose their own minimalist bill, try to pass it, then pledge to fight for universal coverage in the new 1995 Congress.

Of those proposals, the first, seeking a Mitchell-Mainstream com-promise, offered them this dismal prospect: "We could end up with the worst of both worlds; a political defeat and blame for a health bill that doesn't work." As for the second, the no-bill approach, the plus side was this: "We are perilously close to the line now on whether the bill proposed does more harm than good, so this is not a case of allowing the perfect to be the enemy of the good." But the negatives were even more dire: "Democrats," Magaziner warned the Clintons, "could be blamed severely at the polls in 1994 and the President in 1996 for having failed to pass any health bill. The recriminations against the President, the First Lady, the health care team and the Administration in general could be devastating." On the alternative of seeking a "minimalist" health reform bill that "at least could do as much good and little harm as possible," he warned them, gloomily, "This option may also be moot. Congress may not want to take our suggestions."

With deadly accuracy, he had singled out their greatest weakness: they could no longer count on the support of their own Democratic-controlled Congress. That, Magaziner concluded, meant they had lost the battle.

Jason Solomon had no such dramatic flash of intuition, nor a phone call that informed him. But he knew, too. Solomon was the young man who had put his college education on hold to work, first as a campaign volunteer, then as a Delivery Room aide to Bob Boorstin. For months, there had been one crushing disappointment after another — Whitewater, the plunging polls for both the President and health care reform, the problems in Congress, the battering from the interests, the growing disaffection of the public. Yet even that summer he found reasons for hope. At first, the bus tour seemed promising; he and others in the Delivery Room deluded themselves that it would kindle a public outcry for reform. It did not. Then they believed Mitchell and Gephardt would carry the day when they introduced their bills. That hope, too, quickly died. A heavier blow soon followed. "We were always thinking," Solomon said of himself and his young Delivery Room colleagues, "that we'll pull it off even if it's only by one vote. But that loss on the crime bill came out of nowhere. It was devastating."

Now, as Solomon was preparing to return to Harvard, he was invited to talk at the high school in his hometown in New Jersey. He was proud to do so, and after he described the Clinton reform, the teacher spoke to the students on how democracy works — specifically how a bill becomes law. She proceeded to outline the steps, logical and neat, in the legislative process: You propose the bill, there are hearings, opponents and proponents make their cases, the vote is held, the measure passes, a new law goes on the books.

Listening, Solomon found himself wanting to tell the students what he had learned from his Washington experience. Let's stop a second and talk about how The System really works, he thought. Let's talk about interest groups and their money and their campaign contributions. Let's talk about the media, how if you're good at spinning the press you can influence the outcome. That's what really matters. Later, recalling that moment, he said: "I'm pretty cynical now, and my basic conclusion is that we're cheating people who are going through public schools out of an education on how government *really* works. But then I wonder if we *should* tell them, because that [knowledge] would turn them off even more."

*   *   *

John Chafee heard it more and more on those long hot summer days. Something big is coming, his Republican colleagues whispered to each other in the cloakroom, something historic. We're going to control the Senate again, they told each other, maybe even control the House. "We've got this baby now," Chafee heard Republicans tell each other. "We can kill this thing." As Chafee remarked, in typically understated New England manner, "Once people smell blood, it inspires their forces."

Chafee decided to try once more with Bob Dole. "I wish you'd talk to Senator Mitchell about health care," Chafee urged the minority leader. "You've got a bill and he's got a bill. I wish you'd talk." Dole's reply was, "They're not getting anything out of here." Chafee couldn't understand Dole's attitude, any more than he could fathom what was happening in his party. He had voted for the crime bill and he wanted to vote for the right kind of health reform. That made him an exile in his own party. "I and some others do represent a wing of the party that is certainly not in power," he observed dryly.

Bob Bennett, the shrewd Utah Republican who was acting as Dole's emissary to the various GOP factions, had been attending Chafee's Mainstream Coalition meetings regularly and was fascinated by what he viewed as their misunderstanding of political realities. In those closed-door meetings, they kept thinking they could come up with a bill that could pass. "And I kept saying to them," Bennett told us later, " 'Guys, you're not going to get seven Republican votes or seven Democratic votes. I mean, you're the head of the fish, but somebody has cut the fish off behind the eyes. There's no tail back there. You're swimming along back there without a tail.' "

Finally, Bennett told them they weren't going to get *any* Republicans. The reasons had almost nothing to do with the issue, or which proposal had most merit. Now the battle was being driven by the conviction that Republicans, for generations the minority congressional party, were on the verge of an electoral victory of historic proportions. That tantalizing prospect had filtered into the consciousness of every Republican, and was confirmed in every private sounding the party pollsters took as the November elections drew closer. This political dynamic, almost unbelievable considering the losses Republicans had suffered just two years before, drove everything before it, and made the prospects for compromise even dimmer. By August, Bennett stopped attending the Mainstream meetings. "I finally decided it's inappropriate for me to be there, since I am clearly not going to vote for anything they produce."

Bennett was struck by the forces that were combining to kill the Clinton bill. "We had lobbyists from groups we never heard of coming to our Republican Steering Committee meetings," he recalled, "groups coming out of the woodwork. The original herd instinct of the lobbyists was, We're going to have a bill, so I serve my clients best by helping change the bill. As soon as it became clear that there's a chance to kill this whole thing, they realized they could become a hero with their client and the herd instinct really took over."

Looking back on those private meetings of the Republican Steering Committee he attended that summer, Bennett had a sense of wonder at what he witnessed. They were like Amway rallies, he thought: "I can sell more bars of soap than you." One after another, each lobbyist "stood up and pledged more undying opposition than the one before," Bennett said.

Georgia's Paul Coverdell gathered the lobbyists in a room with other GOP senators and kept pushing them to greater efforts at opposition, just as Kennedy had urged his outside allies to mobilize support. Usually, lobbyists urged legislators to act. But in this fight, the *politicians* were pushing the lobbyists for more action. Of course, the groups in the No Name Coalition, who were in the meetings with Coverdell, needed no urging.

Reinforcing them was the conservative talk radio network. "Talk shows, frankly, had a role in helping us sense what was happening in the country," Bennett said. "I remember Connie Mack [the Republican senator from Florida] coming to one of our meetings and saying, 'I have spent two hours on the radio and I can tell you that *nobody* wants any kind of health care bill. A Republican health care bill, a Democratic health care bill — they don't want it.' "

This was the period that most dramatically proved the accuracy of Republican lobbyist Deborah Steelman's observation that the battle was won because of "the lineup of the stars you don't get in politics very often." All elements of the Republican coalition — social conservatives and business lobbyists, talk radio networks and elected officials — combined to kill health care. In the House, of course, Newt Gingrich led the assault with his crime bill ambush. In the Senate, Bob Dole privately discarded any pretense of seeking a compromise. He turned over command of the battle to Bob Packwood of Oregon.

Packwood is one of the more intriguing figures in the story. For decades, he had been a Republican progressive on social issues, including women's rights and health care. Twenty years before, he introduced President Nixon's health bill and touted its employer mandate. But in 1992 things changed for Packwood. Ten women alleged to the *Washington Post* that he had sexually harassed them and made forceful advances, some when they were in their teens, during interviews and hotel visits, at fund-raisers and even in his Senate office. Constituents blasted him for abusing his power. Colleagues called for his resignation. As the number of accusers multiplied and the cameras invaded, Packwood drew inward and took refuge among conservatives. He hoped they would stand by him when the time came for a Senate judgment on ethical misconduct charges that could end his Senate career.

In public, he seemed almost frantic, pacing the Senate floor. But privately Packwood was Eisenhower on the beaches of Normandy, as Bennett put it, employing a World War II analogy, and Dole was FDR, the commander in chief. Packwood divided the Republican senators into teams. Each was assigned to work on specific issues — first-tier issues, second-tier issues — and each team had a designated leader. Bennett was appointed leader of the issue deemed most critical to opponents: employer mandates. He and his team produced a thick briefing book to use in Senate floor debate. The goal was to frustrate and crush any Democratic bill. Don't let *any* Democratic measure come to a vote.

As Bennett said, "Dole made it very clear: No bill is the strategy. And the Republicans were as united as they have ever been on anything. Packwood had Dole's mace in his hand and we met twice a day. We met at nine o'clock in the morning and we met at four-thirty in the afternoon to review the vetting. And I had my team up and my briefing book ready and my speech ready." He meant that he was prepared to deliver the assault against employer mandates whenever it surfaced in the Senate.

In Bennett's opinion, Packwood proved to be a superb general in the decisive phases of the war. At an early closed-door conference of Senate Republicans — never leaked, therefore never reported — Packwood made an "absolutely brilliant" strategic comparison that Bennett thought he would always remember. The Oregon senator laid out a scenario by which they would attack and destroy the Democrats' commander, George Mitchell.

Mitchell, Packwood told his colleagues, was like Rommel at El Alamein. Some of the younger senators asked what he was talking about. Packwood explained how the great Nazi general Erwin Rommel, the legendary "Desert Fox," was outmaneuvered and destroyed by his British opponent, Field Marshal Sir Bernard Montgomery, in the crucial Battle of El Alamein in North Africa in 1942. Packwood described Montgomery's tactics to them: Montgomery had destroyed Rommel's gasoline trucks so that Rommel, who wanted to go in *this* direction, refuel, and then maneuver, had to go *that* way to secure vital fuel for his lightning-fast Panzer tank corps. The only path left for Rommel was to go through a mountain pass where Montgomery had dug in his forces on either side. Rommel had no choice but to take that route. Then Packwood said, "And Mitchell has no choice but to march into our guns that are waiting in place for *him*. We've got him just like Montgomery got Rommel at El Alamein."

Recalling that scene to us later, Bennett savored the moment. Having committed himself so publicly to his bill, Mitchell had no alternative than to keep going forward toward the enemy. He knew, figuratively, he was out of ammunition, and his reserves, the supportive Democratic members, were deserting. All he could do was press ahead and hope his bill survived. Though time and terrain were against him, he was determined to battle for a recorded vote; that way, he might salvage something from a total disaster. "And we sat there and watched that happen," Senator Bennett said. "We watched the whole thing disintegrate. And George Mitchell, the brilliant strategist, the smartest guy in the United States Senate, the irreplacable

George Mitchell, just got cut to ribbons. Then the whole thing flew apart. And we went to the people and we were enormously well rewarded for having killed the Clinton health care plan." He paused and gestured around his large new Senate office with its splendid view — one of the perks that went to the Republican Senate majority after the '94 election.

A thousand miles to the west in that summer of political anger, there was no place in America more likely to be above the embittered partisanship of Washington than Minnesota. But by that August, Minnesota was seized by the same passions over health care reform, complete with the same negative attacks, scare tactics, political polarization, and lavish expenditure of money by special interests. In the process, The System at that level of state government and politics was also being shaken to its core.

When the battle began, Minnesota was in the forefront of reform of the health system. Hillary Clinton traveled there frequently, repeatedly citing Minnesota as an example of how The System can best serve the people. And with good reason. Minnesota was probably the most progressive state in the Union, a state where reform flourished, where good government was not a sneering term, and where citizens traditionally respected the leaders they elected. Besides, Minnesota was a leader among states in the effort to provide universal health care. It was one of the birthplaces of managed care, with strong private-sector leaders who believed in using the market to deliver more efficient results but who also recognized the need for government to establish rules and incentives.

In 1987, the Minnesota legislature passed a law to provide basic health care for pregnant women and children under eight. It was available to any uninsured family of four whose annual income was under $21,500. Two years later that coverage was expanded to those up to age eighteen, an extension that was to begin in 1991. By the time Bill Clinton became President, MinnesotaCare was widely heralded as a model for the nation. Under plans then in effect, through bipartisan legislation passed in 1991 and 1992, the state had set a goal of reaching universal coverage by 1997.

Minnesota's governor at the time was a moderate Republican,

Arne Carlson. Like many players in this story, Carlson's commitment to health care reform stemmed from personal experience. When he was about five years old, his brother suffered an attack of acute appendicitis. Carlson's mother, a Swedish immigrant, was told her son would not be operated on unless she paid $400 — which she did not have. Attempts to beg or borrow the money were unsuccessful; the boy's condition worsened. As the governor recalled, "She went into the hospital with a knife and said to that doctor, 'If my son dies, you die.' " The operation was done; he didn't die. "But he's got the damnedest scar you've ever seen," Carlson said. "He was poisoned, a little kid. Why? So the doctor could illegally extract money."

When we first began talking with Carlson, the governor believed Congress would pass a reform bill and Clinton would get the political credit. He knew Clinton well, having worked closely with him on various issues, including health care. But from the beginning, Carlson expressed serious doubts about the way the Clinton plan was fashioned and the people who designed it. He said that Ira Magaziner's policy process exhibited "daunting complexity, well-meant engineering maybe running amok." Magaziner struck him as a "global thinker," operating from the principle of "wreck the world and I'll rebuild it." He also thought "there are a lot of Ira Magaziners in the world and they have left behind enormous difficulties for others to clean up. They justify their existence on the grounds of, 'Well, we solved the crisis, but not everything worked,' and then they invent a new crisis."

Misgivings notwithstanding, Carlson thought the President ultimately would prevail. But 1994 changed Carlson's mind. He saw what toll personal attacks on politicians were taking and how polarized the nation was becoming. "As a society, we're not prone to follow," he said, "and we've come to the point of instant analysis, instant information, talk shows where people with outrageous behavior and outrageous sentiments are paid fantastic sums to divide society in a very harsh way." It was getting worse and worse for political leaders, he thought, partly because "the zealots have decided that 'compromise' is a bad word."

Here, the governor was addressing his own political situation as well as the President's, for by then the far right had mounted an aggressive, well-financed campaign to unseat Carlson. The Minnesota Republican Party convention, dominated by the Christian Coalition, had endorsed an ultraconservative opponent named Allen Quist. They would meet in a September primary. Suddenly, the moderate-conservative Republican governor was being tagged as a far-out liberal, and the Minnesota health plan was being attacked in the same terms as Clinton's. The comparison was explicit: Minnesota reform opponents assailed the "Carlson-Clinton plan" as a government-run health scheme that would drive up costs, limit choices, create a bloated bureaucracy.

As in Washington, NFIB applied heavy pressure against Carlson, warning in a letter to small-business owners in Minnesota that Carlson's plan would bankrupt them. The insurance lobbies also launched a strong, sustained attack, just as in Washington.

Carlson's opponent, Quist, belittled the governor's claim that he was trying to create a market-oriented reform. In one debate, where Carlson's chief of staff, Curt Johnson, stood in for the governor, Johnson was stunned to hear Quist "take the unbelievably extreme position that the government shouldn't be in health care at all — *at all* — notwithstanding the government is the payer for at least forty percent of all health costs."

Johnson was struck by the power of money and by the unprecedented attacks over talk radio. It made him wonder, "How much of the angry voices belong to people who are making money off resentment? I mean the ceaseless parade of talk show tyrants who have found a way to get rich by mining the resentment. We're providing an electronic mirror in many cases for the worst in each of us."

No one, not even the governor, was subjected to more scurrilous attacks than his state health commissioner, Mary Jo O'Brien. The abuse to which she was subjected resembled that inflicted on Sheila Burke, Bob Dole's chief of staff and health care expert. Like Burke in Washington, O'Brien in Minnesota found herself accused of being an ultraliberal Democrat. The irony is that O'Brien, born and raised in Minnesota, the daughter of a Republican district judge, was herself a lifelong Republican who had been recruited for her health commission job by Republicans who wanted to disprove the belief that health care was a Democratic issue. "I am a Republican," O'Brien said that summer. "I have never been called a socialist and a liberal and a bureaucrat with such venom as I have since last spring [of 1994]."

She received death threats. Her husband got anonymous phone calls at night telling him his wife wasn't working late; she was having an affair. As in Washington, it was the groups that saw themselves as most threatened by reform, from small business to insurance agents, that led the assault. "They're in a survival mode," O'Brien said, "and it's getting uglier and uglier." So great was the toll that she decided to leave her public position after the 1994 election. "This is not an honorable profession anymore," she concluded sadly. "We've made 'government' and 'leadership in government' ugly words now. It is not going to serve us well. We can't recruit people. We've got to have thoughtful leadership, but we're driving people out."

O'Brien also worried that despite Minnesota's reputation as a model of democracy, the public was increasingly ill served by the policy debates. "The System isn't serving the people well," she said, "because we've never engaged them so they know what choices they need to make. The debate has been largely a debate among interest groups. It's so complex, so easy to demagogue, so easy to arouse fears. The public is totally confused. People are frightened of what reform would mean. It has become the symbol of their discontent."

By the third week of August, Harris Wofford had scaled back even the tempered hope for reform he had expressed in late spring — "moderately optimistic," he had said then. While Majority Leader Mitchell grimly struggled to reach any compromise, Wofford watched as "the steam was going out of the machine." For weeks that summer, Wofford and a group of pro-reform Democratic senators, numbering between twenty and twenty-eight, were meeting secretly almost every day in the Capitol, usually behind the closed doors of the ornate Senate Foreign Relations Committee hearing room. They called themselves the Universal Coverage Group.

By the closing days of August, they were thoroughly frustrated. Each day, Wofford heard more and more colleagues returning from their states to report constituents didn't want them to act on health reform. "Let's wait until next year," Wofford heard them say. "Let's adjourn and admit we can't do anything now." Not only was reform slipping away, the debate itself was being waged on its weakest point: how to provide coverage for the poorest 15 or 20 percent of the population. That only reinforced in the public mind the idea that the Clinton plan was aimed primarily at helping the poor. "Whereas," Wofford told us, "the power in my election was that the middle class of Pennsylvania, broadly defined as eighty percent of the people, was concerned that if they lost their job, they'd lose their health insurance. And if they *didn't* lose their job, they were afraid that the next year their employer was going to reduce their health insurance benefits or increase their costs."

Finally, unable to contain his frustration yet unwilling to admit defeat, on August 23, with the clock nearing midnight, Wofford sat in his Senate office and composed a lengthy handwritten memo. Just two days before, Republicans and Democrats in the House, having worked day and night, had finally agreed to the crime bill. Now, as the Senate turned to the crime bill, Wofford urged his colleagues not to forsake health reform. The next day his handwritten memo was printed and distributed as "A Midnight Memorandum to Colleagues Seeking a Common Ground for Action on Health Reform This Year."

He was heartened, he wrote, that House Republicans and Democrats had reached agreement on the crime bill. "My heart leapt with new hope that we in this Congress might indeed be remembered in spite of ourselves," Wofford wrote — and this, he added, "in spite of the partisanship of these last months that has reached depths I've not seen in my lifetime." He hoped "a spirit of working together to find common ground will become contagious in the other vital issue before us: health reform."

Don't let this moment pass without *some* action, he implored them. Don't let this Congress become history without taking the first bipartisan step on reform. Go forward, not backward, "because no action helps no one." He recalled the great congressional debate in 1957 over enacting the first civil rights law since Reconstruction; how "the bill that emerged fell so far short of our goals that many

in the civil rights movement rejected it." Lyndon Johnson, then the
Senate majority leader, opposed the activists' reasoning. If that first,
limited bill passed, he said, every Congress thereafter would be under pressure to take further steps until the ultimate goal was reached.
That's how history was affected, Wofford said, and as a central participant in that civil rights battle, he learned "how great goals take
great effort and sometimes a long march."

As with civil rights, so with health reform. None of the proposals
before Congress had a chance of passing, he wrote, and this Congress would not be able to take "a giant leap forward." But even in
the final days of a most difficult session, they need not lose a historic opportunity to take steps that would lead to more fundamental
reform. Break the gridlock, he urged. Concentrate on what Congress can do now. Agree on reform elements that "can begin sooner
rather than later." He made specific proposals: provide coverage for
all children; open the Federal insurance plan to small businesses and
individuals; ensure that proposed Medicare savings go first to such
critical needs as helping older citizens receive long-term home care;
end discriminatory insurance practices that deny coverage for those
with preexisting conditions.

Join him, he concluded, "not only in the steps we take this year,
but in building on that foundation next year, and the year after that."

It was a brave, honorable, old-fashioned appeal, eloquent and
stirring. But it came much too late.

That summer, Hillary Clinton used every conceivable opportunity
to influence the process, including dispatching emissaries to Capitol
Hill to talk to Republican senators who were still working with the
Mainstream group. One of those she relied on most in that private
capacity was Dr. C. Everett Koop, the U.S. surgeon general during
the Reagan administration.

Based on his contacts with Republicans, especially Dave
Durenberger and Jack Danforth, Koop told the First Lady during two
of their meetings in August that he was hopeful they would still
achieve a breakthrough before Congress recessed. Those hopes were
dashed by the time Koop met with Hillary in the White House Map
Room on August 24, the day before the Clintons were scheduled

to leave for Martha's Vineyard. By then, both Durenberger and Danforth had turned increasingly pessimistic about the prospects for working something out. The situation seemed hopeless, especially as the atmosphere had become so embittered, so partisan. Hopes for a bipartisan solution were fading.

Even after confronting these realities, the First Lady was still reluctant to abandon the fight. She and Koop, whom she had come to admire, discussed the possibility of appointing a bipartisan commission to elevate the debate above the politics of the moment. No matter how they assessed that possibility, though, it was hard to see how anything the President might offer would win enough Republican votes to pass reform.

It was then the First Lady realized that it was probably dead.

On August 25, the day after Wofford released his "Midnight Memorandum" and Hillary dealt with the knowledge they had lost, Democratic leaders of both congressional chambers gave up. Thoroughly exhausted and dispirited — they had *finally* cleared the crime bill for the President's signature — Democratic leaders announced they were letting their members go home for their much-postponed vacation. They would reconvene September 12, technically, that is; but since the Jewish holiday Yom Kippur fell on Thursday, September 15, they would not actually resume business until Monday, September 19, further intensifying the time pressures upon all members anxious to leave for the elections.

Neither Senate nor House had come close to passing any health bill — or come close even to voting on one.

In the House, a leadership aide described the situation the members faced in those final days as "entropy," which dictionaries describe as "a measure of the unavailable energy in a closed system." The characterization was perfect as applied to the Democrats: The health care battle dramatically demonstrated both their declining energy and their ebbing political ability to act. "It was a process of slow suffocation," one House Democratic leader said privately. "The Senate was sliding down the slippery slope. Public support was eroding. Democrats didn't want to vote for it. They didn't want to vote against it. They just wanted it to go away."

Dick Gephardt put it this way: "The bill was dead. It wasn't going to happen. There was no sense wasting time going out and losing on the floor. It just wasn't worth it."

But John Dingell argued vehemently that they should call up a bill for a floor vote. He said he'd personally like it to be one of the two most liberal bills, the ones that were voted out of his friend Billy Ford's Education and Labor Committee. But he thought the bill fashioned by Pete Stark and Sam Gibbons out of Ways and Means would serve as well. "It was always my thesis that we ought to bring the goddamn bill to the floor," Dingell said, "have a vote on it, and then take the question to the people. I thought that was about as near a way as we could come to winning either way."

Ford and Gibbons agreed. So did Rostenkowski. "We have an obligation to let these SOBs on the floor vote yes or no and go back to their constituents," Rosty stormed. That was the argument he made to the President days before the final crime bill passage. In a phone call to Clinton the evening of August 16, Rosty urged Clinton, "Tell the Congress. 'You've got my bill. You put a bill together. If you don't pass a bill, I'm telling you right now, I won't be there telling people you deserve reelection.' Just bang the Congress!"

That was not the counsel of Speaker Tom Foley. Foley agreed with Gephardt: The votes weren't there, and defeat would be demoralizing. "I didn't think the members wanted to vote," Foley told us later. "There wasn't anything out there they wanted to vote for. We weren't close to a majority on any specific health care plan."

So the U.S. House of Representatives, controlled for most of the last sixty years by Democrats, possessing a majority of 257 to 176 over their Republican counterparts, with one Independent, Vermont Socialist Bernard Sanders, who normally went with the Democrats, failed even to bring a bill to a vote.

So also in the U.S. Senate, where Democrats then outnumbered Republicans by fifty-six to forty-four. On Friday afternoon, August 26, after conferring with other Democratic leaders and White House officials, George Mitchell gave the coup de grâce. Comprehensive health care reform was not possible in that Congress, he solemnly announced, with White House Chief of Staff Leon Panetta at his side, but he and others would continue to work for other reform measures during the recess and resume deliberations when the full Senate returned three weeks later.

20

Pulling the Plug

LONG BEFORE CONGRESS RECESSED, and long before he and Hillary left on their vacation at the end of August, the President knew they had lost. For him, as he told us later, that realization came when John Dingell could not get a bill out of his committee at the end of June, forcing Dingell to admit defeat publicly. The weeks from then through August were times of anguish. "I was sick about it," the President said, "because I knew before it was shut down that even with Chafee, who really believed in it, there might not be more than three Republicans for it."

During those weeks, he and Hillary had many conversations about how they should handle failure. The question they had to answer was how to pull the plug. Should they, as John Glenn had urged his Senate Democratic colleagues, go down "with flags flying" after making their case to the country? Should they wait until Congress adjourned before the fall elections to give a public accounting? Should they offer a public reprise on the battle at all? How could they reach closure on an issue the First Lady had characterized as the Social Security Act of this generation, the reform that would establish the identity of the Democratic Party and be the defining legislation for generations to come?

As with everything else in this story, the signals were seriously mixed. The Clintons received strongly conflicting advice on how — or whether — to pull the plug both from within the White House and from the cabinet, from Capitol Hill, and from the pro-reform groups. John Rother of AARP best expressed the view of those who wanted the President to go out fighting. "One of the questions

I have is why Clinton doesn't give a speech to the country on this issue," Rother said late in the afternoon of August 24, the day before Congress recessed, when it was apparent they had lost the war. "Why let this erode away without at least being clear and naming names and pointing fingers? Tell the American people what's going on. I just don't understand the reticence. The President's got to go to the American public, he's got to make the case."

Many in the White House felt the same way, but, once again, a sharp split developed over the President's course. Once more, it was a case of the political and communications people versus the health policy team.

"We really and truly believed that when this issue got to the floor, it would be crystal clear how right the position was to do something about health care reform, something fundamental," the First Lady's aide, Melanne Verveer, recalled weeks later. "We believed that once debate occurred, there would be this clamor from the folks who wanted to get something done against the folks who were the obstructionists. Now that may have been a naive expectation, especially looking back, because it became such a god-awful thing."

Then, as always, the leaks began. "That was a *very* frustrating part," said Chris Jennings, who worked for the First Lady as a White House liaison with Capitol Hill. "No one knows who they were: unsourced comments out of the White House saying we should be pulling this turkey. It was dead. For three straight days leaks like that happened. It was particularly frustrating for Harold [Ickes] because he was out there publicly fighting, saying we're working with Mitchell, and Harold was being undermined directly by people within the White House. It made us look like unmitigated assholes on the Hill."

Toward the end of August, before the Clintons' vacation, Health and Human Services Secretary Donna Shalala pleaded with the First Lady not to pull the plug. We're not at that point yet, Shalala said, urging her to hang in there; they might still get something worthwhile out of this Congress. Shalala was among those who believed there were people inside the White House who thought their careers would be enhanced if health care collapsed, enabling them to emerge as stronger players when decisions were made about what issues Clinton should emphasize for his reelection campaign. Paul Begala, the political consultant, disagreed with Shalala: Better to pull this bill and get on with other matters, he argued.

Congressional leaders, especially Senate Majority Leader George Mitchell, wanted to continue the battle.

Clinton felt a special obligation to Mitchell. The President later told us, "You know, George Mitchell was ending his service in the Senate. He had been very good to me, very strong for me, very effective as a Senate majority leader. He and some others were really still struggling to try to get something, and thought they had some remote chance, although he was never overly optimistic. So he asked me to be able to keep working for it."

The President consented. Later, he regretted that decision. "I probably should have tried to make a major speech to the country," he told us. That, however, was his retrospective view; at the time, as he and the First Lady left for Martha's Vineyard, he was not going to say anything that might hinder the slim prospect for reform when Congress returned in mid-September.

Hillary agreed that he should remain silent. "My feeling was that even though we knew we were not going to be successful," she told us, "we did not want to be the ones to declare health care dead. We, at least, tried to do everything we could to keep it alive. We had put it on life support time and time again. So we didn't want to say it's dead and then let the Republicans say, 'Well, look, they gave up on it.' So we just kept saying we're going to keep working, we're going to keep working, we're going to keep working."

To that end, she was determined to encourage the efforts of Mitchell, Chafee, Kennedy, and others to achieve what even she acknowledged privately was "sort of the rock bottom of the Mainstream proposal." As she explained, "We kept encouraging that and would not say it was over because we didn't want anybody to have an opportunity to say, 'If only they had done this, we would have gotten something.' We knew there was no real chance, but we wanted everybody basically to reach that judgment on their own and not preempt the process. So eventually it became clear

to Senator Mitchell and Senator Chafee, who were the real stalwarts all the way to the end, that they didn't have the votes for
anything."

The battering they took that summer extracted a heavy toll. It
made both the President and the First Lady extremely wary of pursuing the issue further, particularly during those draining weeks
when the crime bill was in doubt. "The whole thing is so delicate,"
the First Lady said then, explaining how she and the President concluded they should not speak out. Instead, they would wait for a less
polarized moment to present their case — say, in the next State of
the Union message in January 1995. "The timing on that struck all
of us as dangerous," she said, referring to those final weeks of summer and early fall. They wanted to accomplish what they could
before members of Congress went home.

In such a poisonous climate, she was convinced anything the
President could say would only make matters worse. "It was such
a terrible, vitriolic atmosphere," she said, "and the feelings were so
raw that almost no matter what he would have said could have been
misinterpreted, mischaracterized, used in some way. So we thought
it was better to wait and then start fresh."

Another factor complicated the decision on how, when, by
whom — and if — to pull the plug. That was the fragile condition
of the Democratic Party as it approached the midterm elections in
November.

On September 1, Sam Gibbons told hometown reporters in Florida
that "health care reform is dead for now." For the old paratrooper
who had jumped into Normandy on D-Day, it was a bitter defeat.

In less than a month, his hopes for historic reform had turned to
ashes. To add to his frustration, the proud and fiery Gibbons knew
recriminations were already beginning among his fellow Democrats
about the crafting of the bill that came out of his committee and
was introduced to the full House the first week in August by Majority Leader Dick Gephardt. In order to shore up his position on
the floor of the House, Gephardt had made last-minute changes
aimed at solidifying the support of single-payers and other liberals,

at the risk of further alienating business and managed care advocates. Rosty was furious. He was stunned, he said privately, that the bill "went further to the left" in Gephardt's hands. "He surrendered to the Stark left wing. I would have taken it to the right, but at that point I would have had GE, IBM, I would have had 'em all buying full-page ads saying, 'Goddamn it, pass it.' But that didn't happen."

The Gingrich ambush of the crime bill had made Rosty's point moot and Gibbons was forced to acknowledge total defeat. Worse, the internal divisions that had surfaced had exposed the deep fissures within the Democratic Party and helped explain why it was so difficult to reach agreement on how to pull the plug.

The same kinds of divisions plagued the Senate. To allay Democratic House members' fears of being betrayed again as in the BTU tax debacle of a year earlier, it was understood that the Senate would take the lead in determining the strategy; the House would follow. The problem was, the Senate, too, lacked political cohesion, as events that summer proved dramatically. When the time came to decide whether to fight to force a vote, pervasive ambivalence seized the Democrats.

Tom Daschle of South Dakota, Mitchell's deputy and soon to be his successor as Democratic leader, was as devoted as anyone to passage; but, he conceded in conversations with us that August, because the Democrats lacked consensus on whether to fight or let the issue fade, "there is a belief that to have it trail off may be the best approach."

Daschle was among the senators who argued they needed "to force accountability," to "force the Republicans to vote on something." In the end, though, his was a minority view. "There is a feeling," Daschle added, "that we are putting as many Democrats on the line as Republicans" by pressing for a vote on the unpopular bill, and that feeling was even stronger among House Democrats. In recalling his private conversations with House Democratic leaders, Daschle remembered, "They were just really worried about crawling out there on a limb as they've done in the past this close to an election. The votes weren't there for that."

For Democrats, there was a deeper problem. The Republicans

operated with rock-solid unity while privately plotting the death of health reform. The Democrats increasingly performed with less and less unity. House and Senate Democrats alike, as Daschle ruefully observed, behaved like independent operatives, not as a unified political force. "It's much easier for each person to take care of himself or herself than to believe that if they work together they could do it in a much more effective way," Daschle said.

Throughout the entire two years of the debate, no matter how they differed ideologically on what course to pursue — from bigger-government single-payers like Jim McDermott to minimalist reform proponents like Jim Cooper — Democrats in the House were united around one belief: They were the majority party. Whatever happened to the legislation, however badly their own President stood in the polls, even if they were to lose the White House two years later, *they* would retain control of their side of Congress in the coming elections. The Senate might well turn from Democratic to Republican, as it had in the Reagan landslide of 1980; not the House. They would likely lose seats. But not control. Inconceivable! For most Democrats, and for virtually all staff members, the House had been in Democratic hands throughout their lifetime, and would continue to be. So they believed.

As members prepared for the November elections, they were already distancing themselves from their President — and from the reform he had attempted. They had even been given special license to do so. Before their recess, Stan Greenberg, the President's pollster, had written a fourteen-page memo to Democratic candidates advising them to stay away from health care in their campaigns. Talk about something else, Greenberg counseled.

Greenberg advised incumbents to portray themselves as "independent" soldiers for their districts. "There is no reason to highlight [accomplishments] as Clinton or Democratic proposals," the pollster and strategist said. "Voters want to know that you are fighting to get things done for them, not that you are advancing some national agenda." He told them to emphasize the tough new restrictions on crime they had secured. In focus groups, "no other accomplishment even comes close" to the passage of the "three strikes and you're out" crime legislation, Greenberg said. Incumbents need not mention health care, or vow to break gridlock, Greenberg said. "Democrats are seen to share in the problem."

This counsel of political isolation from party, President, and, one might say, even principle, was a boon to Republican operatives and conservative commentators when Greenberg's memo leaked to the press in mid-August. In his *Wall Street Journal* column headed "Stan Recants! Or Why Health Reform Is a Dud," Paul A. Gigot found Greenberg's backpedaling a large and irresistible target. "[With Democrats] having lost the health debate," which Gigot characterized as "the greatest entitlement expansion since Bismarck united Germany by creating the welfare state," he said Republicans "should be unafraid to stop this power play even if it requires a filibuster." He did not need to make the obvious point that Greenberg's memo further highlighted the weaknesses and divisions of the Democrats as a party.

Their "every man for himself" behavior was an example of how quickly political lessons are forgotten in The System. In the 1980 Reagan landslide, the shock of losing the Senate had forced Democrats to unite for self-interest. During those six years in the minority, they learned painfully what it was like not to be committee chairmen, not to have the kind of support staff and perks and powers they had long enjoyed. Under the leadership of George Mitchell, they made their comeback into the majority in the 1986 elections; two years later, they overwhelmingly voted Mitchell their new majority leader, largely, as Daschle remembered, "because there was a belief that. God, we could lose this place again. We better get with it. So that scared the hell out of them. But then it became comfortable again too quickly. You could slowly see this intransigence becoming more and more prevalent. And with that intransigence the possibility of doing something more relevant [like health care] was gone."

Looking back on their collective political failure, and facing what everyone understood was a dire threat for survival in the upcoming November elections now only weeks away, Tom Daschle foresaw even greater problems. He feared that growing disenchantment with the bitterness of political life, and increasing disillusionment with the way The System worked foreshadowed more upheaval. Look what was happening even before this highly polarized session of Congress ended, he said. Some of the most respected and distinguished political players, notably George Mitchell, had already announced they were leaving the Senate after this session. And these were people who almost certainly would have been reelected. Instead, at the peak of their influence and expertise, they chose to leave public life rather than continue to try to serve. It was a discouraging trend, dangerous even for what it signaled about the ability of The System to attract and hold its best and most talented people, Republicans as well as Democrats. Now Daschle feared it would become even worse. Looking ahead, he predicted that "because of the extraordinary frustration a lot of our better members are feeling," there would be a rash of retirements before the 1996 presidential election year.

He was correct. Within a year after the debacle of the midterm elections, eight Democrats (along with five Republicans) had announced their plans to leave the Senate, further weakening their party's future prospects. Daschle had clearly anticipated that dismal potential, but he did not then foresee the dimensions of the imminent election disaster looming for Democrats in both houses, and for their party as a whole.

On September 1, the same day Sam Gibbons conceded defeat on health reform in Florida, Nick Littlefield, Ted Kennedy's most valued adviser, sat alone in his large conference room in the Russell Senate Office Building. It was the Thursday before the long Labor Day weekend, and a fateful moment for reform. Other members of Congress were scattered across the country, increasingly anxious about shoring up support for their critical reelection contests two months away. On the table before Littlefield were stacks upon stacks of papers. He was a chief player, though virtually unknown to the public, in the closing scenes of the story.

Littlefield was chief of staff to Ted Kennedy's Labor and Human Resources Committee. Tall, lean, energetic, a New Englander of old and distinguished lineage, Littlefield was a believer in liberal government. Like Kennedy, he was also a believer in practical

politics. Winning was what counted, and if that meant compromise, so be it. Now he was coordinating the last effort to
salvage passage of the reform before this Congress passed into
history.

There was something surreal about this desperate, doomed effort.
Outside, Washington slumbered in the summer sun, its normally
congested streets deserted, its principal offices closed or operating on
a skeleton force. The record heat wave that bore down mercilessly on
the capital that summer caused pedestrians to gasp from the stifling
humidity, and tourists to flee the city. Judging by all appearances,
the nation's capital had shut down. Yet behind those closed doors
an extraordinary effort was under way. The top aides to Kennedy,
Mitchell, and Chafee were engaged in round-the-clock sessions writing a final compromise bill that would be ready for Congress's return
September 19. Their sessions had begun immediately after Mitchell
announced that while comprehensive reform was not possible, the
effort to produce something significant would continue. Since then,
they had been meeting day after day, late into the night. Twelve of
Littlefield's staff members worked with Mitchell's staff in the Hart
Senate Office Building nearby. They, in turn, met daily with Christy
Ferguson, Chafee's top aide, and with others from the Mainstream
Coalition.

By September 1, a substantial bill numbering about a thousand
pages was already emerging: the Chafee Mainstream bill served as its
base. The new version being born provided, as Littlefield described
it, "real insurance reform, with real subsidies, real choice, and offering federal employee benefits" to other Americans while also making
a start on long-term care.

No one involved in this effort had any illusions about the difficulty they faced. As Littlefield remarked on that September 1, "I'd
say it's about a thirty percent chance we can pull off the Chafee bill."
He also passionately believed, as did all the others involved, that it
was worth trying. They might just succeed.

Littlefield was a cheerleader, as well as a political pragmatist. For
weeks that summer, he had attended the regular evening meetings
with the hundred or more pro-reform groups in the Labor Committee hearing room, where Kennedy rallied the troops. Littlefield

sought to be a constant source of optimism, stirring flagging spirits, imploring participants to "keep the process going, keep the process going." Hearing that refrain yet again one night, someone called out: "Well, Nick, does that mean you think the Democrats are going to start acting like a party?" And Jerry Shea, a top operative of the AFL-CIO, joked that he thought he could make a fortune on a new campaign button saying "The Process Stops Here" from those who'd heard the Littlefield refrain ad nauseum.

Shea reflected the feelings of the many who attended those rallies and had devoted years to health care reform. They were "exhausted people who wanted to have hope but couldn't find it," who found themselves sinking into a state of "paralyzing depression" at losing the best chance for reform in a lifetime. Shea harbored an even greater concern. "I have this sickening feeling," he said that first week in September, thinking of the possible long-term impact of failure, "that we have increased the alienation quotient [of the public] substantially."

Still, none of them gave up entirely, not Nick Littlefield, Christy Ferguson, Mitchell's people, nor John Chafee himself. During one of our conversations with Chafee late in September, he was asked to think aloud about how he would write the obituary of health reform. He stiffened. *If* there's an obituary, he said. For John Chafee, even then it wasn't over.

Labor Day brought another vivid example of the great power shift between the long-dominant old Democratic Party and the highly organized new Republican opposition.

The unions played the old politics. They planned rallies across the country — the President and First Lady attended one in Maine — with balloons, placards, crowds of workers, and speakers shouting out their pleas to act, now, for reform. The opponents played the new politics. While the Labor Day union rallies were staged to ignite enthusiasm for reform, the conservative group Citizens for a Sound Economy used the electronic airwaves to reach a wider audience. That Labor Day weekend, CSE "made a very substantial buy," as its media director Brent Bahler put it, to air its commercials in fifteen states; they ran one spot per hour. The message: yet another attack on "government-run health care." Describing their strategy from the Washington headquarters then, Bahler pointed to a *Washington Post* front-page mock-up that the interest group had specially printed and distributed to its tens of thousands of members across the country. The mock-up was labeled an "Election Day special edition." Under the masthead and the date Thursday, October 13, 1994, a bold banner headline read "MAJOR HEALTH REFORM PACKAGE APPROVED 61–38 DESPITE GOP ASSAULT." Above the fake front-page, this warning was printed: "This can still happen." At the bottom, this message: "Keep up the fight against government-run health care."

CSE had the page printed and distributed after Congress recessed, when most agreed the battle was over and conservatives could relax. They left nothing to chance; they mobilized for the final assault on Election Day.

On Sunday, September 18, the *New York Times* reported remarks — never subsequently denied — that Bob Packwood had made to his Republican senatorial colleagues during those closed-door strategy sessions while Packwood was managing the summer's Republican attack. "We've killed health care reform," Packwood told his fellow Republican senators. "Now we've got to make sure our fingerprints are not on it."

For many, this was the "smoking gun": proof of a carefully plotted, and secret, Republican strategy. The First Lady was disturbed by that quote. She had long thought that Packwood's opposition to a reform he had strongly supported for nearly twenty years was "a symbolic defection," disturbing evidence of how "extremely difficult it was going to be [for Democrats] to come up with something." Just weeks before the Packwood quote was published, she told us Packwood was a prime example of problems they had not anticipated. "When someone like Senator Packwood, who has always stood for something, now decides it's politically impossible," she said, "that was not in our political calculations." The low point in the entire battle, she thought, was seeing "people who know what's right, know what will work, really taking a dive because of political pressure." At a Rose Garden event attended by Democratic and

Republican members of Congress, the First Lady said to Packwood, "Senator, introduce the Nixon bill. We can live with that." Packwood, who had backed that reform, did not reply.

Another who seized on the Packwood quote was Nick Littlefield. He had a big poster made bearing that "no fingerprints" quote and put it in his private office to ponder while he continued the last-minute efforts to craft a bill.

The spotlight fell on the Mainstream Coalition members when senators returned to Washington on Monday, September 19.

Mitchell and Chafee met briefly that day to assess where they stood and where they were going. If they were to get a bill, this was the last moment for it. They both knew how long the odds had become, and knew, too, they faced a greater obstacle than assembling a bipartisan majority of senators behind their bill. Mitchell's hope was that he could set aside four days for Senate debate on the new Mainstream bill that week and then schedule a historic up-or-down vote. The problem was Republicans were mobilizing a filibuster. They did not intend to let any bill reach the floor. The question is, Mitchell told Chafee, can we get enough votes to stop a filibuster? Chafee said he would gather as many members as possible of the Mainstream group later that day and canvass them. He would find out who would vote to break a filibuster, who would not. Mitchell, in turn, would conduct his own poll of Democratic senators not in Chafee's group. They agreed to meet again the next day to assess the results of their private surveys.

Once more, John Chafee called the Mainstream members to order in his hideaway. It was a large turnout, some eighteen senators, Democrats and Republicans, all of whom had worked together for weeks trying to find a bipartisan solution. He told them the reason for the meeting and asked who would vote with him to cut off the inevitable filibuster. The results were disheartening; he could get only four Republican votes for cloture — the parliamentary term for cutting off debate.

It was not enough. Sixty votes would be needed to break a filibuster. Everyone knew that the Democrats could not possibly hold all their fifty-six senators in line — Shelby of Alabama was lost for sure, and others almost certainly.

The next morning was fateful. For George Mitchell, the first order of business was a congressional leadership meeting at the White House with the President.

Newt Gingrich, addressing himself to the President, delivered what Mitchell thought was an atomic bomb blast. Gingrich warned Clinton that if he continued to push for health reform in the closing days of this Congress, he would lose the Republican support needed to pass the GATT (General Agreement on Tariffs and Trade), which the President believed critical to the U.S. economic position as the leader of the Western alliance.

Speaker Tom Foley was also troubled, he told us later. "Gingrich sat in the White House at the end of September and said, 'If you try to do anything on health care, we'll bring down GATT.' He put it slightly more politely than that. It was more like, 'If you try to push through some last-minute health care bill, you will destroy the kind of environment that's necessary to pass GATT.' But it was not hard to read."

Everyone got the message. That threat of Republican opposition to GATT had been looming for nearly three months, leading Pat Moynihan to express his concern privately that if Democrats kept pushing health reform, Republicans would retaliate by killing GATT. Now Gingrich had made that threat to the President's face. He would pull the GATT plug unless the President and the Democrats pulled the health plug.

Early that evening, in the majority leader's office, a solemn George Mitchell relayed Gingrich's threat to four stalwarts of the Mainstream Coalition — two Republicans, Chafee and Durenberger, and two Democrats, Breaux and Kerrey. "Mitchell equated this to an atomic bomb," Chafee told us shortly afterward. "And Dole, to a lesser degree, had said the same thing."

Mitchell had more bad news. He had received a letter from a number of the groups backing reform — the unions, AARP, others — saying they strongly opposed the Mainstream compromise bill. The worst news, though, came from John Chafee.

In his usual direct manner, Chafee gave a candid assessment of where the Mainstream group stood on a vote to cut off a filibuster. He told Mitchell that he could count on only four Republican votes. He could have gotten more, he said, had they more time. But time had run out.

They talked among themselves, soberly, quietly. No one had to say the obvious; they all knew. Times had changed, reform had slipped away. They all felt a sadness about this moment. To John Breaux, who had been so close a personal link between the Clintons and the moderate Democratic and Republican senators, "it was sort of a lonely feeling, realizing this was Mitchell's last hurrah on a subject he cared a great deal about and possibly gave up a Supreme Court seat to work on." Here we are, Breaux thought, sitting around this table, all knowing it's over, but speaking in circles and avoiding saying so. "There was this fat lady on the porch singing," Breaux said. "I thought maybe if we could hear, we would open the doors, but we didn't open the doors and we didn't hear her. But she was there." No one proclaimed it was over; all knew it was.

Mitchell was clear about his now deep reservations. "I don't want to bring out a bill we can't get the votes for," he told them. He wanted to talk to others before making a final decision. He wanted to brood about it. He'd get back to them in the next couple of days.

They all knew what this meeting signaled. Even Chafee, the eternal optimist who liked to quote "the old hymn where it says we have the strength of ten because our hearts are pure," had to acknowledge to himself it was over.

His aide, Christy Ferguson, was waiting outside. Perhaps no one in the entire battle had worked harder and more diligently for reform. Ferguson had put her heart and soul into this search for compromise, and so had those with whom she worked. They had all gone without vacations, had worked against impossible deadlines and pressures, had tried to be realistic about the prospects for success, but all clung, as Ferguson said, "to that hope that we could still pull it off."

Ferguson thought she had prepared herself emotionally for this moment. Since early August, she had gone through at least five stages of grieving over the lost opportunity for reform, and steeled herself for the almost certain knowledge it was going to die. And she still was not prepared for her feelings when Chafee and the others came out of Mitchell's office that night.

She and Chafee went back to his office, sat together, drinking a bourbon and talking about what had happened. "I teared up," Ferguson confessed later, "and I think he teared up a little too. We regretted the fact that it ended this way, but acknowledged it was probably destined to."

Chafee left for his home in McLean, Virginia, driving alone in the rain, and Ferguson returned to her own office in the Chafee suite. There, alone, she wept. Then she composed herself. She was preparing to leave when Nick Littlefield, Kennedy's aide, came into her office. Christy, he said, excitedly, we have to get this done. We have to get something to show. Littlefield exuded optimism.

Ferguson listened. Finally, she said, "Nick, wake up! It's over. It's dead. Forget it."

No, no, no, Littlefield continued. Kennedy's going to be able to deliver this no matter what happens, he said. We're going to get the votes for cloture on our side. You've got to get the votes for cloture on your side.

At that point, Ferguson burst into tears. "Look," she cried, "do you understand what's happened here? Do you understand how stupid you people have been?"

No final word came from Mitchell the next day, Wednesday, but everyone knew he was dealing with another crisis.

Two days before, in a sudden move that dominated the news, the President had dispatched American troops to Haiti. The landings took place even as his special emissaries, former President Jimmy Carter, General Colin Powell, and Senator Sam Nunn of Georgia, were concluding their mission to persuade leaders of the regime to go into exile.

By Wednesday, Mitchell was deeply involved in the congressional skirmish over whether to pass a resolution of support for the President's troop deployment. After a rancorous debate, the resolution passed. Once again, a decision on health care — this, the final one — was postponed.

Twenty-four more hours passed, and still there was no word from Mitchell. Chafee reassembled the Mainstream group in his hideaway on Thursday to brief them about his Tuesday night session with the majority leader. He solicited their views on what course to follow if, as expected, Mitchell told them he would not call up their bill.

Bob Kerrey spoke with passion. He wanted them to introduce their bill regardless of any vote. It drove him berserk, he told them, when he heard Phil Gramm belittle their group as "the Mainstream inside the Beltway." We're Mainstream America, Kerrey exclaimed. When Mainstream America finds out what we've got in this bill, and learns that we haven't passed it, they're going to be upset. If Mitchell decides to go forward with their bill, he's got my vote — for cloture and the rest. If Mitchell didn't, Kerrey still wanted their bill introduced.

The others agreed. "We'd like to have *our* bill out there, the bill we've worked so hard on, which we think is a darn good bill, and have it available for people to study and look at," Chafee recalled to us hours later.

But in the end, they didn't introduce their bill. It was postponed until after the election.

On Friday morning, September 23, Mitchell still had not flashed the final signal, but already the news was circulating throughout Capitol Hill: the majority leader was meeting with the President that afternoon; all that remained was a decision on how, and when, to pull the plug. If not this Friday, then it would be Saturday, or maybe, at the latest, the deed would be done Monday.

Jay Rockefeller knew. For the past two days he had been battling "a deep reservoir of anger, still too deep to come out yet." He was also, oddly, he thought, beginning for the first time to search for answers to what went wrong. Until then, he had been so preoccupied with the daily battle, he had not allowed himself to think more seriously about the meaning and consequences of failure. Rockefeller was in his office where we had talked so often in the last two years.

One thing seemed clear. "The American people always have been deeply skeptical of government," he said. "That's true even of the history of the people of my own state who came as indentured servants to the plantations of Virginia. They weren't meant to be ruled or told what to do. They came on their own for their own reasons, and if they wanted something, they made it known, and if they didn't, they made it known. I think it can be said that the public came to the conclusion that they didn't want health care badly enough."

That wasn't the whole story, he said; it didn't begin to address the many mistakes that had been made, from the White House to the Congress and beyond; and it certainly didn't account for the powerful forces that had been mobilized against reform. As for his judgment on the President, well, Rockefeller's emotions were too tangled this day for that kind of analysis, but he was disappointed. "When you set something out that clearly, you just don't let go of the choke hold," and the President "didn't keep the choke hold." But, then, neither did the Democratic leadership. Even George Mitchell, whom Rockefeller greatly admired, who in all other ways he thought to be "a glorious, model public personality," was reluctant to take on their opponents. "To be more in the face of Dole and the Republicans on this subject as well as others, you do have to *confront*, you do have to have a *showdown*, an O.K. Corral thing. He eschews that."

Laura Quinn, Rockefeller's communications director, who sat in on this conversation, was ardently committed to the cause and for much of the year had been devoting almost full time to helping coordinate the message of the White House Delivery Room. This day, she was in mourning; she wore black to Rockefeller's office — black dress, black headband, black stockings. She, too, knew it was finally over. In her quiet way, she was angry at how it was ending — just trailing off into vapor. At least, Quinn said, they should have given the public "the satisfaction of seeing it win or seeing it lose and knowing who did it. But there was none of that. No bill. No accountability. No understanding of why it happened."

At 3:40 Monday afternoon, September 26, at a news conference in the Capitol, a year and four days after Clinton had formally opened the battle with his address to Congress, George Mitchell pulled the plug. His formal statement, which he read to reporters before taking their questions, contained ten paragraphs. "Under the rules of the Senate," he said, "a minority can obstruct the majority. This is what happened to comprehensive health insurance reform." He briefly recounted his discussions with members of the Mainstream Coalition, reporting that they all agreed "it would serve no purpose to go forward unless we had the necessary votes." Last week, he said, Republican leaders of the House and Senate "said aloud what their colleagues have been saying privately: They will oppose any health care bill this year, modest or not, bipartisan or not. . . . Therefore, it is clear that health insurance reform cannot be enacted this year." He also cited the Packwood boast of how the Republicans had killed reform, and added, "Whether they succeed in making sure their fingerprints are not on it remains to be seen."

In the end, the majority leader said, "the combination of the insurance industry on the outside and a majority of Republicans on the inside proved to be too much to overcome."

Reaction was instantaneous. Bob Dole said, "Something went right for a change; that's how democracy works." Phil Gramm said, "I think America rejoices that the President's health care plan is dead. This is American democracy at its best." Chip Kahn of the Health Insurance Association of America, sponsor of the Harry and Louise ads, said, "We went to the airwaves to raise questions. Our purpose was to change the product, not harm it." John Motley, chief lobbyist of the National Federation of Independent Business, whose small-business armies were credited in a *Wall Street Journal* op-ed column with forging this "seismic and stunning win," said the legacy for his organization would be to enhance its power in future battles because "our reputation precedes us. . . . The perception you have power is often the power to influence." Haley Barbour, the Republican National Committee chairman, said, "We find ourselves in this position because the Clinton administration proposed creation of a government-run health care system. The more people learned about Clintoncare, the less they liked it." The *Wall Street Journal*, in an editorial that ran for an entire two columns, said, "The failure of health reform is a seismic event, the collapse of a political method that was thought could never lose. Yet despite a clever and ambitious liberal president and overwhelming majorities in Congress, Democrats couldn't persuade Americans or even all of their own Members to turn over the health-care system to the government. We may be watching the demise of entitlement politics." Ted Kennedy, in a Senate speech immediately after Mitchell's announcement, vowed to continue the battle. "I will never give up the fight until the working men and women of this country know that years of effort and hard-won savings cannot be wiped out by a sudden illness. The drive for comprehensive health reform will begin again next year."

The President of the United States spoke not a word.

A statement was released in his name, from New York, where he addressed the United Nations General Assembly that day. It was two paragraphs long. "I am very sorry that this means Congress isn't going to reform health care this year," the President's statement read. "But we are not giving up on our mission to cover every American and to control health care costs. This journey is far, far from over. For the sake of those who touched us during this great journey, we are going to keep up the fight and we will prevail."

That afternoon, even as Mitchell delivered the obituary, members of Citizens for a Sound Economy were plotting their next step. In a week Congress would adjourn, as its members prepared to stand for reelection. Republicans, led by Newt Gingrich, were campaigning to enact what they called a "Contract With America" that fall. It was too extreme, too radical, some White House strategists said. Gingrich was nationalizing an off-year election, traditionally determined by local issues. It would backfire at the polls. The American people wouldn't buy it. Difficult though conditions appeared for the Democrats, some in the White House found new hope. This might prove a godsend, one of those political miscalculations that could lessen Democratic losses in the upcoming races.

Citizens for a Sound Economy strategists had a totally different interpretation. "There is little doubt that the makeup of the One Hundred Fourth Congress is going to be remarkably different,"

CSE's Brent Bahler was saying at exactly the moment that Mitchell made his announcement pulling the plug. "It's going to be a more philosophically friendly Congress to what we advocate than what we've had in the past two years." Their private electoral trackings suggested a historic reversal, something on the scale of the Watergate election-year returns of 1974 that saw Republican ranks decimated in the wake of the scandal that forced a President to resign in disgrace for the first time in American history. They expected that Republicans would pick up forty-seven or forty-eight House seats from the Democrats, and had an excellent chance to regain the Senate. "You do that and you've just turned the world upside down," Bahler said. "Without a doubt it's going to be a more friendly Congress for our kind of philosophy in the next few years."

Bob Chlopak saw it coming. As head of the Health Care Reform Project, he had watched them lose fight after fight for more than a year until finally the war itself was lost. On Friday, September 30, when he learned that Congress planned to adjourn the next week, Chlopak made an urgent appeal to Harold Ickes. How can you let them go, he asked, without some kind of a message from the White House? "You're going to get all the blame and there is no message whatsoever," Chlopak said. "You've got to mark these moments with some message from the other side."

Chlopak thought they should say something about the special interests, and all the money expended, and the fact that most Republicans were clearly committed from day one to killing reform. They should assess the blame, point to the obstructionism of the Republican Party. It was an easy argument to make, especially since the Packwood quote had leaked: The only thing these guys are worried about is their fingerprints, Chlopak said; they don't care whether Americans have health care; they don't care what it costs; they don't care that people are being denied quality care. All they care about is politics, and that's why we lost this thing. They had a case to make, and they should make it.

That's what they should say.

But they didn't.

* * *

The day after Mitchell pulled the plug, William Kristol of the Project for the Republican Future spelled out the next stage of the battle plan. "I think we can continue to wrap the Clinton plan around the necks of the Democratic candidates," he gloated.

On Wednesday, October 5, the House of Representatives, controlled for forty years by the Democratic Party, agreed to a demand by House Republican leader Gingrich to delay action on GATT until after the 1994 elections. It was a final sign, if any more were needed, that the Democrats had lost their taste for battle; they wanted to scatter to their home territories, protect their individual seats, and return for other political skirmishes the next year. They allowed GATT to be held hostage to the very end.

Within minutes, in the late afternoon of Friday, October 7, the One Hundred Third Congress of the United States, the health care–battle Congress, would end its business and adjourn. Already, most senators and representatives had departed the capital for their districts. Offices were closed. Not even tourists or lobbyists prowled the halls.

In his office in the Hart Building, Tom Daschle was waiting to leave on a late-afternoon flight to South Dakota. He was about to be voted George Mitchell's successor as Senate Democratic leader. Now he was nearing the end of a long, introspective conversation about the politics of Washington past and present, and particularly about the politics of health care. Admiring though he was of the President, Daschle had been thinking about some of the lessons as they applied to political leadership in such a volcanic struggle — particularly about the politics of perseverance. "The President was very good at articulating the health message from time to time," Daschle said, "but I think it was important that he stay with it and say, 'Now here's what *they're* going to tell you,' and say it over and over and over again. Anticipate all these negatives, use his bully pulpit, use the kind of, you know, boom box that he's got all across the country. Never get off of it."

He stopped and thought a moment. Then he recalled Harry Truman, not from personal memory, but from political legend. "I don't know what Truman was really like," the senator said, "but my impression of him was that he just put his teeth into something and hung on, like a dog hanging on to your leg for two miles. He just hung in there. I think that's what it takes — a persistence, with incredible focus. If you really want health care, you give up a lot in order to get it."

21

The Country

IT WAS OCTOBER 1994, and David Langness was angry — "angry and irritated," he said, "at the entire System."

A year earlier, Langness had thought "it was inevitable that we're going to see" a major reform. He was head of the Hospital Council of Southern California, and from his long study of public attitudes about health care and his professional background in hospitals, he was convinced, he told us, that legislation would pass Congress. The electoral consequences of not acting "would be severe, because this is higher on the country's agenda" than anything in fifty years, making it "politically intolerable not to do something."

Now, with the 1994 elections about to be held and Congress having adjourned without a vote, Langness was seething about the consequences of failure.

The Hospital Council was the largest and oldest in the nation, representing all the public and private hospitals in southern California, and was already feeling the shocks. We were talking in his downtown Los Angeles office. "The shakeup is so massive," he told us, "that it's forcing huge mergers, consolidations, new networks. We're getting corporatized health care in southern California, and probably it will sweep the rest of the nation. Huge companies will employ thousands of physicians, own hundreds of hospitals, and probably ultimately control the insurance companies as well as the HMOs and the rest. They will control the vast bulk of American health care."

In the closing years of this century, the United States confronted the same question The System had faced at the beginning of it: how to reconcile the conflict between public and private interests.

In the early years of the century, fear of the growing power of private interests spawned the Progressive, New Nationalism, and New Freedom movements led by reformers like Theodore Roosevelt and Woodrow Wilson. They battled the trusts and sought to regulate the private interests through government. Their efforts moved America away from nineteenth-century laissez-faire government to one in which government played, as Theodore Roosevelt put it, "a dynamic, positive role" in society.

Out of that struggle, and through the New Deal, the Fair Deal, and the Great Society administrations of Franklin Roosevelt, Harry Truman, and Lyndon Johnson, the role of the government had greatly expanded, decade after decade. Government became the mediator of national conflicts, the place to which the public looked for resolution of great national issues: racial and sexual discrimination, protecting labor and farmers, regulating business and the environment, guaranteeing bank deposits of citizens, and providing a "safety net" of benefits for the jobless and the homeless, the aged and the ailing.

By the nineties, attitudes about government had turned deeply negative. Americans wanted to limit, not expand, government's role in their lives, as the fate of the health care battle demonstrated so clearly. The dramatic shift from public to private power that Langness described had barely been noticed during the two years of that battle. Opponents of reform in politics and the private sector had successfully diverted public attention by heightening fears that *Big Government* would take over the American health care system, limit choice, and restrict service. Now, in the aftermath of that struggle, *private power* was poised to take over people's health care and therefore their lives.

Consolidation of health services was only part of a dominant national trend, as huge banks merged, blue-chip corporations were swallowed up by larger ones, and mega-conglomerates were formed in publishing, entertainment, and other key industries. With exquisite irony, defeat of the greatest attempt at governmental expansion in sixty years demonstrated that the power of private interests was again on the rise in America. Not only had the public rejected, for better or worse, for sound or false reasons, a greater governmental role in the health care system, but it had also accelerated, though perhaps unwittingly, the move toward greater control by huge, new private "trusts."

These new forces, a powerful symbol of the national trend toward eliminating basic functions of government and privatizing public services, sharply increased the already great divide between America's haves and have-nots and placed greater power in the hands of fewer and fewer. "It's going to sneak up on the American populace so fast, and at such a clip, that our heads are going to reel," Dave Langness said. "By the year 2000, our prediction is that in southern California, eighty-five percent of all health care is going to be controlled by eight to ten corporations. It's on the way now. The little hospital on the corner, the little doctor's office down the street, will disappear. The solo practitioner is almost gone now except in Beverly Hills, where you have a few plastic surgeons still charging rich people. So what you've got is a monopoly. And if the American people like that better than government control, then they're going to get a big taste of it."

The frontline health care people we interviewed in Los Angeles in 1993 and other public officials outside Washington with whom we kept in contact throughout the battle had the most direct stakes in the outcome and were most directly affected by its failure. When we met them again, many of their worst fears were coming true. Some, like Langness, ruefully admitted their predictions about the passage of reform had been wrong. The concerns they had expressed about the failure of reform were sadly being realized.

Tom Priselac, president and chief executive officer of Cedars-Sinai, "the hospital of the stars," had been most worried that *public* hospitals might not survive. Their failure inevitably would place greater pressures on private institutions, already battling soaring costs, to fill the gap in services. That meant further price increases and even greater restructuring. In 1993, when Priselac expressed those concerns, the public institutions were severely strapped for funds and struggled to serve the third of the population of Los Angeles County without insurance. During the year, the strain on public hospitals and clinics had intensified. Waiting lines grew longer; many facilities were forced to close; private health organizations accepted younger and healthier patients with insurance plans while public institutions were forced to expend greater sums to treat the elderly and the ill unable to obtain insurance.

As Dave Langness saw it, these conditions would almost certainly worsen. One of the consequences of the failure of reform, he feared, was its effect on small business, which plays a dominant role in California's economy: The overwhelming majority of California workers were employed by businesses with fewer than a hundred employees. Because the small-business lobby viewed defeat of reform as a big win for them, Langness expected an already-established trend would accelerate: cutting employees out of insurance programs; raising premiums for others; hiring two part-time workers *without* benefits instead of one full-time employee *with* benefits. This would force many more people out of the insurance pool into the uninsured ranks. Already, the numbers of the uninsured were rising dramatically.

The "two-tier" system — splendid for those with coverage, terrible for those without — would become more inequitable. "If you have insurance, you go to Cedars," he said. "If you don't, you go to L.A. County [General Hospital] where you wait for hours, days, and months to get your health care."

Langness told us a personal story. That weekend, he and his wife had been hiking with friends. One of them told Langness about a health problem her housekeeper was having. She was undergoing dialysis for a kidney problem that was becoming more severe, causing her such constant pain that she often cried while at work.

"Is she legal?" Langness asked.

"Yes," his friend replied.

"Does she have health insurance?"

"No."

"Well," Langness said, "has she gone to County?"

She had. Her condition was serious, physicians there told her. The kidney needed to be removed. An appointment was made for the surgery. The earliest date available was November 1995 — thirteen months later. "So that's what people are having to go through," Langness said, "and that's by no means the worst story I've heard.

We've taken our health care system and marginalized a whole third of our population and said, 'You're not going to get health care even if you really need it.' To others who can afford it, we've said, 'You can have it.' That divide between the haves and have-nots will widen, that gulf will deepen."

Chris Klasen was both sad and angry. She is the Los Angeles County General Hospital doctor who chose to work at a huge public hospital because that is where the physician deals most urgently with daily life-and-death emergencies.

A year before, Klasen had looked forward hopefully, if guardedly, to the Clinton plan. Now, she was filled with sharply conflicting emotions — sorrow at the failure to take at least a first step toward reform; anger at apathetic doctors who "care nothing about what's happening in health care"; disgust at special interests "who have enough money to buy Harry and Louise ads"; bewilderment at why The System was unable to deal with an obviously critical national problem. "It just makes me sad — really sad — that as a civilized country we couldn't begin to resolve health care," she said. "I've been around this track for twenty-five years since I graduated from medical school. So health care is my career. And I see it going down the tubes. I mean, I am aware of the importance of market issues, but I thought some kind of publicly sponsored movement was better than nothing at all. Instead, it was a deadlock. There was no movement."

With her in a Los Angeles restaurant were two colleagues from the massive L.A. County–University of Southern California Medical Center whom we had interviewed the previous October. The difficult conditions they faced then had worsened; the hospital hallways were more crowded than ever, the funds to support them increasingly short, the strain on everyone more severe. At the Hudson Clinic, where indigent people come for basic public health services, the problems Julie Delgado, a clinical social worker, described for society's "throwaway people" were even grimmer. "At Hudson, there are not enough chairs for the clients to sit on," she said. "There's just one train coming after the next after the next, and there's no time, there's no physical space to be nice to people."

Delgado expressed a deeper level of anger than Chris Klasen. "I despair," she said. "I'm full of cynicism. If I hear Phil Gramm crow one more time about how cool it is that he killed health care reform I'll throw up. Anybody can kill anything, but that doesn't do the country a whole lot of good. I think these guys in Congress must all have beards. I can't imagine they shave in the morning and look in the mirror. Their performance has been disgraceful. This is not a great thing they've done. If they didn't like it, there must be some-thing better they could do. But just to stall and leave people —" She threw up her hands and said, in disgust, "Oh, maybe I'm just dumb and young, I don't know."

Dr. Ron Kaufman, administrator of L.A. County General, took a more tempered view. The Clinton plan was too big, he thought. It wasn't wrong. It wasn't right. It was just too big. They should have attacked the most important issues first, then moved on to the next.

As for The System itself, Kaufman was not as negative as the oth-ers. In such a diverse, heterogeneous society, you have to forge pub-lic consensus, he believed. That's the role for political leaders; they must create that environment. Obviously, that hadn't happened this time. Without it, people will always resist change; they will stand with the status quo. The Clinton battle even had its positive side, he thought. It had accelerated the pace of marketplace reform in Los Angeles and the nation. But the negative side was all too evident and nowhere more so than in the place Kaufman and his colleagues knew best — the sprawling public L.A. County–USC Med Center, by far the busiest hospital complex in a county of ten million people, a hospital facility where 40 percent of all patients can't pay.

Did you know, Dr. Kaufman asked his colleagues, that the Med Center is the second-busiest bus stop in our entire region? The first is Union Station. The third is LAX [Los Angeles International Air-port]. It's a little-known fact, he added, pleased at surprising them with this knowledge.

Then he became deadly serious, and suddenly sounded as pessi-mistic as the others. We're buffeted, he said, by the rapidity of change in the part of our population that has health insurance and the large, growing population that hasn't. How long can we survive, he asked rhetorically, in a system that requires us to compete with all pro-viders while we have to provide care for which we are inadequately compensated? We have a shadow system called the public system. Because that system has been inadequately funded and faces excess demands on its services, public hospitals and clinics have been forced to subsidize the care they provide by paying low salaries and hiring people who are either willing to accept a lower salary or who cannot be hired anyplace else. Without reform of the entire system, they were now at the additional disadvantage of having to be competitive in the private marketplace without the resources to compete in it.

What it meant, Kaufman said, was that America was accepting a situation in which past commitments to public services would no longer be honored. "We're going to depend on the private system," he said, "which has never served the needy in the past." It's going to be brutal, he said, "brutal in terms of the cost, brutal in terms of the squeezing out of health providers — both facilities and individuals."

It turned out to be even more brutal than Kaufman had feared.

Almost eight months to the day after we spoke, plans were announced to *close* the L.A. County General–USC Medical Center, four comprehensive health centers and clinics (including Julie Delgado's Hudson), and twenty-five neighborhood clinics, eliminating twelve thousand six hundred jobs for a saving of six hundred fifty-five million dollars — part of a total projected county budget cut of one billion two hundred million dollars. These massive cutbacks, prompted by spiraling long-term debt and made worse by a shortfall in federal and state funds threatening the county with bankruptcy, were submitted to the Los Angeles County Board of Supervisors, the governing body of the largest local governmental entity in the nation. If the supervisors approved these proposals, calling for elimination of one of every five county jobs by 1996 and sweeping reductions in a vast array of county services, the only public health facilities in Los Angeles County, which embraces the city of Los Angeles, would be two comprehensive health centers and fourteen community clinics.

This news set off immense shock waves throughout Los Angeles, sparking political controversy and predictions of incalculable damage to the health needs of the region, especially to people least able to afford good care. The cuts vividly underscored the growing national trend to make massive reductions in public services from health and welfare to parks and libraries and courts and sheriff's offices. In Los Angeles, as in other areas, the drastic cutbacks came against a background of the reductions in federal and state spending and amid new political priorities that favored lower taxes, less government, reduced social services, and greater privatization of public services. All of these elements had been central in the great health battle of 1993–94. Now, in late 1995, they had come home with a vengeance to the parts of The System that most directly served the people — local and state governments.

Not surprisingly, the consequences of the failure of reform had hit with particular cruelty in the area of Los Angeles that most typified the problems of urban America — in the Watts section of South Central L.A., where race riots had flared in 1964 and again in 1992. There, in the fall of 1994, Dr. Reed Tuckson was in a state of suppressed fury as he described the effect of that failure on the major public health institution he heads, the Martin Luther King Jr./Charles Drew Medical Center in the heart of Watts. The Center, a huge complex of concrete structures that took form when the Great Society was pouring money into domestic programs and seeking to improve the nation's health and welfare systems, is part of the L.A. County health care system. Even before the Clinton effort, the Medical Center had experienced major cutbacks as it struggled to serve a growing indigent inner-city population with a decrease in funds from the State of California. The result, as the battle began, was that the Center found itself with many more patients to serve with many fewer health professionals to serve them, and forced to operate with fewer resources, medical supplies, and equipment.

Reed Tuckson, a slim, energetic, black professional, was optimistic at the beginning of the health care battle. He was one of the medical experts who traveled back and forth from Los Angeles to Washington to offer advice to the Clinton planners, and, despite all the problems with the plan, Dr. Tuckson felt confident that positive action would result from it. Now he, too, felt enraged about the immense failure.

Surveying that wreckage, he enumerated some of the consequences. As costs continued to escalate, so did the number of the uninsured whose employers, or whose spouse's employers, or whose parents' employers, could no longer provide insurance. That meant more and more people had no place to turn but to a public sector whose resources were dwindling rapidly.

With each passing day, Tuckson said, the public health infrastructure that supports inner-city communities like his in Watts deteriorated. Preventable diseases like tuberculosis continued to be widespread in the poor communities. Instead of providing a unified national approach, in failing, the attempt at reform had produced mass confusion and uncertainty — "chaos in the land" — as hospitals and practitioners jockeyed for their share of a shrinking market increasingly dominated by the rising mega–health conglomerates. "People are not sitting down to figure out how to work together to solve unmet needs," he said. "People are sitting down trying to organize, in a very competitive way, to preserve, maintain, or expand their market share for patients. Those without insurance are not part of these discussions."

Tuckson found this attitude despicable — a sign that Americans were shirking their civic duties, becoming new Social Darwinists trumpeting a belief in survival of the fittest, a belief that society had no special responsibility to those who could not help themselves.

For Tuckson, what he called *the* defining moment came when Phil Gramm *boasted* that he had killed health reform. "I felt pure outrage," Tuckson said, still burning as he recalled that moment. "Anger, embarrassment, and shame for America." He was enraged that Gramm and Gingrich and lobbyists would smugly and self-righteously *brag* about defeating reform.

"What's even worse is the fact that it's not condemned by the nation," he raged, "that we are not angry at those who are happy that little babies are crying in the night. We, the American people, engaged in this two-year process without either understanding or appreciating the human misery, pain, and suffering that accompany so many of our countrymen and -women and children's lives."

Yet even these concerns, passionately felt and expressed to us, did not reflect, he thought, what caused him the most anguish, and anger.

"What scares me about all of this is that when it comes to health care, the consequences of failure are death, human misery, and suffering," he said. "It would be one thing if the consequences were a mere inconvenience in, say, our transportation system, so it took us longer to get home at night. That is frustrating, but not deadly. Here, we're talking about whether people *live or die.*"

The lack of public outrage, or of the passion to address fundamental public questions, perplexed Tuckson, he confessed:

> I'm left with an emotion of real pessimism about how America will ever have the maturity to address complex issues of public policy given the manipulation that is possible, given the talk show mentalities that are so filled with cynicism and pessimism and can't-do, and with two-second sound bites on news that pass for transmission of information. What worries me most is that it's very possible that America does not have the ability, the capacity, the competence, to come together as a unified nation of people who are able and willing to tackle complex problems and work through a logical sequence of solutions. Instead, we will have politicians who find it in their best interests to continue to sub-fragment the political marketplace, to trade on divisions and differences, class, race, geography, and political ideologies, so that we become so fragmented and unable to discuss complex issues that we will get piecework, small incremental changes that will fail in the short run, and, worse, doom us to severe consequences in the long run.

The night before we spoke with him, toward the end of October 1994, Ed Edelman had watched a PBS television documentary on the life of Franklin D. Roosevelt. Now the next day, in his conference room overlooking downtown Los Angeles, Edelman was filled with a strong impression of the powerful, almost painful contrast between those earlier scenes of an America battling a political/economic crisis in the thirties and the present period of disillusionment with all institutions and all leaders, particularly political leaders.

Edelman had good reason to appreciate those public attitudes; as head of the Los Angeles County Board of Supervisors, he faced one crisis after another over crime, housing, courts, transportation, education, immigration, welfare, and, yes, health needs for the ten million people he was charged with serving. "My God, there was something there in that old footage," he exclaimed. "There was something about Roosevelt that comes over — jaunty, buoyant — and here's a guy who was in constant pain. I mean, it was not just retrospective bullshit."

Then Edelman turned to the impact of the reform battle on his level of The System and on the upcoming fall elections. A lifelong Democrat, Edelman had had high hopes for Bill Clinton and his reform when we first spoke a year before. He now believed the President had been "wounded going in," as revelations about his personal life during the election made him vulnerable to suspicions about his character. Then Whitewater further damaged the President's credibility. Edelman was now more critical of the President, and of the way the battle was fought — and lost. Clinton hadn't helped people understand where we are and where we need to go as clearly and sharply as he could have, Edelman thought. He wondered, still thinking about FDR, how that strong President would have handled the issue today. Most critically, he wondered whether even FDR would have made a difference. Probably, he concluded, the outcome would have been the same.

Today's political climate is so different, he said. The country is less united because it doesn't face the threat of a Depression or a war, as it did in FDR's time. There's so much public indifference and lack of concern. Everything's more ideological. There's less willingness to compromise. "Given the present antigovernment feelings and partisanship throughout The System," Edelman said, "leaders may be powerless no matter what their magnetism or their acumen."

But the greatest problem was the spreading sense of disillusionment that lessened respect for leaders and institutions. Clinton had paid dearly in that respect, he thought. Even an FDR would have great difficulties dealing with the complex American problems of the nineties. "In politics, there's a lack of putting the interests of the country first," he said. "That's why the parties are not doing well. People don't trust them. People are maneuvering for their own benefit." Third-party movements headed by outsiders like Ross Perot were becoming stronger. "I see them having more opportunity to gain power," Edelman said. Everyone wants "to get control of Congress. That is the most important thing. They look at every issue in that light."

His critical views of The System were echoed by nearly everyone with whom we spoke in the last days before the 1994 elections. They all sensed tremendous change in the making, change driven by a deep and growing sense of anger with the American way of government and politics. No one foresaw the political consequences more vividly than Dave Langness. "I feel sick at heart about the future of our political system," he said. "Our political system has almost made itself obsolete. It's so ineffectual and so controlled by monied interests that it has become a joke to most American people. I don't know anyone anymore who thinks the political leaders serve their interests except those with large amounts of cash. That's a recipe for growing disaffection and, ultimately, a recipe for chaos. That's what we're fomenting in this country very, very fast."

22

Earthquake

NO ONE WAS LESS surprised at the ignominious death of the Clinton plan than Newt Gingrich. For almost two years, he had predicted that outcome privately and bent every effort to ensure the plan would fail. During those years, he plotted its demise, organized his forces, defined their strategy, provided their martial rhetoric. And he dispersed his guerrilla warriors for what Gingrich had long boasted would be the decisive "ambush" that won the war.

It is one of Gingrich's conceits — a source of what his followers see as self-confidence and his critics as arrogance — that he believes himself to be in league with powerful historical forces, which he has identified and his adversaries have not. In Newt Gingrich's self-portrait, he is the one-eyed king in the land of the blind. Armed with that faith, he waited confidently for the Clinton plan to crash so he could address his next, and grander, goal: restoring Republican control of Congress with himself as its most powerful player.

To Gingrich, the plan was a prime example of how out of touch the Clintons were with the powerful new socioeconomic and political forces of the mid-nineties. "I believe the Clintons so thoroughly misunderstand America they were simply in the wrong world," he told us. "It's like being tone-deaf. Their tactics were fine, but their vision and strategy were crazy and therefore their project was doomed. . . . They were going against the entire tide of Western history. Centralized command bureaucracies are dying. This is the end of that era."

As early as July of 1994, he understood the script for a campaign massacre. "Imagine it's October," he told the *Washington Post*'s

Helen Dewar. "The Democrats are going to get up and make the following case: 'We've run the House for forty years, we've run the Senate for eight years, we have the White House, and the Republicans are so much more clever than we are that they've obstructed. We need you to elect more dumb Democrats so we can overcome these clever Republicans.' " Gingrich sketched out a campaign in which term-limits supporters would join those "afraid of Big Government health care" in forming the "nitroglycerin" that would blow up Democratic control of Congress.

Even so, Gingrich, the master plotter, feared the Clintons could still escape his trap. Had the President and the First Lady come back to him and said, "Okay, *our* version of reform is dead, but let's pass *yours*" — the Rowland-Bilirakis bill, designed by lobbyists, House Republicans, and some conservative Democrats as a stopgap to Clinton — they could have prevailed. "The President could have had a bill-signing," Gingrich told us. "We would have been totally outflanked and we would have helped pass it."

Then, brimming with typical self-assurance, Gingrich contradicted himself. From the beginning, he said, he counted on the President's never abandoning the legislative strategy of forming his winning coalition from a liberal base. Had Clinton tried to endorse a minimalist Republican bill, Democratic liberals like Pete Stark and Henry Waxman "would have gone berserk." So, Gingrich happily concluded, he had the Clintons enclosed in a box. "They were just trapped."

By the time George Mitchell pulled the plug on health care in late September, Gingrich's goal of recapturing Congress was on track, though Democratic strategists, including the President's political advisers, did not believe the midterm election campaign would lead to a Republican takeover. To ensure total political unity — normally close to impossible in a deeply fragmented society — Gingrich got all his troops, incumbents and challengers alike, to sign a ten-point "Contract With America."

The Contract was a solemn pledge from Republicans to voters to act on a specific conservative agenda in the first hundred days of the next Congress — assuming, of course, voters shifted power from Democrats to Republicans in the House of Representatives. Tax cuts, balanced budgets, welfare reform, term limits, massive government cutbacks, all were part of the Contract. Unlike the Democratic strategy, which was to craft their fall campaigns around local issues and the popularity of individual lawmakers, the Republican strategy was to nationalize this election. It would be a referendum on the role of government, liberalism versus conservatism, and on President Clinton's leadership — and also on the role of his wife, Hillary.

Reforming health care was not part of the Contract; nonetheless, it was a key part of the Republican election campaign strategy. Across the country, Republican candidates denounced the Clinton plan in their campaign ads and speeches; they depicted it as the preeminent symbol of the Big Government they opposed. In Republican rhetoric, the Clinton plan was "the mother of all entitlements," something that would force higher taxes and produce even greater deficits. It was "bureaucracy run amok." It was a threat to the American way of life.

Repeatedly raising the specter of a "government-run health plan" accomplished many things for Republicans, Gingrich said, in a rare burst of understatement. First, it "scared everybody. If you were a senior, you got scared. If you were a doctor, you got scared. Suddenly, everybody is driven to us," he said, "and you have this huge, grand coalition forming. Combined with the tax increase of 'ninety-three, gays in the military, [it gave voters the sense] that these folks were committed to a government-controlled, left-wing vision of America."

From the beginning, these were the themes that Gingrich and his troops had brilliantly employed to bring about their Republican Revolution. Playing on mistrust and fears of government enabled Gingrich to use the health care battle as a powerful symbol of the failings of the liberal welfare state. So, as we have seen, even a full year before Bill Clinton was nominated for President, Gingrich had plotted to defeat *any* Democratic attempt to provide universal health care for Americans. Only by defeating what Gingrich was convinced would be this next great domestic policy of the Democrats could he fulfill the goals of the Revolution: win back control of Congress, with himself as its dominant figure. He was determined to break the public dependency on Democratic tax-funded government programs. He dreamed of replacing them with a new, antigovernment, antitax, entrepreneurial nation. The stakes were immense; so were the consequences of victory, or defeat. And the health care battle symbolized it all. As Grover Norquist, a top Gingrich conservative strategist, later put it, for the Democrats the loss of the health care battle became "their Stalingrad, their Gettysburg, their Waterloo."

Gingrich, better than anyone, anticipated these results and the effect they would have on the 1994 elections. As Gingrich boasted, not only had the opponents succeeded brilliantly in "scaring everybody"; the long battle had another more subtle but equally important result for the Democrats. The fight, Gingrich said, had "totally exhausted their elites. People like Mitchell and Gephardt were just devoured. They were demoralized. They've never recovered the energy level they had prior to this fight."

That gap between the energy and enthusiasm of Gingrich's Contract candidates and the lethargy of the Democrats was vividly displayed in the fall of 1994. Democrats dragged through their schedules: Republicans added more and more events. The main Democratic support groups, especially organized labor, exhibited the same striking lack of enthusiasm; emotionally, they were bankrupt. The unions, the teachers, the nurses, the entire liberal coalition, in fact, had expended millions of dollars and countless hours trying to build grassroots support for reform. Yet at the end — nothing. They were deprived of even a floor vote in the House or Senate to identify "enemies" or rally support for "friends."

By Tuesday, November 8, 1994, a fateful Election Day, the Democrats knew from their private polls that they were in trouble. They anticipated a dramatic drop in Democratic turnout from the last off-year election four years before. Republicans, exuding confidence, knew their own voter rolls were soaring, and Newt Gingrich knew that his time had come.

Outside Atlanta, in a shopping mall ballroom, little girls marched through the Election Night crowds waving placards reading "Liberals, your time is up!" Beyond the doors, vendors were selling T-shirts. "Rush Limbaugh for President," was the message printed on one, "Clinocchio" on another. As the returns poured in, the Newt Gingrich victory party became a celebration of the new conservative tide engulfing America that night. "The air," as Maureen Dowd reported from the scene in next morning's *New York Times*, "was filled with vengeful glee."

An Atlanta conservative talk show host, Sean Hannity, master of ceremonies for the celebration, exulted in the toppling of a Democratic Party liberal icon, Governor Mario Cuomo, by the voters of New York. Hannity sneered as he mispronounced the governor's name, "Coo-mo." Then he joked that a Federal Express delivery had just brought Tylenol for President Clinton, who was "about to feel the pain."

In the sea of euphoric faces, all eyes were on Newt Gingrich, not only in that Atlanta ballroom but in living rooms across the nation, where millions watched this moment live on television. The most pugnacious of politicians, the architect of the Revolution, who, as Dowd noted, had in recent days campaigned against Clinton Democrats as "the enemy of normal Americans," had linked the drowning murder of two young boys by their mother in South Carolina with Democratic liberalism, and had vowed an all-out congressional investigation of what he called White House corruption, was now a picture of soothing nonpartisanship. Beaming, his eyes sparkling, his NEWT button gleaming on his suit jacket, Gingrich pledged a new era of cooperation, not confrontation. He wanted "to try to reach out to every Democrat who wants to work with us," he said into the massed microphones. His intention was to be "Speaker of the House, not Speaker of the Republican Party."

He had the band play "Happy Days Are Here Again," the bouncy political anthem that was the theme song for Franklin D. Roosevelt's New Deal sixty-two years before. Now, in that victory ballroom, they were saying America was about to get "the Newt Deal."

On the corner of Broad Street, in South Philadelphia, across from a tailor shop, Harris Wofford made a final campaign stop at a diner packed with people. It was about an hour before the polls closed in Pennsylvania. A couple of hours earlier, around 4:30, Wofford had received bad news: a private exit poll of voters who had already cast their ballots showed Wofford losing to his young challenger, Congressman Rick Santorum, by four percentage points. Now, Wofford was greeted with the cheers of people wishing him well, pledging their support, saying they were for him. He left buoyed, his hopes rising; then he went to a downtown athletic club for a swim and a sauna, and back to his hotel suite to await the outcome. By then, the exit polls had narrowed; he was only two points down. As the actual returns began coming in, he was ahead by five. There it stayed until nearly 91 percent of the precincts had reported; but already, he knew. The counties still unreported were almost solidly Republican.

About eleven o'clock, Wofford began drafting, in longhand, two statements: one for victory, one for concession. By midnight, the time for decision had arrived. He entered the hotel ballroom, where his victory party was fast becoming a wake, and began his concession speech. Halfway through his remarks, still thanking his supporters but not yet giving his formal concession, the TV stations cut him off. The cameras switched to a ballroom in Pittsburgh where Rick Santorum, the thirty-seven-year-old Republican congressman whose campaign had been given $784,000 by the health and insurance industries for consistently voting and speaking against the administration reform bill in the Ways and Means Committee, was about to declare victory.

In a special election just three years before, it was Harris Wofford who had put health reform on the political map. In the closing days of his Senate service, Wofford offered a symbolic bill that would have stopped the federal government from offering health insurance policies to members of Congress while other Americans remained uninsured. He tried to convince his constituents that Republicans like Santorum were to blame for the inaction. Instead, they blamed the man — and the party — that had promised and not delivered. Harris Wofford lost by two percentage points.*

---

*Fourteen months later, Wofford's wife, Clare, whom he had cited to us at the beginning of the health reform battle as an example of someone with a preexisting medical condition who could be denied health insurance, died of leukemia.

* * *

Across the continent, in the Pacific Northwest, Tom Foley met his doom in typical style: quietly and with dignity. His Fifth Congressional District — which lay on the eastern border of Washington State, an area of arid farmland and piney foothills with a nearly all-white population, conservative in temperament but far more dependent than most for federal agricultural supports and defense spending — was one of the last in the nation to be decided this Election Day.

It was nine o'clock Pacific Time, midnight in the nation's capital, when a somber Foley emerged from his Spokane campaign headquarters to give his first public reaction to the electoral shock waves rolling across America. He had campaigned in the same courtly, gentlemanly style that won him election to the House for thirty years. Though urged to go negative to combat aggressive grassroots efforts against him by the National Rifle Association, the Christian Coalition, the National Taxpayers Union, and other conservative groups, Foley refused to do so. The night before, in his final rally, he said quietly that he was "sick and tired of the negativism and pessimism." Now, in his reaction to news of the Republican takeover of Congress, he said, "It will be, I think, unfortunate if the result of this election is more a sense of frustration, more a sense of gridlock and indecision that is still at the heart of public dissatisfaction."

At that time, Foley's race was too close to call; he went to bed still not knowing whether he had won or lost. By mid-morning of the next day, the race had still not been officially determined. Only a scattered thousand or so swing votes separated Foley from his challenger, George Nethercutt, a former U.S. Senate aide and local Republican leader. But they were enough, and Foley, seated at a table in his district office, joined by his wife, Heather, and aides with long faces, calmly conceded the election. He gave no farewell blast, or call to arms. He ended with a defense of, and tribute to, The System. "Despite what some people think," he said, "the overwhelming membership of the Congress, Republican and Democrat, are wonderful, upstanding, talented people who carry on the service of their constituents with honor and effectiveness." He praised all the Presidents with whom he had served, Republicans and Democrats: Nixon and Johnson, Ford, Carter, Reagan, Bush, Clinton. All of them had "sought to move our country forward. Men of honor and integrity," he said. "I have tried to give them my best service and counsel and assistance."

Tom Foley lost by two points. He became the first sitting Speaker of the House of Representatives to be defeated for reelection since 1862, when America was in the midst of its Civil War.

When it was over, voters had delivered the worst midterm repudiation of a President since Harry Truman in 1946 and signaled the most decisive shift in the role and direction of government since Franklin Roosevelt and the New Deal. They broke the forty-year hold of the Democrats on Congress, restored Republicans to power at every level of government, and set the stage for a further great test over the nation's ideological future in 1996, the last presidential election of the century. David Wilhelm, the outgoing Democratic Party chairman, a pleasant, ineffectual young man — a disaster, many thought, as party strategist, especially on the health care battle — offered no excuses. "Well, we made history last night," he told Adam Clymer of the *New York Times*. "Call it what you want: an earthquake, a tidal wave, a blowout. We got our butts kicked."

The Republican tide was strong and deep and historic — a tsunami, it was immediately called by pundits groping for an adequate term to describe the magnitude of this political earthquake, settling on the Japanese term for a huge wave, produced by an undersea volcanic eruption, that crashes upon the shores and alters everything in its path. Journalistic exaggeration aside, superlatives were deserved.

In two years, Democrats had gone from a controlling majority of two hundred fifty-eight seats in the House of Representatives to a minority of two hundred four. For the first time, Republicans won a majority of House seats from the South. Earlier, signs of the final breakup of the old solid South had appeared in the border state of Kentucky. A conservative Republican, Ron Lewis, won the seat of the late William Natcher, a longtime congressional powerhouse, in a special election by portraying his Democratic opponent, Joe Prather, as a clone of Bill Clinton. Democrats had held that congressional seat for the last one hundred twenty-nine years. In the Senate, Democrats saw their numbers decrease from fifty-seven to forty-seven, and within a few months, two Democrats defected to the Republican side, further strengthening the GOP majority. In gubernatorial races, the Democrats saw their numbers reversed. In 1992, they held thirty governors' seats. Two years later they held nineteen, and thirty Republicans occupied the statehouses. (There was one Independent.)

Most important, Republicans now governed nine of the ten most populous states, a critical factor in determining which party's nominee wins the White House: Massachusetts, New York, New Jersey, Pennsylvania, Ohio, Michigan, Illinois, Texas, California. Three of those states — California, New York, Texas — control 40 percent of the 270 electoral votes needed to win the presidency. Only one of the nation's ten megastates, Florida, remained in Democratic hands. Republicans also won in many of the smaller swing states, including Minnesota, where pro-reform Governor Arne Carlson survived in the Republican primary against ultraconservative Allen Quist and then clobbered his Democratic opponent in November.

Not only had Republicans broken the Democratic hold on the great industrial states that were traditionally the stronghold of the most loyal and powerful Democratic constituency, organized labor; they also strengthened their grip on the once solidly Democratic South and Southwest, defeating Democratic gubernatorial candidates in Alabama, Tennessee, Texas, and Oklahoma.

Nor did the Republican surge end there. Their party gained control of eighteen state legislative chambers, bringing them to virtual parity with the Democrats. In 1992, Democrats had a more than two-to-one margin, sixty-six to twenty-nine, in those state legislatures. After the 1994 election, Republicans controlled forty-seven and the Democrats forty-eight. The shift in numbers of state legislators was equally dramatic: Republicans gained nearly five hundred new seats from Democrats across the nation. More telling was the remarkable turnaround in the number of states where both legislative chambers and the governor were from the same party. In 1992, Democrats enjoyed total control in sixteen of those states, while the Republicans held only three. Two years later, Republicans controlled fifteen states; the Democratic number had shrunk to seven.

Even these stunning statistics don't tell the most significant story of the 1994 earthquake: In all the contests for House, Senate, and gubernatorial seats, not a single Republican seeking reelection lost. Across the nation, in every region, *only* Democratic incumbents were defeated, forty-one of them in all. Seldom, if ever, in American elections have voters delivered such an unmistakably strong and clear verdict of disapproval against members of one of the two major parties.

Historically, there are few precedents for such a startling shakeup of The System. The 1994 upheaval ranks with the four most significant off-year elections in the century. In 1938, FDR's New Deal was dealt a mortal blow when Democrats lost eighty-one House and eight Senate seats. In 1946, Harry Truman's plans to continue liberal Roosevelt policies into the post–World War II era were seemingly crushed when Republicans regained control of Congress by winning fifty-five House and thirteen Senate seats. In 1966, Lyndon Johnson's Great Society was dashed when Democrats lost thirty-six House and four Senate seats. In 1974, Richard Nixon's conservative era ended when Republicans lost forty-seven House and five Senate seats. But fateful though those elections proved, they were all dominated by specific issues that led to the electoral shocks. In the cases of Johnson and Nixon, the war in Vietnam and the Watergate scandal sparked a great voter reaction. In Truman's, it was fear over crime and communism; in FDR's, his plan to pack the Supreme Court.

In 1994, policy and ideology drove the voters — and drove them with such uniformity of purpose that they singled out Democratic incumbent candidates for defeat across the entire System while sparing every Republican seeking reelection.

In the aftermath of the election, conservative groups — the gun lobby, the pro-life groups, the Christian Coalition, the antitaxers — hailed the results, justifiably, as powerful evidence that voters were supporting their causes. So they did. In 1992, the designated Year of the Woman, *pro-choice* candidates were in the ascendancy. Two years later, six new women *pro-life* candidates were elected to Congress, all Republicans, all fitting the strongly conservative ideological profile that characterized new members of Congress and state legislatures. The election data demonstrated that, indeed, the voters of 1994 viewed their ballots in far more ideological terms. As the respected Times Mirror Center for the People & the Press noted, in a careful analysis completed five months after the election, "Last year, while cynicism and discontent with government were major factors in the GOP victory, the Republicans scored a major tactical victory. They turned out conservatives who knew what they were voting for."

That was the key. Although the total voter turnout on November 8, 1994, was barely higher than the low turnout of the last off-year election in 1990 — 38 percent of eligible voters in 1994 compared to 37 percent in 1990 — it was the Republicans who were most committed to voting. Democratic turnout dropped precipitously, falling a million votes below 1990. At the same time, Republican candidates drew nine million more votes than they had in 1990. The result was devastating to the Democrats: the political earthquake that ended their long rule of Congress and of many of the states.

Of those who did vote, the portrait that emerged was of a sharply polarized electorate. While voter surveys showed virtually no change in the party identification of voters between 1992 and 1994 — Democrats favored by 38 percent in '92 and 37 percent in '94, with Republicans holding to exactly the same 35 percent in both years — there was a dramatic shift in those identifying themselves as "conservatives." Seven percent more of those voting in 1994 called themselves conservative. Of those, 80 percent voted Republican. In contrast, sharply highlighting the electoral polarization, 82 percent of those identifying themselves as liberals voted for Democrats. The demographic breakdown depicted similar sharp differences among American voters: 57 percent of men voted Republican, 54 percent of women Democratic; 58 percent of whites voted Republican, 92 percent of blacks, 60 percent of Hispanics, and 55 percent of Asians for Democrats; 60 percent of Protestants voted Republican; 85 percent of conservative white men voted Republican, 83 percent of liberal white men, Democratic.

Among those who voted, antigovernment ads and rhetoric still resonated in the nineties; "trust in government" hit an all-time low in 1994, the continuation of a long trend. In the 1950s, nearly three-fourths of the American population told pollsters they trusted government "to do what is right" all or most of the time. In 1994, only a fourth of the population felt that way.

Voters' feelings about government were crystallized by the health care battle, and Republicans exploited those emotions brilliantly. Phil Gramm, who made defeat of the Clinton plan a personal crusade, told us "it was the dominant factor in this election." Admitting, "I'm not sure to this day that I fully understand everything that went into the remarkable transformation that occurred on this issue," he compared it to "a near-death experience." Clinton, he said, came so close to selling the country on what Gramm called "socialized medicine," that when the voters realized it, they asked themselves, "How the hell did I get here? Do I want to stay on this road?" The chorus of nos, Gramm said, translated into a tide of Republican votes.

Less biased observers agreed. Everett Carll Ladd, director of the Roper Center for Public Opinion Research at the University of Connecticut, said, "The message of this election is a call for curbs, a worry about excesses in government, but not an end to government. The health care debate was the definitive debate in describing this era." Stan Greenberg, the President's pollster, said the main reason that Independents swung to the GOP in 1994 was their "disappointment that Clinton proposed Big Government solutions like health care reform."

The lobbyists' powerful campaigns against reform were vindicated at the polls. Not only Tom Foley, whose advice on the issue was influential with the Clintons, and Harris Wofford, whose Senate career symbolized the fight, were defeated. Other players, closely identified with the battle, became notable losers. In the House, the formidable Danny Rostenkowski lost to an unknown Chicago Republican, Michael Patrick Flanagan. Peter Hoagland was soundly beaten in Nebraska by Jon Christensen, the Republican who had taunted him from his front-row seat while Hoagland voted to keep the employer mandate provision in the House Ways and Means Committee bill.*

---

*Christensen, widely publicized as a "family values" House Republican freshman, became involved in a nasty divorce suit in 1995 involving allegations of adultery.

In Tennessee, Jim Cooper's bid for an open Senate seat failed. He was beaten by Fred Thompson, a Republican lawyer-lobbyist with a second career as an occasional movie actor. Cooper collected nearly $753,000 in campaign contributions from the insurance and health industry and — despite John Dingell's efforts to stir up trouble for him at home — held on to much of the labor and minority vote. In TV ads, Cooper portrayed himself as a congressional David fighting the White House Goliath of his own party. "The Washington power structure was so frightened by the Cooper plan that they never allowed a vote on it," the TV narrator said, boldly rewriting history. "But they couldn't kill his idea or intimidate him. He stood like a rock. And a President retreated."

But Thompson took the "Clinton Lite" label that Cooper had placed on his own plan and gave it a negative twist. At the end of an ad assailing Cooper's record and positions as models of hypocrisy, Thompson's campaign commercial aired across Tennessee said, "Career politician Jim Cooper. No wonder they call him Clinton Lite." Thompson effectively hung Cooper with a noose the young Democratic congressman had placed around his own neck.

In Kansas, Jim Slattery, who had joined Cooper in denying Dingell the votes to report the Clinton bill from Energy and Commerce, found himself facing a similar problem. He lost the governor's race by a landslide, to Republican Bill Graves, and came away believing that his opposition to Clinton was "a lose-lose proposition." In the spring, he said, "the supporters of the Clinton plan ran full-page ads against me in Kansas that told the people of Kansas that I had this great health care plan as a member of Congress and I was basically an unsympathetic bastard because I was taking care of myself and to hell with the rest of the country." In the fall, "the health care debate defined our party in a very negative context for the American public. It was perceived to be this huge government plan to be funded by higher taxes and cuts in Medicare and as something that would possibly threaten the quality of health care for those who currently have good coverage."

The same reverse twist happened in dozens of other races, as Democrats found themselves on the wrong side of a boomerang issue. The *Wall Street Journal*'s Hilary Stout told the tale of Sheila

McGuire's Iowa congressional race against her Republican opponent, Tom Latham. McGuire, an epidemiologist, had been a member of one of Ira Magaziner's health care task force review panels. Latham ran radio ads saying, "Professor McGuire helped write the Clinton health care plan that would put a bureaucrat between you and your doctor, raise your taxes, and close many rural hospitals. Everyone agrees the Clinton-McGuire plan was a bad idea."

Latham won Fred Grandy's old seat by a three-to-two margin.

In addition to figuring in numerous congressional races, the health care issue resounded in California. There a ballot initiative for a state-run single-payer system was crushed at the polls, failing by an almost three-to-one margin, after a free-spending opposition campaign led by many of the same interest groups that helped defeat the Clinton plan in Congress. Fear of too much government involvement at the state level was the main reason cited for opposition to the measure.

Watching the disaster overtaking their party, some of the survivors reacted with uncharacteristic bitterness. John Breaux of Louisiana, one of the most frustrated would-be deal makers in the Senate, a confidant of the Clintons from the beginning, and one who worked until the end to fashion the bipartisan Mainstream Coalition plan, complained that "instead of debating the welfare system that everyone agrees serves no one well, we spent our time on a 'do it all at once' health proposal that many Americans felt was a 'take from me and give to them' redistribution regime mandated by Washington."

Breaux had not changed his mind about the need for health care reform, or his conviction that The System would still have to deal with it for America's future well-being. The experience left him bemused and bewildered, however. He was walking through the New Orleans airport, returning home, when an elderly female constituent approached him. "Senator, Senator," she said, plucking emotionally at his sleeve. "Now don't you let the government get a hold of my Medicare." Breaux, ever the charmer, smiled and said reassuringly of this greatest of government entitlement programs, "Oh, no, we won't let the government touch your Medicare."

* * *

The election shook The System to its roots and altered the power structure in Washington and across the nation, but it did not, with breathtaking irony, change the high priority the public placed on health care reform.

An Election Night survey for the Kaiser Family Foundation and Harvard University found voters actually ranking health care as *the* most important issue to affect their vote that day, ahead of crime and taxes, and also as the most important issue for the new Congress. Two other results from that poll reflected the conservative electoral swing, however. By a substantial margin, these voters said they wanted modest changes rather than a major reform. As many wanted the system left alone (a fourth of a sample) as wanted a major overhaul. Most wanted Congress, not the President, to take the lead in improving the system.

By the end of the year, as the Gingrich Revolution Congress was about to assume office, a Gallup poll showed the power the issue still held. At that point, 72 percent of the public listed major health care reform as a top or high priority for the new One Hundred Fourth Congress of the United States. Only crime and deficit reduction ranked higher.

23

Aftershocks

NOT SINCE THE NEW DEAL had Washington witnessed such a spectacle. They poured into the capital, eager, determined — conservative crusaders who all believed *their* time finally had arrived. Ideologically, they were the heirs of Barry Goldwater and Ronald Reagan, who thirty years before had begun the national movement to replace the liberal welfare state with a radically more conservative model. By the nineties, their movement had evolved into a powerful "leave us alone" coalition. Now, for the first time, they were America's political majority.

Newt Gingrich arrived by plane from Atlanta on Tuesday afternoon, January 3, 1995, four weeks after having been nominated by Republicans to become the fiftieth Speaker of the House of Representatives. He was surrounded by followers and an army of reporters and TV technicians. So crowded was the flight, and so occupied by jostling newspeople, that stewards were unable to force their way back down the aisles with snacks to the rear, where his wife, Marianne, was sitting in 28E. En route, a friend handed a King James Bible to a seatmate, instructing her to look up Proverbs 2:10 for this week's lesson: "When wisdom entereth into thine heart, and knowledge is pleasant unto thy soul."

Gingrich and his entourage immediately headed for the Capitol, and history. Soon he was standing above the well of the House, before the high-backed Speaker's chair framed by the huge American flag, listening as outgoing Majority Leader Dick Gephardt, clearly emotional, but tightly composed, turned and handed the gavel to Gingrich. "So ends forty years of Democratic control," Gephardt said. His words were drowned out by a roar from the aisles occupied by the new majority Republicans. Then, after conciliatory words in which he praised Democratic liberals for their civil rights efforts in the sixties, Gingrich banged down the gavel and began the Revolution with a demonstration of unified power and ideology the House had not witnessed in anyone's memory.

Fourteen hours and fifteen roll calls later, at 2:23 in the morning of Wednesday, January 4, the Gingrich-led House had rammed through every bill they introduced. Not a single Republican voted against any of them. No defections: total unity, total victory. The conservative steamroller had begun.

During those votes, Peggy Noonan, the Reagan speechwriter and ardent conservative, who was commissioned to do a book on the first hundred days of the new Congress, talked to Grover Norquist, the conservative activist central to Gingrich's plans to "defund the government." Noonan asked Norquist, whom she called the "Contract With America co-conspirator," for his impressions of what had just happened. "It was fun," Norquist replied. "We were nice to the other team while we beat them. That was in one day the next forty years. We're gonna be cheerful, and we're gonna beat them, we're gonna be polite, and we're gonna beat them. For the next forty years."

In a way, Norquist was paraphrasing the famous comment of Harry Hopkins, FDR's right-hand man and most committed New Dealer, which Republicans had been citing for decades since as a warning of liberal power run wild: "We will tax and tax, spend and spend, and elect and elect."

Now, sixty years later, it was the conservatives' turn. They would cut and cut, slash and slash, and elect and elect. It was a revolution, after all, and they were the revolutionaries.

The Gingrich legions differed from the New Dealers in other respects. For all the conservative belief that Roosevelt was a radical, and his New Dealers agents of the destruction of the American Way of Life, in reality FDR's New Deal was far less rigid ideologically. The New Dealers were innovators, tinkerers, who toiled to perfect, reform, and save The System. The new conservatives could hardly be called political pragmatists, as could FDR and many New Dealers; the Gingrich Republicans were, both in self-image and in reality, far more ideologically motivated. They were the real radicals of American politics, and the assault they led on the federal government's social welfare programs was unprecedented for the breadth of its goals and the zeal of its operatives.

As political analyst Michael Barone noted on ABC-TV's Sunday morning show *This Week with David Brinkley* just before the election, "We are going to have more Reagan Republicans in the House and the Senate than we had when Ronald Reagan was President." He was right, and the new Republican majorities reveled in that fact. It was Reagan II that was beginning, they liked to boast, the final political wave that would wash away the remnants of the long, discredited liberal era, leaving in place the shining new America of privatization of public services and deregulation of the markets and the environment.

While the new generation conservatives who took power under Newt Gingrich invoked Ronald Reagan as their spiritual leader, important differences distinguished them from that earlier conservative capture of Washington. Ideologically, their goals were the same — less government through tax cuts and reduced services, spurring greater free-market enterprise — but in style, method, and manner they were notably different.

Though Reagan preached from the same text, espousing such priority social agenda issues of the right as school prayer, anti-abortion, anti–gun control, anti–gay rights, in practice he was a far more benign figure; he never waged aggressive political war to achieve *those* ends. Fighting communism, increasing defense, cutting taxes were his real priorities. Reagan adopted more of a live-and-let-live attitude than was generally understood at the time. Nor, in personal style, did Reagan come over as a stern, polarizing force. His greatest gift as a political leader was his ability to seem soothing, positive, cheering, while pursuing highly conservative goals.

Furthermore, for all the talk about the "Reagan Revolution" during his presidency, his administration was staffed and backed by many "country club Republicans" — conservative, yes, but rich, content, and socially eager to bask in the glow of power. Nor did

Reagan ever enjoy total command of the Congress. His 1980 election had provided the coattails for Republican control of the Senate, but though Republicans picked up thirty-two House seats that year, numerically the Democrats still had fifty-two more members when Reagan took office. Two years later, in the midterm elections of 1982, Republicans lost twenty-four House seats. Four years later, the Democrats regained the Senate, putting them again solidly in control of Congress, as they had been for most of the time since FDR.

The Gingrich-era Republicans who came to power in 1994 were younger, even more determined, and more sure of their mission and their opportunity. They truly believed themselves to be the vanguards of the Revolution and approached their role of disbanding the liberal social programs with passion, conviction, and a relentless determination not to be diverted. When they boasted of their movement being "Reagan II," they meant much more than a continuation of Reagan policies; they were intent on not missing a historic opportunity, as many of them privately believed Reagan had, to radically shrink the role of the federal government in America.

In Gingrich, they had a perfect leader: confident to a point of arrogance, energetic, driven to become one of the rare political figures who actually shapes history through force of action and power of ideas. To this end, Gingrich immediately asserted iron control over the process of the House. To a remarkable degree, the Republicans who took power with him believed they owed him their seats, and agreed with his ideological goals. If they didn't, they quickly got the message of the New Order as Gingrich discarded seniority rules of the past and appointed his own people as committee chairmen.

It was Newt Gingrich's House. He established the rules. He set the timetable. It was his idea of a Contract With America that determined the initial agenda. Gingrich dominated the American political scene as few other House Speakers since Henry Clay had. In the all-encompassing electronic media age, he was, in fact, treated as *the* dominant American leader, eclipsing even the President, by a press fascinated with his combustible political personality and, as ever, eager to focus on the new, the different, the controversial. As Gingrich's House of Representatives pressed at breakneck speed to fulfill the campaign pledge to bring all ten of the Contract With

America promises to a vote within the first hundred days, the new Republican majority operated in lockstep, displaying remarkable political unity and ideological conformity.

That was not so in the Senate, where the Republicans also now reigned. The barons of the Senate often did not agree with Gingrich and his "Newtoids," as they were called by critics. We didn't sign any Contract With America, said Bob Dole, once again exercising power as Senate majority leader, and once again seeking as he had twice before to become the Republican presidential nominee.

Gingrich himself had a long history of personal differences with Dole. When Gingrich was rising out of his status as a fiery back-bencher in the House, he had gone out of his way repeatedly to pick fights with Dole. At one point in the 1980s, he disparagingly called Dole "the tax collector for the welfare state." Those conflicts were sharpened during the early months of the new Congress by the far more radical brand of political change Gingrich was leading in the House, in contrast to the more traditional brand of conservatism practiced by Dole. Complicating this relationship was the prospect, which Gingrich himself encouraged through public comments, that the Speaker might seek the Republican presidential nomination against Dole in 1996. But there was more to their differences than personal political ambition; these two players, one the last of the old World War II generation in national leadership, the other the first baby boomer to lead Congress, represented profoundly different views of the role of government at century's end. At the same time, Gingrich and Dole knew they had a strong common interest in establishing a working relationship; despite their personal and political differences, they did so.

Still, the Right remained suspicious of a Bob Dole who proudly called himself an Eisenhower Republican. They remembered how he had helped George McGovern, the liberal Democratic senator and presidential nominee in 1972, strengthen the food stamp program. They exchanged stories of how Dole, too, had supported the move to honor Martin Luther King Jr. by declaring King's birthday a national holiday. They recalled how, as Senate Finance Committee chairman, Dole had taken a leading hand in the $100 billion tax increase of 1982 followed by a $50 billion tax hike two years later. If this were not heretical enough for conservative true believers, they could cite Dole's refusal to join George Bush in pledging not to raise taxes during the 1988 Republican primaries — a position that prompted Bush campaign ads attacking Dole as "Senator Straddle."

Not surprisingly, given the basic rivalries and resentments being stirred by the new exercise of power, Dole's chief of staff, Sheila Burke, once more was subjected to the same kinds of public attacks from right-wing commentators and polemicists that she had endured during the health care battle over the previous two years. Again, she was accused of being an unduly liberal influence on Dole, someone who would thwart the true conservative agenda should Dole reach the White House. The criticisms of Burke, which Dole again dismissed, were one of many signs of the growing ideological strains in this new Senate — a trend that was accelerated by the election of more conservative senators in the 1994 earthquake. When moderate Republican Senator Mark Hatfield of Oregon refused to provide the sixty-seventh vote needed to pass the balanced budget constitutional amendment in the Senate, Dole had to intervene to quash a move by young conservatives to strip Hatfield of his Appropriations Committee chairmanship. Later in the year, Hatfield announced his plans to retire.

Even Gingrich was dissected for flaws by ideological purists. In her search for perspective on the outcome of the Revolution, and particularly on the chief revolutionary, Peggy Noonan encountered discord over Gingrich's leadership role even on the night when he was sworn in as Speaker. Someone whom she described as "a conservative intellectual" told her then, "I will make a wager that exactly a year from now we will be talking about the end of Newt, and who will replace him. I'm telling you, he is not suited temperamentally or just in terms of his style to day-to-day leadership." Two other conservatives who joined in that conversation disagreed, and took the bet. You watch, one of them said. He'll be one of the rare Trotsky-Bolshie-type opposition leaders in history who can govern and go the distance.

Immediately, the Gingrich House passed a flood of legislation intended to reduce the role of the federal government. It would deregulate the environment and commerce, privatize public facilities, shift

control of many domestic programs out of Washington and back
to the states and local communities. Block grants giving the states
broad discretion on income and nutrition programs would replace
the federal guarantees of welfare and school lunches.

The new conservative majority began this great political reversal
together with the interest groups allied with the Republican Right
working to make sure the candidates they had backed actually carried out the Revolution. They had a special claim on those candidates. As they boasted, the overwhelming majority had been elected
through their support.

Nor was this an idle boast. The Christian Coalition cited figures showing that forty-four of the winning Republican freshmen
enjoyed the strong support of "pro-family, pro-life" groups. They
also claimed similar influence in electing Republican senators and
governors. So did the National Rifle Association, and the small-
business lobby, and the antitax groups, among others, all of whom
crowed about the list of candidates elected through their support.

In truth, they were a markedly different group of lawmakers.
Their profile, drawn by a careful *Congressional Quarterly* analysis
the week of the election, showed them to be notably younger, whiter,
and less well educated than the previous Congress, with significant
numbers of newcomers boasting of having no prior elective experience before coming to Congress. Just over half of the new House
freshmen, of whom an astonishing seven out of eight were Republicans, had held previous office. By comparison, just two years before,
72 percent of newcomers had elective experience.

The youth of the new group was even more striking: 59 percent
of them were under the age of forty-five. Educationally, only 56
percent of the House freshmen held advanced degrees as opposed to
65 percent of House members who were reelected. Also significantly,
far more of the newcomers came from business or banking careers;
and, a notable dropoff, only thirty-six new members of House and
Senate were lawyers. (In the previous Congress, law was the dominant occupation; there were two hundred thirty-six lawyers.) There
were also far fewer who came from academic backgrounds: a total
of seventeen of the new House and Senate members compared to
eighty-two in the last Congress.

In terms of race and gender, the new members were also dramatically different. In the last Congress, women, blacks, Hispanics, and Asians had all sharply increased in numbers. Two years before, the number of blacks in the House jumped from twenty-six to thirty-nine; Hispanics from twelve to nineteen; Asians from seven to eight. In 1994, there were no gains in total numbers of blacks, Hispanics, and Asians. As for women, who had been gaining in numbers strongly in recent elections — quadrupling in the Senate, rising from twenty-nine to forty-eight in the House — there were virtually no changes. All this meant the new class was significantly *less* reflective of America's diverse racial, ethnic, sexual background — to say nothing of the sternly more conservative cast of mind of the new members.

Once these ideological forces assumed power, the interest groups joined forces with Republican leaders to guarantee that their electoral efforts were rewarded by legislative action. They were not disappointed. For them, and for the new Republican majorities, it was payback and cash-in time: payback time to the Democrats for the long years the Republicans had suffered in the minority, cash-in time for the opportunity to enact *their* ideological and economic agenda.

Nothing more dramatically signaled how great a change had occurred than the boldness with which special-interest lobbyists openly worked with Republicans to pass their bills. Not that Democrats were innocent of directly dealing with lobbyists; when they were trying to pass the Clinton plan, Democratic congressional leaders met daily with lobbying groups working for the same goal. But what was occurring in the Gingrich Era Congress went far beyond that alliance. It was the very *brazenness* of the relationship between the Republicans and lobbyists that was so striking. No longer did groups like the No Name Coalition that had played a key role in defeating the Clinton plan feel compelled to hide from public scrutiny; now they were in the open, and they gloried in it. Politically and economically, two themes unified them: belief in small business — and big profits. To those ends, they worked hand in hand with Gingrich forces to pass the Contract With America provisions within the first hundred days.

So confident of their new position of power and influence were they that they even permitted reporters and photographers to attend what previously would have been highly private sessions. After one, a *Time* writer, Jeffrey H. Birnbaum, gave a revealing portrait of the way the lobbyists and the lawmakers collaborated. Birnbaum, co-author with Alan Murray of a fine book on Washington high-stakes lobbying, *Showdown at Gucci Gulch*, described the meeting of the "Thursday Group," which assembled each week around a large conference room table in an office beneath the Capitol dome.

Presiding were Representative John Boehner of Ohio and Senator Paul Coverdell of Georgia. Those gathered around the table were not fellow Republican lawmakers or even GOP congressional aides. They were all lobbyists representing some of the richest special interests in the country. Boehner, the chairman of the House Republican Conference, the fourth-ranking leadership post, treated the group, Birnbaum noted, with the business-as-usual familiarity of a colleague. "Okay, let's get going," Boehner said crisply, as he called them to order, then listened as the lobbyists began reporting on their efforts to pass the Contract With America bills.

Each of the lobbyists had been assigned specific provisions of the Contract and headed task forces, commanding other groups and lobbyists operating in Washington and around the country. The largest of these lobbying groups was headed by John Motley of the National Federation of Independent Business (NFIB), who oversaw a coalition of more than a hundred groups doing everything from fund-raising to grassroots lobbying — just as they had done so successfully in the health care wars.

As Birnbaum commented, "Welcome to the underside of the Republican revolution. To an extent unusual even for parasitic Washington, the House GOP leadership has attached its fortunes to private lobbyists, and is relying on their far-flung influence to pass its agenda. Boehner's Thursday Group is the top of the pyramid of that sophisticated effort, serving as command central for a series of multimillion-dollar campaigns on behalf of the Contract With America. The stakes of the enterprise — and the potential rewards for the lobbyists — are huge."

Even more revealing was the photo *Time* ran of the lobbyists who regularly sat around that table plotting legislative strategy with the lawmakers. They were familiar: In addition to the NFIB small-business lobby, their members included representatives of Citizens for a Sound Economy, the Christian Coalition, the Americans for Tax Reform, the National Restaurant Association, the Chamber of Commerce of the U.S. All had been part of the powerful coalition formed to kill health care. Now, in the Gingrich era, they, and additional groups, were meeting and forming new coalitions to further their ideological and economic interests.

Nor were these the only efforts under way. Each Wednesday, in what the *Wall Street Journal's* Paul Gigot described as "the Grand Central Station of this coalition," people representing conservative think tanks, the National Rifle Association, the Christian Coalition, and small-business, term-limits, property rights, and antitax groups assembled in the Washington offices of Grover Norquist to plot strategy and trade intelligence.

Gigot gave a telling example of Norquist's readiness "in effect (if unofficially) to help Mr. Gingrich enforce party discipline." When Fred Upton, a moderate Republican congressman from Michigan, threatened to oppose the proposed tax cuts, Norquist's antitax group peppered Upton's Kalamazoo district with direct mail and faxes. Another group bought radio ads. Both tactics, as we have seen, had been perfected and employed to great effect during the health care battle. Once again, they worked. Upton voted for the tax cut bill. (The Senate also voted for the House-passed tax cut bill but it languished during the ensuing budget deadlock.)

It was not consensus politics being practiced in Washington, or even conservative politics as previously defined. This was ideological warfare, a battle to destroy the remnants of the liberal, progressive brand of politics that had governed America throughout most of the twentieth century.

So rapid was the legislative pace, so hastily were the new measures stitched together, so skimpy the details and limited the public hearings on them, that few legislators — to say nothing of the public affected — could say with certainty what specific provisions the new bills contained. But that didn't matter. This was a political revolution, and the new revolutionaries were rapidly dismantling the welfare state. Not only were they seeking to "defund" the federal government; they were determined to break the centralized power of Washington and disperse its functions to the states. No more micromanaging or unfunded mandates from Washington, they vowed. Now they would let the states decide how to set standards, if any, for federal appropriations by giving the states block grants with few strings attached. The health and safety protections and the welfare guarantees that Democrats and progressive Republicans had established gradually throughout the entire century were being swept aside.

No one better expressed the flavor, and the fervor, of the new revolutionaries than Rush Limbaugh, the bombastic talk show host whose daily efforts in stirring conservative legions had earned him election by the newly installed Republicans as an honorary member of the Class of 1995. In the wake of the election, Limbaugh offered his advice to the revolutionaries. "Never moderate your tone," he urged them in the pages of the *Wall Street Journal*. "Never attempt to be liked by those you defeated."

Health care was not part of the Contract With America, the set of bills the Republicans promised to bring to a vote within a hundred days. Too complicated to fit that time schedule, Gingrich said. Only 17 percent of voters polled during the 1994 campaign said they knew anything about the Contract. But Gingrich and the freshmen took it seriously, and for three months the effort to pass it dominated the news. Gingrich dramatized the Contract brilliantly as the vehicle of political change, holding up a laminated copy at every opportunity. Progress reports on the Contract led network newscasts and became the subject of constant examination and speculation on radio and TV talk shows. Throughout the winter, Gingrich's stature increased while that of Bill Clinton diminished. So weak was Clinton considered to be that conservatives began openly disparaging him as irrelevant. That the President of the United States could be so regarded by so many leading players was only one of many signs of the earthquake's aftershocks.

House Republicans made their hundred-day deadline with a week to spare. They won approval for every one of their promises except a term-limits constitutional amendment.During those initial months of the new Congress, while the spotlight blazed unceasingly on the Contract, the issue that had brought Clinton and the Democrats so low and elevated Gingrich and the Republicans to such intoxicating heights merely flickered backstage.

But as soon as the Republicans in April of 1995 turned to writing a budget, health care reform proved to be as powerful and vexatious an issue as ever. This time, however, the shoe was on the other foot. Now Republicans discovered they could not achieve their objectives without addressing the very same questions over which the Clinton administration had fought and nearly died for two years. They even adopted some of the same arguments, asserting that managed care and health maintenance organizations would make the system more efficient and less costly.

That deeply ironic situation appeared to be all right with Bill Clinton As the shock of the election defeat sank in with the President, he complained to advisers about the fickleness of the public. Republicans had spent two years saying no, he said, and here they were, rewarded with virtually every prize the voters could give them. The President thought he had taken on the hard issues; in return, he got nothing but abuse.

Some who listened to these complaints — among them Democrats whose own careers had been derailed by the 1994 debacle — found them more than a little self-pitying and self-serving. They could offer a long list of political mistakes for which the President could blame no one but himself. But there was an element of truth in what the President was saying. Bill Clinton had fought his heart out to get a deficit-reducing budget through Congress. He succeeded only by the barest possible minimum — a single vote in each congressional chamber — and that in the face of unanimous Republican opposition. Not one Republican had voted for *his* plan to reduce the budget. When it came to the next great obstacle to balancing the budget, controlling health care costs nationally, once again Republicans were solidly against the Clinton plan.

Even though he never formally closed the circle on the great health care war by addressing the nation on the consequences of its defeat and singling out those responsible. Clinton had promised not to let the effort die altogether. "I fully intend to keep after [health care reform]," he told a news conference just a month before the election. At that time, he reiterated his belief that "we'll have to address this comprehensively" if health costs are to be controlled. That means "having a mechanism to cover everybody," he said. "I intend to come back full force trying to do that."

Hillary Clinton had made the same pledge. "Health reform is not a boxing match that goes fifteen rounds and suddenly is over," the First Lady told a George Washington University medical school audience at the end of September.

That resolve melted with the election returns. When the President turned to drafting his third budget for submission to the new Congress, there were rumors that he would propose a first step of reform guaranteeing insurance for all pregnant women and children in the country — a so-called Kiddiecare, parallel to Medicare for all retirees, to be financed by a forty-five-cents-a-pack cigarette tax that had been part of the 1994 Ways and Means bill. There was also speculation that Clinton might renew his plan to find savings in the Medicare program and recycle them into new prescription drug benefits and a start on instituting a broad-based long-term care for senior citizens.

In the end, the President did nothing. His budget projected no savings for Medicare. It contained no new health care proposals. The deficit was projected to continue at $200 billion a year for five years — then increase. Of two hundred pages of budget proposals, only six were devoted to health care. They referred to a letter the President had sent the new congressional leadership a week before they took power, saying, "We can pass legislation that includes measures to address the unfairness in the insurance market, make coverage more affordable for working families and children, assure quality and efficiency in the Medicare and Medicaid programs, and reduce the long-term federal deficit." If nothing is done, Clinton's letter warned, health costs per person will rise 50 percent by 2000, more Americans will lose coverage, living standards will suffer, and business and government budgets will be increasingly burdened.

Clinton was walking away from the problem, Republicans now complained. What he was really doing was forcing them to take the first step — and now it was their shoe that pinched. Republicans resented being placed in that position, even though they had profited when Democrats failed at their reforms the year before.

*   *   *

The first sign of trouble — this time for the Republicans, initiating the second wave of the battle — came on February 14, 1995, when Senate Majority Leader Dole announced that in order to meet the Republican goal of balancing the budget within seven years, "savings" of $146 billion in Medicare spending and another $75 billion in Medicaid would have to be achieved. At that point no significant health care legislation was moving through the new Republican-controlled Congress. In the first few months only minimal, and noncontroversial, measures were being acted upon, such as those extending and improving the tax deductibility of health insurance premiums paid by the self-employed and expanding the "Medicare Select" program from fifteen to all fifty states. That program encouraged Medicare recipients to purchase supplemental insurance policies voluntarily from HMOs. Nancy Johnson of Connecticut, the Republican House sponsor, accurately described this as "a very, very little step forward."

Although several of the new Republican chairmen introduced modest health insurance reform bills — building on incremental plans cobbled together in 1994 — it was not until the House and Senate budget committees took up their spending plans that the 1995 political debate on health care began. It proved to be even more explosive than the battle launched by Clinton in 1993.

When Senate and House Republican budget chairmen Pete Domenici of New Mexico and John Kasich of Ohio unveiled their plans, they asserted that they could balance the budget by 2002 without a tax increase. Indeed, the initial Kasich House budget version called for a huge tax *cut* for families with children and for investors eager to cash in their capital gains.

Balancing the budget within seven years without a tax increase, even substantially *reducing* taxes, all the while calling for additional federal spending on defense, was a political wizard's trick rivaling the sleight-of-hand maneuvers during the early Reagan years of supply-side economics. At that time Reagan and his budget director, David Stockman, promised to balance the federal budget within three years, producing an actual surplus in the fourth, while at the same time sharply cutting taxes, massively increasing defense spending, and not cutting such "entitlements" as Social Security, Medicare, and Medicaid.

It was a wonderfully seductive theory. The taxes were cut, defense spending rose, spending on entitlements continued to increase — and the budget ballooned out of control. Annual deficits soared. In the eight years of Reagan's presidency, the national debt tripled, rising from $1 trillion to $3 trillion. "Magic asterisks," placed in the Reagan budget projections to indicate savings that would be achieved through unspecified means in the "out years," proved to be just that — magic, puffs of smoke, political promises easily made and easily broken.

Now, fourteen years later, in an even more strongly ideological period, with the central players even more determined to carry out the Revolution and with the national debt having increased fivefold since 1981, the same kinds of promises were being made and the same kinds of rhetoric advanced to justify major changes.

The Republicans promised to balance the budget within seven years. Gingrich later said he chose the period "by intuition." A similar promise was made in George Bush's reelection campaign because it would supposedly end the deficits in the symbolic millennium year of 2000. To reach that goal, both Republican budget chairmen asked for unprecedented reductions in the two largest federal health care programs, Medicare and Medicaid. They proposed taking more than $250 billion from Medicare, reducing its annual growth rate by a third, and more than $175 billion from Medicaid, with even sharper curbs on its projected growth.

Bob Blendon, the Harvard health care policy and public opinion expert, understated the case when he said "the Republicans have really struck into a political hornets' nest." Tom Scully, a spokesman for for-profit hospitals and a former Bush administration official, warned that "there is no policy that can get them to two hundred fifty billion dollars in Medicare cuts that doesn't kill them in the next election." His group and many others immediately mobilized for the new battle. And Judy Feder, still bearing the scars from the Clinton plan war, said the administration "will oppose all cuts in the absence of real health care reform."

Once again, the battle lines had formed. Less than a year after the Republicans had boasted to each other of having killed health care reform, and after their victory had helped produce the greatest electoral turnover in decades, they found themselves facing the same intractable problems that the Democrats had tried, and failed, to address. Only this time, the pressure was on the Republicans to persuade a doubtful public that *their* plan would save and strengthen, not weaken and destroy, the public-sector health care system.

The Republicans recognized the danger. They tried to ward it off by demanding that Clinton act responsibly with them to save the health care system. Join us in creating a bipartisan commission to suggest needed changes in Medicare, Gingrich and Dole publicly urged the President. The White House declined, and Chief of Staff Leon Panetta responded to the Republican leaders in writing. No matter how you disguise it, he said, "no one can hide the reality that you are essentially calling for the largest Medicare cut in history to pay for tax cuts for the well off."

It was a powerful political argument, and the Republicans knew it. Now the Democrats were on the offensive. They trumpeted that the Republicans' plan would "cost every Medicare recipient an extra thousand dollars a year" in higher co-payments. They warned that seniors would be forced into HMOs, unless they were willing to pay much higher premiums to stay with doctors and hospitals they knew. They pointed, gleefully for once, to polls showing that most of the public — and an overwhelming majority of seniors — thought preserving Medicare more important than balancing the budget within a specific time period. Those same polls showed eroding approval for the new Republican majority in Congress.

Faced with an attack that threatened their entire agenda, Republicans mounted a counteroffensive, as they had so successfully done in the past two years. They singled out an April 3 report from the trustees of the Medicare Trust Fund — technically, the Hospital Insurance Trust Fund — warning that beginning in 1996, the fund would start paying out more for benefits than it collected in payroll taxes. Unless changes were made, the fund would be exhausted by 2002 — the very year the budget was supposed to be in balance.

Such warnings were not new. Nine times since 1970, the trustees had warned that Medicare would approach "bankruptcy" within seven years. As was the case with similar warnings about Social Security trust funds going broke, every time The System had responded in a bipartisan way to save it. Impending Medicare insolvency had always been solved by trimming payment schedules to health care providers and by either increasing the Medicare tax rate or raising the amount of income on which the tax was levied. In fact, in 1994, just a year before, the trustees had issued a similar warning of bankruptcy. Then, with many Republicans vigorously denying there was a "crisis" in any part of the health care system, the trustee report created scarcely a ripple. Now, the trustees said, it would require about $100 billion over ten years — an expenditure barely felt in the multitrillion-dollar American economy — to remedy the shortfall forecast in 1995. But this time, the Republicans had ruled out higher Medicare taxes to safeguard the program and were reluctant to state exactly how their economies would be achieved.

Haley Barbour, the chairman of the Republican National Committee, thought the new trustees' report was "manna from heaven." As he later confessed to Michael Weisskopf and David Maraniss of the *Washington Post*, he had argued against making any changes in Medicare before the 1996 election for fear of the political backlash. Now, he and Gingrich seized on the trustee report and elevated it to a dire threat to all thirty-seven and a half million Medicare beneficiaries. Suddenly, Gingrich was out front warning about the impending Medicare bankruptcy, as affirmed by a trustee report signed by members of Clinton's own administration (the secretaries of Health and Human Services, Treasury, and Labor are, by law, trustees). The Speaker coupled his repeated warnings about the calamity facing Medicare with a strong appeal for public support of the Republican alternative to "save" Medicare through major reforms — none spelled out explicitly.

Frank Luntz, the Republican pollster, circulated an eight-page private memo among House Republicans entitled "Everything You

Ever Wanted to Know About Communicating Medicare."* Luntz
warned Republicans that senior citizens would never accept changes
in Medicare until they were "convinced the system's going broke."
He added, "If we can't prove that Medicare is going bankrupt, we'll
never be able to sell our solutions." He also urged them, "Remind
your audience that Republicans want to 'increase spending but at a
slower rate.' This language works."

Go on the attack, he advised the new Republican House. Accuse
Democrats of "using 'scare tactics' by allowing a program to go
broke . . . just to score political points."

As in the earlier health care battle, that strategic advice was
followed with singular unanimity. From Gingrich down, Republicans attempted to deflect Democratic attacks by passionately arguing they weren't cutting Medicare spending; notwithstanding that
their plan called for spending a quarter of a trillion dollars less on
Medicare than the last Democratic budget projected for the next
seven years, they were merely reducing the rate of increase in the
growth of spending over the years — growth that would be driven
by increasing numbers of older Americans, inflation, and ever-
higher costs of new medical technology, although these factors were
not mentioned. They were saving the program, not dismembering
it. They never used the word "cuts," instead agreeing in their private strategy meetings to speak always of the "savings" they would
make.

As early as April, Bill McInturff, the pollster whose work had
guided so much of the earlier strategy, and Linda DiVall, Gingrich's
pollster, gave Gingrich and Barbour a focus group report suggesting that the best formulation was to claim that "Republicans want
to protect, improve and preserve Medicare." According to the careful retrospective reporting of Weisskopf and Maraniss, Gingrich
edited the phrase only to change the word order so it more closely
echoed the Constitution's language to "preserve, protect and defend the Constitution of the United States." From now on, Gingrich
said, Republicans will speak only of their intent to "preserve,

---

*The Luntz memo was later cited at length in a Sept. 25, 1995, *New Yorker* article by Sidney
Blumenthal, "Medicine Show: The Republicans' script leads them into trouble."

protect and improve" Medicare. Later, Frank Luntz suggested another editing change to make it more credible to those who doubted Republicans would really "improve" Medicare. In its amended form, it became "preserve, protect and strengthen Medicare." When the Republicans saw a need to distinguish their long-term plan from what they called the "short-run" fix offered by Clinton, they added a few more words. In its final form, it became a pledge to "preserve, protect and strengthen Medicare for the next generation."

Their counteroffensive was politically effective, but it was not as one-sided a struggle as the battle two years before. This time they faced unified opposition from congressional Democrats who pummeled them for "destroying" Medicare, and whose attacks were rewarded with sharp drops in public approval for the new Republican congressional majority.

Five months after the Revolution began, Democrats thought they had found the key to their political comeback.

Then, unexpectedly, Bill Clinton seemed to pull the rug from under them. On June 13, the President announced that he had decided to join the Republicans in the quest to erase the budget deficit. His balanced budget target date was ten years, not seven as with Republicans, he said in a brief, nationally televised address, but he conceded that his plan, like the Republicans', would require major savings in Medicare and Medicaid.

The President said he was putting $124 billion of Medicare and $54 billion of Medicaid savings on the table. Consternation, outrage, from Democrats. Relief, though not publicly expressed, from Republicans, who quickly struck back by charging that Clinton was overestimating the effect of his own proposals — and leaving himself well short of balancing the budget, which they were determined to do through *their* plan.

For Democrats, this sudden action of the President was a bitter blow. The President had abandoned a strategy that was *working*. "Opening the door to deep Medicare cuts while the Republicans are struggling to pay for their huge tax breaks threatens to make Medicare a political football," fumed Dick Gephardt, now the House minority leader. More pointedly, Dave Obey, a liberal Democrat from

Wisconsin, said sardonically, "Most of us learned some time ago that if you don't like the President's position on a particular issue, you simply need to wait a few weeks."

That was a public reaction; privately, many Democrats were so furious with Clinton that they muttered about either not supporting him for reelection or encouraging others to oppose him for their party's nomination.

Once again, an internal White House struggle had caused a sudden shift in the President's course, and once again the question of how to proceed on health care policy lay at the center of it.

When the new Republican Congress began, Clinton had adopted a political strategy that would, he hoped, force Republicans to pay the political price for making unpopular budget cuts to achieve their twin goals of tax reduction and a balanced budget. His decision relied on tactical advice of Stan Greenberg, his pollster, and George Stephanopoulos and Harold Ickes, his two liberal White House advisers.

As they looked ahead to the 1996 reelection campaign, their first concern was to minimize the prospect that Clinton would face a Democratic primary challenge for renomination. This was not an idle threat. Presidents Lyndon Johnson and Jimmy Carter, both sitting Democrats, had been opposed by challengers from their party's liberal wing, with disastrous results for them. Eugene McCarthy's strong showing in the early 1968 primaries was a major factor in Johnson's decision not to seek reelection. Twelve years later, Ted Kennedy's challenge to Carter sowed Democratic divisions that made Ronald Reagan's path to the White House easier. To keep Clinton from becoming the third incumbent Democratic victim in a row, his liberal advisers believed it imperative to position him as the defender of programs cherished by Democratic loyalists. No constituency group was more important than senior citizens. They regarded LBJ's Medicare, along with FDR's Social Security, as the Democratic Party's most precious legacies.

Liberal tacticians like the Gephardts and Obeys on Capitol Hill understood that, in the end, Clinton would have to negotiate with congressional Republicans the best budget he could get for the last year of his first term. But the liberals thought the time for dealing would be the fall of 1995, not the spring. By autumn, it would almost be too late for a challenger to mount a serious effort against Clinton in presidential primaries beginning in February 1996. By autumn, the Democrats would have had three more months to bash the Republicans' Medicare and Medicaid plans.

They knew that in the end, Clinton could veto Republican budget plans — and probably win on his vetoes. But that strategy entailed major risks, both politically for him and practically for the nation. Unless the President was prepared to accept responsibility for a "train wreck" — a shutdown of government, creating havoc in countless programs and essential services — because Congress failed to approve operating funds for the new fiscal year beginning October 1, Clinton would have to make a deal. From the beginning, Newt Gingrich had repeatedly raised that threat of a government shutdown as a means of forcing Clinton to accept the Republican budget. Unlike during the previous health care battle, in which he had kept his hand hidden most of the time, Gingrich now made no effort to disguise his intentions. Flushed with their victory, exulting in their congressional dominance, convinced of their ideological mandate, Gingrich and the House Republicans dismissed Clinton as a weak, irrelevant President who would cave under their pressure. They could bend and break him; he would be compelled to accept their budget demands.

The reason for Clinton's stunning shift in direction, and for moving his negotiating timetable up to June instead of waiting for the fall, was advice he accepted from someone new to the White House, Dick Morris, a Connecticut-based pollster and media adviser. Though Morris was a stranger to most of Clinton's aides, and to much of the media/political world inside the Beltway, he had a long and important relationship with the two players who counted most: Bill and Hillary Clinton. Years before, in plotting Clinton's 1980 comeback to the Arkansas governor's mansion, Morris had worked closely with Clinton. They were so alike, especially in their volatile temperaments, that their relationship was one of constant quarrels and reconciliations. But when Bill Clinton was in trouble, it was to Dick Morris that he turned. And in 1995 both he and Hillary saw themselves drowning in a sea of troubles.

Morris was no liberal. Unlike most political consultants, he played both sides of the street, working more often for Republicans than Democrats. One of his most recent clients was Senator Trent Lott of Mississippi, now the second-ranking Republican in the Senate. During the health care battles of 1993–94, in yet another of many ironies in this story, Trent Lott had been one of the most powerful and effective opponents of the Clinton reform plan, all the while getting advice from Dick Morris.

Now Morris told Clinton that his courting of the constituencies of the Left in the Democratic Party had gone on long enough. The President needed to focus on the people who would decide the 1996 presidential election — particularly, the 19 percent who had supported Ross Perot's Independent candidacy in 1992. More than anyone else in that race, Perot had emphasized ending the budget deficits. If Clinton was going to compete for Perot voters, Morris argued, he had to demonstrate he shared their concern about stopping the red ink.

On a wide variety of issues — including Medicare — Morris argued that swing voters agreed with Clinton. They would not, however, give his views a hearing until the President first in effect told them, "You're right. We have to get rid of the deficit."

That is what Clinton did. In essence, he agreed with the Republicans' overall objective of balancing the budget and agreed that would require Medicare and Medicaid economies. It was just a matter of degree, he said, thus separating himself from the Democratic leadership and from much of the rank-and-file of his party in Congress.

The President's about-face strengthened, not weakened, his hand. By agreeing with the goal of a balanced budget, Clinton undercut the Republican claim to be the real defenders of fiscal responsibility and put himself in a better position to fight "excessive cuts" in health care and other programs.

In June, Republican budget writers completed their House-Senate conference and reaffirmed their goal of reaching a balance in seven years, 2002. To do so, "savings" of $270 billion in Medicare

($20 billion more than in their early projections) and $182 billion in Medicaid were proposed — Draconian reductions in both programs, representing cuts of 20 percent in the projected future Medicare spending for elderly Americans and 30 percent in Medicaid for the nation's poor and disabled.

In many ways, Medicaid provides a metaphor for how much The System may change during the next several years. If restructured into block grants to the states with few requirements, Medicaid's current federal guarantees of comprehensive health services for the vulnerable poor, elderly, and disabled who qualify would cease to exist. Instead, under the terms of the GOP block-grant plan, states would be charged with creating their own safety-net programs, the basic requirement being to spend a targeted amount of money (tied to a percentage of historical average spending) on Medicaid's distinct populations during their first few years. Only immunization and family planning services would be mandated as benefits by the federal government — which, if not expanded substantially by states, would not constitute a health insurance program. The Clinton administration argued that unless Medicaid remained a federal entitlement for eligible individuals to receive a range of health services, as needed, the number of uninsured would rise rapidly. The White House and other health experts also argued that most states did not have the infrastructure to establish quickly good-quality programs for individuals formerly eligible for Medicaid.

The Medicaid quagmire raises key federal-state issues that were at the heart of both the 1993–94 health care reform debate and the ensuing bitter budget impasse between the Clinton administration and the Republican Congress. Both turn on what is the most appropriate role for The System. A revealing insight into the dimensions of that conflict came in a 1995 book, *The People's Budget*, by GOP pollster Frank Luntz and others, featuring a foreword by the new House Budget Committee chairman, John Kasich of Ohio, and a strong endorsement by Speaker Gingrich. The authors assert that the proper conclusion to the Medicaid debate is that the federal government would no longer provide *any* money for the program. The logic is that federal taxes must be dramatically lowered, and that safety-net programs are the responsibility of the states to fund and provide for their own residents. Parenthetically, many experts believe that if Medicaid, which now pays for over half of *all* nursing home care, ceases to be a federal entitlement, any significant commitment by either the federal government or states to funding long-term care for an ever rising number of seniors will not be re-created.

According to Harvard's Bob Blendon, polls indicate the public has virtually no understanding of how Medicaid is structured now or of what the implications are of giving the states the freedom to rewrite the program almost completely. Most people, Blendon says, believe that states are as capable of running social welfare programs as the federal government is. But most people also do not have direct personal experience with safety-net programs such as Medicaid, or welfare programs such as aid to families with dependent children (AFDC) and Social Security supplemental income assistance for the poor (SSI). This strongly suggests that the public barely grasps the stakes involved in the battle over Medicaid, one of The System's fundamental safety-net programs.

Though they continued to claim their overall budget reduction of nearly half a trillion dollars was not a cut but only a reduction in the rate of growth of the programs, the Republicans offered no specifics on how these changes would be achieved — at what cost and to whom. Meantime, they were also proposing a tax cut of $245 billion. It didn't require a mathematician to make the connection between a Medicare cut of $270 billion and a tax cut of $245 billion. The Republicans had handed the Democrats a powerful weapon, and Democrats swiftly employed it. The true purpose of the massive health care cuts, they argued, was to permit Republicans to give a tax cut to the wealthiest Americans.

What the Democrats chose to ignore, for the moment, was something that Clinton and all the rest of them knew to be the case: The growth in Medicare spending was unsustainable. In 1970, five years after it began, it accounted for only 3 percent of the budget. In 1994, it was 11 percent. By 2005, the Congressional Budget Office said, it would reach 17 percent. After that, it would get much worse, because from 2010 on through 2025 the baby boomer retirement wave would vastly expand the number of seniors claiming medical benefits.

President Clinton was right in 1993 and 1994 in saying that runaway health costs were robbing America of its future. Republicans foiled his solution. Now, it appeared he was going to try to foil theirs. It was exactly the kind of behavior that was destroying public faith in The System.

In Washington in those last days of September 1995, exactly a year after the plug was pulled on the Clinton reform, a rout of historic proportions was being completed: Sixty years of United States domestic social policy was being reversed. To accomplish the goal of a balanced budget and tax cuts within seven years, scores of programs enacted during administrations from Franklin Roosevelt's to Richard Nixon's were being hobbled or entirely eliminated. These actions alone marked the One Hundred Fourth Congress as one of the most significant in more than half a century; but the most dramatic evidence of how ambitious this effort was to reverse decades of growing federal government responsibility and power came in the closing weeks of the congressional session.

On September 19 the Senate voted eighty-seven to twelve to join the House in transferring control of basic welfare programs from Washington to the state capitals by repealing a section of the Social Security Act of 1935 that provided aid to dependent children of indigent families.

Watching this remarkable unraveling of social policy, Pat Moynihan arose on the Senate floor to give voice to the shame he felt about what was occurring and to heap scorn both on his Senate colleagues and on a Democratic administration "that abandoned, eagerly abandoned, the national commitment to dependent children." Speaking in tones of anguish, Moynihan told the Senate, "I had no idea how profoundly what used to be known as liberalism was shaken by the last election. No President, Republican or Democrat in history, or sixty years' history, would dream of agreeing to repeal of Title IV of Social Security. . . . I cannot understand how this is happening. It has never happened before."

Ending the federal welfare system set the stage for a final assault on the two biggest government health programs, Medicare and Medicaid. As already described, the Republicans would attempt to restructure them to give the private sector and the states far more control over services received by millions upon millions of the beneficiaries of those programs. By that third week in September, the final clashes in the new health care wars were engaging the very same players who had fought the last time. Once again, the television airwaves were flooded with commercials either extolling the correctness of the Republican approach or warning of its grave dangers.

But this time, the roles were reversed. Now it was the Republicans who inveighed against scare tactics, which they themselves had employed so effectively for two years. Now they charged their opponents with trying to frighten the elderly, and keep them from understanding how the GOP plan would reform and save Medicare; "it's the responsible thing to do," their commercial said. Now the Democrats and their allies adopted the "Harry and Louise" approach. They aired commercials showing a couple in a kitchen worrying about the harsh impact of *Republican* cuts on their aging mother in the living room. "Think about it," the TV actors say sadly. "What would your parents be reduced to if their health care collapsed?" The TV actors didn't add — and didn't have to — the old punch line: There has to be a better way.

In the hearing rooms and halls of Congress, tempers were so raw that shouting legislators actually came close to fistfights. In a scene repeatedly shown on TV newscasts, Sam Gibbons of Florida, who in 1994 led the House Ways and Means Committee in its effort to enact the Democratic reform, was seen erupting in rage during a committee meeting now led by Republicans. His face beet red, the veteran of the Normandy invasion suddenly rose from his seat, balled up a piece of paper, threw it onto the table, and stalked out. Every few steps he paused to denounce what was taking place as a "railroad" and the people leading it as "dictators" and "fascists."

More than phony political theatrics prompted such extraordinary flashes of temper. Gibbons was reacting to yet another Republican delay in making public details of their Medicare plan. He and other Democrats complained that Republicans intended to force a vote on their plan — still not fully disclosed — after just a *single day* of hearings the following week.

To Gibbons, this was an outrage. In 1994, his committee had conducted hearings day after day on the merits and defects of the Clinton plan, long available to public scrutiny. Now a fundamental restructuring of the nation's health care system was about to be voted on just one day after a bill had finally been drafted. This deliberate Republican strategy was part of the lesson learned from watching the Clinton plan founder. They would keep specific details of their plan hidden, they agreed privately. They would keep public hearings to a minimum in order to lessen the ability of lobbyists and the press to pick them apart. "We're very pleased to do the exact opposite of what was done with the Clinton plan, both in terms of process and substance," Ari Fleischer, spokesman for the Republican Ways and Means leadership, told Robin Toner of the *New York Times* after Gibbons's outpouring of rage. John Rother, the AARP lobbyist, said, "They absolutely want to get it done before anybody has a chance to know what's in there."

Nor was this the only significant difference between 1994 and 1995. Gingrich fundamentally reversed the Democrats' strategy for dealing with the issue — both in Congress and with the interest groups. Instead of having the Medicare and Medicaid proposals drafted in the conventional fashion, starting in subcommittees of Ways and Means and Energy and Commerce, then moving to the full committees, and only then bringing them through the leadership-controlled Rules Committee and from there to the floor, Gingrich in effect wrote the bills in his own office.

"The contrast could not have been more stark," John Rother said. In the previous Congress, the Democratic leaders found themselves "herding cats," Rother said, "and they couldn't overcome the different factions. Here, you had one key decision-maker [Gingrich] with unquestioned authority to make everybody else fall into line in the House and, to some extent, in the Senate as well. It was quite remarkable."

In effect, Gingrich adopted the "supercommittee" that Hillary Clinton had asked Foley and Gephardt to employ for health care reform and that they rejected as impractical. Gingrich didn't call it a supercommittee; he called it a task force, one of many that he created to bypass the formal structure of the House standing committees.

The rationale was to allow more of the freshmen — who were the shock troops of his Revolution — to participate in the real work of legislation. But it also gave Gingrich and his leadership team more leverage, because they could determine the makeup of the task force and ensure that loyalists would predominate. Gingrich named others to head most of the task forces, but kept the health care one for himself. He realized health care posed the greatest political dangers for his party, and he did not want to delegate that responsibility to anyone else. He "invited" the top two Republicans on the committees with jurisdiction to join his tight circle of leadership aides in figuring out the bill they would offer. It was an invitation they could not refuse.

At the same time, Gingrich negotiated an understanding with Dole that they would stay closely in touch and mesh the Senate operation — both substantively and in timing — with the House. They wanted no repetition of the disjointed and unsuccessful operation the Democrats had run the previous year: no Moynihan tantrums, no Stark end runs. This was going to be tough; they could not afford internal battles.

They relied for technical assistance on committee staff, of whom none was more important than Chip Kahn, the same Chip Kahn who had been the right hand of Bill Gradison at the Health Insurance Association of America (HIAA) all through the Harry and Louise campaign. Kahn left HIAA when Republicans captured the House and became chief counsel to the Ways and Means Health Subcommittee, working for Bill Thomas of California, the subcommittee chairman, Bill Archer of Texas, the full committee chairman, and ultimately for Gingrich.

Kahn's crossover was not unique. Unlike the Clintons, who wrote the plan first and then sought to negotiate for support from the stakeholder groups, Gingrich brought the major provider and business groups into the room at an early stage of discussion and essentially bargained for their support as he framed the proposal. Gradison told us that Gingrich launched "a genuine outreach to find the hot buttons of a wide variety of interest groups and accommodate them sufficiently to either gain their support or neutralize them so that they would not be strong opponents."

As early as May, Gingrich told representatives of hospitals, physicians, insurers, and other business groups that they should accept as a given that the $450 billion in medical program savings called for in the Republican budget would be achieved. Don't waste your breath protesting that. But tell us how we can make those cuts in ways that are least damaging to you, and we will listen. And we are prepared to help you in other ways you suggest — as long as it doesn't require new spending.

It was precisely the strategy that Dan Rostenkowski had recommended to the Clintons — and had practiced himself, until his indictment took him out of the game. The side effect of the dealing was also exactly what Rosty had worked out, temporarily, with Bill Gradison and the health insurers: a cease-fire in the public-relations war. While they were dealing with Gingrich, the groups did not mount advertising or grassroots campaigns against the Republican initiative. Gingrich "has done a brilliant job of making sure everyone sits on their hands," Tom Scully, the for-profit hospitals' lobbyist, told Paul Gigot of the *Wall Street Journal*. The American Hospital Association started a campaign, was admonished by Gingrich, and stopped. The American Association of Retired Persons (AARP) held its fire for months, while it negotiated. Horace Deets, the group's president, even appeared on a Republican National Committee cable television show on Medicare reform and offered only bland comments about the importance of preserving the program — something that host Haley Barbour assured him the Republicans would do.

The Republicans also played hardball when it was necessary. John Rother said there was "a two-pronged approach" to AARP. Gingrich and his allies communicated the message that "we know we have to talk to you. We understand that you guys have power to torpedo this, and we don't want that." At the same time, the Republicans flexed their muscle; the enforcer was Senator Alan Simpson of Wyoming, who announced plans for hearings on AARP's financing and its tax-exempt status. Shortly before the hearings were to begin, Rother said, Simpson paid a call to the AARP board and said, "I want you to know that the intensity of my investigation of AARP will vary directly with the intensity of your efforts to fight the Medicare changes." Rother insisted that AARP was not intimidated, but it waited until very late in the fall to announce its opposition to the Republican plan.

The Republican proposal that emerged was a cleverly constructed hybrid, so craftily designed that even health care specialists took some time to discern what the drafters had done. For thirty years, Medicare had been a "defined benefit" plan in which all recipients were guaranteed a uniform and generous set of hospital and doctor benefits. There were co-payments for some services and paid monthly premiums for the physicians' services, but the biggest part of the bill went to the government, which used both payroll and general taxes to support the program. When costs exploded, as they did from the start, the government squeezed the providers and, less willingly, raised the taxes, premiums, and co-payments.

Instead of a "defined benefit" plan, the new Gingrich version became a "defined payment" system, in which the government allocated a certain amount of money for each Medicare recipient and encouraged the individual to use it to procure the best coverage he or she could find in the marketplace. No longer would everyone be guaranteed the same package of benefits. Instead, as Laurie McGinley and Christopher Georges reported in the *Wall Street Journal*, "Benefits, particularly the freedom to choose physicians, will vary more than they do now. Most likely, the wealthy would come out ahead, the poor might be hurt, and those in the middle could get better benefits in return for certain restrictions — on choosing a doctor, for instance."

The Republicans described the new system as offering greater "choice" to the individual. (Ironically, it was the same claim the Clintons had made — not for the Medicare population, but for all others, who could pick their plan from a menu of options, rather than accept their employer's choice. When the Clintons claimed this as a benefit of managed competition, the Republicans had ridiculed the notion.) Now the Republicans talked of giving senior citizens the option of using their Medicare dollars to join HMOs, which might offer free prescriptions and no co-payments. They said healthy retirees could put their Medicare money into Medical Savings Accounts (or MSAs), and if they didn't get sick, withdraw the money and take a Caribbean cruise. To make it sound even better, Gingrich told everyone that over the next seven years, the value of a Medicare policy would increase from $4800 per person to $6700. What a deal! (He neglected to say that under previous estimates, when taking in inflation and the increasing number of older Americans entering the Medicare program, spending had been projected to rise to $8400.)

They also promised that anyone now in Medicare could keep the same doctors and hospitals they were accustomed to using. But there were a number of things they didn't say when it came to explaining how they were going to do all this and still save $270 billion in the next seven years. Both individual doctors and independent hospitals would face increased competition from HMOs and decreased reimbursements from the government — a combination that experts said would push many of them into joining one of the burgeoning managed care networks. The same would be true of trying to make it on their own. As a sweetener for those doctors and hospitals, and designed to neutralize their political opposition, Gingrich and Co. offered a change in antitrust laws that would allow medical providers to set up their own managed care companies, without insurance companies, and capture a share of the market for themselves.

Even with this new competition, HMOs could look forward to a big expansion as more and more of the thirty-seven million Medicare recipients turned to them to make their Medicare dollars stretch further. Insurers, in turn, were promised access to a huge new market of senior citizens who would be converting Medicare money into their own insurance policies or managed care contracts, purchased on the open market. The risk was that costs might well outrun the fixed sums allocated for Medicare, leaving some seniors without coverage when they most needed it. Republicans said they would deal with that by including a "look-back" provision requiring administration officials — not Congress — to make further cuts in programs. In essence, they said: If Medicare runs out of money, the players and providers and patients will have to take their belts in a notch or two.

When the Congressional Budget Office (CBO) put the Republican plan under the microscope, it reported that the overall goal of saving $270 billion could be achieved within seven years, but *not* by the supposedly innovative new health policies Republicans claimed would reform the health system. Savings of that magnitude would have to be achieved the old, and painful, way: by raising costs to beneficiaries and cutting payments to doctors and hospitals. CBO also dashed claims that Medical Savings Accounts would help reduce costs. Rather than saving, CBO found that new plan would cost the government an additional two billion three hundred million dollars over seven years, by handing money to healthy seniors who run up minimal costs under the current system.

One of the implications of the CBO report was that costs of the uninsured or the underinsured elderly would be shifted to the private sector, to the employers who pay the bulk of the premiums for workers with insurance. In late October, a study by the Lewin-VHI, Inc. consulting firm estimated that employers and insured workers would face an extra $91 billion in health care costs because of this transfer of responsibility. But the business lobbies did not waver, suggesting that Hillary Clinton may have been right when she argued a year earlier that ideology was more important to them than the bottom-line economic interests of their members. A spokesman for the National Association of Manufacturers was quoted by the *Washington Post* as saying that the organization was a strong supporter of the Republican reform "and we've had zero pressure from our members to take a different stand."

As for Gradison and HIAA, even though they objected to the very favorable terms for doctors and hospitals who chose to form their own networks and compete with insurers for managed care contracts, there was never a thought of putting Harry and Louise back on the air — even when the White House asked them to consider it. "We respectfully declined" that request, Gradison told us. When the Clinton plan was on the table in 1993–94, "our members thought they were fighting for survival; that is why they sent us all that money. Now, the thrust we see in Congress on Medicare and Medicaid is toward privatization. That creates enormous opportunity to offer our services to literally tens of millions of people who are not in the insurance market today."

In addition to the major benefits, Gingrich rewarded business backers in many small but significant ways. Doctors would face fewer restrictions on referring patients to labs in which they had a financial interest. Their office labs would be freed from onerous regulation. Punitive damages would be reduced. Pharmaceutical companies would no longer be required to give discounts to public hospitals and community health centers.

As we have noted, the Republicans' Medicaid proposal was similar to — but more stringent than — the Medicare reform. But once again, Republicans defended the plan as providing much greater flexibility and choice — this time for states, not individuals. Republican governors, now running three-fifths of the states, said they were eager to be freed of hobbling federal regulation and of the obligation to keep pumping more and more of their own tax dollars into medical assistance for the needy.

These were vital issues, but complicated to explain. Congressional Democrats and the White House, now playing opposition-party politics, took a leaf from the Republicans' 1993–94 playbook and brushed past the serious debate to the demagogic appeals that rang emotional alarm bells with easily frightened senior citizens. Once more they insisted that the Republicans' "savings" were really "cuts," and argued that the $270 billion being taken out of Medicare was being shifted to $245 billion of "tax cuts for the wealthiest Americans." When Gingrich incautiously suggested that the changes being proposed would eventually cause Medicare "to wither on the vine," Democrats immediately ran an ad saying the plot had been exposed. Gingrich's insistence that he was talking about the agency that runs the program, not the program itself, did little to mitigate the damage.

The fleshed-out Medicare and Medicaid plans passed the House on October 18 on an almost strictly party-line vote. Only four Democrats voted with the Republicans, who suffered only six defections in their own ranks. Action in the Senate followed within a few days and on a similarly sharp partisan line. The President promised to veto the bill — and did so, knowing he would not be overridden. There the matter stood as debate on an even larger fiscal policy reached its climax.

By 1995, the economic forces that combined to make health care so explosive an issue had intensified. A continuing wave of major corporate restructurings — mergers, acquisitions, downsizings — including such giants as AT&T, ITT, Chase Manhattan, and Chemical Bank, had thrown hundreds of thousands of Americans out of work, threatening their ability to provide basic health care for themselves and their families. By the time of the showdown over the Republican budget cuts, an additional two million Americans had fallen into the ranks of those without health insurance. By then, too, fears of many health care experts about lasting damage to the system were being realized.

Across the country, the nation's preeminent teaching hospitals were battling for survival in a more competitive medical marketplace that forced them to compete with health maintenance organizations and other for-profit managed care operations. The teaching hospitals, long viewed as the crown jewels of American medicine, had achieved some of the century's greatest medical breakthroughs through basic research and experimentation; many of America's best doctors were trained, and health techniques perfected, in them. Now these hospitals were faced with a financial crisis that threatened the ability of the best universities to fund their research and teaching missions.

At stake was the foundational medical research that led the search for cures to cancer, AIDS, and Alzheimer's disease. In just a year, thirty of the nation's one hundred twenty-six academic medical centers had registered a drop in revenues — nearly double the figure of three years before — and that trend was expected to accelerate, driving a number of the centers out of business. Already, some top academic medical centers had been forced to eliminate hundreds of jobs to cut costs. Others, including Georgetown, George Washington, and Howard universities in the nation's capital, also had to take the drastic step of selling off all or parts of their hospitals.

The Medicare and Medicaid changes proposed in the Republican budget further imperiled their operations. They would eliminate between half and two-thirds of the federal subsidies their medical centers received. This crisis came hand in hand with another even more immediate one that endangered the nation's basic public health systems.

Nowhere were those signs more evident than in Los Angeles. On September 21, the same day that Sam Gibbons erupted in rage over failure to obtain health hearings in Washington, Dr. Chris Klasen of the L.A. County General–USC Medical Center told us of the shock waves then rolling over the hospital where she had worked so long. Just six days earlier, as the final skirmishing began in Washington over the new health care battle, layoff notices had gone out to thousands of public-health workers in L.A. County. "It is one of the darkest days of my county career," Mike Henry, L.A. County's personnel director, told the *Los Angeles Times*, "to know that some six thousand seven hundred notices of layoffs are going out to county employees. There has never been anything like this in the history of the county."

Among the cuts already announced — with more to come — were 50 percent of all nurses assigned to the operating rooms, emergency rooms, and intensive care units. Desperate patients were being turned away. "I just feel devastated," said L.A. County's Klasen. "It's a total meltdown of the public health care system. And don't think that's not going to have a great impact on the hospitals that stay open. People who have insurance are going to find emergency rooms flooded with new patients when they have to go there, and this isn't going to be limited to Los Angeles. This is going to happen everywhere." Their only hope, she said, was for a federal bailout to save total destruction of the county public health system. One day later, on September 22, while on a fund-raising swing in California, President Clinton announced a $364 million emergency assistant grant to the L.A. County public health system, an action taken, he announced after last-minute consultations with state officials, because "it would have been criminal to allow all those clinics to close." His action eased the immediate crisis but did not solve the long-term threat to that public system and others like it.

* * *

In Washington, as 1995 neared its end, there was an immediate crisis that underlined the long-term health care problem. The new fiscal year would begin on October 1, and the President and Congress remained at loggerheads on the financing of government. The "train wreck" that could shut down the functions of government loomed. And Newt Gingrich added a new threat to The System by telling an audience of security analysts that if Clinton did not satisfy the Republican demands for a balanced budget and a tax cut, they were ready to force the United States to default on its debt for the first time in history.

Unless Congress voted to raise the federal debt ceiling, then rapidly approaching its nearly $5 trillion statutory limit, the government would be unable to meet many of its obligations, starting with the $25 billion in interest payments due on November 15. Such a failure could jeopardize confidence in the world's strongest reserve currency and sow chaos in markets around the globe. But Gingrich insisted he was not bluffing. "What we are saying to Clinton is, 'Do not assume that we will flinch, because we won't,' " the Speaker said.

Gingrich's plan represented a breathtakingly bold political gamble. He assumed that he would force the President to balance the budget on the Speaker's terms — and that even if Clinton refused, and a train wreck occurred, the American people would blame the President, not the Republican Congress, for it.

But a *Wall Street Journal*/NBC News poll published the morning after Gingrich's speech showed a sharp drop in public support for the Republican Revolution. In contrast to positive ratings in the spring, by the end of September Americans by a margin of 58 to 30 percent disapproved of the job Congress was doing. For the first time since the takeover of Congress, more people "disagree with the Republicans' overall agenda than agree," reported pollsters Peter Hart and Robert Teeter. Their national survey also showed that by more than two to one, Americans blamed Republicans rather than Clinton for the budget wrangles.

That survey strongly suggested that the public was worried that the conservatives had gone too far. Certainly, commentators thought so. Russell Baker's column in the *New York Times* captured the moment best. On September 23, after watching the Gingrich forces work their will during the remarkable preceding days, Baker wrote, suddenly "the fun time" of the Revolution was over:

> [W]e are finally seeing where it's been carrying us from the first. Dr. Kevorkian is now waiting in the parlor. He's about to be shown upstairs to finish off the government we have known for sixty years. . . . Do the designers of the post-government age know what they're doing? In a matter of days they have been dismantling and redesigning structures that took years to put up. Who knows what is in these hastily sketched plans. The sound-bite artists will fill the air with reassuring bushwah about it, but who really has the vaguest idea what the results will be? Best bet: nobody.

By the end of September 1995, one year after House Republicans had signed their Contract With America, Congress had failed to pass eleven of thirteen appropriations bills to keep the federal government operating, and half of the Contract's provisions were stalled by opposition or inaction. All this provided further evidence, as if more were needed, of the increasing inability of government to work cooperatively on national problems.

In Washington, growing disgust and disillusionment with the way The System was working — with its polarization, its bitterness, its extremism — prompted one leading Democrat, Bill Bradley of New Jersey, to announce he was leaving the Senate. He did so, he said, because he believed The System was "broken."

Bradley's belief, widely shared among both Democratic and Republican moderates, was reinforced when a leading Republican possibility for Bradley's Senate seat, Thomas H. Kean, announced he would not seek it because he was repelled by the growing influence of "right-wing radicals" in his Republican Party. Kean, who had enjoyed broad popularity as New Jersey's governor from 1981 to 1989, said he had concluded that his moderate views would not be welcomed, or given a voice, within the Republican Party and Republican Senate, as then constituted. He criticized a "lack of civility" and meanness in national politics and his own party's "green eyeshade mentality," which he said had shortchanged the environment, education, and the disadvantaged. "If the whole priority is just reducing the budget," he told Dale Russakoff of the *Washington Post*, "you're just crunching numbers and you don't have a guiding philosophy, and that's not governing."

Kean's and Bradley's comments came against a backdrop of growing public disaffection with politics and government, and amid strong signs of renewed interest in independent or third-party candidates. This hunger was dramatically highlighted by the sudden emergence that fall of Colin Powell, the former chairman of the Joint Chiefs of Staff, as a prospective presidential candidate. Powell's national book tour to promote his autobiography, *My American Journey*, attracted extraordinary media and public attention. In a matter of weeks, Powell vaulted to the top in national presidential polls, topping Clinton, Dole, Gingrich, and other potential rivals. His emergence as a possible candidate, which he did not discourage, came as the nation was given another disturbing example of its racial divisions after a predominantly African-American jury swiftly acquitted O. J. Simpson of all murder charges, triggering an emotional national debate about the fairness of the criminal justice system. This latest example of America's racial polarization made Powell, an African-American himself, even more appealing as a public figure who might have the capacity to bridge the racial divide and diminish other tensions. In the end, Powell announced he would not be a candidate for any political office in 1996, but the acclaim he received provided powerful evidence of the public's hunger for someone who might breathe new life into The System. Not coincidentally, in that same period Ross Perot again stepped into the public spotlight, announcing plans to form the Independence Party to back a candidate against President Clinton and the Republican nominee in the 1996 presidential election. The two-party system was fragmenting along with other pieces of The System.

The breakdown began in stages and steadily grew more destructive. First came the shutdown of major parts of the government in mid-November after a temporary extension of funding expired, with Congress and the President locked in bitter dispute over a budget agreement. Once more, inability to agree on how to fund and re-form the nation's health care programs — to "cut" or "save" in or-der to provide both tax relief and a balanced budget — was at the center of the difficulties. Federal workers deemed "essential" came into their offices; those who were not "essential" suffered the stigma of irrelevance and got an early start on their Christmas shopping, knowing that they would be granted back pay for the days they missed by politicians who did not want to anger such a large group of voters. Americans watching the scenes on television saw citizens be-ing turned away from the national parks, from the Grand Canyon to Yosemite. The great national memorials — the Statue of Liberty, the Washington Monument, the Lincoln Memorial — worldwide sym-bols for American democracy, were closed. They saw, too, more vivid evidence of the increasing bitterness that enveloped The System. Capitol police had to intervene when opposing congressmen were about to come to blows. The political rhetoric, already venomous, became more so. A Republican House member, John Mica of Florida, boasted on the House floor of "nailing the little bugger," referring to the President of the United States. Newt Gingrich's public standing sank even lower after he complained to reporters that his supposed discourteous treatment by the President on an Air Force One flight to attend the state funeral for the assassinated Israeli leader Yitzhak Rabin strengthened his determination to force a shutdown of the government. He had been humiliated by being forced to leave from the rear of the aircraft, Gingrich said sourly, and berated the Presi-dent for failing to use that flight to consult with him. Gingrich's po-sition was weakened when the White House produced photographs showing him chatting with the President aboard Air Force One. It was all petty, and stirred further negative reactions among a public already dismayed by the ever more embittered partisan wrangling in Washington.

Government contractors and those needing government services were not as fortunate as the furloughed federal workers. Bills went unpaid and contracts unfulfilled. Television and newspapers car-ried poignant stories of travelers needing passports to cope with family emergencies frustrated because the passport offices were deemed nonessential. Both Gingrich and Clinton remained adamant

for seventy-two hours, then found that the rising tide of public anger threatened both of them. So a new temporary spending bill was
passed, this one due to expire on December 15. And, the public
learned, this political brinksmanship in the capital came with a cost:
The bill to the taxpayers for shutting down the government for that
week came to nearly three-quarters of a billion dollars.

The second, even more serious phase in the breakdown came
in mid-December after the latest temporary spending bill deadline
expired with the Republican Congress and the Democratic President still far from agreement on the budget and amid vociferous
arguments over health care versus the tax cut. By then, the President
had submitted another budget proposal, his third of the year. This
narrowed the dollar differences between the White House and the
Republicans on Medicare (where they had never been as far apart as
the rhetoric suggested) and on domestic programs. But the President
drew the line on the proposal to end federal responsibility for Medicaid and turn that program over to the states — and Republicans
remained adamant in their insistence that the shift take place.

Against that acrimonious background, the second partial government shutdown began. This one stretched day after day through
the Christmas holidays, barring thousands of visitors to Washington
from the museums and monuments on the Mall. The partisan rhetoric grew even more furious. Not even a highly publicized "handshake
agreement" between the President, Speaker Gingrich, and Senate
Majority Leader Dole to reopen the government while negotiations
continued could break the deadlock. Freshmen House Republicans
rebelled, calling Gingrich onto the carpet for making that concession to practicality. So Congress went home for Christmas leaving a
fractured government behind it, and its federal workers hostage to
this embittered breakdown in The System.

When Congress returned after the New Year, the rancor and
name-calling grew even worse. By then the public was becoming aware of the human and financial consequences of this longest
shutdown of the federal government in American history.

The cost to the taxpayers was $40 million a day, all added
to the national debt; more personal, and more devastating, was the
cost to federal workers who missed mortgage payments, saw their

credit ratings endangered, and watched those they served, from veterans hospitals to federal research centers for disease, suffer. By then, departments and agencies were a quarter of the way through the fiscal year. No budget had yet been enacted. The bitterness intensified. Whitewater resurfaced, with still more congressional hearings focusing on Hillary Clinton's and other players' roles in the land deals and the firing of White House Travel Office employees in the spring of 1993, reaching a new level of vituperation when *New York Times* columnist William Safire called the First Lady "a congenital liar." This was followed by the extraordinary — and unprecedented — spectacle of the First Lady being forced to appear before a Whitewater grand jury. This development came after a Clinton aide found long-missing, and long-sought, legal billing documents involving the Whitewater development mysteriously lying on a table in the White House family quarters. Republicans experienced their own internal problems: House Republicans even turned on Bob Dole and accused him of "caving in" after he led the Senate in passing a resolution to reopen the government while talks continued. "Enough is enough," Dole said.

But the breakdown continued. Even the temporary return of federal workers that January did not solve the destructive polarization that had enveloped Washington and brought the functions of the federal government to a halt, with long-term consequences in morale for U.S. employees at home and abroad, and for future government operations. The budget impasse still had not been broken; no final agreement was reached after days and days of intense meetings between the President and Republican congressional leaders. Nor, more pointedly for our story, did the return of federal workers resolve the future of Medicare and Medicaid — not only in the short term for the 1996 congressional session, but in the longer term in the way those programs ultimately serve the people.

The governmental breakdown becomes a metaphor for this story. When the President tried his reform, The System failed. When Republicans tried to achieve their changes, the failure was even greater.

24

Lessons:
Lost Opportunities

I N ONE OF OUR early interviews, Secretary of Health and
Human Services Donna Shalala described the battle launched
by President Bill Clinton and his wife, Hillary Rodham Clinton, as
one for "the last great social policy of this century." Enumerating the
programs passed during the previous decades, she said, "This is
the last piece, the country focusing on improving the quality of life
for its people at the turn of the century."

She was correct in those judgments, but the battle represented
much more than an attempt to forge a major policy. It became a
fundamental test of the clashing elements in The System. As Shalala
pointed out in that interview, for the first time in a dozen years one
party had been entrusted by the voters with control of the executive
and legislative branches of government. "If this Democratic Party
doesn't move to cover people who get up in the morning and go to
work in minimum-wage jobs," she said, "then it's not only lost its
soul, it's lost its political coalition for the future."

When she spoke, she and others in the Clinton administration
were optimistic. But in the end, the Democratic Congress adjourned
without even a roll call on reform, and the Clinton White House
barely addressed its demise — an outcome that no one, including its
most determined opponents, thought possible when the fight began.
As Shalala feared, the Democratic coalition collapsed in the historic
midterm election of 1994; a widely recognized public need went
unfulfilled; Republicans ended forty years of Democratic control of

Congress and initiated the great struggle over the role and purpose of the federal government that will continue through the 1996 presidential election and beyond. Thus the story of the life and death of health reform shines a harsh light on the way The System — and the men and women in it — succeeds or fails. As Paul Starr, the Princeton scholar and author who played a major part in designing the Clinton health care reform, ruefully said later, "The collapse of health care reform in the first two years of the Clinton administration will go down as one of the great lost political opportunities in American history. It is a story of compromises that never happened, of deals that were never closed, of Republicans, moderate Democrats, and key interest groups that backpedaled from proposals they themselves had earlier co-sponsored or endorsed. It is also a story of strategic miscalculations on the part of the President and those of us who advised him."

He also accurately said, "The Republicans enjoyed a double triumph, killing reform and then watching jurors find the President guilty. It was the political equivalent of the perfect crime."

It is easy in retrospect to say that this kind of fundamental change was too much for The System to resolve. But another ambitious proposal, the tax reform bill of 1986, was enacted in a divided government, and there were many moments when different decisions could have produced a different result. As we have seen, the lessons of that earlier tax reform battle and the 1989 fiasco with Medicare catastrophic health insurance were either ignored or forgotten. They are instructive not only for our story, but also for future attempts to achieve major reform on controversial issues.

First and foremost, tax reform succeeded because it had bipartisan support. While interest groups modified the final bill, sufficient interest-group support remained to keep it alive. In the Congress, instead of diffusing responsibility for its passage through many competing committees, the tax bill was clearly the responsibility of two principal committees: House Ways and Means and Senate Finance. Leaders of those committees imposed structure on the legislative process and maintained discipline in the debate. Perhaps most critical of all, the tax bill, even though lengthy and complex, was based on

a simple, easy to communicate idea that all Americans could readily understand. No complex media explanation was necessary. Also
critically important, tax reform did not directly threaten average
Americans. Virtually every citizen understood that taxes, which of
course no one likes, were nonetheless fundamental to government.
By contrast, the federal government's large role in health care, providing about $4 of every $10 spent nationally, is often hidden and
not well understood by the public.

Some of our players, notably Newt Gingrich, contend that The
System "worked" on health care. Government inaction, they argue, was the best outcome. The trillion-dollar health care industry,
prodded by powerful market forces, began to restructure itself long
before the Clinton plan was unveiled, and, after it failed, the pace of
change continued to escalate. Already, the health care system is dramatically different. Whether these changes result in better-quality
care for all Americans is a far different question.

A year after the battle over the Clinton plan had ended, at a time
when it was not clear whether Gingrich's Medicare and Medicaid
changes would become law, we talked again with Bill Gradison, the
head of the Health Insurance Association of America (HIAA). Like
Gingrich, he observed that "from a private sector point of view, one
could argue that the inability of the government to bring about significant change gives the private market a chance to develop without
major hurdles. On the other hand, there are actions which only the
government can take which are really needed."

Gradison added: "I told my members when Congress went home
in 1994 that there were no winners and a lot of losers in the great
health care debate. The problems were still there. The number of
uninsured was already at unacceptable levels and was going to rise.
The level of health care inflation, while moderating, was still too
high. These things require action. That is still my view."

It is our view, as well, that in this great test The System failed
the people it was designed to serve. The goal of providing affordable
quality health care for all — more substantially addressed, if not
fully achieved, by every other advanced industrial country in the
world — is farther from realization in the United States in 1996 than
it was at the beginning of the decade. When the debate began, a broad

public bipartisan consensus had developed on the need for fundamental reform, although not on the best policy to pursue or on the
solutions people were ready to support. The battle was fought amid
the most favorable conditions in this century. Paul Starr's epitaph is
correct: The loss of this battle will be recorded as one of the great lost
opportunities in American history.

How great a failure this turned out to be became clear over the
next year. Many of the problems that prompted the Clinton initiative remain, and one of them, the number of uninsured Americans,
grows steadily larger. Medical inflation continues. Public health services for the poorest Americans rapidly erode, and older Americans
in need of health care find themselves threatened with higher costs
for reduced services. States, counties, and cities, which face sharply
reduced federal support, search in vain for local tax dollars to maintain basic services. Major public hospitals close. The already great
chasm separating America's haves from its have-nots continues to
widen. At the end of 1995, a year after the Clinton effort crashed,
the triumphant Republican majorities in Congress struggled with the
same runaway costs of the largest federal health programs, Medicare
and Medicaid, that led Clinton to try to reform them. The increasingly fractious battle between the Democratic President and the Republican Congress over the federal budget that resulted in the longest
shutdown of the federal government in history exposes the greater
struggle that health care symbolizes: over two conflicting visions of
the role of American government and the values of the society at
century's end.

The failure of The System on health care reform might not
loom so large if other great challenges facing the society were being
met. They are not. Personal safety, economic opportunity, international peace, and health care are the four great security questions
by which the American people judge the quality of their lives.
On all but one of these, international peace, the last quarter of
the twentieth century has witnessed the failure of The System to
meet the legitimate expectations of the people it is supposed to be
serving.

The exception becomes important for the standard of success it
set. In the span of a generation, there were bitter debates over ending

the war in Vietnam, over relinquishing control of the Panama Canal, and over a number of arms control agreements, as well as strong conflicts over U.S. policy in Afghanistan, Nicaragua, El Salvador, the Philippines, South Africa, China, Iraq, Iran, Kuwait, Somalia, Haiti — to say nothing of the former Soviet Union. In the early 1980s, there were battles over the great expansion of our armed forces. In the 1990s, more battles were fought over the proposals to reduce the size of those same forces. In the midst of these conflicts, a major scandal rocked the heart of American policy-making, the President's National Security Council, over secretly trading arms for hostages in the Iran-Contra affair.

Despite these many disagreements, the main course of American foreign policy and military doctrine was clear and constant, not only to allies and adversaries, but to U.S. citizens who gave those policies broad and continuing support. Though Democrats controlled the House of Representatives, and Republicans occupied the White House for most of those years, with control of the Senate switching back and forth between the two parties, partisanship did not thwart basic agreement on national policies. Leaders of both parties helped the American people understand the challenges and the sacrifices of lives and treasure that might be required. The press and television, though often at odds with politicians in power, and despite their natural instinct to highlight controversy and conflict, portrayed the situation in sufficiently clear and compelling terms, so that what President Kennedy had called "the long, twilight struggle" was sustained until the moment of victory.

Throughout that quarter of a century and the quarter century that preceded it, the United States organized and led an international coalition that rebuilt Western Europe and Japan after the destruction of World War II, contained the aggression of the Soviet Union, and applied such economic and military pressure that the Soviet empire crumbled. A new Russia, with newly independent states, arose to begin the struggle for democratic reform.

It was a historic achievement for freedom and democracy, a victory in nearly a half century of Cold War struggle, and vindication of the governing institutions of the United States — all that comprise The System.

That record stands in stark contrast to the American scene at home. By the time the Berlin Wall came down and Boris Yeltsin stood atop a Russian tank, defying the last remnants of the old regime, Americans had a strong sense that The System has been far less successful in dealing with domestic problems than with foreign ones.

They are right. The sense of personal safety, linchpin of a stable society, has been shattered by the spread of random violence. No area is immune: The specter of violent crime haunts farm communities as well as urban centers. Drug dealers now operate in rural Iowa and Alabama as well as in metropolitan New York, Chicago, and Los Angeles. Between 1968, when urban riots made "law and order" a major theme of Richard Nixon's successful presidential campaign, and the beginning of 1996, Congress passed and Presidents signed no fewer than seven major crime and drug bills. State legislatures and governors have been at least as busy proclaiming and producing battle plans for their own "wars" on crime. But in that same period the threat of serious crime has increased as "drive-by shootings" and gang assaults become metaphors for the times. A pervasive sense of personal insecurity has been heightened.

So also when it comes to economic insecurity. Confidence in government's ability to protect people against the vagaries of a rapidly changing economy has been shaken. Beginning with the "oil shocks" of the 1970s and continuing through the computer revolution that fundamentally altered the character and demands of the workplace in the 1980s and '90s, the American standard of living has stagnated. After growing rapidly in the first quarter century following World War II, median family income stalled. Measured in constant dollars, that typical family earned $34,523 in 1970 and only $36,959 in 1993.

Even discounting for inflation and the overall growth of the U.S. economy, more and more of the financial rewards are going to the wealthiest portion of the society. For millions in the middle class, the American Dream is receding. Inequality, in everything from incomes to health care, becomes the new norm. The addition of two-income parents to the workplace, a necessity by the nineties, fails to persuade these better-educated Americans that they are enjoying the lifestyle their father's single income had provided, or even living as well as their grandparents had. They struggle merely to hold their own.

Emergence of an urban underclass with spiraling rates of out-of-wedlock births and attendant rises in juvenile crime add to their fear that America has lost its way. Optimism, hallmark of middle-class American society, turns into persistent pessimism. For blue-collar workers, the sense of dashed hopes is even more profound. High-income production jobs have moved overseas as companies employ lower-wage workers in underdeveloped Third World econo-mies. Many Americans have been forced into "givebacks" of benefits in their health and pension plans in order to retain their jobs. Good-paying jobs for unskilled workers are virtually disappearing; keep-ing a factory floor job requires computer skills beyond the training of many middle-aged workers. Automation renders many of those in middle management expendable as their higher-echelon supervisors are able to monitor sales, production, and inventories directly from their desktop computers. Entire layers of good white-collar jobs are being eliminated. The "downsizing" wave sweeps through even the biggest and most stable companies, the IBMs and General Motors and AT&Ts. Previously, a young college graduate who secured an entry-level job in these bluest of blue chip American corporations could count on lifetime employment. No longer.

To these increasingly anxious workers, the government appears either indifferent or incompetent in assisting them through the im-mense structural changes in the American economy. From Washington, they hear much talk but see little action to ease the pressures on their lives. Increasingly embittered debates over such intensely divisive issues as Vietnam and Watergate have added to the feeling that confrontation, not consensus, drives The System. More and more Americans now view both Democrats and Republicans as intent on tearing down opponents rather than building up the coun-try. Energy policy fails to ensure conservation of natural resources or sufficient protection of the environment. Tax policy produces be-wildering complexities. Crime policy involves more posturing than policing. In the most glaring failure, government has been unable to put its fiscal house in order. Annual deficits on a previously un-imaginable scale accumulate; future generations are burdened with a geometrically rising national debt that threatens their personal prospects and the American future.

It was in this context that the battle between the President and the Congress over health reform was waged. Difficult and complex as that battle proved to be, restoring a sense of personal safety and fostering economic security are far more daunting. The twin scourges of crime and drugs are fed by powerful sociological forces that include the breakdown of the family structure and the disappearance, in many neighborhoods, of adult males capable of imposing discipline and establishing role models for a generation of alienated and increasingly violent teenagers. The Information Age transforms the entire marketplace from one with primary dependence on the creation and distribution of tangible goods to one relying mainly on the generation and transmission of data. In a time when billions of dollars of currency and investment whiz around the world in fractions of a second of microchip activity, debates about tariffs and trade seem antique. Clearly, education and training are even more important keys to individual prosperity than in the past. Yet Americans entering the workplace face a formidable new problem: No one knows how many and what kinds of jobs there will be and where they will be located. There are no easy solutions; most of the problems are structural, having developed over decades. They present long-term challenges to a System, and a society, fixated on the immediate moment.

In contrast to these immensely complex challenges, the goal of providing access to quality health care for everyone was not an impossible dream. No doubt the credibility of the Clintons would have been enhanced had they admitted from the beginning that hard choices were involved — and acknowledged, too, that some people would have to pay a price in dollars, convenience, or freedom of choice for a new system that enabled everyone, not just the 85 percent with insurance, to receive care. There were reasons to be skeptical of Ira Magaziner's belief that waste in the existing health care system was so great that fine-tuning could produce sufficient savings to finance universal care, but no one seriously challenged his assertion about its enormous inefficiencies. Shortchanging such preventive measures as immunization has resulted in millions of people seeking expensive, unreimbursed care in hospital emergency rooms for

conditions that could — and should — be treated far more cheaply
and humanely at earlier stages of the illness. The administrative
costs of competing insurance companies could — and should — be
cut significantly by some mechanism, whether termed a purchasing
cooperative or an alliance, that draws small groups or individuals into larger blocks of health care consumers. Real competition
could — and should — limit medical inflation even more than private business was beginning to experience when the Clintons began
their effort. Even if one rejects the government-financed single-
payer plan, which the Congressional Budget Office says would provide health insurance for everyone at lower overall total cost, room
clearly existed for reforms that made practical economic and social
sense.

Failure to achieve any of those possible changes was a failure of
The System and every one of its parts: the presidency, the Congress,
the political parties, the interest groups, and the press.

We cannot render a tougher judgment on Bill Clinton and his administration than the one he pronounced on himself: "I set the
Congress up for failure." The errors of judgment, of omission and
execution, that he and First Lady Hillary Clinton and their associates made were critical. While they deserve great credit for tack-
ling a problem that Presidents had found reason to postpone for six
decades or more, and for placing it at the center of national debate
and consciousness, they cannot avoid blame for the ultimate failure. Though many factors contributed to that end, we agree with
Paul Starr's retrospective judgment: The lesson for the next time in
health care reform is faster, smaller. "We made the error of trying to
do too much, took too long, and ended up achieving nothing." Even
worse, Starr said, is the ultimate irony that appears to be coming
true a year after the end of the Clinton attempt: a movement that
began with liberal proposals to control costs and expand coverage
has produced conservative legislation that raises costs and reduces
coverage.

Of all the mistakes, the greatest was the failure to recognize the
limits on the President's authority imposed by the election returns.
Conventional wisdom holds that you do not build bold agendas on

small majorities, and Bill Clinton had no majority at all. He won with 43 percent of the popular vote, while his party lost ten seats in the House and just held its own in the Senate. Clinton limped into Washington, trailing the popular vote district by district of almost every member of Congress and with few longtime political alliances on which to draw. Moreover, health care reform was not the only item on his agenda or, to a majority of his advisers, the most important. During his presidential transition discussions in Little Rock, the highest priority, understandably and inevitably, was placed on dealing with the soaring budget deficit he had inherited. By reducing the deficit, he hoped to stimulate the economic growth he had promised in the campaign.

In the euphoria of victory, Clinton and his advisers grossly underestimated how much time and political capital it would take to get their budget and economic plan through a Congress in which Republicans possessed almost unlimited power to block legislation. Clinton, by his own testimony to us, was forewarned by Senate Minority Leader Bob Dole not to expect a single Republican vote for the budget. Even if the President underestimated the difficulties he would face in his own Democratic ranks, he should have held no illusions about the problems he faced from Republicans. Given that reality, he clearly would have been well advised to take the counsel some gave him to "make haste slowly."

Despite all the warning signals, the Clintons marched ahead, fortified by a belief that the rightness of their cause and the hard work they were prepared to expend on it would overcome all obstacles. They did not. Indeed, the Clintons compounded their problems by the structure they themselves designed.

The decision to create the special White House task force headed by Hillary Rodham Clinton and Ira Magaziner was a major mistake. Magaziner did a thorough job of devising a plan that was internally consistent and that addressed as many of the complex problems as any public policy could. The First Lady was an eloquent, tireless, and, for the most part, effective advocate for the cause. But the consequences of the President's decision to entrust the task to them were overwhelmingly negative. Having Hillary at the head of the task force inhibited the political debate within the administration. The secrecy under which it operated alienated not only important congressional leaders but others in the administration whose support was critical for its success. These people, in significant instances, resorted to the classic Washington tactic of making their objections public by leaking damaging (and often inaccurate) information to a press corps thoroughly frustrated by the curtain of silence erected by Hillary Clinton and Ira Magaziner. Leaks that plagued the project reflected an extraordinary lack of discipline and cohesion in the heart of the government. These repeated and destructive leaks exposed a larger problem: Despite the obvious importance both the President and the First Lady attached to health care reform, it remained something of an orphan within their administration. The White House staff for domestic policy, budget, politics, and lobbying, to say nothing of aides at Treasury, Health and Human Services, and other departments, were never fully committed to a project from which they felt excluded. The task force joke about living on "Planet Ira" contained a hard truth: Many in the White House said of the reform group, "They're so smart. Let them figure out how to pass it." That attitude was echoed, and amplified, on Capitol Hill.

All these were political mistakes, and the ultimate responsibility for them goes to the man in charge, who, as we have seen, was more than ready to take the blame. We've already explored two of these errors: first, the mismatch between the scale of reform and the political capital available to achieve it; second, the decision to place responsibility for devising the plan on a small group within the White House in a way that made other officials with expertise feel circumvented and that cast doubt on the President's claim to policy flexibility. A third set of errors involves the Congress.

The White House never resolved the contradiction between a House strategy based on the Democratic Left and a Senate strategy aimed at achieving consensus on a bill by winning moderates of both parties. Even within the Senate, the chairmen of the two committees, each believing he had White House backing, operated under very different assumptions about what served the President's interests. And there was another problem: Few on Capitol Hill could claim any expertise on the subject; fewer were even vaguely familiar with the program he chose to support, and many of them disagreed with Clinton's version as they examined it.

These contradictions contributed to what the President told us he believed to be his greatest blunder. His first strategy was to bypass the legislative roadblocks to passage by making reform part of the budget reconciliation bill on which time for debate is limited and no Senate filibuster can be mounted. Robert C. Byrd of West Virginia, a Democrat whose passion for rules and precedents exceeds his enthusiasm for any new program, blocked that approach. Byrd was serving as guardian of one of The System's genuine foundations: lengthy Senate debate that allows the public to understand and react to controversial bills. Those who condemn him ignore some of the follies that have gained transient popularity in the past. But the President is right in saying that once Senator Byrd slammed shut the door to the reconciliation bill, Clinton should have immediately reached out to Senate Republicans and moderate Democrats who had proposed their own versions of health reform. He did not. Instead, he continued to lobby for his own proposal and, in his 1994 State of the Union address, pledged to veto any bill that would not guarantee a short timetable to achieve universal coverage. By appearing to rule out any compromise at that point, even as his political support was waning alarmingly, the President doomed whatever small chance remained to salvage some kind of victory.

In dwelling on the mistakes and shortcomings of the principal White House players, we know there is the danger of exaggerating the impact that individuals have on large events and of minimizing the institutional obstacles and historical forces they face. Certainly, the President understood this. He knew from the beginning, as he told us, how difficult the battle would be, that "it was an issue with a lot of downside and a high probability of failure." Both he and Hillary had studied the previous record of presidential failures with health care. "When Harry Truman tried to do it, he went from eighty percent approval in the polls after he dropped the bomb on Japan down to, I think, thirty-six when he sent health care to the Congress for the second time," the President said. Hillary, in a separate conversation, would detail chapter and verse how opposition interest groups had prevailed in earlier battles. Still, neither of the Clintons was prepared for the magnitude of the problems they encountered. As the President said, simply, "It turned out to be even more difficult than I thought it would be."

Our story sheds light on at least three of the ways in which large historical forces have weakened the presidency as a vehicle for change. In the era of "the perpetual campaign," as some have called it, the politics of governing have been all but overwhelmed by the demands of seeking and retaining office. The 1992 campaign, and the need to dramatize his differences with President George Bush, impelled Clinton to pledge to have his entire health care reform plan ready for Congress within one hundred days of taking office. This FDR emulation, common to nearly all Presidents since FDR, bore no relationship to the legislative timetable or to the reasonable expectations of what a new government can produce in its first three months. It was an easy applause line. Period. (The same political posturing led the Gingrich Congress to its hundred-day Contract: The easy items won House approval, but nearly six months later, the serious work had not been accomplished as the new Congress failed to complete even one of thirteen appropriation bills legally required to keep the government functioning before the end of the fiscal year, a dismal record for a determined, newly empowered majority.) But Clinton's hundred-day pledge *did* have major consequences. It forced the President to attempt to shortcut the bureaucracy, set up his own health care task force, and turn it over to two of the most indefatigable workers he knew — Hillary and Ira. The hundred-day pledge also quickly collided with another campaign promise: to cut his White House staff by 25 percent. As a result, the Clinton staff was all but overwhelmed by the work involved in his ambitious first-year agenda. Because nearly all the people he had available were committed to the budget battle, political support for the health care plan was nonexistent almost until the moment it was announced. Even then, the White House had been operating for months without a day-to-day coordinator of lobbying, media, and grassroots support for the most ambitious and most vulnerable of the President's initiatives. When the opponents launched their all-out attacks, lack of staff support crippled the administration effort. It was a high price to pay for a cheap and easily forgotten campaign promise, but typical of what happens in today's System. George Bush was bedeviled by the same problems after his "no new taxes" pledge, Ronald Reagan was impaled by his own words during the Iran-Contra affair, and, most spectacularly, Richard Nixon lost his presidency through his stupid plan to disconcert the Democratic opposition during the 1972 campaign.

The presidential campaign also affects the presidency by personalizing campaign figures and creating obligations to them, sometimes to the detriment of the ensuing administration. Hillary Clinton's role as head of the health care battle represented an unprecedented leap in visible authority for any First Lady, including Eleanor Roosevelt, but one that was implied in the campaign when Clinton, the candidate, told audiences, "Buy one — get one free." Ira Magaziner's subsequent role provides another example. Magaziner won Clinton's trust by functioning as his health care guru during the campaign. Bonds forged then were so strong that Magaziner later prevailed with Clinton the President on issue after issue, even when Magaziner's judgment was challenged by people who had not experienced the snows of New Hampshire or the dark days of June when Ross Perot's rise threatened to doom Clinton to a third-place finish. Lloyd Bentsen had written more health care legislation than anyone in the Clinton administration, but as Treasury Secretary he was an outsider. Donna Shalala had more expertise in her Health and Human Services Department than anyone else but had not been part of the campaign team. The same was true of Leon Panetta at the Office of Management and Budget, another experienced legislator, and of Alice Rivlin, his deputy and former head of the Congressional Budget Office, and of Laura D'Andrea Tyson at the Council of Economic Advisers. Issues these people raised inside the administration were the same ones that later undermined the credibility of the Clinton plan on Capitol Hill. But because they lacked those campaign battle stars, their advice was not heeded.

Finally, the overlap of the campaign into government gives a powerful impetus to the inclination to politicize every issue the President faces. The entire mind-set of the Clinton White House was to treat the passage of health care reform as the campaign of 1994. As

Chip Kahn of HIAA remarked, the "Harry and Louise" commercials would have made no sense if the Clintons had been running an ordinary legislative strategy for passage of their plan. When they made it a political campaign, driven by the same polling and media consultants who had steered the 1992 presidential campaign, they made the battlefield both more partisan and more public, enabling their opponents to use the tactics they did. It need hardly be said that some of those opponents — Newt Gingrich from the start and Bob Dole by the end — saw the policy battle almost entirely as a prelude to the 1994 midterm campaign and the 1996 presidential election.

That the Clintons fell into their campaign mode and then failed to muster adequate resources for the battle or to find someone with the skill and time to run the campaign just compounded the problem. But the fundamental flaw was the one pointed out, in pungent language, by Lawrence O'Donnell, Pat Moynihan's aide. When your purpose is legislation, you don't set up War Rooms and you don't believe that you are going to vanquish the opposition. It was "campaign-think" that clouded the Clintons' ability to see that fact.

A third institutional problem our story illuminates is the loss of the credibility that enables a President to communicate with the American people on complex subjects. The power of the presidency, as Richard Neustadt has written, lies almost entirely in the President's ability to persuade other people to do what he thinks right. It is no accident that the great moments of the modern presidency are closely associated with memorable presidential addresses. When a difficult challenge presents itself, the President has to be able, figuratively speaking, to take people by the hand and lead them through it. That is what Harry Truman did when he persuaded a war-weary nation to take up the burdens of the Marshall Plan and the NATO Alliance in order to combat a new threat from the Soviet Union. It is what John Kennedy did during the Cuban Missile Crisis.

For anyone who remembers those Presidents, Bill Clinton was at least their equal — and probably their superior — when it came to eloquence, articulateness, and grasp of subject. He might not have been able to tug the heartstrings as effectively as Ronald Reagan, but he spoke with passion and force about subjects like health care, as he showed on the night of September 22, 1993, when, despite his problems with a TelePrompTer, he delivered his magnificent address to a joint session of Congress and the nation. But that was the only time the President moved the nation with him in this fight. From then on, though he spoke often and well, the path was downhill. The problem was not with his speeches; the problem was that the platform from which he spoke was splintering beneath him.

Americans have learned, from bitter experience, not to take their Presidents at their word. The phrase "credibility gap" entered the language with Lyndon Johnson and Vietnam; the phenomenon it described grew with every successive President. From Watergate to "read my lips," Americans have been disillusioned again and again and again. Whitewater, and a host of lesser stories, shattered Clinton's credibility — and Hillary's as well — during the time health care was on the national agenda. Trust was destroyed. In the end, Hillary was literally driven offstage by near-fanatical opponents, and the President was forced to participate in a political charade when he supposedly removed his name from the health care bill.

Finally, our story illustrates how this overly politicized, personalized, weakened, and less credible presidency has been fenced off from the rest of the government, its occupant forced to improvise in order to maintain a leading role. In recent years, the typical route to the presidency has been to adopt the role of the outsider. Except for George Bush, who was elevated from the vice presidency, recent Presidents have stressed their "apartness" from official Washington and their intention to scourge The System rather than fit into it. Jimmy Carter promised to make government "as good as the American people." Ronald Reagan jabbed at "Disneyland on the Potomac." Bill Clinton condemned "the brain-dead politics of Washington."

Whether they meant these words or not, the result has been to convey a belief that these Presidents seek power for themselves and expect to win by exposing those inside The System. Upon election, Reagan immediately enlisted the insiders, bringing in several consummate Washington players — notably Jim Baker, Dick Darman, and congressional liaison chief Kenneth Duberstein — to manage his domestic business. Carter did not do that, and Clinton began his presidency with no one — literally no one — outside the National Security Council staff who had ever worked in the White House. Only those who regard governing as a simple task were surprised that Clinton's first year produced personnel problems, mixed messages, and lost opportunities, of which health care reform was the greatest. These problems, and others he faced with interest groups and with Congress, were not just Clinton's fault. They typified the state of the presidency in the last years of the century.

Another fateful decision Clinton made early in his presidency was to rely heavily on the advice and judgment of the Democratic congressional leaders to pass his program. As we have noted, Clinton ran against Washington and constantly pressed Magaziner and others to get beyond "conventional Washington thinking" on the substance of his health care program.

But at a dinner in Little Rock, during his transition period, Clinton listened attentively as Vice President Gore, Speaker Foley, House Majority Leader Gephardt, and Senate Majority Leader Mitchell begged him not to repeat the "error" Jimmy Carter had made by holding himself aloof from the congressional Democrats. Let us be your foot soldiers, they said. Gephardt and Mitchell were particularly forceful in warning that Carter's legislative program had been crippled by the early divorce between him and the congressional Democrats. This miscalculation left him vulnerable to a serious renomination challenge from an esteemed legislator, Senator Edward M. Kennedy, and ultimately led to his defeat by Reagan.

No matter how narrow Clinton's victory, no matter how slim the congressional majorities, the leaders assured the new President that the congressional Democrats would deliver for him — if he gave them a chance. Gephardt said many Democrats like himself, who were newcomers when Carter became President, had learned their lesson: Failure to back your President opens the White House door to the Republicans. They would not make that mistake again, Gephardt said. But, please, Mr. President, he added, once you've given us our marching orders, let us carry them out *our* way.

Clinton cannot be seriously faulted for listening to them, even though none of them had been a close ally in helping him win the nomination or the election. They were the veterans. They knew The System. It hardly made sense to begin his term by refusing to agree to cooperate with his own party leaders, especially given the hostile signals from the Republicans.

The congressional leaders meant no duplicity. They were not setting Clinton up for a fall. They all genuinely believed that Congress was prepared to help make this Democratic President a success, including Speaker Tom Foley, perhaps the most privately skeptical of the feasibility of Clinton's legislative ambitions, a view he held because he painfully remembered how the great Lyndon Johnson landslide of 1964 soon was consumed in a protracted public backlash against the Great Society. What they all underestimated, probably because they had been part of a process of slow erosion for so long, was the extent to which the authority of congressional leaders had diminished. All of them — and the whole country — were about to learn how the structure of Congress as a legislative body had been atomized during the long period of Democratic control. During that time, senators and representatives had increasingly become individual political entrepreneurs. They picked out the office they wanted and ran their own campaigns for it. They hired their own pollsters, media advisers, and campaign consultants. They raised their own funds, recruited their own volunteers, chose their own issues. If they were successful, they found themselves in Washington in January raising their hands to take the oath to "protect and defend the Constitution of the United States." Then they looked around at the other ninety-nine senators or four hundred thirty-four House members. Suddenly, it dawned on them that they were to govern collectively.

When The System grappled with the consuming problems of the Great Depression, World War II, and the start of the Cold War, new members of Congress were assimilated into Congress very much as apprentices were brought into the studios of the great Renaissance artists and craftsmen. They were assigned to a working group — the committee — headed by a senior specialist in that field. They were instructed to watch and listen and say as little as possible for the first few years; and they were expected to follow their elders' example when it came to voting. In time, they might be asked to tackle a few simple chores on their own: examining a particular witness or handling a minor bill on the floor. As the years passed, their chores became more difficult, their discretion greater. If they played their expected congressional roles and "took care of" their districts well enough to be reelected year after year, eventually they would be the masters (or committee chairmen) indoctrinating the apprentices in the workings of The System.

That Congress disappeared long before Bill Clinton came to Washington. In the Senate, it was overthrown by television and by the new form of lone-wolf, entrepreneurial politics. When the televised hearings on organized crime made a not-much-liked junior senator, Estes Kefauver of Tennessee, a national figure in 1951 and launched him into presidential politics, the old system shuddered. When another junior senator, John F. Kennedy, actually won the presidential nomination over a field that included Senate Majority Leader Lyndon B. Johnson, the message was unmistakable: Use the Senate or its committees as the stage for building a national television constituency, and you can go as far in politics as you like.

Increasingly, the apprenticeship system gave way to the entrepreneurial senator — each looking for an issue, a hearing, a political device to draw attention to himself. Even the Senate schedule became hostage to the independent activities of individual senators, inside and outside the chamber. Lyndon Johnson, as majority leader, kept the Senate in session for twenty-four hours for days to break civil rights filibusters. Gentlemanly Mike Mansfield of Montana, who succeeded him, would not risk the health of his colleagues by doing that. Consequently, delaying tactics by small groups of opponents became more prevalent and effective. By the time George Mitchell became majority leader in 1989, the threat of filibuster had become as lethal to legislative action as the filibuster itself — and it was employed far more frequently.

The same process unfolded in the House of Representatives, and for many of the same reasons. House members, too, became independent entrepreneurs as the old party "machines" declined in the Democratic cities and the Republican suburbs along with the rise of the ubiquitous TV campaign. Once elected, the members found that the perks of incumbency — multiple home-district offices, newsletters mailed at public expense, regular appearances on local TV and radio shows and, perhaps most important, easy access to campaign funds from political action committees (PACs) — gave them enormous advantages in gaining reelection. They did not have to vote as their elders wished; if they chose, they could thumb their noses and appear strong and independent in the eyes of their constituents.

Like the senators, some of them began looking at Congress mainly as a platform from which to rise to more prominent office: senator, governor, even President. After Morris Udall of Arizona became runner-up for the Democratic nomination in 1976, a House member almost always sought the presidential nomination of one party or the other.

In addition, the cultural and generational changes in House membership undermined the old system of deference and discipline. Speaker Sam Rayburn — "Mister Sam" — the venerable embodiment of that system who told entering freshmen they would "get along by going along," died two years before the teenage Bill Clinton came to Washington as a delegate to a Boy's Nation conference where his famous handshake with President Kennedy became capital for his future political campaigns. No successor in the Speakership, not even Newt Gingrich, had as much authority as Rayburn wielded. The huge freshman Democratic classes of 1964 and 1974 contained dozens of bright, ambitious, reform-minded legislators who were ready to "change The System." And they did. The "Watergate babies" elected in 1974 were especially antagonistic to the old regime; they voted some committee chairmen out of office and stripped others of their unilateral control over the committee agendas. The result of the rule changes they put through was to disperse power outward and downward. Scores of subcommittees began operating as autonomous centers of legislative initiative, each with its own entrepreneur in charge. If you did not remember a congressional Democrat's name, you could safely get by by asking, "How are you, Mr. Chairman?"

In the 1980s, facing Republican Presidents, Democrats in Congress realized that they might have gone too far in democratizing their institution and began to strengthen their leadership. They gave the Speaker and the two majority leaders more say in committee assignments; they beefed up their policy and communications staffs; occasionally they even disciplined a notable defector, like Phil Gramm, by removing him from an influential committee. But these steps did not alter the basic fact that when the health care battle began, the centrifugal forces of personal ambition and predilection were far more powerful in both houses of Congress than the cohesive forces of party loyalty.

Forming a unified, disciplined political front was nearly impossible in that Congress. Because the Clintons' health care reform would touch the jurisdictions of at least five major committees of the House and Senate in major ways, and an additional eight or nine in peripheral ways, some thought was given to creation of an ad hoc supercommittee in each chamber that could move the bill promptly to the floor. As we have seen, the First Lady ardently sought this approach. Gephardt, Foley, and Mitchell immediately rejected the idea; the members of the committees with jurisdiction would never yield that much power to a select group appointed by the leaders.

And, as we have also seen, the obstacles in the multicommittee approach proved to be so formidable that the leaders were unable to get a measure to the point of being voted up or down in either the House or the Senate. Responsibility was hopelessly, destructively, fragmented.

One House subcommittee chairman (Pete Stark) blithely discarded the Clinton plan and substituted a bill that he had been promoting personally for years. That bill, which envisaged a much larger role for the federal government than anything the President had in mind, became the main vehicle in the House — and could not be passed. Another House subcommittee chairman (Henry Waxman) was unable to make the compromises to get anything out of his panel and turned over the job to the full committee chairman (John Dingell), who had no better luck. Dingell found himself frustrated by two members (Jim Cooper and Jim Slattery) who were driven in large part by the political imperatives of the statewide races they were making. On the third House committee, the makeup was so liberal that the bills they reported were of no use to the leadership as vehicles for floor action.

In the Senate, one committee chairman (Ted Kennedy) was

obsessed by the need for speedy action, yet he delayed again and again in reporting the measure in what turned out to be a futile hope that he would get more than one Republican to come aboard. The other chairman (Pat Moynihan) was so indiscreet about his qualms about the Clinton plan that he may have done more to damage the legislation than any of its avowed opponents. His committee dithered and delayed and ultimately was supplanted by two ad hoc efforts, one conducted by the bipartisan Mainstream Coalition and the other by Majority Leader Mitchell acting on his own. Both efforts came to naught.

The health care battle exposed as clearly as any recent legislative effort the infirmities that had developed in Congress under the long period of Democratic control. Clinton was not to blame for them; he was their victim. And when he had to sit and watch, in August of 1994, as the very leaders he had trusted to deliver for him squabbled for weeks over petty, parochial jurisdictional questions while health care reform went down the tubes, he must have wondered whether he had made a mistake in trying to move this broken system.

The fight also exposed the weakness of the Democratic Party — and led directly to its further dismemberment in the election of 1994. What Donna Shalala told us was the simple truth: Bringing health insurance within reach of every American family was the final piece of the Social Security system the Democrats had begun assembling under Franklin Roosevelt. It represented the single most important unfulfilled commitment of that party to its working-class and middle-class base. The very rich and the very poor had health care coverage. So did the elderly. The millions of ordinary working Americans without coverage were the people for whom the Democrats supposedly stood.

The most stunning fact about this entire effort is that when the Democrats controlled both houses of Congress and had in the White House in Bill and Hillary Clinton the two most knowledgeable and committed advocates of universal health care coverage in history, they failed over two years even to bring the measure to a vote.

This failure spoke to weaknesses in both the presidency and in

Congress. But it screamed to the world that the Democratic Party, the oldest and arguably most successful political institution in the free world, had lost its core, lost its heart, lost its soul.

David Wilhelm, the chairman of the Democratic National Committee during this battle, observed when it was over that Democrats were up against the fact that "the easiest thing in the world to do is organize the status quo."

"I mean," he said, "if you have money in your pocket and you know you're going to be affected, you're easy to organize. But if you're a checkout clerk at WalMart or Kmart, and you work part-time and you don't have coverage, you're a hard person to organize. So we had this challenge of organizing on behalf of people who may have been only dimly aware that they were going to benefit."

Wilhelm's point is valid. But the boast of the Democratic Party through its history was its readiness to fight the forces of smug complacency and to mobilize on behalf of the checkout clerks and others who are struggling to feed, house, and educate their families — and protect them against the ravages of disease. In this battle, the Democrats' mobilization was pitiful. At its peak, the party had perhaps two dozen organizers in the field, building support for the Clinton bill. In contrast, Wilhelm said, there were three hundred paid organizers working for Democratic candidates in California alone during the 1994 campaign.

Two clear messages emerge from that contrast. The Democratic Party is far more motivated to gain or keep political jobs than to deliver essential programs for its constituents. And the people who pay the party's bills, the contributors, care much more about keeping their friends in office than they do about fulfilling what the party claims to be its policy objectives.

During the many decades that they controlled Congress, Democrats built a closer and closer relationship with the contributors who gave money in order to gain access to the men and women who wrote the laws. Particularly from 1980 onward, when a California congressman named Tony Coelho was head of the Democratic Congressional Campaign Committee, the incumbents on Capitol Hill successfully put the arm on business and industry lobbyists to finance their reelection campaigns. PAC contributions became the price of admission to their committee rooms and personal offices. Thus, when business turned against the Clinton plan, many Democrats lost their enthusiasm for the project. And that made it easier for the outnumbered Republican opponents to prevail.

The health care battle also revealed with stark clarity the fundamental policy and political divisions that have crippled the Democrats. The New Deal wing of the party — symbolized by John Dingell and Pete Stark — favored a single-payer, Canadian-style, government-run and managed national health system. The New Democrat wing — symbolized by Jim Cooper and John Breaux — wanted to rely on a restructured private marketplace, with a minimum of direct government intervention, that was a relatively pure version of managed competition.

Clinton offered a blend of the two that satisfied neither camp. Although his roots were with the Cooper-Breaux wing of the party, he put in enough "sweeteners" for the New Deal side that most of the vocal criticism came from more conservative, market-oriented Democrats. But at a crucial point in the House battle, Jim McDermott, the single-payers' leader, voted against reporting the Ways and Means Committee bill and used his leverage to force Dick Gephardt to rewrite the bill to take it further in the direction of the single-payer plan.

These were more than the battles among a few stubborn individuals. Much of the organizational and financial muscle of the traditional Democratic Party has come from its alliance with organized labor and minority groups. Labor and the Congressional Black Caucus overwhelmingly favored the single-payer approach and were only reluctantly enlisted to fight for the Clinton plan. But much of the intellectual energy of the party in recent years has come from the Democratic Leadership Council, which Clinton once headed. The DLC has close ties to business and has virtually no labor representation in its mix. The DLC favored the Cooper-Breaux version of managed competition over Clinton's hybrid and was more often than not a stumbling block to his attempt at reform.

Many tried to broker these differences — Dingell, Dan Rostenkowski, Sam Gibbons, Ted Kennedy, George Mitchell, John Breaux, even Pat Moynihan, in his way. But they learned, as Clinton himself did, that the divisions within their party even on such a fundamental question as health care were so deep that they could not be mediated. The result was a disaster for the Democratic Party — and a signal that it faces serious, long-term problems.

In many respects, the situation of the Republican Party was the mirror image of the Democrats'. Republicans had lost the White House and were in the minority in Congress after 1992, but they were the beneficiaries of twelve years of growing financial, media, and organizational power in Washington. In many key states, local Republican parties were as inert as their Democratic counterparts when it came to mobilizing workers in the precincts. But over a quarter century, when their hold on the White House was interrupted only by the four Carter years, Republicans had invested heavily in three areas. Their Washington headquarters had a computerized program of small-gift solicitations that kept money flowing into the party coffers in good times and bad. Much of that money had been devoted to a state-of-the-art communications system that constantly relayed Republican messages to networks of television and radio stations and to allied organizations. Presiding over this operation, as the health care fight began, was a genial Mississippi lawyer named Haley Barbour, who unlike his Democratic counterpart, David Wilhelm, had run for major office himself, had managed many campaigns, had served in the White House as political director under Ronald Reagan, and was known and trusted by party leaders around the country and by Republican members of Congress.

When Barbour decided that defeat of the Clinton plan was an integral part of a successful Republican comeback strategy for 1994 and 1996, he had the tools to do the job. True, the decision was not his alone. It was made over a period of months in conjunction with House and Senate party leaders, and it was one all of them eventually embraced.

As we have noted, at the outset of the fight a significant number of Republicans, especially in the Senate, were interested in writing legislation to solve what they saw as a serious national problem: a health care system that cost far too much and still did not serve the needs of millions of Americans. Those who took this view were mainly Republicans who had been on the scene for years: people like John Chafee of Rhode Island, Bob Packwood of Oregon, Dave Durenberger of Minnesota, and Jack Danforth of Missouri. Initially, Bob Dole was with their group, as he had been on health issues during most of his career.

But their Republican Party was changing rapidly. Beginning with Ronald Reagan's election in 1980, each successive class of Republican legislators appeared to be more conservative — more deeply skeptical than the one before of using government leverage and public funds to attack national problems. This was no accident. It was the result of historical forces as profound as any that splintered the Democratic Party. The victory of Ronald Reagan in 1981 was the culmination of a transformation that began in 1964 when Barry Goldwater of Arizona defeated Nelson Rockefeller of New York and William Scranton of Pennsylvania for the presidential nomination. For decades, the center of the party had run from its historical birthplace in the Midwest to the financial centers of the Northeast. Goldwater challenged that control and defeated it by taking the most vehement antigovernment stance of any Republican candidate since Calvin Coolidge. His ideological position won broad support in what had been the Democrats' base, a solid South increasingly uncomfortable with the pro–civil rights stance of the national party. And it resonated in the West.

Although Lyndon Johnson crushed Goldwater, the young people he drew to his campaign became the new cadre of the Republican Party. Ronald Reagan and George Bush both were Goldwater Republicans. So were thousands of lesser-known men and women. Over the next thirty years they filled the seats of Congress, governorships, and state legislatures. They also staffed three successive Republican presidential administrations.

This new Republican Party, interestingly, was a less reliable ally of big business and the banks than the party of Dewey, Eisenhower, Dulles, and Rockefeller had been. It was closer to small business, which was more upset about government regulation, and about union influence, than big business. As we have seen, that small-business alliance was a key to the outcome of the health care battle.

The political strategy the Republicans employed to demolish the

Clinton plan was brilliant in its boldness. If Ira Magaziner thought the administration could "make complexity our ally," the Republican pollsters quickly discovered that the specter of a Big Government health care bureaucracy was their most powerful weapon. They took only a few weeks to recover from the initial favorable wave of stories about the President's speech and Hillary Clinton's round of appearances at congressional committees before they launched a series of ever-stronger attacks on "government health care."

Some of the hard-core conservatives in the party clearly believed the threat was real. For Newt Gingrich, Trent Lott, and Phil Gramm, antigovernment rhetoric was consistent with their overall philosophy. They were sincere when they warned that this expansion of the welfare state would diminish individual freedom and drive up tax rates. That point of view forms the basis for a legitimate debate.

But the same cannot be said of many Republicans who worked to defeat the Clinton plan. The Republican legislators who had done the most substantive work on health care policy — people like Senators Chafee and Durenberger, representatives like William Thomas of California and Nancy Johnson of Connecticut — knew there were real problems that needed fixing. They had legitimate grievances with the way the Clinton administration approached the issue. In some cases, the Clintons' consultation with them was perfunctory, and they had real problems with the specifics of the plan. But these Republicans, who had sought without success to get President Bush engaged with the issue, knew that dealing with Clinton offered the best opportunity to accomplish a needed reform. In the final test, most of them withdrew from the fight, permitting Republicans who had the overriding goal of defeating Clinton to triumph.

It was not an edifying example of political leadership. It was, in fact, the kind of rank political partisanship that disgusts so many citizens.

Republicans were far from alone in playing narrow politics. Dozens of interest groups that the Democrats had counted on also demonstrated how parochial they could be: how fixated on their own agendas, how heedless of the necessity to compromise to achieve a larger goal. At every stage of the story, many of them — from the giant

American Association of Retired Persons to the tiny Foundation for Hospice and Home Care — declined to say flat out, "Help pass the Clinton plan."

Not that the White House was always skillful in negotiating with these interest groups. But administration ineptitude did not justify their holding back their vital support. Talking with their lobbyists and directors after the battle, we heard repeatedly, "We always assumed we would get something through Congress. We just wanted to get the best deal we could." But this was a classic case where the perfect became the enemy of the good — and of the attainable. Thus, these groups must ultimately share the blame for the fact that the country got nothing.

In the end, this battle revealed something even more significant about the interest groups that were so determined to defeat the Clinton reform. On the evidence of this struggle, they have so far outgrown the conceptions and definitions of past interest-group operations that it is necessary to rethink the way The System works.

For many decades, we have known that the schoolbook model of representative democracy obscures the reality. We remember the disillusioned reaction of the dedicated young White House Delivery Room volunteer who, when invited to speak to his hometown high school students about the lessons he had learned about our democracy, would not tell them how The System *really* works for fear it would make them even more cynical. One of those lessons is that the majority does not always — or automatically — prevail. Our system of government is littered with constitutional and political roadblocks that make it hard for huge policy changes like health care reform to be enacted quickly. We agree, up to a point, with those who point this out and who conclude that The System operated exactly as it is supposed to in the health care battle: Where no strong consensus exists, major change should wait.

But that argument ignores a deeper truth about the critical role that public opinion plays in The System. In many respects, the story of the life and death of health care reform is the story of how to manufacture and manipulate public opinion. A fundamental question that emerges from this story is, Why did the anticipated, and needed, great public debate about what kind of health care Americans want never occur? And why did the initially favorable American public become so frightened by the President's reform?

The answer is that "public opinion" was largely an artifact of the groups that mobilized to defeat reform. They created opinion with their grassroots and media efforts. Then they invoked that public opinion to convince, or provide a rationale for, the members of Congress who for reasons of self-interest wanted to vote no.

One of the most striking aspects of this battle is that, from beginning to end, 70 percent or more of those polled said they agreed with two fundamental propositions underlying the Clinton plan: that all American families should have health insurance and that all employers should contribute to paying for their workers' premiums.

Seventy percent–plus agreement on anything is most rare in American politics. It suggests a strong climate for change. Yet when we asked pollsters and lobbyists working to defeat the Clinton plan why these public attitudes did not represent a clear public mandate for reform, the answer we got went like this: "Of course, people want employers to pay for their health insurance. Why wouldn't they? But if you ask a follow-up question, 'Do you want the government to require business to pay for health insurance if it means lower wages and fewer jobs?' the number of those supporting reform turns around."

The interest groups opposing Clinton successfully persuaded much of the public that his plan would mean not only lower wages and fewer jobs but less freedom to choose a doctor, a hospital, or an insurer. It would mean more bureaucracy and lower-quality care. They spread this largely false message relentlessly in a campaign that cost literally hundreds of millions of dollars and involved the use of every technique developed for the modern high-tech election campaign.

Operations of some of those groups, notably the National Federation of Independent Business and the Health Insurance Association of America, have already been described in detail; but they were far from alone. Dozens of others spread similar messages on parallel networks to their members and their customers.

We want to reiterate an earlier point. For more than two decades,

reformers have argued that our method of private campaign contributions is corrupting The System and distorting policy outcomes.
There's no question that opponents of health care reform showered
more money into the campaigns of members of Congress, especially
on the key committees, than did the supporters. But we agree with
the point made by many of Clinton's chief congressional allies: You
could sweep all private and PAC money out of campaigns and the
outcome of this battle, and others like it, would not be changed.

The reason is that pro-business groups of all kinds have gone
immeasurably beyond the old methods of financing campaigns in
order to prevail. They have become crypto-political parties of their
own — unelected and unaccountable — employing skilled operatives who at other times run presidential and senatorial campaigns.
This is the development that reformers need to address. The shift in
control of Congress to the Republicans in 1995 vividly underscored
the growing power of these new interest group–political coalitions. In
the late 1990s, they have become the eight-hundred-pound gorillas
of our politics. Republican lobbyist Deborah Steelman's remark
about the "political moon and the stars being in alignment" during
the health care battle, describing how groups from the Christian Coalition to the National Restaurant Association met in the office of the
House Republican leader to plot the downfall of the Clinton plan,
was a memorable expression of this new reality. A year later those
same groups — and dozens more — again were meeting weekly with
the House Republican leadership to push through the Contract With
America, and indeed even actually writing the legislation themselves.

Unless you have a simplistic notion of democracy and argue that
people with common interests should not attempt to sway government policy, operations of these lobbying-political coalitions cannot be rejected as improper. We are not interested in prohibiting
grassroots lobbying and media campaigns. But the problems they
pose for The System cannot be disposed of that easily. In most major political races, a rough parity of resources is available to the
opposing sides. Presidential campaigns, financed by public funds,
give each major party candidate the same amount. In most states,
Democrats and Republicans campaigning for governor and senator are able to deliver their messages. But there is no balance of

power when business and its allies line up against organized labor, consumer groups, and other liberal organizations. The latter are almost always out-organized, out-spent, out-gunned.

The problem is doubly compounded. The Republican Party, usually allied with business, is far more professional and single-minded in its operations than the badly divided Democrats. And, perhaps most important, as David Wilhelm pointed out, those with an economic stake in the status quo are more easily influenced by interest groups than those who would benefit most from change. In both this fight and the earlier battle over Medicare catastrophic insurance, the ability of the opposition to mobilize a small minority of people who feared losing some of their advantages carried the day.

Patients at Cedars-Sinai were much more attuned to the battle than those at Los Angeles General. Or, to cite another example that deeply impressed us, we talked with Representative Frank Tejeda, a freshman Texas Democrat and Vietnam veteran, after the Easter recess in 1994, when grassroots lobbying was at its most intense. What had he heard from home? we asked Tejeda. "People are really scared of this Clinton plan," he said. What people? we asked. "Everyone I talked to at my Rotary and Kiwanis and Chamber meetings said they were scared as hell."

Earlier in our conversation Tejeda had described his district, which covers a swath of thirteen counties running from the south side of San Antonio to the Rio Grande Valley. Five of the thirteen counties, he said, are officially on the list of "medically underserved" areas: That is, no hospital or clinics are available to the people who live there. One of the counties was officially ranked as the second-poorest in the nation.

What did you hear from those people? we asked.

"I didn't hear anything," he answered.

We are tempted to leave the story there, but another institution that plays a critical part in The System was also found wanting in this battle. It is the press — or, if you prefer, the media. Many reporters and news organizations made a heroic effort to explain to their audiences what was going on. To cite but one example, NBC-TV in June of 1994 ran a two-hour, prime-time, commercial-free program on health care, financed by a $2.5 million grant from the Robert Wood Johnson Foundation but produced by the network's news division. Hillary Rodham Clinton, Bob Dole, and many other key players participated in the exchange of views. The audience size was respectable, but later survey research found little lasting gain in understanding by the viewers.

In the same month, the *New York Times* published a sixteen-page special section on health care reform, including explanatory articles by experts and pieces advocating various solutions. Similar projects were undertaken by many other news organizations.

They produced some distinguished journalism. But the evidence is overwhelming that we — for this is our institution — failed to convey to most of the American people what was at stake. Regardless of what they thought the outcome of the battle should be, no one was satisfied with the way it emerged in the media — or in the public mind. Jim McDermott, the single-payer advocate, was so angered by the short shrift he thought the press gave his preferred plan that he suggested a conspiracy. Too many television reporters and anchors were "pocketing big checks from insurance companies in exchange for speeches," he complained.

Herb Berkowitz, the publicist for the conservative Heritage Foundation, which tried in vain to promote a "consumer-choice health plan," similar to the federal employees' program, said "the media's overall performance was terrible," citing particularly "their refusal to give any significant attention to reform plans not at the center of the political maelstrom."

And from the White House, former journalist and presidential counselor David Gergen said that "neither the press nor academia has helped inform the public debate. Even if we passed a bill, there would have been little public understanding of what had been done."

Newspeople themselves, as we have previously noted, were as disturbed as anyone by the evident lack of public understanding. Hilary Stout was a lead reporter for the *Wall Street Journal*, whose news pages were models of clear, conscientious reporting on this subject. (The editorial page was something else again.) When it was over, she said, "The total failure of communication was very depressing to me." Stout wrote the story that was the classic demonstration of the problem. In the spring of 1994, the *Journal* assembled a focus group in York, Pennsylvania, to discuss the reform. "People were totally ignorant of the [Clinton] plan," Stout recalled, "but they knew they hated it. It was too expensive, too complicated. They thought the government would employ the doctors, that you'd go to jail if you went to a doctor other than the one you d been assigned. These people were a walking illustration of what was wrong with our health care system, but they were terrified of changing it."

When Peter D. Hart, the pollster employed to run the focus group, asked them what they wanted, they responded that they wanted everyone covered, with a choice of doctors and hospitals, protection on quality and cost, and a sharing of insurance premiums between employers and workers. "I remember thinking, This is amazing, because it's what Clinton is proposing, and they didn't know it," Stout said. "You could blame the administration in large part. But it was clear to me we hadn't done our job either."

Study after study showed that public understanding of the Clinton plan actually declined from September of 1993, when the President made his first speech to Congress on the issue, until it was declared dead a year later. Drew Altman, the head of the Kaiser Family Foundation, observed that the "media went from hyping the problem to hyping the problem with the solutions." The focus clearly shifted from the character and seriousness of the crisis that had spurred both Republicans and Democrats in Congress to move on this issue before the Clintons arrived to the politics of the increasingly partisan battle over the administration proposal.

Less and less attention was devoted to explaining the consequences of the Clinton plan — and the major alternatives — for the consumers whose views should have shaped the decision. When the opponents of change began flooding the airwaves and the mail with warnings of dire consequences and mobilizing their grassroots campaigns to frighten people, the press reported their efforts but did not try to debunk them. It was not a matter of ideology. A year later, in 1995, when it was Republicans and conservatives proposing changes in the Medicare and Medicaid systems, and the White House and Democrats running the negative campaigns, much the same thing happened. Exaggerated charges were repeated in orchestrated waves from the floor of the House and Senate and amplified by interest groups into a chorus of frightening rhetoric. And again, the media left the public so ill-informed that the scare stories were believed.

The public cannot avoid some of the blame for letting itself be duped. Uwe Reinhardt, the Princeton University expert on health matters, wrote of the 1993–94 battle that "the staff reporters of the major newspapers deserve high marks for their ceaseless efforts at digging out the relevant facts on the Clinton plan and other health care reform plans. They also deserve high marks for their skill in presenting these facts to the public." But this kind of "one-way, top-down communication" does not reach very far into the mass public, which increasingly relies on television news for its information. As Reinhardt said, "It is not clear that the general public even had the patience to digest the lengthier, excellent articles on health reform in the major dailies."

Too much of the debate was dominated by negative sound bites, by the importunings of "spin doctors" with their misleading arguments, false analogies, and statistics crafted for the convenience of the argument, not the truth of the case. As a result, the public, for excellent reasons, was confused and frightened throughout. In a classic sense, the people were woefully uninformed. The manufactured, and manipulated, "public opinion" prevailed.

James Fallows, a talented journalist himself, has described the health care reform battle as "the press's Vietnam War," arguing that "the media failed in a historic way to help Americans understand and decide on this issue." That is arguably an overstatement. The press did not kill the reform effort, nor did it significantly impede the process of policy formulation or legislative action. Except for a handful of people, like Elizabeth McCaughey — a policy advocate, not a journalist — there was little mendacity in the coverage.

But the battle did reveal shortcomings that are built into today's journalism and that ill serve the society. The journalistic culture — both its professional mind-set and its commercial, competitive pressures — nudges the coverage strongly to emphasize conflict and dissent rather than clarification of alternatives and the search for consensus.

That tendency showed in the speed and eagerness with which the press focus shifted from explanation of the problem and the proposed solutions to an emphasis on what might be called the mugging of the Clinton plan. Health care reform became the prize in a classic power game, and the press was caught up quickly in gauging and guessing who would win, not in exploring what the consequences would be for the country.

The emphasis reflects the "insider" perspective that is the bane of today's journalism: a tone and focus that leaves millions of ordinary citizens feeling that they have been excluded from the conversation. What people *really* wanted to know was how the various plans would affect them and their families, and the media did not answer those questions well.

Today's journalism, geared to the reality of a fleeting public attention span, looked at the complexity of the issue and threw up its hands in horror. The basic task of exposition was done at the beginning of the process, but not repeated nearly as often as would have been necessary for even conscientious readers to grasp the unfamiliar concepts and shifting designs. As for television, this was rarely a picture story, so its interest waned early.

In the end, the public got much of its information — or misinformation — from partisan or special-interest sources. Those intent on stopping reform were far better organized than its proponents. To use a Vietnam-era term, the press was left looking like "a pitiful, helpless giant."

If this failure were unique, it would be disappointing but not all that disquieting. But more and more journalists and elected officials are coming to realize that public opinion — in the sense of a somewhat informed or reasoned reaction — is more often than not a myth in this democracy. For a nation that rests on the premise that The System helps public opinion become the arbiter of public policy, this may be the most dangerous discovery of all.

Epilogue

The System

JOHN KENNEDY'S *Profiles in Courage* tells the story of eight of his Senate predecessors who met the test of their times with conspicuous acts of political courage, often at risk of their careers and reputations. Busts of those senators now stand in an honored place off the Senate floor in the Capitol, mute reminders that the greatest challenge of political life is to follow one's conscience and make the hard choices in the public interest — what Kennedy called "grace under pressure," the moral courage of those who do what they must "in spite of personal consequences, in spite of obstacles and dangers and pressures." Kennedy's theme, as expressed in his handwritten notes for *Profiles*, deals with the inherent difficulties of public life and of the politician caught in what he called the "jungle" of politics, "torn between doing the right thing & staying in office — between the local interest & the national interest — between the private good of the politician & the general good."

In our story a number of elected officials and staff members successfully met those tests. Senators like John Chafee withstood enormous pressures from conservatives in his own party determined to kill health care reform by any means necessary. He, Jack Danforth, Dave Durenberger, and staff members like Christy Ferguson, to cite Republican examples, and George Mitchell, Ted Kennedy, Jay Rockefeller, Tom Daschle, Harris Wofford, and Nick Littlefield, among Democrats, battled to the end even when there was no hope. Bureaucrats like Robert Reischauer risked jobs and careers to remain true to the highest standards of public service.

At the same time, the story shows how private interest can triumph over the public interest, how a powerful minority can manipulate opinion to defeat a reform desired by the majority, how hope for needed change can result in more cynicism about the workings of The System.

After the battle was over, one of the most thoughtful players in it, John Rother of AARP, worried that our story would reinforce already deeply held public feelings of distrust about government and politics. "It is important not to be too negative about the lessons learned from health care or from our collective failure to stage even a constructive national debate," Rother told us. "There are many ways to make The System work, even if it failed in 1994. I know it will be many years before we will have another chance at comprehensive health reform, but when we get there I would like to use this painful experience as a road map for how to get it."

Rother added, "I hope I won't only read why the effort is inevitably futile under our fragmented, frustrating, and often fumbling system of democratic government."

We agree. We did not begin this story as cynics, nor do we end it so. We continue to subscribe to Al Smith's famous adage that the only cure to the ails of democracy is more democracy. Yet only the most naive American could be reassured by the way the battle over health care reform was fought, or by the even more dismaying aftermath resulting in the senseless shutdown of the federal government twice in a matter of weeks that caused needless suffering for millions of Americans, or by the deeper problems about the workings of government it exposed. Even John Rother, who wants to draw the most positive lesson from the experience of the health care battle, betrays an underlying pessimism in the wake of the failure to achieve reform.

It's hard to be upbeat, as Rother says, when the United States already has passed the forty-million mark of people without health insurance, a condition that almost certainly will worsen as the wave of economic downsizing throws increasing numbers of Americans into the ranks of the uninsured. Already many Americans are facing a crisis over health care as public hospitals that have been operating for years are forced to close. Those conditions almost certainly will continue as health costs become more and more expensive and the aggressive emergence of HMOs leaves increasing numbers of citizens feeling the health care system is not their friend, that they will have to fight to get needed treatment. It is a grim picture and suggests a more polarized, class-based society, where people with money are going to be fine but people without money are going to be much worse off. As we have seen personally in our reporting of this story, the health care battle suggests a hardening of public attitudes toward people who are most vulnerable and most in need of assistance, with the poor being most dramatically affected. If that is the case, then we're headed toward a social Darwinist society rather than toward the Western European models — "toward the Third World," as John Rother puts it, "where there are explosive sanctioned differences between classes in the basic opportunities of life: education, health care, welfare, you name it." All of this comes down to American values, raising the question of whether our handling of public programs reflects those values of charity and compassion or suggests a sharp change in attitudes is occurring. It sets the stage for the most fundamental debate about national values America has had in decades.

From the beginning, the health care struggle was about much more than a single issue, however important health care is in the lives of all citizens and the functioning of the U.S. economy. It was about the health of The System and the values it represents.

Founders of The System, as we have noted several times, made it difficult for major changes to occur. But they surely did not foresee the self-destructiveness and distrust that now hobble American government and politics: the hatred of government; the demonization of elected officials from President down; the belittling of career civil servants who do the public's business, sometimes at risk of their lives. The bombing of the federal center in Oklahoma City in the spring of 1995 provides a warning of how strong those antigovernment feelings are becoming — and of the dangers from those who deliberately foment them. It was this acrimonious backdrop to the health care debate that led Dr. Reed Tuckson of the King/Drew Medical Center in the Watts section of Los Angeles to rail against those who fragment the political marketplace by trading on societal divisions and differences of class, race, ethnicity, religion, and political ideologies. The danger we face, Dr. Tuckson said, is that "we will become so fragmented and unable to discuss complex issues" that we will be incapable as a nation of addressing the major long-term problems facing the society.

Not that the instinct to fragment and divide power is a recent phenomenon, nor necessarily a bad one. Americans have always distrusted government, often for good historical reasons. They have also distrusted all "isms," including at times capitalism. So they divide power, create joint authorities — private/public, city/county, state/federal, House/Senate, courts/press — and display continuing ambivalence about the role of government in their lives. Sometimes they reflect the sentiments of a Jefferson (government governs best that governs least), at other times, those of an FDR (better a government that lives in the spirit of charity than one mired in the ice of its own indifference). And, always, they are reluctant to place too much faith in any one leader, or any one institution. Therefore, they seek ways to check power and the inevitable abuses from those who wield it. These conflicting attitudes produce an exceedingly complicated system. But at no point, we believe, has the cumulative assault on the *idea* of responsible government been so destructive of the very faith in the democratic system as now. A thoroughly cynical society, deeply distrustful of its institutions and leaders and the reliability of information it receives, is a society in peril of breaking apart.

All these factors came strongly into play during the health care reform battle. They became even more notable over the next year in the bitter struggle between President and Congress about two starkly different visions of the purpose and values of government, and are certain to be important in 1996, when the American people choose which path to follow in the last presidential election of the century. We say "certain to be important" because the difficulties that both Democrats and Republicans encountered over how to address a genuine unmet public need still exist.

In historical terms, what President Clinton told us is correct: "This kind of sweeping reform is rare in our country's history." As he said, only the strongest Presidents have succeeded in getting Congress to pass such fundamental reforms or to take action on their own to make major controversial changes. And in those rare cases the President almost always has been assisted by a national crisis created during wartime, during economic collapse, or during a tragedy: Lincoln and

the suspension of habeas corpus during the Civil War; FDR and the
New Deal in the depths of the Depression and in World War II; LBJ
and civil rights and the Great Society in the wake of the Kennedy
assassination. Against these examples, health care reform was an
anomaly. As the President put it, "People basically want less government, or at least a government that is less centralized, less bureaucratic. Yet [health care reform] was a problem, in my judgment, that
could not be comprehensively solved *without* government. So it was
an anomalous problem." Viewed from that perspective, the President
retrospectively concluded, "We shouldn't overdraw the lessons that
The System won't work."

He went on to say this:

On the other hand, it is clear that The System, as much as it
ever has been, is more responsive to those that are organized
and very wealthy. . . . We know that a majority of the electorate, if they're engaged and they understand what the options
are, will make decisions which will essentially keep America
moving economically and coming together as a society; that
they swing from being slightly more conservative to slightly
less conservative in philosophical terms. They change their
positions on some of the issues over time. But, basically, we
know that the American people are passionately devoted to the
Constitution and are ultimately pragmatic.

He challenged us to address the question of whether The System
can be made to work amid the present proliferation of more and more
highly organized lobby groups that "splinter the public interest more
than ever before," even as the explosion and fragmentation of communications technology make it more difficult for substantive issues
to be fully explained and debated. "The question is," the President
said, "can the people get a coherent enough view of the central issues
of our time to not only hold the American political system in the middle of the road but keep pushing it down the road?" He worried most
that the health care reform battle would become "a metaphor for
people's experiences in other areas: That it will become a metaphor
for what's happening to people economically. That it will become a
metaphor for what's happening to people in terms of public safety.
That it will become a metaphor in terms of what's going to happen

to people in education. That we will literally see the splintering apart of our national community. That is the darkest view of this."

The brightest view, he thought, was the evidence of young people coming back into The System in 1992, reversing the long decline in voting turnout, and the clear hunger of Americans since then for genuine political change, even change that represents a rejection of his own reform attempt. In the end, he was optimistic: The American people will get it straight. At the same time, the greatest tests for The System still lie ahead. "We're having debates here in the Congress about the role of government and the responsibilities of government that are more profound than the ones we had at the dawn of the Depression," the President said. "In fact, we are ending this century with debates about who we are as a people and what public purposes there are that are as profound as the ones we began the century with. And nothing in the middle, including the Great Depression and the New Deal, approaches the depth of the debate in terms of the differences."

In this, the President is surely correct, and in this, at least, his view would surely be shared by his political and philosophical adversary Newt Gingrich. As Gingrich repeatedly has said, the battle he and his ideological opponents have been waging represents much more than a debate over programs and numbers. It offers fundamentally different visions about the future.

In the end, the challenge of repairing the problems afflicting government is not one just for the political players, however powerful they may be. Ultimately, the people must make the critical decisions about what kind of society they want, what they are willing to work and sacrifice for, what kind of people Americans have become as they approach a new century. As we write, those decisions have not been made. The shocks that had begun to shake The System when we started this story have not abated. They are certain to continue, possibly with greater force, until the central question — how well America's great experiment in self-government serves its people — is resolved.

Notes

The basic sources for this book are the principal players in our story and our own reporting of the events described herein. Over a nearly three-year period, we conducted lengthy tape-recorded interviews with these players; with some individuals, we had ten or more separate conversations. The list of those interviewed formally, excepting the names of some people excluded here at their request, follows: David Abernethy; Michael A. Andrews; Brent Bahler; Robert Ball; Arnold Bennett; Bob Bennett; Duane Benson; Lloyd Bentson; Karen Bernstein; Roger Berry; Michael A. Bilirakis; Bob Blendon; Thomas J. Bliley; Linda Blumberg; Jack Bonner; Robert O. Boorstin; Molly Bostrom; John Breaux; Sheila Burke; Robert C. Byrd; Benjamin L. Cardin; Arne Carlson; Richard Celeste; John Chafee; Lawton Chiles; Robert Chlopak; Bill Clinton; Hillary Rodham Clinton; William S. Cohen; Douglas Cook; Jim Cooper; David Cutler; Ellen Dadisman; Geraldine Dallek; Tom Daschle; Richard Davidson; Julie Delgado; Butler Derrick; Joel Derringer; John Dingell; Bob Dole; David Dreyer; John Dunlop; Dave Durenberger; Ed Edelman; Jeff Eller; Jack Faris; Judy Feder; Carl Feldbaum; Christine Ferguson; Dave Flores; Hector Flores; Tom Foley; Susan Foote; Bruce Fried; Kathy Gardner; Atul Gawande; Richard A. Gephardt; Sam Gibbons; Newt Gingrich; Ellen Globocar; John Gomperts; Bill Gradison; Phil Gramm; Fred Grandy; Stan Greenberg; Patrick J. Griffin; Dennis Hastert; Peter Hoagland; Kathy Hurwit; Harold Ickes; Karen Ignagni; Mark Isakowitz; Andy Jacobs; William Jefferson; Chris Jennings; Darryl Jodrey; Curt Johnson; Nancy Johnson; Charles Kahn III; Edward M. Kennedy; Barbara Kennelly; Bob Kerrey; Andrea King; Lane

Kirkland; Christine Klasen; Gerald Kleczka; Jerry Klepner; Mike Kopetski; Michael Kuzenow; David Langness; Bonnie Lawry; Philip Lee; Sander Levin; John Lewis; Nick Littlefield; Bill Lukhart; Ira C. Magaziner; Greg Marchilden; Lynn Margherio; Marjorie Margolies-Mezvinsky; Robert Matsui; Jim McCrery; Jim McDermott; Gerald McEntee; Bill McInturff; George J. Mitchell; Gerry Mossinghoff; John Motley; Daniel Patrick Moynihan; Richard Neal; Susan Neely; David Nexon; Len Nichols; Mary Jo O'Brien; Lawrence O'Donnell; John Ong; Carl Parks; Howard Paster; L. F. Payne; Billy Pitts; Mike Podhorzer; Tom Priselac; Robert Reischauer; Steve Ricchetti; John D. Rockefeller IV; Jeremy Rosner; Dan Rostenkowski; Ed Rothchild; John Rother; Mike Roush; J. Roy Rowland; Elizabeth Sauer; Lynn Schenk; Donna Shalala; Jerry Shea; Kazne Shibata; Jim Slattery; Jason Solomon; Deborah Steelman; George Stephanopoulos; Mike Synar; Bill Thomas; Ken Thorpe; James Todd; Cindy Toth; Reed Tuckson; Laura D'Andrea Tyson; Fred Upton; Vivek Varma; Melanne Verveer; Jeffrey Warren; Henry Waxman; David Wilhelm; Marina Weiss; Anne Wexler; Harris Wofford; Ron Wyden; Walter Zelman. Unless otherwise noted in the text, all quotations come from those interviews.

We have tried to keep footnotes to a minimum and have also attempted, whenever possible, to indicate the source of any other quoted material in the main text. Sources for some other quotations follow: The John F. Kennedy "victory has one hundred fathers and defeat is an orphan" remark on page vi was made by President Kennedy at a Washington, D.C., news conference April 21, 1961, after the failure of the Bay of Pigs invasion. The Machiavelli quote immediately after it comes from Niccolò Machiavelli, *The Prince* (New York: Mentor/New American Library, 1952). In chapter 3, "The Players," Jay Rockefeller's remarks about his mother and Alzheimer's disease were part of a health care reform speech before some three thousand AFL-CIO building trades leaders, reported by James Gannon in the *Detroit News* April 24, 1994. In chapter 10, "The Interests," the Hugo Black quote is cited in the Center for Public Integrity's report *Well-Heeled: Inside Lobbying for Health Care Reform* (Washington, D.C., 1994). In chapter 13, "Waves of Whitewater," Rush Limbaugh's remark "Whitewater is about health care" was made during a special edition of the ABC-TV program *Nightline* April 19, 1994, moderated by Ted Koppel and broadcast from the campus of Drake University, Ames, Iowa (*Nightline* transcript no. 3357). In chapter 15, "Make a Deal," we relied on Jake H. Thompson's *Bob Dole: The Republican Man for All Seasons* (New York: Donald I. Fine, 1994) for our account of Bob Dole's World War II combat wounds. In that same chapter, James Mongan's extensive remarks about "who pays" come from a transcript of a health care panel discussion at the Brookings Institution in 1994. In chapter 19, "Summer of Discontent," Paul Starr's statement that for all its flaws, the Mainstream Coalition reform bill would have represented "a historic advance," is from Starr's brilliant retrospective analysis, "What Happened to Health Care Reform," *The American Prospect* (winter 1995, 20–31). In chapter 22, "Earthquake," Grover Norquist's depiction of the Clinton health plan's defeat as "their Stalingrad, their Gettysburg, their Waterloo" was made during an American Enterprise Institute panel discussion in Washington September 6, 1995, on the topic "Republicans, Democrats: Who Owns the Future of America?" It was televised on C-SPAN, which made transcripts. The account of how Tom Foley met defeat in Spokane, Washington, draws upon reporting from there in the *Los Angeles Times* by Melissa Healy and Doug Connor on November 9, 1994, and by John Balzar and Connor the next day, November 10. In that same chapter, the Everett Carll Ladd remark about the health care debate's being definitive in the campaign came from an interview with Ladd conducted by Ann Devroy of the *Washington Post* on Election Day. In chapter 23, "Aftershocks," Peggy Noonan's observations about the beginnings of the Gingrich speakership and the comments made to her by Grover Norquist and others comes from her article on the *Wall Street Journal* editorial page, January 9, 1995. In that same chapter, Rush Limbaugh's postelection advice to Republicans, "never moderate your tone. Never attempt to be liked by those you defeated," was reported on the *Wall Street Journal*'s editorial page December 15, 1994. In chapter 24, "Lessons: Lost Opportunities," Paul Starr's analysis of why health reform failed and its lessons ("trying to do too much, took too long, and ended up achieving nothing") is from his *American Prospect* winter 1995 article cited above. In the epilogue, John F. Kennedy's handwritten notes for *Profiles in Courage* are quoted in Arthur M. Schlesinger Jr.'s *A Thousand Days: John F. Kennedy in the White House* (Boston: Houghton Mifflin Co., 1965), pp. 94, 100–101.

Bibliography

In addition to our interviews and daily reporting of the health care reform battle over three years, we had access to a vast amount of documentary material in the form of official and private memoranda, diaries of participants, and numerous official and private studies. Limited space prevents any attempt to list all of this material; the literature of health care reform alone is so extensive, and growing, that it becomes virtually impossible even to keep up with the outpouring. We do want to cite a few of the many works we found particularly helpful. First is Paul Starr's indispensable *The Social Transformation of American Medicine: The Rise of a Sovereign Profession and the Making of a Vast Industry* (New York: Basic Books, 1982). This was the book that won the Pulitzer Prize for general nonfiction. Starr's *The Logic of Health Care Reform: Why and How the President's Plan Will Work* (Whittle/Penguin, 1992–94) is instructive, in retrospect, of the dimensions of the failure. It was Starr, too, who gave the best analysis of the debacle in his already cited winter 1995 *American Prospect* article, "What Happened to Health Care Reform." The best analysis of the lobbying battle, with the amounts expended and the groups involved, is the carefully documented *Well-Heeled: Inside Lobbying for Health Care Reform* by the Center for Public Integrity (Washington, D.C., 1994). We also relied upon, and admired, the Brookings Institution study *Intensive Care: How Congress Shapes Health Policy*, edited by Thomas E. Mann and Norman J. Ornstein (Washington, 1995). For our account of the problems of Los Angeles County, we found "Closing the Gap," Report to the Los Angeles County Board of Supervisors by the Task

Force for Health Care Access in Los Angeles County, November 24, 1992, most helpful and revealing. Among other studies we found useful were *The Politics of Health Care Reform: Lessons from the Past, Prospects for the Future*, edited by James A. Morone and Gary S. Belkin (Duke University Press, 1994); Peter A. Corning's *The Evolution of Medicare . . . From Idea to Law* (Research report no. 29 of the U.S. Department of Health, Education, and Welfare, Social Security Administration, Office of Research and Statistics) was valuable for an overall history on the background of the long effort to provide universal health insurance. Among political books focusing on Bill Clinton's presidency, the best to date are Elizabeth Drew's *On the Edge: The Clinton Presidency;* Bob Woodward's *The Agenda;* and David Maraniss's *First in His Class*, all published in 1994 by Simon & Schuster. One of our own works, Haynes Johnson's *Divided We Fall: Gambling with History in the Nineties* (Norton, 1994), deals with American values and attitudes during the 1992 presidential election year and Clinton's first year as President.

Acknowledgments

We owe a heavy debt to many more people than we can acknowledge here, especially to those who gave unstintingly of their time during our lengthy interviews. Most of their names have already been cited. We also wish to acknowledge the special contribution made by James H. Silberman, a great editor, and friend. Kate Nash and Nina Evtuhov, his editorial assistants at Little, Brown, helped in numerous ways. Pamela Marshall, our copyeditor there, was splendid. Thanks also to Amanda Murray of Little, Brown. Our agent, Bill Leigh, and his assistant, Wes Neff, were supportive throughout this long project. In addition, we want to acknowledge the contribution made by some of our colleagues, especially Gloria Borger and Ann Montgomery, whose great help far exceeded the bounds of collegial courtesy. We are also grateful to Dana Priest, Julie Rovner, and Hilary Stout; to Kathleen Hall Jamieson, dean of the Annenberg School of Communications, for generous support and sharp counsel; and to Tanya Hands of Annenberg for research assistance. Jason Weintraub of the Stanford-in-Washington program also assisted with research. Once again, Adrienne Jamieson, director of the Stanford program, was a source of valuable help and ideas. At the *Washington Post*, we are grateful to Executive Editor Leonard Downie Jr., Managing Editor Robert G. Kaiser, and Assistant Managing Editor/National Karen DeYoung, and to researchers Anne O'Hanlon (later a staff reporter) and Barbara J. Saffir. Olwen Price, Marilee Steele Stevens, Kerri Toppel, Carol Von Horn, and Deborah Walden processed our tape-recorded interviews and produced verbatim transcripts from them. Our friends and colleagues at *Congressional Quarterly* were helpful throughout. Michelle Von Euw performed many manuscript deadline tasks efficiently and always with good humor. Maria George of the National Center for Communications Studies at George Washington University was a lifesaver in last-minute deadline crises. To our family and friends, and especially to Ann Broder, Marcia L. Hale, Carol Houck Smith, Christie Basham, and Jonathan Rinehart, we are grateful beyond words for sustained support and encouragement. Finally, and foremost, we want to acknowledge the indispensable role played by Ilyse Veron, our principal editorial assistant and researcher, whom we were fortunate to hire away from *Congressional Quarterly*. For more than two years, she arranged our interviews, conducting some on her own, organized our burgeoning files, provided basic research and editorial criticism, pushed us to raise deeper, more substantive questions, and in numerous ways contributed immeasurably to the final product. Quite simply, we could not have accomplished this project without her.

H.J. and D.S.B.
February 1996
Washington, D.C.

Index

Aaron, Henry, 81
ABC-TV, 181, 562
Abernethy, David S., 172, 396, 399–400,
    401, 407, 411
  and Clinton plan, 172, 396, 399–400
abortion issue, 454, 554
advertising campaigns
  business, 342
  Democratic Party, 60, 291, 293–294,
    338, 585
  insurance industry, 199, 203–204, 207
  lobbying group, 386
  Republican Party, 289
  See also "Harry and Louise" ads; lobbyists;
    news media
Aetna Insurance Company, 199
AFL-CIO (American Federation of
    Labor–Congress of Industrial
    Organizations), 12, 81, 86, 292, 331,
    355, 356n, 418, 520
AFSCME (American Federation of State,
    County and Municipal Employees), 50,
    164, 165, 177, 290, 331–332, 472
AFT (American Federation of Teachers), 306
Agenda, The (Woodward), 79
Aid to Families with Dependent Children
    (AFDC), 238, 583, 584
Alexander, Lamar, 160
Alliance for Managed Competition. *See* Big
    Five insurance companies
Altman, Drew, 633
Altman, Roger, 20, 151, 154, 261, 320,
    321, 411
Alzheimer's Association, 417
American Academy of Pediatricians, 209
American Association of Retired Persons
    (AARP), 418, 426
  lack of support from, 480–481, 523,
    538–589, 628
  See also Rother, John

American Cancer Society, 426
American Dental Association, 90–91
American Farm Bureau Federation, 66
American Hospital Association, 168, 588
American Medical Association (AMA), 66, 67, 93
  AMA *Journal*, 65
Americans for Tax Reform, 569
American Spectator, 255, 281, 384, 465n
Anderson, M.D., Cancer Center, 403, 429
Andrews, Mike (Michael A.), 400, 401, 407,
    423, 430–435 *passim*
  and tobacco tax, 402–403, 427, 429
Arafat, Yasir, 19
Archer, Bill, 587
Arkansas Children's Hospital, 99
Arkansas Securities Department, 259
Armey, Dick (Richard K.), 184–185
Atlantic, The, 272
Atwater, H. Bruce Jr., 320
automobile industry, 166, 288, 307, 320

Bahler, Brent, 467, 520–521, 530
Bailey, John M., 432
Baker, Cissy, 309
Baker, Howard H. Jr., 309, 383
Baker, Jim (James A. III), 176, 177, 616
Baker, Russell, 595–596
Baltimore Sun, 391
Barbour, Haley, 37, 528, 576, 577, 588,
    625
Barone, Michael, 562
Baucus, Max, 221, 366, 368, 378, 390
Baumol, William J., and "Baumol's Disease,"
    354–356
Begala, Paul, 8, 26, 90, 124, 292, 293, 513
Bennett, Arnold, 152–153, 154, 471
Bennett, Bob, 48–49, 234–235, 271, 272, 383,
    447–448, 469–470, 498–502 *passim*
Bennett, William J., 186, 233, 386
Bentsen, Lloyd, 61, 137–138, 345, 352, 400

and Clinton plan, 22, 68, 138–139, 148,
        151, 157, 161, 162, 320, 410–411, 614
    and deficit reduction, 119, 122
Berkowitz, Herb, 632
Berry, Roger, 128, 130
Bethlehem Steel Corporation, 320
B. F. Goodrich, 318
Bieber, Owen, 474
big business, 210, 389
    and Clinton plan, 166, 197, 288, 316–326,
        335, 382
    First Lady attacks, 202, 318–325 *passim*
    and health care costs, 61, 307, 326, 382
    mandate negotiations with, 413
    tobacco industry, 420–421
    See also health care industry; health insurance
        industry; lobbyists; taxes
Big Five insurance companies, 199, 200,
    214, 318
"Big Government"
    Democrats seen as, *see* Democratic Party
    public fears of, 264, 271, 466–467, 483,
        534, 546, 627
Bilheimer, Linda, 488
Bilirakis, Michael, 192, 333–334
Bingaman, Jeff, 349
biotech industry, 335, 336
bipartisanship
    bills passed, 254, 287, 345, 348, 602
    in crime bill, 477–478
    in health care reform, 61, 125, 199, 330
        bipartisan/compromise bills, *see* health
            care plans
        Clinton's view, 160, 167, 192, 255,
            301, 394
        Republican position, 328, 330, 375, 575
    political consensus, 302, 366–377, 378–382,
        386, 390, 440–446, 452, 487, 611
        (*see also* Mainstream Coalition)
    public consensus, 604
    Senate hostility toward, 375, 382–386 (*see
        also* partisanship)
Birnbaum, Jeffrey H., 568
Bismarck, Otto von, 64*n*, 517
Black, Hugo, 194
Blackmun, Harry, 296
Blackwell, Morton C., 373
Blair, Jim, 273
Blauwet, Roger, 419
Blendon, Bob (Robert J.), 91, 94, 152, 177,
    273, 583
Bliley, Thomas J. Jr., 327*n*, 343–344
Blueberry Donut Group, 70, 79, 81, 95, 108,
    109, 171, 474
Blue Cross and Blue Shield, 66
Blumenthal, Sidney, 577*n*
Blythe, Bill (William Jefferson Clinton), 58
Boehner, John, 568
Bond, Kit (Christopher), 378, 379
Bonior, David, 421–422, 433, 454, 474
Bonner, Jack, 214–215
Boorstin, Bob, 26–27, 148, 152, 153, 186,
    229, 497
    and Clinton's health care speech, 27, 31,
        49, 51, 52

and task force, 111–112, 114
Boren, David, 146, 367, 371, 378, 390, 443
Borger, Gloria, 395
Bosnia crises, 254, 275, 471
Boston Globe, 75, 76
Bozell, L. Brent, 373
Bradley, Bill, 367, 368, 378, 386, 390, 443
    leaves Senate, 596, 597
Brady bill, 254, 269, 449
Branstad, Terry E., 427
Breaux, John, 301–302, 378, 443, 475,
        523, 624
    and Clinton plan, 228, 336–337
    and compromise/bipartisan bills, 367, 371,
        377, 380, 386, 390, 524, 558
    co-sponsors Cooper bill, 302, 313, 315,
        337, 367
Brewster, Bill K., 186, 423, 433, 435
Britain, health care system in, 71
Brock, David, 255
Brooke, Edward W., 444
Brookings Institution, 81, 115, 116
Brophy, Susan, 82
Brown, Jerry (Edmund Gerald Jr.), 78
Brownell, Tom, 464
Bruck, Connie, 108
BTU tax. *See* taxes
budget
    balancing, 565, 573–574, 578, 581, 595
    Clinton and, 121–122, 124, 143–149
        passim, 154, 155–156, 160, 163, 572,
        578–580, 610
        government shutdown, 580, 595,
            597–600, 604
    Clinton plan derailed by, 137, 143, 146–150,
        154, 155–156, 324, 394, 613
    deficit reduction, 119, 121–122, 143, 173,
        228, 449, 571, 610
    reconciliation bill, 119–120, 123, 143,
        146, 345, 450
        Byrd blocks, 125–127, 174, 468–469, 612
    Republicans and, 35, 125, 156, 160,
        174, 238–239, 367, 571, 572–581,
        583–584
    See also taxes
Bull Moose Party, 257
Burger King, 197
Burke, Sheila, 64, 133, 173, 360–361, 363,
        372, 373, 374
    attacks on, 385–386, 504, 565
    and Dole-Packwood bill, 391, 448–449
Bush, George, and administration, 19, 43,
        48, 261, 404–405, 552, 616, 626
    and budget/taxes, 122, 574, 614
    in campaigns, 60, 82–92 *passim,* 95, 390,
        400, 565, 574, 613
    and health care, 38, 82–83, 89–92 *passim,*
        131, 354, 359–360, 390, 428, 441
    indifference toward, 41, 60, 68, 97, 173,
        431, 627
Business Council, 318
business interests. *See* big business; health care
        industry; health insurance industry;
        lobbyists; small business
Business Roundtable, 196, 316, 318–324, 389

Butler, Sandra, 474
Byrd, Robert C., 118, 125–127, 174, 330,
    468–469, 612

"Cadillac" plans. *See* health care plans
Califano, Joseph A. Jr., 41
California
    fiscal situation of, 238–240
    managed competition plan in, 77–78
    mandate defeated, 203
    See also Los Angeles County
California Medical Association, 203
Calio, Nicholas E., 204
CALPERS (California pension fund), 74*n*
Canadian health care system, 71, 77, 153,
    164, 438
Cardin, Ben (Benjamin L.), 400, 402, 408,
    425, 432, 454
Carlson, Arne, 503–504, 553
Carper, Roger, 464
Carter, Jimmy, and administration, 19, 67,
    525, 552, 579, 616, 617, 625
    and health care, 38, 41, 68, 155, 370
    staff members, 104, 116
Carter, Rosalyn, 182
Carville, James ("Ragin' Cajun"), 51, 60, 97,
    98, 123, 210, 293
    and health care plan, 90, 124
Case, Clifford, 444
Casey, Robert P., 58–59
Casey, William J., 353
Cassidy, Edith, 58
Castle, Mike (Michael N.), 160
catastrophic-illness insurance. *See* Medicare
Catholic Church, 66
Catholic Hospitals Association, 91
Cato Institute. 465*n*
CAT scan, cost of, 242
CBS Evening News, 464, 470
CBS This Morning, 494
Cedars-Sinai Medical Center (Los Angeles),
    241–244, 245, 535, 536, 631
Celeste, Dick (Richard F.), 47, 208–209,
    293–294
Center for Public Integrity, 212
Central Intelligence Agency (CIA), 206, 353
Chafee, John, 36–37, 273, 349, 357–358,
    364–371 *passim*, 385, 444, 514,
    626, 636
    and Clinton plan, 132–133, 375, 511
    and consensus, 375–379 *passim*, 390, 392,
        445–446, 498
    health plans of, 132–133, 266, 302, 305,
        337, 362–365 *passim*, 368–373
        passim, 394, 424, 441, 519, 523,
        527 (*see also* Mainstream Coalition)
Chamberlain, Joshua Lawrence, 36
Chamber of Commerce, U.S., 66, 188, 316,
    322–323, 324, 489, 569
checks and balances, 118, 127, 484
Children's Defense Fund, 99, 115
Children's Hospital (Washington), 30
Chiles, Lawton, 375
Chlopak, Bob, 288, 289–290, 291, 338, 530
Christensen, Jon, 419, 556

Christian Coalition, 53, 197, 466, 504, 551,
    554, 566, 569, 630
Chrysler Corporation, 288
Chung, Connie, 47, 464
Cigna Insurance Company, 199
Citizen Action, 412
Citizens for a Sound Economy (CSE), 52, 197,
    386, 464–467, 520–521, 529–530, 569
civil rights movement, 152, 257, 348, 403,
    460, 506–507, 561, 640
Claussen, Rick, 203, 204, 205
Clay, Henry, 563
Clean Air Act, 348
Clean Water Act, 449
Clinton, Bill (William Jefferson)
    background, 57–58, 105, 620
    on bipartisanship, 160, 192
    and budget, *see* budget
    and catastrophic insurance, 69–70
    compared to FDR, 40, 155
    and compromise plans, 380–381
    Congress addressed by, 120, 121, 264
        (*see also* Clinton health care plan, his
        speeches on)
    congressional process misunderstood by, 208
    criticism of, 19, 44–45, 276
    cuts staff, 232
    economic plan rejected, 17, 139, 345
    and government shutdown, 580, 595,
        598–599
    as governor of Arkansas, 100, 259
    and health care reform, *see* Clinton health
        care plan; task force
    legislative victories, 449
    and Magaziner, *see* Magaziner, Ira C.
    Medicaid and Medicare as viewed by, 97,
        98, 99, 398
    and NAFTA, 19, 269, 292, 324, 326, 394,
        407, 408, 449, 453, 458
    1992 campaign, 70–85 *passim*, 87–95,
        100, 109, 152–154 *passim*, 202, 257,
        259–260, 311, 469, 493, 613
    inaugurated, 95
    personal allegations against, 78, 255–256, 274
    personal lobbying of, 217–218
    political strategy established, 90, 301
    poll ratings of, *see* polls
    problems of presidency, 17, 33, 44, 145,
        254, 255, 262, 282–287
        international crises, 188–189, 254,
            471–472
        L.A. County crisis, 594
        (*see also* and Whitewater, *below*)
    reelection plans, 124, 144, 227, 581, 597
    State of the Union address (1994), 264,
        267–270, 347, 357, 363, 612
    on "the System," 639–641
    temper outbursts, 20, 145, 157, 158
    and Whitewater, 235, 256, 259–263 *passim*,
        270, 273, 278–281, 442, 616
Clinton, Hillary Rodham, 581
    compared to Eleanor Roosevelt, 102–103,
        182, 184, 186
    criticism of, 19, 167, 176, 186, 225–226,
        273–274, 281–282

Clinton, Hillary Rodham (*continued*)
  criticism of, (*continued*)
    personal attacks, 102, 277, 312, 460–462,
      600, 616
  father's illness and death, 135–136
  news media treatment of, 231, 277, 281,
    460, 600
    New Yorker profile, 108
    New York Times, 182, 185, 187, 210, 600
  as partner in law firm, 259, 260
  poll ratings of, 255, 265, 274
  power/policy making of, 9, 16–17, 93–103,
    120, 182–187, 210, 226, 547
  praise and popularity of, 34, 101, 108, 131,
    133, 173, 183–186, 255, 274, 411
  and Whitewater, 235, 256, 259–263 *passim*,
    270, 273, 278, 280–281, 600, 616
Clinton, Hillary Rodham, and health care
  plan, 26, 229, 327, 383, 457, 480, 612
  appears before Congress, *see* Congress, U.S.
  attacks big business, 202, 318–325 *passim*
  and catastrophic-insurance fiasco, 69
  and compromise plans, 302–303, 311, 312,
    315, 433, 437–438, 439, 456, 496
  denounces, parodies TV ads, 209–211
  and draft bill, 167, 170, 173–178
  failure of plan accepted by, 508, 513–514
  and Health Care Reform Project, 288
  meetings with press, 23–25, 632
  meets with congressmen, 341, 454
  and MinnesotaCare, 502
  and Mitchell's departure from Senate,
    296, 299
  and Moynihan, 352, 354
  and President's speeches, 9, 16–23 *passim*,
    29, 30, 49, 52, 269
  and Reform Riders, 460, 461–462, 469,
    471, 473
  speeches by, 166–167, 190, 209, 225,
    324–325, 330, 387–389 *passim*, 474,
    478, 572
    protested, 461–462
  supercommittee plan urged by, 305, 451,
    586, 621
  and task force, 10, 114, 129–133 *passim*,
    139, 146, 381
    appointed to head, 96, 98–103, 111–112,
      149–150, 610–611, 613, 614
    and budget plan, 121, 125
    and financing, 122, 217, 308, 381
    and Magaziner as co-worker, 14, 108,
      134, 136, 148, 154, 157, 161–163,
      165, 293, 375
    and secrecy, 140, 141–142, 145
    and time constraints, 119–120, 137,
      143, 147, 155
Clinton health care plan
  budget issue vs., *see* budget
  business and, *see* big business; small business
  "Clintoncare," 52, 218, 220, 461, 528
  complexity of, 16, 230–231
    Clinton's grasp of, 411
    public understanding of, 53–54, 154,
      175, 231, 506, 631–635 (*see also*
      public view of, *below*)

compromise plans vs., 303, 307–308,
    311–316 (*see also* health care plans)
  concessions suggested, 369
  and cost of care, 141, 287 (*see also* health
    care costs)
  decisions on, 26, 160–163, 169 (*see also*
    task force)
  Democratic doubts/criticism of, 37–38,
    40–41, 44–45, 117–119 *passim*,
    137–140 *passim*, 161–163, 172–173,
    176, 228–229, 351, 353, 433, 451, 622
  Dole and, *see* Dole, Bob
  draft lacking, 191
  draft presented to Congress, 167–178
  early prospects for, 62, 132
  failure of, 238, 344, 459, 508, 511–532, 546
    responsibility for, x, 10, 70, 127–128,
      142, 198, 232, 609–612, 622
    unworkability recognized, 381
  false or misleading reports on, 141, 145,
    272, 340, 611
  First Lady and, *see* Clinton, Hillary Rodham,
    and health care plan
  formulation of, and Clintons' role in,
    108–111, 173–178
  Gingrich and, *see* Gingrich, Newt
  grassroots effort attempted, 291–294
  hospital personnel hopes for, 237, 240,
    244–245, 252, 537
  internal debates/infighting about, 80,
    144–145, 153, 161, 291–297
  international crises vs., 188–189
  Kennedy version, *see* Kennedy, Ted
  labor unions and, *see* labor unions
  lobbying for and against, *see* lobbyists
  and long-term care, 418, 572
  and managed competition, 77–78, 79–80,
    87, 91, 168, 589
  Moynihan's variation on, 377, 390,
    391–393, 424
  organizations opposing, 46, 52–53, 159,
    188, 196–224 (*see also* Republican
    Party and health care)
  organizations supporting, 12, 152–153,
    168, 213, 338
  pay-or-play system, 75–76, 81, 86
  and prescription benefits, 80, 418, 572
  and preventive care, 80
  public view of, 231, 363, 506, 631–635
    doubts and fears, ix–x, 12, 15–16, 18,
      53–54, 91–92, 153–154, 234–235,
      264, 375, 491 (*see also* polls)
  "rescue" bills, *see* Gephardt, Dick;
    Mitchell, George
  secrecy surrounding, 140–143, 145, 611
  Senate Finance Committee jurisdiction
    over, 347
  single-payer plan changed, 76–77
  speeches on, *see* Clinton health care plan,
    his speeches on, *below*
  sponsors and co-sponsors of, 390, 416
  Stark version of ("Medicare C"), *see* Stark, Pete
  strategy for, 16, 301–304, 324
  supercommittee plan, 305–306, 451,
    586, 621

support withdrawn, 148, 363, 374
task force on, *see* task force
time constraints on, 100, 119–120, 123,
139, 143, 147, 149, 178, 191, 233
and trust vs. issues, 263–264, 265, 273,
322, 326
universal coverage as part of, *see* health
insurance, national
"vacuum" in planning, 225–226, 232
and veto threat, 267, 268–269, 270
warnings ignored, 93, 107, 110–111, 118
weaknesses of, 85
white paper on (1992), 75–76
Whitewater and, *see* Whitewater case
Clinton health care plan, his speeches on
September 1992 (at Merck & Co.
Pharmaceuticals), 39, 95, 109, 322
February 1993 (before Congress), 120–122, 123
August 1993 (before National Governors'
Association), 159–160
September 1993 (before Congress), 3–10,
14–23, 25–31, 34, 41, 45, 48–54,
159, 169
follow-up to, 181–186, 225, 231, 616
Republican response, 313, 465, 627
October 1993 (before Congress), 190–191, 225
January 1994 (State of the Union), 267–271
August 1994 (at rally and at White House),
472–473
Clymer, Adam, 392
CNN (Cable News Network), 204, 255–256
Coalition for Health Insurance Choices,
204, 213
Coats, Dan, 305, 349, 364
Cochran, Thad, 349
Coehlo, Tony, 623
Cohen, Bill (William S.), 133, 375, 378, 379,
383–384, 444, 445
Cohen, Wilbur J., 65
Cold War, 353, 605, 618
Collins, Mac, 276
Columbia Journalism Review, 230
Computervision (firm), 153
Congress, U.S.
as center of The System, 300
change in attitude of, 445, 620
Clinton's strategy toward, 301, 611–612
defeats health insurance bills, 34, 44, 62,
65–69 *passim*, 306, 333, 375–376, 622
draft of Clinton plan presented to, 167–178
First Lady appears before, sends aides to,
123, 151, 167, 182–186, 187, 190,
222, 231, 507, 627
health insurance for members, 289–291,
338, 432
news media coverage of, 298–299, 426, 482, 619
party control of, *see* Democratic Party;
Republican Party
polarization and bitterness of, 38, 156,
596, 598–600, 619–621
President speaks before, *see* Clinton, Bill
public perception of, 297–298
special-interest/PAC contributions to, 165,
212–213, 422, 620, 623, 630 (*see*
also lobbyists)

See also elections, congressional (1994); House
of Representatives, U.S.; Senate, U.S.
Congressional Black Caucus, 421, 483,
485, 624
Congressional Budget Office (CBO), 115, 116,
583, 609
and Clinton plan, 171, 282–287, 324, 381
and compromise plans, 487–489, 492, 591
Congressional Office of Legislative Counsel, 169
Congressional Quarterly, 131, 397, 405
Conrad, Kent, 367–368, 378, 390, 443
Conrad, Paul, 481
conservative groups, 465n. *See also* lobbyists
Conservative Political Action Conference, 274
Conservative Victory Committee, 373
Contract With America. *See* Gingrich, Newt
Coolidge, Calvin, 626
Cooper, Jim, 74, 84, 309–310, 319, 344,
408, 427, 516, 621
and Clinton plan, 311–313, 325, 336–337
Cooper plans, 302, 309, 310, 311, 313,
420, 524
Cooper-Grandy, 313–322 *passim*,
330–334 *passim*, 337, 342–343, 367,
400–402, 419, 428, 452, 487, 557
Cooper, Prentice, 309
Cooper, William Prentice, 310
costs. *See* health care costs
Council of Economic Advisers, 134, 614
Coverdell, Paul, 365, 489, 499, 568
Cox, John and Jan, 473, 474
Cranston, Alan, 227
credibility gap, 616
crime, "war" on, 606
crime bill, 449, 477–478, 480, 498, 506,
508, 509, 516–517
defeated, 482–486, 489–490, 494, 497,
500, 515
C-SPAN, 426, 457, 482
Cuomo, Mario, 549

Daley, Richard J., 292, 404
D'Amato, Al (Alfonse M.), 358
Danforth, Jack (John C.), 133, 184, 362, 392,
507–508, 626, 636
and consensus, 375–380 *passim*, 390, 443,
444, 445
Darman, Richard, 176, 177, 384–385, 616
Daschle, Tom (Thomas A.), 161, 336, 367, 383,
490, 515–518 *passim*, 530–531, 636
Davis, Michele, 52
Dayton "deal group," 10, 267–268
Deadly Force (O'Donnell), 265
Dean, Howard, 374
Dean, Thomas, 54
Deaver, Mike, 287
DeConcini, Dennis, 492
Deets, Horace, 588
Delgado, Julie, 247–248, 537–538, 539
"Delivery Room," 52, 278, 497, 527
Democratic Leadership Council (DLC), 70,
77, 228, 302, 624
Democratic National Committee (DNC), 47,
82, 208, 209, 291–294, 332, 387
Democratic National Convention, 71, 81

Democratic Party, 59, 106, 113, 143, 174
    ad campaigns by, 60, 291, 293–294,
        338, 585
    as Big Government, 229, 384, 467, 474,
        483, 547, 627
    "BTU-ed," 146, 269, 424, 438, 515
    division and weakness of, 301, 310–311, 332,
        366, 392, 483, 485–486, 492–494,
        515–516, 621, 622–625
    in election campaigns, 60, 70–83 passim,
        86, 95, 548
    and health care, 41, 43, 60–74 passim,
        124, 153, 173, 269, 301, 505–506
    Health Care Reform Project, 50, 287–291,
        338, 480, 494, 530
    loyalty to, as issue, 426–427, 429
    as majority party, 427, 509, 516, 517, 531,
        532–533, 563, 623
        loses control, 124 (see also Republican
            Party [in Congress])
    New Deal wing, 624
    "New" or "Yellow Pages" Democrats, 77,
        310–311, 493, 624
    and social spending, 122, 139
    See also partisanship
Deukmejian, George, 248
Dewar, Helen, 546
Dingell, Debbie, 307
Dingell, John D. Sr., 42, 45, 65, 184, 306,
        307
    Dingell, John D. Jr. ("Johnny," "Big John"),
        72, 123, 184, 330, 430
    and Clinton plan, 45, 307–309, 311,
        323, 329
    and compromise bills, 327, 332, 333,
        335–344 passim, 371, 414, 509, 511
    and Cooper, 310, 316, 331, 342–343,
        427, 557
    and Democratic Party split, 621, 624
    and H.R. 16, 306
    power of, 41–42, 310, 334–335
Dinkins, David, 227
DiVall, Linda, 577
Divinity, Karen, 474–475
Dodd, Chris (Christopher J.), 349, 492
Dole, Bob (Robert J.), 64, 337, 345, 379, 380,
        383, 395, 396
    attacks on, 385–386, 474
    bipartisan (Moynihan-Dole) plan, 266, 270,
        345–346, 350, 358, 372–373, 395
    and budget, 125, 573, 610
    and Clinton plan, 35, 125, 222, 270, 302,
        305, 351, 632
        Mitchell variant, 479, 495, 498, 500,
            527, 528
    and compromise plans, 305, 365–366,
        372–378 passim, 391, 392, 394, 500
        disparages Mainstream group, 446
        and mandates, 366, 371
    filibuster mounted by, 345, 350
    and Gingrich, 564, 587
    and government shutdown, 599, 600
    and Medicare, 575
    "no-crisis," "no bill" strategy, 270, 500
    presidential ambitions, 36, 227, 347, 361,

        364, 371, 384, 386, 395, 445, 472,
            565, 515
    and Republican health care plans, 132,
        305, 359, 363, 364, 441, 447, 626
        Dole-Packwood, 390–391, 448–449
Domenici, Pete, 573
Dority, Douglas, 356
Douglass, Linda, 464
Dowd, Maureen, 182, 186, 549
Downey, Tom, 415–416
Dreyer, David, 6–7, 8–10, 22–23, 25, 28, 31
Duberstein, Kenneth, 616
Dukakis, Michael, 26, 30, 138, 451
Durenberger, Dave, 131, 362, 495, 507–508,
        523
    and consensus, 369, 375–382 passim, 390,
        443–446 passim
    supports health care reform, 133, 349, 392,
        626, 627, 636
Duvall, Frank, 193

Eagle Forum, 373
economic conditions
    Clinton's economic plans, 17, 139, 345
    Great Depression, 65, 144, 310, 618,
        640, 641
    growth, 124
    health care costs affecting, 61–62, 124
    1990s, 62–63, 606–608
        California, 238–240
        downsizing, 593–594, 607
    See also budget; health care costs; taxes
Edelman, Ed, 542–544
Edelstein, Steve, 303
education reform bill, 298, 350
Eisenhower, Dwight, 66, 346, 626
elections, congressional (1994), 106, 428,
        449, 531, 548–549, 554, 601, 623
    and breakdown of System, 505, 544, 547,
        565, 622
    demographics of, 555, 566–567
    failure of health bill and, 496
    See also Republican Party (in Congress)
elections, presidential campaigns
    1992, 60, 390, 400, 469 (see also Clinton, Bill)
    1996, 124, 144, 227, 496, 581, 597 (see
        also Dole, Bob)
Eller, Jeff, 52, 154, 315
Ellwood, Paul, 73, 148
"Elmer's Glue" amendment. See Jefferson,
        William L., and Jefferson amendment
Emanuel, Rahm, 10
"employer mandate." See mandates, employer
Empower America, 386
energy tax. See taxes
Enthoven, Alain C., 72, 74, 148
Evans & Novak, 385

Faircloth, Lauch, 489
Fair Deal, 534
Fallows, James, 272, 634
Falwell, Jerry, 281
Families USA, 152–153, 213, 470, 471
Faris, Jack (S. Jackson), 46, 47, 217–219,
        223–224, 341, 489

"farmers' markets," 319
"Far Side" cartoon, 172
Faulty Diagnosis: Public Misconceptions About Health Care Reform (Public Agenda Foundation), 90
Fazio, Vic, 454
Feder, Judy, 47, 70, 81, 109–111, 118, 128, 370
Federal Bureau of Investigation (FBI), 206, 260
Federal Election Commission, 212
Federal Employee Health Benefits program, 482
Federal Home Loan Bank Board, 259
Federal Reserve Board, 122
Feingold, Russ (Russell D.), 492
Feinstein, Dianne, 374, 378
Ferguson, Christy, 133, 273, 636
    attacks on, 385
    and bipartisan and compromise bills, 372, 378, 379, 443, 519, 520, 524–525
filibusters. *See* Senate, U.S.
Fischer, Celia, 292, 293
Fischer, Richard, 434
Fiske, Robert, 489
Flanagan, Michael Patrick, 556
Fleischer, Ari, 586
Florida, 221, 415
    health plan defeated, 375
Flowers, Gennifer, 78
Foley, Tom (Thomas S.), 40–41, 344, 425, 438, 449, 452, 453, 523, 617
    and Clinton plan, 41, 146, 151, 305, 338, 450–451, 453, 586, 618, 621
    "rescue" bills, 437, 458, 479–480, 509
    and committee jurisdiction, 454–455
    and consensus (within party), 417
    and crime bill, 484–485
    defeated, 551–552, 556
    and veto threat, 268–269
Food and Commercial Workers' Union, 356
Forand, Aime, 66
Ford, Billy (William D.), 123, 344, 509
Ford, Gerald, 19, 21, 552
Ford, Wendell, 491
foreign policy, U.S., 605–606
    international crises, 188–189, 254, 275, 471–472
48 Hours (TV show), 47
Foster, Vincent, 235, 260–261, 263, 275, 277, 281, 465n
Foundation for Hospice and Home Care, 628
Freeh, Louis J., 260
Fried, Bruce M., 70, 79, 81, 88–90 *passim*, 109, 171, 173, 474
Friendly, Andrew, 7
Fulbright, J. William, 57, 259

Gallipoli (movie), 45
Gallup polls, 371, 559
Garamendi, John, 77–78, 80
Gawande, Atul, 83–89 *passim*, 93–95, 109, 144, 155, 309
Gearan, Mark, 30, 31, 456
General Agreement on Tariffs and Trade (GATT), 449–450, 523, 531

General Mills Corporation, 320
General Motors Corporation, 307
Georges, Christopher, 589
Georgia, lobbying tactics in, 221
Gephardt, Dick (Richard A.), 8, 340, 400, 421, 433, 449, 450, 548, 560, 578, 617
    and budget, 123, 145, 579
    and Clinton plan, 120, 123, 124, 128, 151, 169, 195, 269, 288, 305, 451, 452–454, 586, 621, 624
    "rescue" bill, 437, 438, 458, 476–480 *passim*, 487, 497, 509
    and consensus (within party), 417, 452
    and crime bill, 484–485
    and health care reform, 12, 41, 60–61, 173, 316, 514–515
Gergen, David, 21–22, 26, 209, 217, 268
    and health care plans, 149, 155, 301, 315, 632
Germany, health care in, 61, 64n
Gibbons, Sam, 427, 514, 518, 585–586, 594, 624
    replaces Rostenkowski as Committee chairman, 414–418, 421, 432, 454
    and Stark-Gibbons bill, *see* Stark, Pete
Gigot, Paul A., 517, 569, 588
Gingrich, Newt, 57, 301, 316, 383, 445, 620
    comments on Clinton plan, 272, 275–276, 314
    and debt default, 595
    and GATT, 531
    and government shutdown, 580, 598–599
    health care reform opposed by, 366, 373, 424, 447, 474, 541
    health care reform plan of, 430, 575–578, 582–593, 603
    ideology of, 627, 641
    legislative strategy, 580, 586–590, 595–596
    opposition strategy, 11, 38–40, 186–187, 195, 304–305, 327–328, 343, 364, 425–429 *passim*, 447, 462–463, 545–549, 615
        conservative groups, 464–467
        Contract With America, 234, 529, 546–547, 561–570 *passim*, 596, 613, 630
        crime bill attacked by, 482–486, 500, 515
        "no bill," 366
    poll rating of, 597, 598
    staff of, 131, 184
    takes power, 560–565, 569
Ginsburg, Ruth Bader, 260, 355
Glenn, John, 492, 511
"global budgets" ("premium caps"), 74. *See also* health care costs (insurance rates)
Globocar, Ellen, 50–51, 290–291, 331–332, 338
Goddard, Ben, 203, 204, 205
Golden Rule Insurance Company, 430
Goldwater, Barry, 67, 626
Goodin, Steve, 48
Goodwin, Doris Kearns, 102
Gordon, Slade, 469
Gore, Al (Albert Jr.), 70, 83, 158, 268, 318, 337, 357, 471, 617
    and budget bill, 119, 143, 146, 156, 174
    and Clinton plan, 5–6, 22, 49, 119, 140, 217, 342, 457

Goss, Porter, 468
Gradison, Bill (A. Willis Jr.), 53, 69, 435
   with HIAA, 198–199, 200–204, 207,
      210, 219, 603 (*see also* advertising
      campaigns)
   Rostenkowski-Gradison deal, 411–414,
      417, 432, 588
Gramm, Phil, 37, 364, 430, 478, 621
   and Democratic health plans, 36, 131,
      277, 305, 486, 494, 526, 528, 541,
      556, 627
Grandy, Fred, 131, 313–314, 431, 558
   and bipartisan bills, 313–316, 401–402,
      419, 426–428, 429 (*see also* Cooper, Jim)
Grassley, Charles E., 362
Graves, Bill, 557
Great Depression. *See* economic conditions
Great Society, 40, 67, 270, 311, 534, 554,
      618, 640
Greenberg, Stan, 17–18, 26, 159, 293
   and Dayton "dial group," 10, 267–268
   polls by, 82, 189, 264, 556
   and strategy, 90, 152, 229, 289, 516–517,
      579
Greenhouse Compact, The, 106, 107
Greenspan, Alan, 122
Gridiron Club, 211
Griffin, Pat, 322, 330, 374, 375, 434
Grunwald, Henry, 26
Grunwald, Mandy, 26, 90, 124, 144, 159,
      229, 292, 293, 294
   and Health Care Reform Project, 289, 290,
      291, 338
Guinier, Lani, 17, 145
Gunderson, Steve, 434
Guthrie, Woody, 475

Haight-Asbury Medical Clinic, 399
Haiti crisis, 189, 225, 254, 525
Hallmark Cards, 339, 342
Hamilton, Bill, 203, 204
Hannity, Sean, 549
Harkin, Tom, 72, 78, 202–203, 209
Harrison, Christine, 54
Harrold, Kathryn, 265
"Harry and Louise" ads, 16, 46, 205–213
      passim, 225, 229, 288, 328, 343,
      537, 615
   discontinued, returned to air, 47, 209,
      386–387, 411, 417, 489, 591
Hart, Gary, 22, 83
Hart, Peter D., 595, 633
Hastert, Denny (J. Dennis), 328, 334
Hatch, Orrin G., 363
Hatch Act, 449
Hatfield, Mark, 133, 375, 378, 379, 565
Head Start program, 415
Health, Education and Welfare, U.S. Department
      of, 65, 115
Health and Human Services (HHS), U.S.
      Department of, 82, 112, 115, 116,
      128, 140, 169, 398, 456, 576
health care alliances, 87, 253, 289, 319
   California and Florida, 157, 382
   disparaged, doomed, 399–400, 411, 453

See also HIPCs
health care costs
   business battle against, 61, 307, 326, 382
   Clinton plan
      business view of, 382
      and cost containment, 170
      falsely reported, 141
      financing of, *see* financing, *below*
      reported by CBO, 287
   Committee on (1920s), 65
   cost-cutting devices, 382
   economic gains cut by, 61–62, 124
   financing
      bipartisan/compromise plans, 69, 72,
         333, 391
      Clinton plan, 80, 82, 85, 110, 122, 172,
         217, 370–371, 608
      Clinton plan variants, 377, 391, 402,
         408–409
      (*see also* mandates, employer; mandates,
         individual; taxes)
   First Lady's view, 135–136
   hospital
      Maryland cost containment plan, 400, 402
      1977 bill defeated, 41
   insurance administration, waste in, 242–243
   insurance costs paid by individual, 63, 126
   insurance rates, 62, 73*n*, 74*n*, 382
      price controls ("premium caps") on, 74,
         110, 161, 162, 167, 201, 214, 319,
         420, 431
   malpractice case limits, 402
   Medicaid and Medicare, 25, 77, 97, 242,
      243, 354, 583–584
   as policy issue, 94, 157, 160, 318
   public view, 90, 152, 153, 329
   in Republican plan, 591
   rise in, predicted, 572, 583–584
Health Care Financing Agency (HCFA), 99
health care industry, 62, 331
   corporate control of, 533, 535, 603
   financial crisis in, 593–594
      hospitals close, 239–240, 539, 594,
         604, 637
   Gingrich rewards, 592
   hospital personnel hopes for Clinton plan,
      237, 240, 244–245, 252, 537
   lobbies, 12, 46, 90–91
   medical profession, 65, 66, 67
   pharmaceutical companies, 89, 90, 322,
      413, 417
   size, 12, 45, 64, 603
   See also health insurance industry; health
      maintenance organizations (HMOs)
Healthcare Leadership Council, 196
health care plans
   bipartisan, 376–377, 434 (*see also* Cooper,
      Jim [Cooper-Grandy]; Mainstream
      Coalition; Moynihan, Pat [Moynihan-Dole];
      Rowland-Bilirakis bill)
   "Cadillac," 309–310, 316
   Canadian, 71, 77, 153, 164, 438
   Clinton, *see* Clinton health care plan
   Democrat compromise/alternative, 328
      (*see also* Breaux, John; Gephardt,

Dick; Kennedy, Ted; Mitchell, George;
Stark, Pete)
Heritage Foundation, 365
"Kiddicare," 572
lobbies for and against, *see* lobbyists
long-term care, 69, 165, 418, 423, 572, 583
managed care, *see* health maintenance
organizations (HMOs)
managed competition concept, 72–74,
77–80 *passim*, 86–91 *passim*, 152,
168, 201, 381, 589, 624
Jackson Hole Plan, 73–74, 84–85, 148,
309, 319, 396, 419
and mandates, *see* mandates, employer;
mandates, individual
Medicaid, Medicare, *see* Medicaid; Medicare
medical IRAs, 430
"Medicare C" (Stark-Gibbons), *see* Stark, Pete
"no bill" approach, 448, 496, 500
pay-or-play, 75–76, 80, 81, 85, 86
President threatens veto, 267–270, 357,
387, 388, 402
Republican, 123, 150, 273, 359, 428–429,
430, 448, 573
Chafee, *see* Chafee, John
Dole, *see* Dole, Bob
Gingrich, 430, 575–578, 582–593, 603
Michel, 43, 316, 328
Nixon, 67, 269, 370, 376, 500, 521, 522
vetoed, 592–593
single-payer system, 71–72, 80, 609
Clinton plan and, 76–77, 150, 311,
326, 438
proponents of, 43, 86, 308, 344, 400,
416, 426, 433, 624
public support of, 91
Social Security and, 45, 65, 66, 306, 310, 622
state plans defeated or passed, 374–375,
400, 502–505, 558
subsidized, 39, 91, 160, 369
See also health insurance, national; health
insurance industry
Health Care Reform Project. *See* Democratic Party
health insurance, national
Congress defeats, 34, 44, 62, 65–69 *passim*,
306, 333, 375–376, 622
cost and financing of, *see* health care costs
and the uninsured, 90, 153, 247–252,
329, 373
cutbacks and, 62–63, 240, 637
number of, 266, 382, 420, 421, 536,
593, 603, 607, 637–638
universal coverage
Clinton plan and, 44, 82, 87, 170, 202,
313, 402, 433, 438, 456–457
joint bill suggested, 377
opposed, 66, 386
public view of concept, 219, 333, 370, 375
Republican plans, 132, 313, 368, 394, 424
supported, 200, 202, 387, 421, 505
World War II and, 65
See also health care plans; Medicaid;
Medicare
Health Insurance Association of America
(HIAA), 199, 219, 428, 603

in Coalition group, 53, 188, 196, 198
"Harry and Louise" campaign, *see* advertising
campaigns
lobbying by, 90, 204, 214, 332
Rostenkowski and, 411–414, 417, 419
supports universal coverage, 200, 202, 387
health insurance industry
ads by, *see* advertising campaigns
Big Five companies, 199, 200, 214, 318
Blue Cross and Blue Shield, 66
"cherry picking" by, 66
"community rating," 80, 201–202
concessions to, 412, 417, 423, 432
corporate control of, 533
and employer mandate, 200, 214, 219
expands, 66
First Lady attacks, 202, 324
Gingrich and, 588
lobbies of, *see* lobbyists
managed competition concept, *see* health
care plans
opposes health plans, 67, 71, 188, 200,
228, 253, 322, 341
public distrust of, 204
retrenchment by, 240
unmanaged competition, 73–74
health maintenance organizations (HMOs),
73n, 81, 271, 381–382, 396, 533,
573, 575
bill passed, 67
expansion of, 589–590, 637
versions of managed care, 139, 166, 313
HealthRIGHT, 470
Health Security card, 53, 169, 465–466
Healthtrust, Inc., 331
Heclo, Hugh, 112
Hedleton, Tracy, 193
Heinz, John, 50, 58–59
Henry, Mike, 594
Herblock cartoon, 392
Heritage Foundation plan, 365, 465n, 632
Hesburgh, Theodore, 59
Hilley, John, 123
Himmelfarb, Gertrude, 233
HIPCs ("Hippicks"), 73–74, 80, 87. *See also*
health care alliances
Hoagland, Peter, 418–419, 423, 433, 435, 556
Hoover, J. Edgar, 206
Hopkins, Harry, 561
Horton, Willie, 152
Hosler, Karen, 391
hospital closings. *See* health care industry
Hospital Council of Southern California, 239,
248, 533
Hospital Insurance Trust Fund, 575
Hospital of the Good Samaritan (Los
Angeles), 251
Houghton, Amo, 106
House of Representatives, U.S.
Budget Committee, 199
changes in membership, 619–620
Conservative Democratic Forum, 311
Democratic majority in, 509, 531
Education and Labor Committee, 306, 344,
433, 453, 455, 509

House of Representatives, U.S. (*continued*)
  Energy and Commerce Committee, 42,
      306–307, 309, 310, 329, 427, 455
    and Clinton plan, 192, 557
    and compromise plan, 341, 342, 414
    Republicans on, 287, 307, 327*n*, 328
    Gingrich heads, 560–565
    and health care bill, 509, 621
    jurisdiction battles, 454–456
    lobbyists at, 216, 220, 340, 386
    Republican "Theme Team," 275–276,
      467, 482
  Small Business Committee, 222
  Ways and Means Committee, 42, 176, 284,
      337, 386, 401, 414, 455
    and budget bill, 143
    and Clinton plan, 172, 214
    contributions to, 404
    Democratic majority on, 427
    First Lady appears before, 167, 183, 186
    Gibbons takes over as chairman,
      414–418, 421
    and health care, 66, 68, 131, 287, 306,
      509
    Health Subcommittee, 199, 397, 399
  See also Congress, U.S.
House Republican Conference, 199, 568
Housing and Urban Development (HUD),
    U.S. Department of, 116
Hudson Comprehensive Health Center (Los
    Angeles), 247–248, 537, 539
Hurd, G. David, 202–203, 208–209
Hurwit, Cathy, 412

Iacocca, Lee, 59
IBM (International Business Machines), 413
Ickes, Harold Sr., 257, 258
Ickes, Harold Jr., 154, 226–227, 232–233,
    256–258, 268, 274–275, 278, 393
  and Health Care Reform Project, 289, 290,
    291, 530
  and strategy, 375, 411, 456–457, 485–486,
    512, 579
  and trust vs. issues, 263–264, 322, 326
Ignagni, Karen, 81, 86
Immerwahr, John, 90
In Critical Condition (Kennedy), 348
Independent voters, 556, 581, 597
insurance. *See* health insurance, national;
    health insurance industry
interest groups, 123–124, 149, 169, 177,
    207, 537, 627–631 *passim*, 635
  See also Congress, U.S.; lobbyists
Internal Revenue Service, 175
Iran-Contra affair, 353, 605, 614
Isakowitz, Mark, 341
Israel-PLO peace accord ceremony, 19, 22

Jackson, Jesse, 257
Jackson, "Scoop" (Henry Martin), 383
Jackson Hole Group, 73, 84, 148, 309, 325,
    396, 419
  "Jackson Hole Plan," *see* health care plans
    (managed competition concept)
Jacobs, Andrew, 425, 427, 429–430, 433

Jamieson, Kathleen Hall, 211
Jasinowski, Jerry, 317–318, 321
Javits, Jacob K., 50, 444
Jefferson, Thomas, 60, 639
Jefferson, William J., and Jefferson amendment,
    421–425, 431, 435
Jeffords, Jim (James M.), 133, 184, 349, 351,
    390, 444
  and consensus, 375, 378, 379
Jennings, Chris, 122–123, 303, 324, 398,
    512
Johnson, Andrew, 156
Johnson, Curt, 504
Johnson, Lyndon B., and administration,
    138, 148, 206, 432, 481, 552, 579,
    619, 626
  and civil rights, 507
  special programs of, 32, 415, 449, 471 (*see
    also* Great Society)
  staff members, 101, 115
  and Vietnam War, 67, 397, 493, 554, 616
Johnson, Nancy, 401, 431, 573, 627
Johnson, Ralph, 319, 320
Johnson & Johnson, 319
Johnston, Harry, 128, 475
Jones, Paula Corbin, 274
Justice Department, U.S., 43, 261, 362

Kahn, Chip (Charles N. III), 199, 203, 204,
    212, 219, 411–412
  and "Harry and Louise" ads, 207–208,
    209, 417, 528, 587, 615
Kaiser Family Foundation, 82, 91, 230,
    559, 633
Kasich, John, 573, 582
Kassebaum, Nancy, 349, 375, 378, 379
Kaufman, Dr. Ron, 538–539
Kaus, Mickey, 272
Kean, Thomas H., 596–597
Kefauver, Estes, 619
Kemp, Jack, 386
Kennedy, John F., and administration, 32,
    117, 206, 605, 615, 620, 636, 640
  cabinet and staff members, 35, 59
  campaign (1960), 4, 138, 432, 619
  and health care, 66–67, 68
Kennedy, Robert F., 206
Kennedy, Ted (Edward Moore), 3, 4, 106,
    257, 518, 579, 617, 524
  and Clinton plan, 124, 183, 284–285, 302,
    347–351
    variant on, 347, 351, 374, 390, 393,
      439, 446–447, 621–622
  and crime bill, 478
  health care battle by, 34, 68, 72, 499,
    529, 636
  Mitchell bill, 491, 513, 519
Kennelly, Barbara Bailey, 426–427, 431–432,
    434, 435
Kerrey, Bob, 75, 78, 155–156, 378, 433
  health care plan of, 71–72, 80
  and Mitchell plan, 490–492, 523, 526
Kerry, John, 492
Kevorkian, Dr. Jack, 185, 596
King, Andie (Andrea), 128, 453

King, Coretta Scott, 4
King, Martin Luther Jr., 14, 206, 564
King/Drew Medical Center (Los Angeles),
    540, 638
Kinsley, Michael, 272
Kirkland, Lane, 12–13, 42, 348–349, 356n
Klasen, Chris (Dr. Christine), 236, 237, 239,
    244–247, 250, 252–253, 537, 594
Kleczka, Gerald D., 401, 403
Klein, Joe, 351
Knox, Richard A., 75
Kodak, 320
Kohl, Herbert, 486
Koop, Dr. C. Everett, 507–508
Kopetski, Mike, 214, 408, 423–427 passim,
    432–433, 434–435
Kranowitz, Alan, 333
Kristol, Bill (William), 233–234, 270, 363,
    371, 385, 446, 531
Kristol, Irving, 233
Kroger, John, 109
Kuntz, Phil, 465n

Labor, U.S. Department of, 169, 576
labor unions
    and Clinton plan, 12–13, 50, 86, 164,
        348–349, 356, 470, 624
    and Cooper bill, 309–310, 311, 331
    and health care, 356
    lobbying by, see lobbyists
    and NAFTA, 292, 321
    oppose compromise bill, 523
Ladd, Everett Carll, 556
Lake, Celinda, 152
Langness, David, 239–240, 248–249, 533–537
    passim, 544
Larson, Gary, 172
Latham, Tom, 558
Leadership Institute Press, 373
leaks to press. See news media
Lee, Philip, 100–101
Levin, Carl, 400
Levin, Sandy (Sander M.), 400–401, 402,
    403
Lewin, Tamar, 185
Lewin-VHI, Inc. consulting firm, 591
Lewis, John, 183–184, 400, 401, 403, 423,
    424, 454
Lewis, Ron, 552
Liddy, G. Gordon, 384
Lieberman, Joseph, 378
Limbaugh, Rush, 24, 197, 256, 276–277,
    384, 467, 549, 570
Lincoln, Abraham, 639
Lindsay, Bruce, 261
Lippmann, Walter, 196
Littlefield, Nick, 350, 518–520, 522, 525, 636
lobbyists, 82, 105, 426, 499, 628
    AARP, 418, 423, 426 (see also Rother,
        John)
    big business, 197, 316–318 passim, 325,
        339, 342, 343, 489, 591
    Chamber of Commerce, 66, 188, 316,
        322–323, 324, 489, 569
    Clean Air Act, 348

compromise bill amendments submitted
    by, 417–418
conservative group, 66, 569 (see also
    Christian Coalition; Citizens for a
    Sound Economy [CSE])
Democratic Party, 70, 387, 567
effectiveness of, 154, 194–224
health care industry, 12, 66, 90–91, 196, 418
insurance industry, 46–47, 340–342,
    439, 504 (see also Health Insurance
    Association of America [HIAA])
labor union, 331–332, 338, 418, 474, 520
mandates opposed by, 204, 371
money spent by, 194–195, 212–213, 430
National Rifle Association, 483, 484,
    485, 569
President approached by, 217–218
progressive organization, 152–153, 213,
    470, 471
and Reform Riders, 460–475
representation imbalance, 631
Republican Party, and relationship with,
    501, 567–570
    Gingrich and, 488–489
small business, 47, 225, 569 (see also
    National Federation of Independent
    Business [NFIB])
tobacco, 343, 422
See also advertising campaigns; interest groups
long-term care. See health care plans
Los Angeles County, 237–253, 535, 539,
    540, 542, 594
    Medicare and Medicaid enrollment in, 249
Los Angeles County General Hospital–University
    of Southern California Medical Center,
    236–251 passim, 536–540, 594, 631
Los Angeles Times, 230, 256, 333, 481, 594
Lott, Trent, 304, 364, 581, 627
Louisiana, lobbying tactics in, 221
Lugar, Richard G., 447–448
Lumley, Daniel, 473
Luntz, Frank, 576–577, 578, 582
Lux, Mike, 177, 213

McCarthy, Eugene, 257, 579
McCaughey, Betsy (Elizabeth), 271–272, 634
McCormack, John W., 306
McCrery, Jim, 401
McDermott, Jim (James A.), 43, 171–172,
    176, 275, 284, 516, 632
    and Clinton plan, 44–46, 173, 400, 433, 457
    and compromise plan, 423, 424, 624
    and party loyalty as issue, 426–427
    and Stark bill, 397, 400–403 passim, 431,
        433, 435
McDougal, Jim and Susan, 259
McEntee, Jerry (Gerald W.), 164–165, 177,
    178, 288, 332, 472, 473
McGinley, Laurie, 589
McGovern, George, 564
McGuire, Sheila, 557–558
McInturff, Bill (William), 91–92, 189–190,
    197, 198, 203–208 passim
    and Gingrich's strategy, 196, 234, 428–429, 577
Mack, Connie, 499

McLarty, "Mack," 20, 21, 268, 293–294,
    318, 398
  and strategy, 301, 315, 320, 456
  and task force, 146, 149, 227, 375
McLean Hospital, 27
McWhorter, Clayton, 331
Madison Guaranty, 259, 260, 261, 262
Magaziner, Ira C., 186–189 passim, 226,
    227, 356, 411, 459, 627
  background, 15, 78, 105–108
  and business interests, 317–322 passim
  Clintons' support of, 103–104, 107–108,
    160–163, 614
  and compromise bills, 311–313, 393,
    438–440 passim, 495–496
  concessions suggested by, 369–370
  and decision making, 130, 136, 164, 165
  dislike/distrust of, 81–87 passim, 107,
    133–134, 171–172, 186, 209, 266, 503
  and draft plans, 83, 121, 167–173 passim
  Gradison and, 200–201, 202
  and health costs, 80, 85, 122, 124, 162,
    217, 410, 608
  and managed competition concept, 78, 79,
    80, 85, 381
  President briefed by, 95, 134, 140, 145–146,
    157, 213, 267, 301–303 passim, 617
  last-ditch efforts, 375–377
  and President's health care plan speech,
    14–18 passim, 26, 31, 49
  and secrecy policy, 140, 142, 611
  Stark and, 167, 172, 396–399 passim
  task force run by, 96, 103–118 passim,
    131–139 passim, 233, 420, 610–611, 613
  and time constraints, 119, 120, 123, 128,
    129, 143, 147, 149
Mainstream Coalition, 440–446 passim,
    487–491 passim, 494–499 passim,
    513, 519, 523–528 passim, 558, 622
managed care. See health maintenance
    organizations (HMOs)
managed competition concept. See health
    care plans
mandates, employer
  big business support sought, 413
  in bipartisan plans, 69, 314, 316,
    333
  in Clinton plan, 160, 216–217, 289,
    313, 323, 377, 381, 409, 438,
    453
  in compromise plans, 313, 366, 377, 386,
    391, 401, 423
  and congressional benefits, 289–291,
    338, 482
  deadlock on issue, 424
  defeated in California, 203
  Nixon plan, 500
  opposition to
    conservative group, 386
    Democratic Party, 342, 403, 408,
      420, 424
    insurance industry, 214, 219
    Republican Party, 313, 373, 377, 391,
      402, 501
    small business (and NFIB), 204,

      216, 218–223 passim, 418, 419,
        422
    public view of, 371
    supported, 200, 204, 323, 418, 419
mandates, individual, 337, 363, 371, 394,
    424
  opposition to, 373
Manhattan Institute, 271
Manhattan Project, 117
Mansfield, Mike, 619
Maraniss, David, 576, 577
Marchildon, Greg, 470
Margolies-Mezvinsky, Marjorie, 336
Marlboro cigarettes, 343
Marmor, Theodore, 272
Marshall Plan, 117, 615
Marx, Karl, and Marxism, 185
Maryland cost-containment plan, 400, 402
Mathias, Charles McC. Jr., 444
Matsui, Bob (Robert T.), 408, 424, 435, 436,
    457–568
May, Dr. Richard, 245
Mayo Clinic, 158
Mays, Janice, 415
Medicaid, 67, 306, 359, 474, 600
  abolition of, under compromise plan, 477
  in California, 236, 249
  Clinton and, 77, 82–83, 97–99 passim,
    161, 572, 599
  costs, 77, 97, 354
  cuts in, 97, 122, 173, 373, 573, 574, 578,
    581–583
  inefficiency of, 85, 114, 192
  Republican plan, 580, 582–583, 591–594
    passim, 599, 603, 633
Medi-Cal, 238, 250
medical IRAs, 430
medical profession. See health care industry
Medicare, 306, 326, 359, 558, 572, 579,
    600
  in California, 249
  catastrophic-illness bill, 68–70, 93, 144,
    157, 175, 301, 397, 480, 602, 630
  cost, cost variations, 25, 242, 243, 583–584
  cuts in, 97, 122, 161, 162, 167, 173, 373,
    410, 427, 494, 573–578 passim,
    581–583 passim, 592
  Dole and, 359, 573
  enacted, 33, 66–67, 101, 301, 306
  expansion plans, 68–69, 80, 144, 154,
    168, 398, 399
  impending insolvency, 575–577
  and managed care, 139, 166
  "Medicare C" (Stark-Gibbons bill), see
    Stark, Pete
  and "Medigap," 69
  Republican plan, 580–586 passim, 589–592,
    593–594, 603, 633
  See also health insurance, national
"Medigap," 69
Meet the Press (TV show), 172, 351, 366, 371
Merck & Co. Pharmaceuticals, 89, 95,
    109, 322
Metropolitan Life Insurance Company,
    199

Metzenbaum, Howard, 349
Mica, John, 598
Michel, Bob (Robert H.), 38, 191–192, 197,
    270, 329, 333, 334
  health care bill of, 43, 316, 328
Mikulski, Barbara, 349
Minding America's Business (Magaziner and
    Reich), 106
MinnesotaCare, 502–505
Mitchell, George, 4, 358, 517, 548, 617,
    619, 636
  and budget bill, 123, 125, 126, 145
  and Clean Air Act, 348
  and Clinton plan, 119–120, 124, 151, 173,
    233, 302, 305, 336, 367–370, 379,
    383, 621
    doubts about, 37–38
    Kennedy version, 347, 351, 393
    and mandate, 371
    "rescue" bill, 437–440, 442, 454–459
      passim, 476–480, 486–502 *passim*,
      505, 509, 513–522 *passim*, 523–531
      passim, 546, 622
    threatens to keep Congress open,
      486–487, 489
  and Democratic Party split, 624
  health reform bills, 296, 391, 448
    Bush administration, 60–61, 173
  leaves Senate, 294–299, 518, 531
Mondale, Walter, 257, 337, 445
Mongan, James, 370
Montana, lobbying tactics in, 220–221
Moon, Marilyn, 70
Moorhead, Carlos, 327
Morris, Dick, 580–581
Motley, John, 159, 160, 215–222, 224, 340,
    528, 568
Moynihan, Liz, 352, 355
Moynihan, Maura, 266
Moynihan, Pat (Daniel Patrick), 35, 349,
    353, 523, 584
  and budget bill, 345
  and CBO, 284
  and Clinton plan, 265, 302, 348, 379–380,
    414, 457
    ambivalence about, 396, 454
    denigrates, 172, 351, 622
    GATT vs., 450
    lack of commitment, 347, 353–354,
      366, 368, 372, 378, 393–394
    support expected, 161
    variation of, 377, 390, 391–393, 424
  and compromise/bipartisan bills, 270, 376,
    378, 390, 391
    Moynihan-Dole, 266, 270, 345–346,
      350, 358, 372–373, 395
  and Democratic Party split, 624
  and NAFTA, 345, 352
  relations with Clintons, 351–352, 354–358
Murray, Alan, 568
Murray, James, 65
Muskie, Edmund, 257, 383
Mutual of Omaha, 66
My American Journey (Powell), 597
Myers, Dee Dee, 456

NAFTA (North American Free Trade
    Agreement), 159, 189, 210, 228,
    352, 457
  bipartisan support of, 254, 287, 345
  Clinton's fight for, *see* Clinton, Bill
  Rostenkowski and, 407, 410
  union opposition to, 292, 321
Natcher, William, 552
National Association of Community Health
    Centers, 91
National Association of Life Underwriters
    (NALU), 340
National Association of Manufacturers (NAM),
    316, 317–318, 489, 591
National Association of Wholesalers, 333
National Center for Public Policy Research,
    373
National Economic Council, 134, 143
National Education Association, 306
National Federation of Independent Business
    (NFIB), 46, 159, 196–197, 204,
    215–224, 228, 409, 426
  in coalition, 53, 188, 198, 323
  and Cooper bill, 316
  "endgame" of, 223–224
  power of/pressure by, 216, 220–222,
    339–343 *passim*, 371, 390, 439, 467,
    489, 504, 528, 568
National Governors' Association, 30, 77,
    159–160, 216, 436
National Health Care Campaign, 70
National Institutes of Health (NIH), 241–242
National Press Club, 452
National Restaurant Association, 343, 371,
    569, 630
National Rifle Association (NRA), 254, 269,
    308, 483, 484, 485, 551, 566, 569
National Security Council, 605, 617
National Service Corps, 350, 449
National Taxpayers Union, 53, 551
NBC-TV, 172, 631
Neal, Richard, 432, 435
Neeley, Jim, 331
Nelson, Ben, 456
Nethercutt, George, 551
Neustadt, Richard, 615
New Deal era, 102, 194, 270, 306, 310, 311.
    See also Roosevelt, Franklin
New England Journal of Medicine, 72
New Left, 346
New Republic magazine, 271, 272
news media, 324, 456–457, 563
  attacks Clintons, 255–256, 273, 277,
    281–282, 600
  battle for coverage, 298, 466–472
  coverage of Congress, 298–299, 426,
    482, 619
  First Lady's meetings with, 23–25, 632
  leaks to, 145, 261, 521, 530
    on drafts of plan, 15, 120, 140, 149,
      151, 167–168, 317, 512, 517, 611
    misleading or destructive, 140–141, 145,
      151, 512, 611
  lobbying and, 221–222, 520–521
  on Mitchell bill, 479

news media (*continued*)
    and public understanding of Clinton plan,
        230–231, 631–635
    and public view of government, 206–207,
        297–298, 384
    reports on Reform Riders, 463, 464
    secrecy policy and, 142–143
    talk shows, 282, 460, 484, 499, 504, 570
        (*see also* Limbaugh, Rush)
    TV, 19, 47, 60, 82, 231, 255–256, 314,
        470, 635
        effectiveness of, 298, 619–620
    and Whitewater, 258, 259–260, 263, 275,
        276–277, 281
    See also advertising campaigns
Newsweek, 351
New Yorker, The, 108, 577*n*
New York Times, 82, 200, 256, 352, 392, 586
    business survey by, 382
    on Clinton's plan and speeches, 52, 89,
        141, 145, 168
    on First Lady, 182, 185, 187, 210, 600
    on Gingrich, 462, 549
    leaks to, 141, 145, 521
    Russell Baker's column, 595–596
    on state health plans, 77, 314
    on Whitewater, 259, 262, 263
Nexon, David, 349
Nichols, Len, 144
Nickles, Don, 365
Nixon, Richard, and administration, 21, 35,
        263, 384, 397, 418, 441, 481, 551,
        584, 606
    and health care plan, 67, 269, 370, 376,
        500, 521, 522
    and Watergate, 206, 277, 418, 530, 554, 614
No Name Coalition, 53, 188, 197, 198, 323,
        328, 464, 499, 567
Noonan, Peggy, 561, 565
No Ordinary Time (Goodwin), 102
Norquist, Grover G., 384–385, 548, 561, 569
Norrell, Judy, 204
Nunn, Sam, 525
Nussbaum, Bernard, 261, 263
Nuttle, Marc, 223, 224

Obey, Dave, 578–579
O'Brien, Lawrence F. III, 204
O'Brien, Mary Jo, 504–505
"October of Opposition," 189
O'Donnell, Kirk, 104
O'Donnell, Lawrence Jr., 265–267, 355, 360,
        372–373, 450, 491, 492, 493
    on "War Room," 356, 615
Office of Management and Budget (OMB),
        112, 115, 116, 139, 162, 410
Oklahoma City bombing, 638
Omaha World-Herald, 419
O'Neill, Patrick, 461
O'Neill, Tip (Thomas P.), 104
Ong, John, 318–320, 321–322
Oregon, lobbying tactics in, 221

Packwood, Bob (Robert W.), 133, 362, 369,
        371, 500–501, 626

boasts of killing plan, 521–522, 528, 530
    and consensus, 375, 376, 378–380, 386, 390
    Dole-Packwood bill, 390–391, 448–449
    and Nixon plan/employer mandate, 376,
        424, 500, 521–522
PACs (political action committees), 165, 620,
        623, 630. *See also* lobbyists
Pakula, Alan, 27
Panetta, Leon, 115, 144, 211, 318, 510, 575
    and Clinton plan, 161, 177, 485, 614
"paper hospital," 80
partisanship, 36–40, 304–305, 375, 382–386,
        434, 445, 598, 627
    polarization of Congress, *see* Congress, U.S.
    See also bipartisanship
Paster, Howard, 8, 125, 303, 305, 330,
        396, 398
Patinkin, Mark, 107
Patricelli, Robert, 323
Payne, L. F., 409, 420–421, 422, 424, 429, 435
pay-or-play system, 75–76, 81, 86
payroll tax. *See* taxes
Peace Corps, 32, 72, 116, 293
Pear, Robert, 82
Pell, Claiborne, 486
Pennsylvania, lobbying tactics in, 221
People's Budget, The (Luntz), 582
Pepper, Claude, 69
Pepper-Rockefeller Commission, 70, 109, 221,
        398
Pepsico, 197, 339, 342
Perot, Ross, 78–79, 121, 268, 451, 543, 581,
        597, 614
pharmaceutical companies. *See* health care
        industry
Pickle, Jake (J. J.), 432
Pines, Burt Y., 373
Pitts, Billy (William R.), 197, 198, 270, 333
"policy networks," 112–113
Pollack, Ron, 153
polls
    on Clinton, 10, 82, 145, 149, 189–190,
        254, 256, 274, 384, 489, 597
    on Clinton plan, 192–193, 205, 219, 264,
        274, 371
    on First Lady, 255, 265, 274
    on Gingrich, 597, 598
    on health insurance and care, 62, 82, 90,
        152, 333, 559, 575, 583, 629, 633
    on mandates, 371
    NFIB, 220
    on Powell, 597
    on Reagan, 254, 347
    on Republican Party, 575, 578, 595
    on Truman, 612
    on trust in government, 556
Portland Oregonian, 461
Powell, Gen. Colin, 525, 597
Prather, Joe, 552
prescription benefits, 80, 165, 418, 572
President's Task Force on National Health
        Reform. *See* task force
press, the. *See* news media
Pressler, Larry, 222
preventive care, 80, 246, 421, 608–609

price controls, insurance. *See* health care costs
      (insurance rates)
Priest, Dana, 134, 142, 230, 417, 426, 429
Principal Financial Group, 202
Priselac, Tom (Thomas M.), 242, 243–244,
      252, 535
Profiles in Courage (Kennedy), 636
Progressive era, 63, 534
Project for the Republican Future, 234, 531
Proposition 166 (California), 203
Prudential Insurance Company, 199, 318,
      322, 323
Pryor, David, 122, 367
Public Agenda Foundation, 90, 91, 94
"public opinion," 629. *See also* news media; polls
purchasing cooperatives, 319. *See also* health
      care alliances
Purdum, Todd, 352
Putting People First (policy staff booklet),
      79–80, 81

Quayle, Dan (J. Danforth), 85, 138, 233–234,
      364
Quinn, Laura, 527
Quist, Allen, 504, 553

Rabin, Yitzhak, 19, 598
Randolph, A. Philip, 403
Rangel, Charles B., 417
Rasco, Carol, 109, 456
Rather, Dan, 47
Ratliff, Cathy, 53
Rayburn, Sam ("Mister Sam"), 620
Reagan, Ronald, and administration, 30,
      57–58, 261, 400, 457, 479, 481, 615
   aides and officials, 21, 186, 287, 329,
      552, 625
   budget and tax reform, 119, 175–176,
      352, 404, 573–574
   election of, 44, 195, 206, 337, 516, 517,
      579, 616, 617, 626
   and health care, 38, 68, 354, 359, 360
   and Iran-Contra, 353, 614
   as "model" for Gingrich followers, 562–563
   poll ratings, 254, 347
reconciliation bill. *See* budget
Reed, Bruce, 70, 75, 79
Reform Riders, 460–475, 476, 479
Regan, Donald E., 175, 176, 177
Reich, Robert, 78, 106, 158
Reinecke, Dr. Bob, 59
Reinhardt, Uwe, 634
"reinventing government," 158
Reischauer, Edwin O., 116, 285
Reischauer, Bob (Robert), 116–118, 171,
      282–287, 324, 487–489, 636
Reno, Janet, 263, 277
Republican National Committee, 196, 386,
      391, 428, 528, 576, 588
Republican Party
   ads by, 289 (*see also* advertising campaigns)
   and budget, *see* budget
   changes in, 11–12, 38, 625–627
      ideological shift, 444–445, 448, 627
   in Congress (1930s, 1940s), 66, 67

in Congress (wins control), 11, 124, 155,
      215, 224, 227, 238, 304, 498–499,
      502, 505, 552–558, 622, 630
   demographic breakdown, 566–567
   Gingrich heads House, 560–565
   on House committees, 287, 307, 327n, 328
Congress denigrated by, 297
conservative tradition of, 37, 346, 626
defeats Clinton's economic plans, 17, 139
divisions within, 366, 596
filibusters by, *see* Senate, U.S.
in Florida, 415
pressure from right wing of, 373, 376
response to State of Union Message, 270
and Senate Finance Committee, 362–363
Steering Committee, 409
tax increases opposed by, 370, 409
and Whitewater, 261–262, 263, 275
See also partisanship
Republican Party and health care
   Democratic coalition vs., 287–289 (*see
      also* Democratic Party)
   Dole and, 35–36, 270 (*see also* Dole, Bob)
   excluded from discussions, 131–132,
      142, 627
   health care reform opposed, 327, 330,
      462–463, 521
      bipartisan plans, 423, 474
      Clinton plan, 69, 169, 191–192, 197,
         233–234, 283, 284, 323, 328–330
         passim, 375, 376, 384, 386, 446–447,
         449, 625
      "no crisis," "no bill" strategy, 270,
         363–364, 448, 500, 515–516, 576
   health care reform supported, 62, 64, 68,
      133, 625–626 (*see also* health care
      plans [Republican Party])
   political strategy, 626–627
   Truman and, 66
   See also Gingrich, Newt; Medicaid; Medicare
Resolution Trust Corporation (RTC),
      260, 261
Rhode Island, 106, 107
Ribicoff, Abraham, 383
Ricchetti, Steve, 255
Riegle, Don (Donald W. Jr.), 111, 367
Rivlin, Alice, 115, 116, 139, 144, 161,
      614
Robertson, Pat, 197
Robert Wood Johnson Foundation, 632
Rockefeller, Jay (John D IV), 3, 32–34, 69,
      315, 366, 383, 442
   and budget bill, 125, 126
   and Clinton plan, 144, 447, 636
      comments on, 109, 114, 136, 152,
         167, 168–169, 257, 275, 323,
         526–527
      and "planning vacuum," 225–227,
         231–233
      supports, 86, 92–93
   and compromise or variant bills, 371–372,
      377, 392
   and consensus, 367, 494–495
   and Health Care Reform Project, 50,
      288, 289

Rockefeller, Jay (*continued*)
  Pepper-Rockefeller Commission, 70, 109,
    221, 398
Rockefeller, John D., 32, 168
Rockefeller, Nelson, 626
Rodham, Hugh, 135–136
Rolling Stone magazine, 227
Romney, Mitt, 106
Rooney, Patrick, 430
Roosevelt, Eleanor, 102, 103, 182, 184,
    186, 614
Roosevelt, Franklin, 315, 392, 419, 429, 438,
    542–543, 554, 613, 639
  Clinton compared to, 40, 155
  and health care, 24, 44, 65
  New Deal of, 44, 117, 257, 346, 534, 549,
    554, 561, 640, 641
  and Social Security, 12, 42, 44, 65, 144, 155
  See also New Deal era
Roosevelt, Theodore, 63, 257, 346, 534
Roper Center for Public Opinion Research, 556
Rose Law Firm (Little Rock), 259, 275
Rosenbaum, David E., 462, 463
Rosner, Jeremy, 21–22, 23, 25, 28–29
Rosoff, Arnold, 175
Rostenkowski, Dan ("Rosty"), 285, 357, 403,
    404–406, 455–456, 556
  and budget bill, 123
  and Clinton plan, 171, 172, 202
    comments on, 111, 177, 191, 321, 324,
      493
    supports, 68, 173, 322
  and Democratic Party split, 624
  and health alliances, 399–400
  investigation/indictment of, 42–43, 406–407,
    411, 414–416, 434–435, 588
  and Jefferson amendment (tobacco tax),
    421, 422, 425, 431
  power of, 416
  relations with Clintons, 183, 186, 411,
    412–413, 414
  Rostenkowski-Gradison deal, 411–414,
    417, 432, 588
  and Stark bill ("Medicare C"), 407–414,
    419, 434, 509, 515
Roth, Toby, 276
Roth, Bill (William V.), 362
Rother, John, 50, 289, 322, 423, 447, 458,
    588–589
  doubts and worries of, 154, 168, 273,
    388–389, 457, 480–481, 511–512, 586,
    637–638
Roush, Mike, 222–223
Rowland, J. Roy "Doc," 192
Rowland-Bilirakis bill, 192, 333–334, 344,
    366, 373, 390, 487, 546
Rubin, Alissa J., 131, 397
Rubin, Bob (Robert), 22, 122, 134–135, 138,
    143, 161, 162, 318
  and Business Roundtable, 320, 321
Rucker, Jamarkus, 54
"rump group," 378–380, 390, 440
Russakoff, Dale, 597
Russian crisis, 189, 254
Russo, Martin A., 422

Safire, William, 600
Sanders, Bernard, 509
San Francisco Bay Area Business Group on
    Health, 382
Santorum, Rick, 550
Sasser, Jim (James R.), 332
Sauer, Elizabeth, 466, 467
Scaife, Richard Mellon, 465n
Schenk, Lynn, 184, 335–336
Schlafly, Phyllis, 373
Schramm, Carl J., 200
Scranton, William, 626
Scully, Tom, 588
Senate, U.S.
  Aging Committee, 122
  Appropriations Committee, 125, 565
  Ethics Committee, 362, 425
  filibusters
    Democratic health plans stalled by, 302,
      305, 345, 350, 375, 448, 484, 489,
      522, 524
    economic plan defeated by, 17, 139
    number and use of, 297, 619
  Finance Committee
    and budget, 146
    and Clinton plan, 111, 266, 336, 347,
      358, 370, 374, 380, 392–393, 414
    and compromise bills or no bill, 270,
      366, 380, 386, 390
    and consensus/bipartisanship, 302,
      366–370, 376, 378–380, 390, 440
    Democratic chairmen of, 61, 138, 172,
      345
    Dole as chairman, 564
    Health Subcommittee, 369
    hearings before, 161
    and mandates, 221, 371
    media and, 469, 619
    Republican side, 360, 362–363, 450,
      564 (*see also* filibusters, *above*)
    and "Treasury I," 176
  and health care bill, 509–510
  Intelligence Committee, 353
  Labor and Human Resources Committee,
    347, 349, 439, 447, 518
  lobbying of, 220 (*see also* lobbyists)
  members leave, 294–299, 518
  partisanship of, 304–305, 375, 382–386
  and TV constituency, 619
  Universal Coverage Group, 505
Service Employees' International Union
    (SEIU), 356
Shalala, Donna, 101, 115, 128, 144, 274
  and Clinton plan, 22, 116, 140, 145, 148,
    177, 456, 512–513, 614, 622
  doubts about, 116, 139, 157, 161,
    177
Shea, Jerry, 520
Shelby, Richard, 523
Showdown at Gucci Gulch (Birnbaum and
    Murray), 568
Simpson, Alan, 427–428, 588
Simpson, O. J., 472, 597
"single-payer" system. *See* health care
    plans

Slattery, Jim, 337–339, 340–342, 344, 427, 557, 621
small business, 85, 166, 253, 338, 339, 389. *See also* lobbyists; National Federation of Independent Business (NFIB)
Smith, Adam, 158
Smith, J. Brian, 200
Smith, Lamar, 275–276, 467
Smith, Robert C., 305
Social Security, 33, 94, 579, 583, 584
  enacted, 12, 42, 51, 144, 155, 301
  health care as part of, 44, 65, 66, 306, 310, 622
  rescue operation, 301, 346
Social Transformation of American Medicine, The (Starr), 64n
Solomon, Jason, 278, 495, 497
Somalia crisis, 188–189, 225, 254
Southern California Edison, 288
space program, 117
Specter, Arlen, 271
Stark, Deborah, 398
Stark, Pete (Fortney Pete), 69, 219, 415, 430, 431–432, 457, 546, 624
  and Cooper bill, 316, 452
  and Magaziner/Clinton plan, 167, 172, 396–399 *passim*
  and "Medicare C" (Stark-Gibbons bill), 399–404 *passim*, 411–419 *passim*, 430, 433, 434–436, 453–454, 509, 514–515, 621
    Jefferson amendment to, 423, 424, 425, 431
Starr, Kenneth, 489
Starr, Paul, 64n, 316, 494, 602, 604, 609
State, U.S. Department of, 44
Steelman, Deborah, 197–198, 223, 333, 334, 499–500, 630
Stephanopoulos, George, 51, 268, 273, 293, 411, 494
  and Clinton plan, 22, 94, 122, 146, 149, 229, 322, 375
    speech on, 5–7, 8–10, 25–26, 29, 43
  and strategy, 450, 579
Stockman, David, 329, 573
Stout, Hilary, 103, 557, 632–633
Sullivan, Dr. Louis W., 82
Sununu, John, 360
Superfund toxic waste cleanups, 449
Sweeney, John, 356
Sweet, Bonnie, 329
Synar, Mike (Michael L.), 129, 195, 336, 337, 337n, 343

talk shows. *See* news media
task force, 96, 98–136, 216, 420
  vs. budget issue, 137, 147–150
  Clinton forms, briefed by, 96–100 *passim*, 112, 134, 145–146, 149–150, 610–611
  decision making by, 19, 113, 129–131, 134, 136, 164, 165, 177
  disbanded, 146

doubted/challenged, 115, 116–118, 139, 161, 361
draft plan produced by, 167–172
information leaked to press, 140, 145, 149
lawsuit against, 111–112, 172
"managed chaos," 113–114
process questioned, 173–178
secrecy policy, 140–143, 611
size, 10, 113, 319
time constraints, 100, 119–120, 123, 128–129, 143, 147, 149, 453
See also Clinton, Hillary Rodham, and health care plans; Magaziner, Ira C.
Tauzin, Billy (W. J.), 210, 336
taxes
  energy (BTU), 145, 146, 269, 367, 424, 438, 515
  on guns and ammunition, 308, 377, 391, 392
  on health benefits, 164, 418
  on health insurance premiums, 377, 391
  increases in (1980s), 564–565
  payroll, 72, 88, 145, 332, 342, 377, 398, 403, 409
  Republicans oppose increase in, 370, 409
  suggested, protest against, 151
  tax cut, 569, 583
  tax reform, 175–176, 177, 404, 602–603
  on tobacco, 151, 172, 308, 377, 391, 402, 403, 409–410, 420–429 *passim*, 494, 572
  value-added, 140
  on wine and liquor, 151
Teeter, Robert, 595
Tejeda, Frank, 631
Templeton, Carol, 54, 193
"Theme Team" (Republican). *See* House of Representatives, U.S.
This Week with David Brinkley (TV show), 562
Thomas, Bill (William M.), 401, 420, 423–425, 434, 587, 627
Thomases, Susan, 154
Thomasson, Patsy, 261
Thompson, Fred, 331, 557
Thornburgh, Dick (Richard), 58, 59, 60
Thorpe, Ken, 70, 144, 145
Thurmond, Strom, 349
Tighe, Peggy, 214
Time magazine, 26, 230, 568
Times Mirror Center for the People & the Press, 230
tobacco industry, 343, 421–422. *See also* taxes
Toner, Robin, 586
Trafford, Abigail, 463
Travelers Insurance Company, 199
Treasury, U.S. Department of, 138, 154, 261, 576
  and Clinton plan, 139, 169
  savings from Medicare cutbacks, 162, 410
  "Treasury I" (1986 tax reform), *see* taxes
"Troopergate," 256, 258, 261, 262, 274
Truman, Harry, 67, 138, 314, 531–532, 534, 552, 554, 612, 615
  battles for health care, 66, 269, 471
TRW, 320
Tsongas, Paul, 72, 74, 75, 77–78, 121
Tuckson, Dr. Reed, 540–542, 638
Tumulty, Karen, 230
TV. *See* advertising campaigns; news media

Tyson, Laura D'Andrea, 134–135, 138–139, 144, 158, 161–163 *passim*, 614
Tyson Foods Inc., 273, 356

Udall, Morris K., 257, 620
Ukockis, James R., 162
United Auto Workers, 474
United Nations, 181, 189
United Paperworkers International Union, 331
United Seniors Association, 373
universal coverage. *See* health insurance, national
unmanaged competition, 73–74
Upjohn pharmaceuticals, 90, 417
Upton, Fred, 329–330, 431, 569
Urban Institute, 70, 116
USA Today, 140, 382
U.S. News & World Report, 395

Vagelos, Dr. P. Roy, 89, 322
Van Dyke, Mike, 340
Varma, Vivek, 129
Vermont health plan defeated, 374
Verveer, Melanne, 210, 281, 462, 512
Vietnam War, 71, 78, 84
    anger over/opposition to, 43, 67, 152, 206, 257, 348, 397, 493, 554, 605, 607
    Johnson and, 67, 397, 493, 554, 616
Viguerie, Richard, 373
Villers, Philippe, 153

Wagner, Robert, 65
Wagner-Murray-Dingell bill, 184
Walker, Robert S., 131
Wallop, Malcolm, 362, 486
Wall Street Journal, 103, 222, 322, 385
    editorials, 197, 271, 323, 632
    news stories, 216, 263, 465n, 557, 569
        on Clinton plan, 153, 517, 528, 632–633
        on Gingrich/Gingrich plan, 570, 588, 589
"War Room," 51–52, 154, 356, 615
Washington, State of, lobbying tactics in, 221
Washington Post, 134, 230, 263, 298, 334, 342, 392, 412, 417, 463, 500, 545, 591
    Blue Ash, Ohio, focus group of, 53, 193
    on Clinton plan, 142, 145, 168, 317
    on compromise bills, 417, 426–427, 479
    mock-up of, 521
Washington Post/ABC News surveys, 62, 192

Washington Times, 261, 385
Watergate, 206, 261, 262, 277, 418, 530, 554, 607, 616
"Watergate babies," 620
Watts riots, 540
Waxman, Henry A., 123, 307, 316, 335, 336, 344, 546, 621
Weicker, Lowell, 444
Weiss, Marina, 151
Weisskopf, Michael, 340–341, 576, 577
welfare programs repealed, 584–585
Wellford, Harrison, 104
Well-Heeled: Inside Lobbying for Health Care Reform (Center for Public Integrity), 212
Wellstone, Paul, 349
Wexler, Anne, and Wexler Group, 70, 81, 90
Whirlpool Corporation, 329
Whitewater case, 235, 256, 258–264, 273–282, 351, 356, 376, 442, 600
    effect of, on Clinton plan, 264, 270, 273, 275–278, 279, 543, 616
    news media and, 258, 259–260, 263, 275, 276–277, 281
    ultraconservative groups and, 465n
Wilhelm, David, 291–293, 552, 623, 625, 631
Will, George, 111
Williams, Maggie, 261, 281
Wilson, Pete, 248, 397
Wilson, Woodrow, 63–64, 126, 534
Winters, Robert, 318, 319, 320, 321, 323
Wofford, Harris, 3–4, 34, 58–61, 72, 93, 199, 277, 549–550, 556
    and health care plans, 62, 349, 505–507, 508, 550, 636
Woodruff Savings and Loan, 259
Woodward, Bob, 79
World War II, 65, 102, 117, 310, 618, 640
    lobbying "war" compared to, 196, 501
Wyden, Ron, 340

Xerox, 320

Yarrow, Peter, 475
Yeltsin, Boris, 189, 606

Zelman, Walter, 77, 78, 114, 128, 270

About the Authors

Haynes Johnson and David S. Broder have worked together for more than thirty years as reporters and columnists at the *Washington Post* and earlier the *Washington Star*. In addition to their newspaper work, the authors have written, individually or in collaboration with others, more than a dozen books, a number of them bestsellers. These include histories of the civil rights revolution and the Reagan years and studies of the political party system and the emerging generation of young political leaders. Both men are familiar to television viewers of such programs as *Washington Week in Review*, *Meet the Press*, and *The NewsHour with Jim Lehrer*. Broder, a native of Chicago Heights, Illinois, holds a master's degree in political science from the University of Chicago. He won the Pulitzer Prize for distinguished commentary in 1973. Johnson, a native of New York, holds a master's degree in American history from the University of Wisconsin. He won the Pulitzer Prize in 1966 for distinguished national reporting of the civil rights struggle in Selma, Alabama. Though the authors have collaborated on numerous major newspaper series, *The System* is their first book-length project together.